Visions of Culture

Visions of Culture

Visions of Culture

An Annotated Reader

Edited by
Jerry D. Moore

ALTAMIRA
PRESS

A Division of

ROWMAN & LITTLEFIELD PUBLISHERS, INC.
Lanham • New York • Toronto • Plymouth, UK

AltaMira Press
A division of Rowman & Littlefield Publishers, Inc.
A wholly owned subsidary of The Rowman & Littlefield Publishing Group, Inc.
4501 Forbes Boulevard, Suite 200
Lanham, MD 20706
www.altamirapress.com

Estover Road
Plymouth PL6 7PY
United Kingdom

British Library Cataloguing in Publication Information Available

Library of Congress Cataloging-in-Publication Data:

Visions of culture : an annotated reader / edited by Jerry D. Moore.
    p. cm.
  Includes bibliographical references and index.
  ISBN-13: 978-0-7591-1854-6 (cloth : alk. paper)
  ISBN-10: 0-7591-1854-X (cloth : alk. paper)
  ISBN-13: 978-0-7591-1855-3 (pbk. : alk. paper)
  ISBN-10: 0-7591-1855-8 (pbk. : alk. paper)
  eISBN-13: 978-0-7591-1856-0
  eISBN-10: 0-7591-1856-6

  1. Culture. 2. Anthropology. 3. Ethnology. I. Moore, Jerry D.
  GN357.V57 2009
  306—dc22   2008043779

Printed in the United States of America

™
∞ The paper used in this publication meets the minimum requirements of American National Standard for Information Sciences—Permanence of Paper for Printed Library Materials, ANSI/NISO Z39.48-1992.

Contents

Part IV: Evolutionary, Adaptionist, and Materialist Theories

Part V: Structures, Symbols, and Meaning

Part VI: Structures, Practice, Agency, and Power

Introduction

Visions of Culture: An Annotated Reader is an edited anthology of articles by twenty-five anthropologists—Edward Tylor, Lewis Henry Morgan, Franz Boas, Émile Durkheim, Alfred Kroeber, Ruth Benedict, Edward Sapir, Margaret Mead, Marcel Mauss, Bronislaw Malinowski, A. R. Radcliffe-Brown, Leslie White, Julian Steward, Marvin Harris, Eleanor Burke Leacock, Edward Evans-Pritchard, Victor Turner, Mary Douglas, Claude Lévi-Strauss, Clifford Geertz, James Fernandez, Sherry Ortner, Pierre Bourdieu, Eric Wolf, and Marshall Sahlins. This anthology is designed to complement the text, *Visions of Culture: An Introduction to Anthropological Theories and Theorists* (Moore 2008 [3rd edition]). For that reason this volume, *Visions of Culture: An Annotated Reader*, reflects the assumptions and concerns that motivated my original book.

First, the original articles are intellectual waypoints in the development of anthropology in the United States, Great Britain, and France from the mid-19th to the early 21st century. In each article we encounter a scholar, limited and enabled by the state of anthropological knowledge in her or his time, who is attempting to understand cultural differences. Repeatedly we encounter an anthropologist engaged in a debate with other anthropologists, predecessors and contemporaries. Marshall Sahlins, writing in the 1990s, "debates" with Alfred Kroeber (1876–1960), Julian Steward (1902–1972), and Claude Lévi-Strauss (b. 1908) among other anthropologists—not to engage in some sterile intellectual exercise, but because Sahlins understands that his own anthropological insights are indebted to those of earlier scholars, even in disagreement. E. E. Evans-Pritchard distinguishes his concept of anthropology from those of his former professor, A. R. Radcliffe-Brown. Radcliffe-Brown delineates his ideas from those of his contemporary rival Bronislaw Malinowski, and the American cultural anthropologists—such as

Franz Boas, Margaret Mead, and Ruth Benedict—whom he held in a disdain verging on pity. Ruth Benedict distances her ideas from those of a prior generation (for example, Sir James Frazier) and from other scholars of her own era. Pierre Bourdieu responds to Claude Lévi-Strauss. Eric Wolf in an address to the American Anthropological Association delivered in 1990 responds to Boasian particularism, the interpretive anthropology of Clifford Geertz, the theoretical shortcomings of Julian Steward's research program in Puerto Rico (in which Wolf participated), and a broad array of other social theorists from Sherry Ortner to Karl Marx and Friedrich Engels.

Anthropology students easily become distracted by this theoretical clamor, taking as cacophony what is actually a conversation stretching over decades. Central to that conversation are a set of key issues: What is the nature of culture? How can anyone understand or explain the complex and often-subtle variations of the human experience? To what extent is cultural behavior adaptive and utilitarian or inherently symbolic and irreducible to pragmatics? How can we understand people from cultural traditions different from our own? Is anthropology a search for scientific laws or an exploration of diverse culturally specific meanings?

Visions of Culture: An Annotated Reader encourages students to eavesdrop on that conversation—with the idea that someday, some of them will participate in it.

While the articles selected here are all texts about anthropological theory, they are simultaneously texts dealing with ethnographic data. As I discuss elsewhere (Moore 2008:xiii–xiv), I am convinced that there is an important dynamic between anthropological theory and ethnographic data. I do not mean to suggest that theoretical positions arise from ethnographic observations in some mystical or uncritical process, nor am I suggesting that individual anthropologists were not influenced by broader intellectual currents. What I contend, however, is that anthropologists tend to write about and modify their theoretical positions in the process of exploring specific sets of ethnographic data, and conversely they will choose lines of ethnographic research to examine certain theoretical propositions.

For that reason, I have chosen articles that combine ethnographic cases as exemplifying theoretical propositions. For example, I think that Geertz's "Ritual and Social Change: A Javanese Example" gives us a much better insight into interpretive anthropology than his later, much-praised and oft-reprinted "Thick Description: Toward an Interpretive Theory of Culture." Radcliffe-Brown's extended discussion of kinship in Australia and elsewhere, which comprises about 80 percent of the article "The Comparative Method in Social Anthropology" gives a much clearer sense of his idea of "social structure" than does his article "On Social Structure." As Radcliffe-Brown observed, "The only really satisfactory way of explaining a method is by means of illustration"—which I consider very good advice. Leacock's analysis of women in egalitarian societies grounds her theoretical perspective, simultaneously feminist and Marxist, in fundamental ethnographic detail. In each article in this collection, I have chosen texts that demonstrate—to paraphrase Lévi-Strauss—that anthropological theories are not only important *to think about*, they are important *to think with*.

As I mentioned above, this collection—like the companion volume, *Visions of Culture: An Introduction to Anthropological Theories and Theorists* (Moore 2008)—is written for students. The companion volume provides profiles of each anthropologist and the intellectual milieu in which they lived. *Visions of Culture: An Annotated Reader* intentionally does not repeat the material found in the companion volume; they are designed to be used together.

In this volume, each selection is prefaced with a brief introduction about the anthropologist and the text, referring the reader to relevant sections in *Visions of Culture: An Introduction to Anthropological Theories and Theorists*. This is followed by one or more primary texts, complete versions or edited excerpts of original anthropological writings. (When selections have been edited for length, the missing section is indicated by a trio of asterisks, "***".) Each primary text is followed by a section titled "Queries and Connections," a series of questions designed to help students focus on central issues in a given text and the intersections between those ideas and concepts explored by other anthropologists in other readings. While original footnotes have been maintained in general, sometimes it has been necessary to modify or edit them; in addition, I have added editor's notes to clarify specific issues or phrases in the texts.

A brief word about the selection of certain anthropologists and of specific texts. The twenty-five anthropologists included here represent a cross-section of major contributors to anthropological theory. Obviously, many other scholars have contributed to theoretical discussions, but they simply cannot all be included in a single volume. As the 3rd edition of *Visions of Cultue: An Introduction to Anthropological Theories and Theorists* was in preparation, my editor, Alan McClare and his staff at AltaMira Press, sent a questionnaire out to professors across the United States who use the text in their classes, asking for their advice about including or dropping anthropologists from the book. The survey results were less than informative. The only consensus was the need to include Marshall Sahlins in the texts, excellent advice and an excellent addition to the new edition. Beyond that, chaos reigned: one professor recommended dropping all the French theorists (Durkheim, Mauss, Lévi-Strauss, Bourdieu), another suggested eliminating all the materialists (White, Steward, Harris, and Leacock), while another proposed deleting anyone who worked before 1950. What we concluded from this exercise in public opinion survey is that there was no consensus.

Again, this is a text written for students, and no one who either teaches at a university or writes for a student audience can ignore the skyrocketing cost of textbooks. Frankly, one of the factors influencing the selection of original texts is the cost of reprint rights. This is a problem that anyone editing anthologies must face: as Mark Bauerlein recently noted for the field of literary criticism, "If publishers do charge high [reprint] fees, in effect they make these works disappear" (Bauerlein 2007). For that reason, I attempted to choose exemplary articles available from nonprofit associations and publishers or works that are in the public domain, rather than use materials whose copyrights are held by trade-book publishers, simply to keep down the cost of *Visions of Culture: An Annotated Reader*.

A final note: since 1993 I have taught a class each semester in anthropological theory at my university, California State University, Dominguez Hills; as of this writing I have taught this course twenty-five times to more than five hundred students. *Visions of Culture: An Annotated Reader* and *Visions of Culture: An Introduction to Anthropological Theories and Theorists* are the products of that experience, and I want to thank my students who have contributed to my understanding of anthropological theory. I hope that these books will be of use to my future students and to students elsewhere as they explore the diverse visions of culture that anthropology provides.

BIBLIOGRAPHY

Bauerlein, Mark
    2007   What We Owe the New Critics. Chronicle of Higher Education 54(17):B6.

I

FOUNDERS

1

Edward Tylor

INTRODUCTION

The following excerpts written by British anthropologist Edward Tylor (1832–1917) come from the opening chapter of the foundational text *Primitive Culture*. The first professor of anthropology at Oxford University and the author of the first anthropology textbook, Edward Tylor introduced a series of influential concepts and approaches (see Moore 2008:5–17).

Arguably the most significant idea is his definition of culture, found in the very first paragraph. This definition points to several essential aspects of culture. First, culture is learned. This has several immediate implications. Culture is acquired by learning, which implies that it is not genetically inherited. For this reason, Tylor can assert "possible and desirable to eliminate considerations of hereditary varieties or races of man, and to treat mankind as homogenous in nature." Second, culture is knowledge shared among members of a group. This implies that culture is transmitted between generations through the use of symbols, which leads to anthropological interest in language, indigenous systems of knowledge, and the processes of "acquiring" culture (enculturation and acculturation). Third, culture "taken in its wide ethnographic sense, is that complex whole" of human experience. "Culture" is not limited to "high culture"—arts, fashion, *haute cuisine*, design—but encompasses the broad domain of human experience. Further—although tucked away in the definition—is the implication that culture is complex and interconnected, implying the need for a "holistic" approach to culture.

Throughout this selection, we encounter fundamental concepts that shaped 19th-century anthropology—and the 20th-century response. For example, Tylor argues that there are broad similarities in cultural practices among human societies otherwise unconnected by historical ties or interactions. The evidence of these "similarity and consistency of phenomena," Tylor concludes, indicates the existence of "different grades of civilization," a progressive model of cultural evolution that Tylor develops in his 1881 textbook, *Anthropology* (see Moore 2008:14–15). Tylor's ideas are paralleled by the works of Lewis Henry Morgan (see chapter 2), and these two scholars shaped a view of human history referred to as Victorian unilineal evolution.

Since archaeology was in its infancy, Tylor had little data to work with about the long-term development of human societies. Instead, Tylor relied on analogy and inference. First, Tylor argued that there was a general principle of human thought-processes, moving from the simple to the complex. Just as innovations in firearms and navigational instruments became increasingly complex (to cite two of Tylor's examples), so too would other forms of human knowledge: mathematics, religion, subsistence, all cultural knowledge. All cultural knowledge, Tylor asserted, is characterized by progressive acquisition and addition. Yet, some practices are carried on by force of habit into new situations even though their original meanings may be lost; these cultural practices Tylor termed "survivals" (see Moore 2008:12–13). These practices, originally created in earlier periods, serve as intriguing echoes of previous cultural patterns, and thus are a source of data for the anthropologist interested in reconstructing the past stages of human experience.

PRIMARY TEXT: *PRIMITIVE CULTURE* (EXCERPTS)

Editor's note: Originally published 1871, John Murray & Sons, London.

Culture or Civilization, taken in its wide ethnographic sense, is that complex whole which includes knowledge, belief, art, morals, law, custom, and any other capabilities and habits acquired by man as a member of society. The condition of culture among the various societies of mankind, in so far as it is capable of being investigated on general principles, is a subject apt for the study of laws of human thought and action. On the one hand, the uniformity which so largely pervades civilization may be ascribed, in great measure, to the uniform causes: while on the other hand its various grades may be regarded as stages of development or evolution, each the outcome of previous history, and about to do its proper part in shaping the history of the future. To the investigation of these two great principles in several departments of ethnography, with especial consideration of the civilization of the lower tribes as related to the civilization of the higher nations, the present volumes are devoted.

* * *

"One event is always the son of another, and we must never forget the parentage," was a remark made by a Bechuana chief to Casalis the African missionary. Thus at all times historians, so far as they have aimed at being more than mere chroniclers, have done their best to show not merely succession, but connexion, among the events upon their record. Moreover, they have striven to elicit general principles of human action, and by these to explain particular events, stating expressly or taking tacitly for granted the existence of a philosophy of history. Should any one deny the possibility of thus establishing historical laws, the answer is ready with which Boswell in such a case turned on Johnson: "Then, sir, you would reduce all history to no better than an almanack." That nevertheless the labours of so many eminent thinkers should have as yet brought history only to the threshold of science, need cause no wonder to those who consider the bewildering complexity of the problems which come before the general historian.

* * *

Yet there are departments of it which, though difficult enough, seem comparatively accessible. If the field of enquiry be narrowed from History as a whole to that branch of it which is here called Culture, the history, not of tribes or nations, but of the condition of knowledge, religion, art, custom, and the like among them, the task of investigation proves to lie within far more moderate compass. We suffer still from the same kind of difficulties which beset the wider argument, but they are more diminished. The evidence is no longer so wildly heterogenous, but may be more simply classified and compared, while the power of getting rid of extraneous matter, and treating each issue on its own proper set of facts, makes close reasoning on the whole more available than in general history. This may appear from a brief preliminary examination of the problem, how the phenomena of a Culture may be classified and arranged, stage by stage, in a probable order of evolution.

Surveyed in a broad view, the character and habit of mankind at once display that similarity and consistency of phenomena which led the Italian proverb-maker to declare that "all the world is one country," "tutto il mondo è paese." To general likeness in human nature on the one hand, and to general likeness in the circumstances of life on the other, this similarity and consistency may no doubt be traced, and they may be studied with especial fitness in comparing races near the same grade of civilization. Little respect need be had in such comparisons for date in history or for place on the map; the ancient Swiss lake-dweller may be set beside the medieval Aztec, and the Ojibwa of North America beside the Zulu of South Africa. As

Dr. Johnson contemptuously said when he had read about Patagonians and South Sea Islanders in Hawkesworth's Voyages, "one set of savages is like another." How true a generalization this really is, any Ethnological Museum may show. Examine for instance the edged and pointed instruments in such a collection; the inventory includes hatchet, adze, chisel, knife, saw, scraper, awl, needle, spear and arrow-head, and of these most or all belong with only differences of detail to races the most various. So it is with savage occupations; the wood chopping, fishing with net and line, shooting and spearing game, fire-making, cooking, twisting cord and plaiting baskets, repeat themselves with wonderful uniformity in the museum shelves which illustrate the life of the lower races from Kamchatka to Tierra del Fuego, and from Dahome to Hawaii. Even when it comes to comparing barbarous hordes with civilized nations, the consideration thrusts itself upon our minds, how far item after item of the life of the lower races passes into analogous proceedings of the higher, in forms not too far changed to be recognized, and sometimes hardly changed at all. Look at the modern European peasant using his hatchet and his hoe, see his food boiling or roasting over the log fire, observe the exact place which beer holds in his calculation of happiness, hear his tale of the ghost in the nearest haunted house, and of the farmer's niece who was bewitched with knots in her inside till she fell into fits and died. If we choose out in this way things which have altered little in a long course of centuries, we may draw a picture where there shall be scarce a hand's breadth difference between an English ploughman and a negro of Central Africa. These pages will be so crowded with evidence of such correspondence among mankind, that there is no need to dwell upon its details here, but it may be used at once to override a problem which would complicate the argument, namely, the question of race. For the present purpose it appears both possible and desirable to eliminate considerations of hereditary varieties or races of man, and to treat mankind as homogenous in nature, though placed in different grades of civilization. The details of the enquiry will, I think, prove that stages of culture may be compared without taking into account how far tribes who use the same implement, follow the same custom, or believe the same myth, may differ in their bodily configuration and the colour of their skin and hair.

*   *   *

That a whole nation should have a special dress, special tools and weapons, special laws of marriage and property, special moral and religious doctrines, is a remarkable fact, which we notice so little because we have lived all our lives in the midst of it. It is with such general qualities of organized bodies of men that ethnography has especially to deal. Yet, while generalizing on the culture of a tribe or nation, and setting aside the peculiarities of the individuals composing it as unimportant to the main result, we must be careful not to forget what makes up this main result. There are people so intent on the separate life of individuals that they cannot grasp a notion of the action of the community as a whole—such an observer, incapable of a wide view of society, is aptly described in the saying that he "cannot see the forest for the trees." But, on the other hand, the philosopher may be so intent upon his own general laws of society as to neglect the individual actors of whom that society is made up, and of him it may be said that he cannot see the trees for the forest. We know how arts, customs, and ideas are shaped among ourselves by the combined actions of many individuals, of which actions both motive and effect often come quite distinctly within our view. The history of an invention, an opinion, a ceremony, is a history of suggestion and modification, encouragement and opposition, personal gain and party prejudice, and the individuals concerned act each according to his own motives, as determined by his character and circumstances. Thus sometimes we watch individuals acting for their own ends with little thought of their effect on society at large, and sometimes we have to study movements of national life as a whole, where the individuals co-operating in them are utterly beyond our observation. But seeing that collective social action is the mere resultant of many individual actions, it is clear that these two methods of enquiry, if rightly followed, must be absolutely consistent.

In studying both the recurrence of special habits or ideas in several districts, and their prevalence within each district, there come before us ever-reiterated proofs of regular causation producing the phenomena of human life, and of laws of maintenance and diffusion according to which these phenomena settle into permanent standard conditions of society, at definite stages of culture. But, while giving full importance to the evidence bearing on these standard conditions of society, let us be careful to avoid a pitfall which may entrap the unwary student. Of course the opinions and habits belonging in common to masses of mankind are to a great extent the results of sound judgment and practical wisdom. But to a great extent it is not so. That many numerous societies of men should have believed in the influence of the evil eye and the existence of a firmament, should have sacrificed slaves and goods to the ghosts of the departed, should have handed down traditions of giants slaying monsters and men turning into beasts—all this is ground for holding that such ideas were indeed produced in men's minds by efficient causes, but it is not ground for holding that the rites in question are profitable, the beliefs sound, and the history authentic.

* * *

It being shown that the details of Culture are capable of being classified in a great number of ethnographic groups of arts, beliefs, customs, and the rest, the consideration comes next how far the facts arranged in these groups are produced by evolution from one another.

* * *

Mechanical invention supplies apt examples of the kind of development which affects civilization at large. In the history of fire arms, the clumsy wheel-lock, in which a notched steel wheel revolved by means of a spring against a piece of pyrites till a spark caught the priming, led to the invention of the more serviceable flint-lock, of which a few still hang in the kitchens of our farm houses for the boys to shoot small birds with at Christmas; the flint-lock in time passed by modification into the percussion-lock, which is now changing its old-fashioned arrangement to be adapted from muzzle-loading to breech-loading. The medieval astrolabe passed into the quadrant, now discarded in its turn by the seaman, who uses the more delicate sextant, and so it is through the history of one art and instrument after another. Such examples of progression are known to us as direct history, but so thoroughly is this notion of development at home in our minds, that by means of it we reconstruct lost history without scruple, trusting to general knowledge of the principles of human thought and action as a guide in putting the facts in their proper order. Whether chronicle speaks or is silent on the point, no one comparing a long-bow and a cross-bow would doubt that the cross-bow was a development arising from the simpler instrument.

* * *

And thus, in the other branches of our history, there will come again and again into view series of facts which may be consistently arranged as having followed one another in a particular order of development, but which will hardly bear being turned round and made to follow in reversed order. Such for instance are the facts I have here brought forward in a chapter on the Art of Counting, which tend to prove that as to this point of culture at least, savage tribes reached their position by learning and not by unlearning, by elevation from a lower rather than by degradation from a higher state.

Among evidence aiding us to trace the course which the civilization of the world has actually followed, is that great class of facts to denote which I have found it convenient to introduce the term "survivals." These are processes, customs, opinions, and so forth, which have been carried on by force of habit into a new state of society different from that which they had in their original home, and they thus remain as proofs and examples of an older condition of culture out of which has never been evolved.

* * *

The serious business of ancient society may be seen to sink into the sport of later generations, and its serious belief to linger on in nursery folk-lore, while superseded habits of old-world life may be modified into new-world forms still powerful for good and evil. Sometimes old thoughts and practices will burst out afresh, to the amazement of a world that thought them, long since dead or dying; here survival passes into revival, as has lately happened in so remarkable a way in the history of modern spiritualism, a subject full of instruction from the ethnographer's point of view. The study of the principles of survival has, indeed, no small practical importance, for most of what we call superstition is included within survival, and in this way lies open to the attack of its deadliest enemy, a reasonable explanation. Insignificant, moreover, as multitudes of the facts of survival are in themselves, their study is so effective for tracing the course of the historical development through which alone it is possible to understand their meaning, that it becomes a vital point of ethnographic research to gain the clearest possible insight into their nature. This importance must justify the detail here devoted to an examination of survival, on the evidence of such games, popular sayings, customs, superstitions, and the like, as may serve well to bring into view the manner of its operation.

Progress, degradation, survival, revival, modification, are all modes of the connexion that binds together the complex network of civilization. It needs but a glance into the trivial details of our own daily life to set us thinking how far we are really in its originators, and how far but the transmitters and modifiers of the results of long past ages.

* * *

Nowhere, perhaps, are broad views of historical development more needed than in the study of religion. Notwithstanding all that has been written to make the world acquainted with the lower theologies, the popular ideas of their place in history and their relation to the faiths of higher nations are still of the medieval type. It is wonderful to contrast some missionary journals with Max Muller's Essays, and to set the unappreciating hatred and ridicule that is lavished by narrow hostile zeal on Brahmanism, Buddhism, Zoroastrism, besides the catholic sympathy with which deep and wide knowledge can survey those ancient and noble phases of man's religious consciousness; nor, because the religions of savage tribes may be rude and primitive compared with the great Asiatic systems, do they lie too low for interest and even for respect. The question really lies between understanding and misunderstanding them. Few who will give their minds to master the general principles of savage religion will ever again think it ridiculous, or the knowledge of it superfluous to the rest of mankind. Far from its beliefs and practices being a rubbish-heap of miscellaneous folly, they are consistent and logical in so high a degree as to begin, as soon as even roughly classified, to display the principles of their formation and development; and these principles prove to be essentially rational, though working in a mental condition of intense and inveterate ignorance. It is with a sense of attempting an investigation which bears very closely on the current theology of our own day, that I have set myself to examine systematically, among the lower races, the development of Animism; that is to say, the doctrine of souls and other spiritual beings in general. More than half of the present work is occupied with a mass of evidence from all religions of the world, displaying the nature and meaning of this great element of the Philosophy of Religion, and tracing its transmission, expansion, restriction, modification, along the course of history into the midst of our own modern thought. Nor are the questions of small practical moment which have to be raised in a similar attempt to trace the development of certain prominent Rites and Ceremonies—customs so full of instruction as to the inmost powers of religion, whose outward expression and practical result they are.

* * *

Not merely as a matter of curious research, but as an important practical guide to the understanding of the present and the shaping of the future, the investigation into the origin and early development of civilization must be pushed on zealously. Every possible avenue of knowledge must be explored, every door tried to see if it is open. No kind of evidence need be left untouched on the score of remoteness or complexity, of minuteness or triviality. The tendency of modern enquiry is more and more towards the conclusion that if law is anywhere, it is everywhere. To despair of what a conscientious collection and study of facts may lead to, and to declare any problem insoluble because difficult and far off, is distinctly to be on the wrong side in science; and he who will choose a hopeless task may set himself to discover the limits of discovery. One remembers Comte starting in his account of astronomy with a remark on the necessary limitation of our knowledge of the stars; we conceive, he tells us, the possibility of determining their form, distance, size, and movement, whilst we should never by any method be able to study their chemical composition, their mineralogical structure, &c. Had the philosopher lived to see the application of spectrum analysis to this very problem, his proclamation of the dispiriting doctrine of necessary ignorance would perhaps have been recanted in favour of a more hopeful view. And it seems to be with the philosophy of remote human life somewhat as with the study of the nature of the celestial bodies.

The process to be made out in the early stages of our mental evolution lie distant from us in time as the stars lie distant from us in space, but the laws of the universe are not limited with the direct observation of our senses. There is vast material to be used in our enquiry; many workers are now busied in bringing this material into shape, though little may have yet been done in proportion to what remains to do; and already it seems not too much to say that the vague outlines of a philosophy of primeval history are beginning to come within our view.

QUERIES

- What are the reasons Tylor presents for the "uniformities" of culture?
- Why does Tylor assert that the cultural correspondences of mankind undercut racial explanations of human behavioral differences?
- Tylor provides an interesting discussion regarding the relationship between culture and the individual (see pp. 6–7). What does this imply for anthropological inquiry?
- Define "survivals." What are some examples of survivals in modern American culture? According to Tylor, why are survivals important sources of information for anthropology?

CONNECTIONS

- How would Franz Boas respond to Tylor's assertion that similar cultural practices in different human societies indicated the existence of "uniform causes"?
- Contrast Tylor's definition of culture with the model of culture presented by Leslie White.
- How would Marvin Harris react to Tylor's attempt to explain the evolution of religious concepts?

2

Lewis Henry Morgan

INTRODUCTION

The following selection from *Ancient Society* written by American anthropologist Lewis Henry Morgan (1818–1881) is a classic example of 19th century cultural evolution, with all its virtues and failings (Moore 2008:25–29). Morgan presents a vision of human society as having progressed through prehistory through stages of development or what he called "ethnical periods" consisting of three major stages: Savagery, Barbarism, and Civilization. Savagery and Barbarism are further divided into subphases—"lower," "middle," and "upper"—used in a geological sense to denote a relative sequence of progressive changes. Although such terms may imply prejudice to a modern reader, Morgan intended terms like "Savagery" and "Barbarism" to imply a specific set of associated traits rather than gross bigotries. In fact, a careful reading of *Ancient Society* leads to understanding it as a progressive vision of human variations.

Ancient Society is progressive on multiple levels. First, Morgan views human history as marked by the "slow accumulations" of knowledge and innovations gained through experience. Instead of a decline from Eden or similar past Golden Age, Morgan argues that history is marked by the cumulative developments and is characterized by progress. Second, our ancestors employed a brain that is essentially the same as that of modern humans. (When Morgan wrote, there were no known fossils of any recognized hominids other than that of Homo sapiens.) More importantly, all living humans have essentially the same brain—and this is one of Morgan's important points—including members of different races. In an era when variations in human societies were frequently explained in terms of race, Morgan dismissed such racial explanations. Therefore Morgan discounts two sets of theories of human behavioral differences: theories of degradation and racial theories.

What, then, accounts for the differences in human societies? Morgan argues that all human societies have passed through different stages of cultural progress; the ancestors of the most civilized humans were once savages and barbarians. (As Morgan observes, even with the 19th century's limited archaeological record, one could infer this from certain historical cases—such as the fact the civilization of Victorian England was derived in part from the barbaric tribes of Britons the Romans encountered in the first century AD.) Some societies have progressed through the entire evolutionary sequence, while others have developed only to certain stages. Morgan does not really explain why some societies have progressed to civilization and others have not, but the important point is this: All societies—savage, barbarian or civilized—are representatives of the history of human progress.

This progress occurred along multiple dimensions, as Morgan enumerates: (1) subsistence, (2) government, (3) language, (4) the family (or kinship), (5) religion, (6) house life and architecture, and (7) property. These dimensions are causally linked. For example, the development of agriculture results in changes in ideas about property, leading to modifications in kinship systems that emphasize lineal descent and the inheritance of property (see Moore 2008:21–25). Changes in concepts of property result in new territorially-based forms of government. Even religious ideas may be linked to changes in subsistence. (The Christian concept "The Lord is my Shepherd" is meaningless unless you have domesticated sheep.) In such ways, Morgan offers a theoretical model that is progressive and materialist.

These are some of the virtues of Morgan's approach; what, then, are its failings? There are several, but the major one is this: Morgan assumed that different societies were fossilized remnants of earlier stages of cultural evolution (see Moore 2008:28–29). Rather than interpreting such differences as the product of different historical circumstances, environmental variations, or other factors, Morgan assumed that social differences were the remnants of stages of unilineal cultural evolution. This analytical flaw was seized upon by Franz Boas and his students (Moore 2008:34, 40–41), and it is the major reason that evolutionary approaches in anthropology would be discredited until the mid-20th century.

PRIMARY TEXT: *ANCIENT SOCIETY*

Editor's note: Originally published 1877.

Ethnical Periods

The latest investigations respecting the early condition of the human race are tending to the conclusion that mankind commenced their career at the bottom of the scale and worked their way up from savagery to civilization through the slow accumulations of experimental knowledge.

As it is undeniable that portions of the human family have existed in a state of savagery, other portions in a state of barbarism, and still other portions in a state of civilization, it seems equally so that these three distinct conditions are connected with each other in a natural as well as necessary sequence of progress. Moreover, that this sequence has been historically true of the entire human family, up to the status attained by each branch respectively, is rendered probable by the conditions under which all progress occurs, and by the known advancement of several branches of the family through two or more of these conditions. An attempt will be made in the following pages to bring forward additional evidence of the rudeness of the early condition of mankind, of the gradual evolution of their mental and moral powers through experience, and of their protracted struggle with opposing obstacles while winning their way to civilization. It will be drawn in part, from the great sequence of inventions and discoveries which stretches along the entire pathway of human progress; but chiefly from domestic institutions, which express the growth of certain ideas and passions. As we re-ascend along the several lines of progress toward the primitive ages of mankind, and eliminate one after the other, in the order in which they appeared, inventions and discoveries on the one hand, and institutions on the other, we are enabled to perceive that the former stand to each other in progressive, and the latter in unfolding relations. While the former class have had a connection, more or less direct, the latter have been developed from a few primary germs of thought. Modern institutions plant their roots in the period of barbarism, into which their germs were transmitted from the previous period of savagery. They have had a lineal descent through the ages, with the streams of the blood, as well as a logical development. Two independent lines of investigations thus invite our attention. The one leads through inventions and discoveries, and the other through primary institutions. With the knowledge gained therefrom, we may hope to indicate the principal stages of human development. The proofs to be adduced will be drawn chiefly from domestic institutions; the references to achievements more strictly intellectual being general as well as subordinate.

The facts indicate the gradual formation and subsequent development of certain ideas, passions, and aspirations. Those which hold the most prominent positions may be generalized as growths of the particular ideas with which they severally stand connected. Apart from inventions and discoveries they are the following:

I.	Subsistence	IV.	The Family	VII.	Property
II.	Government	V.	Religion		
III.	Language	VI.	House Life and Architecture		

First. Subsistence has been increased and perfected by a series of successive arts, introduced at long intervals of time, and connected more or less directly with inventions and discoveries.

Second. The germ of government must be sought in the organization into gentes in the Status of savagery; and followed down, through advancing forms of this institution, to the establishment of political society.

Third. Human speech seems to have been developed from the rudest and simplest forms of expression. Gesture or sign language, as intimated by Lucretius, must have preceded articulate language, as thought preceded speech. The monosyllabical preceded the syllabical, as the latter did that of concrete words. Human intelligence, unconscious of design, evolved articulate language by utilizing the vocal sounds. This great subject, a department of knowledge by itself, does not fall within the scope of the present investigation.

Fourth. With respect to the family, the stages of its growth are embodied in systems of consanguinity and affinity, and in usages relating to marriage, by means of which, collectively, the family can be definitely traced through several successive forms.

Fifth. The growth of religious ideas is environed with such intrinsic difficulties that it may never receive a perfectly satisfactory exposition. Religion deals so largely with the imaginative and emotional nature, and consequently with such uncertain elements of knowledge, that all primitive religions are grotesque and to some extent unintelligible. This subject also falls without the plan of this work excepting as it may prompt incidental suggestions.

Sixth. House architecture, which connects itself with the form of the family and the plan of domestic life, affords a tolerably complete illustration of progress from savagery to civilization. Its growth can be traced from the hut of the savage, through the communal houses of the barbarians, to the house of the single family of civilized nations, with all the successive links by which one extreme is connected with the other. This subject will be noticed incidentally.

Lastly. The idea of property was slowly formed in the human mind, remaining nascent and feeble through immense periods of time. Springing into life in savagery, it required all the experience of this period and of the subsequent period of barbarism to develop the germ, and to prepare the human brain for the acceptance of its controlling influence. Its dominance as passion over all other passions marks the commencement of civilization. It not only led mankind to overcome the obstacles which delayed civilization, but to establish political society on the basis of territory and property. A critical knowledge of the evolution of the idea of property would embody, in some respects, the most remarkable portion of the mental history of mankind.

It will be my object to present some evidence of human progress along these several lines, and through successive ethnical periods, as it is revealed by inventions and discoveries, and by the growth of the ideas of government, of the family, and of property.

It may be here premised that all forms of government are reducible to two general plans, using the word plan in its scientific sense. In their bases the two are fundamentally distinct. The first, in the order of time, is founded upon persons, and upon relations purely personal, and may be distinguished as a society (*societas*). The gens is the unit of this organization; giving as the successive stages of integration, in the archaic period, the gens, the phratry, the tribe, and the confederacy of tribes, which constituted a people or nation (*populus*). At a later period a coalescence of tribes in the same area into a nation took the place of a confederacy of tribes occupying independent areas. Such, through prolonged ages, after the gens appeared, was the substantially universal organization of ancient society; and it remained among the Greeks and Romans after civilization supervened. The second is founded upon territory and upon property, and may be distinguished as a state (*civitas*). The township or ward, circumscribed by metes and bounds, with the property it contains, is the basis or unit of the latter, and political society is the result. Political society is organized upon territorial areas, and deals with property as well as with persons through territorial relations. The successive stages of integration are the township or ward, which is the unit of organization; the county or province, which is an aggregation of townships or wards; and the national domain or territory, which is an aggregation of counties or provinces; the people of each of which are organized into a body politic. It taxed the Greeks and Romans to the extent of their capacities, after they had gained civilization, to invent the deme or township and the city ward; and thus inaugurate the second great plan of government, which remains among civilized nations to the present hour. In ancient society this territorial plan was unknown. When it came in it fixed the boundary line between ancient and modern society as the distinction will be recognized in these pages.

It may be further observed that the domestic institutions of the barbarous, and even of the savage ancestors of man-kind, are still exemplified in portions of the human family with such completeness that, with the exception of the strictly primitive period, the several stages of this progress are tolerably well preserved. They are seen in the organization of society upon the basis of sex, then upon the basis of kin, and finally upon the basis of territory; through the successive forms of marriage and of the family, with the systems of consanguinity thereby created; through house life and architecture; and through progress in usages with respect to the ownership and inheritance of property.

The theory of human degradation to explain the existence of savages and of barbarians is no longer tenable. It came in as a corollary from the Mosaic cosmogony, and was acquiesced in from a supposed necessity which no longer exists. As a theory, it is not only incapable of explaining the existence of savages, but it is without support in the facts of human experience.

The remote ancestors of the Aryan nations presumptively passed through an experience similar to that of existing barbarous and savage tribes. Though the experience of these nations embodies all the information necessary to illustrate the periods of civilization, both ancient and modern, together with a part of that in the later period of barbarism, their anterior experience must be deduced, in the main, from the traceable connection between the elements of their existing institutions and inventions, and similar elements still preserved in those of savage and barbarous tribes.

It may be remarked finally that the experience of mankind has run in nearly uniform channels; that human necessities in similar conditions have been substantially the same; and that the operations of the mental principle have been uniform in virtue of the specific identity of the brain of all the races of mankind. This, however, is but a part of the explanation of uniformity in results. The germs of the principal institutions and arts of life were developed while man was still a savage. To a very great extent the experience of the subsequent periods of barbarism and of civilization has been expended in the further development of these original conceptions. Wherever a connection can be traced on different continents between a present institution and a common germ, the derivation of the people themselves from a common original stock is implied.

The discussion of these several classes of facts will be facilitated by the establishment of a certain number of Ethnical Periods; each representing a distinct condition of society, and distinguishable by a mode of life peculiar to itself. The terms "Age of Stone," "of Bronze," and "of Iron," introduced by Danish archaeologists, have been extremely useful for certain purposes, and will remain so for the classification of objects of ancient art; but the progress of knowledge has rendered other and different subdivisions necessary. Stone implements were not entirely laid aside with the introduction of tools of iron, nor of those of bronze. The invention of the process of smelting iron ore created an ethnical epoch, yet we could scarcely date another from the production of bronze. Moreover, since the period of stone implements overlaps those of bronze and of iron, and since that of bronze also overlaps that of iron, they are not capable of a circumscription that would have each independent and distinct.

It is probable that the successive arts of subsistence which arose at long intervals will ultimately, from the great influence they must have exercised upon the condition of mankind, afford the most satisfactory bases for these divisions. But investigation has not been carried far enough in this direction to yield the necessary information. With our present knowledge the main result can be attained by selecting such other inventions or discoveries as will afford sufficient tests of progress to characterize the commencement of successive ethnical periods. Even though accepted as provisional, these periods will he found convenient, and useful. Each of those about to be proposed will be found to cover a distinct culture, and to represent a particular mode of life.

The period of savagery, of the early part of which very little is known, may be divided, provisionally, into three sub-periods. These may be named respectively the Older, the Middle, and the Later period of savagery; and the condition of society in each, respectively, may be distinguished as the Lower, the Middle, and the Upper Status of savagery.

In like manner, the period of barbarism divides naturally into three sub-periods, which will be called, respectively, the Older, the Middle, and the Later period of barbarism; and the condition of society in each, respectively, will be distinguished as the Lower, the Middle, and the Upper Status of barbarism.

It is difficult, if not impossible, to find such tests of progress to mark the commencement of these several periods as will be found absolute in their application, and without exceptions upon all the continents. Neither is it necessary, for the purpose in hand, that exceptions should not exist. It will be sufficient if the principal tribes of mankind can be classified, according to the degree of their relative progress, into conditions which can be recognized as distinct.

I. *Lower Status of Savagery.* This period commenced with the infancy of the human race, and may be said to have ended with the acquisition of fish subsistence and of knowledge of the use of fire. Mankind were then living in their original restricted habitat and subsisting upon fruits and nuts. The commencement of articulate speech belongs to this period. No exemplification of tribes of mankind in this condition remained to the historical period.

II. *Middle Status of Savagery*. It commenced with the acquisition of fish subsistence and knowledge of the use of fire, and ended with the invention of the bow and arrow. Mankind, while in this condition, spread from their original habitat over the greater portion of the earth's surface. Among tribes still existing, it will leave in the Middle Status of savagery, for example, the Australians and the greater part of the Polynesians when discovered. It will be sufficient to give one or more exemplifications of each status.

III. *Upper Status of Savagery*. It commenced with the invention of the bow and arrow, and ended with the invention of the art of pottery. It leaves in the Upper Status of Savagery the Athapascan tribes of the Hudson's Bay Territory, the tribes of the valley of the Columbia, and certain coast tribes of North and South America; but with relation to the time of their discovery. This closes the period of Savagery.

IV. *Lower Status of Barbarism*. The invention or practice of the art of pottery, all things considered, is probably the most effective and conclusive test that can be selected to fix a boundary line, necessarily arbitrary, between savagery and barbarism. The distinctness of the two conditions has long been recognized, but no criterion of progress out of the former into the latter has hitherto been brought forward. All such tribes, then, as never attained to the art of pottery will be classed as savages, and those possessing this art, but who never attained a phonetic alphabet and the use of writing will be classed as barbarians. The first sub-period of barbarism commenced with the manufacture of pottery, whether by original invention or adoption. In finding its termination, and the commencement of the Middle Status, a difficulty is encountered in the unequal endowments of the two hemispheres, which began to be influential upon human affairs after the period of savagery, had passed. It may be met, however, by the adoption of equivalents. In the Eastern hemisphere, the domestication of animals, and the Western, the cultivation of maize and plants by irrigation, together with the use of adobe-brick and stone in house building have been selected as sufficient evidence of progress to work a transition out of the Lower and into the Middle Status of barbarism. It leaves, for example, in the Lower Status, the Indian tribes of the United States east of the Missouri River, and such tribes of Europe and Asia as practiced the art of pottery, but, were without domestic animals.

V. *Middle Status of Barbarism*. It commenced with the domestication of animals in the Eastern hemisphere, and in the Western with cultivation by irrigation and with the use of adobe brick and stone in architecture, as shown. Its termination may be fixed with the invention of the process of smelting iron ore. This places in the Middle Status, for example, the Village Indians of New Mexico, Mexico, Central America and Peru, and such tribes in the Eastern hemisphere as possessed domestic animals, but were without a knowledge of iron. The ancient Britons, although familiar with the use of iron, fairly belong in this connection. The vicinity of more advanced continental tribes had advanced the arts of life among them far beyond the state of development of their domestic institutions.

VI. *Upper Status of Barbarism.* It commenced with the manufacture of iron, and ended with the invention of a phonetic alphabet and the use of writing in literary composition. Here civilization begins. This leaves in the Upper Status, for example, the Grecian tribes of the Homeric age, the Italian tribes shortly before the founding of Rome, and the Germanic tribes of the time of Cesar.

VII. *Status of Civilization.* It commenced, as stated, with the use of a phonetic alphabet and the production of literary records, and divides into Ancient and Modern. As an equivalent, hieroglyphical writing upon stone may be admitted.

Recapitulation

Periods

I. Older Period of Savagery
II. Middle Period of Savagery
III. Later Period of Savagery
IV. Older Period of Barbarism
V. Middle Period of Barbarism
VI. Later Period of Barbarism

Conditions

I. Lower Status of Savagery
II. Middle Status of Savagery
III. Upper Status of Savagery
IV. Lower Status of Barbarism
V. Middle Status of Barbarism
VI. Upper Status of Barbarism
VII. Status of Civilization

I. *Lower Status of Savagery, from the Infancy of the Human Race to the commencement of the next Period.*

II. *Middle Status of Savagery, from the acquisition of a fish subsistence and a knowledge of the use of fire to etc.*

III. *Upper Status of Savagery, from the Invention of the Bow and Arrow, to etc.*

IV. *Lower Status of Barbarism, from the Invention of the Art of Pottery, to etc.*

V. *Middle Status of Barbarism, from the Domestication of animals on the Eastern hemisphere, and in the Western from the cultivation of maize and plants by Irrigation, with the use of adobe-brick and stone, to etc.*

VI. *Upper Status of Barbarism, from the Invention of the process of Smelting Iron Ore, with the use of iron tools, to etc.*

VII. *Status of Civilization, from the Invention of a Phonetic Alphabet, with the use of writing, to the present time.*

Each of these periods has a distinct culture and exhibits a mode of life more or less special and peculiar to itself. This specialization of ethnical periods renders it possible to treat a particular society according to its condition of relative advancement, and to make it a subject of independent study and discussion. It does not affect the main result that different tribes and nations on the same continent, and even of the same linguistic family, are

in different conditions at the same time, since for our purpose the condition of each is the material fact, the time being immaterial.

* * *

Another advantage of fixing definite ethnical periods is the direction of special
investigation to those tribes and nations which afford the best exemplification
of each status, with the view of making each both standard and illustrative.
Some tribes and families have been left in geographical isolation to work out
the problems of progress by original mental effort; and have, consequently, retained their arts and institutions pure and homogeneous; while those of other
tribes and nations have been adulterated through external influence. Thus,
while Africa was and is an ethnical chaos of savagery and barbarism, Australia
and Polynesia were in savagery, pure and simple, with the arts and institutions
belonging to that condition. In the like manner, the Indian family of America,
unlike any other existing family, exemplified the condition of mankind in
three successive ethnical periods. In the undisturbed possession of a great, continent, of common descent, and with homogeneous institutions, they illustrated, when discovered, each of these conditions, and especially those of the
Lower and of the Middle Status of barbarism, more elaborately and completely
than any other portion of mankind. The far northern Indians and some of the
coast tribes of North and South America were in the Upper Status of savagery;
the partially Village Indians east of the Mississippi were in the Lower Status of
barbarism, and the Village Indians of North and South America were in the
Middle Status. Such an opportunity to recover full and minute information of
the course of human experience and progress in developing their arts and institutions through these successive conditions has not been offered within the
historical period. It must be added that it has been indifferently improved. Our
greatest deficiencies relate to the last period named.

Differences in the culture of the same period in the Eastern and Western
hemispheres undoubtedly existed in consequence of the unequal endowments of the continents; but the condition of society in the corresponding
status must have been, in the main, substantially similar.

The ancestors of the Grecian, Roman, and German tribes passed through
the stages we have indicated, in the midst of the last of which the light of
history fell upon them. Their differentiation from the undistinguishable
mass of barbarians did not occur, probably, earlier than the commencement of the Middle Period of barbarism. The experience of these tribes has
been lost, with the exception of so much as is represented by the institutions, inventions and discoveries which they had brought with them, and
possessed when they first came under historical observation. The Grecian,
and Latin tribes of the Homeric and Romulian periods afford the highest
exemplification of the Upper Status of barbarism. Their institutions were

and other methods. The assemblage of these on his original map makes this bewildering in its complexity. Of particular interest are the frequent limitations of a particular method to a particular social class, so that several methods coexist in one tribe, and the same method has different applications in successive tribes. Thus, river burial is sometimes reserved for chiefs, sometimes for the drowned, sometimes is the normal practice of a group. Tree and platform burial is in certain populations restricted respectively to musicians, magicians, the bewitched, the lightning struck, criminals, and kings; cremation is generally reserved for criminals, but also occurs as the usual practice; exposure is variously in usage, according to tribe, for the corpses of criminals, slaves, children, the common people, the entire population. These variations between adjacent peoples, and the numerous instances of coexistence of several practices within one population, constitute a powerful argument for instability. They virtually prove change where ordinary intertribal distributions only indicate it. A tribe following three or four methods, and in contact with tribes that follow other methods or employ the same methods for different populational groups, can scarcely be likely to adhere long to its customs of the moment without alteration.

These instances perhaps suffice to establish that disposal of the dead often shows a fluctuating history instead of the relative stability which at first judgment might attribute to it. From this follows the generalization that intensity of feeling regarding any institution is likely to be a poor criterion, if any, of its permanence. Emotion evidently attaches secondarily to social behavior much as thought does. The completeness and plausibility of a rationalization are no index of the reality of its purported motivation; the immediacy and intensity of emotion concerning a cultural practice are no index of the origin or durability of that practice. The stimulus of such an emotion may be a physiologic or "natural" situation, to which a social practice also relates. The emotion or some of it promptly adheres to the practice. But it has not caused the practice; it evidently does not maintain it; and it attaches itself to a new practice as soon as this, from causes which may be relatively uncharged with emotion, displaces the older practice.

The further question whether affect-laden practices are not perhaps actually more unstable than emotionally low-toned ones, cannot be answered summarily. There are certainly instances of mortuary habits that have continued for long times with only minor modification: in dynastic Egypt, for instance; in most of Europe during most of the Neolithic; in all but the fringe of Pueblo culture.[6]

More fruitful, perhaps, is a consideration of the type of motivation or historic causality that influences modes of disposal of the dead. Here it appears

---

[6] A. V. Kidder, An Introduction to the Study of Southwestern Archaeology, Phillips Academy, Andover, 1924.

that a feature which is pretty likely to characterize mortuary practices is their dissociation from certain large blocks of cultural activity, especially those having to do with material and economic life, its subsistence and mechanical aspects. That is, disposal of the dead has little connection with that part of behavior which relates to the biological or primary social necessities, with those activities which are a frequent or constant portion of living and therefore tend to become interadapted and dependent one on the other. On the other hand, disposal of the dead also does not lend itself to any great degree of integration with domains of behavior which are susceptible of formalization and codification, like law, much of religion, and social organization. Standing apart, therefore, both from the basic type of activities which mostly regulate themselves unconsciously, and from those which largely involve relations of persons and therefore become socially conscious and systematized, disposal of the dead falls rather into a class with fashions, than with either customs or folkways on the one hand, or institutions on the other. It does not readily enter intrinsically into the inevitable integrations of the bases of life nor into attempts at wider systems. In their relative isolation or detachment from the remainder of culture, their rather high degree of entry into consciousness, and their tendency to strong emotional toning, social practices of disposing of the dead are of a kind with fashions of dress, luxury, and etiquette.

It may be added that in so far as mortuary practices may be accepted as partaking of the nature of fashions, they will tend to discredit certain interpretations based on them. Rivers' contention that the variety of Australian practices is to be construed as due to intrusion of migrant groups certainly falls to the ground. Schmidt's employment of such practices as indicative of the spread of hypothetical blocks or complexes of culture becomes less convincing. And Küsters' inquiry into motivation, objectively founded as part of it is, can hardly be followed all the way if fashion impulses have moulded methods of disposing of the dead as extensively as it would seem they have.

QUERIES

- Kroeber observes that in Native California, the geographical distribution of burial vs. cremation practices did not correlate with other regional differences such as topography, climate, or biogeographical variations. Does the distribution of burying vs. cremating correlate with any spatial patterns?
- Kroeber discusses the hypothesis that the more significant a culture practice the less it will tend to vary, what he calls a "positive relation between . . . the intensity of an emotion and its manifestation in behavior." What does Kroeber conclude about this hypothesis?

- Concluding that "disposal of the dead falls rather into a class with fashions," Kroeber concludes that funerary practices are not tightly integrated with other dimensions of culture. Consider the variations in funerary practices in modern American culture (for example, coffin burials in cemeteries, organ donation and partial burials, cremation with ashes in urns, burial at sea, cremation and spreading the ashes); do you think Kroeber was correct?

CONNECTIONS

- How does Kroeber's approach to variations in funerary customs differ from Edward Tylor's discussion of survivals and their implications for reconstructing earlier stages of cultural development?
- If Kroeber argues that funerary customs are simply matters of fashion, how would this contrast with Ruth Benedict's idea that cultures are "more or less coherent" integrated wholes?
- Drawing on his theory of cultural materialism, how would Marvin Harris explain the variation in funerary practices that Kroeber describes?

PRIMARY TEXT: *EIGHTEEN PROFESSIONS*

Reproduced by permission of the American Anthropological Association from *American Anthropologist*, Vol. 17 (2) Apr.–Jun. 1915, pp. 283–288. www.aaanet.org. Not for sale or further reproduction.

Anthropology today includes two studies which fundamental differences of aim and method render irreconcilable. One of these branches is biological and psychological; the other, social or historical.

There is a third field, the special province of anthropology, concerned with the relation of biological and social factors. This is no-man's-land, and therefore used as a picnic-ground by whosoever prefers pleasure excursions to the work of cultivating a patch of understanding. Some day this tract will also be surveyed, fenced, and improved. Biological science already claims it; but the title remains to be established. For the present, the labor in hand is the delimitation of the scope of history from that of science.

In what follows, historical anthropology, history, and sociology are referred to as history. Physical anthropology and psychology are included in biology.

1. *The aim of history is to know the relations of social facts to the whole of civilization.* Civilization means civilization itself, not its impulses. Relation is actual connection, not cause.

2. *The material studied by history is not man, but his works.* It is not men, but the results of their deeds, the manifestations of their activities, that are the subject of historical inquiry.

3. *Civilization, though carried by men and existing through them, is an entity in itself, and of another order from life.* History is not concerned with the agencies producing civilization, but with civilization as such. The causes are the business of the psychologist. The entity civilization has intrinsically nothing to do with individual men nor with the aggregates of men on whom it rests. It springs from the organic, but is independent of it. The mental processes of groups of men are, after all, only the collected processes of individuals reacting under certain special stimuli. Collective psychology is therefore ultimately resolvable into individual human psychology, just as this in turn is resolvable into organic psychology and physiology. But history deals with material which is essentially non-individual and integrally social. History is not concerned with the relations of civilization to men or organisms, but with the interrelations of civilization. The psychic organization of man in the abstract does not exist for it, save as something given directly and more or less completely to the student's consciousness. The uncivilized man does not exist; if he did, he would mean nothing to the historian. Even civilized man is none of history's business; its sphere is the civilization of which man is the necessary basis but which is inevitable once this basis exists.

4. *A certain mental constitution of man must be assumed by the historian, but may not be used by him as a resolution of social phenomena.* The historian can and should obtain for himself the needed interpretation of man's mind from familiarity with social facts and the direct application to them of his own psychic activities. This interpretation is likely to be of service in proportion as it emanates immediately from himself and not from the formulated laws of the biological psychologist. Whether an understanding of civilization will or will not help the psychologist is for the latter to determine.

5. *True instincts lie at the bottom and origin of social phenomena, but cannot be considered or dealt with by history.* History begins where instincts commence to be expressed in social facts.

6. *The personal or individual has no historical value save as illustration.* Ethnological genealogies are valuable material. So are the actions of conspicuous historical personages. But their dramatic, anecdotic, or biographic recital is biographic or fictional art, or possibly psychology, not history.

7. *Geography, or physical environment, is material made use of by civilization, not a factor shaping or explaining civilization.* Civilization reacts to civilization, not to geography. For the historian, geography does not act

on civilization, but civilization incorporates geographical circumstances. Agriculture presupposes a climate able to sustain agriculture, and modifies itself according to climatic conditions. It is not caused by climate. The understanding of agricultural activity is to be sought in the other phenomena of civilization affecting it.

8. *The absolute equality and identity of all human races and strains as carriers of civilization must be assumed by the historian.* The identity has not been proved nor has it been disproved. It remains to be established, or to be limited, by observations directed to this end, perhaps only by experiments. The historical and social influences affecting every race and every large group of persons are closely intertwined with the alleged biological and hereditary ones, and have never yet been sufficiently separated to allow demonstration of the actual efficiency of either. All opinions on this point are only convictions falsely fortified by subjectively interpreted evidence. The biologist dealing with man must assume at least some hereditary differences, and often does assume biological factors as the only ones existent. The historian, until such differences are established and exactly defined, must assume their non-existence. If he does not base his studies on this assumption, his work becomes a vitiated mixture of history and biology.

9. *Heredity cannot be allowed to have acted any part in history.* Individual hereditary differences undoubtedly exist, but are not historical material because they are individual. Hereditary differences between human groups may ultimately be established, but like geography must in that event be converted into material acted upon by the force of civilization, not treated as causes of civilization.

10. *Heredity by acquirement is equally a biological and historical monstrosity.* This naive explanation may be eliminated on the findings of biology; but should biology ever determine that such heredity operates through a mechanism as yet undiscovered, this heredity must nevertheless be disregarded by history together with congenital heredity. In the present stage of understanding, heredity by acquirement is only too often the cherished inclination of those who confuse their biological thinking by the introduction of social aspects, and of those who confound history by deceiving themselves that they are turning it into biology.

11. *Selection and other factors of organic evolution cannot be admitted as affecting civilization.* It is actually unproved that the processes of organic evolution are materially influencing civilization or that they have influenced it. Civilization obviously introduces an important factor which is practically or entirely lacking in the existence of animals and plants, and which must at least largely neutralize the operation of any kind of selection. Prehistoric archeology shows with certainty that civilization has changed profoundly without accompanying material

alterations in the human organism. Even so far as biological evolution may ultimately be proved in greater or less degree for man, a correspondence between organic types and civilizational forms will have to be definitely established before history can concern itself with these organic types or their changes.

12. *The so-called savage is no transition between the animal and the scientifically educated man. All men are totally civilized.* All animals are totally uncivilized because they are almost totally uncivilizable. The connecting condition, which it is universally believed must have existed, is entirely unknown. If ever it becomes known, it can furnish to the historian only an introduction to history. There is no higher and lower in civilization for the historian. The ranging of the portions of civilization in any sequence, save the actual one of time, place, and connection, is normally misleading and always valueless. The estimation of the adult savage as similar to the modern European child is superficial and prevents his proper appreciation either biologically or historically.

13. *There are no social species or standard cultural types or stages.* A social species in history rests on false analogy with organic species. A stage in civilization is merely a preconception made plausible by arbitrarily selected facts.

14. *There is no ethnic mind, but only civilization.* There are only individual minds. When these react on each other cumulatively, the process is merely physiological. The single ethnic or social existence is civilization, which biologically is resolvable purely into a product of physiological forces, and historically is the only and untranscendable entity.

15. *There are no laws in history similar to the laws of physico-chemical science.* All asserted civilizational laws are at most tendencies, which, however determinable, are not permanent quantitative expressions. Nor are such tendencies the substitute which history has for the laws of science. History need not deny them and may have to recognize them, but their formulation is not its end.

16. *History deals with conditions sine qua non, not with causes.* The relations between civilizational phenomena are relations of sequence, not of effect. The principles of mechanical causality, emanating from the underlying biological sciences, are applicable to individual and collective psychology. Applied to history, they convert it into psychology. An insistence that all treatment of civilizational data should be by the methods of mechanical causality is equivalent to a denial of the valid existence of history as a subject of study. The only antecedents of historical phenomena are historical phenomena.

17. *The causality of history is teleological.* Psychological causes are mechanical. For history, psychology is assumable, not demonstrable. To

make the object of historical study the proving of the fundamental identity of the human mind by endless examples is as tedious as barren. If the process of civilization seems the worthwhile end of knowledge of civilization, it must be sought as a process distinct from that of mechanical causality, or the result will be a reintegration that is not history. Teleology of course does not suggest theology to those free from the influence of theology. The teleology of history involves the absolute conditioning of historical events by other historical events. This causality of history is as completely unknown and unused as chemical causality was a thousand and physical causality three thousand years ago.

18. *In fine,*[1] *the determinations and methods of biological, psychological, or natural science do not exist for history, just as the results and the manner of operation of history are disregarded by consistent biological practice.* Most biologists have implicitly followed their aspect of this doctrine, but their consequent success has tempted many historians, especially sociologists, anthropologists, and theorists, to imitate them instead of pursuing their proper complementary method.

QUERIES

- What does Kroeber mean when he asserts, "The causality of history is teleological"?
- "All men are totally civilized," Kroeber wrote; explain what this implies for earlier theories of cultural evolution.
- According to Kroeber, why are the principles of natural selection irrelevant to understanding human culture?
- Kroeber insists that there are no stages in culture; on what grounds does he make this assertion?

CONNECTIONS

- Kroeber insists that cultural practices cannot be explained by reference to "the laws of physico-chemical science." How would—and did—Leslie White respond to such a theoretical position?
- Considering anthropology as a form of history, Kroeber proclaims that "the determinations and methods of biological, psychological, or natural science do not exist for history." How does this position contrast with Radcliffe-Brown's view of the methods and logics of social anthropology?

---

[1] Editor's note: For "In conclusion."

6

Ruth Benedict

INTRODUCTION

In the following article, American anthropologist Ruth Benedict (1887–1948) introduces a set of theoretical concepts she subsequently elaborated in her 1934 best-selling book, *Patterns of Culture* (see Moore 2008:78–87). Benedict argues that since its emergence in the mid-19th century, anthropology had obtained more complete sets of ethnographic data and these had implications for anthropological theory. In the beginning, anthropology relied on sketchy sources of ethnographic details—missionaries' letters, explorers' accounts, and diplomats' reports—that rarely presented a complete or unbiased view of another culture. Such accounts were mined by early anthropologists—like Tylor, Morgan, and others—for ethnographic details, presented as isolated traits with little cultural context. Such isolated traits could be arrayed conveniently into the evolutionary stages proposed by the Victorian evolutionists.

But in the early 20th century, more coherent programs of anthropological fieldwork began (see Moore 2008:62, 67–69, 135–36). With the development of rigorous standards and practices of anthropological research, Benedict observes, more complete ethnographic portraits emerged. These studies indicated that cultures had distinctive patterns or configurations, rather than merely being a hodgepodge of isolated traits.

Benedict argues that cultures are integrated according to central ideals or principles. Rather than a random assortment of isolated traits or functionally articulated by complementary purposes, cultures achieve a "more or less successful attainment of integrated behavior." Such values are encoded in distinctive worldviews and expressed in specific cultural practices, resulting in a cultural configuration or pattern.

As Benedict observes, such configurational approaches had been used by other scholars, but Benedict borrows two key concepts from philosopher Friedrich Nietzche: the Apollonian worldview—"the cultural pursuit of sobriety"—versus the Dionysian worldview, which "values excess as escape to an order of existence beyond that of the five senses." Drawing on her research among North American Indian groups, Benedict argues that the cultural practices of the so-called Pueblo Indians (the Hopi and Zuni) reflect an Apollonian worldview, whereas the Plains Indians (Blackfoot and Cheyenne) are Dionysian in their conceptions of existence. Such different configurations are based on core values that articulate and integrate cultural practices into more or less coherent patterns. For example, auto-sacrifice (what Benedict labels "self-torture") is pervasive in Plains ceremonies (mourning, vision quests), yet absent among the Pueblos—not because these ceremonial practices are different "traits" but because these practices reflect different worldviews. The Pueblos value the communality of the group, reject individual displays of power, and avoid disruptive impulses. The Plains embrace individual and violent displays of glory and loss, actively seek the transformative experience of visions, and honor the individual "will to power."

Of course, some individuals may find their personalities at cross-purposes with the core values of their own society. Such individuals are seen as deviants, but the self-aggrandizing individual classified as a deviant in Pueblo society could be a mainstream exemplary member in Plains society. It all depends on the core values, Benedict argues, that provide a coherent pattern to a culture. Such configurations must become the focus of anthropological investigation, Benedict insists, and this is what she did during the balance of her anthropological career (Moore 2008:78–80, 85–86).

PRIMARY TEXT: *CONFIGURATIONS OF CULTURE IN NORTH AMERICA*

Reproduced by permission of the American Anthropological Association from *American Anthropologist*, vol. 34 (1), 1932, pp. 1–27. www.aaanet.org. Not for sale or further reproduction.

In the past twenty-five years the fact of prime importance in anthropology has without doubt been the accumulation of a few full-length portraits of primitive peoples. It is hard to think back to a time when as yet the chance of reconstructing even a passable picture of any primitive tribe was limited to two or three regions, each of them beset with difficulties. The best accounts that were available were not the outcome of any purposeful inquiry on the part of students of custom, but of the lucky chances that had brought together a good observer and a striking culture, the records of Sahagun, for instance, or Codrington in Melanesia.[1]

The vast amount of available anthropological material was frankly anecdotal as in travelers' accounts, or schematically dissected and tabulated as in many ethnologists'. Under the circumstances general anthropological discussion of necessity had recourse, as in Tylor's day, to the comparative method, which is by definition anecdotal and schematic. It sought by collecting great series of observations detached from their context to build up "the" primitive mind, or "the" development of religion, or "the" history of marriage.

Out of the necessities of the same situation there flourished also the schools of strict diffusionists who made a virtue out of the limitations of materials at their disposal and operated solely with detached objects, never with their setting or function in the culture from which they came.

The growing dissatisfaction with these two dominant theoretical approaches of what we may well call the anecdotal period of ethnology has always been explicit in Boas' insistence upon exhaustive study of any primitive culture, and is today most clearly voiced by Malinowski. His vigor is directed against the diffusionist group rather than against the Frazers and the Westermarcks of the comparative method, but in his own work he insists always that anthropological theory must take into account not detached items but human cultures as organic and functioning wholes. He would have us realize that when a museum collection has been installed from the Niam-Niam or a monograph of like type has been published we still know in reality exactly nothing about them unless we know the way in which the arrangement of the house, the articles of dress, the rules of avoidance or of marriage, the ideas of the supernatural—how each object and culture trait, in other words, is employed in their native life. Malinowski, somewhat disappointingly, does not go on to the examination of these cultural wholes, but is content to conclude his argument with pointing out in each context that each trait functions in the total cultural complex, a conclusion which seems increasingly the beginning of inquiry rather than its peroration. For it is a position that leads directly to the necessity of investigating in what sort of a whole these traits are functioning, and what reference they bear to the total culture. In how far do the traits achieve an organic interrelation? Are the Leitmotivs in the world by which they may be integrated many or few? These questions the functionalists do not ask.

---

[1] Editor's note: Fray Bernardo Sahagun (1499–1590) was a Franciscan priest who provided detailed accounts of Aztec life immediately after the Spanish Conquest. R. H. Codrington (1830–1922) was a Church of England missionary and author of The Melanesians: Studies of Their Anthropology and Folklore (1891).

Now the fact that becomes increasingly apparent as full-length accounts of primitive peoples come from the press is that these cultures, though they are so overwhelmingly made up of disparate elements fortuitously assembled from all directions by diffusion, are none the less over and over again in different tribes integrated according to very different and individual patterns. The order that is achieved is not merely the reflection of the fact that each trait has a pragmatic function that it performs—which is much like a great discovery in physiology that the normal eye sees and the normally muscled hand grasps, or, still more exactly, the discovery that nothing exists in human life that mankind has not espoused and rationalized. The order is due rather to the circumstance that in these societies a principle has been set up according to which the assembled cultural material is made over into consistent patterns in accordance with certain inner necessities that have developed within the group. These syntheses are of various sorts. For some of them we have convenient terminology and for some we have not. But they are in each case the more or less successful attainment of integrated behavior, an attainment that is all the more striking for the anthropologist because of his knowledge of the scattered and hybrid materials out of which the integration has been achieved.

The proposition that cultures must be studied from this point of view and that it is crucial in an understanding even of our own cultural history has been put forward by the German school headed by Wilhelm Dilthey and popularly represented in English-speaking countries by Oswald Spengler in his *Untergang des Abendlandes*.[2] For this philosophical school, history is the succession of culturally organized philosophies of life, and philosophy is the study of these great readings of life. For Dilthey himself the emphasis is only secondarily and as it were accidentally on the configuration of culture itself to express these varied readings of life. His primary emphasis is upon these great interpretations as expressing the variety of existence and is directed against the assumption that any one of them can be final. He argues vigorously that essential configurations in philosophy are incommensurable and that their fundamental categories cannot be resolved the one into the other.

His most systematic study, the *Einleitung in die Geisteswissenschaften*,[3] is frankly historically descriptive. When he does become systematic, his groupings are not configurations at all but personality types in philosophy; he groups Democritus, Epicurus, Hobbes, and the French Encyclopedists as ex-

---

[2] Editor's note: Wilhem Dilthey (1833–1911) was a German philosopher who wrote on the natural and social sciences. Oswald Spengler (1880–1936) was a German philosopher and historian who argued for cyclical patterns in history; Spengler's work was translated into English as Decline of the West.

[3] Editor's note: Translated as Introduction to the Human Sciences (1989), R. Betranzos, trans. Detroit: Wayne State University Press.

emplifying his "materialist-positivist" type, over against which he sets a type of objective idealist and the idealist of freedom, both of them as eclectically selected from different nations and ages. He has, however, in his less systematic essays well characterized certain cultural attitudes significant in the period of Frederick the Great and in the medieval period, and he often makes use of cultural points. E. Spranger's elaboration of types is a priori and subjective, not drawn from the study of history.[4] He presents as his types the man of theory, economic man, aesthetic man, man as gregarious, man as exemplifying a will to power, man as religious.

Spengler, however, has elaborated the cultural aspect of the philosophy of his school. He has avoided their attempt to define and limit "the" types that may occur. For him the "destiny ideas" whatever they may be that evolve within a culture and give it individuality are what is dynamic and challenging in human life. These have differed profoundly one from another, and they condition their carriers so that certain beliefs and certain blindnesses are inevitable to them. Each great culture has taken a certain direction not taken by another, it has developed beliefs and institutions until they are the expression of this fundamental orientation, and the full working out of this unique and highly individualized attitude toward life is what is significant in that cultural epoch. His study makes a confused impression owing to its discursiveness and the unresolved complexities of the civilizations with which he deals. From an anthropological point of view the fundamental criticism of his work is that it involves treating modern stratified civilization as if it had the essential homogeneity of a primitive culture. His picture, especially of the modern worldview which he calls the Faustian, is only one of the integrated pictures that could validly be drawn for modern man. It needs to be balanced by a picture of a Babbitt or a Roosevelt, for instance. Even at that, what with his rather mystic consideration of numbers, of architecture, of music, of painting, of will, space, and time, the definition of his types becomes confused, and the identification of his different Faustian "destiny ideas" in mathematics, finance, philosophy, and morals hard to make out.

The fundamental principle of the philosophy of Dilthey and his school has remained in its application to the civilization of Western Europe stimulating and provocative rather than convincing. The difficulty, which Dilthey himself largely avoided by stressing primarily the dominant drives in philosophy instead of in cultures at large, in Spengler is very clear; historical data of western Europe are too complex and cultural stratification too thoroughgoing to yield itself in our present state of historical knowledge to the necessary analysis.

It is one of the philosophical justifications for the study of primitive peoples that ethnological data may make clear fundamental social facts that are otherwise confused and not open to demonstration. Of these none seem to

---

[4] Eduard Spranger, Types of Men. English translation by Paul J. W. Pigors. Halle, 1928.

me more important than this of fundamental and distinctive configurations in culture that so pattern existence and condition the emotional and cognitive reactions of its carriers that they become incommensurables, each specializing in certain selected types of behavior and each ruling out the behavior proper to its opposites.

I have recently examined from this point of view two types of cultures represented in the Southwest, that of the Pueblo contrasted with those of the various surrounding peoples.[5] I have called the ethos of the Pueblo Apollonian in Nietzsche's sense of the cultural pursuit of sobriety, of measure, of the distrust of excess and orgy. On the other hand Nietzsche's contrasted type, the Dionysian, is abundantly illustrated in all the surrounding cultures. It values excess as escape to an order of existence beyond that of the five senses, and finds its expression in the creation in culture of painful and dangerous experiences, and in the cultivation of emotional and psychic excesses, in drunkenness, in dreams, and in trance.

The situation in the Southwest gives an exceptionally good opportunity for the study of the extent to which contrasted psychological sets of this sort, once they have become institutionalized, can shape the resulting cultures. The Pueblo are a clearly marked-off civilization of very considerable known antiquity, islanded in the midst of highly divergent cultures. But this islanding of their culture cannot be set down as in Oceania to the facts of the physical environment. There are no mountain ranges, no impassable deserts, not even many miles that separate them from their neighbors. It is a cultural islanding achieved almost in the face of geographical conditions.

The eastern Pueblo went regularly to the plains for the buffalo hunt, and the center of the Pima country is within a day's run on foot of Hopi and Zuni. The fact therefore that they have a complex culture set off as strikingly as any in North America from that of their impinging neighbors makes the situation unmistakable. The resistance that has kept out of the Pueblos[6] such traits as that of the guardian spirit and the vision, the shaman, the torture, the orgy, the cultural use of intoxicants, the ideas of mystic danger associated with sex, initiative of the individual and personal authority in social affairs, is a cultural resistance, not the result of an isolation due to physical facts of the environment.

The culture of the southwest Pueblo, as I have pointed out in the article referred to above, is a thoroughgoing, institutionalized elaboration of the theme of sobriety and restraint in behavior. This dominating theme has effectually prevented the development of those typical Dionysian situations which most North American tribes elaborate out of every phase of life, cultivating abandon and emotional excesses, and making birth, adolescence,

---

[5] Psychological Types in the Cultures of the American Southwest, International Congress of Americanists 23:572–581, 1928.

[6] Op. cit., p. 573ff.

menstruation, the dead, the taking of life, and any other life crises ambivalently charged occasions fraught with danger and with power. It has likewise refused such traits of surrounding cultures as self-torture, ceremonially used drugs, and the inspirational vision, along with all the authority that is usually derived from personal contact with the supernatural, i.e., shamanism. It hates disruptive impulses in the individual—I speak in animistic shorthand, meaning that their cultural bias is opposed to and finally pares down to a minimum the potential human impulses to see visions and experiment in indulgences and work off its energy in excesses of the flesh.

Among these disruptive impulses the Pueblo ethos counts also the will to power. Just as surely as it has acted to obliterate self-torture it has acted to obliterate the human impulse toward the exercise of authority. Their ideal man avoids authority in the home or in public office. He has office at last thrust upon him, but even at that the culture has already taken away from the position he has to occupy anything that approaches personal authority in our sense; it remains a position of trust, a center of reference in planning the communal program, not much more.

Sanction for all acts comes always from the formal structure, not from the individual. He may not kill unless he has the power of the scalp or is planning to be initiated into it—that is, into the organized war society. He may not doctor because he knows how or acquires sanction from any personal encounter with the supernatural, but because he has bought his way up to the highest rank in the curing societies. Even if he is the chief priest he will not plant a prayer stick except at the institutionally prescribed seasons; if he does he will be regarded as practicing sorcery, as, according to the point of tales in which this situation occurs, he is indeed. The individual devotes himself therefore to the constituted forms of his society. He takes part in all cult activity, and according to his means will increase the number of masks possessed in Zuni by having one made for him—which involves feasting and considerable expense. He will undertake to sponsor the calendric kachina dances; he will entertain them at the great winter dance by building them a new house and assuming the expenses of his share of the ceremony. But he does all this with an anonymity that is hard to duplicate from other cultures. He does not undertake them as bids for personal prestige. Socially the good man never raises himself above his neighbor by displaying authority. He sets everyone at his ease, he "talks lots," he gives no occasion for offense. He is never violent, nor at the mercy of his emotions.

The whole interest of the culture is directed toward providing for every situation sets of rules and practices by means of which one gets by without resort to the violence and disruption that their culture distrusts. Even fertility practices, associated so universally in other cultures with excess and orgy, though they make them the leading motif of their religion[7]: are non-erotic rites based on analogies and sympathetic magic. I shall discuss later the thoroughness with which their rites of mourning are designed to this same end.

Such configurations of culture, built around certain selected human traits and working toward the obliteration of others are of first-rate importance in the understanding of culture. Traits objectively similar and genetically allied may be utilized in different configurations; it may be, without change in detail. The relevant facts are the emotional background against which the act takes place in the two cultures. It will illustrate this if we imagine the Pueblo snake dance in the setting of our own society. Among the western Pueblo, at least, repulsion is hardly felt for the snake. They have no physiological shudder at the touch of its body; in the ceremony, they are not flying in the face of a deep antipathy and horror. When we identify ourselves with them we are emotionally poles apart, though we put ourselves meticulously into the pattern of their behavior. For them, the poison of the rattlesnakes being removed, the whole procedure is upon the level of a dance with eagles or with kittens. It is a completely characteristic Apollonian dance expression, whereas with us, with our emotional reaction to the snake, the dance is not possible upon this level. Without changing an item of the outward behavior of the dance, its emotional significance and its functioning in the culture are reversed. And yet often enough, in ethnographic monographs, we are at a loss to know this emotional background even in traits where it becomes of first-rate importance, as for instance in the feeling directed toward the corpse. We need much more relevant data from the field in order to evaluate the emotional background.

The more usual situation is the one in which the trait is reworked to express the different emotional patterning characteristic of the culture that has adopted it. This reworking of widespread behavior traits into different configurations of culture can only be adequately described when there is a much greater body of field data presented from this angle, and a much greater agreement has been arrived at among anthropologists as to the relevant patternings. There are however certain configurations of culture that are clear from the existing monographs, and not only, nor chiefly perhaps, from America. However in order to establish the validity of the argument I am presenting, I shall limit myself to traits diffused over this continent and discuss only well-known North American cultural traits and the way in which they have been shaped by the dominant drives of certain contrasted cultures.

I have already referred to death practices. There are two aspects involved in death practices which I shall consider separately: on the one hand, the

---

[7] H. K. Haeberlin, The Idea of Fertilization in the Culture of the Pueblo Indians. American Anthropological Association Memoir 3, no. 1, 1916.

bereavement situation, and on the other, the situation of the individual
who has killed another.

The bereavement situation is characteristically handled in Dionysian and
in Apollonian cultures according to their bias. Dionysian behavior for the
bereaved has found several different channels of expression in the region
we are discussing in North America. Among the western Plains it was a violent expression of loss and upheaval. Abandon took the form of self-
mutilation, especially for women. They gashed their heads, their calves,
they cut off fingers. Long lines of women marched through camp after the
death of an important person, their legs bare and bleeding. The blood on
their heads and legs they let cake and did not remove. When the body was
taken out for burial everything in the lodge was thrown on the ground for
any that were not relatives to possess themselves of it. The lodge was pulled
down and given to another. Soon everything was gone and the widow had
nothing left but the blanket about her. At the grave the man's favorite horses
were killed and both men and women wailed for the dead. A wife or daughter might remain at the grave, wailing and refusing to eat, for twenty-four
hours, until her relatives dragged her away. At intervals, even twenty years
after a death had occurred, on passing the grave they cried for the dead.[8]

On the death of children especially, abandon of grief is described as being indulged. Suicide is often resorted to by one parent or the other. According to Denig, among the Assiniboine:

> should anyone offend the parent during this time his death would most cer-
> tainly follow, as the man, being in profound sorrow, seeks something on which
> to wreak his revenge, and he soon after goes to war, to kill or be killed, either
> being immaterial to him in that state.[9]

Such descriptions are characteristic of Plains mourning. They have in
common fundamental social patterns of violent and uninhibited grief.
This has nothing to do, of course, with the question of whether this is the
emotion called up in all those who participate in the rites; the point at issue is only that in this region institutionalized behavior at this crisis is patterned upon free emotional indulgence.

In such a typical Apollonian culture as the pueblo of Isleta, on the other
hand, Plains mourning is unthinkable. Isleta, like any other Apollonian society provides itself with rules by which to outlaw violence and aggressive
moods of any kind. Strong feeling is repulsive to it and even at death, which
is the most stubbornly unescapable of the tragic occasions of life, their whole
emphasis is to provide a routine for getting by with the least possible upheaval. In Isleta a priest who is known as the Black Corn Mother and who is

---

[8] George Bird Grinnell, The Cheyenne Indians, 2:162, New Haven, CT: Yale University Press,
1923.

[9] Denig, The Assiniboine. Bureau of American Ethnology Report 46:573.

a functionary of one of the four "Corn" divisions of the Pueblo, officiates at death. He is called immediately and prepares the corpse, brushing the hair and washing and painting the face with identification marks to indicate the social affiliation of the dead. After this the relatives come in, bringing each a candle to the dead, and the Corn Mother prays and sends the people away again. When they have gone him and his helpers "feed" the dead man ceremonially with the left hand—associated with ghosts—and make an altar in the room. Only once again during all this ritual tending of the dead are the relatives admitted, and that is when the priest has ready a small smudge from the combings of the dead man's hair. The bereaved breathe this in and will thereby cease to grieve over the dead person. The burial takes place the following day, but the family and relatives are ceremonially taboo for four days and remain in retreat in the house of the dead man, receiving certain ritual washings from the priest. The formalities that more nearly correspond to burial in other regions are performed over the burial of food for the deceased on the fourth day. They go outside the village for this, and after it is over, they break the pot in which water was carried, and the hairbrush that was used to prepare the body for burial, and on their return cut their trail with a deep incision with a flint knife. They listen and hear the dead man come, far off, to the place where they buried food for him. The house is filled with people awaiting their return, and the Black Corn Mother preaches to them, telling them this is the last time they need be afraid of the dead man's returning. The four days has been as four years to him and therefore those who remain will be the readier to forget. The relatives go to their houses but the housemates observe the ordinary taboos for ceremonial purity for eight days more, after which everything is over. The Black Corn Mother goes to the cacique and returns to him the power he received from him and must always receive from him for every death, but which he has this means of disposing of when he is not compelled to exercise it. It is a characteristic Apollonian touch, and very common in the Southwest.[10]

There is here no frank institutionalized indulgence in grief, no cutting off of fingers—not even of hair—nor gashing of bodies, no destruction of property, not even a show of its distribution. Instead of insistence upon prolonged mourning by the most closely bereaved, the emphasis is all upon immediate forgetting. The two pictures are of course familiar types of contrasted behavior, and they are here institutionalized for two contrasted cultures.

In the face of the evident opposition of these two institutionalized types of behavior it is at first sight somewhat bizarre to group them together over against another type in contrast to which they are at one. It is true nevertheless. In their different contexts, the Southwest and the Plains are alike in not capitalizing ideas of pollution and dread. This is not to say that fear of con-

---

[10] Esther Schiff Goldfrank, Isleta mss.

tamination or of the dangerous power of the dead are never to be detected in these regions; they are humanly potential attitudes and no culture is perhaps hermetically sealed against them. But the culture does not capitalize them. In contrast with the non-Pueblo Southwest, for instance, these two are alike in realistically directing their behavior toward the loss-situation instead of romantically elaborating the danger situation. In Isleta the clan head officiating at death does not have to be purified and the curse of contact with the dead lifted from him when the rites are over; he lays aside his official prerogatives as undertaker as he would his stole. He has not been polluted by his office. Nor is the smudge for the relatives designed to put them beyond the pursuit of vengefulness of the dead, but rather to make them forget quickly.[11] They break his hairbrush, not the bones of his legs, because what they are symbolizing is the ending of this man's life not precautions against his envy and vindictiveness. Similarly on the Plains[12] the giving away of property and the demeaning of one's self in personal appearance, which is so commonly a ruse for forestalling the jealousy of the deceased, is here a gesture of grief and associated with such other manifestations of oblivion of one's self and ordinary routine as going off mourning alone on the prairies, or starting off "to kill or be killed, either being immaterial to him" in his grief. They do not destroy the tipi and all the man's horses, for they are neither concerned with the contamination of the corpse nor with the malice of the ghost toward those who continue to enjoy them. On the contrary their one thought is to give them away. Neither do they capitalize that common theme for patterning a danger situation, the fear and hatred of the person who has used supernatural power to kill the deceased.

These themes however are the very basis of the mourning ceremony in surrounding regions. It is no uncommon thing to find that death rites are hardly directed at all toward the loss-situation but wholly preoccupied with contamination. The Navaho are by no means extreme examples. The Franciscan Fathers[13] tell us that in former times slaves were employed to prepare and carry the corpse and they were killed at the grave. Now members of the family must expose themselves to this defilement. Men and women strip themselves to a breechcloth for the duty and leave the hair flowing so that not even a hair string may be exposed. To the Navaho either type of behavior we have just been describing would be unthinkable. Only those who because of their close kinship cannot avoid the duty accompany the body. Four are necessary, one to lead the favorite horse which is to be killed on the grave of his master, two to carry the corpse, and one to warn any travelers along the way that they may turn aside and save themselves from defilement. To protect themselves

---

[11] In Zuñi however certain scalp dance attitudes are explicitly associated with the widow and widower.

[12] In this entire discussion I exclude the Southern Sioux.

[13] An Ethnologic Dictionary of the Navajo Language, 454. St. Michael's, Arizona, 1910.

the mourners keep strict silence. Meantime the hogan in which death occurred has been burnt to the ground. All the members of the family fast for
four days and during this time a guard warns all comers off the trail between
the hogan and the grave lest they incur danger.[14]

Besides the dominating fear of pollution, the Navaho have a strong fear
also of the return of the ghost. If a woman fails in fasting or breaks silence,
it will show the dead the way back and the ghost will harm the offender.
This discomfort of the living before the dead is nearly universal, though it
assumes very different proportions in different cultures.

On the other hand, the dreaded vengefulness of the ghost and his malice
toward those who have been spared by death is not as popular in North
America in the elaboration of the horror situation as it is in South America
and in other parts of the world. It is a theme that for Crawley,[15] for example, is fundamental in death practices, and it is striking that it should play
so slight a role in North America. One of the clearest examples on this continent is from the Fox. The Central Algonkin have a strong belief in cruel antagonists which the dead must overcome along their route, and the custom
of burying weapons with the body was in order that they might be armed
against them. With the Winnebago,[16] too, war hatchets were buried with
the dead so that they might kill animals they met along their way, and their
relatives in this world be blessed in like fashion. But Jones records that
among the Fox it was a frequent request of the dying that they might be provided in the grave with a war hatchet to protect themselves against Cracker
of Skulls; but this living would not do because the dead were feared and it
was desirable that they be weaponless. Therefore they are helpless before
Cracker of Skulls who scoops from each a fingerful of brain.[17]

The Mohave on the other hand made much of the fear and blame of the
medicine-man who had supernaturally caused the death. A seer was employed
to visit the land of the dead after a death. If the deceased was not there, it was
known that the doctor who attended him was guilty of malpractice. "It is the
nature of these doctors to kill people in this way just as it is the nature of hawks
to kill little birds for a living," according to a Mohave in the 80's. A rich man
remained rich in the other world and all those a medicine-man killed were under his chieftainship. He desired a large rich band. "I've killed only two. When
I die I want to rule a bigger band than that."[18] When blame was attached to
any medicine-man, anyone might take it upon himself to kill him.

The medicine-man openly avowed his complicity. He might hand a stick
to a man and say, "I killed your father." Or he might come and tell a sick

[14] Gladys A. Reichard, Social Life of the Navajo Indians. CU-CA 7:142.
[15] Editor's note: A Reference to the Ideas of British Scholar, A. E. Crawley.
[16] Paul Radin, JAFL 22:312.
[17] Wm. Jones, ICA 15:266.
[18] John J. Bourke, Journal of American Folklore 2:175, 1889.

person, "Don't you know that it is I that am killing you? Must I grasp you and despatch you with my hands before you will try to kill me?"[19] The point is that this is supernatural killing. There has never been any intimation that it was the custom for a medicine-man to use poison or knife. It is a blame- and terror-situation open and declared, a situation more familiar in Africa than in North America.

It is well to contrast this Mohave attitude with the Pueblo witchcraft the- ories. In Zuni the bereavement situation is not lost in a situation of sorcery and of vengeance taken upon sorcery; bereavement is handled as bereave- ment, however clearly the emphasis is upon putting it by as soon as possi- ble. In spite of the great amount of anxiety about witches which is always present among the Pueblo, at an actual death little attention is paid to the possibility of their complicity. Only in an epidemic when death becomes a public menace is the witch theory ordinarily acted upon. And it is a com- munity anxiety neurosis, not a Dionysian situation depending like the Mo- have on the exercise of the shaman's will to supernatural power, and the ambivalent attitude of the group toward this power. I doubt whether any- one in Zuni has any witch techniques which he actually practices; no one defies another over a dead or dying man. It is never the medicine-man who by virtue of his medicine powers is also the death bringer and embodies in his one person the characteristic Dionysian double aspects of power. Death is not dramatized as a duel between a shaman, thought of as a bird of prey and his victim. Even the existence of all the necessary ideas among the Pueblo—it is interesting that they are overwhelmingly European in their detail—does not lead to this Dionysian interpretation of death.

There are other themes upon which danger situations can be and have been built up around death in different cultures. The point we need for our discussion is that the Dionysian indulgence in emotion at death can be in- stitutionalized around realistic grief at the loss of a member of the com- munity, or around various constructs such as contamination, guilt, and the vengefulness of the dead. The contrast between cultures which indulge in danger constructs of this sort in every situation in life and those that do not is as striking as that between the Apollonian-Dionysian types. The fullest collections of primitive material on the danger situation are of course the various works of Crawley. This was his outstanding subject throughout his work, and he interpreted it as a universal drive in human society. It is cer- tainly one that is common in institutional behavior, but it is for all its wide distribution a particular configuration of culture, and contrasting configu- rations develop their contrasting behaviors.

Where human contacts, the crises of life, and a wide range of acts are re- garded realistically in any culture, and especially without the metamorphosis

---

[19] A. L. Kroeber, Handbook of the Indians of California. BAE-B 78:778.

that passes over them in consequence of the fear- and contamination-constructs we have been discussing, and this is institutionalized in culture, I shall call them realists. Cultures of the opposite type I shall call simply non-realists. It is admittedly poor terminology. James's antithesis of the tough and tender-minded approaches also the distinction I wish to make, but his substitute for these of healthy-mindedness and the sick soul brings in an implication I wish to avoid.

We must be content to say, I think, that those cultures that institutionalize death as loss, adolescence as an individual's growing up, mating as sex choice, killing as success in a fight, and so on, contrast strongly with those who live in an Aladdin's cave where all the vegetation is something else. It is certainly one of the most striking facts of anthropology that primary life situations are so seldom read off culturally in this direct and realistic fashion.

Indeed it is the realistic institutions that would seem to be the less thoroughly carried through. Human culture as a whole throughout its history has been based on certain non-realistic notions, of which animism and incest are the ones which will occur to every anthropologist. The fear of the ghost—not of his enmity or vengefulness, which is found only locally, but of his mere wraith—is another. These notions appear to have conditioned the human race from the beginning, and it is obviously impossible to go back to their beginnings or discuss the attitudes that gave them birth. For the purposes of this discussion we must accept them as we have to accept the fact that we have five fingers. Even the realistic Plains have not discarded them, though they use them more realistically than other cultures.

In the region we are discussing, the Dionysian cultures are cross-sectioned by this realist-nonrealist antithesis, the Plains institutionalizing excess and abandon without elaborating danger-situations, and the non-Pueblo Southwest, the Shoshoneans, and the Northwest Coast carrying these danger-situations to extremes. The realist cultures likewise are Dionysian among the Plains and Apollonian among the Pueblo. The two categories operate at a different level and cross-section each other. It is difficult, however, to imagine an Apollonian culture maintaining itself on the basis of fundamental danger-constructs, and certainly this type does not occur in the region we are considering.

It is impossible to do justice here to the consistency of this realist configuration among the western Plains; it would be necessary first to differentiate their institutional behavior from the Apollonian Pueblo and then from the romantics about them. So far as the people directly to the west, the Shoshoneans, are concerned, the differences in behavior which I wish to stress have already been pointed out by Lowie.[20] He notices the change in

---

[20] The Cultural Connection of California and Plateau Shoshonean Tribes. UC-PAAE 20:145–156.

affect in menstrual taboos[21] and the dropping out of the relevant customs. Childbirth and the menstruating woman have been two of the great points of departure for the tender-minded elaboration of horror and the uncanny. The Plains, like the Pueblo, do not share the trait. Lowie points out also how the Plains, again like the Pueblo, stand contrasted with the western groups in ignoring the non-realistic involvement of the husband in his wife's confinement. Attenuated forms of couvade are the rule for Shoshoneans, Plateau peoples, and Californians. It is not a Plains trait.

The same disinclination is evident in the contrasting attitude toward the name. Plains names are not mystic part and parcel of one's personality; they are realistic appellations much in our own sense. It is not a grievous insult to ask another's name. Even more, it is not an affair of life and death to use the name of another after his death. Among the Karok, for instance, the same retribution must be visited upon this act as upon having taken the man's life.[22] It is a fiction that is alien on the Plains.

There are therefore a considerable number of reasons for thinking that the cultural attitude we have noted in Plains mourning ceremonies over against those to the west and south (Navaho and Pima) are characteristic for their culture. Most striking of all perhaps, Lowie points out that among the western Plains vengeance upon the medicine man is atypical whereas it is reported among the Shoshoneans and the central Californians. I believe this can be put very much more strongly. In any other part of the world than North America we should frankly refer to the attitude that is constantly reported from British Columbia to the Pima as sorcery, and the killing of the shaman as vengeance taken on the sorcerer. The Plains simply do not make anything of this pattern. They use supernatural power to further their own exploits as warriors, they do not use it to build up threats. Sorcery is the prime institutionalization of the neurotic's fear world, and it does not find place from the Blackfoot to the Cheyenne.

Before we continue with further examples of mourning practices in other configurations, it will be clearer to illustrate the configurations we have just discussed by another situation—the situation of the man who has killed another. It throws into relief the attitudes we have been discussing.

The Cheyenne scalp dance is characteristic of Plains configuration. Tremendous Dionysian exaltation is achieved, but not by way of horror or contamination ideas connected with the corpse; it is an uninhibited triumph, a gloating over the enemy who has been put out of the way. There is no intimation of a curse lying upon the scalper which it is the function of the dance to remove. There is no idea of the fearful potency of the scalp. It

---

[21] Lowie, ibid., 149.
[22] Stephen Powers, Tribes of California. CNAE 3:33, 1877.

is a completely joyous occasion, a celebration of triumph and the answer to a prayer that had been made with tears.

Before setting out upon a warpath everything is solemn and prayerful, even sorrowful, in order to gain pity from the supernatural.[23] On the return with the scalps, however, all is changed. The party falls upon the home camp by surprise at daybreak, the favorite hour for Indian attack, their faces blackened in triumph

> . . . shooting off their guns and waving the poles on which were the scalps that had been taken. The people were excited and welcomed them with shouts and yells. All was joy. The women sang songs of victory. . . . In the front rank were those who had . . . counted coups. . . . Some threw their arms around the successful warriors. Old men and women sang songs in which the names were mentioned. The relatives of those who rode in the first rank . . . testified to their joy by making gifts to friends or to poor people. The whole crowd might go to where some brave man lived or to where his father lived, and there dance in his honor. They were likely to prepare to dance all night, and perhaps to keep up this dancing for two days and two nights.[24]

Grinnell speaks especially of the fact that there was no ceremonial recognition of the priest or of his services on their return. The scalp was an emblem of victory and something to rejoice over. If members of the war party had been killed the scalps were thrown away and there was no scalp dance. But if the warrior who had been killed had counted coup before he died there was no occasion for grief, so great was the honor, and the victory celebration over the scalp went forward. Everyone joined in the scalp dance. In keeping with its social character it was in charge of berdaches who were here matchmakers and "good company" and who took the place of the female relative who usually has so conspicuous a role. They called out the dances and carried the scalps. Old men and women came out as clowns, and as if anything wanted to emphasize the absence among the Cheyenne of dread and danger in relation to the slain enemy, Grinnell says that some of these were dressed to represent the very warriors whose scalps were the center of the ceremony.[25]

This Plains behavior was unthinkable over a great part of the continent. In the southern belt of the United States, from the Natchez to the Mohave— excluding the Pueblo for the moment—the opposite attitude is at its height. Over this whole area the point of the scalp dance was the great dangerous supernatural potency of the scalp and the curse that must be removed from the slayer. It belonged to their whole tender-minded awe before dark and uncanny forces.

---

[23] Powers, ibid., 22.
[24] Grinnell, op. cit., 6–22.
[25] ibid., 39–44.

* * *

As I pointed out in a previous discussion of the Southwest, there is no culture trait in Zuni that presents so many unmodified likenesses to institutions outside the Pueblo as the scalp dance. From the point of view of Pueblo cultural attitudes it presents strikingly atypical elements which are well-known for the central region of North America and at home there. One such is the biting of the scalp, reported from Laguna[26] and Zuni. This act is performed in the face of a strong feeling of contamination from the scalp. In Zuni they say that the woman upon whom this act devolves is free of the curse because she rises to the point of "acting like an animal." It is an almost unique recognition in this culture of the state of ecstasy, and is an instance of a diffused culture trait, the scalp dance, which has been accepted among the Pueblo without the reconstruction that would have been necessary to bring it into line with their dominant attitudes.

Accepting this fact, we may examine the Zuni scalp dance to see in what directions it has been modified at their hands. In the first place, they have rephrased the release from the curse so that it is no longer, as with the Pima and Papago, a dramatization of ambivalent attitudes toward the sacred—on the one hand, the polluting, on the other, the powerful—but belongs with any retreat undertaken to gain membership in a society. The scalp dance in Zuni is an initiation into the policing society of the bow priesthood. It is taken up into their pattern of providing formal fraternal organizations for handling every situation. The bow priesthood is an elaborate organization with special responsibilities, functioning for life. The curse of the slayer and the release from it are dwarfed by the pattern of initiation into a new set of social functions.

* * *

Both the bereavement situation and the murder situation show therefore strong contrasts in the three North American cultural configurations we have considered. I shall arbitrarily select one other contrasting configuration that is perhaps nowhere in the world more strikingly illustrated than in North America. The pursuit of personal aggrandizement on the Northwest Coast is carried out in such a way that it approaches an institutionalization of the megalomaniac personality type. The censorship which is insisted upon in civilizations like our own is absent in such self-glorifications as a Kwakiutl public address, and when censorship functions, as among the tribes of the gulf of Georgia, their self-abasements are patently not expressions of humility but

---

[26] Franz Boas, Keres Texts. AES-P 8:290 (pt. 1).

equivalents of the familiar self-glorification of the Kwakiutl. Any of their songs illustrate the usual tenor:

> *I am the great chief who makes people ashamed.*
> *I am the great chief who makes people ashamed.*
> *Our chief brings shame to the faces.*
> *Our chief brings jealousy to the faces. Our chief makes people cover their faces by what*
> *he is continually doing in this world. Giving again and again oil feasts to all the tribes.*[27]
> *I began at the upper end of the tribes. Serves them right! Serves them right!*
> *I came downstream setting fire to the tribes with my fire-bringer.*
> *Serves them right! Serves them right!*
> *My name, just my name, killed them, I, the great Mover of the world. Serves them*
> *right! Serves them right!*[28]

The energy of the culture is frankly given to competition in a game of raising one's personal status and of entrenching oneself by the humiliation of one's fellows. In a lesser degree this pursuit of personal prestige is characteristic of the Plains. But the picture is sharply contrasted. The Plains do not institutionalize the inferiority complex and its compensations. They do not preoccupy themselves with the discovery of insults in every situation. They are anything but paranoid. But it is in terms of these particular psychological sets that the pursuit of personal aggrandizement is carried out in the culture of the North Pacific coast. Probably the inferiority complex has never been so blatantly institutionalized. The greatest range of acts are regarded as insults, not only personal derogatory acts, but all untoward events like a cut from an axe or the overturning of a canoe. All such events threaten the ego security of the members of this paranoid-like civilization, and according to their pattern may be wiped out by the distribution of property. If they cannot be, the response is perfectly in character: the bubble of self-esteem is pricked and the man retires to his pallet for weeks at a time, or, it may be, takes his life. This extreme of negative self feeling is far removed from the exhibitions of shame due to indecent exposures or breaking of taboo in other regions. It is plain sulking, the behavior of a person whose self-esteem is all he has and who has been wounded in his pride.

All the circumstances of life are regarded on the Northwest Coast, not as occasions for violent grief or equally violent jubilation, occasions for freely expending energy in differentiated ways, but primarily as furthering, all of them alike, this insult contest. They are occasions for the required fight for prestige. Sex, the life cycle, death, warfare, are all almost equivalent raw material for cultural patterning to this end. A girl's adolescence is an event for which her father gathers property for ten years in order to demonstrate his

---

[27] Franz Boas, Ethnology of the Kwakiutl. BAE-R 35:1291.
[28] Boas, op. cit., 1381.

greatness by a great distribution of wealth; it is not as a fact in the girl's sex life that it figures in their culture, but as a rung of her father's ladder toward higher social standing, therefore also of her own. For since in this region all property that is distributed must be paid back with usury (else the recipient will entirely lose face), to make oneself poor is the prime act in acquiring wealth. Even a quarrel with one's wife is something only a great man may indulge in, for it entails the distribution of all his property, even to the rafters of his house. But if the chief has enough wealth for this distribution of property, he welcomes the occasion as he does his daughter's puberty as a rung in the ladder of advancement.[29]

This comes out clearly in the reinterpretation of the bereavement situation in this region. Even the cutting of the hair in mourning has become not an act of grief on the part of near relatives, but the service of the opposite phratry signifying their tribute to the greatness of the deceased, and the fact that the relatives of the dead are able to recompense them. Similarly it also is another step upward in the pursuit of prestige and the acquisition of wealth. All the services for the dead are carried out in like manner. The emphasis of the society at death fell upon the distribution of property by the bereaved phratry to the officiating opposite phratry. Without reference to its character as a loss- or danger-situation, it was used just as the occasion of the girl's first menstruation or a domestic quarrel to demonstrate the solvency of the family group and to put down rival claimants to like wealth. Among the Haida[30] the great funeral potlatch, a year after the death, where this property was distributed, was organized around the transfer of winter-dance society membership to members of the host's phratry from members of the guests' phratry, in return for the property that was being distributed to them—an activity of course that has reference to ideas of ownership and prestige and winter ceremonial among the Haida but not to the loss involved in death nor yet to the danger associated with the corpse or the ghost. As the Kwakiutl say "they fight with property"—i.e., to achieve and maintain status based on wealth and inherited prerogatives; therefore "they fight," also, with a funeral.

This reinterpretation of the bereavement situation in terms of the "fight with property" is, however, only a part of the Northwest Coast pattern of behavior. It is assimilated as well to the insult preoccupation. The death of a relative, not only in a war but by sickness or accident, was an affront to be wiped out by the death of a person of another tribe. One was shamed until the score had been settled. The bereaved was dangerous in the way any man was who had been grievously shamed. When the chief Neqapenkem's sister and her daughter did not come back from Victoria either, people said,

---

[29] Boas, op. cit., 1359.
[30] John R. Swanton, The Haida, Jessup Expedition Report 5:176, 179.

because their boat capsized or they drank bad whiskey, he called together the warriors. "Now I ask you tribes, who shall wail? Shall I do it or shall another?" The foremost responded, "Not you, Chief, let some other of the tribes." They set up the war pole, and the others came forward saying, "We came here to ask you to go to war that someone else may wail on account of our deceased sister." So they started out with full war rites to "pull under" the Sanetch for the chief's dead relatives. They found seven men and two children asleep and killed all except one girl whom they took captive.[31]

Again, the chief Qaselas' son died, and he and his brother and uncle set out to wipe out the stain. They were entertained by Nengemalis at their first stop. After they had eaten, "Now I will tell you the news, Chief," Qaselas said. "My prince died today and you will go with him." So they killed their host and his wife. "Then Qaselas and his crew felt good when they arrived at Sebaa in the evening. . . . It is not called war, but 'to die with those that are dead.'"[32]

This is pure head hunting, a paranoid reading of bereavement that stands almost alone in North America. Here death is institutionalized in such practices as this as the major instance of the countless untoward events of life which confound a man's pride and are treated as insults.

Both the preoccupation with prestige and the preoccupation with insults underlie also the behavior centered around the killing of an enemy. The victory dance has become permanent, graded societies institutionalizing the most fiercely guarded prerogatives of these tribes; they constitute one of the most elaborate prestige organizations we know anything about. The original trait upon which they were built is preserved among the tribes to the south. It was a victory dance with the head of the enemy held in the teeth. As Professor Boas has shown, this became, as it was worked up into the Northwest Coast configuration, the cannibal dance[33] and the pattern of the secret societies. The dancers of the Kwakuitl secret societies are still considered "warriors," and the societies, which are normally in operation only during the winter season, always function on a war party no matter what the season. Now these secret societies are the great validations of prestige and of wealth through the distribution of property, and the final Northwest Coast form of the germinal idea of the victory dance is therefore that of enormously elaborate, rigidly prescribed secret societies, membership in which establishes and validates social status.

The dominant drive being the competition for prerogatives, another turn is given to the situation of the person who has killed another. One can get prerogatives, according to their idea, not only through the death of relatives,

---

[31] Boas, op. cit., 1363.

[32] Boas, op. cit., 1385.

[33] 12th and Final Report on the North-Western Tribes. British Association for the Advancement of Science 51, 1898.

but through that of a victim, so that if a person has been killed at my hands I may claim his prerogatives. The slayer's situation is therefore not one of circumventing a dread curse or of celebrating a triumph of personal prowess; it is one of distributing large amounts of wealth to validate the privileges he has taken by violence at the moment when, incidentally so far as institutional behavior goes, he took also the life of the owner. That is, the taking of life is dwarfed behind the immense edifice of behavior proper to the Northwest Coast configuration.

* * *

There are of course aspects of culture, especially of material culture, which are independent of many of the aims and virtues a society may make for itself. I do not mean to imply that the fortunes of the sinew-backed bow will depend upon whether the culture is Dionysian or Apollonian. But the range of applicability of the point I am making is nevertheless greater than is generally supposed. Radin has for instance argued very cogently from Winnebago material for the great importance of individuality and individual initiative "among primitive."[34] Now the Plains and the Winnebago are among our great primitive examples, according to all observers, of high cultural evaluation of the individual. He is allowed institutionally guaranteed initiative in his life such as one cannot easily duplicate from other regions. One has only to compare it with the Pueblo to realize that Radin's point of very great personal initiative is a prime fact among the Winnebago and the western Plains, but not coextensive with primitive culture. It is an attitude to be studied independently in each area.

The same is also true of Malinowski's picture of the way in which the Trobrianders—and Melanesia generally, we may well add—have made reciprocity a basic behavior trait of their culture. He describes the reciprocal obligations of sea and land peoples, of chief and subjects, of the two sides of the house, of husband and wife and other selected reciprocating relatives, and he deduces from this that "tradition" is a weak word invoked by the anthropologist to cover our ignorance of what really holds "society" together, a function that is performed by reciprocity. But this organization of society here is of a definite type, highly uncharacteristic, say, of Siberia, and fundamental in any description of Melanesia. In what way it ties up with fundamental attitudes in that region is still to be defined.

Cultural configurations stand to the understanding of group behavior in the relation that personality types stand to the understanding of individual behavior. In the psychological field, behavior is no longer given the same interpretation, say, for the cycloid and the schizoid type. It is recognized

---

[34] Primitive Man as Philosopher, 32 ff.

that the organization of the total personality is crucial in the understanding or even in the mere description of individual behavior.[35] If this is true in individual psychology where individual differentiation must be limited always by the cultural forms and by the short span of a human lifetime, it is even more imperative in social psychology where the limitations of time and of conformity are transcended. The degree of integration that may be attained is of course incomparably greater than can ever be found in individual psychology. Cultures from this point of view are individual psychology thrown large upon the screen, given gigantic proportions and a long time span.

* * *

This involves another aspect of the problem of cultural configurations, that which concerns the adjustment of the individual to his society. As we have said, it is probable that about the same range of individual temperaments are found in any group. But the group has already made its cultural choice of those human endowments and peculiarities it will put to use. Out of small leanings in one direction or another it has bent itself so far toward some point of the compass that no manipulation can change its direction. Most of the persons born into the culture will take its bent and very likely incline it further. Those are most fortunate whose native dispositions are in accord with the culture they happen to be born into—those of realistic tendencies who are born among the western Plains, those who are liable to delusions of reference who are born on the Northwest Coast, the Apollonians who are born among the Pueblo, the Dionysians who are born among the American Indians outside the Pueblo. In the particular situation we have been discussing, the person to whom violent indulgence in grief is congenial is well provided for culturally among the Cheyenne; the one who dreads violent expression and wishes to get the painful situation over with a minimum of expression, in Isleta. The person who easily feels personal reference in any situation of life, even in death, finds his paranoid tendencies well channeled among the Kwakiutl.

Contrariwise, the misfit is the person whose disposition is not capitalized by his culture. The Dionysian who is born among the Pueblo must re-educate himself or go for nothing in the culture. The Apollonian, likewise, in California is shut out of social activity in so far as he cannot learn to take to himself the institutionalized behavior of the locality. The person who does not readily read insults into external events can only function with extreme difficulty on the north Pacific Coast or in northwestern California.

---

[35] William Stern, Die menschliche Personlichkeit, Johann Ambrosius Barth, Leipzig, 1919.

It is clear that there is not possible any generalized description of "the" deviant—he is the representative of that arc of human capacities that is not capitalized in his culture. In proportion as his civilization has committed itself to a direction alien to him, he will be the sufferer. The intelligent understanding of the relation of the individual to his society, therefore, involves always the understanding of the types of human motivations and capacities capitalized in his society and the congruity or incongruity of these with those that are native to the individual under discussion or are the result of early familial conditioning. It can always be unquestioningly assumed that by far the majority of any population will be thoroughly assimilated to the standards of their culture—they will learn to read life in terms of violence, or of sobriety, or of insults as the case may be. But the person who is at a loss in his society, the unavailable person, is not some one type to be specified and described on the basis of a universally valid abnormal psychology, but he represents the type not capitalized in the society to which he was born.

All this has a most important bearing on the formation and functioning of culture traits. We are too much in the habit of studying religion, let us say, or property complexes, as if the fundamental fact about them were a dependable human response: like awe, for example, or the "acquisitive instinct," from which they stemmed. Now there have been human institutions that do show this direct correspondence to simple human emotions—death practices that express grief, mating customs that express sex preference, agricultural practices that begin and end with the provisioning of the tribe. But even to list them in this fashion makes forcibly clear how difficult it is to find such examples. As a matter of fact, agriculture and economic life in general usually sets itself other ends than the satisfaction of the food quest, marriage usually expresses other things more strikingly than sex preference, and mourning notoriously does not stress grief. The more intimately we know the inner workings of different cultures the more readily we can see that the almost infinite variability in any cultural trait if it is followed around the globe is not a mere ringing of the changes upon some simple underlying human response. Another and greater force has been at work that has used the recurring situations of mating, death, provisioning, and the rest almost as raw material and elaborated them to express its own intent. This force that bends occasions to its purposes and fashions them to its own idiom we can call within that society its dominant drive. Some societies have brought all this raw material into conspicuous harmony with this dominant drive, the societies to which on an a priori basis Sapir would allow the appellation of "genuine cultures."[36] Many have not.

---

[36] E. Sapir, Culture, Genuine and Spurious. American Journal Soc. 29:401–17, 1924.

Sapir holds that an honest self-consistency that rules out hypocritical pretensions is the mark of a genuine culture. It seems to me that cultures may be built solidly and harmoniously upon fantasies, fear-constructs, or inferiority complexes and indulges to the limit in hypocrisy and pretensions. The person who has an ineradicable drive to face the facts and avoid hypocrisy may be the outlaw of a culture that is nevertheless on its own basis symmetrical and harmonious. Because a configuration is well-defined it is not therefore honest.

It is, however, the reality of such configurations that is in question. I do not see that the development of these configurations in different societies is more mystic or difficult to understand than, for example, the development of an art style. In both if we have the available material we can see the gradual integration of elements, and growing dominance of some few stylistic drives. In both, also if we had the material, we could without doubt trace the influence of gifted individuals who have bent the culture in the direction of their own capacities. But the configuration of the culture nevertheless always transcends the individual elements that have gone to its making. The cultural configuration builds itself up over generations, discarding, as no individual may, the traits that are uncongenial to it. It takes to itself ritual and artistic and activational modes of expression that solidify its attitude and make it explicit. Many cultures have never achieved this thorough-going harmony. There are peoples who seem to shift back and forth between different types of behavior. Like our own civilization they may have received too many contradictory influences from different outside sources and been unable to reduce them to a common denominator. But the fact that certain people have not done so, no more makes it unnecessary to study culture from this angle than the fact that some languages shift back and forth between different fundamental grammatical devices in forming the plural or in designating tense, makes it unnecessary to study grammatical forms.

These dominant drives are as characteristic for individual areas as are house forms or the regulations of inheritance. We are too handicapped yet by lack of relevant descriptions of culture to know whether these drive-distributions are often coextensive with distribution of material culture, or whether in some regions there are many such to one culture area defined from more objective traits. Descriptions of culture from this point of view must include much that older fieldwork ignored, and without the relevant fieldwork all our propositions are pure romancing.

QUERIES

- According to Benedict, how did the development of systematic ethnography change the study of culture? Why should anthropologists reject a view of culture as a set of traits?

- Define the Dionysian and Apollonian worldviews. Why does Benedict consider the "Pueblo Indians" to be Apollonian and the "Plains Indians" Dionysian? How are these different configurations reflected in different aspects of Native American cultural practices (such as mourning ceremonies?)
- Discuss the different conceptions of individual power among the Pueblo Indians versus the natives of the Northwest Coast.
- According to Benedict, what defines a "deviant" in a given society?
- Benedict suggests that the cultural configurations develop in ways similar to art styles. Explain this analogy.

CONNECTIONS

- On what grounds would Benedict criticize Morgan's evolutionary model?
- How would Marvin Harris respond to Benedict's ideas that cultural patterns are the response to core values?
- Based on her historical analyses of the ways "traditional" societies have been changed through the spread of capitalism, how would Eleanor Leacock criticize Benedict's summaries of the "patterns" of native culture in North America?

7

Edward Sapir

INTRODUCTION

The American linguist and cultural anthropologist Edward Sapir (1884–1939) made numerous contributions to the study of language and culture. Sapir authored a series of groundbreaking studies of American Indian languages, he contributed to a field of anthropological inquiry known as "culture and personality" or psychological anthropology, and he published a flurry of reviews, poems, and articles—a diverse array of scholarship anchored by his fascination with language (see Moore 2008:88–103). In this, Sapir followed on Franz Boas's insight that mastery of a native language provided essential entry into another culture, but Sapir advanced that insight, arguing that language was a cultural construction and encoded the basic frameworks of social life.

Expanded by his student, Benjamin Whorf, this idea—that there is a relationship between the categories of meaning within a language and the mental categories its speakers use to conceptualize the world—is referred to as the Sapir-Whorf hypothesis or "linguistic relativity." This hypothesis has several elements, several of which are presented in the following selections from two of Sapir's works: his 1921 book, *Language: An Introduction to the Study of Speech*, and his 1912 article, "Language and Environment." First, language is learned behavior; while human language may be based on the physical elements of vocal cords, larynx, and lungs and limited by the innate range of human hearing, nothing about language is inherited. Second, language is always artificial and based on convention. Even the simplest of words—for example, words that imitate natural sounds—are not simply renderings of nature but are culturally prescribed conventions, which is why a rooster cries "cock-a-doodle-do!" in English, but "cocorico!" in French. Third, words reflect the environments in which they are used, and not just the natural environments but the social environments as well. Languages employ specific words because the associated things and concepts are socially useful. (For example, Sapir points out that a modern American looking at a vacant lot might see the various plants as "weeds" while a traditional hunter-gatherer would have very precise and distinguishing terms for the same plants.) Finally, languages thus distinctively encode different ways of conceiving and perceiving the world, and speakers of different languages occupy conceptually distinct universes.

The Sapir-Whorf hypothesis has been criticized severely on different grounds and some argue that it has never been adequately tested. Yet, Sapir's ideas represent an effort to understand a basic question—what gives a culture its internal coherence?—and Sapir proposed that this coherence derives from the conceptions of the cosmos shared by speakers of the same language.

PRIMARY TEXT: *LANGUAGE: AN INTRODUCTION TO THE STUDY OF SPEECH*

Editor's note: First published 1921, New York: Harcourt, Brace.

Speech is so familiar a feature of daily life that we rarely pause to define it. It seems as natural to man as walking, and only less so than breathing. Yet it needs but a moment's reflection to convince us that this naturalness of speech is but an illusory feeling. The process of acquiring speech is, in sober fact, an utterly different sort of thing from the process of learning to walk. In the case of the latter function, culture, in other words, the traditional body of social usage, is not seriously brought into play. The child is individually equipped, by the complex set of factors that we term biological heredity, to make all the needed muscular and nervous adjustments that result in walking. Indeed, the very conformation of these muscles and of the appropriate parts of the nervous system may be said to be primarily adapted to the movements made in walking and in similar activities. In a very real sense the normal human being is predestined to walk, not because his elders will assist him to learn the art, but because his organism is prepared from birth, or even from the moment of conception, to take on all those expenditures of nervous energy and all those muscular adaptations that result in walking. To put it concisely, walking is an inherent, biological function of man.

Not so language. It is of course true that in a certain sense the individual is predestined to talk, but that is due entirely to the circumstance that he is born not merely in nature, but in the lap of a society that is certain, reasonably certain, to lead him to its traditions. Eliminate society and there is every reason to believe that he will learn to walk, if, indeed, he survives at all. But it is just as certain that he will never learn to talk, that is, to communicate ideas according to the traditional system of a particular society. Or, again, remove the new-born individual from the social environment into which he has come and transplant him to an utterly alien one. He will develop the art of walking in his new environment very much as he would have developed it in the old. But his speech will be completely at variance with the speech of his native environment. Walking, then, is a general human activity that varies only within circumscribed limits as we pass from individual to individual. Its variability is involuntary and purposeless. Speech is a human activity that varies without assignable limit as we pass from social group to social group, because it is a purely historical heritage of the group, the product of long-continued social usage. It varies as all creative effort varies—not as consciously, perhaps, but none the less as truly as do the religions, the beliefs, the customs, and the arts of different peoples. Walking is an organic, an instinctive, function (not, of course, itself an instinct); speech is a non-instinctive, acquired, "cultural" function.

There is one fact that has frequently tended to prevent the recognition of language as a merely conventional system of sound symbols, that has seduced the popular mind into attributing to it an instinctive basis that it does not really possess. This is the well-known observation that under the stress of emotion, say of a sudden twinge of pain or of unbridled joy, we do involuntarily give utterance to sounds that the hearer interprets as indicative of the emotion itself. But there is all the difference in the world between such involuntary expression of feeling and the normal type of communication of ideas that is speech. The former kind of utterance is indeed instinctive, but it is non-symbolic; in other words, the sound of pain or the sound of joy does not, as such, indicate the emotion, it does not stand aloof, as it were, and announce that such and such an emotion is being felt. What it does is to serve as a more or less automatic overflow of the emotional energy; in a sense, it is part and parcel of the emotion itself. Moreover, such instinctive cries hardly constitute communication in any strict sense. They are not addressed to any one, they are merely overheard, if heard at all, as the bark of a dog, the sound of approaching footsteps, or the rustling of the wind is heard. If they convey certain ideas to the hearer, it is only in the very general sense in which any and every sound or even any phenomenon in our environment may be said to convey an idea to the perceiving mind. If the involuntary cry of pain which is conventionally represented by "Oh!" be looked upon as a true speech symbol equivalent to some such idea as "I am in great pain," it is just as allowable to interpret the appearance of clouds as an equivalent symbol that carries the definite message "It is likely to rain." A definition of language, however, that is so extended as to cover every type of inference becomes utterly meaningless.

The mistake must not be made of identifying our conventional interjections (our oh! and ah! and sh!) with the instinctive cries themselves. These interjections are merely conventional fixations of the natural sounds. They therefore differ widely in various languages in accordance with the specific phonetic genius of each of these. As such they may be considered an integral portion of speech, in the properly cultural sense of the term, being no more identical with the instinctive cries themselves than such words as "cuckoo" and "kill-deer" are identical with the cries of the birds they denote or than Rossini's treatment of a storm in the overture to "William Tell" is in fact a storm. In other words, the interjections and sound-imitative words of normal speech are related to their natural prototypes as is art, a purely social or cultural thing, to nature. It may be objected that, though the interjections differ somewhat as we pass from language to language, they do nevertheless offer striking family resemblances and may therefore be looked upon as having grown up out of a common instinctive base. But their case is nowise different from that, say, of the varying national modes of pictorial representation. A Japanese picture of a hill both differs from and resembles a typical modern European painting of the same kind of hill. Both are suggested by and both "imitate" the same natural feature. Neither the one nor the other is the same thing as, or, in any intelligible sense, a direct outgrowth of, this natural feature. The two modes of representation are not identical because they proceed from differing historical traditions, are executed with differing pictorial techniques. The interjections of Japanese and English are, just so, suggested by a common natural prototype, the instinctive cries, and are thus unavoidably suggestive of each other. They differ, now greatly, now but little, because they are builded out of historically diverse materials or techniques, the respective linguistic traditions, phonetic systems, speech habits of the two peoples. Yet the instinctive cries as such are practically identical for all humanity, just as the human skeleton or nervous system is to all intents and purposes a "fixed," that is, an only slightly and "accidentally" variable, feature of man's organism.

Interjections are among the least important of speech elements. Their discussion is valuable mainly because it can be shown that even they, avowedly the nearest of all language sounds to instinctive utterance, are only superficially of an instinctive nature. Were it therefore possible to demonstrate that the whole of language is traceable, in its ultimate historical and psychological foundations, to the interjections, it would still not follow that language is an instinctive activity. But, as a matter of fact, all attempts to explain the origin of speech have been fruitless. There is no tangible evidence, historical or otherwise, tending to show that the mass of speech elements and speech processes has evolved out of the interjections. These are a very small and functionally insignificant proportion of the vocabulary of language; at no time and in no linguistic province that we have record of do we see a noticeable tendency towards their elaboration into the primary warp and woof of language. They are never more, at best, than a decorative edging to the ample, complex fabric.

* * *

The way is now cleared for a serviceable definition of language. Language is a purely human and non-instinctive method of communicating ideas, emotions, and desires by means of a system of voluntarily produced symbols. These symbols are, in the first instance, auditory and they are produced by the so-called "organs of speech." There is no discernible instinctive basis in human speech as such, however much instinctive expressions and the natural environment may serve as a stimulus for the development of certain elements of speech, however much instinctive tendencies, motor and other, may give a predetermined range or mold to linguistic expression. Such human or animal communication, if "communication" it may be called, as is brought about by involuntary, instinctive cries is not, in our sense, language at all.

* * *

We can profitably discuss the intention, the form, and the history of speech, precisely as we discuss the nature of any other phase of human culture—say art or religion—as an institutional or cultural entity, leaving the organic and psychological mechanisms back of it as something to be taken for granted. Accordingly, it must be clearly understood that this introduction to the study of speech is not concerned with those aspects of physiology and of physiological psychology that underlie speech. Our study of language is not to be one of the genesis and operation of a concrete mechanism; it is, rather, to be an inquiry into the function and form of the arbitrary systems of symbolism that we term languages.

* * *

Language is primarily an auditory system of symbols. In so far as it is articulated it is also a motor system, but the motor aspect of speech is clearly secondary to the auditory. In normal individuals the impulse to speech first takes effect in the sphere of auditory imagery and is then transmitted to the motor nerves that control the organs of speech. The motor processes and the accompanying motor feelings are not, however, the end, the final resting point. They are merely a means and a control leading to auditory perception in both speaker and hearer. Communication, which is the very object of speech, is successfully effected only when the hearer's auditory perceptions are translated into the appropriate and intended flow of imagery or thought or both combined. Hence the cycle of speech, in so far as we may look upon it as a purely external instrument, begins and ends in the realm of sounds. The concordance between the initial auditory imagery and the final auditory perceptions is the social seal or warrant of the successful issue of the process. As we have already seen, the typical course of this process may undergo endless modifications or transfers into equivalent systems without thereby losing its essential formal characteristics.

There is no more striking general fact about language than its universality. One may argue as to whether a particular tribe engages in activities that are worthy of the name of religion or of art, but we know of no people that is not possessed of a fully developed language. The lowliest South African Bushman speaks in the forms of a rich symbolic system that is in essence perfectly comparable to the speech of the cultivated Frenchman. It goes without saying that the more abstract concepts are not nearly so plentifully represented in the language of the savage, nor is there the rich terminology and the finer definition of nuances that reflect the higher culture. Yet the sort of linguistic development that parallels the historic growth of culture and which, in its later stages, we associate with literature is, at best, but a superficial thing. The fundamental groundwork of language—the development of a clear-cut phonetic system, the specific association of speech elements with concepts, and the delicate provision for the formal expression of all manner of relations—all this meets us rigidly perfected and systematized in every language known to us. Many primitive languages have a formal richness, a latent luxuriance of expression, that eclipses anything known to the languages of modern civilization. Even in the mere matter of the inventory of speech the layman must be prepared for strange surprises. Popular statements as to the extreme poverty of expression to which primitive languages are doomed are simply myths. Scarcely less impressive than the universality of speech is its almost incredible diversity. Those of us that have studied French or German, or, better yet, Latin or Greek, know in what varied forms a thought may run. The formal divergences between the English plan and the Latin plan, however, are comparatively slight in the perspective of what we know of more exotic linguistic patterns. The universality and the diversity of speech lead to a significant inference. We are forced to believe that language is an immensely ancient heritage of the human race, whether or not all forms of speech are the historical outgrowth of a single pristine form. It is doubtful if any other cultural asset of man, be it the art of drilling for fire or of chipping stone, may lay claim to a greater age. I am inclined to believe that it antedated even the lowliest developments of material culture, that these developments, in fact, were not strictly possible until language, the tool of significant expression, had itself taken shape.

* * *

Language and our thought-grooves are inextricably interwoven, are, in a sense, one and the same. As there is nothing to show that there are significant racial differences in the fundamental conformation of thought, it follows that the infinite variability of linguistic form, another name for the infinite variability of the actual process of thought, cannot be an index of such significant racial differences. This is only apparently a paradox. The latent content of all languages is the same—the intuitive *science* of experience. It is the manifest form that is never twice the same, for this form, which we call linguistic morphology, is nothing more nor less than a collective *art* of thought, an art denuded of the irrelevancies of individual sentiment. At last analysis, then, language can no more flow from race as such than can the sonnet form.

Nor can I believe that culture and language are in any true sense causally related. Culture may be defined as *what* a society does and thinks. Language is a particular *how* of thought. It is difficult to see what particular causal relations may be expected to subsist between a selected inventory of experience (culture, a significant selection made by society) and the particular manner in which the society expresses all experience. The drift of culture, another way of saying history, is a complex series of changes in society's selected inventory—additions, losses, changes of emphasis and relation. The drift of language is not properly concerned with changes of content at all, merely with changes in formal expression. It is possible, in thought, to change every sound, word, and concrete concept of a language without changing its inner actuality in the least, just as one can pour into a fixed mold water or plaster or molten gold. If it can be shown that culture has an innate form, a series of contours, quite apart from subject-matter of any description whatsoever, we have a something in culture that may serve as a term of comparison with and possibly a means of relating it to language. But until such purely formal patterns of culture are discovered and laid bare, we shall do well to hold the drifts of language and of culture to be non-comparable and unrelated processes. From this it follows that all attempts to connect particular types of linguistic morphology with certain correlated stages of cultural development are vain. Rightly understood, such correlations are rubbish. The merest *coup d'oeil* verifies our theoretical argument on this point. Both simple and complex types of language of an indefinite number of varieties may be found spoken at any desired level of cultural advance. When it comes to linguistic form, Plato walks with the Macedonian swineherd, Confucius with the head-hunting savage of Assam.

It goes without saying that the mere content of language is intimately related to culture. A society that has no knowledge of theosophy need have no name for it; aborigines that had never seen or heard of a horse were compelled to invent or borrow a word for the animal when they made his acquaintance. In the sense that the vocabulary of a language more or less faithfully reflects the culture whose purposes it serves it is perfectly true that the history of language and the history of culture move along parallel lines. But this superficial and extraneous kind of parallelism is of no real interest to the linguist except in so far as the growth or borrowing of new words incidentally throws light on the formal trends of the language. The linguistic student should never make the mistake of identifying a language with its dictionary.

If both this and the preceding chapter have been largely negative in their contentions, I believe that they have been healthily so. There is perhaps no better way to learn the essential nature of speech than to realize what it is not and what it does not do. Its superficial connections with other historic processes are so close that it needs to be shaken free of them if we are to see it in its own right. Everything that we have so far seen to be true of language points to the fact that it is the most significant and colossal work that the human spirit has evolved—nothing short of a finished form of expression for all communicable experience. This form may be endlessly varied by the individual without thereby losing its distinctive contours; and it is constantly reshaping itself as is all art. Language is the most massive and inclusive art we know, a mountainous and anonymous work of unconscious generations.

QUERIES

- Sapir argues that language, although based on human biology, is not derived from nature. How do humans acquire language?
- Sapir distinguishes "instinctive cries" of pain or pleasure from real speech, asserting that language is not derived from such utterances and interjections. What is the defining quality of language?
- "We know of no people that is not possessed of a fully developed language," Sapir concludes. What does this imply about the antiquity of human language?

CONNECTIONS

- Compare Sapir's discussion of words as spoken symbols to Sherry Ortner's discussion of key symbols (see chapter 22). How are these different sets of symbols similarly defined by the social contexts in which they are used?

PRIMARY TEXT: *LANGUAGE AND ENVIRONMENT* (EXCERPTS)

Reproduced by permission of the American Anthropological Association from *American Anthropologist*, vol. 14 (2), 1912, pp. 226–242. www.aaanet.org. Not for sale or further reproduction.

There is a strong tendency to ascribe many elements of human culture to the influence of the environment in which the sharers of that culture are placed, some even taking the extreme position of reducing practically all manifestations of human life and thought to environmental influences. I shall not attempt to argue for or against the importance of the influence had by forces of environment on traits of culture, nor shall I attempt to show in how far the influence of environment is crossed by that of other factors. To explain any one trait of human culture as due solely to the force of physical environment, however, seems to me to rest on a fallacy. Properly speaking, environment can act directly only on an individual, and in those cases where we find that a purely environmental influence is responsible for a communal trait, this common trait must be interpreted as a summation of distinct processes of environmental influences on individuals. Such, however, is obviously not the typical form in which we find the forces of environment at work on human groups. In these it is enough that a single individual may react directly to his environment and bring the rest of the group to share consciously or unconsciously in the influence exerted upon him. Whether even a single individual can be truthfully said to be capable of environmental influence uncombined with influences of another character is doubtful, but we may at least assume the possibility. The important point remains that in actual society even the simplest environmental influence is either supported or transformed by social force. Hence any attempt to consider even the simplest element of culture as due solely to the influence of environment must be termed misleading. The social forces which thus transform the purely environmental influences may themselves be looked upon as environmental in character in so far as a given individual is placed in, and therefore reacts to, a set of social factors. On the other hand, the social forces may be looked upon, somewhat metaphorically, as parallel in their influence to those of heredity in so far as they are handed down from generation to generation. That these traditional social forces are themselves subject to environmental, among other, changes, illustrates the complexity of the problem of cultural origins and development. On the whole one does better to employ the term "environment" only when reference is had to such influences, chiefly physical in character, as lie outside the will of man. Yet in speaking of language, which may be considered a complex of symbols reflecting the whole physical and social background in which a group of men is placed, it is advantageous to comprise within the term environment both physical and social factors. Under physical environment are comprised geographical characters, such as the topography of the country (whether coast, valley, plain, plateau, or mountain), climate, and amount of rainfall, and what may be called the economic basis of human life, under which terms are comprised the fauna, flora, and mineral resources of the region. Under social environment are comprised the various forces of society that mold the life and thought of each individual. Among the more important of these social forces are religion, ethical standards, form of political organization, and art.

According to this classification of environmental influences, we may expect to find two sets of environmental factors reflected in language, assuming for the moment that language is materially influenced by the environmental background of its speakers. Properly speaking, of course, the physical environment is reflected in language only in so far as it has been influenced by social factors. The mere existence, for instance, of a certain type of animal in the physical environment of a people does not suffice to give rise to a linguistic symbol referring to it. It is necessary that the animal be known by the members of the group in common and that they have some interest, however slight, in it before the language of the community is called upon to make reference to this particular element of the physical environment. In other words, so far as language is concerned, all environmental influence reduces at last analysis to the influence of social environment.

Nevertheless it is practical to keep apart such social influences as proceed more or less directly from the physical environment, and those that can not be easily connected with it. Language may be influenced in one of three ways: in regard to its subject matter or content, i.e., in regard to the vocabulary; in regard to its phonetic system, i.e., the system of sounds with which it operates in the building of words; and in regard to its grammatical form, i.e., in regard to the formal processes and the logical or psychological classifications made use of in speech. Morphology, or the formal structure of words, and syntax, or the methods employed in combining words into larger units or sentences, are the two main aspects of grammatical form.

It is the vocabulary of a language that most clearly reflects the physical and social environment of its speakers. The complete vocabulary of a language may indeed be looked upon as a complex inventory of all the ideas, interests, and occupations that take up the attention of the community, and were such a complete thesaurus of the language of a given tribe at our disposal, we might to a large extent infer the character of the physical environment and the characteristics of the culture of the people making use of it. It is not difficult to find examples of languages whose vocabulary thus bears the stamp of the physical environment in which the speakers are placed. This is particularly true of the languages of primitive peoples, for among these culture has not attained such a degree of complexity as to imply practically universal interests. From this point of view the vocabulary of primitive languages may be compared to the vocabularies of particular sections of the population of civilized peoples. The characteristic vocabulary of a coast tribe, such as the Nootka Indians, with its precise terms for many species of marine animals, vertebrate and invertebrate, might be compared to the vocabulary of such European fisher-folk as the Basques of southwestern France and northern Spain. In contrast to such coast peoples may be mentioned the inhabitants of a desert plateau, like the Southern Paiute of Arizona, Nevada, and Utah. In the vocabulary of this tribe we find adequate provision made for many topographical features that would in some cases seem almost too precise to be of practical value. Some of the topographical terms of this language that have been collected are: divide, ledge, sand flat, semicircular valley, circular valley or hollow, spot of level ground in mountains surrounded by ridges, plain valley surrounded by mountains, plain, desert, knoll, plateau, canyon without water, canyon with creek, wash or gutter, gulch, slope of mountain or canyon wall receiving sunlight, shaded slope of mountain or canyon wall, rolling country intersected by several small hill-ridges, and many others.

In the case of the specialized vocabularies of both Nootka and Southern Paiute, it is important to note that it is not merely the fauna or topographical features of the country as such that are reflected, but rather the interest of the people in such environmental features. Were the Nootka Indians dependent for their food supply primarily on land hunting and vegetable products, despite their proximity to the sea, there is little doubt that their vocabulary would not be as thoroughly saturated as it is with sea lore. Similarly it is quite evident from the presence in Paiute of such topographical terms as have been listed, that accurate reference to topography is a necessary thing to dwellers in an inhospitable semi-arid region; so purely practical a need as definitely locating a spring might well require reference to several features of topographical detail. How far the interest in the physical environment rather than its mere presence affects the character of a vocabulary may be made apparent by a converse case in English. One who is not a botanist, or is not particularly interested for purposes of folk medicine or otherwise in plant lore, would not know how to refer to numberless plants that make up part of his environment except merely as "weeds", whereas an Indian tribe very largely dependent for its food supply on wild roots, seeds of wild plants, and other vegetable products, might have precise terms for each and every one of these nondescript weeds. In many cases distinct terms would even be in use for various conditions of a single plant species, distinct reference being made as to whether it is raw or cooked, or of this or that color, or in this or that stage of growth. In this way special vocabularies having reference to acorns or camass might be collected from various tribes of California or Oregon. Another instructive example of how largely interest determines the character of a vocabulary is afforded by the terms in several Indian languages for sun and moon. While we find it necessary to distinguish sun and moon, not a few tribes content themselves with a single word for both, the exact reference being left to the context. If we complain that so vague a term fails to do justice to an essential natural difference, the Indian might well retaliate by pointing to the omnium gatherum character of our term "weed" as contrasted with his own more precise plant vocabulary. Everything naturally depends on the point of view as determined by interest. Bearing this in mind, it becomes evident that the presence or absence of general terms is to a large extent dependent on the negative or positive character of the interest in the elements of environment involved. The more necessary a particular culture finds it to make distinctions within a given range of phenomena, the less likely the existence of a general term covering the range. On the other hand, the more indifferent culturally are the elements, the more likely that they will all be embraced in a single term of general application. The case may be summarized, if example can summarize, by saying that to the layman every animal form that is neither human being, quadruped, fish, nor bird, is a bug or worm. To this same type of layman the concept and corresponding word "mammal" would, for a converse reason, be quite unfamiliar.

There is an obvious difference between words that are merely words, incapable of further analysis, and such words as are so evidently secondary in formation as to yield analysis to even superficial reflection. A lion is merely a lion, but a mountain-lion suggests something more than the animal referred to. Where a transparent descriptive term is in use for a simple concept, it seems fair in most cases to conclude that the knowledge of the environmental element referred to is comparatively recent, or at any rate that the present naming has taken place at a comparatively recent time. The destructive agencies of phonetic change would in the long run wear down originally descriptive terms to mere labels or unanalyzable words pure and simple. I speak of this matter here because the transparent or untransparent character of a vocabulary may lead us to infer, if somewhat vaguely, the length of time that a group of people has been familiar with a particular concept. People who speak of lions have evidently been familiar with that animal for many generations. Those who speak of mountain lions would seem to date their knowledge of these from yesterday. The case is even clearer when we turn to a consideration of placenames. Only the student of language history is able to analyze such names as Essex, Norfolk, and Sutton into their component elements as East Saxon, North Folk, and South Town, while to the lay consciousness these names are etymological units as purely as are "butter" and "cheese". The contrast between a country inhabited by an historically homogeneous group for a long time, full of etymologically obscure place-names, and a newly settled country with its New-towns, Wildwoods, and Mill Creeks, is apparent. Naturally much depends on the grammatical character of the language itself; such highly synthetic forms of speech as are many American Indian languages seem to lose hold of the descriptive character of their terms less readily than does English, for instance.

* * *

If the characteristic physical environment of a people is to a large extent reflected in its language, this is true to an even greater extent of its social environment. A large number, if not most, of the elements that make up a physical environment are found universally distributed in time and place, so that there are natural limits set to the variability of lexical materials in so far as they give expression to concepts derived from the physical world. A culture, however, develops in numberless ways and may reach any degree of complexity. Hence we need not be surprised to find that the vocabularies of peoples that differ widely in character or degree of culture share this wide difference. There is a difference between the rich, conceptually ramified vocabulary of a language like English or French and that of any typical primitive group, corresponding in large measure to that which obtains between the complex culture of the English-speaking or French-speaking peoples of Europe and America with its vast array of specialized interests, and the relatively simple undifferentiated culture of the primitive group. Such variability of vocabulary, as reflecting social environment, obtains in time as well as place; in other words, the stock of cultural concepts and therefore also the corresponding vocabulary become constantly enriched and ramified with the increase within a group of cultural complexity. That a vocabulary should thus to a great degree reflect cultural complexity is practically self-evident, for a vocabulary, that is, the subject matter of a language, aims at any given time to serve as a set of symbols referring to the culture background of the group. If by complexity of language is meant the range of interests implied in its vocabulary, it goes without saying that there is a constant correlation between complexity of language and culture. If, however, as is more usual, linguistic complexity be used to refer to degree of morphologic and syntactic development, it is by no means true that such a correlation exists. In fact, one might almost make a case for an inverse correlation and maintain that morphologic development tends to decrease with increase of cultural complexity. Examples of this tendency are so easy to find that it is hardly worth our while going into the matter here. It need merely be pointed out that the history of English and French shows a constant loss in elaborateness of grammatical structure from their earliest recorded forms to the present. On the other hand, too much must not be made of this. The existence of numerous relatively simple forms of speech among primitive peoples discourages the idea of any tangible correlation between degree or form of culture and form of speech.

* * *

We seem, then, perhaps reluctantly, forced to admit that, apart from the reflection of environment in the vocabulary of a language, there is nothing in the language itself that can be shown to be directly associated with environment. One wonders why, if such be the case, so large a number of distinct phonetic systems and types of linguistic morphology are found in various parts of the world. Perhaps the whole problem of the relation between culture and environment generally, on the one hand, and language, on the other, may be furthered somewhat by a consideration simply of the rate of change or development of both. Linguistic features are necessarily less capable of rising into the consciousness of the speakers than traits of culture. Without here attempting to go into an analysis of this psychological difference between the two sets of phenomena, it would seem to follow that changes in culture are the result, to at least a considerable extent, of conscious processes or of processes more easily made conscious, whereas those of language are to be explained, if explained at all, as due to the more minute action of psychological factors beyond the control of will or reflection. If this is true, and there seems every reason to believe that it is, we must conclude that cultural change and linguistic change do not move along parallel lines and hence do not tend to stand in a close causal relation. This point of view makes it quite legitimate to grant, if necessary, the existence at some primitive stage in the past of a more definite association between environment and linguistic form than can now be posited anywhere, for the different character and rate of change in linguistic and cultural phenomena, conditioned by the very nature of those phenomena, would in the long run very materially disturb and ultimately entirely eliminate such an association.

We may conceive, somewhat schematically, the development of culture and language to have taken place as follows: A primitive group, among whom even the beginnings of culture and language are as yet hardly in evidence, may nevertheless be supposed to behave in accordance with a fairly definite group psychology, determined, we will suppose, partly by race mind, partly by physical environment. On the basis of this group psychology, whatever tendencies it may possess, a language and a culture will slowly develop. As both of these are directly determined, to begin with, by fundamental factors of race and physical environment, they will parallel each other somewhat closely, so that the forms of cultural activity will be reflected in the grammatical system of the language. In other words, not only will the words themselves of a language serve as symbols of detached cultural elements, as is true of languages at all periods of development, but we may suppose the grammatical categories and processes themselves to symbolize corresponding types of thought and activity of cultural significance. To some extent culture and language may then be conceived of as in a constant state of interaction and definite association for a considerable lapse of time. This state of correlation, however, cannot continue indefinitely. With gradual change of group psychology and physical environment more or less profound changes must be effected in the form and content of both language and culture. Language and culture, however, are obviously not the direct expression of racial psychology and physical environment, but depend for their existence and continuance primarily on the forces of tradition. Hence, despite necessary modifications in either with the lapse of time, a conservative tendency will always make itself felt as a check to those tendencies that make for change. And here we come to the crux of the matter. Cultural elements, as more definitely serving the immediate needs of society and entering more clearly into consciousness, will not only change more rapidly than those of language, but the form itself of culture, giving each element its relative significance, will be continually shaping itself anew. Linguistic elements, on the other hand, while they may and do readily change in themselves, do not so easily lend themselves to regroupings, owing to the subconscious character of grammatical classification. A grammatical system as such tends to persist: indefinitely. In other words, the conservative tendency makes itself felt more profoundly in the formal groundwork of language than in that of culture. One necessary consequence of this is that the forms of language will in course of time cease to symbolize those of culture, and this is our main thesis. Another consequence is that the forms of language may be thought to more accurately reflect those of a remotely past stage of culture than the present ones of culture itself. It is not claimed that a stage is ever reached at which language and culture stand in no sort of relation to each other, but simply that the relative rates of change of the two differ so materially as to make it practically impossible to detect the relationship.

Though the forms of language may not change as rapidly as those of culture, it is doubtless true that an unusual rate of cultural change is accompanied by a corresponding accelerated rate of change in language. If this point of view be pushed to its legitimate conclusion, we must be led to believe that rapidly increasing complexity of culture necessitates correspondingly, though not equally rapid, changes in linguistic form and content. This view is the direct opposite of the one generally held with respect to the greater conservatism of language in civilized communities than among primitive peoples. To be sure, the tendency to rapid linguistic change with increasingly rapid complexity of culture may be checked by one of the most important elements of an advanced culture itself, namely, the use of a secondary set of language symbols necessarily possessing greater conservatism than the primarily spoken set of symbols and exerting a conservative influence on the latter. I refer to the use of writing. In spite of this, however, it seems to me that the apparent paradox that we have arrived at contains a liberal element of truth. I am not inclined to consider it an accident that the rapid development of culture in western Europe during the last 2,000 years has been synchronous with what seems to be unusually rapid changes in language. Though it is impossible to prove the matter definitely, I am inclined to doubt whether many languages of primitive peoples have undergone as rapid modification in a corresponding period of time as has the English language.

We have no time at our disposal to go more fully into this purely hypothetical explanation of our failure to bring environment and language into causal relation, but a metaphor may help us to grasp it. Two men start on a journey on condition that each shift for himself, depending on his own resources, yet traveling in the same general direction. For a considerable time the two men, both as yet unwearied, will keep pretty well together. In course of time, however, the varying degrees of physical strength, resourcefulness, ability to orient oneself, and many other factors, will begin to manifest themselves. The actual course traveled by each in reference to the other and to the course originally planned will diverge more and more, while the absolute distance between the two will also tend to become greater and greater. And so with many sets of historic sequences which, at one time causally associated, tend in course of time to diverge.

QUERIES

- In discussing the relationships between language and environment, Sapir writes that "even the simplest environmental influence is either supported or transformed by social force." What are some of the social forces Sapir has in mind, and how would they influence languages?
- According to Sapir, the physical and social environments have the greatest impact on the vocabularies of different languages—not only the words used but also the classifications employed. What is the basic reason that such different classifications reflect the social environment?
- In his discussion of culture and language, Sapir argues that language always is more conservative and resistant to change than culture. Why is this the case?

CONNECTIONS

- Sapir argues that linguistic forms may reflect earlier forms of culture. Compare this observation to Tylor's doctrine of survivals (chapter 1), and then apply these ideas to the common phrase in American English, "dialing the phone."
- Contrast Sapir's notion that the influences of environment on language and culture are, in essence, always social influences to Julian Steward's (chapter 14) ideas about the influence of environment on culture.

8

Margaret Mead

INTRODUCTION

Margaret Mead (1901–1978) was the most widely known anthropologist in America, the author of nearly 1,500 books and scientific journals, as well as hundreds of newspaper and magazine articles. Many of these publications dealt with Mead's central observation: the various ways children are raised is pivotal for understanding cultural differences (see Moore 2008:104–16). This insight was presented in Mead's early books, *Coming of Age in Samoa* (1928)—an instant classic and bestseller—*Growing up in New Guinea* (1930), and in the article reprinted below.

Despite Mead's early public successes, her emphasis on the importance of detailed studies of childrearing met with some resistance from other anthropologists. In this article, Mead argues that such studies are essential to ethnographic understanding. On one level Mead's point seems fairly obvious: anthropologists cannot understand different cultures without documenting the transformations from birth to adulthood. At another level, Mead's argument is more subtle. Ethnographers are attracted by and observe elaborated and stylized cultural practices: public festivals, initiation rites surrounded by taboos, calendar-based ceremonies, and so on. Yet some societies emphasize other, less formulaic cultural practices—essential cultural practices that the ethnographer may overlook.

This uneven ethnographic attention to formalized and nonformalized cultural practices means that comparative studies are impossible. And yet, as Mead writes, "The facts of birth, child training, family life, marriage, widowhood, old age, death are of as great importance in the life of every individual in the culture, whether that culture has seized upon them for externalization in ceremonial or not."

This point has implications for ethnographic research. Societies that employ a highly formalized ceremonial cycle can be studied through a straightforward (at least in theory) research program: the anthropologist interviews "expert" informants, observes the individual ceremonies, and then recasts and summarizes the data into an ethnography. But what about research in a society where cultural practices are less formalized? In such cultures, "the study of an unformalized part of culture, a knowledge of the language, a much more extended entrée into the lives of the people, a much more complete participation in their lives" are required.

This challenge is even greater when the ethnographer studies children. In many societies the rules governing children's lives are less explicit than those about adult behavior; in fact, "growing up" is, in part, the process of learning those rules. Further, there may be significant differences between the rules surrounding children and those relevant to adults. And yet, Mead writes, "for an adequate understanding of human culture, it is absolutely essential to study carefully all parts of a culture, and not merely those which present the superficial appearance of having greatest form."

Mead not only outlines ethnographic field methods, but also argues that subtle and inexplicit aspects of cultural practice cannot be overlooked. This position has theoretical implications that contrast with other visions of culture (see "Connections" below).

PRIMARY TEXT: *MORE COMPREHENSIVE FIELD METHODS*

Reproduced by permission of the American Anthropological Association from *American Anthropologist*, Vol. 35 (1), 1933, pp. 1–15. www.aaanet.org. Not for sale or further reproduction.

The history of ethnographic field work has been also the history of widening definition of which departments of human life are to be regarded as culture, which are to be classified, and which ignored, under the heading of "psychology" or "private life."[1] In the traditional monograph it is still regarded as adequate to dismiss "Family relations" with a paragraph and "child training" with a page. Accidents of early choice have also determined which questions all good ethnographers ask; for example, a monograph would be condemned which betrayed the fact that the ethnographer has failed to find out whether there was circumcision or what disposition was

---

[1] This paper is based upon the combined field experience of Mr. Fortune and myself; on Mr. Fortune's experience in Dobu and Basima, my experience in Samoa, our joint experience in Manus of the Admiralties, and among a North American Indian tribe.

made of the umbilical cord. But a complete ignorance of the way in which a child is weaned or the position in which a child is held while being suckled, although just as culturally standardized and possibly far more significant in the life of the child, may be omitted with a clear ethnographic conscience. Emphases such as these are purely accidental, having no essential relevance to the line drawn between those fields which are essentially the province of the ethnographer and those which are not. It is, however, advisable to scrutinize critically such fashions in field work and point out how inconsistent and disjointed present standards of inquiry are.

One turns, however, from these merely fortuitous omissions which any traditional ethnographer will admit as nevertheless appropriate for study, to a more elaborate problem, the problem of how unformalized aspects of culture are to be studied. Traditionally, puberty has been studied from the standpoint of ceremonial. If there are periods of segregation, mutilations, instructions, taboos, rituals surrounding puberty, the ethnologist sets them down with conscientious regard for detail. If, however, the particular culture under consideration makes no formal point of puberty, stresses it by no ceremonial, no taboo, the ethnologist has in the past simply ignored the subject, counting his duty well done if he sets down: "These people have no puberty ceremonials." Yet a serious consideration of the problem will show that though the absence of a type of behavior inquired about because characteristic of other primitive societies is of historical interest, the mere recording of its absence is hardly an adequate statement about the society in question. The young people of Dobu and Samoa have to grow up just as certainly as do the young people of Manus or of the Orokaiva. Their own attitudes towards the increasing responsibilities of maturity, their behavior towards each other, towards their parents, towards members of the opposite sex, is just as much a fact of culture as if it were rendered explicit and conspicuous by ceremonial and taboo.

What can be said of puberty can be said with equal justice of childbirth, which is dismissed with a sentence if there are no religious or social rites, or immediately observable and striking customs; of marriage, to which pages are given only if the particular culture has happened to seize upon marriage for obvious elaboration. The field ethnographer in the past has too often been prone to describe culture only in terms of the conspicuous, the conventional, and the bizarre. It is at his door that many of the most characteristic errors of the arm-chair theorizer must be laid; there is small wonder that Lévy-Bruhl sees the native as pre-logical, or Crawley as obsessed by ideas of sex, when only the cultural elaborations of the unusual are presented for their consideration.

In addition to this tendency to neglect whole aspects of culture, there has also been a failure, very often, to distinguish methodologically between the forms under which various aspects of culture appear in different societies.

The religion of a people like the Zuni, with their fixed calendrical ceremonial lends itself to a different type of analysis than does the religion of the Western Plains. In one case, the ground-plan of the culture is laid down and individuals pass through it, their experience is subsidiary, at least for a general understanding of the culture, to the plan itself. In the other there is no such ground-plan; only from the records of individual visions, from a running record of the lives of individuals, can an adequate picture of the structure of religion be gained. This contrast can be drawn equally well between any other calendrical and non-calendrical people: in Hawaii the chief religious festivals occurred at stated seasons each year; the gods marched through the districts and each district presented tribute; among the Maori, on the contrary, it was an occasion, like the building of a great house or of a war canoe which called for important religious ceremonies; without the occasion, there was no ceremony. The observer of one year among the Maori might come away without having seen most of the ceremonies; this would have been impossible among the ancient Hawaiians, where the ground-plan, laid down in time, instead of the running current of events, was the cultural theme.

Again, if the comparison is made between those people who depend upon formulas and those who depend upon extemporaneous speech or invocation, the field worker is confronted with the same problem. The Dobuan who recites a spell, makes every effort to recite it unchanged; unless the student is primarily interested in those slight variations which occur in the transfer of an oral tradition, it will not make much difference whether he learns the charm from father or from son; and one text will give him the form of the spell as perfectly as would five renderings of the same spell by different people, if so be it the spell was shared by that number of individuals. It is otherwise, however, with the speeches which a Manus man makes to his guardian ghost whenever he gives a feast. These are extemporaneous, follow no such set verbal scheme; one man will complain of his recent bad luck with his crab baskets, another remark upon the recent illness and recovery of a child, a third comment gratefully upon rescue from a shipwreck, a fourth may wax facetious and almost discourteous to his supernatural. One of these speeches will not do as well as another; only by carefully recording a series of them may the cultural pattern, as firm, although more varyingly embodied in words, be derived.

In studies of leadership and political life, a great deal will depend upon whether the individual takes a fixed place in a hierarchical society, in which the person is only a temporary pawn, as in Samoa or among the Iroquois, or whether the headman owes his position, not to an inherited or acquired place in a permanent scheme, but to his own exploits which stand as his only claim to position. The contrast between the position of peace chiefs and war leaders among the Iroquois or in the Southern Plains is an example of this difference. A count of Iroquois sachems, of how they were chosen, of their various defined functions and duties, gives a formally complete picture of that aspect of Iroquois political life. The war leader, with an unstylized position based upon his personality, the number of personal adherents he could muster, accidents of success or failure on a war party, could not be studied in any such cursory fashion, in fact in most American Indian tribes was not studied at all. Where the pattern was explicit it was recorded; where any comparable statement would have entailed observations of the personality of war leader after war leader, and the fortunes of war party after war party, it was ignored. And yet would any one seriously argue that the sachem was of more actual importance in Iroquois life than the leader of the war party which finally vanquished the Susquehannocks?

The study of kinship shows particularly sharply the effect upon investigators of formulated and unformulated kinship ideas. Rivers' insistence that wherever there was a special kinship term, there the investigator should look for kinship function, could be paralleled by a statement, that wherever there is no special kinship term, the average investigator does not think of looking for a special function. Yet the facts of patrilocal or matrilocal residence may make either a maternal or a paternal grandmother stand out more sharply in the life of a child, without any difference in terminology. There may be one term for parents-in-law, used by husband or wife indifferently, yet residence arrangements may make a great difference as to which in-law relationship, parents to son's wife or parents to daughter's husband, is the more significant in the life of the people. In Samoa there is one word for younger sibling, *tei*. A formal account of the kinship would merely state that this is "younger sibling, either sex, regardless of sex of speaker." Actual observation of conditions reveals the fact that this is a term which is very seldom used by males and used particularly seldom by grown men. Its real usage, aside from its formal origins, which it shares with other Polynesian kinship systems, is intimately connected with the fostering relationship between a girl-child and her younger siblings.

Upon these very real differences in cultural explicitness there rest several points of method. In the first place, only the formal points can be obtained from informants in a dead culture. Students of American Indian cultures today, with the exception of the Southwest, will have to content themselves in most part with recording those aspects of a people's lives which the culture had elaborated and formalized, either in myth, kinship terminology, or ceremonial. But it should be realized at the outset that such material is merely data upon cultural emphases, a series of partially complete skeletons which must often, if not always, give a most distorted view of any given culture. The facts of birth, child training, family life, marriage, widowhood, old age, death are of as great importance in the life of every individual in the culture, whether that culture has seized upon them for externalization in ceremonial or not. It is impossible adequately to discuss the form of a culture which is only known at various obtrusive and often accidentally chosen points, with whole areas of the human lives lived within it unknown.

This point of view may be submitted to a test by selecting a culture where the explicit aspects of the culture have been perfectly recorded with a fine feeling for form and structure, but where there has been no record given of all the unformulated cultural attitudes which give that form meaning. The Banaro[2] is a case in point. Thurnwald presents the reader with a description of a situation which would seem to provide for an endless amount of conflict; a woman has to stand aside while her husband initiates a young girl, a man while his wife initiates a young man. Here the traditional setting for jealousy which comes with age and failing powers is explicit, but we are given no material on the attitudes which make the situation bearable or possibly desirable to the Banaro. Similarly, the young husband has to forego not only his bride's first favors but all her favors until she has born a goblin child to her goblin father. What is the attitude of the husband to this goblin child, as compared with his attitude towards the children which he believes are his? Is this a point which is made or ignored or differently phrased? What is the effect upon marital happiness when both men and women are formally initiated by experienced elders? Into what category does the bride fit the goblin father, into that of husband or of father-substitute? Thurnwald has given us only one clue: he remarks that the Banaro boys are so absorbed in their system that it is difficult to find work boys among them. This is evidence that the system works, for willingness to sign on as indentured labor is a good index of the degree to which the young men's lives are integrated at home—at least this is so in other parts of Melanesia.

In contrast, take the kinship structure of Dobu. Set down in formal ethnographic terms, it could be phrased as bi-local residence, the married couples spending alternate years in their respective villages, the villages being coterminous with the sub-clan group. The wife has a house in her village and the husband has a house in his. Such a statement would give no clue to the fact that in Dobu, as Mr. Fortune has demonstrated with careful documentation,[3] the bi-local residence is a festering point in the social life, a device by which a woman may betray her husband with her clan brothers, and he in turn, the following year, betray her; a continual reminder of the fear of sorcery, because all affinal relatives are witches and sorcerers; a form of social organization so rife with difficult situations that individuals in order to stabilize their marriages frequently attempt a usually unsuccessful suicide.

Again in the matter of name taboos and their role in the group life: Williams states of the Orokaiva,[4]

---

[2] Thurnwald, R. Banaro Society. Social Organization and Kinship System of a Tribe in the Interior of New Guinea. AAA-M 111, no. 4.

[3] Sorcerers of Dobu, London: George Routledge and Sons, 1931.

[4] Williams, F. E. Orokaiva Society, Oxford University Press, 1930.

When he takes a wife she is economically absorbed into his clan and her life in all important respects belongs to that clan; and he by certain elaborate precautions, of which name taboos are an instance, takes good care to remain on good terms with his relatives by marriage.

But what does this mean? In Manus, where a man also observes name taboos towards his affinal relatives, they are a most effective way of keeping affinal relatives apart, for—and this is inexplicit, hence would escape conventional study—a woman may not discuss her husband with her relatives, nor discuss her relatives with her husband. If she does so, even obliquely, she is violating the spirit of the taboo, although only the name taboo is explicit. When relatives draw together, the affinal relatives must be completely excluded from the circle of attention or reference. This may act to prevent intimacy in marriage, as in Manus; it may, as Williams lightly suggests, cement marriage, but it is impossible to tell which from a mere statement of form.

This might seem to be a mere reiteration of the functional point of view, but it adds to the contention that the form of institutions must be illuminated by study of their function, the contention that there are wide areas of human life which, inexplicit in a given culture, nevertheless have both form and function in the society. Attitudes towards a child, attitudes towards the aged, standards of friendship, habits of direct or indirect statement of desired ends, conceptions of motivation—all of these are fit and appropriate subjects for the detailed study of the ethnographer. Studying the Trobriands on this basis, after a careful investigation of the form and function of mothers' brother right, it would be necessary to study in more detail, because it is less explicit, that aspect of the culture which Professor Malinowski has called "father-love." It would be necessary to know how many fathers are real fathers, how many step-fathers; how father love operates in absentia; how often the ties which bind a child to its father are strong enough to survive the father's divorce from its mother; how father's preference and mother's brother's preference may be made to dovetail and supplement each other within a family of several children. Similarly, Professor Malinowski's statement that delayed weaning makes weaning of less psychical moment to the child would have to be supported with case histories of children, actual details of weaning, the child's comments, the mother attitude, the results of aberrant methods or times of weaning, etc.

Moreover, this question of inexplicit aspects of culture has most important bearings upon two other problems of field method, the time necessary to make a study, and the way in which the study is to be made. Again we may disregard for a moment those aspects of life which have been traditionally ignored by ethnologists whenever they were inexplicit in the culture. For the study of a calendrical religion as compared with an episodic religion very different methods must be used. A calendrical religion once followed through its prescribed round with a competent informant at one's side may be formally known. Similarly the Kula, studied once or at most twice to allow for return gifts, would present few surprises. It is formalized, occurs at regular intervals, and in a prescribed way. (This is to leave aside the question of the degree to which the variation in the functioning of a formal institution may be studied in a society.) But a special study of trade in the Admiralty Islands would have to be attacked very differently. Without a set time and place and manner of trading, without definite trading partners, without a defined route by which certain products move always from one island to another, trade in the Admiralties is a bewildering conglomerate of trade relationships between tribal groups and the exigencies of affinal exchange within tribal groups which have then their reverberation in the casual day by day market between land and sea people. Such an unformalized mass of activities must be studied many times; no informant can generalize upon it as an intelligent Dobuan can generalize upon a section of the Kula; the field worker can only understand the pattern after following the trading activities of many individuals in many different places. Furthermore, for the study of an unformalized part of culture, a knowledge of the language, a much more extended entrée into the lives of the people, a much more complete participation in their lives is essential.

When the question is not a matter of unformulated adult behavior, but of the behavior of children, the matter becomes immediately more complicated. The process of education in primitive society is primarily a matter of assimilation to type. More and more of the life of the individual becomes explicit in the culture, casual tussles are replaced by games with recognized form, and finally feud and warfare have their defined rules. The attitudes of a little child towards relatives become codified in a set of formal terms of address, and in rules of respect, avoidance, jesting, or casual behavior. If any of these are to be studied in children before the form of the culture has been conspicuously stamped upon them, a very different method must be employed from that of conventional field work. The relationship between a chief and his talking chief in Samoa is culturally standardized, and any intelligent Samoan can report upon it, but nowhere can one receive explicit information upon the friendships of children, except from actual observation of a large number of individual children through a long period of time.

So it may be said that different aspects of social life will differ from culture to culture as to the degree of external and explicit form which they have been given, and secondly that within any culture there is likely to be found a varying degree of explicitness between the behavior and attitudes of children and the behavior and attitudes of adults. To what degree the formulations of child life will correspond with the adult culture is very probably a matter of emphasis, whether adults are interested in children or not, and whether moments in the child's life have been chosen as points about which the formal life of the culture is organized. At present there seems no justification for assuming any necessary relationship between those aspects of culture which are explicit in adult life and those which are explicit in child life, although one will often be a reflection of the other. As an example of lack of correlation, in the life of the Samoan female child, the locality is of great importance; her friends are chosen from the immediately adjacent households. Upon growing towards maturity this emphasis upon locality gives place to the more important ties of kinship and rank: a girl will seek out her cousins; a chief's wife, the wife of her husband's talking chief. The behavior of children could not be retrospectively derived from an analysis of the companionships of adolescent girls or grown women, nor could the alliances of the latter be set down to childhood friendship patterns. Similarly, there are two types of relationship between boys in Samoa, both of which are called by the same term, *soa*. One type of soa is a companion at circumcision, a prepubertal alliance between small boys who are close comrades; the other is an alliance between young men, one of whom acts as go-between for the other in love affairs. The similarity of terminology alone, not to mention the fact of explicit friendship in both cases, would lead the investigator to think that the same pairing off existed throughout boyhood, and yet a careful investigation revealed that the first soa relationship resulted from the friendships bred in the neighborhood group; the second, which did not correspond in personnel to the first, was a reflection of the rank and kinship patterns which were so much more important in adult life. Nevertheless, this neighborhood group which would seem to have been overridden in many ways in maturity very probably played a dynamic role in the political life, for where large villages split into two political subgroups, the split followed neighborhood lines and occurred first, not among the leaders of the village political life, the titled men, but in the formal young men's group, the Aumaga. The strong habits of childhood, of close solidarity with neighbors and hostility to those who lived at a distance, even though they were kin, reasserted itself when the Aumaga became too large. So a study of children's allegiances,[5] they in themselves inexplicit but as definitely patterned as a fine textile, also served to throw light upon the political processes in the culture.

It has been my fortunate experience to have twice held fellowships which not only permitted, but required that I concentrate upon the study of inexplicit unformulated aspects of culture, the behavior of the adolescent in Samoa, and of young children in Manus. The conditions of my field grants have therefore acted, not as a deterrent, as they so often must when students are sent out with a definite ethnographic commission to fulfill, but as a stimulus to the development of methods for dealing with various forms of cultural inexplicitness. The discussion of particular methods in ethnology

---

[5] See the author's Coming of Age in Samoa, New York: William Morrow, 1928, and Growing up in New Guinea, New York: William Morrow, 1930.

often seems to be a barren occupation because the same method will vary so much in two investigators' hands, and because each culture presents unique problems for the solution of which special methods must be devised. Nevertheless, because I feel that for an adequate understanding of human culture, it is absolutely essential to study carefully all parts of a culture, and not merely those which present the superficial appearance of having greatest form, it may be worth while to go into some detail as to methods which I have found useful.

Reviews of my two studies have revealed very clearly two facts: first, that many anthropologists are far from clearly realizing that child behavior or sex attitudes are as much a part of culture, are as distinctly and as elaborately patterned as are religious observances; and, second, that they have no very definite conception of how such inexplicit aspects of culture are to be studied. For example, Professor Kroeber writes of data upon children's behavior as "clues" and objects because I confined my comparison of methods of education to Manus and Samoa "without even Trobriand." This criticism implies, first, that children's behavior is not a cultural fact which can be studied like any other cultural fact, and from the study of which a careful observer is as justified in drawing conclusions as is, e.g., the student of social organization; and, second, the mention of the Trobriands shows that Professor Kroeber does not realize the difference between studying an inexplicit aspect of culture and merely commenting upon it. If I were to have written up Samoan canoe-building and Manus canoe-building in formal technological style without comparing either to the Trobriand technology, I should have met with no such criticism, for Professor Malinowski has not yet published on the technology of the Trobriands. But because Professor Malinowski's work contains many astute and vivid passing comments upon children, the student of child behavior in another culture in Melanesia is censured for being unhistorically-minded, for not comparing the results of fourteen months' continuous study of a particular subject with the comments of an observer who was in no sense specializing on children and who makes no claim to have studied them individually.

It would seem therefore necessary to state in some detail the methods I have used. In the first place, for a study of children, it is necessary to remain in one community, because the task of establishing rapport with every member of the group chosen for study does not permit of interruptions and absences. The community must be mastered in detail—residence, interrelationships, names, clan affiliations, economic status, and past, existent and projected marriages must be got by heart. The rudimentary materials with which such an investigation operates are: an understanding of the form of the culture, a speaking knowledge of the language, a detailed knowledge of the chosen community, and a special knowledge of every individual within the particular group being studied. From these preliminary requirements various practical counsels flow naturally: the student who has a short time at his disposal or who prefers to concentrate upon a particular problem without spending much time upon the details of other aspects of ethnography than the one under investigation, or the student who works in a bad climate where prolonged residence is not advisable, should work in a known culture or work in collaboration with another investigator who is making a study of the explicit aspects of the culture. It is advisable to choose a language which can be learned quickly and to settle in a community which is not too large or too scattered. Unknown names or unknown faces put the investigator at an immediate disadvantage. Where problems and languages and time available are to be adjusted to each other, the student of children will be less handicapped by a difficult language than will the student of some abstruse point of adult life, for the vocabulary and sentence structure of children is so simple that an investigator will be understanding all that a child says long before a complex discussion with an adult can be satisfactorily carried on.

The method I have followed so far has been to choose a group of children of a definite age range, and in Samoa of only one sex, and to study this group intensively. I have been dealing throughout with aspects of culture which were for the most part unformulated. An adult in Samoa can tell the investigator that boys do not play with girls, that brothers and sisters should avoid each other, that children are afraid of ghosts; he cannot tell one whether children play with elder siblings of the same sex or with friends, along what lines children form friendships, what children's attitudes are towards the adults of the household, in what relationship a girl stands to a headman who is her father as compared with a headman who is not her father; on what grounds children are left free to choose to reside in one household instead of another. Similarly in Manus, adults can tell one that little girls don't learn to shoot fish, but not on what terms children of both sexes play together, nor how the children's group is organized in respect to age—whether there are fixed allegiances between pairs of children, or whether and under what conditions an older boy plays with a younger one. All of these facts, and they are facts of culture just as surely as are the ways in which a canoe is made or a clan organized, have to be derived from a long series of observations, far longer than for canoe or clan.

It will be immediately obvious that the less explicit a cultural fact is, the larger the number of observations, and the more complicated the method of study will become. This is true not only of children but also of adults. In Manus, Mr. Fortune made a careful study of the religion: to do so it was necessary to attend and record a great number of dances, describe all the issues, the social and economic relations which lay back of the dances, the ruses and devices of diviner and medium; to compare the diagnosis of cause of illness given immediately with the diagnosis later adopted generally. It was necessary to record infinitely more instances, in order to present an adequate study of Manus religion, than to make an equally adequate and formal statement of Dobuan magic; one system had explicit form, which the other lacked.

Similarly, in Manus and on the island of Pak, the same formal kinship system obtains in which the grandson of a woman theoretically marries the granddaughter of that woman's brother (with one typical exception which I shall not note here). But on Pak this marriage actually does take place; genealogical records reveal the painstaking care with which the proper marriage is made whenever possible. In Manus, on the other hand, this explicit theory serves to mask a most inexplicit and unformulated practice in which this traditional child of cross-cousin marriage is only a formal way in which men of means succeed in marrying economic wards to one another. To understand the Manus system, which is unformulated, requires the painstaking collection of a great number of marriage records before a generalization can be made.

Behind every general statement about the behavior of children in Manus and Samoa lies a long line of observations, which are not made at random and recorded casually, but are made systematically about a selected group of children, on points which preliminary investigation has shown to be most significant. To take an instance, in Manus I studied the effect of personality of fathers upon the personality of the sons whom they have reared. From the early observation of the group, I saw what any good observer would see, that fathers paid a great deal of attention to their children, that fathers seldom disciplined their children, and that between two or three pairs of fathers and sons there was a close resemblance in external character traits. From the analysis of households and from genealogies I knew that adoption was frequent. Now this is the point at which the specific student of children and the good ethnographer interested in some other point will diverge. The disinterested ethnographer will report:

> Fathers take a great interest in their children, permit them to go everywhere with them, and seldom chastise them. It is amusing to see how closely the behavior of some children corresponds to that of their fathers.

This is the most that one could reasonably expect from a busy observer of other aspects of the culture and it is, as a matter of fact, about a 100 per cent more than one usually gets from the average field worker, on any unformulated point of culture which he is not actively investigating.

But as a student of children particularly, I now proceeded to attack this particular problem in detail. I studied the behavior of fathers towards sons who were still babies; the behavior of older children towards their fathers; the behavior of children whose fathers had died while they were very small, later, or at puberty. Adoptions and blood relationships were tabulated and the true parentage of adopted sons was worked out. The behavior of foster-children and foster-fathers was compared and set beside a comparison of the behavior of these same children and their real fathers of whom they had seen very little. Recently adopted children were studied in relation to past home and present home. As Mr. Fortune's and my joint studies of the social organization revealed that assurance and dominance of manner were definitely related as interdependent cause and effect with economic status, which in turn was partly correlated with age, partly with temperament, the children of men born at different stages of their economic career were studied and compared to one another. Siblings who had been reared by different adults were studied, as were also the children of widows, and children reared in homes where the wife was dominant. Every attempt was made to find out, by observations of normal conditions, by a study of deviant conditions like widowhood and orphanhood and no adoption, by a study of deviant children—like the one small boy who claimed to have seen his dead father—what was the pattern of child-son relationships, at what points it was crucial, what was its role in determining the character of the child, what were the interrelations between economic success and character as derived from type of father or foster-father.

All the details of such an investigation as this cannot be published, any more than can the details which lie back of the final conclusions of any ethnologist upon any aspect of culture. But before the problem can even be grasped, before the importance of any aspect of education or family relations can be evaluated in terms of its relationship to the culture and to the personality of the individual, a great number of minute and consecutive observations must be made. Similar analysis and controlled observations, long records of average behavior, utilization of the deviant situation and the deviant individual, lie back of statements about age groups, types of leadership, kinds of quarrels, types of friendships, etc. And a detailed study of child behavior, or of parental attitude towards children shows that these aspects of culture are as formal, as patterned, as individual to the cultures in which they are found, as are kinship systems or religious forms. They are also as important to the individual who is moulded by and in his turn moulds his cultural forms.

Nor are they without definite historical interest also. The father-child situation—in broad outline one of close and fairly uncritical affection—has been reported for Manus, Dobu, Trobriands, and the Orokaiva. It is thus a Melanesian feature which may be found to be characteristic of a much wider culture area, just as it has already been found to transcend the borders of patriliny or matriliny. But a comparative study of father-son relationships as a basic form of personal relations in Melanesia can only be made upon the basis of detailed studies such as I have described.

It would seem unprofitable to labor further a discussion of my own particular methods, devised to meet definite situations, many of them suitable for only one culture. In Samoa where moral attitudes were inexplicit, I had to resort to the device of getting every girl to name a series of individuals—the best man, the wisest woman, the worst boy, the best girl, etc., in the village. Only by collecting a large number of such judgments could the implicit moral standards of the children be discovered. In Manus the moralistic nature of the society rendered all such attitudes explicit and this device was not necessary.

The relationship of the individual to his society is an aspect of culture which is given varying explicitness in different societies. Where the culture has conventionalized individual religious experiences (Western Plains) or aesthetic gifts (Maori tattooing), or formally makes one person the butt of jesting as among the Okanagan, the aspect of individuality or temperament so selected will be relatively open to investigation. Where all recognition of individual contribution is smothered beneath heavy trappings of traditional behavior as in the Pueblos, the study of individual contributions will have to be approached as deviously as the study of unformulated child behavior. This does not mean, however, that the role permitted the individual innovator, the degree of recognition of the peculiar gifts or limitations of one personality over against the personalities in different societies, the mechanisms by which individual differences are emphasized or minimized, or artificially discounted, are not aspects of culture. But they are aspects of culture which must be studied through detailed analysis of the problem and controlled observation of series of individuals against a known cultural background.

Similarly the problem of social control—what are the mechanisms by which the individual is made to conform to the standard of the group would have to be investigated by a study of a series of individuals of different ages, sex, and social status. A study of the genesis of social control in children of different ages would have to be made, combined with a study of the relative strength or weakness of habits of social conformity in the behavior of marked and undistinguished personalities, and the behavior of individuals away from the home, the village, the tribe—if such a study were possible. For instance, Manus natives abroad preserve their strong respect for property inculcated in early childhood, but their sex standards which are enforced by fear of the resident ancestral spirits disappear in a foreign community.

Only with time can we develop criteria by which the validity of this type of observation can be judged. As a preliminary basis of evaluation I suggest: (1) the degree to which the investigation of any inexplicit aspect of culture shows it to have definite form, so that the type behavior described for one culture differs or is formally similar to the type behavior of another culture;

(2) the degree to which deviations when intensively studied tend to support the formal generalization which has been made; and (3) in special cases the application of the test of the presence or absence of the normal curve of distribution. If an investigator finds size of families in primitive society following a normal distribution, he may assume the difference in size of families is the result of biological factors, but if he should find no family exceeding two children, he would be justified in looking at once for a cultural cause.

In a study of animism among the children of a particular culture, if children were found to vary according to the normal curve, the presence of animism might be suspected to be a fact of psychology, rather than of culture. When, however, animism is found in no child in a society, the investigator may regard its absence in that society, and probably therefore its presence in children of other societies, as a cultural fact. (With an increasing knowledge of cultural processes we may be able to add some test of internal consistency of results on explicit and inexplicit aspects of culture, or of adult and child behavior. At the present time we have not sufficient knowledge to do this.)

The ethnologist has defined his scientific position in terms of a field of study rather than a type of problem, or a delimitation of theoretical inquiry. The cultures of primitive peoples are that field. In order to adequately describe primitive cultures, it is necessary to extend the present narrow, accidental and inadequate rubrics under which most investigators have been accustomed to collect and present their data. It is necessary to realize that the whole of man's life is determined and bounded by his culture and that every aspect of it, the inexplicit, the unformulated, the uninstitutionalized, is as important to an understanding of the whole, as are the traditional institutions about which it has been customary to center inquiry.

QUERIES

- Define Mead's distinction between explicit vs. inexplicit cultural behaviors; drawing on your own religious ideas, give examples of each.
- How does Mead respond to Kroeber's characterization of children's behavior as "clues"?
- Summarize the methods Mead employed for studying children's behavior in Samoa and Manus.

CONNECTIONS

- Given Radcliffe-Brown's emphasis on "social structure," how would he respond to Mead's emphasis on the "inexplicit" aspects of cultural practice?

- Based on Sherry Ortner's discussion of "key symbols," could any aspect of childrearing be a "key symbol" among adolescents in Samoa or young children in Manus?
- How would Leslie White respond to Mead's emphasis on the study of childrearing?

III

THE NATURE OF SOCIETY

9

Marcel Mauss

INTRODUCTION

The French scholar Marcel Mauss (1872–1950) was the nephew of Emile Durkheim and advanced the Durkheimian goal of developing a science of society (Moore 2008:121–33). Famous for the breadth of his scholarship, Mauss trained an entire generation of French anthropologists—including Claude Lévi-Strauss, who once remarked, "Mauss knows all." Mauss mastered a broad array of anthropological topics, ranging from the social logics of sacrifice to seasonal adaptations of hunting societies, but the conceptual intersection of his work was Durkheim's fundamental questions: What holds societies together? What is the basis of social integration?

The inquiry into social integration is central to Durkheim's science of society (Moore 2008:49–55), and it recurs throughout Mauss's diverse writings, including the following excerpt from his best-known work, *The Gift*. In this study, Mauss explores the issue of social integration by focusing on the cultural dimensions of exchange. Rather than a simple function of supply and demand, Mauss shows that certain types of exchange are more than economic transactions and resonate in other domains of social life. Such transactions have multidimensional implications, are "total prestations," and they are surrounded by social rules and conventions. These rules and obligations, Mauss argues, fall into three sets: the obligation to give, the obligation to accept, and the obligation to repay. An exchange that at first appears to be "in theory voluntary, disinterested and spontaneous," in fact is surrounded by specific obligations and consequences, and the "gift" is given to achieve a specific goal. These total prestations may involve a variety of goods—like the dramatic displays of wealth in the potlatch of the Northwest

Coast or the shell beads and arm bands exchanged in the Trobrianders' kula ring—but may also include the "exchange" of ceremonies, rituals, or military alliances. Regardless, total prestations mark the social relationships between the parties involved, and total prestations socially integrate those parties. In short, *The Gift* explores one form of social integration—total prestations— and shows how those exchanges are embedded in the expectations and dialogues of social life.

The second text is from a 1914 speech that Mauss presented to the French Institute of Anthropology, "The Origins of the Idea of Money." This brief note exemplifies Mauss's broad scholarship, the fertile connections that he made between different cultural practices, and his commitment to scholarly cooperation (Moore 2008:121–22). Mauss's discussion of the origins of the idea of money emphasizes the connection between money and social conceptions of the sacred; in many cases the names for money share etymologies with words for the sacred, the spiritual, and the powerful. From this, Mauss argues that money is expressly a social creation—an observation linked to his point in *The Gift* about the social embededness of exchange. Rather than being objects of inherent value, Mauss argues that all currencies—gold, beads, shells, or stock certificates—are based on social conventions, on shared beliefs rooted in social knowledge.

PRIMARY TEXT: *THE GIFT: FORMS AND FUNCTIONS OF EXCHANGE IN ARCHAIC SOCIETIES*

From *The Gift: Forms and Functions of Exchange in Archaic Societies*. Translated by Ian Gunnison. © 1967 [1923], W. W. Norton and Company, pp. 1–5. Reproduced by permission of Taylor & Francis Books UK.

I have never found a man so generous and hospitable that he would not receive a present, nor one so liberal with his money that he would dislike a reward if he could get one.

Friends should rejoice each others' hearts with gifts of weapons and raiment, that is clear from one's own experience That friendship lasts longest—if there is a chance of its being a success—in which friends both give and receive gifts.

A man ought to be a friend to his friend and repay gift with gift. People should meet smiles with smiles and lies with treachery.

Know—if you have a friend in whom you have sure confidence and wish to make use of him, you ought to exchange ideas and gifts with him and go to see him often. If you have another in whom you have no confidence and yet will make use of him, you ought to address him with fair words but crafty heart and repay treachery with lies.

Further, with regard to him in whom you have no confidence and of whose motives you are suspicious, you ought to smile upon him and dissemble your feelings. Gifts ought to be repaid in like coin.

*Generous and bold men have the best time in life and never foster troubles.
But the coward is apprehensive of everything and a miser is always groaning over
his gifts.*

*Better there should be no prayer than excessive offering; a gift always looks for
recompense. Better there should be no sacrifice than an excessive slaughter?*[1]

Gifts and Return Gifts

The foregoing lines from the *Edda* outline our subject matter. In Scandinavian and many other civilizations contracts are fulfilled and exchanges of goods are made by means of gifts. In theory such gifts are voluntary but in fact they are given and repaid under obligation.

This work is part of a wider study. For some years our attention has been drawn to the realm of contract and the system of economic prestations between the component sections or sub-groups of 'primitive' and what we might call 'archaic' societies. On this subject there is a great mass of complex data. For, in these 'early' societies, social phenomena are not discrete; each phenomenon contains all the threads of which the social fabric is composed. In these total social phenomena, as we propose to call them, all kinds of institutions find simultaneous expression: religious, legal, moral, and economic. In addition, the phenomena have their aesthetic aspect and they reveal morphological types.

We intend in this book to isolate one important set of phenomena: namely, prestations which are in theory voluntary, disinterested and spontaneous, but are in fact obligatory and interested. The form usually taken is that of the gift generously offered; but the accompanying behaviour is formal pretence and social deception, while the transaction itself is based on obligation and economic self-interest. We shall note the various principles behind this necessary form of exchange (which is nothing less than the division of labor itself), but we shall confine our detailed study to the enquiry: In primitive or archaic types of society what is the principle whereby the gift received has to be repaid? What force is there in the thing given which compels the recipient to make a return? We hope, by presenting enough data, to be able to answer this question precisely, and also to indicate the direction in which answers to cognate questions might be sought. We shall also pose new problems. Of these, some concern the morality of the contract: for instance, the manner in which today the law of things remains bound up with the law of persons; and some refer to the forms and ideas which have always been present in exchange and which even now are to be seen in the idea of individual interest.

---

[1] *Havamal*, vv. 39, 41–43, 44–46, 48, and 145, from the translation by D. E. Martin Clarke in the *Havamal*, with Selections from other Poems in the Edda, Cambridge, 1923. Editor's note: the Hávámal is a section of the Elder or Poetic Edda, and the maxims quoted were written circa AD 800 but derived from earlier Norse oral traditions.

Thus we have a double aim. We seek a set of more or less archaeological conclusions on the nature of human transactions in the societies which surround us and those which immediately preceded ours, and whose exchange institutions differ from our own. We describe their forms of contract and exchange. It has been suggested that these societies lack the economic market, but this is not true; for the market is a human phenomenon which we believe to be familiar to every known society. Markets are found before the development of merchants, and before their most important innovation, currency as we know it. They functioned before they took the modern forms (Semitic, Hellenic, Hellenistic, and Roman) of contract and sale and capital. We shall take note of the moral and economic features of these institutions.

We contend that the same morality and economy are at work, albeit less noticeably, in our own societies, and we believe that in them we have discovered one of the bases of social life and thus we may draw conclusions of a moral nature about some of the problems confronting us in our present economic crisis. These pages of social history, theoretical sociology, political economy and morality do no more than lead us to old problems which are constantly turning up under new guises.

The Method Followed

Our method is one of careful comparison. We confine the study to certain chosen areas, Polynesia, Melanesia, and north-West America, and to certain well-known codes. Again, since we are concerned with words and their meanings, we choose only areas where we have access to the minds of the societies through documentation and philological research. This further limits our field of comparison. Each particular study has a bearing on the systems we set out to describe and is presented in its logical place. In this way we avoid that method of haphazard comparison in which institutions lose their local color and documents their value.

Prestation, Gift, and Potlatch

This work is part of the wider research carried out by M. Davy and myself upon archaic forms of contract, so we may start by summarizing what we have found so far. It appears that there has never existed, either in the past or in modern primitive societies, anything like a 'natural' economy. By a strange chance the type of that economy was taken to be the one described by Captain Cook when he wrote of exchange and barter among the Polynesians. In our study here of these same Polynesians we shall see how far removed they are from a state of nature in these matters.

In the systems of the past we do not find simple exchange of goods, wealth and produce through markets established among individuals. For it is groups, and not individuals, which carry on exchange, make contracts, and are bound by obligations; the persons represented in the contracts are moral persons— clans, tribes, and families; the groups, or the chiefs as intermediaries for the groups, confront and oppose each other. Further, what they exchange is not exclusively goods and wealth, real and personal property, and things of economic value. They exchange rather courtesies, entertainments, ritual military assistance, women, children, dances, and feasts and fairs in which the market is but one element and the circulation of wealth but one part of a wide and enduring contract. Finally, although the prestations and counter-prestations take place under a voluntary guise they are in essence strictly obligatory, and their sanction is private or open warfare. We propose to call this the system of total prestations. Such institutions seem to us to be best represented in the alliance of pairs of phratries in Australian and North American tribes, where ritual, marriages, succession to wealth, community of right and interest, military and religious rank and even games all form part of one system and presuppose the collaboration of the two moieties of the tribe. The Tlingit and Haida of North-West America give a good expression of the nature of these practices when they say that they 'show respect to each other'.

But with the Tlingit and Haida, and in the whole of that region, total prestations appear in a form which, although quite typical, is yet evolved and relatively rare. We propose, following American authors, to call it the potlatch. This Chinook word has passed into the current language of Whites and Indians from Vancouver to Alaska. *Potlatch* meant originally 'to nourish' or 'to consume'. The Tlingit and Haida inhabit the islands, the coast, and the land between the coast and the Rockies; they are very rich, and pass their winters in continuous festival, in banquets, fairs and markets which at the same time are solemn tribal gatherings. The tribes place themselves hierarchically in their fraternities and secret societies. On these occasions are practiced marriages, initiations, shamanistic séances, arid the cults of the great gods, totems, and group or individual ancestors. These are all accompanied by ritual and by prestations by whose means political rank within subgroups, tribes, tribal confederations and nations is settled. But the remarkable thing about these tribes is the spirit of rivalry and antagonism which dominates all their activities. A man is not afraid to challenge an opposing chief or nobleman. Nor does one stop at the purely sumptuous destruction of accumulated wealth in order to eclipse a rival chief (who may be a close relative). We are here confronted with total prestation in the sense that the whole clan, through the intermediacy of its chiefs, makes contracts involving all its members and everything it possesses. But the agonistic character of the prestation is pronounced. Essentially usurious and extravagant, it is above all a struggle among nobles to determine their position in the hierarchy to the ultimate benefit, if they are successful, of their own clans. This agonistic type of total prestation we propose to call the 'potlatch'.

So far in our study Davy and I had found few examples of this institution outside North-West America, Melanesia, and Papua. Everywhere else—in Africa, Polynesia, and Malaya, in South America and (the rest of North America—the basis of exchange seemed to us to be a simpler type of total prestation. However, further research brings to light a number of forms intermediate between exchanges marked by exaggerated rivalry like those of the American north-west and Melanesia, and others more moderate where the contracting parties rival each other with gifts: for instance, the French compete with each other in their ceremonial gifts, parties, weddings, and invitations, and feel bound, as the Germans say, to *revanchieren*[2] themselves. We find some of these intermediate forms in the Indo-European world, notably in Thrace.

Many ideas and principles are to be noted in systems of this type. The most important of these spiritual mechanisms is clearly the one which obliges us to make a return gift for a gift received. The moral and religious reasons for this constraint are nowhere more obvious than in Polynesia; and in approaching the Polynesian data in the following chapter we shall see clearly the power which enforces the repayment of a gift and the fulfillment of contracts of this kind.

QUERIES

- What are "total prestations"? Based on your own experience, discuss an example of a total prestation.
- What are "total social phenomena"? According to Mauss, how can we distinguish such phenomena?
- What does Mauss mean by the phrase "natural economy"? Why does he suggest that such economies do not exist in "past or in modern primitive societies"?
- What are the three sets of obligations surrounding total prestations?

CONNECTIONS

- How does the kula exchange described for the Trobriand Islanders by Malinowski exemplify Mauss's idea of a total prestation?
- How would Radcliffe-Brown's idea of "social structure" include total prestations?
- If we applied Leslie White's tripartite model of culture to Mauss's ideas, where would total social phenomena "fit" into White's scheme?

---

[2] Editor's note: German for "to get one's own back," that is, the anticipated rewards of reciprocity.

PRIMARY TEXT: *THE ORIGINS OF THE CONCEPT OF MONEY*

Originally published as "Les origines de la notion de monnaie," communication faite à l'Institut français d'anthropologie. "Comptes-rendus des séances" II, tome I, supplément à l'Anthropologie, 1914, 25, pp. 14–19. Reproduced in *Oeuvres* 2, "Representations collectives de civilisations," pp. 106–112. Les Editions de Minuit, 1969. Translated by J. Moore. (Footnotes renumbered from original.) Translation by permission of les Editions de Minuit.

In light of the instructions by Monsieur President, I cannot present lengthy considerations, but only the most essential, about the definition of money and the manner which, I think, one can explore the origins of that idea. Before raising those few points and the hypothesis they suggest, allow me to raise some preliminary issues.

In the first place, it is well understood that we are discussing the *concept* of money. Money is never just a material or physical act, it is essentially a social creation; its value is its purchasing power, a measure of confidence in it. It is of the origin of a notion, an institution, of a faith that we are speaking.

In the second place, it is impossible to point to an origin, to speak of an absolute beginning or so to speak of a birth from nothingness. In contrast to received wisdom, you will see that, among known societies or those that we present for the hypothesis, it is uncertain whether there were any notions analogous to those we now imply by "money." We will not attempt to explain here how the initially foreign idea of money occurred to humanity. Rather, we seek the most primitive, the simplest, the most elementary form in order to better state, to be able to better represent, the idea of money among simpler societies which have been documented.

Of course, it is unnecessary here to state that these hypotheses, these indications of my work, are provisional. But a friendly meeting like this allows us to communicate our unfinished ideas, our preliminary and unresolved questions, and thus nourish a scientific work in progress.

During the last four years, I have been working with the excellent documents published by the German missionaries to Togo about the languages of the *Ewhé* nations of that region. Initially, I was not interested in the question of the origins of the idea of money. (I regret that I was unaware then of the excellent brief book by the much-missed Schurtz,[3] so full of facts and ideas.) And I had yet to concern myself with the definition of economic phenomena, with the notion of monetary value in particular. I had not yet made such questions a particular objective of my research.

A reading of the *Ewhé* documents, presented in the translations by Monsieur Spieth and the dictionary by Monsieur Westernmann, supported the ideas about the hypothesis I will present.

---

[3] *Grundiss einer Entstehungsgeschichte des Geldes*, Weimar, 1898.

I specifically studied the concept of *dzó* equivalent to *mana*, which is the power of substances involved in the Ewhé's magic. Among the derivations of the root morpheme *dzó*, I found in the Westermann dictionary the word *dzonú* (Zauberding), "magical thing," "All forms of beads or thing in the shape of a bead, et cetera." It is one of the common names given to cowry shells used in the magic and religions of the African nations in general.[4]

Around this fact, other details readily crystallized, becoming somewhat systematic. In this process different things become more clearly themselves.

The idea of *mana* in Melanesia is directly linked to the idea of money.[5] In the Banks Islands of Santa Cruz, they call shell bead money *rongo* ("holy red") that elsewhere is referred to by the name *diwarra*.[6]

Another example of the idea of magico-religious power is the concept of *manitou* or spirit essence (or more precisely *manido*) of the Algonquins. Now Father Thavent[7] notes that trade beads used by the Algonquins (probably the Sauteux) are said to be the scales of the manitou fish.[8]

The idea of money is specifically linked to the idea of the sacred. In New Guinea in the Bismark Archipelago, money, guarded in the men's houses, is called *tambu* [or holy]. This point is treated in the work by Schurz.[9]

Elsewhere money is more clearly linked with idea of a talisman. This is particularly the case among the tribes of Northwest America, especially among the Kwakiutl, where the name *logwa* or talisman, specifically a supernatural object, is the actual name for the clan paraphernalia, the coppers and copper emblems that are the money used in the exchanges between clans.[10] The original sense of the word *logwa* is linked to the root *lògu* which Monsieur Boas translates as "supernatural power."[11]

In each of these cases, the religious and magical character of money is strongly evident and the names people give to money expressly connect it to magical power.

Since then we have continued our research in a systematic spirit: we have not found a society, sufficiently close to its origins, where religion and magic are not the true sources of the value given to stones, of shells, or precious met-

---

[4] The cowry necklaces are not worn by priests, magicians nor by the twin children of priests or magicians (see Westermann, Ewe-Deut., p. 230, col. 1 s. v. *hotsui to-to*).

[5] Codrington, The Melanesians, p. 103, etc.

[6] Codrington, The Melanesians, p. 325, sq.

[7] Tesa Studi del Thavenet, Pise, 1881, p. 18.

[8] The word mi'gis designates the talismans, and especially the large oyster shells that are synonymous with beads. (Cf. Hoffman, The Mide wiwin of the Ojibwa, VIIth Ann. Rep. of the Bur. of Ethno, 1891, pp. 215, 219, 220). Furthermore Father Cuoq (Lexique de la langue algonquine, p. 220), identifies mikis as wampum, the string-bead money of the Iroquois.

[9] Preuss. Jabrbücher, 1895, p. 50 sq.

[10] See for example, F. Boas, The Social Organization and the Secret Societies of the Kwakiutl, 1897, 3 vers de la p. 373; cf. Kwakiutl Texts, Memoirs of the Am. Mus. Nat. Hist. Jesup Expedit. 1re série, 1, p. 355, 1. 18–19.

[11] See Boas and Hunt, Kwakiutl Texts, III, p. 527, cf. I, p. I. 2.

als. The religious usages of gold in antiquity, the semiprecious stones used in all the civilizations of the Ancient World, the name for pearl in Arabic, *barakà* (meaning a benediction or holy gift), all these are well-known examples.

Considering less complex societies, we have been impressed by the importance and prominence given to crystal and particularly quartz crystal by various societies, whether very primitive or very civilized. We have been intrigued by the attention given to the acquisition of crystals by Australian sorcerers.[12] Then, in a very bad book, in the old story of an encounter between an elderly sorcerer and the lieutenant of a voyaging English vessel,[13] we have found confirmation of our hypothesis, that the reason for the impact on the primitive imagination is that the crystal distorts light: water changes to fire by passing through a frigid solid, and that is one of the first mysteries that man recognizes. . . .

Variations on this abstract concept further support the hypothesis. Isn't it striking that the myth of quartz, of the mountain of quartz, the source of talismans,[14] is found in Northwest America in terms nearly identical to those found in Australia?

On the other hand, in Australia we not only find the acts that are equivalent to those purely on the order of magic and religion, but also of economic acts. To begin with, the trade in quartz crystals and other talismans indicates to us their value. Thus, among the Aruntas, Messrs. Spencer and Gillen record the use of *lonka-lonka*, large shell ornaments from the Gulf of Carpinteria where they are thought to descend from thunder.[15] The word *lonka-lonka* is derived from the [English] "long away, long away."[16]

And another remarkable thing is that among the same tribes, magical talismans are not the only trade items, but also the sacred emblems of individuals—the *churinga*[17]—are exchange objects. And now we can see that not only are these religious acts but also economic events as part of the pilgrimages that include the exchange and trade of totemic emblems whose movements Spencer and Gillen have described;[18] these visits involve numerous prestations: feastings, the exchange of women, et cetera, all of which occur at the same time.[19] Furthermore, another witness of

---

[12] Hubert and Mauss, Mélange d'histoire des religions, p. 155, p. 167 suiv.

[13] Leigh, Reconnoitering Voyages, in the New Colonies of South Australia, London, 1839, p. 160.

[14] Cf. Boas, Social Organization, p. 405; Boas and Hunt, Kwakiutl Texts, I, p. 111, 15, 20, 2e série, p. 29, I. 25–30, etc.

[15] See these authors about Arunta ritual in Native Tribes of Central Australia, p. 545, the rite is poorly translated and almost surely relates to thunder over water.

[16] Cf. Kempe, "Vocabulary of the Tribes Inhabiting the Macdonnell Ranges." Transact. Royal Society of South Australia, XIV. s. v.

[17] Regarding these see Durkheim, Formes élémentaires de la vie religieuse, p. 168 sq.

[18] Nat. Tribes, p. 159 sq., Northern Tribes of Central Australia, p. 259 sq.

[19] Cf. the Arunta ritual, Northern Tribes, p. 263.

Messrs. Spencer and Gillen, a Monsieur Eylmann, expressly states—and without having a preconceived idea about this matter—that the *churinga*, the sacred objects (which is the essence of the word) serve as a measure of value for these tribes.[20] He recounts an anecdote in which his guides, coming from distant nations, spontaneously told him that [the *churinga*] are "black people's money."

This is, perhaps, the basis on which one can define the primitive forms of the idea of money. Money, as I have defined it, is a standard value, a use-value that is not divisible but is permanent, transmissible, and although the object involved in the transactions and usages may deteriorate, the medium can acquire other values from usage and gift-giving that are fungible and transformational. Undoubtedly, we think it is undeniable that in most primitive societies the talisman and its ownership becomes equivalent, becoming an object desired by all but conferring on its owner a power readily transformed into purchasing power.

And, as to surplus, does this also come from the nature of societies? Let's take an example. The word *mana* in the Malayo-Polynesian languages designates the power of magical substances and rites greater than the authority of men.[21] It is equally applied to precious objects, to tribal talismans,[22] from which one knows of the exchanges, the battles, and the history associated with the object. This does not seem irrational; if we understand that it is representing the spiritual state on which the institutions function. The purchasing power of money is not natural, when it is attached to a talisman that, if absolutely necessary, can compel the subordinates of chiefs or the clients of magical specialists to provide prestations upon demand. And inversely, but not necessarily, from the intervening notion of wealth, as vague as that concept may be, that the wealth of the chief and of the magician resides above all in the emblems that embody their magical powers, in a word their authority that symbolizes the power of the clan.

Schurtz mentioned this,[23] in light of Kubary's observation that in the Palau Islands[24] that primitive money was not used as a means to acquire consumable goods, but to acquire luxury items and to gain authority over men. The purchasing power of primitive money is above all, to our way of thinking, the prestige that the talisman conveys to those that possess it and those who use it to command others.

But isn't this a well established sense among ourselves? It is the deep faith we nourish regarding gold or the all the things of value that come from our esteem, isn't that a large part of the confidence that we have in them comes

---

[20] Die Eingeborenen Süd-Australiens, 1908, p. 179.

[21] See Tregear, Maori Comparative Dictionary, s. v.

[22] Compare for example the texts translated by Percy Smith, "The Aotea Canoe," Journal of the Polynesian Society, IX, 1900, p. 220.

[23] Entstehungsgeschichte, p. 19.

[24] Etnogr. Beiträge, p. 9.

from their power? The essential faith in the value of gold resides in the belief that, thanks to it, we can obtain gifts—in goods and services—from our contemporaries, and from this idea the market can exist.

These are, gentlemen, a few reflections that I am able to present with all the reservations involved in basic working hypotheses, a work in which I invite you to collaborate with your questions and criticisms.

QUERIES

- What does Mauss mean when he states that money is unnatural?
- According to Mauss, what gives money its value?
- In the potlatch of the Northwest Coast, what social units are engaged in exchange of coppers and metal objects? How do these prestations reflect Mauss's ideas about the potlatch discussed in *The Gift*?

CONNECTIONS

- How do Mauss's ideas about the origins of money reflect Durkheim's concepts about the social origins of collective representations?
- How does Mauss's discussion of the origins of money differ from Malinowski's discussion of money and exchange among the Trobriand Islanders?

10

Bronislaw Malinowski

INTRODUCTION

The Polish-born anthropologist Bronislaw Malinowski (1884–1942) was one of the pivotal figures in transforming anthropology in the early 20th century. His signal contribution was to develop rigorous standards and approaches to ethnographic fieldwork, innovations that he developed and systematized during extended research projects among the people of the Trobriand Islands located off the east coast of Papua New Guinea (for an overview, see Moore 2008:135–38). Malinowski was one of the first anthropologists to conduct sustained fieldwork lasting six or more months at a time, and these projects resulted in ethnographic classics, such as the 1922 book, *Argonauts of the Western Pacific*. Malinowski's research also led him to develop systematic strategies for ethnographic research, and his research was marked by an exploration of the interconnections between different domains of culture—for example, gardening and magic, exchange and social status—that were often discussed as discrete fields of human social life. Rather than write about a single dimension—religion or economics—Malinowski attempted to show the multifaceted nature of culture.

In turn, this ethnographic holism was reflected in Malinowski's theoretical position, functionalism. Malinowski argued that the starting point for anthropological theory should be the individual and the satisfaction of the individual's basic needs for existence (see Moore 2008:139–44). Every human has a basic set of requirements (for food, shelter, safety, and so on) and those needs are met through learned behaviors gained as a member of a social group—in other words, through culture. In turn, the cultural response to those initial individual needs creates new needs, and human history is characterized by the cumulative spiral of needs/cultural response → new needs/new cultural responses. The ethnographer's task, according to Malinowski, was to analytically disentangle these multiple causal connections and thus explain the nature of culture. Malinowski's brand of functionalism was distinct from that proposed by Radcliffe-Brown, who argued that the fundamental function of social structures was the maintenance and perpetuation of human society (see chapter 11). To put it somewhat broadly, Radcliffe-Brown's functionalism was focused on human society while Malinowski's functionalism began with the individual.

In the following article, Malinowski explores economics among the Trobriand Islanders, and it becomes quickly obvious how deeply embedded economics were in other dimensions of Trobriand culture. For example, Malinowski asked the Trobrianders a seemingly simple question: who owns a garden plot? Surprisingly, Malinowski discovered that as many as five different people were identified as the "owners" of a garden plot, but the implications of that answer require understanding a great deal about Trobriand culture, because land tenure is connected to political structure, religion, and cosmology. The discussion of "money" provides another entry into the complexities of Trobriand culture. Trobrianders exchange ceremonial stone axe blades, shell bead necklaces, and armbands made from large conch shells, and these are widely recognized as objects or tokens of wealth. Yet, Malinowski argues, these are not money and Trobriand exchange is not a market economy because those objects and their value are uniquely embedded within other dimensions of Trobriand culture. As always, Malinowski insists that anthropology expose the complex interconnections of human culture.

PRIMARY TEXT: *THE PRIMITIVE ECONOMICS OF THE TROBRIAND ISLANDERS*

"The Primitive Economics of the Trobriand Islanders," in *The Economic Journal*, Vol. 31 (121), 1921, pp. 1–16. Reproduced with permission of Blackwell Publishing Ltd.

Only a very slight acquaintance with ethnological literature is needed to convince us that little attention has been paid so far to the problems of economics among primitive races. A certain amount of speculation has been devoted to origins of economic institutions—more especially to origins of property; to the stages of economic development, and to certain questions of exchange, "primitive money," and rudimentary forms of division of labor. As a rule, however, small results have been achieved, because the amount of serious consideration given by theoretical writers to economic problems is in no way proportional to their complexity and importance, and the field observations extant are scanty. Again, the lack of inspiration from theoretical work has reacted detrimentally on ethnographic field work, and a careful survey of the best records of savage life reveals little or nothing that might be of value to the economist.

A student of economics, in possession of a systematic theory, might be naturally tempted to inquire how far, if at all, his conclusions can be applied to a type of society entirely different from our own. He would attempt in vain, however, to answer this question on the basis of the ethnological data extant, or, if he did, his results could not be correct. In fact, the question has been set forth and an attempt at its solution made by C. Buecher in his *Industrial Evolution*. His conclusions are, in my opinion, a failure, not owing to imperfect reasoning or method, but rather to the defective material on which they are formed. Buecher comes to the conclusion that the savages—he includes among them races as highly developed as the Polynesians—have no economic organization, and that they are in a pre-economic stage—the lowest in that of the individual search for food, the higher ones in the stage of self-sufficient household economy.

In this article I shall try to present some data referring to the economic life of the Trobriand Islanders, a community living on a, coral archipelago off the north-east coast of New Guinea. These natives, typical South Sea Islanders of the Melanesian stock, with a developed institution of chieftainship, great ability in various crafts and a fine decorative art, certainly are not at the lower end of savagery. In their general level of culture, however, they may be taken as representative of the majority of the savage races now in existence, and they are less developed culturally than the Polynesians, the bulk of North American Indians, of Africans, and of Indonesians. If we find, therefore, distinct forms of economic organization among them, we are safe in assuming that even among the lowest savages we might expect to find more facts of economic interest than have been hitherto recorded.

I shall first give an outline of the natural resources of the Trobrianders and a broad survey of the manner in which these are utilized. The natives live on flat coral islands, covered with rich, heavy soil, very well suited for the cultivation of yams and taro, and they also enjoy a good regular rainfall. The coast is surrounded in parts with a fringing reef, in parts it encloses a big, shallow lagoon, teeming with fish. Having such excellent natural inducements, the natives are splendid tillers of the soil and first-rate fishermen, efficient and hard-working in both pursuits. These in turn reward them with a perennial abundance of food, sufficient to support a population very dense, as compared with other tribes of that part of the world. In gardening the natives obtain their fine results in spite of using only the most primitive implement—a pointed stick, made and discarded every time they go to work. In fishing they use big nets, also traps, fish-hooks and poison. As manufacturers they excel in

wood-carving, basket-weaving, and the production of highly-valued shell ornaments. On the other hand, through lack of material, they have to rely on
the importation from other tribes of stone implements and pottery, as, of
course, neither hard stone nor clay are obtainable on a coral island. I have begun by giving this general outline of their resources, pursuits and crafts, in order to indicate the narrow frame within which the current accounts of economics are encompassed. The data would there, no doubt, be given with a
much greater wealth of detail—especially in the technological aspect—but it
would be mainly the successive description of the various activities, connected with the quest for food and the manufacture of objects, without any
attempt being made at a discussion of the more complex problems, referring
to organization of production, apportionment, and to the mechanism of
tribal life in its economic aspect.

This will be done here, beginning with production, and taking agriculture
as an example.

The questions before us are, first, the important problem of land tenure;
next, the less obvious problems of the organization of production. Is the
work in the gardens carried out by each family or each person individually
and independently? Or is there any general co-ordination of this work, any
social organization of their efforts, and, if so, how is it done, and by whom?
Are the successive stages of the work integrated into any organic whole, by
any supervision, by any personal guidance, or any social or psychological
force?

Land tenure among the Trobriand natives is rather complex, and it shows
well the difficulties of solving ethnographic field problems of this type and
the dangers of being misled into some inadequate approximation. When I
began to inquire into this subject, I first received from my native informant
a series of general statements, such as that the chief is the owner of all land,
or that each garden plot has its owner, or that all the men of a village community own the land jointly. Then I tried to answer the question by the
method of concrete investigation: taking a definite plot, I inquired successively, from several independent informants, who was the owner of it. In
some cases I had mentioned to me successively as many as five different
"owners" to one plot—each answer, as I found out later on, containing part
of the truth, but none being correct by itself. It was only after I had drawn
up complete plans of the garden land of several village communities, and
inquired successively into the details, not only of each separate garden unit,
but also into the details of each of the alleged forms of "ownership," that I
was able to reach a satisfactory conclusion. The main difficulty in this, as in
ever so many similar questions, lies in our giving our own meaning of
"ownership" to the corresponding native word. In doing this we overlook
the fact that to the natives the word "ownership " not only has a different
significance, but that they use one word to denote several legal and eco-

nomic relationships, between which it is absolutely necessary for us to distinguish.

The chief (Guya'u) has in the Trobriands a definite over-right over all the garden land within the district. This consists in the title of "master" or "owner" (Toli), and in the exercise of certain ceremonial rights and privileges, such as the decision on which lands the gardens are to be made, arbitration in garden disputes, and several minor privileges. The garden magician (Towosi) also calls himself the "master of the garden" and is considered as such, in virtue of his complex magical and other functions, fulfilled in the course of gardening. Again, in certain cases, and over certain portions of the land, the same title is given to notables or sub-chiefs, who carry out certain minor offices in connection with it. Finally, each garden plot belongs to some individual or other in the village community, and, when the gardens are made on this particular land, this owner either uses his plot himself or leases it to someone else under a rather complicated system of payment. The chief, the magician and the notables also own individually a number of garden plots each, independently of their general over-rights.

Now the reason why an economist cannot ignore such over-rights and complications is that the natives value them extremely, and, what is more important, that such over-rights carry with them definite functions and wield definite influences of economic importance.

Thus the complex conditions of land tenure, the not infrequent quarrels about gardening, and the need for summoning and maintaining communal labor require a social authority, and this is supplied by the chief with the assistance of the notables. On the other hand, the Towosi, the hereditary garden magician of each village community, has to a great extent the control over the initiative in the more detailed proceedings of the work. Each stage of gardening is inaugurated by a magical rite performed by him. He also orders the work to be done, looks after the way in which it is carried out, and imposes the periods of taboo, which punctuate it.

The proceedings of gardening are opened by a conference, summoned by the chief and held in front of the magician's house, at which all arrangements and the allotment of garden plots are decided upon. Immediately after that, the members of the village community bring a gift of selected food to the garden magician, who at night sacrificially offers a portion of it to the ancestral spirits, with an invocation, and at the same time utters a lengthy spell over some special leaves. Next morning, the magician repairs to the garden, accompanied by the men of the village, each of whom carries an axe with the, charmed leaves wrapped around its blade. While the villagers stand around, the Towosi (magician) strikes the ground with a ceremonial staff, uttering a formula. This he does on each garden plot successively, and on each the men cut a few saplings with their axes. After that, for a month or so, the scrub is cut in the prospective gardens by men only, and communal labor is often resorted to. The Towosi has to decide when the next stage, the burning of scrub and the clearing of soil, has to begin. When he thinks that the cut scrub is sufficiently dry, he imposes a taboo on garden work, so that any belated cutting has to be suspended. In a series of rites, lasting, as a rule, for about three days, he inaugurates the work of clearing the garden plot; this afterwards is carried on by men and women jointly, working in families, each on its own plot, without the help of communal labor. The planting of yams is inaugurated by a very elaborate ceremony, also extending over a few days, during which no further garden work is done at all. A magical rite of its own inaugurates each further stage, the erection of supports for the yam vine; the weeding of the gardens, done by female communal labor; the cleaning of the yam roots and tubers; the preliminary harvest of early yams; and finally the main harvest of late yams.

When the plants begin to grow a series of magical rites, parallel with the inaugural ones, is performed, in which the magician is supposed to give an impulse to the growth and development of the plant at each of its successive stages. Thus, one rite is performed to make the seed tuber sprout; another drives up the sprouting shoot; another lifts it out of the ground; yet another makes it twine round the support; then, with yet other rites, the leaves are made to bud, to open, to expand, respectively.

The Towosi (garden magician) always performs a rite first or one of the four garden plots selected for the purpose each season, and called Leywota. In certain ceremonies he afterwards carries the magic on into each garden plot, in others the magic is performed on the selected plots only. The Leywota are important from the economic point of view, because the owner of such a plot is bound to keep pace with the progress of magic, that is, he may not lag behind with his work. Also, the Leywota plots are always worked with a special care, and they are kept up to a very high standard of gardening. Thus, both in the regularity and in the quality of the work done, these plots set a definite pattern to all the others.

Besides the indirect influence which the Towasi exercises on garden work by giving the initiative and inaugurating the successive stages, by imposing taboos, and by setting the standard by means of the Leywota plots, he also directly supervises certain activities of general importance to all the gardens. Thus, for example, he keeps his eye on the work done in fencing round the garden. All the plots are placed within a common enclosing fence, of which everyone has to make his share, corresponding to his plot or plots. Thus, the neglect of one careless individual might result in damage to all, for bush pigs or wallabies might find their way in and destroy the new crops. If this happens, the garden magician gets up in front of his house in the evening and harangues the village, often mentioning the culprit by name and heaping blame on him—a proceeding which seldom fails to take effect.

It is easy to see that the magician performs manifold and complex functions, and that his claim to be the "master of the garden" is not an empty one! What is now the economic importance of his functions? The natives believe deeply that through his magic the Towosi controls the forces of Nature, and they also believe that he ought to control the work of man. To start a new stage of gardening without a magical inauguration is, for them, unthinkable. Thus, his magical power, exercised side by side with their work, his magical co-operation, so to speak, inspires them with confidence in success and gives them a powerful impulse to work. Their implicit belief in magic also supplies them with a leader, whose initiative and command they are ready to accept in all matters, where it is needed. It is obvious that the series of magical rites—punctuating the progress of activities at regular intervals, imposing a series of rest periods, and, in the institution of standard plots (Leywota), establishing a model to the whole community—is of extreme importance. It acts as a psychological force, making for a more highly organized system of work, than it would be possible to achieve at this stage of culture by an appeal to force or to reason.

Thus, we can answer the questions, referring to the organization of production, by summing up our results and saying that the authority of the chief, the belief in magic, and the prestige of the magician are the social and psychological forces which regulate and organize production; that this latter, far from being just the sum of uncorrelated individual efforts, is a complex and organically united tribal enterprise.

Finally, a few words must be said about the character of native labor in the Trobriands. We would see their economic activities in an entirely wrong perspective, if we were to imagine that these natives are temperamentally lazy and can work only under some outside pressure. They have a keen interest in their gardens, work with spirit, and can do sustained and efficient work, both when they do it individually and communally. There are different systems of communal work on various scales; sometimes the several village communities join together, sometimes the whole community, sometimes a few households. Distinctive native names are given to the various kinds of communal work, and payment in food also differs. In the more extensive kinds of work, it is the chief's duty to feed the workers.

An interesting institution of ceremonial enterprise deserves special attention. This is known as the Kayasa, and might be described as a period when all activities, whether gardening, fishing, industrial or even merely tribal sports and merrymaking, are carried out with special intensity. When the season is good, and the time is felt by the whole community to be propitious, the chief announces the Kayasa, and inaugurates it by giving a big feast. The whole period of the Kayasa is punctuated by other feasts, also provided for by the chief, and everyone who takes part is under an implicit obligation to do his best, and work his hardest, so that the Kayasa may be a success.

We have discussed their production on the example of gardening. The same conclusions, however, could have been drawn from a discussion of fishing, building of houses or canoes, or from a description of their big trading expeditions. All these activities are dependent upon the social power of the chief and the influence of the respective magicians. In all of them the quantity of the produce, the nature of the work and the manner in which it is carried out—all of which are essentially economic features— are highly modified by the social organization of the tribe and by their magical belief. Customary and legal norms, magical and mythological ideas, introduce system into their economic efforts and organize them on a social basis. On the other hand, it is clear that if an ethnologist proposes to describe any aspect of tribal life, without approaching it also from the economic point of view, his account would be bound to be a failure.

This will be still more evident after a description of the manner in which they apportion the produce and utilize it in what could be called the financing of tribal enterprise. Here, again, I shall speak, for simplicity's sake, mainly of the garden produce. As each man has allotted to him for each season one or several garden plots, we might expect that, following the principle of "closed household economy," each family would by themselves consume the results of their labor. As a matter of fact, the apportionment or distribution, far from following such a simple scheme, is again full of intricacies and presents many economically interesting features. Of these the two most important are: the obligations, imposed by rules of kinship and relationship-in-law, and the dues and tributes paid to the chief.

The first-named obligations involve a very complex redistribution of garden produce, resulting in a state of things in which everybody is working for somebody else. The main rule is that a man is obliged to distribute almost all his garden produce among his sisters; in fact, to maintain his sisters and their families. I must pass over all the complications and consequences implied by this system, and only notice that it means an enormous amount of additional labor in handling and transporting the produce, and that it enmeshes the whole community into a network of reciprocal obligations and dues, one constant flow of gift and counter-gift.

This constant economic undertow to all public and private activities— this materialistic streak which runs through all their doings—gives a special and unexpected color to the existence of the natives, and shows the immense importance to them of the economic aspect of everything. Economic considerations pervade their social life, economic difficulties constantly face them. Whenever the native moves—to a feast, to an expedition, or in warfare—he will have to deal with the problems of giving and counter-giving. The detailed analysis of this state of affairs would lead us to interesting results, but it would be a side issue from our main theme—the public economy of the tribe.

To return to this, we must first consider what part of the whole tribal income is apportioned to the chief. By various channels, by dues and tributes, and especially through the effect of polygamy, with its resulting obligations of his relatives-in-law, about 30 per cent of the whole food production of his district finds its way into the large, finely-decorated yam houses of the chief. Now to the natives the possession and display of food are of immense value and importance in themselves. Pride in possessing abundant food is one of their leading characteristics. One of the greatest insults that can be uttered is to call someone "Man with no food," and it would be bitterly resented, and probably a quarrel would ensue. To be able to boast of having food is one of their chief glories and ambitions. Their whole conduct, in the matter of eating in public, is guided by the rule that no suspicion of scarcity of food can possibly be attached to the eater. For example, to eat publicly in a strange village would be considered humiliating, and is never done.

Their ambitions in this direction are also shown by the keen interest taken in the display of food. On all possible occasions—at harvest time, when there is an interchange of gifts, or when the enormous food distributions (Sagali) take place—the display of the food is one of the main features of interest. And there are even special food exhibitions, in which two villages compete against each other, and which in the old days used to be taken so seriously that often war was the result.

The chief is the only person who owns a big yam house, which is made with open interstices between the beams so that all may look through and admire the yams, of which the finest are always placed to the front. The chief is, as a matter of fact, also the only person who can accumulate, and, as a matter of privilege, the only one who is allowed to own and display large quantities. This gives him a definite status, is a sign of high rank, and satisfies his ambition. Finally, it enhances his power, broadly speaking, in the same manner as possession of wealth does with us.

Another important privilege of the chief, is his power to transform food into objects of permanent wealth. Here again, he is the only man rich enough to do it, but he also jealously guards his right, and would punish anyone who might attempt to emulate him, even on a small scale.

The Vaygua—objects or tokens of wealth—consist of several classes of highly-valued articles, mainly big ceremonial axe-blades, necklaces of red shell discs, and armshells of the Conus millepunctatus shell. These objects are hardly ever put to any real use, but they are extremely highly valued in themselves by the natives. The material of which they are made is rare and difficult to obtain, and much time and labor must be spent in working it. Once made, however, the objects are very durable, almost indestructible. Their main economic function is to be owned as signs of wealth, and consequently of power, and from time to time to change hands as ceremonial gifts. As such, they are the foundation of certain kinds of native trade, and they constitute an indispensable element of the social organization of the natives. For, as mentioned above, all their social life is accompanied by gift and counter-gift. These are, as a rule, arranged so that one party has to give a substantial present of food, when the other offers one of the tokens of wealth.

The chief, as said, has the means and the customary privilege of producing these objects. He also, in definite circumstances, frequently acquires them in exchange for food. In any case, about 80 per cent of these objects remain in his possession (or at least this was the proportion before the chief's power and all their tribal law had been undermined by white man's influence). This acquisition of valuables, side by side with possession of food, is the basis of his power and a mark of his dignity and rank.

The chief finally is (or, more correctly, in olden days was) the owner of about three-quarters of all the pigs, coconuts and betel nuts in the district. By a system of métayage,[1] there are in the various villages certain people, who look after his right over these three classes of things; they also receive their share, but have to bring him the bulk of the produce.

Thus, the possession of the beautiful yam houses, always ready to receive the crops, and often filled with them; the acquisition of a large amount of Vaygua (tokens of wealth), and of the greater part of the pigs, coconuts and betel nuts, give the chief a static basis of power, prestige and rank. But also the control over all these classes of wealth allows him to exercise his power dynamically.

For in a society where everything has to be accompanied by gift and payment, even the chief, the highest and most powerful individual in the community, though, according to customary rule, he can command the services of all, still must pay for them. He enjoys many personal services, such as being carried about on his journeys, sending people on errands, having all forms of magic performed for him. For such services, rendered by retainers and picked specialists, a chief must pay immediately, sometimes in Vaygua, sometimes in food, more especially in pigs, coconuts and betel nuts.

The essential of power is, of course, the possibility of enforcing orders and commanding obedience by means of punishment. The chief has special henchmen to carry out his verdicts directly by inflicting capital punishment, and they must be paid by Vaygua. More often, however, the punishment is meted out by means of evil magic. How often the sorcerers in the Trobriands use poison, it would be difficult to say. But the enormous dread of them, and the deep belief in their power, renders their magic efficient enough. And if the chief were known to have given a Vaygua to a powerful sorcerer in order to kill a man, I should say that man was doomed.

---

[1] Editors' note: *Métayage* is a form of land tenure similar to sharecropping in which a farmer works land owned by another in which the "rent" is paid for in kind.

Even more important than the exercise of personal power, is the command, already mentioned once or twice, which wealth gives the chief over the organization of tribal enterprises. The chief has the power of initiative, the customary right to organize all big tribal affairs, and conduct them in the character of master of ceremonies. But there are two conditions incidental to the role he has to play. The leading men, such as the headmen of dependent villages, the main performers, the always indispensable magicians, the technical specialists, have all to be paid, and are, as usual, paid in objects of wealth, and the bulk of the participants have to be fed.

Both these conditions can be fulfilled by the chief in virtue of his control over a considerable portion of the consumable and condensed wealth of the tribe.

As a concrete example of big tribal affairs, organized and financed by the chief, we can quote first of all the above-mentioned Kayasa, a term embracing several kinds of ceremonial enterprises. In these, as we saw, the chief, by means of gifts, imposes a binding obligation on the participants to carry out the undertaking, and by means of periodical distributions he keeps everyone going during the time of dancing, merry-making or communal working. In former times during war, when the inhabitants of two hostile districts used to forgather in their respective chiefs' villages, the chief had to summon his vassal headmen by gifts of Vaygua.[2] Then at an initial ceremonial gathering, there would be a distribution of food, in particular the specially coveted pig's flesh, coconuts and betel nuts. And, later on, when during the progress of hostilities large numbers had to camp in or near the chief's village, his yam houses would be severely taxed in order to keep the warriors provided with food. Again, there is an important feature of their tribal life—the Sagali, or ceremonial distributions of food from one clan to another, associated with their mortuary ritual. In these the chief's wealth often had to be called upon to a considerable extent if the nominal giver of the feast had any claim on him as his kinsman, clansman, or relative-in-law.

We see, therefore, that in following up the various channels through which produce flows, and in studying the transformations it undergoes, we find a new and extremely interesting field for ethnological and economic interest. The chief's economic role in public life can be pointedly described as that of "tribal banker," without, of course, giving this term its literal meaning. His position, his privileges, allow him to collect a considerable portion of tribal yield and to store it, also to transform part of it into permanent condensed wealth, by the accumulation of which he gives himself a still bigger fund of power. Thus, on the one hand, the chief's economic function is to create objects of wealth, and to accumulate provisions for

---

[2] For a general description of the Kiriwinian war customs, which are a thing of the past, see the article by the writer in Man, January 1920.

tribal use, thus making big tribal enterprises possible. On the other hand, in doing so, he enhances his prestige and influence, which he also exercises through economic means.

It would be idle to generalize from one example, or to draw strained parallels—to speak of the chief as "capitalist" or to use the expression "tribal banker" in any but the most unpretentious way. If we had more accounts of native economics similar to this—that is, going more into detail and giving an economic synthesis of facts—we might be able to arrive, by comparative treatment, at some interesting results. We might be able to grasp the nature of the economic mechanism of savage life, and incidentally we might be able to answer many questions referring to the origins and development of economic institutions. Again, nothing stimulates and broadens our views so much as wide comparison and sharp contrast, and the study of extremely primitive economic institutions would no doubt prove very refreshing and fertilizing to theory.

It is necessary to point out that, in such a short article, where the broad outline of the institutions and customs has to be given with a few strokes, I have had to summarize certain things. Thus I speak of "the chief," whereas in a more detailed account I would have shown that there are several chieftainships in the tribe with a varying range and amount of power. In each case the economic, as well as the other social conditions, are slightly different, and to these differences I have not been able to do justice in this article. I have tried to present the general features which, in a manner are common to all the districts of Kiriwina. A greater wealth of detail, though it might blur certain outlines and certainly would make things look less simple, would have allowed us to draw our conclusions even more forcibly and convincingly.

To sum up the results so far obtained, we may say that both the production and its apportionment in the native communities are by no means as simple as is usually assumed. They are both based on a special form of organization, both are intertwined with other tribal aspects, depending and reacting on other social and psychological forces.

Through the institution of chieftainship and the belief in magic, their production is integrated into a systematic effort of the whole community. By this a considerable amount of consumable wealth is produced, a great part of which is controlled by the chief, who transforms some of it into permanent wealth and keeps the rest in store. This, again, coupled with the natives' regard for wealth, and the importance of material give-and-take in their social institutions, allows the chief to wield his power to organize and finance tribal life.

We have not spoken of exchange yet, and, indeed, it is such a vast subject in the Trobriands—that is, if treated in the light of a more precise analysis—that in this paper I shall not attempt to deal with it exhaustively. There is, however, one point to which I want to draw attention. The tokens of wealth have often been called "money." It is at first sight evident that "money" in our sense cannot exist among the Trobrianders. The word "currency"— differentiated from "money" in that it is an object of use as well as a means of exchange—does not help us much here, as the articles in question are not utilities. Any article which can be classed as "money" or "currency" must fulfill certain essential conditions; it must function as a medium of exchange and as a common measure of value, and it must be the instrument of condensing wealth, the means by which value can be accumulated. Money also, as a rule, serves as the standard of deferred payments. It is obvious at once that in economic conditions such as obtain among the Trobrianders, there can be no question of a standard of deferred payments, as payments are never deferred. It is equally clear that the Vaygua do serve as a means of condensing wealth—in fact, that this is their essential role.

The questions of a common measure of value and a measure of exchange require, however, some consideration. Exchange of useful articles against one another does exist in Kiriwina, both in internal and external trade. Indeed, barter among the natives is very well developed. Their exchange sometimes takes the form of free gift and following counter-gift—always repaid according to definite rules of equivalence. Sometimes it is real barter (for which they have a term—Gimwali), where one article is traded against another, with direct assessment of equivalence and even with haggling.

But in all cases trade follows customary rules, which determine what and how much shall be exchanged for any given article. Thus the villagers of Bwoitalu are the professional carvers in hard wood and produce excellent carved dishes. They are, on the other hand, in need of coconuts and yam food, and they like to acquire certain ornaments. Whenever one of them has a few dishes of certain dimensions on hand, he knows that in the village of Oburaku he can get about forty coconuts for one grade, twenty for another, ten for another, and so on; in the central villages of Kiriwina, he can obtain a definite number of yam baskets; in some other villages, he can get a few red shell discs or turtle-shell ear-rings. Again, some coastal villages need a special kind of strong creeper for lashing their canoes. This they know can be obtained from villages near swamps for a definite payment—that is, one coil of creeper for one coconut or betel nut, or ten coils for a small basketful of yams.

All the trade is carried on in exactly the same way—given the article, and the communities between which it is traded, anyone would know its equivalent, rigidly prescribed by custom. In fact, the narrow range of exchangeable articles and the inertia of custom leave no room for any free exchange, in which there would be a need for comparing a number of articles by means of a common measure. Still less is there a need for a medium of exchange, since, whenever something changes hands, it does so always because the barterers directly require the other article.

This leads us first of all to the conclusion that we cannot think of Vaygua in terms of "money." Moreover, what is more important still, we see that in Kiriwina the character of the exchange does not admit of any article becoming money. Certain things, no doubt, more especially basketsful of yams, bundles of taro and coconuts are very frequently exchanged, and against a wide range of other articles, and in economic considerations they may serve us as measures of value; but they are not regarded or purposely used as such by the natives.

When reading ethnological accounts about native "money"—such, for example, as those about the diwarra shells in New Britain or about the big stones in the Carolines—the statements appear to me singularly unconvincing. Unless it is shown that the mechanism of exchange among the natives there requires or even allows of the existence of an article, used as a common measure of value or medium of exchange, all the data given about an article, however much they might lend it a superficial resemblance to money must be considered worthless. Of course, when a savage community comes into commercial relations with a higher culture—as in Africa, where trading between Arabs and Europeans has long taken place—then money can and even must exist. Some forms of the so-called South Sea "money" may have acquired this character recently under European influence, and the diwarra may possibly be a case in point.

The discussion of the problem of money among primitive peoples shows very clearly how necessary it is in ethnology to analyze the economic background of the conditions indispensable to the existence of certain complex phenomena. The existence of "money" or "currency" so easily assumed, so glibly introduced by the use of these terms, proves with close analysis to be an hypothesis extremely bold and probably equally misleading.

One further function of the tokens of value should be mentioned here, that is, their exchange in the form of circular trading, called by the natives Kula, which takes place over a wide area amongst the islands and coasts of this part of British New Guinea. This peculiar form of circular trade presents many interesting economic features, but as it has been described elsewhere I shall not enter into the subject now.[3]

All the facts adduced in this article lead us to the conclusion that primitive economics are not by any means the simple matter we are generally led to suppose. In savage societies national economy certainly does not exist, if we mean by the term a system of free competitive exchange of goods and services, with the interplay of supply and demand determining value and regulating all economic life. But there is a long step between this and Buecher's assumption that the only alternative is a preeconomic stage, where an individual person

---

[3] See article by the writer, Kula: Circulating Exchange of Valuables in the Archipelagoes of Eastern New Guinea, Man, July 1920.

or a single household satisfy their primary wants as best they can, without any more elaborate mechanism than division of labor according to sex, and an occasional spasmodic bit of barter. Instead, we find a state of affairs where production, exchange and consumption are socially organized and regulated by custom, and where a special system of traditional economic values governs their activities and spurs them on to efforts. This state of affairs might be called—as a new conception requires a new term—Tribal Economy.

The analysis of the natives' own economic conceptions of value, ownership, equivalence, commercial honor and morals opens a new vista of economic research, indispensable for any deeper understanding of a native community. Economic elements enter into tribal life in all its aspects—social, customary, legal and magico-religious—and are in turn controlled by these. It is not for the observer in the field to answer or to contemplate the metaphysical question as to what is the cause and effect—the economic or the other aspects. To study their interplay and correlation is, however, his duty. For to overlook the relation between two or several aspects of native life is as much an error of omission as to overlook any one aspect.

QUERIES

- Who owns a garden plot in Trobriand society? How is land tenure connected to other dimensions of Trobriand culture?
- Discuss the authority of a Trobriand chief. What are the bases of his authority? What are some of its limits?
- What are Malinowski's reasons for insisting that Vaygua are not money?

CONNECTIONS

- Given Malinowski's discussion of the political power of Trobriand chiefs, how would you classify them in terms of Sahlins's ideas in "Poor Man, Rich Man, Big Man, Chief?"
- How would Mauss interpret Malinowski's discussion of gift-giving by Trobriand chiefs?

11

A. R. Radcliffe-Brown

INTRODUCTION

In the following article, originally a lecture given to the Royal Anthropological Institute in 1951, A. R. Radcliffe-Brown (1881–1955) defines and defends his concept of social anthropology as a science based on the comparative method. Responding to Franz Boas's historical particularism (Moore 2008:40–42), Radcliffe-Brown distinguishes social anthropology from American cultural anthropology. Radcliffe-Brown rejects Boas's call to study individual cultures, to "reconstruct" those cultures if they were no longer independent and cohesive units, and to explain their practices within their specific contexts.

Rather, Radcliffe-Brown argues, social anthropology should be "the study of discoverable regularities in the development of human society in so far as these can be illustrated or demonstrated by the study of primitive peoples." It was Radcliffe-Brown's objective to advance Durkheim's goal of developing a "science of society" that identified cross-cultural regularities or scientific laws (for a discussion, see Moore 2008:150–52). This endeavor was based on several principles. First, Radcliffe-Brown argued, social life was built upon regularly recurring interactions between individuals with different roles; those interactions are "social structures." (Some obvious examples of social structures in the United States might include parent/child, husband/wife, employer/employee, and so on.) Social structures have various functions, but their fundamental function is the maintenance and perpetuation of society. (Thus, the social structure of judge/defendant/jury functions to determine guilt or innocence and penalty; the function of that social structure is to maintain social order.) If similar social structures are shown to have similar functions in different societies, then one can arrive at a generalization or scientific law about society. In that, the Durkheimian goal has been advanced.

Radcliffe-Brown demonstrates his theoretical position and analytical approach through an extended analysis of social organization based on the moiety, exogamy, and totemism. *Moieties* refers to the division of members of a society into one of two groups, usually based on kinship (one is born into Moiety A or Moiety B). *Exogamy* is the social prescription that one must marry a spouse from a group other than one's own. *Totemism* refers to the mythic association of an animal or natural feature with a social group; the affiliate animal is considered "sacred" by the members of that group, but not necessarily by other people. Moieties are simultaneously halves of the same society, but poised in opposition. A member of one moiety "takes" someone from another moiety as a spouse. Myths may recount battles or conflicts between the totemic creatures associated with the different moieties. Public rituals may oppose moieties and play on old rivalries. Beginning with an example of exogamous moieties in indigenous groups of southeastern Australia, Radcliffe-Brown finds similar cases elsewhere in Australia, in North America, and in Africa. These cases are characterized by "the union of opposites." What begins as a somewhat esoteric ethnographic case emerges as a recurrent practice in human societies: solidarity characterized by opposition. For Radcliffe-Brown, this exemplifies how social anthropology can arrive at broad principles about human society.

PRIMARY TEXT: *THE COMPARATIVE METHOD IN SOCIAL ANTHROPOLOGY*

"The Comparative Method in Social Anthropology," in *The Journal of the Royal Anthropological Institute*, Vol. 81 (1/2), 1951, pp. 15–22. Reproduced with permission of Blackwell Publishing Ltd.

What is meant when one speaks of "the comparative method" in anthropology is the method used by such a writer as Frazer in his *Golden Bough*. But comparisons of particular features of social life can be made for either of two very different purposes, which correspond to the distinction now commonly made in England between ethnology and social anthropology. The existence of similar institutions, customs or beliefs in two or more societies may in certain instances be taken by the ethnologist as pointing to some historical connection. What is aimed at is some sort of reconstruction of the history of a society or people or region. In comparative sociology or social anthropology the purpose of comparison is different, the aim being to explore the varieties of forms of social life as a basis for the theoretical study of human social phenomena.

Franz Boas, writing in 1888 and 1896, pointed out that in anthropology there are two tasks to be undertaken. One kind of task is to 'reconstruct' the history of particular regions or peoples, and this he spoke of as being "the first task." The second task he describes as follows: "A comparison of the social life of different peoples proves that the foundations of their cultural development are remarkably uniform. It follows from this that there are laws to which this development is subject. Their discovery is the second, perhaps the more important aim of our science. . . . In the pursuit of these studies we find that the same custom, the same idea, occurs among peoples for whom we cannot establish any historical connection, so that a common historical origin cannot be assumed and it becomes necessary to decide whether there are laws that result in the same, or at least similar, phenomena independently of historical causes. Thus develops the second important task of ethnology, the investigation of the laws governing social life." "The frequent occurrence of similar phenomena in cultural areas that have no historical contact suggests that important results may be obtained from their study, for it shows that the human mind develops everywhere according to the same laws."

Boas included these two tasks in the single discipline which he called sometimes 'anthropology,' sometimes 'ethnology.' To some of us in this country it seems more convenient to refer to those investigations that are concerned with the reconstruction of history as belonging to ethnology and to keep the term social anthropology for the study of discoverable regularities in the development of human society in so far as these can be illustrated or demonstrated by the study of primitive peoples.

Thus, the comparative method in social anthropology is the method of those who have been called 'arm-chair anthropologists' since they work in libraries. Their first task is to look for what used to be called 'parallels,' similar social features appearing in different societies, in the present or in the past. At Cambridge sixty years ago Frazer represented armchair anthropology using the comparative method, while Haddon urged the need of 'intensive' studies of particular societies by systematic field studies of competent observers. The development of field studies has led to a relative neglect of studies making use of the comparative method. This is both understandable and excusable, but it does have some regrettable effects. The student is told that he must consider any feature of social life in its context, in its relation to the other features of the particular social system in which it is found. But he is often not taught to look at it in the wider context of human societies in general. The teaching of the Cambridge school of anthropology forty-five years ago was not that arm-chair anthropology was to be abandoned but that it must be combined with intensive studies of particular primitive societies in which any particular institution, custom, or belief of the society should be examined in relation to the total social system of which it was a part or item. Without systematic comparative studies anthropology will become only historiography and ethnography. Sociological theory must be based on, and continually tested by, systematic comparison.

The only really satisfactory way of explaining a method is by means of illustration. Let us therefore consider how the method can be applied in a particular instance. We may take our start with a particular feature of some tribes in the interior of New South Wales. In these tribes there is a division of the population into two parts, which are named after the eaglehawk and the crow (Kilpara and Makwara). There is a rule by which a man should only take a wife from the division other than his own, and that the children will belong to the same division as their mother. The system is described in technical terms as one of totemically represented exogamous matrilineal moieties.

One way of explaining why a particular society has the features that it does have is by its history. As we have no authentic history of these or other Australian tribes the historical anthropologists are reduced to offering us imaginary histories. Thus the Rev. John Mathew would explain these divisions and their names by supposing that two different peoples, one called Eaglehawks and the other Crows, met in this part of Australia and fought with each other. Ultimately they decided to make peace and agreed that in the future Eaglehawk men would only marry Crow women and *vice versa*.

Let us begin looking for parallels. There is a very close parallel to be found amongst the Haida of north-west America, who also have a division into two exogamous matrilineal moieties which are named after the eagle and the raven, two species which correspond very closely indeed to the eaglehawk and crow of Australia. The Haida have a legend that in the beginning only the eagle possessed fresh water which he kept in a basket. The raven discovered this and succeeded in stealing the water from the eagle. But as he flew with the basket over Queen Charlotte Island the water was spilled from the heavy basket and formed the lakes and rivers from which all birds can now drink; and salmon made their way into the streams and now furnish food for men.

In some parts of Australia there are similar legends about the eaglehawk and the crow. One is to the effect that in the beginning only the eaglehawk possessed a supply of fresh water, which he kept under a large stone. The crow, spying on him, saw him lift the stone and take a drink, then replace the stone. The crow proceeded to lift the stone, and after he had taken a drink of fresh water scratched the lice from his head into the water and did not replace the stone. The result was that the water escaped and formed the rivers of eastern Australia in which the lice became the Murray cod that were an important item of food for the aborigines just as salmon are in northwest America. If we accept the criteria formulated by the diffusionists, such as Graebner, we have here what they would say is evidence of a historical connection between Australia and the Pacific coast of North America.

Once we begin looking for parallels to the Eaglehawk-Crow division of Australia we find many instances of exogamous moieties, in some instances matrilineal, in others patrilineal, in the rest of Australia, and frequently the divisions are named after or represented by birds. In Victoria we find black cockatoo and white cockatoo, in Western Australia white cockatoo and crow. In New Ireland there is a similar system in which the moieties are associated with the sea-eagle and the fish-hawk. At this point we may feel inclined to ask why these social divisions should be identified by reference to two species of birds.

In Eastern Australia the division of the population into two sexes is represented by what is called sex totemism. In tribes of New South Wales the men have for their 'brother' the bat, and the women have for their 'sister' the night owl in some tribes and the owlet nightjar in others. In the northern part of New South Wales the totems are the bat for men and the treecreeper for women. (It must be remembered that the Australian aborigines classify the bat as a 'bird.') So we find another dichotomy of society in which the divisions are represented by birds.

Throughout most of Australia there is a very important social division into two alternating generation divisions or endogamous moieties. One division consists of all the persons of a single generation together with those of the generation of their grandparents and the generation of their grandchildren, while the other division includes all those of the generation of their parents and the generation of their children. These divisions are rarely given names but in some tribes may be referred to by terms, one of which a man applies to his own division and its members while the other is applied to the other division. But in one part of Western Australia these endogamous moieties are named after the kingfisher and the bee-eater, while in another part they are named after a little red bird and a little black bird.

Our question "Why all these birds?" is thus widened in its scope. It is not only the exogamous moieties, but also dual divisions of other kinds that are identified by connection with a pair of birds. It is, however, not always a question of birds. In Australia the moieties may be associated with other pairs of animals, with two species of kangaroo in one part, with two species of bee in another. In California one moiety is associated with the coyote and the other with the wild cat.

Our collection of parallels could be extended to other instances in which a social group or division is given an identity and distinguished from others by association with a natural species. The Australian moieties are merely one instance of a widely spread social phenomenon. From the particular phenomenon we are led, by the comparative method, to a much more general problem—How can we understand the customs by which social groups and divisions are distinguished by associating a particular group or division with a particular natural species? This is the general problem of totemism, as it has been designated. I do not offer you a solution of this problem, as it seems to me to be the resultant of two other problems. One is the problem of the way in which in a particular society the relation of human beings to natural species is represented, and as a contribution to this problem I have offered an analysis of the non-totemic Andaman Islanders. The other is the problem of how social groups come to be identified by connection with some emblem, symbol, or object having symbolic or emblematic reference. A nation identified by its flag, a family identified by its coat of arms, a particular congregation of a church identified by its relation to a particular saint, a clan identified by its relation to a totemic species; these are all so many examples of a single class of phenomena for which we have to look for, a general theory.

The problem to which it is desired to draw your attention here is a different one. Granted that it is for some reason appropriate to identify social divisions by association with natural species, what is the principle by which such pairs as eaglehawk and crow, eagle and raven, coyote and wild cat are chosen as representing the moieties of a dual division? The reason for asking this question is not idle curiosity. We may, it can be held, suppose that an understanding of the principle in question will give us an important insight into the way in which the natives themselves think about the dual division as a part of their social structure. In other words, instead of asking "Why all these birds?" we can ask "Why particularly eaglehawk and crow, and other pairs?"

I have collected many tales about Eaglehawk and Crow in different parts of Australia, and in all of them the two are represented as opponents in some sort of conflict. A single example must suffice and it comes from Western Australia. Eaglehawk was the mother's brother of Crow. In these tribes a man marries the daughter of a mother's brother so that Eaglehawk was the possible father-in-law of Crow, to whom therefore he owed obligations such as that of providing him with food. Eaglehawk told his nephew to go and hunt wallaby. Crow, having killed a wallaby, ate it himself, an extremely reprehensible action in terms of native morality. On his return to the camp his uncle asked him what he had brought, and Crow, being a liar, said that he had succeeded in getting nothing. Eaglehawk then said, "But what is in your belly, since your hunger-belt is no longer tight?" Crow replied that to stay the pangs of hunger he had filled his belly with the gum from the acacia. The uncle replied that he did not believe him and would tickle him until he vomited. (This incident is given in the legend in the form of a song of Eaglehawk—*Balmanangabalu ngabarina, kidji-kidji malidyala*.) The crow vomited the wallaby that he had eaten. Thereupon Eaglehawk seized him and rolled him in the fire; his eyes became red with the fire, he was blackened by the charcoal, and he called out in pain "Wa! Wa! Wa!" Eaglehawk pronounced what was to be the law "You will never be a hunter, but you will for ever be a thief." And that is how things now are.

To interpret this tale we have to consider how these birds appear to the aborigines. In the first place they are the two chief meat-eating birds and the Australian aborigine thinks of himself as a meat-eater. One method of hunting in this region is for a number of men and women to come together at an appropriate season for a collective hunt. A fire across a stretch of country is started in such a way that it will be spread by the wind. The men advance in front of the fire killing with spear or throwing stick the animals that are fleeing from it, while the women follow the fire to dig out such animals as bandicoots that have taken refuge underground. When such a hunt has been started it will not be long before first one and then another eaglehawk makes its appearance to join in the hunting of the animals in flight from the advancing flames. Eaglehawk is the hunter. The crow does not join in this or any other kind of hunt, but when a camp fire is started it is rarely very long before a crow makes his appearance to settle in a tree out of reach of a throwing stick and wait for the chance of thieving a piece of meat for his dinner.

Amongst the tales told by the Australians about animals we can find an immense number of parallels to this tale of Eaglehawk and Crow. Here, as an example, is one about the wombat and the kangaroo from the region where South Australia adjoins Victoria. In this region the wombat and the kangaroo are the two largest meat animals. In the beginning Wombat and Kangaroo lived together as friends. One day Wombat began to make a 'house' for himself. (The wombat lives in a burrow in the ground.) Kangaroo jeered at him and thus annoyed him. Then one day it rained. (It is to be remembered that in these tales whatever happens is thought of as happening for the first time in the history of the world.) Wombat went into his 'house' out of the rain. Kangaroo asked Wombat to make room for him, but the latter explained that there was only room for one. Thus Wombat and Kangaroo quarreled and fought. Kangaroo hit Wombat on the head with a big stone, flattening his skull; Wombat threw a spear at Kangaroo which fixed itself at the base of the backbone. The wombat has a flattened skull to this day and the kangaroo has a tail; the former lives in a burrow while the kangaroo lives in the open; they are no longer friends.

This is, of course, a 'just-so' story which you may think is childish. It amuses the listeners when it is told with the suitable dramatic expressions. But if we examine some dozens of these tales we find that they have a single theme. The resemblances and differences of animal species are translated into terms of friendship and conflict, solidarity and opposition. In other words the world of animal life is represented in terms of social relations similar to those of human society.

One may find legends which relate not to particular species or pairs of species but to animals in general. There is a legend in New South Wales according to which in the beginning all the animals formed a single society.

Then the bat was responsible for introducing death into the world by killing his two wives. His brothers-in-law called all the animals to a corroborree, and catching the bat unawares threw him into the fire. This started a general fight in which the animals attacked each other with fire, and of this fight all the animals now show the marks. The various species no longer form one society of friends.

There is a very similar tale in the Andaman Islands. The various species of animals originally formed a single society. At a meeting one of them brought fire. There was a general quarrel in which they all threw fire at each other. Some fled into the sea and became fishes, others escaped into the trees and became birds, and birds and fishes still show the marks of the burns they suffered.

A comparative study therefore reveals to us the fact that the Australian ideas about the eaglehawk and the crow are only a particular instance of a widespread phenomenon. First, these tales interpret the resemblances and differences of animal species in terms of social relationships of friendship and antagonism as they are known in the social life of human beings. Secondly, natural species are placed in pairs of opposites. They can only be so regarded if there is some respect in which they resemble each other. Thus eaglehawk and crow resemble each other in being the two prominent meat-eating birds. When I first investigated the sex totems of New South Wales I supposed, quite wrongly, that what was the basic resemblance of the bat and the night owl or nightjar was that they both fly about at night. But the tree-creeper does not fly at night and is the totem of the women in the northern part of New South Wales. As I was sitting in the region of the Macleay River with a native a tree-creeper made its appearance, and I asked him to tell me about it. "That is the bird that taught women how to climb trees" he told me. After some conversation I asked "What resemblance is there between the bat and the tree creeper?" and with an expression on his face that showed surprise that I should ask such a question he replied, "But of course they both live in holes in trees." I realised that the night owl and the nightjar also live in trees. The fact that certain animals eat meat constitutes a sort of social similarity, as of eaglehawk and crow or dingo and wild cat. Similarly the habit of living in holes in trees.

We can now answer the question "Why eaglehawk and crow?" by saying that these are selected as representing a certain kind of relationship which we may call one of 'opposition.'

The Australian idea of what is here called 'opposition' is a particular application of that association by contrariety that is a universal feature of human thinking, so that we think by pairs of contraries, upwards and downwards, strong and weak, black and white. But the Australian conception of 'opposition' combines the idea of a pair of contraries with that of a pair of opponents. In the tales about eaglehawk and crow the two birds are opponents in the sense of being antagonists. They are also contraries by reason of their difference of character, Eaglehawk the hunter, Crow the thief. Black cockatoo and white cockatoo which represent the moieties in Western Victoria are another example of contrariety, the birds being essentially similar except for the contrast of colour. In America the moieties are referred to by other pairs of contraries, Heaven and Earth, war and peace, up-stream and down-stream, red and white. After a lengthy comparative study I think I am fully justified in stating a general law, that wherever, in Australia, Melanesia or America, there exists a social structure of exogamous moieties, the moieties are thought of as being in a relation of what is here called 'opposition.'

Obviously the next step in a comparative study is to attempt to discover what are the various forms that the opposition between the moieties of a dual division takes in actual social life. In the literature there are occasional references to a certain hostility between the two divisions described as existing or reported to have existed in the past. All the available evidence is that there is no real hostility in the proper sense of the term but only a conventional attitude which finds expression in some customary mode of behaviour. Certainly in Australia, although in some instances where there is a dispute it is possible to observe the members of the two patrilineal moieties forming separate 'sides,' real hostility, of the kind that may lead to violent action is not between the moieties but between local groups, and two local groups of the same patrilineal moiety seem to be just as frequently in conflict as two groups belonging to different moieties. Indeed, since a common source of actual conflict is the taking by one man of a woman married to or betrothed to another the two antagonists or groups of antagonists in such instances will both belong to the same patrilineal moiety.

The expression of opposition between the moieties may take various forms. One is the institution to which anthropologists have given the not very satisfactory name of 'the joking relationship.' Members of opposite divisions are permitted or expected to indulge in teasing each other, in verbal abuse or in exchange of insults. Kroeber (*Handbook of Indians of California*) writes that amongst the Cupeño "a sort of good natured opposition is recognized between the moieties, whose members frequently taunt each other with being unsteady and slow-witted respectively." Strong (*Aboriginal Society in Southern California*) reports the same thing. "A good-natured antagonism between the moieties exhibits itself in joking between persons of the one and the other. The coyote people taunt the wild cat people with being slow-witted and lazy like their animal representative and the wild cat people retaliate by accusing their opponents with being unsteady. There are indications that this teasing of one moiety by another entered into their serious ceremonies. There were songs of a satirical kind that could be sung by one moiety against the other. However, the opposition between the moieties seems to have been much strong less than between certain pairs of clans, sometimes belonging to the same moiety, which were traditionally 'enemies.' These clans, on certain occasions would sing 'enemy songs' against each other."

This institution, for which it is to be hoped that some one will find a better name than 'joking relationship,' is found in a variety of forms in a number of different societies, and calls for systematic comparative study. It has for its function to maintain a continuous relationship between two persons, or two groups, of apparent but factitious hostility or antagonism. I have offered a suggestion towards a comparative study of this institution in a paper published in the journal *Africa*.

Another significant custom in which is expressed the relation of opposition between the two moieties is that by which, in some tribes of Australia and in some of North America the moieties provide the 'sides' in games such as football. Competitive games provide a social occasion on which two persons or two groups of persons are opponents. Two continuing groups in a social structure can be maintained in a relation in which they are regularly opponents. An example is provided by the two universities of Oxford and Cambridge.

There are other customs in which the opposition of moieties is expressed. For example, in the Omaha tribe of North America the camp circle was divided into two semi-circles, and when a boy of the one half crossed into the other he took companions with him and there was a fight with the boys of the other moiety. We need not and can not here examine these various customs.

Let us consider briefly the institution of moiety exogamy, by which every marriage, where the rule is observed, is between persons belonging to opposite moieties. There are innumerable customs which that in many primitive societies the taking of a woman in marriage is represented symbolically as an act of hostility against her family or group. Every anthropologist is familiar with the custom by which it is represented that the bride is captured or taken by force from her kinsfolk. A first collection of instances of this custom was made by McLennan, who interpreted them historically as being survivals from the earliest condition of human society in which the only way to obtain a wife was to steal or capture a woman from another tribe.

An illuminating example of this kind of custom is provided by the people of the Marquesas. When a marriage has been arranged the kinsmen of the bridegroom take the gifts which are to be offered to the kinsfolk of the bride and proceed towards the bride's home. On the way they are ambushed and attacked by the bride's kin who seize by force the goods that they are conveying. The first act of violence comes from the kin of the bride. By the Polynesian principle of *utu* those who suffer an injury are entitled to retaliate by inflicting an injury. So the bridegroom's kinsmen exercise this right by carrying off the bride. No example could better illustrate the fact that these customary actions are symbolic.

Viewed in relation to social structure the meaning or symbolic reference of these customs ought to be obvious. The solidarity of a group requires that the loss of one of its members shall be recognized as an injury to the group. Some expression of this is therefore called for. The taking of a woman in marriage is represented as in some sense an act of hostility against her kin. This is what is meant by the saying of the Gusii of East Africa "Those whom we marry are those whom we fight."

It is in the light of this that we must interpret the custom of marriage by exchange. The group or kin of a woman lose her when she marries; they are compensated for their loss if they receive another who will become the wife of one of them. In Australian tribes, with a few exceptions, the custom is that when a man takes a wife he should give a sister to replace her. In the Yaralde tribe of South Australia, which did not have a system of moieties, when a man married a woman of another local clan, his own clan was expected to provide a wife for some member of the clan from which the bride came. Otherwise the marriage was regarded as irregular, improper, or we might almost say illegal. It has been reported from the tribes of the eastern part of Victoria (Gippsland) that the only proper form of marriage was by exchange. The system of exogamous moieties provides a system of generalisation of marriage by exchange, since every marriage is one incident in the continual process by which the men of one moiety get their wives from the other.

A comparative study shows that in many primitive societies the relation established between two groups of kin by a marriage between a man of one group and a woman of the other is one which is expressed by customs of avoidance and by the joking relationship. In many societies a man is required to avoid any close social contact with the mother of his wife, frequently also with her father, and with other persons of that generation amongst his wife's kin. With this custom there is frequently associated the custom called the 'joking relationship' by which a man is permitted or even required to use insulting behaviour to some of his wife's kin of his own generation. I have elsewhere suggested that these customs can be understood as being the conventional means by which a relationship of a peculiar kind, which can be described as a compound of friendship or solidarity with hostility or opposition is established and maintained.

In a complete study there are other features of the dual organization that would need to be taken into consideration. There are instances in which there are regular exchanges of goods or services between the two moieties. In that competitive exchange of food and valuables known as 'potlatch' in North America, the moieties may be significant. Amongst the Tlingit, for example, it is members of one moiety who potlatch against members of the other moiety. The two moieties provide the 'sides' for what is a sort of competitive game in which men 'fight with property.'

Our comparative study enables us to see the Eaglehawk-Crow division of the Darling River tribes as one particular example of a widespread type of the application of a certain structural principle. The relation between the two divisions, which has here been spoken of by the term 'opposition' is one which separates and also unites, and which therefore gives us a rather special kind of social integration which deserves systematic study. But the term 'opposition' which I have been obliged to use because I cannot find a better, is not wholly appropriate, for it stresses too much what is only one side of the relationship, that of separation and difference. The more correct description would be to say that the kind of structure with which we are concerned is one of the union of opposites.

The idea of a unity of contraries was one of the leading ideas of the philosophy of Heraclitus. It is summed up in his statement, "Polemos is king, rules all things." The Greek word polemos is sometimes translated as 'strife', but the appropriate translation would be 'opposition' in the sense in which that word has been used in this lecture. Heraclitus uses as one example the mortise and the tenon; these are not at strife; they are contraries or opposites which combine to make a unity when they are joined together.

There is some evidence that this idea of the union of opposites was derived by Heraclitus and the Pythagoreans from the East. At any rate the most complete elaboration of the idea is to be found in the Yin-Yang philosophy of ancient China. The phrase in which this is summed up is *"Yi yin yi yang wei tze tao."* One yin and one yang make an order. Yin is the feminine principle, Yang the masculine. The word 'tao' can here be best translated as 'an ordered whole.' One man (yang) and his wife (yin) likely constitute the unity of a married couple. One day (yang) and one night (yin) make a unified whole or unity of time. Similarly one summer (yang) and one winter (yin) make up the unity we call a year. Activity is yang and passivity is yin and a relation of two tribe entities or persons of which one is active and the other passive is also conceived as a unity of opposites. In this ancient Chinese philosophy this idea of the unity of opposites is given the widest possible extention. The whole universe including human society is interpreted as an 'order' based on this.

There is historical evidence that this philosophy was developed many centuries ago in the region of the Yellow River, the 'Middle Kingdom.' There is also evidence that the social organization of this region was one of paired intermarrying clans, the two clans meeting together at the Spring and Autumn Festivals, and competing in the singing of odes, so that the men of the one clan could find wives amongst the daughters of the other. The evidence is that the system of marriage was one where a man married his mother's brother's daughter, or a woman of the appropriate generation of his mother's clan. According to my information this kind of organization, which apparently existed forty centuries ago in that region, still survived there in 1935, but the investigation of it that I had planned to be carried out by Li Yu I was unfortunately prevented by the Japanese attack on China. It may still not be too late for this to be done; it would enable us to evaluate more exactly the historical reconstruction of Marcel Granet.

This Yin-Yang philosophy of ancient China is the systematic elaboration of the principle that can be used to define the social structure of moieties in Australian tribes, for the structure of moieties is, as may be seen from the brief account here given, one of a unity of opposing groups, in the double sense that the two groups are friendly opponents, and that they are represented as being in some sense opposites, in the way in which eaglehawk and crow or black and white are opposites

Light can be thrown on this by the consideration of another instance of opposition in Australian societies. An Australian camp includes men of a certain local clan and their wives who, by the rule of exogamy, have come from other clans. In New South Wales there is a system of sex totemism, by which one animal species is the 'brother' of the men, and another species is the 'sister' of the women. Occasionally there arises within a native camp a condition of tension between the sexes. What is then to happen, according to the accounts of the aborigines, is that the women will go out and kill a bat, the 'brother' or sex totem of the men, and leave it lying in the camp for the men to see. The men then retaliate by killing the bird which in that is the sex totem of the women. The women then utter abuse against the men and this leads to a fight with sticks (digging sticks for the women, throwing sticks for the men) between the two sex groups in which a good many bruises are inflicted. After the fight peace is restored and the tension is eliminated. The Australian aborigines have the idea that where there is a quarrel between two persons or two groups which is likely to smoulder the thing to do is for them to fight it out and then make friends. The symbolic use of the totem is very significant. This custom shows us that the idea of the opposition of groups, and the union of opposites is not confined to the exogamous moieties. The two sex groups provide a structure of a similar kind; so sometimes do the two groups formed by the alternating generation divisions. The group of the fathers, and the group of their sons are in a relation of opposition, not dissimilar from relation between husbands and their wives.

We can say that in the relatively simple social structure of Australian tribes we can recognize three principal types of relationship between persons or groups. There is the relationship of enmity and strife; at the other extreme there is the relationship of simple solidarity, and in the Australian system this ought to exist between brothers, and between persons of the same generation in the local group; such persons may not fight, though in certain circumstances it is thought to be legitimate for one person to 'growl' against the other, to express in the camp a complaint against the action of the other. There is thirdly the relationship of opposition, which is not at all the same thing as strife or enmity, but is a combination of agreement and disagreement, of solidarity and difference.

We began with a particular feature of a particular region in Australia, the existence of exogamous moieties named after the eaglehawk and the crow. By making comparisons amongst other societies, some of them not Australian, we are enabled to see that this is not something particular or peculiar to one region, but is one instance of certain widespread general tendencies in human societies. We thus substitute for a particular problem of the kind that calls for a historical explanation, certain general problems. There is, for example, the problem of totemism as a social phenomenon in which there is a special association of a social group with a natural species. Another, and perhaps more important, problem that has been raised, is that of the nature and functioning of social relationships and social structures based on what has here been called 'opposition.' This is a much more general problem than that of totemism for it is the problem of how opposition can be used as a mode of social integration. The comparative method is therefore one by which we pass from the particular to the general, from the general to the more general, with the end in view that we may in this way arrive at the universal, at characteristics which can be found in different forms in all human societies.

But the comparative method does not only formulate problems, though the formulation of the right problems is extremely important in any science; it also provides material by which the first steps may be made towards the solution. A study of the system of moieties in Australia can give us results that should have considerable value for the theory of human society.

At the beginning of this lecture I quoted Franz Boas as having distinguished two tasks with which an anthropologist can concern himself in the study of primitive society, and these two tasks call for two different methods. One is the 'historical' method, by which the existence of a particular feature in a particular society is 'explained' as the result of a particular sequence of events. The other is the comparative method by which we seek, not to 'explain,' but to understand a particular feature of a particular society by first seeing it as a particular instance of a general kind or class of social phenomena, and then by relating it to a certain general, or preferably a universal, tendency in human societies. Such a tendency is what is called in certain instances a law. Anthropology as the study of primitive society includes both methods, and I have myself consistently used both in the teaching of ethnology and social anthropology in a number of universities. But there must be discrimination. The historical method will give us particular propositions, only the comparative method can give us general propositions. In primitive societies historical evidence is always lacking or inadequate. There is no historical evidence as to how the Eaglehawk-Crow division in Australia came into existence, and guesses about it seem to me of no significance whatever. How the Australian aborigines arrived at their present social systems is, and forever must be, entirely unknown. The supposition that by the comparative method we might arrive at valid conclusions about the 'origins' of those systems shows a complete disregard for the nature of historical evidence. Anthropology, as the study of primitive societies, includes both historical (ethnographical and ethnological) studies and also the generalizing study known as social anthropology which is a special branch of comparative sociology. It is desirable that the aims and methods should be distinguished. History, in the proper sense of the term, as an authentic account of the succession of events in a particular region over a particular period of time, cannot give us generalizations. The comparative method as a generalising study of the features of human societies cannot give us particular histories. The two studies can only be combined and adjusted when their difference is properly recognized and it is for this reason that thirty years ago I urged that there should be a clear distinction between ethnology as the historical study of primitive societies and social anthropology as that branch of comparative sociology that concerns itself specially with the societies we call primitive. We can leave all questions of historical reconstruction to ethnology. For social anthropology the task is to formulate and validate statements about the conditions of existence of social systems (laws of social statics) and the regularities that are observable in social change (laws of social dynamics). This can only be done by the systematic use of the comparative method, and the only justification of that method is the expectation that it will provide us with results of this kind, or, as Boas stated it, will provide us with knowledge of the laws of social development. It will be only in an integrated and organized study in which historical studies and sociological studies are combined that we shall be able to reach a real understanding of the development of human society, and this we do not yet have.

QUERIES

- How does Radcliffe-Brown's research agenda differ from the historical method outlined by Boas in "The Methods of Ethnology"?
- Define moieties. Summarize the examples of moieties that Radcliffe-Brown describes and explain how they serve as examples of a "social structure."
- Review the various creation myths Radcliffe-Brown summarizes about totemic animals at the beginning of time: what is the common moral or social problem addressed by those myths?
- How does Radcliffe-Brown's comparative study of moiety organization lead to our understanding of a general principle about human society?

CONNECTIONS

- There is a functional argument implicit in this article (such as, moieties serve to unify society through opposition). How would this argument differ from a functionalist argument as outlined by Malinowski (Moore 2008:139–42) or Leslie White (Moore 2008:182–83)?
- How does Radcliffe-Brown advance the goals of the Durkheimian "science of society" compared to Marcel Mauss's essay, *The Gift*? At what point do those two scholars share similar objectives?
- How does Radcliffe-Brown's 1951 view of explanation in social anthropology differ from that outlined by E. E. Evans-Pritchard's 1950 article, "Social Anthropology: Past and Present"?

12

Edward E. Evans-Pritchard

INTRODUCTION

Edward E. Evans-Pritchard (1902–1973) was an anthropologist shaped by the tenets of British social anthropology who later rejected them (for an overview, see Moore 2008:161–72). A highly-esteemed Africanist whose writings—such as *Witchcraft, Oracles and Magic Among the Azande* (1937), *The Nuer* (1940), among others—were considered models of British social anthropology, Evans-Pritchard ultimately rejected the notion that anthropology should be modeled on the natural sciences. Instead, Evans-Pritchard argued that social anthropology should be modeled on history and thus belong among the humanities.

This argument is presented in the following selection, given as a public lecture in 1950 at Oxford University, just a year before Radcliffe-Brown's 1951 lecture on a similar topic to the Royal Anthropological Institute (RAI) of Great Britain and Ireland. Both lectures were published in the *Journal of the RAI*, but the two anthropologists' positions could not have been more different. Radcliffe-Brown insisted that social anthropology should be modeled on the natural sciences, and should search for lawlike regularities in human social life. Evans-Pritchard countered that the view that anthropology should be a natural science was based on a flawed assumption that society was like an organism (Moore 2008:113, 146–47), a natural system—which it is not—and that the so-called laws about human society were mere speculations. Instead, Evans-Pritchard argued, social anthropology has more in common with the humanities than the natural sciences, specifically sharing goals and practices with history. These contrasting positions—anthropology as a natural science vs. anthropology as one of the humanities—represent polar positions that thread through anthropological theory to the present, and they are clearly articulated in Evans-Pritchard's article.

PRIMARY TEXT: *SOCIAL ANTHROPOLOGY: PAST AND PRESENT*

"Social Anthropology: Past and Present" in *Man*, Vol. 50, Sept. 1950, pp. 118–124. Reproduced with permission of Blackwell Publishing Ltd.

Mr. Rector, Fellows and Scholars, I have been greatly honoured by your invitation to deliver this lecture in commemoration of Rector Marett, a great teacher of social anthropology and my friend and counselor for over twenty years. I am touched also, Mr. Rector, at delivering it in this familiar hall.

I have chosen to discuss a few very broad questions of method. The considerable advances made in social anthropology during the last thirty years and the creation of new departments in several universities would seem to require some reflection on what the subject is, and which direction it is taking, or ought to take, for anthropology has now ceased to be an amateur pursuit and has become a profession. There is a division of opinion on these matters among anthropologists themselves, broadly between those who regard the subject as a natural science and those who, like myself, regard it as one of the humanities, and this division, which reflects quite different sentiments and values, is apparent whenever there arises a discussion about the methods and aims of the discipline. It is perhaps at its sharpest when the relations between anthropology and history are being discussed, and since consideration of this difficult question, brings out the issues most clearly, I shall devote a large part of my lecture to it. To perceive how these issues have come about it is necessary to cast our eyes back over the period of the genesis and early development of the subject.

Eighteenth-Century Origins

A subject of scholarship can hardly be said to have autonomy before it is taught in the universities. In that sense social anthropology is a very new subject. In another sense it may be said to have begun with the earliest speculations of mankind, for everywhere and at all times men have propounded theories about the nature of human society. In this sense there is no definite point at which social anthropology can be said to have begun. Nevertheless, there is a point beyond which it is hardly profitable to trace back its development. This nascent period of our subject was the middle and late eighteenth century. It is a child of the Enlightenment and bears throughout its history and today many of the characteristic features of its ancestry.

In France its lineage runs from Montesquieu and such writers as D'Alembert, Condorcet, Turgot, and in general the Encyclopediasts to Saint Simon, who was the first to propose clearly a science of society, and to his one-time disciple Comte, who named the science sociology. This stream of French philosophical rationalism was later, through the writings of Durkheim and his students and Lévy-Bruhl, who were in the direct line of Saint-Simonian tradition, to colour English anthropology strongly.

Our forebears were the Scottish moral philosophers, whose writings were typical of the eighteenth century: David Hume, Adam Smith, Thomas Reid, Frances Hutcheson, Dugald Stewart, Adam Ferguson, Lord Kames and Lord Monboddo. These writers took their inspiration from Bacon, Newton and Locke, though they were also much influenced by Descartes. They insisted that the study of societies, which they regarded as natural systems or organisms, must be empirical, and that by the use of the inductive method it would be possible to explain them in terms of general principles or laws in the same way as physical phenomena had been explained by the physicists. It must also be normative. Natural law is derived from a study of human nature, which is in all societies and at all times the same. These writers also believed in limitless progress and in laws of progress. Man, being everywhere alike, must advance along certain lines through set stages of development, and these stages can be hypothetically reconstructed by what Dugald Stewart called conjectural history, and what later became known as the comparative method. Here we have all the ingredients of anthropological theory in the nineteenth century and even at the present day.

The writers I have mentioned, both in France and England, were of course in the sense of their time philosophers and so regarded themselves. In spite of all their talk about empiricism they relied more on introspection and a priori reasoning than on observation of actual societies. For the most part they used facts to illustrate or corroborate theories reached by speculation. It was not till the middle of the nineteenth century that systematic studies of social institutions were conducted with some attempt at scientific rigour. In the decade between 1861 and 1871 there appeared books which we regard as our early classics: Maine's *Ancient Law* (1861), Bachofen's *Das Mutterrecht* (1861), Fustel de Coulanges' *La Cité antique* (1864), McLennan's *Primitive Marriage* (1865), Tylor's *Researches into the Early History of Mankind* (1865), and Morgan's *The Systems of Consanguinity* (1871). Not all these books were concerned primarily with primitive societies, though those that were least concerned with them, like *Ancient Law*, were dealing with comparable institutions at early periods in the development of historical societies. It was McLennan and Tylor in this country, and Morgan in America, who first treated primitive societies as a subject which might in itself engage the attention of serious scholars.

Nineteenth-Century Anthropology

The authors of this decade, like those of the generation before them, were anxious to rid the study of social institutions of mere speculation. They, also, thought that they could do this by being strictly empirical and by rigorous use of the comparative historical method. Using this method they, and those who followed them, wrote many large volumes purporting to show the origin and development of social institutions: the development of monogamous marriage from promiscuity, of property from communism, of contract from status, of industry from nomadism, of positive science from theology, of monotheism from animism. Sometimes, especially when treating religion, explanations were sought in terms of psychological origins as well as in terms of historical origins.

These Victorian anthropologists were men of outstanding ability, wide learning and obvious integrity. If they overemphasized resemblances in custom and belief and paid insufficient attention to diversities, they were investigating a real and not an imaginary problem when they attempted to account for remarkable similarities in societies widely separated in space and time; and much of permanent value has come out of their researches. Nevertheless, it is difficult to read their theoretical constructions today without irritation, and at times we feel embarrassed at what seems complacency. We see now that though their use of the comparative method allowed them to separate the general from the particular, and so to classify social phenomena, the explanations of these phenomena which they put forward amounted to little more than hypothetical scales of progress, at one end of which were placed forms of institutions or beliefs as they were in nineteenth-century Europe and America, while at the other end were placed their antitheses. An order of stages was then worked out to show what logically might have been the history of development from one end of the scale to the other. All that remained to be done was to hunt through ethnological literature for examples to illustrate each of these stages. It is evident that such reconstructions not only imply moral judgments but must always be conjectural; and that in any case an institution is not to be understood, far less explained, in terms of its origins, whether these are conceived of as beginnings, causes or merely, in a logical sense, its simplest forms. For all their insistence on empiricism in the study of social institutions the nineteenth-century anthropologists were hardly less dialectical, speculative and dogmatic than the moral philosophers of the preceding century, though they at least felt that they had to support their constructions with a wealth of factual evidence, a need scarcely felt by the moral philosophers, so that a very great amount of original literary research was undertaken and vast repositories of ethnological detail were stocked and systematically arranged, as, to mention the largest of these storehouses, in *The Golden Bough.*

It is not surprising that the anthropologists of the last century wrote what they regarded as history, for all contemporaneous learning was radically historical, and at a time when history in England was still a literary art. The genetic approach which had borne impressive fruits in philology, was, as Lord Acton has emphasized, apparent in law, economics, science, theology and philosophy. There was everywhere a passionate endeavour to discover the origins of everything—the origin of species, the origin of religion, the origin of law and so on—an endeavour always to explain the nearer by the farther which, in reference to history proper, Marc Bloch calls 'la hantise des origines.'

In any case, I do not think that the real cause of confusion was, as is generally supposed, that the nineteenth-century anthropologists believed in progress and sought a method by which they might reconstruct how it had come about, for they were well aware that their schemata were hypotheses which could not be finally or fully verified. The cause of confusion in most of their writings is rather to be looked for in the assumption they had inherited from the Enlightenment that societies are natural systems or organisms which have a necessary course of development that can be reduced to general principles or laws. Logical consistencies were in consequence presented as real and necessary connexions and typological classifications as both historical and inevitable courses of development. It will readily be seen how a combination of the notion of scientific law and that of progress leads in anthropology, as in the philosophy of history, to procrustean stages, the presumed inevitability of which gives them a normative character.

The Twentieth Century

The reaction against the attempt to explain social institutions in terms of parallel, seen ideally as unilinear, development came at the end of the century; and though this so-called evolutionary anthropology was recast and re-presented in the writings of Westermarck and Hobhouse it had finally lost its appeal. It had in any case ceased to stimulate research, because once the stages of human development had been marked out further investigation on these lines offered nothing more exciting than attachment of labels written by dead hands. Some anthropologists, and in varying degrees, now turned for inspiration to psychology, which at the time seemed to provide satisfactory solutions of many of their problems without recourse to hypothetical history. This has proved to be, then and since, an attempt to build a house on shifting sands. If I say no more in this lecture about the relation between psychology and anthropology it is not because I do not consider it important, but because it would require more time than I can spare, and also more knowledge of psychology than I possess, to treat adequately.

Apart from the criticism of evolutionary theory implied in the ignoring of it by those, including Rector Marett, who sought psychological explanations of customs and beliefs, it was attacked from two directions, the diffusionist and the functionalist. Diffusionist criticism was based on the very obvious fact that culture is often borrowed and does not emerge by spontaneous growth due to certain common social potentialities and common human nature. To suppose otherwise and to discuss social change without reference to events is to lapse into Cartesian scholasticism. This approach had, unfortunately, little lasting influence in England, partly, no doubt, on account of its uncritical use by Elliot Smith, Perry and Rivers. The other form of attack, the functionalist, has been far more influential, as it has been far more radical. It condemned equally evolutionary anthropology and diffusionist anthropology, not merely on the grounds that their historical reconstructions were unverifiable, but also, and simply, because both were historical approaches, for in the view of writers of this persuasion the history of a society is irrelevant to a study of it as a natural system.

The same kind of development was taking place at the same time in other fields of learning. There were functional biology, functional psychology, functional law, functional economics and so forth. The point of view was the more readily accepted by many social anthropologists because anthropologists generally study societies the history of which cannot be known. Their ready acceptance was also partly due to the influence from across the Channel of the philosophical rationalism of Durkheim and his school. This influence has had, on the whole, not only a profound but a beneficial effect on English anthropology. It injected a tradition which was concerned with broad general questions into the more piecemeal empirical English tradition, exemplified by the way in which theoretical writers like Tylor and Frazer used their material and by both the many firsthand accounts of primitive peoples written by travelers, missionaries and administrators and the early social surveys in this country. On the other hand, if students are not firmly anchored by a heavy weight of ethnographic fact, they are easily led by it into airy discussions about words, into arid classifications, and into either pretentiousness or total scepticism.

The Functional Theory

The functional or organismic theory of society which reigns in social anthropology in England today is not new. We have seen that it was held in their several ways by the early and mid-Victorian anthropologists and by the moral philosophers before them, and it has, of course, a very much longer pedigree in political philosophy. In its modern and more mechanistic form it was set forth at great length by Durkheim and, with special reference to social evolution, by Herbert Spencer. In yet more recent times it has been most clearly and consistently stated by Professor Radcliffe-Brown. Human societies are natural systems in which all the parts are interdependent, each serving in a complex of necessary relations to maintain the whole. The aim of social anthropology is to reduce all social life to laws or general statements about the nature of society which allow prediction. What is new in this restatement of the theory is the insistence that a society can be understood satisfactorily without reference to its past. Almost without exception the eighteenth-century moral philosophers presented their conception of social systems and sociological laws in the form of history in the grand style—a natural history of human societies; and, as we have seen, the enduring passion of their Victorian successors was seeking for origins from which every institution has developed through the working of laws of progress. The modern version of a naturalistic study of society, even if lip-service is sometimes paid to the possibility of a scientific study of social change, claims that for an understanding of the functioning of a society there is no need for the student of it to know anything about its history, any more than there is need for a physiologist to know the history of an organism to understand it. Both are natural systems and can be described in terms of natural law without recourse to history.

The functional orientation, by its insistence on the interrelatedness of things, has been largely responsible for the comprehensive and detailed professional field studies of modern anthropology, such as were entirely unknown to the anthropologists of the nineteenth century, who were content to let laymen collect the facts on which they based their theories. It is also largely due to it that the anthropologist of today sees more clearly than his predecessors that an understanding of human behaviour can only be reached by viewing it in its full social setting. All social anthropologists now accept that the entire activities of primitive societies must be systematically studied in the field, and all have the same holistic approach when they come to set down and interpret their observations.

But a theory may have heuristic value without being sound, and there are many objections to the functional theory. It is no more than an assumption that human societies are systems of the kind they are alleged to be. Indeed in the case of Malinowski the functional theory, in spite of the wide claims he made for it, was little more than a literary device. The theory assumes, moreover, that in the given circumstances no part of social life can be other than what it is and that every custom has social value, thus adding to a naive determinism a crude teleology and pragmatism. It is easy to define the aim of social anthropology to be the establishment of sociological laws, but nothing even remotely resembling a law of the natural sciences has yet been adduced. What general statements have been made are for the most part speculative, and are in any case too general to be of value. Often they are little more than guesses on a common-sense or *post factum* level, and they sometimes degenerate into mere tautologies or even platitudes. Also, it is difficult to reconcile the assertion that a society has come to be what it is by a succession of unique events with the claim that what it is can be comprehensively stated in terms of natural law. In its extreme form functional determinism leads to absolute relativism and makes nonsense not only of the theory itself but of all thought.

If for these and other reasons I cannot accept, without many qualifications, the functional theory dominant in English anthropology today, I do not assert, as you will see, that societies are unintelligible or that they are not in some sense systems. What I am objecting to is what appears to me to be still the same doctrinaire philosophy of the Enlightenment and of the stage-making anthropologists of the nineteenth century, with only the concept of evolution substituted for that of progress. Its constructions are still posited dialectically and imposed on the facts. I attribute this to anthropologists always having tried to model themselves on the natural sciences instead of on the historical sciences, and it is to this important issue that I now turn. I must apologize to historians if, in considering it, what I say may seem obvious to them. My observations would be hotly disputed by most of my anthropological colleagues in England.

Anthropology and History

In discussing the relations between history and social anthropology it is necessary, if the discussion is to be profitable, to perceive that several quite different questions are being asked. The first is whether a knowledge of how a particular social system has come to be what it is helps one to understand its present constitution. We must here distinguish between history in two different senses, though in literate society it is not so easy to maintain the distinction as when speaking of non-literate societies. In the first sense history is part of the conscious tradition of a people and is operative in their social life. It is the collective representation of events as distinct from events themselves. This is what the social anthropologist calls myth. The functionalist anthropologists regard history in this sense, usually a mixture of fact and fancy, as highly relevant to a study of the culture of which it forms part.

On the other hand they have totally rejected the reconstruction from circumstantial evidences of the history of primitive peoples for whose past documents and monuments are totally, or almost totally, lacking. A case can be made out for this rejection, though not in my opinion so strong a case as is usually supposed, for all history is of necessity a reconstruction, the degree of probability attending a particular reconstruction depending on the evidence available. The fact that nineteenth-century anthropologists were uncritical in their reconstructions ought not to lead to the conclusion that all effort expended in this direction is a waste of time.

But with the bath water of presumptive history the functionalists have also thrown out the baby of valid history. They say, Malinowski the most vociferously, that even when the history of a society is recorded it is irrelevant to a functional study of it. I find this point of view unacceptable. The claim that one can understand the functioning of institutions at a certain point of time without knowing how they have come to be what they are, or what they were later to become, as well as a person who, in addition to having studied their constitution at that point of time, has also studied their past and future is to me an absurdity. Moreover, so it seems to me, neglect of the history of institutions prevents the functionalist anthropologist not only from studying diachronic problems but also from testing the very functional constructions to which he attaches most importance, for it is precisely history which provides him with an experimental situation.

The problem here raised is becoming a pressing one because anthropologists are now studying communities which, if still fairly simple in structure, are enclosed in, and form part of, great historical societies, such as Irish and Indian rural communities, Bedouin Arab tribes, or ethnic minorities in America and other parts of the world. They can no longer ignore history, making a virtue out of necessity, but must explicitly reject it or admit its relevance. As anthropologists turn their attention more to complex civilized communities the issue will become more acute, and the direction of theoretical development in the subject will largely depend on its outcome.

A second question is of a different kind. We ask now, not whether in studying a particular society its history forms an integral part of the study, but whether in making comparative sociological studies, for example of political or religious institutions, we ought to include in them societies as resented to us by historians. In spite of their claim that social anthropology aims at being; a natural history of human societies, that is, of all human societies, functionalist anthropologists, at any rate in England, have, in their "general distaste for historical method, almost completely ignored historical writings. They have thereby denied themselves access in their comparative studies to the valuable material provided by historical societies structurally comparable to many of the contemporaneous barbarous societies which they regard as being within their province.

A third, and to me the most important, question is a methodological one: whether social anthropology, for all its present disregard of history, is not itself a kind of historiography. To answer this question we have first to observe what the anthropologist does. He goes to live for some months or years among a primitive people. He lives among them as intimately as he can, and he learns to speak their language, to think in their concepts and to feel in their values. He then lives the experiences over again critically and interpretatively in the conceptual categories and values of his own culture and in terms of the general body of knowledge of his discipline. In other words, he translates from one culture into another.

At this level social anthropology remains a literary and impressionistic art. But even in a single ethnographic study the anthropologist seeks to do more than understand the thought and values of a primitive people and translate them into his own culture. He seeks also to discover the structural order of the society, the patterns which, once established, enable him to see it as a whole, as a set of interrelated abstractions. Then the society is not only culturally intelligible, as it is, at the level of consciousness and action, for one of its members or for the foreigner who has learnt its mores and participates in its life, but also becomes sociologically intelligible.

The historian, or at any rate the social historian, and perhaps the economic historian in particular, will, I think, know what I mean by sociologically intelligible. After all, English society in the eleventh century was understood by Vinogradoff in quite a different way from the way it would have been understood by a Norman or Anglo-Saxon or by a foreigner who had learnt the native languages and was living the life of the natives. Similarly, the social anthropologist discovers in a native society what no native can explain to him and what no layman, however conversant with the culture, can perceive—its basic structure. This structure cannot be seen. It is a set of abstractions, each of which, though derived, it is true, from analysis of observed behaviour, is fundamentally an imaginative construct of the anthropologist himself. By relating these abstractions to one another logically so that they present a pattern he can see the society in its essentials and as a single whole.

What I am trying to say can perhaps be best illustrated by the example of language. A native understands his own language and it can be learnt by a stranger. But certainly neither the native himself nor the stranger can tell you what are its phonological and grammatical systems. These can only be discovered by a trained linguist. By analysis he can reduce the complexity of a language to certain abstractions and show how these abstractions can be interrelated in a logical system or pattern. This is what the social anthropologist also tries to do. He tries to disclose the structural patterns of a society. Having isolated these patterns in one society he compares them with patterns in other societies. The study of each new society enlarges his knowledge of the range of basic social structures and enables him better to construct a typology of forms, and to determine their essential features and the reasons for their variations.

I have tried to show that the work of the social anthropologist is in three main phases or, otherwise expressed, at three levels of abstraction. First he seeks to understand the significant overt features of a culture and to translate them into terms of his own culture. This is precisely what the historian does. There is no fundamental difference here in aim or method between the two disciplines, and both are equally selective in their use of material. The similarity between them has been obscured by the fact that the social anthropologist makes a direct study of social life while the historian makes an indirect study of it through documents and other surviving evidences. This is a technical, not a methodological, difference. The historicity of an-

thropology has also been obscured by its pre-occupation with primitive societies which lack recorded history. But this again is not a methodological
difference. I agree with Professor Kroeber that the fundamental characteristic of the historical method is not a chronological relation of events but descriptive integration of them; and this characteristic historiography shares
with social anthropology. What social anthropologists have in fact chiefly
been doing is to write cross-sections of history, integrative descriptive accounts of primitive peoples at a moment of time which are in other respects
like the accounts written by historians about peoples over a period of time,
for the historian does not just record sequences of events but seeks to establish connexions between them. Nor does the anthropologist's determination to view every institution as a functioning part of a whole society
make a methodological difference. Any good modern historian aims—if I
may be allowed to judge the matter—at the same kind of synthesis.

In my view, therefore, the fact that the anthropologist's problems are
generally synchronic while the historian's problems are generally diachronic is a difference of emphasis in the rather peculiar conditions prevailing and not a real divergence of interest. When the historian fixes his
attention exclusively on a particular culture at a particular and limited period of history he writes what we would call an ethnographic monograph
(Burckhardt's *Culture of the Renaissance* is a striking example). When, on
the other hand, a social anthropologist writes about a society developing
in time he writes a history book, different, it is true, from the ordinary narrative and political history but in all essentials the same as social history.
In the absence of another, I must cite my own book *The Sanusi of Cyrenaica*
as an example.

In the second phase of his work the social anthropologist goes a step farther and seeks by analysis to disclose the latent underlying form of a society or culture. In doing so, he goes farther than the more timorous and conservative historians, but many historians do the same. I am not thinking of
philosophers of history like Vico, Hegel, Marx, Spengler and Toynbee, not
of those who can be exclusively particularized as social historians or writers
of the *Kulturgeschichte* school like Max Weber, Tawney, and Sombart or
Adam Smith, Savigny and Buckle but of historians in the stricter and more
orthodox sense like Fustel de Coulanges, Vinogradoff, Pirenne, Maitland, or
Professor Powicke. It is perhaps worth noting that those historical writings
which we anthropologists regard as examples of sociological method generally deal with early periods of history, where the societies described are
more like primitive societies than the societies of later periods of history,
and where the historical documents are not too vast to be grasped and assimilated by a single mind; so that the total culture can be studied as a
whole and contained in a single mind, as primitive cultures can be studied
and contained. When we read the works of these historians we feel that we

and they are studying the same things in the same way and are reaching out for the same kind of understanding of them.

In the third phase of his work the anthropologist compares the social structures his analysis has revealed in a wide range of societies. When a historian attempts a similar study in his own field he is dubbed a philosopher, but it is not, I think, true to say, as it is often said, that history is a study of the particular and social anthropology of the general. In some historical writers comparison and classification are quite explicit; always they are implicit, for history cannot be written except against a standard of some kind, by comparison with the culture of a different time or people, if only with the writer's own.

I conclude therefore, following Professor Kroeber, that while there are, of course, many differences between social anthropology and historiography they are differences of technique, of emphasis and of perspective, and not differences of method and aim. I believe also that a clearer understanding that this is so will lead to a closer connexion between historical and anthropological studies than is at present provided by their meeting points in ethnology and prehistoric archaeology, and that this will be greatly to the benefit of both disciplines. Historians can supply social anthropologists with invaluable material, sifted and vouched for by critical techniques of testing and interpretation. Social anthropologists can provide the historian of the future with some of his best records, based on careful and detailed observations, and they can shed on history, by their discovery of latent structural forms, the light of universals. The value of each discipline to the other will, I believe, be recognized when anthropologists begin to devote themselves more to historical scholarship and show how knowledge of anthropology often illuminates historical problems.

Social Anthropology as One of the Humanities

The thesis I have put before you, that social anthropology is a kind of historiography, and therefore ultimately of philosophy or art, implies that it studies societies as moral systems and not as natural systems, that it is interested in design rather than in process, and that it therefore seeks patterns and not scientific laws and interprets rather than explains. These are conceptual, and not merely verbal, differences. The concepts of natural system and natural law, modeled on the constructs of the natural sciences, have dominated anthropology from its beginnings, and as we look back over the course of its growth I think we can see that they have been responsible for a false scholasticism which has led to one rigid and ambitious formulation after another. Regarded as a special kind of historiography, that is as one of the humanities, social anthropology is released from these essentially philosophical dogmas and given the opportunity, though it may seem paradoxical to say so, to be really empirical and, in the true sense of the word, scientific. This, I presume, is what Maitland had in mind when he said that 'by and by anthropology will have the choice between becoming history or nothing.'

I have found, both in England and America, that students are often perturbed at these implications. There is no need for them to be, for it does not follow from regarding social anthropology as a special kind of historiography rather than as a special kind of natural science that its researches and theory are any the less systematic. When therefore I am asked how I think that social anthropology should proceed in the future I reply that it must proceed along much the same lines as do social history or the history of institutions, as distinct from purely narrative and political history. For example, the social historian seeking to understand feudal institutions would first study them in one country of Europe and get to know all he can about them there. He would then study them in other European societies to discover which features were common to European civilization at that time and which were local variations, and he would try to see each particular form as a variation of a general pattern and to account for the variations. He would not seek for laws but for significant patterns.

What more do we do, can we do or should we want to do in social anthropology than this? We study witchcraft or a kinship system in a particular primitive society. If we want to know more about these social phenomena we can study them in a second society, and then in a third society, and so on, each study reaching, as our knowledge increases and new problems emerge, a deeper level of investigation and teaching us the essential characteristics of the thing we are inquiring into, so that particular studies are given a new meaning and perspective. This will always happen if one necessary condition is observed: that the conclusions of each study are clearly formulated in such a way that they not only test the conclusions reached by earlier studies but advance new hypotheses which can be broken down into fieldwork problems.

However, the uneasiness I have noted is not, I think, on this score, because it must be evident to any student who has given thought to the matter that those who have most strongly urged that social anthropology should model itself on the natural sciences have done neither better research than those who take the opposite view nor a different kind of research. It is rather due to the feeling that any discipline that does not aim at formulating laws and hence predicting and planning is not worth the labour of a lifetime. This normative element in anthropology is, as we have seen, like the concepts of natural law and progress from which it derives, part of its philosophical heritage. In recent times the natural-science approach has constantly stressed the application of its findings to affairs, the emphasis in England being on colonial problems and in America on political and industrial problems. Its more cautious advocates have held that there can only be applied anthropology when the science is much more advanced than it is today, but the less cautious have made far-reaching claims for the immediate application of anthropological knowledge in social planning; though, whether more or less cautious, both have justified anthropology by appeal to utility. Needless to say, I do not share their enthusiasm and regard the attitude that gives rise to it as naive. A full discussion of it would take too long, but I cannot resist the observation that, as the history of anthropology shows, positivism leads very easily to a misguided ethics, anemic scientific humanism or—Saint Simon and Comte are cases in point—*ersatz* religion.

I conclude by summarizing very briefly the argument I have tried to develop in this lecture and by stating what I believe is likely to be the direction taken by social anthropology in the future. Social anthropologists, dominated consciously or unconsciously, from the beginnings of their subject, by positivist philosophy, have aimed, explicitly or implicitly, and for the most part still aim—for this is what it comes to—at proving that man is an automaton and at discovering the sociological laws in terms of which his actions, ideas and beliefs can be explained and in the light of which they can be planned and controlled. This approach implies that human societies are natural systems which can be reduced to variables. Anthropologists have therefore taken one or other of the natural sciences as their model and have turned their backs on history, which sees men in a different way and eschews, in the light of experience, rigid formulations of any kind.

There is, however, an older tradition than that of the Enlightenment with a different approach to the study of human societies, in which they are seen as systems only because social life must have a pattern of some kind, inasmuch as man, being a reasonable creature, has to live in a world in which his relations with those around him are ordered and intelligible. Naturally I think that those who see things in this way have a clearer understanding of social reality than the others, but whether this is so or not they are increasing in number, and this is likely to continue because the vast majority of students of anthropology today have been trained in one or other of the humanities and not, as was the case thirty years ago, in one or other of the natural sciences. This being so, I expect that in the future there will be a turning towards humanistic disciplines, especially towards history, and particularly towards social history or the history of institutions, of cultures and of ideas. In this change of orientation social anthropology will retain its individuality because it has its own special problems, techniques and traditions. Though it is likely to continue for some time to devote its attention chiefly to primitive societies, I believe that during this second half of the century it will give far more attention than in the past to more complex cultures and especially to the civilizations of the Far and Near East and become, in a very general sense, the counterpart to Oriental Studies, in so far as these are conceived of as primarily linguistic and literary—that is to say, it will take as its province the cultures and societies, past as well as present, of the non-European peoples of the world.

QUERIES

- Evans-Pritchard argues that the functional approach in social anthropology is flawed; what are his reasons for this conclusion?
- Evans-Pritchard offers an alternative vision of social anthropology, distinct from a model based on the natural sciences. What is Evans-Pritchard's alternative?
- Evans-Pritchard argues that the historian and the social anthropologist engage in parallel practices; what are they?
- At the close of the article, Evans-Pritchard concludes that social anthropology is not one of the sciences: what is it instead?

CONNECTIONS

- Contrast Evans-Pritchard's vision of social anthropology with Radcliffe-Brown's concept of social anthropology.
- Evans-Pritchard's historical overview of the development of anthropological theory is similar to Marshall Sahlins's discussion in "What is Anthropological Enlightenment?" and yet those two historical summaries are used to make different theoretical points. What is the point of Evans-Pritchard's summary and how does it differ from Sahlins's?
- Evans-Pritchard argues that Malinowski's functionalism was "little more than a literary device" resulting in little more than broad speculations rather than scientific laws. How would this criticism apply, for example, to Malinowski's discussion of the function of magic (Moore 2008:142–44)?
- Evans-Pritchard argues that a cause of confusion in social anthropology is the idea "that societies are natural systems or organisms which have a necessary course of development that can be reduced to general principles or laws." How is this assumption present in the writings of Morgan, White, and Radcliffe-Brown?
- What does Evans-Pritchard mean when he states that the anthropologist's goal is to render another culture "sociologically intelligible"? How does this position compare with Clifford Geertz's interpretive approach to ethnographic explanation (Moore 2008:263–66)?

IV

EVOLUTIONARY, ADAPTIONIST, AND MATERIALIST THEORIES

13

Leslie A. White

INTRODUCTION

The evolutionary theory proposed by American anthropologist Leslie A. White (1900–1975) offers a materialist explanation of cultural evolution, but—unlike Marvin Harris's cultural materialism—a materialism that never mentions the dialectical materialism of Karl Marx. This is intriguing, especially since White held socialist political views and allegedly wrote a column for the weekly paper of the Socialist Labor Party during the Depression and afterwards (for an overview of White's career, see Moore 2008:179–81). But beyond matters of political position, White's theory of cultural evolution was based on a very 20th-century American notion: technology is the solution to human problems.

Actually, White's model is more sophisticated than this. First, White argues that culture is transmitted based on symbols. Like most anthropologists from Tylor on, White disavows any genetic or hereditary basis to culture: culture is learned and transmitted via symbols, not DNA. Second, culture is the principal means by which humans adapt to the cosmos. Culture is the way humans solve the problems of existence. These problems of existence fall into three sets: the problems of adapting to the physical environment, problems that derive from the challenges of human social life, and problems concerning our efforts to understand the nature of the cosmos and the meanings of existence. Third (and not surprisingly), our cultural responses fall into three corresponding realms: the technological realm, the sociological realm, and the ideological realm (see Moore 2008:182–84). So far, so good.

But why, White asks, do cultures differ in such fundamental ways? Why do some cultures live in small, highly mobile bands while others live in permanent metropolitan cities? Why are some cultures relatively egalitarian while others are stratified into classes and/or castes? Why do some cultures believe in animism while other societies practice monotheism? Why do cultures evolve in different ways?

The answer, White contends, is energy. Through natural selection, the development of new lifeforms has relied on organisms' evolved abilities to acquire more energy and/or to use it more efficiently: an elephant eats more than an amoeba and is correspondingly a more complex organism. Similarly, different forms of human social life rely on the acquisition or efficient use of new quantities of energy,

In the following article, White summarizes this idea with a formula in which the amount of energy expended annually per capita (E) and the efficiency with which energy is used (F) determines the product (P) of goods and services created and considered as an indirect index of levels of cultural development. (In a later publication, White recast this formula to show that the level of per capita energy (E) and the technological efficiency (T) of its use determines cultural development: (C) or E X T =>C; see Moore 2008:186.)

After summarizing this central formula, White presents a broad-brush historical overview of human cultural evolution, first discussing changes in the technological realm, and then outlining ways social patterns reflect and are correlated with specific technological patterns. While changes in the technological system often shape the social system, it is possible for the social system to put a brake on technological advances and cultural evolution stagnates. Yet in either case the level of cultural development is directly explicable by the acquisition of energy and the efficiency of its use, a theory of cultural evolution that White connects to the evolutionary ideas of Tylor and Morgan—and not to Marx.

PRIMARY TEXT: *ENERGY AND THE EVOLUTION OF CULTURE*

Reproduced by permission of the American Anthropological Association from *American Anthropologist*, Vol. 45 (3), Part 1, 1943, pp. 335–356. www.aaanet.org. Not for sale or further reproduction.

Everything in the universe may be described in terms of energy. Galaxies, stars, molecules, and atoms may be regarded as organizations of energy.[1] Living organisms may be looked upon as engines which operate by means of energy derived directly or indirectly from the sun. The civilizations, or cultures of mankind, also, may be regarded as a form or organization of energy. Culture is an organization of phenomena—material objects, bodily

---

[1] By "energy" we mean "the capacity for performing work."

acts, ideas, and sentiments—which consists of or is dependent upon the use of symbols. Man, being the only animal capable of symbol-behavior, is the only creature to possess culture.[2] Culture is a kind of behavior. And behavior, whether of man, mule, plant, comet or molecule, may be treated as a manifestation of energy. Thus we see, on all levels of reality[3] that phenomena lend themselves to description and interpretation in terms of energy. Cultural anthropology is that branch of natural science[4] which deals with matter-and-motion, i.e., energy, phenomena in cultural form, as biology deals with them in cellular, and physics in atomic, form.

The purpose of culture is to serve the needs of man. These needs are of two kinds: (1) those which can be served or satisfied by drawing upon resources within the human organism alone. Singing, dancing, myth-making, forming clubs or associations for the sake of companionship, etc., illustrate this kind of need and ways of satisfying them. (2) The second class of needs can be satisfied only by drawing upon the resources of the external world, outside the human organism. Man must get his food from the external world. The tools, weapons, and other materials with which man provides himself with food, shelter from the elements, protection from his enemies, must likewise come from the external world. The satisfaction of spiritual and esthetic needs through singing, dancing, myth-making, etc., is possible, however, only if man's bodily needs for food, shelter, and defense are met. Thus the whole cultural structure depends upon the material, mechanical means with which man articulates himself with the earth. Furthermore, the satisfaction of human needs from "inner resources" may be regarded as a constant[5] the satisfaction of needs from the outer resources a variable. Therefore, in our discussion of cultural development we may omit consideration of the constant factor and deal only with the variable—the material, mechanical means with which man exploits the resources of nature.

The articulation-of-man-with-the-earth process may be analyzed and resolved into the following five factors: (1) the human organism, (2) the habitat, (3) the amount of energy controlled and expended by man, (4) the ways and means in which energy is expended, and (5) the human-need-serving product which accrues from the expenditure of energy. This is but another

---

[2] Cf. Leslie A. White, The Symbol: The Origin and Basis of Human Behavior (Philosophy of Science, Vol. 7, October 1940), pp. 451–63.

[3] See Leslie A. White. Science Is Sciencing (Philosophy of Science, Vol. 5, October, 1938), pp. 369–89, for a discussion of this general point of view.

[4] "Natural science" is a redundancy. All science is natural; if it is not natural it is not science.

[5] Actually, of course, it is not wholly constant; there may be progress in music, myth-making, etc., regardless of technology. A men's club, however, is still a men's club, whether the underlying technology be simple and crude or highly developed. But, since the overwhelming portion of cultural development is due to technological progress, we may legitimately ignore that small portion which is not so dependent by regarding it a constant.

way of saying that human beings, like all other living creatures, exploit the resources of their habitat, in one way or another in order to sustain life and to perpetuate their kind. Of the above factors, we may regard the organic factor as a constant. Although peoples obviously differ from each other physically, we are not able to attribute differences in culture to differences in physique (or "mentality"). In our study of culture, therefore, we may regard the human race as of uniform quality, i.e., as a constant, and, hence, we may eliminate it from our study.

No two habitats are alike; every habitat varies in time. Yet, in a study of culture as a whole,[6] we may regard the factor of habitat as a constant: we simply reduce the need-serving, welfare-promoting resources of all particular habitats to an average. (In a consideration of particular manifestations of culture we would of course have to deal with their respective particular habitats.) Since we may regard habitat as a constant, we exclude it, along with the human organism, from our study of the development of culture.

This leaves us, then, three factors to be considered in any cultural situation: (1) the amount of energy per capita per unit of time harnessed and put to work within the culture, (2) the technological means with which this energy is expended, and (3) the human need-serving product that accrues from the expenditure of energy. We may express the relationship between these factors in the following simple formula: $E \times T = P$, in which E represents the amount of energy expended per capita per unit of time, T the technological means of its expenditure, and P the magnitude of the product per unit of time. This may be illustrated concretely with the following simple example: A man cuts wood with an axe. Assuming the quality of the wood and the skill of the workman to be constant, the amount of wood cut in a given period of time, an hour say, depends, on the one hand upon the amount of energy the man expends during this time: the more energy expended, the more wood cut. On the other hand, the amount of wood cut in an hour depends upon the kind of axe used. Other things being equal, the amount of wood cut varies with the quality of the axe: the better the axe the more wood cut. Our workman can cut more wood with an iron, or steel, axe than with a stone axe.

The efficiency with which human energy is expended mechanically depends upon the bodily skills of the persons involved, and upon the nature of the tools employed. In the following discussion we shall deal with skill in terms of averages. It is obvious, of course, that, other things being equal, the product of the expenditure of human energy varies directly as the skill employed in the expenditure of this energy. But we may reduce all particular skills, in any given situation, to an average, which, being constant may be

---

[6] "There is only one cultural reality that is not artificial, to wit: the culture of all humanity at all periods and in all places," R. H. Lowie, Cultural Anthropology: A Science (American Journal of Sociology, Vol. 42, 1936), p. 305.

eliminated from our consideration of culture growth. Hereafter, then, when we concern ourselves with the efficiency with which human energy is expended mechanically, we shall be dealing with the efficiency of tools only.

With reference to tools, man can increase the efficiency of the expenditure of his bodily energy in two ways: by improving a tool, or by substituting a better tool for an inferior one. But with regard to any given kind of tool, it must be noted that there is a point beyond which it cannot be improved. The efficiency of various tools of a certain kind varies; some bows are better than others. A bow, or any other implement, may vary in efficiency between 0 per cent and 100 per cent. But there is a maximum, theoretically as well as actually, which cannot be exceeded. Thus, the efficiency of a canoe paddle can be raised or lowered by altering its length, breadth, thickness, shape, etc. Certain proportions or dimensions would render it useless, in which case its efficiency would be 0 per cent. But, in the direction of improvement, a point is reached, ideally as well as practically, when no further progress can be made—any further change would be a detriment. Its efficiency is now at its maximum (100 per cent). So it is with a canoe, arrow, axe, dynamo, locomotive, or any other tool or machine.

We are now ready for some generalizations about cultural development. Let us return to our formula, but this time let us write it E X F = P, in which E and P have the same values as before—E, the amount of energy expended; P the product produced—while F stands for the efficiency of the mechanical means with which the energy is expended. Since culture is a mechanism for serving human needs, cultural development may be measured by the extent to which, and the efficiency with which, need-serving goods or services are provided. P, in our formula, may thus stand for the total amount of goods or services produced in any given cultural situation. Hence P represents the status of culture, or, more accurately, the degree of cultural development. If, then, F, the efficiency with which human energy is expended, remains constant, then P, the degree of cultural development, will vary as E, the amount of energy expended per capita per year[7] varies:

$$\frac{E_1 \times F}{E_2 \times F} = \frac{P_1}{P_2}$$

Thus we obtain the first important law of cultural development: Other things being equal, the degree of cultural development varies directly as the amount of energy per capita per year harnessed and put to work.

---

[7] We say "per year" although "per unit of time" would serve as well, because in concrete cultural situations a year would embrace the full round of the seasons and the occupations and actions appropriate thereto.

Secondly, if the amount of energy expended per capita per unit of time remains constant, then P varies as F:

$$\frac{E \times F_1}{E \times F_2} = \frac{P_1}{P_2}$$

and we get the second law of cultural development: Other things being equal, the degree of cultural development varies directly as the efficiency of the technological means with which the harnessed energy is put to work.

It is obvious, of course, that E and F may vary simultaneously, and in the same or in opposite directions. If E and F increase simultaneously P will increase faster, naturally, than if only one increased while the other remained unchanged. If E and F decrease simultaneously P will decrease more rapidly than if only one decreased while the other remained constant. If E increases while F decreases, or vice versa, then P will vary or remain unchanged, depending upon the magnitude of the changes of these two factors and upon the proportion of one magnitude to the other. If an increase in E is balanced by a decrease in F, or vice versa, then P will remain unchanged. But should E increase faster than F decreases, or vice versa, then P would increase; if E decreases faster than F increases, or vice versa, then P would decrease.

We have, in the above generalizations the law of cultural evolution: culture develops when the amount of energy harnessed by man per capita per year is increased; or as the efficiency of the technological means of putting this energy to work is increased; or, as both factors are simultaneously increased.

All living beings struggle to live, to perpetuate their respective kinds. In the human species the struggle for survival assumes the cultural form. The human struggle for existence expresses itself in a never-ending attempt to make of culture a more effective instrument with which to provide security of life and survival of the species. And one of the ways of making culture a more powerful instrument is to harness and to put to work within it more energy per capita per year. Thus, wind, and water, and fire are harnessed; animals are domesticated, plants cultivated; steam engines are built. The other way of improving culture as an instrument of adjustment and control is to invent new and better tools and to improve old ones. Thus energy for culture-living and culture-building is augmented in quantity, is expended more efficiently, and culture advances.

Thus we know, not only how culture evolves, but why, as well. The urge, inherent in all living species, to live, to make life more secure, more rich, more full, to insure the perpetuation of the species, seizes upon, when it does not produce a better[8] (i.e., more effective) means of living and surviving. In the case of man, the biological urge to live, the power to invent and to discover, the ability to select and use the better of two tools or ways of doing something—these are the factors of cultural evolution. Darwin could tell us the consequences of variations, but he could not tell us how these variations were produced. We know the motive force as well as the means of cultural evolution. The culturologist knows more about cultural evolution than the biologist, even today, knows about biological evolution.[9]

A word about man's motives with regard to cultural development. We do not say that man deliberately set about to improve his culture. It may well have been, as Morgan[10] suggested, decades before Lowie[11] emphasized the same point, that animals were first domesticated through whim or caprice rather than for practical, utilitarian reasons. Perhaps agriculture came about through accident. Hero's steam engine was a plaything. Gunpowder was first used to make pretty fireworks. The compass began as a toy. More than this, we know that peoples often resolutely oppose technological advances with a passionate devotion to the past and to the gods of their fathers. But all of this does not alter the fact that domesticated animals and cultivated plants have been used to make life more secure. Whatever may have been the intentions and motives (if any) of the inventors or discoverers of the bow and arrow, the wheel, the furnace and forge, the steam engine, the microscope, etc., the fact remains that these things have been seized upon by mankind and employed to make life more secure, comfortable, pleasant, and permanent. So we may disregard the psychological circumstances under which new cultural devices were brought into being. What is significant to the cultural evolutionist is that inventions and discoveries have been made, new tools invented, better ways of doings things found, and that these improved tools and techniques are kept and used until they are in turn replaced.

---

[8] The cultural evolutionists have been criticized for identifying progress with evolution by pointing out that these two words are not synonymous. It is as true as it is obvious that they are not synonymous—in the dictionary. But by and large, in the history of human culture, progress and evolution have gone hand in hand.

[9] See Tylor, Primitive Culture, Vol. 1, p. 14 (London, 1929 printing) for another respect in which, in theory of evolution, "the student of the habits of mankind has a great advantage over the student of the species of plants and animals."

[10] "Commencing probably with the dog . . . followed . . . by the capture of the young of other animals and rearing them, not unlikely, from the merest freak offancy, it required time and experience to discover the utility of each . . . " (emphasis ours). Morgan, Ancient Society, p. 42 (Holt, ed.).

[11] Introduction to Cultural Anthropology (New York, 1940 ed.), pp. 51–52. In this argument Lowie leans heavily upon Eduard Hahn, whose work, incidentally, appeared many years after Ancient Society ("Subsistence," p. 303, in General Anthropology, F. Boas, ed., New York, 1938; History of Ethnological Theory, p. 112 ff., New York, 1937).

So much for the laws, or generalizations derived from our basic formula. Let us turn now to concrete facts and see how the history of culture is illuminated and made intelligible by these laws.

In the beginning of culture history, man had only the energy of his own body under his control and at his disposal for culture-living and culture-building. And for a very long period of time this was almost the only source of energy available to him. Wind, water, and fire were but rarely used as forms of energy. Thus we see that, in the first stage of cultural development, the only source of energy under man's control and at his disposal for culture-building was, except for the insignificant and limited use of wind, water and fire, his own body.

The amount of energy that could be derived from this source was very small. The amount of energy at the disposal of a community of 50, 100, or 300 persons would be 50, 100, or 300 times the energy of the average member of the community, which, when infants, the sick, the old and feeble are considered, would be considerably less than one "man-power" per capita. Since one "man-power" is about one-tenth of one horsepower, we see that the amount of energy per capita in the earliest stage of cultural development was very small indeed—perhaps 1/20th horsepower per person.

Since the amount of energy available for culture building in this stage was finite and limited, the extent to which culture could develop was limited. As we have seen, when the energy factor is a constant, cultural progress is made possible only by improvements in the means with which the energy is expended, namely, the technology. Thus, in the human-energy stage of cultural development progress is achieved only by inventing new tools—the bow and arrow, harpoon, needle, etc., or by improving old ones—new techniques of chipping flint implements, for example. But when man has achieved maximum efficiency in the expenditure of energy, and when he has reached the limits of his finite bodily energy resources, then his culture can develop no further. Unless he can harness additional quantities of energy—by tapping new sources—cultural development will come to an end. Man would have remained on the level of savagery[12] indefinitely if he had not learned to augment the amount of energy under his control and at his disposal for culture-building by harnessing new sources of energy. This was first accomplished by the domestication of animals and by the cultivation of plants.

Man added greatly to the amount of energy under his control and at his disposal for culture-building when he domesticated animals and brought plants under cultivation. To be sure, man nourished himself with meat and

---

[12] Following Morgan and Tylor, we use "savagery" to designate cultures resting upon a wild-food basis, "barbarism" for cultures with a domestic food basis. Our use of "civilization," however, differs from that of Tylor and Morgan (see p. 355).

grain and clothed himself with hides and fibers long before animal husbandry and agriculture came into being. But there is a vast difference between merely exploiting the resources of nature and of harnessing the forces
of nature. In a wild food economy, a person, under given environmental
conditions, expends a certain amount of energy (we will assume it is an average person so that the question of skill may be ignored) and in return he
will secure, on the average, so much meat, fish, or plant food. But the food
which he secures is itself a form and a magnitude of energy. Thus the hunter
or wild plant-food gatherer exchanges one magnitude of energy for another:
m units of labor for n calories of food. The ratio between the magnitude of
energy obtained in the form of food and the magnitude expended in hunting and gathering may vary. The amount obtained may be greater than, less
than (in which case the hunter-gatherer would eventually perish), or equal
to, the amount expended. But although the ratio may vary from one situation to another, it is in any particular instance fixed: that is, the magnitude
of energy—value of the game taken or plant-food gathered remains constant between the time that it is obtained and the time of its consumption.
(At least it does not increase, it may in some instances decrease through natural deterioration.)

In a wild food economy, an animal or a plant is of value to man only after it has ceased to be an animal or a plant, i.e., a living organism. The
hunter kills his game, the gatherer digs his roots and bulbs, plucks the fruit
and seeds. It is different with the herdsman and the farmer. These persons
make plants and animals work for them.

Living plants and animals are biochemical mechanisms which, of themselves, accumulate and store up energy derived originally from the sun. Under agriculture and animal husbandry these accumulations can be appropriated and utilized by man periodically in the form of milk, wool, eggs, fruits,
nuts, seeds, sap, and so on. In the case of animals, energy generated by them
may be utilized by man in the form of work, more or less continuously
throughout their lifetime. Thus, when man domesticated animals and
brought plants under cultivation, he harnessed powerful forces of nature,
brought them under his control, and made them work for him just as he has
harnessed rivers and made them run mills and dynamos, just as he has harnessed the tremendous reservoirs of solar energy that are coal and oil. Thus
the difference between a wild plant and animal economy and a domestic
economy is that in the former the return for an expenditure of human energy,
no matter how large, is fixed, limited, whereas in agriculture and animal husbandry the initial return for the expenditure of human labor, augments itself
indefinitely. And so it has come about that with the development and perfec-
tion of the arts of animal husbandry and agriculture—selective breeding, protection from their competitors in the Darwinian struggle for survival, feeding,
fertilizer, irrigation, drainage, etc.—a given quantity of human labor produces

much more than it could before these forces were harnessed. It is true, of course, that a given amount of human labor will produce more food in a wild economy under exceptionally favorable circumstances, such, for example, as in the Northwest Coast of America where salmon could be taken in vast numbers with little labor, or in the Great Plains of North America where, after the introduction of the horse and in favorable circumstances, a large quantity of bison meat could be procured with but little labor, than could be produced by a feeble development of agriculture in unfavorable circumstances. But history and archeology prove that, by and large, the ability of man to procure the first necessity of life, food, was tremendously increased by the domestication of animals and by the cultivation of plants. Cultural progress was extremely rapid after the origin of agriculture.[13] The great civilizations of China, India, Mesopotamia, Egypt, Mexico, and Peru sprang up quickly after the agricultural arts had attained to some degree of development and maturity. This was due, as we have already observed, to the fact that, by means of agriculture man was able to harness, control, and put to work for himself powerful forces of nature. With greatly augmented energy resources man was able to expand and develop his way of life, i.e., his culture.

In the development of culture agriculture is a much more important and powerful factor than animal husbandry.[14] This is because man's control over the forces of nature is more immediate and more complete in agriculture than in animal husbandry. In a pastoral economy man exerts control over the animals only, he merely harnesses solar energy in animal form. But the animals themselves are dependent upon wild plants. Thus pastoral man is still dependent to a great extent upon the forces and caprices of nature. But in agriculture, his control is more intimate, direct, and, above all, greater. Plants receive and store up energy directly from the sun. Man's control over plants is direct and immediate. Further independence of nature is achieved by means of irrigation, drainage, and fertilizer. To be sure, man is always dependent upon nature to a greater or less extent; his control is never complete. But his dependence is less, his control greater, in agriculture than in animal husbandry. The extent to which man may harness natural forces in animal husbandry is limited. No matter how much animals are improved by selective breeding, no matter how carefully they are tended—defended from beasts of prey, protected from the elements—so long as they are dependent upon wild plant food, there is a limit, imposed by nature, to the extent to which man can receive profitable returns from

---

[13] "Finds in the Near East seem to indicate that the domestication of plants and animals in that region was followed by an extraordinary flowering of culture," Ralph Linton, The Present Status of Anthropology (Science, Vol. 87, 1938), p. 245.

[14] But this does not mean that agriculture must be preceded by a pastoral economy in the course of cultural development. Contrary to a notion current nowadays, none of the major evolutionists ever maintained that farming must be preceded by herding.

his efforts expended on his herds. When this limit has been reached no further progress can be made. It is not until man controls also the growth of the plants upon which his animals feed that progress in animal husbandry can advance to higher levels. In agriculture, on the other hand, while there may be a limit to the increase of yield per unit of human labor, this limit has not yet been reached, and, indeed it is not yet even in sight. Thus there appears to be a limit to the return from the expenditure of a given amount of human labor in animal husbandry. But in agriculture this technological limit, if one be assumed to exist, lies so far ahead of us that we cannot see it or imagine where it might lie.

Added to all of the above, is the familiar fact that a nomadic life, which is customary in a pastoral economy, is not conducive to the development of advanced cultures. The sedentary life that goes with agriculture is much more conducive to the development of the arts and crafts, to the accumulation of wealth and surpluses, to urban life.

Agriculture increased tremendously the amount of energy per capita available for culture-building, and, as a consequence of the maturation of the agricultural arts, a tremendous growth of culture was experienced. Cultural progress was very slow during Eolithic and Paleolithic times. But after a relatively brief period in the Neolithic age, during which the agricultural arts were being developed, there was a tremendous acceleration of culture growth, and the great cultures of China, India, Mesopotamia, Egypt, Mexico, and Peru, came rapidly into being.

The sequence of events was somewhat as follows: agriculture transformed a roaming population into a sedentary one. It greatly increased the food supply, which in turn increased the population. As human labor became more productive in agriculture, an increasing portion of society became divorced from the task of food-getting, and was devoted to other occupations. Thus society becomes organized into occupational groups: masons, metal workers, jade carvers, weavers, scribes, priests. This has the effect of accelerating progress in the arts, crafts, and sciences (astronomy, mathematics, etc.), since they are now in the hands of specialists, rather than jacks-of-all-trades. With an increase in manufacturing, added to division of society into occupational groups, comes production for exchange and sale (instead of primarily for use as in tribal society), mediums of exchange, money, merchants, banks, mortgages, debtors, slaves. An accumulation of wealth and competition for favored regions provoke wars of conquest, and produce professional military and ruling classes, slavery and serfdom. Thus agriculture wrought a profound change in the life-and-culture of man as it had existed in the human-energy stage of development.

But the advance of culture was not continuous and without limit. Civilization had, in the main, reached the limit of its development on the basis of a merely agricultural and animal husbandry technology long before the next great cultural advance was initiated by the industrial revolution. As a matter of fact, marked cultural recessions took place in Mesopotamia, Egypt, Greece, Rome, perhaps in India, possibly in China. This is not to say that no cultural progress whatsoever was made; we are well aware of many steps forward from time to time in various places. But so far as general type of culture is concerned, there is no fundamental difference between the culture of Greece during the time of Archimedes and that of Western Europe at the beginning of the eighteenth century.

After the agricultural arts had become relatively mature, some six, eight or ten thousand years before the beginning of the Christian era, there was little cultural advance until the nineteenth century A.D. Agricultural methods in Europe and the United States in 1850 differed very little from those of Egypt of 2000 B.C. The Egyptians did not have an iron plow, but otherwise there was little difference in mode of production. Even today in many places in the United States and in Europe we can find agricultural practices which, the use of iron accepted, are essentially like those of dynastic Egypt. Production in other fields was essentially the same in western Europe at the beginning of the eighteenth (we might almost say nineteenth) century as in ancient Rome, Greece, or Egypt. Man, as freeman, serf, or slave, and beasts of burden and draft animals, supplemented to a meager extent by wind and waterpower, were the sources of energy. The Europeans had gunpowder whereas the ancients did not. But gunpowder cannot be said to be a culture-builder.[15] There was no essential difference in type of social-political and economic institutions. Banks, merchants, the political state, great land-owners, guilds of workmen, and so on were found in ancient Mesopotamia, Greece, and Rome.

Thus we may conclude that culture had developed about as far as it could upon the basis of an agricultural-animal husbandry economy, and that there were recessions from peaks attained in Mesopotamia, Egypt, Greece and Rome long before the beginning of the eighteenth century A.D. We may conclude further, that civilization would never have advanced substantially beyond the levels already reached in the great cultures of antiquity if a way had not been found to harness a greater magnitude of energy per capita per unit of time, by tapping a new source of energy: fuel.

The invention of the steam engine, and of all subsequent engines which derive power from fuels, inaugurated a new era in culture history. When man

---

[15] It is true, of course, that powder is used in blasting in quarries, etc., and is to this extent a motive force in culture building. But energy employed in this way is relatively insignificant quantitatively.

The bow and arrow inaugurated cultural advance because in its economic context it provided man with food in greater quantity or with less effort. The gun, in its hunting context, has had the opposite effect, that of reducing the food supply by killing off the game. In their military contexts, neither the bow and arrow or the gun has been a culture-builder. The mere conquest or extermination of one tribe or nation by another, the mere change from one dynasty or set of office holders to another, is not culture building.

learned to harness energy in the form of fuel he opened the door of a vast treasure house of energy. Fuels and engines tremendously increased the amount of energy under man's control and at his disposal for culture-building. The extent to which energy has been thus harnessed in the modern world is indicated by the eminent physicist, Robert A. Millikan as follows:[16]

> In this country [the U.S.A.] there is now expended about 13.5 horsepower hours per day per capita—the equivalent of 100 human slaves for each of us; in England the figure is 6.7, in Germany 6.0, in France 4.5, in Japan 1.8, in Russia 0.9, in China, 0.5.

Let us return now, for a moment, to our basic principle—culture develops as (1) the amount of energy harnessed and put to work per capita per unit of time increases, and (2) as the efficiency of the means with which this energy is expended increases and consider the evolution of culture from a slightly different angle. In the course of human history various sources of energy are tapped and harnessed by man and put to work at culture-living and culture-building. The original source of energy was, as we have seen, the human organism. Subsequently, energy has been harnessed in other forms—agriculture, animal husbandry, fire,[17] wind, water, fuel. Energy is energy, and from the point of view of technology it makes no difference whether the energy with which a bushel of wheat is ground comes from a free man, a slave,[18] an ox, the flowing stream or a pile of coal. But it makes a big difference to human beings where the energy comes from,[19] and an important index of cultural development is derived from this fact.

To refer once more to our basic equation: On the one hand we have energy expended; on the other, human need-serving goods and services are produced. Culture advances as these two factors increase, hand in hand. But the energy component is resolvable into two factors: the human energy, and the non-human energy, factors. Of these, the human energy factor is a constant; the non-human energy factor, a variable. The increase in quantity of need-serving goods goes hand in hand with an increase in the amount of

---

[16] Science and the World Tomorrow (Scientific Monthly, Sept. 1939), p. 211. These figures do not, however, tell the whole story for they ignore the vast amount of energy harnessed in the form of cultivated plants and domestic animals.

[17] We may be permitted thus to distinguish two different ways of harnessing energy although each involves fire and fuel. By "fire" we indicate such energy uses of fire which preceded the steam engine-clearing forests, burning logs to make dugout canoes, etc. By "fuel" we designate energy harnessed by steam, gasoline, etc., engines.

[18] Technologically a freeman and a slave are equal, both being energy in homo sapiens form. Sociologically, there is, of course, a vast difference between them. Sociologically a slave is not a human being; he is merely a beast of burden who can talk.

[19] According to E. H. Hull, of the General Electric Research Laboratory, the power equivalent of "a groaning and sweating slave" is "75 watts of electricity, which most of us can buy at the rate of two-fifths of a cent an hour." Engineering: Ancient and Modern (Scientific Monthly, November 1939), p. 463.

non-human energy expended. But, since the human energy factor remains constant, an increase in amount of goods and services produced means more goods and services per unit of human labor. Hence, we obtain the law: Other things being equal, culture evolves as the productivity of human labor increases.

In Savagery (wild food economy) the productivity of human labor is low; only a small amount of human need-serving goods and services are produced per unit of human energy. In Barbarism (agriculture, animal husbandry), this productivity is greatly increased. And in Civilization (fuels, engines) it is still further increased.

We must now consider another factor in the process of cultural development, and an important one it is, viz., the social system within which energy is harnessed and put to work.

We may distinguish two kinds of determinants in social organization, two kinds of social groupings. On the one hand we have social groupings which serve those needs of man which can be fed by drawing upon resources within man's own organism: clubs for companionship, classes or castes in so far as they feed the desire for distinction, will serve as examples. On the other hand, social organization is concerned with man's adjustment to the external world; social organization is the way in which human beings organize themselves for the three great processes of adjustment and survival—food getting, defense from enemies, protection from the elements. Thus, we may distinguish two factors in any social system, those elements which are ends in themselves, which we may call E; and elements which are means to ends (food, defense, etc.) which we may term M.

In any social system M is more important than E, because E is dependent upon M. There can be no men's clubs or classes of distinction unless food is provided and enemies guarded against. In the development of culture, moreover, we may regard E as a constant: a men's club is a men's club whether among savage or civilized peoples. Being a constant, we may ignore factor E in our consideration of cultural evolution and deal only with the factor M.

M is a variable factor in the process of cultural evolution. It is, moreover, a dependent variable, dependent upon the technological way in which energy is harnessed and put to work. It is obvious, of course, that it is the technological activities of hunting people that determine, in general, their form of social organization (in so far as that social organization is correlated with hunting rather than with defense against enemies). We of the United States have a certain type of social system (in part) because we have factories, railroads, automobiles, etc.; we do not possess these things as a consequence of a certain kind of social system. Technological systems engender social systems rather than the reverse. Disregarding the factor E, social organization is to be regarded as the way in which human beings organize themselves to wield their respective technologies. Thus we obtain another important law of culture:

The social organization (E excluded) of a people is dependent upon and determined by the mechanical means with which food is secured, shelter provided, and defense maintained. In the process of cultural development, social evolution is a consequence of technological evolution.

But this is not the whole story. While it is true that social systems are engendered by, and dependent upon, their respective underlying technologies, it is also true that social systems condition the operation of the technological systems upon which they rest; the relationship is one of mutual, though not necessarily equal, interaction and influence. A social system may foster the effective operation of its underlying technology or it may tend to restrain and thwart it. In short, in any given situation the social system may play a progressive role or it may play a reactionary role.

We have noted that after the agricultural arts had attained a certain degree of development, the great civilizations of China, India, Egypt, the Near East, Central America and Peru came rapidly into being as a consequence of the greatly augmented energy resources of the peoples of these regions. But these great civilizations did not continue to advance indefinitely. On the contrary they even receded from maximum levels in a number of instances. Why did they not continue progressively to advance? According to our law culture will advance, other things being equal, as long as the amount of energy harnessed and put to work per capita per unit of time increases. The answer to our question, why did not these great cultures continue to advance? is, therefore, that the amount of energy per capita per unit of time, ceased to increase, and, furthermore, the efficiency of the means with which this energy was expended was not advanced beyond a certain limit. In short, there was no fundamental improvement in the agricultural arts from say 2000 B.C. to 1800 A.D.

The next question is, Why did not the agricultural arts advance and improve during this time? We know that the agricultural arts are still capable of tremendous improvement, and the urge of man for plenty, security and efficiency was as great then as now. Why, then, did agriculture fail to progress beyond a certain point in the great civilizations of antiquity? The answer is, the social system, within which these arts functioned, curbed further expansion, thwarted progress.

All great civilizations resting upon intensive agriculture are divided into classes: a ruling class and the masses who are ruled. The masses produced the means of life. But the distribution of these goods is in accordance with rules which are administered by the ruling class. By one method of control or another—by levies, taxes, rents, or some other means—the ruling class takes a portion of the wealth produced by the masses from them, and consumes it according to their liking or as the exigencies of the time dictate.

In this sort of situation cultural advancement may cease at a certain point for lack of incentive. No incentive to progress came from the ruling class in the ancient civilizations of which we are speaking. What they appropriated from their subjects they consumed or wasted. To obtain more wealth the ruling class merely increased taxes, rents, or other levies upon the producers of wealth. This was easier, quicker, and surer than increasing the efficiency of production and thereby augmenting the total product. On the other hand, there was no incentive to progress among the masses—if they produced more by increasing efficiency it would only mean more for the tax-gatherers of the ruling class. The culture history of China during the past few centuries, or indeed, since the Han dynasty, well illustrates situations of this sort.

We come then to the following conclusion: A social system may so condition the operation of a technological system as to impose a limit upon the extent to which it can expand and develop. When this occurs, cultural evolution ceases. Neither evolution nor progress in culture is inevitable (neither Morgan nor Tylor ever said, or even intimated, that they are). When cultural advance has thus been arrested, it can be renewed only by tapping some new source of energy and by harnessing it in sufficient magnitude to burst asunder the social system which binds it. Thus freed, the new technology will form a new social system, one congenial to its growth, and culture will again advance until, perhaps, the social system once more checks it.

It seems quite clear that mankind would never have advanced materially beyond the maximum levels attained by culture between 2000 B.C. and 1700 A.D. had it not tapped a new source of energy (fuel) and harnessed it in substantial magnitudes. The speed with which man could travel, the range of his projectiles, and many other things, could not have advanced beyond a certain point had he not learned to harness more energy in new forms. And so it was with culture as a whole. The steam engine ushered in a new era. With it, and various kinds of internal combustion engines, the energy resources of vast deposits of coal and oil were tapped and harnessed in progressively increasing magnitudes. Hydroelectric plants contributed a substantial amount from rivers. Populations grew, production expanded, wealth increased. The limits of growth of the new technology have not yet been reached; indeed, it is a probably not an exaggeration to say that they have not yet even been foreseen, so vast are the possibilities and so close are we still to the beginning of this new era. But already the new technology has come into conflict with the old social system. The new technology is being curbed and thwarted. The progressive tendencies of the new technology are being held back by a social system that was adapted to the pre-fuel technology. This fact has become commonplace today.

In our present society, goods are produced for sale at a profit. To sell one must have a market. Our market is a world market, but it is, nevertheless, finite in magnitude. When the limit of the market has been reached production ceases to expand: no market, no sale; no sale, no profit; no profit, no production. Drastic curtailment of production, wholesale destruction of surpluses follows. Factories, mills, and mines close; millions of men are divorced from industrial production and thrown upon relief. Population growth recedes. National incomes cease to expand. Stagnation sets in.

When, in the course of cultural development, the expanding technology comes into conflict with the social system, one of two things will happen: either the social system will give way, or technological advance will be arrested. If the latter occurs, cultural evolution will, of course, cease. The outcome of situations such as this is not preordained. The triumph of technology and the continued evolution and progress of culture are not assured merely because we wish it or because it would be better thus. In culture as in mechanics, the greater force prevails. A force is applied to a boulder. If the force were great enough, the rock is moved. If the rock were large enough to withstand the force it will remain stationary. So in the case of technology-institutions conflicts: if the force of the growing technology be great enough the restraining institutions will give way; if this force is not strong enough to overcome institutional opposition, it must submit to it.

There was undoubtedly much institutional resistance to the expanding agricultural technology in late neolithic times. Such staunch institutions as the tribe and clan which had served man well for thousands of years did not give way to the political state without a fight; the "liberty, equality and fraternity" of primitive society were not surrendered for the class-divided, serf and lord, slave and master, society of feudalism without a struggle. But the ancient and time-honored institutions of tribal society could not accommodate the greatly augmented forces of the agricultural technology. Neither could they successfully oppose these new forces. Consequently, tribal institutions gave way and a new social system came into being.

Similarly in our day, our institutions have shown themselves incapable of accommodating the vast technological forces of the Power Age. What the outcome of the present conflict between modern fuel technology and the social system of an earlier era will be, time alone will tell. It seems likely, however, that the old social system is now in the process of destruction. The tremendous forces of the Power Age are not to be denied. The great wars of the twentieth century derive their chief significance from this fact: they are the means by which an old social order is to be scrapped, and a new one to be brought into being. The first World War wiped out the old ruling families of the Hapsburgs, Romanoffs, and Hohenzollerns, hulking relics of Feudalism, and brought Communist and Fascist systems into being. We do not venture to predict the social changes which the present war will bring about. But we may confidently expect them to be as profound and as far-reaching as those effected by World War I.

Thus, in the history of cultural evolution, we have witnessed one complete cultural revolution, and the first stage of a second. The technological transition from a wild food economy to a relatively mature agricultural and animal husbandry economy was followed by an equally profound institutional change: from tribal society to civil society. Thus the first fundamental and all-inclusive cultural change, or revolution, took place. At the present time we are entering upon the second stage of the second great cultural revolution of human history. The Industrial Revolution was but the first stage, the technological stage, of this great cultural revolution. The Industrial Revolution has run its course, and we are now entering upon the second stage, one of profound institutional change, of social revolution. Barring collapse and chaos, which is of course possible, a new social order will emerge. It appears likely that the human race will occupy the earth for some million years to come. It seems probable, also, that man, after having won his way up through savagery and barbarism, is not likely to stop, when at last he finds himself upon the very threshold of civilization.

The key to the future, in any event, lies in the energy situation. If we can continue to harness as much energy per capita per year in the future as we are doing now, there is little doubt but that our old social system will give way to a new one, a new era of civilization. Should, however, the amount of energy that we are able to harness diminish materially, then culture would cease to advance or even recede. A return to a cultural level comparable to that of China during the Ming dynasty is neither inconceivable nor impossible. It all depends upon how man harnesses the forces of nature and the extent to which this is done.

At the present time "the petroleum in sight is only a twelve year supply . . . and new discoveries [of oil] are not keeping pace with use."[20] Coal is more abundant. Even so, many of the best deposits in the United States—which has over half of the world's known coal reserves—will some day be depleted. "Eventually, no matter how much we conserve, this sponging off past ages for fossil energy must cease. . . . What then?"[21] The answer is, of course, that culture will decline unless man is able to maintain the amount of energy harnessed per capita per year by tapping new sources.

Wind, water, waves, tides, solar boilers, photochemical reactions, atomic energy, etc., are sources which might be tapped or further exploited. One of the most intriguing possibilities is that of harnessing atomic energy. When the nucleus of an atom of uranium (U 235) is split it "releases 200,000,000 electron volts, the largest conversion of mass into energy that has yet been produced by terrestrial means."[22] Weight for weight, uranium (as a source

---

[20] C. C. Furnas, Future Sources of Power (Science, Nov. 7, 1941), p. 425.

[21] Ibid., p. 426.

[22] Herbert L. Anderson, Progress in Harnessing Power from Uranium (Scientific Monthly, June 1940).

of energy produced by nuclear fission) is 5,000,000 times as effective as coal.[23] If harnessing sub-atomic energy could be made a practical success, our energy resources would be multiplied a thousand fold. As Dr. R. M. Langer,[24] research associate in physics at California Institute of Technology, has put it:

> The face of the earth will be changed. . . . Privilege and class distinctions . . . will become relics because things that make up the good life will be so abundant and inexpensive. War will become obsolete because of the disappearance of those economic stresses that immemorially have caused it. The kind of civilization we might expect . . . is so different in kind from anything we know that even guesses about it are futile.

To be able to harness sub-atomic energy would, without doubt, create a civilization surpassing sober imagination of today. But not everyone is as confident as Dr. Langer that this advance is imminent. Some experts have their doubts, some think it a possibility. Time alone will tell.

But there is always the sun, from which man has derived all of his energy, directly or indirectly, in the past. And it may be that it will become, directly, our chief source of power in the future. Energy in enormous amounts reaches the earth daily from the sun. "The average intensity of solar energy in this latitude amounts to about 0.1 of a horse power per square foot" (Furnas, p. 426). "Enough energy falls on about 200 square miles of an arid region like the Mojave Desert to supply the [present needs of the] United States" (Furnas, p. 427). But the problem is, of course, to harness it effectively and efficiently.[25] The difficulties do not seem insuperable. It will doubtless be done, and probably before a serious diminution of power from dwindling resources of oil and coal overtakes us. From a power standpoint the outlook for the future is not too dark for optimism.

We turn now to an interesting and important fact, one highly significant to the history of anthropology: The thesis set forth in the preceding pages is substantially the same as that advanced by Lewis H. Morgan and E. B. Tylor many decades ago. We have expounded it in somewhat different form and words; our presentation is, perhaps, more systematic and explicit. At one point we have made a significant change in their theoretical scheme: we begin the third great stage of cultural evolution with engines rather than with writing. But essentially our thesis is that of the Evolutionist school as typified by Morgan and Tylor.

---

[23] Robert D. Potter, Is Atomic Power at Hand? (Scientific Monthly, June 1940), p. 573.

[24] Fast New World (Collier's, July 6, 1940).

[25] See C. C. Abbot, Utilizing Heat from the Sun (Smithsonian Miscellaneous Collections, Vol. 98, No. 5, March 30, 1939).

* * *

In the foregoing we have, we believe, a sound and illuminating theory of cultural evolution. We have hold of principles, fundamental principles, which are operative in all cultures at all times and places. The motive force of cultural evolution is laid bare, the mechanisms of development made clear. The nature of the relationship between social institutions on the one hand and technological instruments on the other is indicated. Understanding that the function of culture is to serve the needs of man, we find that we have an objective criterion for evaluating culture in terms of the extent to which, and the efficiency with which, human needs are satisfied by cultural means. We can measure the amounts of energy expended; we can calculate the efficiency of the expenditure of energy in terms of measurable quantities of goods and services produced. And, finally, as we see, these measurements can be expressed in mathematical terms.

The theory set forth in the preceding pages was, as we have made clear, held by the foremost thinkers of the Evolutionist school of the nineteenth century, both in England and in America. Today they seem to us as sound as they did to Tylor and Morgan, and, if anything, more obvious. It seems almost incredible that anthropologists of the twentieth century could have turned their backs upon and repudiated such a simple, sound, and illuminating generalization, one that makes the vast range of tens of thousands of years of culture history intelligible. But they have done just this.[26] The anti-evolutionists, led in America by Franz Boas, have rejected the theory of evolution in cultural anthropology—and have given us instead a philosophy of "planless hodge-podge-ism."

It is not surprising, therefore, to find at the present time the most impressive recognition of the significance of technological progress in cultural evolution in the writings of a distinguished physicist, the Nobel prize winner, Robert A. Millikan:[27]

> The changes that have occurred within the past hundred years not only in the external conditions under which the average man, at least in this western world, passes life on earth, but in his superstitions . . . his fundamental beliefs, in his philosophy, in his conception of religion, in his whole world outlook, are probably greater than those that occurred during the preceding four thousand years all put together. Life seems to remain static for thousands of years and then to shoot forward with amazing speed. The last century has been one of those periods of extraordinary change, the most amazing in human history.

---

[26] One distinguished anthropologist has gone so far as to declare that "the theory of cultural evolution [is] to my mind the most inane, sterile, and pernicious theory ever conceived in the history of science. . . ." B. Laufer, in a review of Lowie's Culture and Ethnology (American Anthropologist, Vol. 20, 1918), p. 90.

[27] Op.cit., p. 211.

If, then, you ask me to put into one sentence the cause of that recent rapid and enormous change I should reply: "It is found in the discovery and utilization of the means by which heat energy can be made to do man's work for him."

Tucked away in the pages of Volume II of a manual on European archeology, too, we find a similar expression from a distinguished American scholar, George G. MacCurdy:[28]

The *degree of civilization of any epoch, people, or group of peoples is measured by ability to utilize energy for human advancement or needs*. Energy is of two kinds, internal and external or free. Internal energy is that of the human body or machine, and its basis is food. External energy is that outside the human body and its basis is fuel. Man has been able to tap the great storehouse of external energy. Through his internal energy and that acquired from external sources, he has been able to overcome the opposing energy of his natural environment. *The difference between these two opposing forces is the gauge of civilization* (emphasis ours).

Thus, this view is not wholly absent in anthropological theory in America today although extremely rare and lightly regarded. The time will come, we may confidently expect, when the theory of evolution will again prevail in the science of culture as it has in the biological and the physical sciences. It is a significant fact that in cultural anthropology alone among the sciences is a philosophy of anti-evolutionism respectable—a fact we would do well to ponder.

QUERIES

- When White refers to "energy," he is clearly including things other than fossil fuel or electricity. For example, in what ways was the Agricultural Revolution also an energy revolution?
- What is the function of culture? What basic human needs does it satisfy?
- What is White's central formula? How does it predict changes in cultural evolution?
- White writes, "Technological systems engender social systems rather than the reverse," giving an example from the mid-20th century United States. Given the technological systems of the early 21st century, what new forms of social systems now exist in the United States?
- Between approximately 2000 B.C. and A.D. 1800, according to White, there were no fundamental developments in the technology of agriculture. Why not? What does this imply about the causal relationships between the technological and sociological realms?

---

[28] Human Origins (New York, 1933), Vol. 11, pp. 134–35.

CONNECTIONS

- How does White connect his theory of cultural evolution to those offered by Morgan and Tylor? In what fundamental way, however, does White's theory differ from those earlier Victorian evolutionists?
- How do you think Franz Boas would respond to White's theory of cultural evolution?
- In what ways does White's theory parallel and differ from Harris's theory of cultural materialism?

14

Julian Steward

INTRODUCTION

The following excerpts from two articles by Julian Steward (1902–1972) exemplify his complementary approaches to cultural ecology and multilineal evolution (Moore 2008:194–203). On the one hand, Steward argues that cultural patterns were directly shaped by adaptations to the physical environment, and that different societies in similar environments would exhibit similar sociopolitical organizations. For example, the highly mobile foraging societies of the Australian aborigines, the Dobe of the Kalahari, and the Shoshone of the western Great Basin exhibit similarities because they are adapted to similar environments—deserts with unpredictable and disperse food supplies. Alternatively, large and complex societies, such as the archaic civilizations of Mesopotamia and Mesoamerica, developed dense urban populations and hierarchical social organizations because they adapted to other environments—fertile valleys where floodplain and irrigation agriculture was practical. Steward carefully presents the detailed data that connects environment to sociopolitical organization, but the causal relationships are very straightforward: the differences and similarities in the organization of human societies largely reflect distinct adaptations to environmental variations.

This cultural ecological approach is directly connected to Steward's model of cultural evolution (Moore 2008:201–2). If sociopolitical variations at a given time are explained by reference to human adaptations to the environment, then so too are variations through time. Steward's concepts of cultural ecology and cultural evolution are tightly linked, with cultural ecology a synchronic explanation and cultural evolution a diachronic explanation. But it is this link that distinguishes Steward's cultural evolution from earlier evolutionary models proposed by Morgan and Tylor. Steward rejects the idea of universal stages of cultural evolution. Just as different environments set distinct parameters for human adaptation, those parameters will lead to various evolutionary trajectories. Human cultural evolution occurs but not according to the stepladder path that Morgan envisioned ("Middle Status of Barbarism, *then* Upper Status of Barbarism, *then* Civilization"). Instead, according to Steward, cultural evolution is multilinear.

The following selections were written at different points in Steward's career. The first article draws on Steward's extensive research and personal experience in the Great Basin, and it was written during the early phase of his career (see Moore 2008:195–98). The second selection has a somewhat broader scope, written after Steward had edited the multivolume comparative studies found in the *Handbook of South American Indians*. While the first selection compares variations among Great Basin Shoshone groups, the second selection examines broad patterns of the development of civilization in Eurasia and the Americas and presents a critique of 19th-century cultural evolutionists and of the 20th-century anthropologists who insisted that cultural variations could be "explained" by diffusion. As Steward pointedly observes, to say that a cultural trait has "diffused" really explains nothing. To assert, for example, that Japanese anime has diffused to the United States and Europe may describe a pattern, but it does not explain the process (which would minimally include the emergence of global entertainment markets, the role of pop culture in Japanese and American societies, the development of new entertainment media, the messages embodied in anime, and their appeal to viewers of all ages—among many, many other variables). "Diffusion" is a description, not an explanation. Rather, Steward argues, explanations will be found in the causal relationships linking cultural ecological patterns to subsequent sociopolitical organizations.

PRIMARY TEXT: *LINGUISTIC DISTRIBUTIONS AND POLITICAL GROUPS OF THE GREAT BASIN SHOSHONEANS*

Reproduced by permission of the American Anthropological Association from *American Anthropologist*, Vol. 39 (4), 1937, pp. 625–634 . www.aaanet.org. Not for sale or further reproduction. The following is an excerpt from Steward's article. The initial section of the article provided a map and descriptions of where various Native American ethnolinguistic groups were located across the Great Basin. The section reprinted here is Steward's discussion of relationships between sociopolitical organization and environmental constraints, an example of Steward's cultural ecology. Footnotes have been renumbered accordingly.

Political Groups

It is not wholly revealing to record merely that a group had a chief or considered itself a band, for neither the nature and extent of the authority del-
egated to the chief nor the kind of solidarity among members of the band
is self-evident. Moreover, novel conditions and concepts introduced by the
white man often radically altered native groupings, bringing solidarity and
chieftain's authority where it had not previously existed. A definition of
Shoshonean groups in terms of those economic, social, and religious activities which produce group cohesion and of the political control required for
those activities, places some "bands" in a new light and demonstrates that
there were at least two very unlike types of political groups in the area: (1)
village organization, in which habitual association and cooperation was
limited to the inhabitants of a single village; (2) band organization, variable in its social and economic foundation, but always entailing cooperation, some centralized political control, and a sense of solidarity among inhabitants of a well-defined territory.

Village organizations occurred among Shoshoni of Nevada, western
Idaho, western and northwestern Utah, and probably among many Northern Paiute and Southern Paiute. There is reason to suspect that prior to the
introduction of the horse, it may have occurred among some of the eastern
Idaho and Utah Shoshoni and among some of the Ute. Among the Nevada
Shoshoni, restriction of political organization to the village is a function of
social and economic activities. These Shoshoni were primarily gatherers.
Their habitat is a high, semi-arid steppe, which consists of a monotonous
succession of long, sage-covered valleys separated by lofty mountain ranges
which run north and south. The valleys yielded only sparse crops of brush
and grass seeds; the mountains, receiving greater rainfall, supported juniper
and pine nut trees and various species of edible seeds and roots. Game,
everywhere scarce, consisted of rabbits and antelope in the valleys, deer and
mountain sheep in the mountains. The scarcity of foods and the simple devices for procuring, transporting and storing them restricted population to
an average of one person to fifteen or twenty square miles. A few exceptionally fertile localities had one person to two square miles, while abnormally arid regions, like the Great Salt Lake Desert, had one person to fifty
or sixty square miles. Poor transportational facilities made it physically impossible for large aggregates of people to assemble for any considerable
time. Winter villages, consequently, comprised only two to ten or fifteen
families living near their food caches and ordinarily several miles from
neighboring villages. From spring to fall, individual families, or at most two
or three related families, wandered together foraging for food.

It might seem that the inhabitants of each valley, which is an isolated topo-
graphic unit, would tend to associate with one another in such a manner as

to form a band. As a matter of fact, they did associate sufficiently to have slight unity and each area of this kind is indicated on the map as a "district." But the unity was incomplete, people of one valley often cooperating with residents of neighboring valleys for various reasons. Probably the most important factor bringing together people from neighboring areas was the pine nut. The pine nut, which was without question the major food, was erratic in its yield from year to year. A given locality yielded a crop only once in two, three, or four years, but when it did yield, the abundance was many times what the local population could have harvested. People having poor crops in their own region therefore travelled to places of plenty and it would have been absurd for the residents of the favored locality to repel them for poaching. There was, in fact, no concept whatever of group ownership of food territories. The pine nut, therefore, induced a comparatively unsettled life; a family journeyed each year to areas where the crop was most convenient or the harvest most promising. Although it customarily returned to its winter home if economically feasible, it frequently found itself wintering with people from the west one year, with people from the east the following year, in widely separated localities.

Other economic and social activities failed to introduce sufficient regularity in Shoshoni associations to offset the effect of pine nut gathering. The annual communal rabbit drive, usually held in the fall, was undertaken by people who found themselves together at pine nut time and was led by the most experienced and capable person available. Likewise, the spring antelope drive brought together people who had wintered in the proximity of antelope country and was led by whatever antelope shaman was present. Dances usually accompanied these activities, but if they were held at other times, people within convenient distance assembled for a few days. There were no gatherings for purely religious purposes. The difficulties of transporting food to central locations made it impossible to maintain large gatherings for communal activities for more than a few weeks during each year. In fact, most gatherings occurred when cooperative collecting produced an abnormally large food supply for a brief period. The most stable political group among Nevada Shoshoni, therefore, was the small winter village with its somewhat shifting population and its informal headman. But even village cohesion was loose and the head man had little authority except to arrange minor, local dances and to decide when people should go to collect seeds and pine nuts. He might direct hunts, though often a special man led rabbit drives and perhaps some other man took charge of deer or mountain sheep hunts.

The village population naturally comprised many related persons, but, as circumstances of food supply, size of an individual family, choice of residence for various personal reasons, and other factors made postmarital residence variable and entailed frequent changes in residence, each village was not a single lineage. There was no rule of village exogamy. Aggregates of people larger than the village were not only necessarily transient but, in successive years, often brought together very different families under different leaders. From southern Nevada to southern Idaho, consequently, Shoshoni society resembled a vast net, the people of each village being linked to those of villages on all sides by varied economic and social activities as well as by marriage. There were no land-owning bands, no important property rights, no exogamy other than that connected with the bilateral family.

The transformation of Shoshoni political groups wrought by the arrival of the White man contrasts sharply with the native organization. In the Humboldt River Valley, where the racial impact was most severe, the introduction of horses and other features of the White man's economy made possible the amalgamation of formerly independent villages, and warfare, which was unknown in aboriginal days, provided a motive for banding together. A loose organization developed and Tümok, a former nonentity, became chief. When the wars were over, however, this band was dissolved, the Indians became attached to White communities, and Tümok promptly lost all authority. Indians now speak of Tümok as a great chief who led a large band, but careful inquiry shows clearly that his sole functions pertained to matters incident to the arrival of the White man and that so vast a band could not have existed under native conditions—a fact demonstrating the need of careful investigation of the dynamic aspects of native political institutions.

Western Idaho, though north of the habitat of the pine nut, maintained a type of Shoshoni society very similar to that of Nevada. Salmon, the principal food, was very abundant in the Snake River and supported a series of small villages which were slightly more stable than those in Nevada. Also, fish weirs and traps, used only by their builders who were members of the same village, tended to fix group ownership of fishing places. But seed areas, like those in Nevada, were free to all. The Snake River Shoshoni had no bands, for there were no factors to give cohesion to groups larger than the village. Communal hunts were much less important than in Nevada and dances which were sometimes attended by the inhabitants of several different villages gave only a very temporary alliance. Throughout most of this area of village organization, people were designated only as inhabitants of a named locality. In the north, however, there was some tendency to name people after a conspicuous food of their area, e.g., Salmon Eaters on the Snake River, though a given locality was often named differently by its various neighbors.

Present evidence suggests that most of the Northern Paiute had village rather than true band groups, though none have been described in terms which permit classifying them according to present definitions. Band organizations rests upon somewhat different conditions in the western and eastern portions of the Great Basin. In Owens Valley, California, where the population was unusually dense—one person to two square miles—the terrain was divided into small areas, each owned and defended against trespass by its inhabitants. Solidarity was produced among band members by the proximity of their more or less permanent habitations and by habitual cooperation in rabbit drives, deer hunts, antelope hunts, irrigation, much seed gathering and dances. The main function of the band chief was to arrange these communal functions and to send invitations to outsiders to join. Actual direction of each activity usually fell to some person of special ability.

Shoshoni of the Death Valley and Little Lake regions had a somewhat similar organization, though the concept of band ownership of land rapidly disappears among Shoshoni. To some extent, a sense of solidarity among inhabitants of a given region may have diffused from Owens Valley. In the Death Valley region, however, habitual cooperation with one's neighbors was virtually a necessity caused by the physical impossibility of traversing the wide, waterless deserts for frequent association with other people. In like manner, some of the Gosiute Shoshoni inhabiting oases in the vast deserts south of Great Salt Lake approximated band organization. Among eastern Shoshoneans, activities pertaining to band life usually involve the horse. There is reason to suspect that, with the exception of groups occupying country with abundant buffalo, many eastern Shoshoni were once very similar to Nevada Shoshoni, and that the early introduction of the horse brought a changed ecology which provided a basis for band organization. In 1832, Bonneville noted a contrast between the Shoshoni above and below Twin Falls on the Snake River, expressing amazement at the impoverished and disorganized condition of the latter.[1] Twin Falls is the eastern limit of salmon and the western limit of bottom lands where horses could be grazed. Horses were already common in the Fort Hall region at the time of Bonneville's visit. Other travelers have noted the extraordinary differences between the Ute and Gosiute. Escalante, in 1776, seems to have encountered horses among many Ute and definite bands and chiefs in the vicinity of Utah Lake.[2] By the arrival of the Mormon pioneers in 1847, Ute were travelling widely over the country on horseback.

The importance of the horse in primitive economy and the consequent social and political effects should not be underestimated. The horse makes it possible either to transport food to a central point where a large population may assemble and live more or less permanently or for members of separate villages to communicate and cooperate with one another. It is an empirical fact that the western limit of the horse also was the western limit of true bands.

---

[1] Washington Irving, The Adventures of Captain Bonneville, U.S.A., in the Rocky Mountains and the Far West (Pawnee Edition, 2 vols., New York, 1898), Vol. 1, pp. 329–34.

[2] Diary and Travels of Fray Francisco Antanasio Dominguez and Fray Silvestre Velez de Escalante to Discover a Route from the Presidio of Santa Fe, New Mexico, to Monterey in Southern California (in W. R. Harris, The Catholic Church in Utah, Salt Lake City, 1909, pp. 136–84).

Bands of the eastern Shoshoneans are bilateral or composite, that is, consist of many families which, being unrelated, permit band endogamy.[3] Political control is vested in one or more chiefs, certain men having special authority for warfare, hunting, dancing, and other activities. Thanks to strong Plains influence, war honors carried great prestige value and gave their possessors considerable civil as well as military authority. Although each band occupied a fairly well defined territory within which it usually ranged for food, there was little if any band ownership of territory. In fact, the great distances travelled seasonally on horseback entailed frequent association of neighboring bands (as of Idaho and Wyoming Shoshoni bands, which sometimes united temporarily), much traversing of neighbors' territories, and, indeed, invasion, even by Idaho Shoshoni and Utah Ute of buffalo country east of the Rocky Mountains, sometimes within the range of hostile tribes. Fairly exact information is now available on the location of most of the eastern Shoshoni bands. The Salmon River Shoshoni (Salmon Eaters, Mountain Sheep Eaters, or, more commonly, Lemhi Shoshoni) were aboriginally similar to the peoples of the lower Snake River. They lived in five or more independent villages, isolated in the mountains, and became welded into a single band only when, at the instigation of the government and after the acquisition of many horses, they settled on the Lemhi River, where a small band, possessing a few horses had previously lived.[4] Even then, however, many families remained in the mountains.

The greater part of southern Idaho was occupied by the Bohogue' (bohovi, sage brush + gue', butte) band, which consisted of Northern Paiute (Bannock) and Shoshoni, wintering in the vicinity of Fort Hall, and travelling on horseback as far as Camas Prairie to the west, Wyoming to the east. A single chief, usually a Bannock, directed these movements, aided by various other men who took charge of different activities. Raids by Blackfoot and some warfare with Ute further welded the unity of this band. Other smaller, but similar bands of Shoshoni were the Rabbit Eaters (Kamu düka) of the Port Neuf River and vicinity, the Huki Eaters (Hükün düka, from hüki, a wild seed) of the Bear River, Utah, the Fish Eaters (Paŋwidüka) of Cache Valley and vicinity, and the "Weber Ute" of the region of Salt Lake City. It is possible that there were other, small bands in this general area.

Wyoming Shoshoni within historic times seemed to have formed a single band under the chieftainship of Washakie, though it is probable that several distinct native bands were united when Plains warfare, which was intensified

---

[3] In The Economic and Social Basis of Primitive Bands (Essays in Anthropology in Honor of Alfred Louis Kroeber, Berkeley, 1936, pp. 331–50) I contrasted this type with patrilineal, localized, exogamous bands.

[4] Lewis and Clark (op. cit., Vol. 2, p. 347) observed a small band with about four hundred horses on the Lemhi River.

by dislocation of tribes, the introduction of fire arms and other factors incident to the coming of the White man, made amalgamation a virtual necessity.

It is now possible to map Ute bands only in central Utah and southwestern Colorado. There is little question, however, that, excepting a few small, scattered groups which were isolated in some of the inaccessible by-ways of the almost impenetrable portions of the upper Colorado plateau, the Ute ranged on horseback in strong bands. Warfare, especially with Arapaho and Crow, stimulated band growth.

Some of the Ute bands are: Utah Lake (Tiimpanagots, from tümbi, stone, panagots, canyon mouth); Sevier Lake (Pavandiits or Pahvant Ute, "water people"); Sampits (probably named from a chief); Pavogogwunsiŋ, of the upper Sevier River and Fish Lake Regions; the Uintah, of the Uintah Basin;[5] the White River Utes, probably to their east in Colorado; the Uncompahgre Utes, probably to their southeast in Colorado; the Pa-Utes (water Utes) in southeastern Utah, northeastern Arizona, southwestern Colorado; the Wi'-namanute, in the valleys of the Animas, Los Pinos, and Piedra Rivers in southwestern Colorado; the Kapota on the headwaters of the Rio Grande east of the last in Colorado and northern New Mexico. An amalgamation of most of the Colorado bands, including the Uncompahgres, took place under the leadership of Ouray within historic times.

The Southern Paiute must remain in some doubt until Kelly's full data are published. Although she has mapped fifteen "bands," defined as "dialectic units with political concomitants," it is not certain that a more complete definition would correspond with that used here. So long as the Southern Paiute remained on foot, it is difficult to see how people inhabiting so vast a region as that allotted to some of the bands could possibly have cooperated with one another in a sufficient number of enterprises to produce a truly centralized political control and a sense of solidarity with other occupants of the territory. Data have not been advanced to show that the bands were functional in other respects.

My own investigations among Kelly's "Las Vegas band," show that it actually comprised at least three bands of the kind defined here (. . .).[6] These bands were not unlike those of the Shoshoni of the Death Valley region, except that the villages were given somewhat greater fixity by the practise of a small amount of horticulture. It is likely that a greater number of political units existed among pre-horse Southern Paiute than the fifteen bands

---

[5] The Ashley-Smith Explorations and the Discovery of a Central Route to the Pacific, 1822–1829 (Cleveland, 1918, p. 151) records meeting Ute with horses at the mouth of the Uintah River. The Indians claimed a territory 150 miles long, 100 miles wide, the mouth of the river being its center.

[6] Baldwin Möllhausen (Dairy of a Journey from the Mississippi to the Coast of the Pacific, London, 1858, Vol. 2, p. 296) noted that Southern Paiute in the Mohave Desert region did not have horses in 1858.

recorded by Kelly and that Powell's and Ingall's list of thirty-one "tribes" may have been more nearly correct. There are indisputable records that political groups were consolidated into larger units among all other Shoshoneans after the influence of the White man was felt.

QUERIES

- According to Steward, what are the two major types of political groups in the Great Basin? How do these two political groups differ in terms of group size, cooperation among its members, political control, and territoriality?
- What environmental factors limited political organization to the village level in Nevada Shoshone?
- According to Steward, what was the most important factor bringing together people from different areas?
- What was the most stable sociopolitical unit in the Great Basin? Why?
- According to Steward, band societies existed in the western Great Basin, such as the Owens Valley of eastern California. What factors caused this exception to the basic Great Basin pattern?

CONNECTIONS

- Given the cultural patterns associated with the village pattern in the Great Basin—for example, variations in residence patterns, the lack of village exogamy, the limited power of village headmen, and so on— how would Steward's explanation differ from one that Alfred Kroeber would propose?
- Compare Steward's ideas about the relationships between environment and political authority to Marshall Sahlins's hypotheses in "Poor Man, Rich Man, Big-Man, Chief: Political Types in Melanesia and Polynesia."
- How would Lewis Henry Morgan interpret the sociopolitical patterns of the Great Basin?

PRIMARY TEXT: *CULTURAL CAUSALITY AND LAW: A TRIAL FORMULATION OF THE DEVELOPMENT OF EARLY CIVILIZATIONS* (EXCERPTS)

Reproduced by permission of the American Anthropological Association from *American Anthropologist*, Vol. 51 (1), 1949, pp. 1–27. www.aaanet.org. Not for sale or further reproduction.

Methodological Assumptions

It is about three-quarters of a century since the early anthropologists and sociologists attempted to formulate cultural regularities in generalized or scientific terms. The specific evolutionary formulations of such writers as Morgan[7] and Tylor[8] and the functional or sociological formulations of Durkheim and others were largely repudiated by the 20th century anthropologists, especially by those of the so-called "Boas" school, whose field work tested and cast doubt on their validity. Today, despite an enormous and ever-increasing stock-pile of cultural data, little effort has been made to devise new formulations or even to develop a methodology for doing so, except as White and Childe have kept alive the tradition of Morgan, as Radcliffe-Brown and Redfield have continued in the spirit of Durkheim, and as Malinowski has attempted to reconcile diverse schools of anthropology through a "scientific theory of culture."

Reaction to evolutionism and scientific functionalism has very nearly amounted to a denial that regularities exist; that is, to a claim that history never repeats itself. While it is theoretically admitted that cause and effect operate in cultural phenomena, it is considered somewhat rash to mention causality, let alone "law," in specific cases. Attention is centered on cultural differences, particulars, and peculiarities, and culture is often treated as if it developed quixotically, without determinable causes, or else appeared full-blown.

It is unfortunate that the two approaches are so widely thought of as theoretically irreconcilable rather than as expressions of different purposes or interests. The 19th century writers had the perfectly legitimate purpose of making scientific generalizations from what they considered recurrent cultural patterns, sequences, and processes in different cultures, while the more recent school has the equally legitimate purpose of examining the distinctive or non-recurrent features of cultures. As all cultures, though unique in many respects, nonetheless share certain traits and patterns with other cultures, an interest in either or both is entirely defensible. In fact, the analyses of cultural particulars provide the data necessary for any generalizations. If the 19th century formulations were wrong, it was not because their purpose was inadmissible or their objective impossible, but because the data were inadequate and insufficient, the methodology weak, and the application of the schemes too broad.

In spite of a half century of skepticism concerning the possibility of formulating cultural regularities, the conviction is widely held that the discovery of cultural laws is an ultimate goal of anthropology, to be attained when fact-collecting and detailed analyses of particular cultures and sequences are

---

[7] Morgan, 1877.
[8] Tylor, 1865, 1871.

sufficiently advanced. White has already offered some general formulations concerning the relationship of energy to cultural development, and he has argued for the importance of formulations of all kinds.[9] Even some members of the so-called "Boas" school expressly advocate a search for regularities. Lowie, for example, remarks that cultural phenomena "do point toward certain regularities, and these it is certainly our duty to ascertain as rigorously as possible."[10] Lesser cites several trial formulations of regularities, which have been made by various persons, including Boas, and calls for more explicit statement of the regularities which, in the course of his work and thinking, every social scientist assumes to exist.[11] The author has attempted to formulate regularities pertaining to the occurrence of patrilineal bands among hunting and gathering tribes[12] and has suggested others that may occur in the origin and development of clans.[13] In reality, hundreds of formulations appear in the literature—for example, correlations of kinship terminologies with forms of social organization—and the possibility of recognizing the general in the particular is implicit in the very terminology of anthropology. The routine use of such concepts, or typological categories, as "clans," "castes," "classes," "priests," "shamans," "men's tribal societies," "cities," and the like, are tacit recognition that these and scores of other features are common to a large number of cultures, despite the peculiarities of their local patterning.

The present need is not to achieve a world scheme of culture development or a set of universally valid laws, though no doubt many such laws can even now be postulated, but to establish a genuine interest in the scientific objective and a clear conceptualization of what is meant by regularities. It does not matter whether the formulations are sequential (diachronic) or functional (synchronic), on a large scale or a small scale. It is more important that comparative cultural studies should interest themselves in recurrent phenomena as well as in unique phenomena, and that anthropology explicitly recognize that a legitimate and ultimate objective is to see through the differences of cultures to the similarities, to ascertain processes that are duplicated independently in cultural sequences, and to recognize cause and effect in both temporal and functional relationships. Such scientific endeavor need not be ridden by the requirement that cultural laws or regularities be formulated in terms comparable to those of the biological or physical sciences, that they be absolutes and universals, or that they provide ultimate explanations. Any formulations of cultural data are valid provided

[9] White, 1943.
[10] Lowie, 1936, pp. 3, 7.
[11] Lesser, 1930.
[12] Steward, 1936.
[13] Steward 1937.

the procedure is empirical, hypotheses arising from interpretations of fact and being revised as new facts become available.

Three requirements for formulating cultural regularities may be stated in a rough and preliminary way as follows:

(1) *There must be a typology of cultures, patterns, and institutions.* Types represent abstractions, which disregard peculiarities while isolating and comparing similarities. To use Tylor's classic example, the mother-in-law tabu and matrilocal residence, though in each case unique in their local setting, are recurrent types, the cause and effect relationships of which may be compared and formulated. Anthropological terminology demonstrates that hundreds of types of culture elements, patterns, and total configurations are recognized, despite the peculiarities attaching to each in its local occurrence.

(2) *Causal interrelationship of types must be established in sequential or synchronic terms, or both.* Any reconstruction of the history of a particular culture implies, though it may not explicitly state, that certain causes produced certain effects. Insights into causes are deeper when the interrelationships of historical phenomena are analyzed functionally. Functional analysis of archeological data has not been lacking, though archeology has used an atomistic and taxonomic approach[14] far more than has conventional history. Gordon Childe[15] is exceptional in his effort to treat archeological materials functionally. Wittfogel[16] has been outstanding in his use of historical data to make functional-historical analyses of the socio-economic structure of early civilizations.

Where historical data are not available, only the synchronic approach to cause and effect is possible. Radcliffe-Brown, Redfield, and Malinowski, despite important differences in their thinking, are distinctive for their functional analyses.

(3) *The formulation of the independent recurrence of synchronic and/or sequential interrelationships of cultural phenomena is a scientific statement of cause and effect, regularities, or laws.* The particularists, though conceding that such formulations are theoretically possible and even desirable, are inclined to hold that in practice it is virtually impossible to isolate identifiable cause-and-effect relationships that operate in independent cases. Similarities between cultures are interpreted as the result of a single origin and diffusion, provided the obstacles to diffusion do not seem too great. If the obstacles are very great, differences are emphasized. Thus, most American anthropologists explain similarities between the early civilizations of the New World as a case of single origin and diffusion, but, impressed by the obstacles to

---

[14] See Steward and Setzler, 1938.
[15] Childe, 1934, 1946.
[16] Wittfogel, 1935, 1938, 1939–1940.

trans-oceanic culture contacts, they stress the dissimilarities between the civilizations of the Old and New Worlds. Some writers, however, like Elliot-Smith, Perry, and Gladwin[17] recognize the similarities between the two hemispheres and, unimpressed by barriers to diffusion, use the similarities as proof of a single world origin.

The use of diffusion to avoid coming to grips with problems of cause and effect not only fails to provide a consistent approach to culture history, but it gives an explanation of cultural origins that really explains nothing. Diffusion becomes a mechanical and unintelligible, though universal, cause, and it is employed, as if in contrast to other kinds of causes, to account for about 90 per cent of the world's culture. One may fairly ask whether, each time a society accepts diffused culture, it is not an independent recurrence of cause and effect. Malinowski[18] states: "Diffusion . . . is not an act, but a process closely akin in its working to the evolutionary process. For evolution deals above all with the influence of any type of 'origins'; and origins do not differ fundamentally whether they occur by invention or by diffusion."[19] For example, the civilizations of the Andes and Mexico were based on dense, sedentary populations, which in turn were supported by intensive irrigation farming. In both cases, the early societies were integrated by a theocratic hierarchy, which controlled communal endeavor and enlisted labor for the construction of religious centers. It is not sufficient to say that the agricultural, social, and religious institutions merely diffused as a unit, for that would be merely stating distributions in historical terms but failing to explain process. Incipient farming appeared first, and it diffused before the other complexes developed. The latter have a functional dependence on intensive farming. They could not have been accepted anywhere until it developed, and in the course of its development similar patterns would undoubtedly have emerged, whether or not they were diffused. The increasing population and the growing need for political integration very probably would have created small states in each area, and these states would almost certainly have been strongly theocratic, because the supernatural aspects of farming—for example, fertility concepts, the need to reckon seasons and to forecast the rise and fall of rivers, and the like—would have placed power in the hands of religious leaders. Diffusion may have hastened the development of theocratic states, but in each case the new developments were within determinable limits, and independently involved the same functional or cause-and-effect relationships.

It is true, of course, that many peculiar features common to New World civilizations do not represent a logical outgrowth of basic patterns and that

---

[17] Gladwin, 1947.
[18] Malinowski, 1944, pp. 214–15.
[19] See also Wittfogel, 1939–1940, pp. 175–76.

they can be disposed of with the superficial explanation that they diffused. Thus, the wide distribution of such concepts as the plumed serpent or the jaguar god, or of such constructions as terraced pyramids, may be explained in this manner, though deeper analysis might reveal the reasons for their wide acceptance. In general, it is the rather arbitrary, specific, or stylized features, that is, those features which have the least functional dependence on the basic patterns, that provide the greatest evidence of diffusion. These, in other words, are the particulars, which distinguish tribes or areas and which obscure regularities.

Another means of denying the possibility of isolating cultural regularities is to stress that the complexity or multiplicity of the antecedents or functional correlates of any institution makes it virtually impossible to isolate the true causes of the institution; convergent evolution rather than parallel evolution is generally used to explain similarities that seem not to be the result of diffusion. The answer to this is simply that in dealing with cultural phenomena, as in dealing with all the complex phenomena of nature, regularities can be found only by looking for them, and they will be valid only if a rigorous methodology underlies the framing of hypotheses.

It is not necessary that any formulation of cultural regularities provide an ultimate explanation of culture change. In the physical and biological sciences, formulations are merely approximations of observed regularities, and they are valid as working hypotheses despite their failure to deal with ultimate realities. So long as a cultural law formulates recurrences of similar interrelationships of phenomena, it expresses cause and effect in the same way that the law of gravity formulates but does not ultimately explain the attraction between masses of matter. Moreover, like the law of gravity, which has been greatly modified by the theory of relativity, any formulation of cultural data may be useful as a working hypothesis, even though further research requires that it be qualified or reformulated.

Cultural regularities may be formulated on different levels, each in its own terms. At present, the greatest possibilities lie in the purely cultural or superorganic level, for anthropology's traditional primary concern with culture has provided far more data of this kind. Moreover, the greater part of culture history is susceptible to treatment only in superorganic terms. Both sequential or diachronic formulations and synchronic formulations are superorganic, and they may be functional to the extent that the data permit. Redfield's tentative formulation that urban culture contrasts with folk culture in being more individualized, secularized, heterogeneous, and disorganized is synchronic, superorganic, and functional.[20] Morgan's evolutionary schemes[21] and White's formulation concerning the relationship of energy to cultural development[22] are sequential and somewhat functional.

[20] Redfield, 1941.
[21] Morgan, 1877.
[22] White, 1943.

Neither type, however, is wholly one or the other. A time-dimension is implied in Redfield's formulation, and synchronic, functional relationships are implied in White's.

Superorganic formulations do not, of course, provide the deeper explanations of culture change that may come from a psychological level or a biological level. Research on these latter levels may profitably run concurrently with the other, but for the present their formulations will be more applicable to synchronic, functional studies than to sequential ones. Thus, to advocate search for regularities in cultural terms is not at all in conflict with those who state that "culture does not exist apart from the individual, its human carrier." To hope for basic and ultimate explanations of behavior that will interrelate cultural, psychological, neurological, physiological, and even physical phenomena is not to deny the desirability of doing what now seems possible and, in view of anthropology's traditional and primary concern with culture, of doing first things first.

The present statement of scientific purpose and methodology rests on a conception of culture that needs clarification. *If the more important institutions of culture can be isolated from their unique setting so as to be typed, classified, and related to recurring antecedents or functional correlates, it follows that it is possible to consider the institutions in question as the basic or constant ones, whereas the features that lend uniqueness are the secondary or variable ones.* For example, the American high civilizations had agriculture, social classes, and a priest-temple-idol cult. As types, these institutions are abstractions of what was actually present in each area, and they do not take into account the particular crops grown, the precise patterning of the social classes, or the conceptualization of deities, details of ritual, and other religious features of each culture center. The latter are secondary and variable so far as the institutions in question are concerned. In a more comprehensive analysis, however, they would serve to distinguish subtypes, which would require more specific formulations.

This conception of culture is in conflict with an extreme organic view, which regards culture as a closed system in which all parts are of equal importance and are equally fixed. It holds that some features of culture are more basic and more fixed than others and that the problem is to ascertain those which are primary and basic and to explain their origin and development. It assumes that, although the secondary features must be consistent and functionally integrated with the primary ones, it is these that are more susceptible to fortuitous influences from inside or outside the culture, that change most readily, and that acquire such a variety of aspects that they give the impression that history never repeats itself.[23]

---

[23] This proposition has been developed in detail in Steward, 1940: pp. 479–98; 1938: pp. 1–3, 230–62.

For the present, it is not necessary to state criteria for ascertaining the primary features. In general, they are the ones which individual scientists are most interested in studying and which the anthropological record shows to have recurred again and again in independent situations. A procedure which attempts to give equal weight to all features of culture amounts to a negation of typing and of making formulations, for it must include all the unique features, which obscure similarities between cultures.

* * *

Summary and Conclusions

The above analysis may be briefly summarized.

In arid and semi-arid regions, agriculture may be carried on by means of flood-plain and irrigation farming, which does not require metal tools. As irrigation works are developed, population will increase until the limits of water are reached. Political controls become necessary to manage irrigation and other communal projects. As early societies were strongly religious, individuals with supernatural powers—lineage heads, shamans, or special priests—formed a theocratic ruling class, which governed first multi-house-cluster communities and later multi-community states.

The increasing productivity of farming released considerable labor from subsistence activities, and new technologies were developed—basketry, loomweaving, pottery, metallurgy, domestic and religious construction, and transportational facilities. Products made for home use were simple and utilitarian; those made for the theocratic class and for religious purposes became increasingly rich and varied, and they required an increasing proportion of total productive efforts.

When the limits of agricultural productivity under a given system of irrigation were reached, population pressures developed and interstate competition for land and for produce of all kinds began. The resulting warfare led to the creation of empires, warrior classes, and military leaders. It also led to enlargement of irrigation works and to a further increase of population. But the powerful military empires regimented all aspects of culture, and few new inventions were made. Consequently, each culture entered an era of rising and falling empires, each empire achieving a peak of irrigation, population, and political organization and a temporary florescence, but giving way to a subsequent period of dark ages.

The Iron Age gave the Old World a revolutionary technology, but, as iron tools cannot increase water supply, the irrigation areas were little affected, except as they fell under the empires of the north Mediterranean. Iron Age cultures developed in the forested areas of Europe, which had been exploited only with difficulty under the old technology. The New World never reached an Iron Age in precolumbian times. Instead, the Spanish Conquest brought it an Iron Age culture from the Old World, and native culture development was abruptly ended just after it had entered the Era of Cyclical Conquests.

The above formulation is rough, cursory, and tentative. It applies only to the early centers of world civilization. The eras are not "stages," which in a world evolutionary scheme would apply equally to desert, arctic, grassland, and woodland areas. In these other kinds of areas, the functional interrelationship of subsistence patterns, population, settlements, social structure, cooperative work, warfare, and religion had distinctive forms and requires special formulations.

The principal grounds for questioning the present formulation will, I suspect, be that diffusion between the centers of civilization in each hemisphere can be demonstrated. The relative chronology of the eras fits a diffusionist explanation perfectly. The essential question, however, is just what diffusion amounts to as an explanation. There is no doubt about the spread of domesticated plants and animals and little doubt about the diffusion of many technologies, art styles, and details of both material and non-material culture. Proof of diffusion, however, lies in the unique qualities of secondary features, not in the basic types of social, economic, and religious patterns. The latter could be attributed to diffusion only by postulating mass migration or far-flung conquests.

If people borrow domesticated plants and agricultural patterns, it is evident that population will increase in favorable areas. How shall dense, stable populations organize their sociopolitical relations? Obviously, they will not remain inchoate mobs until diffused patterns have taught them how to live together. (And even diffused patterns had to originate somewhere for good and sufficient reasons.) In densely settled areas, internal needs will produce an orderly interrelationship of environment, subsistence patterns, social groupings, occupational specialization, and over-all political, religious, and perhaps military integrating factors. These interrelated institutions do not have unlimited variability, for they must be adapted to the requirements of subsistence patterns established in particular environments; they involve a cultural ecology. Traits whose uniqueness is proof of their diffusion are acceptable if they are congruent with the basic socio-economic institutions. They give uniqueness and local color, and they may help crystallize local patterns in distinctive ways, but they cannot per se produce the underlying conditions of or the need for greater social and political organization. It is therefore possible to concede wide diffusion of particulars within the hemispheres and even between the hemispheres without having to rely upon diffusion as the principal explanation of cultural development.

We have attempted here to present a conception of culture and a methodology for formulating the regularities of cultural data which are consistent with scientific purpose. The data are those painstakingly gathered and arranged spacially and temporally by culture history. Thorough attention to cultural differences and particulars is necessary if typology is to be adequate and valid, but historical reconstructions need not be the sole objective of anthropology. Strong observed that "The time is coming when the rich ethnological and archeological record of the New World can be compared in full detail and time perspective with similar records from Europe, Egypt, Mesopotamia, India, China, and Siberia. When such comparative data are in hand the generalizations that will emerge may well revolutionize our concept of culture history and culture process over the millennia."[24] Any generalizations or formulations must be subject to frequent revision by new data, for, as Kroeber remarks, "Detailed case-by-case analyses are . . . called for if interpretations are not to become vitiated over generalizations which more and more approach formulas."[25] At the same time, it is obvious that the minutiae of culture history will never be completely known and that there is no need to defer formulations until all archeologists have laid down their shovels and all ethnologists have put away their notebooks. Unless anthropology is to interest itself mainly in the unique, exotic, and non-recurrent particulars, it is necessary that formulations be attempted no matter how tentative they may be. It is formulations that will enable us to state new kinds of problems and to direct attention to new kinds of data which have been slighted in the past. Fact-collecting of itself is insufficient scientific procedure; facts exist only as they are related to theories, and theories are not destroyed by facts— they are replaced by new theories which better explain the facts. Therefore, criticisms of this paper which concern facts alone and which fail to offer better formulations are of no interest.

BIBLIOGRAPHY

Childe, V. Gordon
    1934   New Light on the Most Ancient East. New York: Kegan Paul.
    1946   What Happened in History. New York: Pelican Books.
Gladwin, Harold S.
    1947   Men Out of Asia. New York: McGraw Hill.
Kroeber, A. L.
    1940   The Present Status of Americanistic Problems. *In* The Maya and Their
            Neighbors. Pp. 460–487. New York: D. Appleton-Century.
    1944   Peruvian Archaeology in 1942. Viking Fund Publ. Anthrop., No. 4.
Lesser, Alexander
    1939   Research Procedure and Laws of Culture. Philosophy of Science 6:345–
            355.

[24] Strong, 1943, p. 34.
[25] Kroeber, 1940, p. 477.

Lowie, Robert H.
1936   Cultural Anthropology: A Science. Amer. Journ. Soc. 42:301–320.
Malinowski, Bronislaw
1944   A Scientific Theory of Culture. University of North Carolina Press.
Morgan, Lewis H.
1910[1877]   Ancient Society. Chicago.
Redfield, Robert
1941   The Folk Culture of Yucatan. Chicago: University of Chicago Press.
1947   The Folk Culture. Journ. Amer. Soc. 52:293–308.
Steward, Julian H.
1936   The Economic and Social Basis of Primitive Bands. *In* Essays in Honor of
       A. L. Kroeber. Berkeley: University of California Press.
1937   Ecological Aspects of Southwestern Society. Anthropos 32:87–104.
1938   Basin-Plateau Aboriginal Socio-political Groups. Bur. Amer. Ethnol. Bull.
       120.
1940   Native Cultures of the Intermontane (Great Basin) Area. Essays in Histor-
       ical Anthropology of North America. Smithsonian Misc. Coll. 100:
       445–498.
Steward, Julian H. and Frank M. Setzler
1938   Function and Configuration in Archaeology. Amer. Antiquity 4:4–10.
Strong, Wm. Duncan
1943   Cross Sections of New World Prehistory. Smithsonian Misc. Coll. 104(2).
White, Leslie A.
1943   Energy and the Evolution of Culture. Amer. Anthropologist 45:335–356.
1945   Diffusion vs. Evolution: An Anti-Evolutionist Fallacy. Ibid. 47:339–356.
1947   Evolutionary Stages, Progress, and the Evaluation of Cultures. Southwest
       Journ. Anthrop. 3:165–192.
1947   The Expansion of the Scope of Science. Journ. Washington Acad. Sci.
       37:181–210.
Wittfogel, Karl A.
1935   The Foundations and Stages of Chinese Economic History. Zeitschriftfiir
       Sozialforschung 4:26–60. Paris.
1938   Die Theorie der Orientalischen Gesellschaft. Ibid. 7(1–2). Paris.
1939–1940   The Society of Prehistoric China. Studies in Philosophy and Social
       Science. Institute of Soc. Research 8:138–186.
1946   General Introduction to History of Chinese Society: Liao (907–1125), by
       Karl A. Wittfogel and Feng Chia-Sheng. Amer. Philos. Soc., trans. 36:1–35.

QUERIES

- According to Steward, what was the basic response to issues of "causality" by 20th-century American anthropologists?
- What are three essential requirements for a comparative study of cultural regularities?
- Summarize Steward's attack on "diffusion" as a causal explanation.

CONNECTIONS

- Steward argues that anthropology should "see through the differences of cultures to the similarities, to ascertain processes that are duplicated independently in cultural sequences, and to recognize cause and effect in both temporal and functional relationships." How does Steward's idea, however, differ from Radcliffe-Brown's call for a "scientific model" of social anthropology?
- In his discussion of Mesoamerican and Andean civilizations, Steward distinguishes between primary and basic features (for example, intensive farming) versus other secondary features (such as, worshipping a "jaguar god"). How would Marvin Harris explain these different sets of cultural practice?
- Contrast Steward's model of the development of New World civilizations with Leslie White's ideas about the evolution of culture.

15

Marvin Harris

INTRODUCTION

The American anthropologist Marvin Harris (1927–2001) articulated a consistent theoretical position throughout his career, a position he referred to as cultural materialism. Building on the insight in Karl Marx's *Critique of Political Economy* that "the mode of production in material life determines the general character of the social, political, and spiritual processes of life. It is not the consciousness of men that determines their existence, but, on the contrary, their social existence determines their consciousness," Harris argues that the material conditions of existence determined social relationships that, in turn, are reflected and reinforced by the realm of ideas, such as religion, worldview, and ideology. The material realm determined other dimensions of culture, which is the central concept to Harris's theory of cultural materialism (Moore 2008:204–16).

The application of Harris's theory of cultural materialism rests on a tripartite model. First, Harris argues that what anthropologists study are specific human populations interacting as members of society and sharing (and creating) a culture; this intersection of population/society/culture is referred to as a *sociocultural system*. Although articulated, each domain encompasses distinct sets of issues. For example, population is shaped by the mode of production (for example, matters linked to food-getting, adaptation to the environment, technology, and work patterns), and the mode of reproduction (issues that relate to birth and mortality, such as fertility, birth control, and longevity). The mode of production and mode of reproduction are combined into *infrastructure*. At the next level in Harris's model, the organization of people and goods occurs in two settings—the domestic economy (which relates to the order *within* units of consumption) and the political economy (which relates to the patterns of organization *between* units of consumption). Domestic economy and political economy are conflated under the term *structure*. Finally, the ideational realm—religion, worldview, cosmology, etc.—is referred to as *superstructure*. Because infrastructure is the essential way humans solve the essential problems of existence—getting food, maintaining their populations—infrastructure is the fundamental realm. Infrastructure determines structure, and structure determines superstructure, just as Marx had argued.

Harris's position is brilliantly deployed in the following article in which he uses the theory of cultural materialism to analyze the "fall" of the Soviet Union in 1985–1991. Arguing that anthropologists had an intellectual responsibility to address such an important social process, Harris insists that the fall of the Soviet Union had little to do with the incompetence of Soviet leadership, the "triumph of Democracy," or the cleverness of American foreign policy under then-presidents Ronald Reagan and George H. Bush. Instead, the Soviet Empire collapsed because its infrastructure collapsed (an argument documented in the section "Declining Efficiency of Soviet Infrastructure"). As infrastructure collapsed, the domestic economy and political economy unraveled, for example, leading to political unrest within Russia and nationalistic independence movements in distant republics and regions within the now-weakened Soviet empire. And while many commentators concluded that the collapse of the Soviet Empire indicated Marxism was "dead," Harris argues that Marx's central observation—the material conditions of existence determine the social, political, and spiritual dimensions of human life—accurately leads us to understand the collapse of the Soviet Union in terms of a theory of cultural materialism.

PRIMARY TEXT: *ANTHROPOLOGY AND THE THEORETICAL AND PARADIGMATIC SIGNIFICANCE OF THE COLLAPSE OF SOVIET AND EAST EUROPEAN COMMUNISM*

Reproduced by permission of the American Anthropological Association from *American Anthropologist*, Vol. 94 (2), 1992, pp. 295–305. www.aaanet.org. Not for sale or further reproduction. This essay was delivered as the Distinguished Lecture at the 90th annual meeting of the American Anthropological Association, November 23, 1991, in Chicago, Illinois. Footnotes edited from original.

Over the past decade, the political economy of state communism has been threatened with extinction throughout the former Soviet bloc.[1] The appara-

---

[1] According to the official line of the Communist party of the Soviet Union, the former USSR had attained the level of socialism in its ascent toward communism. I shall use the phrase "state communism" rather than "state socialism" or just plain "socialism," in order to emphasize the difference between the Soviet system and Western democratic socialist parties and governments.

tus of central planning and pricing; state ownership of the means of production; subsidies and redistributive entitlements; one-party rule; and state censorship have either been repudiated, eliminated, or substantially weakened and transformed. Currently, the members of the former Soviet bloc are frantically searching for ways to enlarge the sphere of profit-oriented market transactions and augment decentered forms of ownership (such as leasing, cooperatives, and outright privatization). This turn of events has led to a spectacle that few observers, West or East, ever expected to see in their lifetimes: Soviet leaders begging Japan and the West to buy up plants and facilities at fire-sale prices; apostate communists standing hat-in-hand outside of the International Monetary Fund, or traveling from one erstwhile capitalist enemy to another to plead for emergency food donations needed to ward off famine in the coming winter. Equally astonishing has been the destruction of the Soviet empire, shattered not by nuclear warheads from abroad but by explosive ethnic politics among its own peoples.

What do anthropologists have to say about all this? A branch of the human sciences that ignores these immense events, that interprets them exclusively in terms of relativized "local knowledge," or that derides the attempt to understand them in terms of nomothetic principles runs the risk of being confined to the backwaters of contemporary intellectual life. The purpose of this essay is to initiate a discussion among anthropologists of some salient theoretical and paradigmatic issues implicated by the abrupt end of state communism and Soviet hegemony. Of overriding interest in this connection is the impact of these events on Marxism and alternative forms of materialism.

Strategies for Saving Marxism

The collapse of state communism has understandably created the widespread conviction that Marxism is dead (e.g., Hollander 1990). Few would deny that the end of Soviet-style authoritarian state communism will exacerbate the problems of every government, party, or movement that identifies itself as following a Marxist, communist, or even a socialist program whether or not it is Marxist in origin (Heilbronner 1990; Howe 1990). But for many Marxists, these actual or impending political defeats do not necessarily translate into the refutation of classical (pre-Leninist) Marxist theories of history.

For some Western Marxists the collapse of the Soviet bloc does not even signify a serious challenge to Leninist versions of Marxism. They blame the collapse on political incompetence rather than on systemic failure. For example, according to Victor Perlo (1991:11), chairman of the Economics Commission of the Communist party (U.S.), the major problem is not Marxist theory but the breakdown in the unity of the Soviet Communist party. "Indeed, *without that division, the crisis could not have arisen*" (Perlo 1991:17, emphasis in original).

Other attempts to save Marxism contend in effect that state communism represents a distortion of Marx's program for achieving the transition to genuine communism. For example, while Marx and Engels envisioned a "dictatorship of the proletariat" as a phase in the transition from capitalism to communism (Draper 1987:26), the dictatorship they anticipated was that of the rule of proletarians as a class over their enemies, not the dictatorship of a ruling party over the proletariat. It is certainly difficult to find in the writings of Marx and Engels the idea that the transition to communism could only be achieved by a one-party dictatorship imposed on the workers.[2] In the words of the Executive Committee of the Socialist Party of Great Britain (1990:5):

> Something certainly has crumbled in Eastern Europe, but it has not been socialism, communism, or Marxism. For this to have happened, these would have had to exist there in the first place, but they did not. What did exist there—and what has crumbled—is Leninism and totalitarian state capitalism.

Similarly, one can reject the collapse of the Soviet bloc as a test of Marxist theories on the grounds that the Russian revolution itself violated Marx's fundamental prescription for a successful transition to communism. Russia, with its huge semifeudal peasantry, was the least appropriate locus for acting out Marx's revolutionary scenario. Thus, Marxists may argue that from its inception, Russian "communism" was an aberration, a terrible mistake. Since its rise and its despotic nature were neither advocated nor predicted by Marx, its fall can scarcely be regarded as a refutation of Marxism. In the words of economist Samuel Bowles, the recent revolutions in the former Soviet bloc "have removed a millstone from the neck of leftist economists in the West" (quoted in Wallich and Corcoran 1991:135). This line of reasoning even leads some Western Marxists to the verge of euphoria. They reason that Leninism-Stalinism was not merely a degenerate form of communism but its very negation. Its collapse therefore may allow "the authentic Marxist tradition, long driven underground, to return to the light of day" (Callinicos 1991:136). Now that the "muck" has been cleared away, real Marxism, which since the 1920s has been "persecuted and derided," can come into its own. "Now classical Marxism can finally shake itself free of the Stalinist incubus and seize the opportunities offered by a world experiencing greater uncertainty and agitation than for many decades" (Callinicos 1991:136).

In a similar mood, others see the collapse of state communism as but the latest in a series of temporary setbacks that have marked the history of Marxism, but from which the paradigm has always emerged, core principles

---

[2] If anything is established, it is that our party and the working class can come to power only under the form of the democratic republic. This is even the specific form for the dictatorship of the proletariat. [Engels quoted in Draper 1987:26.]

intact, and more compelling than ever. Sociologist Michael Burawoy, for example, argues that since Marxism provides a "fecund" understanding of capitalism's inherent contradictions and dynamics, the more capitalism flourishes throughout the world, the more Marxism will flourish with it: "With the ascendancy of capitalism on a world scale, Marxism will therefore, once more, come into its own . . . the longevity of capitalism guarantees the longevity of Marxism" (Burawoy 1990:791–92).

All of these attempts to insulate classical Marxist theories of history from the history of the Soviet Union have a hollow ring. Marx's most important historical theory, after all, was that capitalism was soon (certainly by the end of the 20th century) to be replaced by communism or a system that was transitional to communism. While it is virtually certain that the political economy toward which the former members of the Soviet bloc are evolving will not be the fictional, unrestrained, unregulated, free-market system promoted by capitalist ideologues, the revolutionary changes of the past decade cannot realistically be regarded as a harbinger of communism.[3] Indeed in the present political milieu the very word itself is as much of an electoral liability in the former Soviet bloc as in the West. Thus, 1990–91 must be added to the already extensive list of unanticipated and nonconforming events that falsify most of Marx's specific theories of history (for more examples, see below).

The Collapse and Cultural Materialism

Some may conclude that the crisis of Marxism (which I equate here with dialectical materialism or historical materialism), affects the credibility of materialist approaches in general. But, for cultural materialism, the transformations taking place have the opposite implication since its basic theoretical principle—the primacy of infrastructure—provides a cogent processual interpretation of the events in question. I shall state this principle as concisely as I can before applying it to the Soviet bloc collapse.

Let me begin with a reassurance: infrastructural, structural, and symbolic-ideational features are equally necessary components of human social life.[4] It

---

[3] "It cannot be denied that while a powerful popular commitment to socialist values remains, there are few signs that this commitment is the basis of any significant movement for the construction of a new form of democratic socialism. The widespread rejection of statism, and widespread demands for autonomy and for democratic accountability, take the predominant form of the demand for the restoration of the market, rather than for the democratisation of systems of planning, and for the democratisation of the state, rather than for its abolition" [Clarke 1990:21–22].

[4] In substituting the phrase "symbolic-ideational" for the term "superstructure," I do not intend to introduce any substantial changes in cultural-materialist principles. The change is purely literary and tactical: literary, because people get bored by the incantational refrain, "infrastructure, structure, and superstructure"; and tactical, because "superstructure" tends to encourage critics in their mistaken belief that the symbolic-ideational components are being relegated to a superficial or superfluous role in human social life.

is no more possible to imagine a human society without a symbolic-ideational or structural sector than it is possible to imagine one without a mode of production and reproduction. Nonetheless, these sectors do not play a symmetrical role in influencing the retention or extinction of sociocultural innovations (see Harris 1991, 1992 for a review of relevant principles and studies). Infrastructure here (in contrast to Marxist formulations of "base") encompasses technological, economic, demographic, and environmental activities and conditions directly linked to sustaining health and well-being through the social control of production and reproduction. Innovations that arise in the infrastructural sector are likely to be preserved and propagated if they enhance productive and reproductive efficiency under specific environmental conditions. And innovations that meet these conditions are likely to be selected for, even if there is a marked incompatibility between them and preexisting structural relationships or symbolic-ideational themes. Moreover, the resolution of any deep incompatibility between an adaptive infrastructural innovation and the preexisting features of the other sectors will predictably consist of substantial changes in those other sectors. In contrast, innovations of a structural or symbolic-ideational nature are likely to be selected against if there is any deep incompatibility between them and infrastructure—that is to say, if they reduce the efficiency of the productive and reproductive processes that sustain health and well-being.

A logical entailment of this principle is that, given similar evolved infrastructural conditions in different societies, one can expect convergence toward similar structural relationships and symbolic-ideational features.

Let me quickly add the proviso that I do not believe that all structural and symbolic-ideational features are subject to infrastructural cost-benefit reckonings. Clearly there are many instances in which structural and symbolic-ideational features are adaptively neutral or functionally equivalent, and capable of persisting tenaciously across the most fundamental sorts of infrastructural transformations and of influencing each other without feedback to infrastructure. Even in infrastructure there is more than one way to shape an effective projectile, fashion a serviceable pot, design a computer program, or in the vernacular, skin a cat. I have never denied that there are specific structural relationships and symbolic-ideational features whose understanding is best provided by historical, idiographic, interpretive, or hermeneutical studies. Rather, I have argued that such relationships and features cannot be identified a priori and that, therefore, claims for their existence must be subjected to rigorous scrutiny.

Declining Efficiency of Soviet Infrastructure

The immediately relevant portion of the principle of the primacy of infrastructure—which I have presented here in a necessarily compressed and,

I hope, merciful manner—is that the political-economic (i.e., structural) and symbolic-ideational innovations introduced in the name of Marxist materialism are in the process of being selected against because they resulted in a stagnant, declining, or increasingly inefficient infrastructure.

State communism failed because it decreased the efficiency of its smoke-stack-type infrastructure and inhibited the application of high-tech innovations to the solution of a deepening technological, demographic, environmental, and economic crisis.

The general outlines of this failure are well known and I shall limit myself to just a few highlights. On the eve of perestroika, the Soviet Union's basic energy supply was in deep trouble (Kuhnert 1991:493). Coal and oil production were stagnant during 1980–84 (Kuhnert 1991:494). Generating plants and transmission lines were antiquated and in a state of disrepair as manifested in frequent breakdowns and blackouts (not to mention Chernobyl). In the agricultural sector, grain production, adjusted for weather conditions, remained about the same in the 1980s as in the previous decade, despite heavy investment (IMF 1990:138). Two-thirds of agricultural processing equipment in use during the 1980s was worn out, with much of it dating back to the 1950s and 1960s (IMF 1990:51).

From 20 per cent to 50 per cent of the grain, potato, sugar beet, and fruit crops were lost before they got to the store (Goldman 1987:37). Even where supplies were adequate, delays in delivery resulted in temporary shortages, resulting in long lines, hoarding, and spot rationing.

Between 1970 and 1987, output per unit of input declined at a rate of more than 1 per cent per year (Gregory and Stuart 1990:147). On the eve of perestroika, there was general agreement from Gorbachev on down that economic growth per capita was zero or negative (Nove 1989:394).

An even more dismal view of the performance of the Soviet infrastructure emerges when the costs of pollution and environmental depletions are subtracted from the national product. Every conceivable form of pollution and resource depletion exists in life-threatening amounts, ranging from uncontrolled sulfur dioxide emissions, to nuclear and other forms of hazardous waste sites, oil erosion, poisoning of Lake Baikal, the Black, Baltic, and Caspian Seas, and the drying up of the Aaral Sea (IMF 1990). It is probably not a coincidence that, as Feshbach (1983) reports, life expectancy for Soviet males was also declining on the eve of perestroika.

Moreover, the Soviet bloc lagged far behind the West in the application of high-tech innovations to the production of nonmilitary goods. By the 1980s, diffusion of technological innovations throughout the economy was taking three times longer in the Soviet Union than in the West (Gregory and Stuart 1990:411). Civilian telecommunications, information processing, and biotechnology remained in a rudimentary state. A telling statistic in this regard is that more than 100,000 villages in the Soviet Union still have no telephone service (IMF 1990:125). The Soviet Union's civilian economy not only lacked computers, but industrial robots, electronic copiers, optical scanners, and many other information-processing devices that had already become the dominant features of Japanese and Western industrialism fifteen or more years earlier.

Structural Incompatibilities

How state communism impeded the development of Soviet bloc infrastructures is also well known and I shall assume that a brief summary is sufficient to make the point. A prime source of infrastructural malfunctioning derived from the inherent limitations of the centrally planned and centrally administered command economy and its immense bureaucracy. At the enterprise level, managers were kept under close scrutiny by bureau chiefs in order to assure conformity with a massive list of rules and regulations that had various unintended consequences. The amount of money made available to an enterprise for incentive bonuses was determined by the number of workers it employed and this led to the hiring of large numbers of unneeded workers (IMF 1990:31). Quotas were also stipulated in crude quantitative terms, resulting in the production of poor-quality goods.

Crude quantitative indices were also an invitation to fulfill quotas by fakery. "Since salaries, bonuses and promotions depend on achieving the plan, the temptation, indeed the pressure, of the centrally planned system is to fake the output" (Armstrong 1989:24). A persistent source of inefficiency in the state communist command structure, as recently described by Katherine Verdery (1991:422) for Eastern Europe, are the "soft budgets" enjoyed by firms and enterprises. This means that the penalties for inefficient and irrational management, such as excess inventory, overemployment, and excess investment, were minimal and did not lead to the extinction of an enterprise. Firms that operated at a loss could always count on subsidies that would bail them out (Verdery 1991:422).

> Because of this, and because central plans usually overstate productive capacities and raise output targets higher and higher each year, firms learn to hoard materials and labor. They overstate their material requirements for production, and they overstate their investment needs, in hopes of having enough to meet or even surpass their assigned production targets. (Verdery 1991:422)

These practices locked up productive resources which could have been put to better use by other enterprises and contributed to the peculiar economy of shortages and interminable queuing that beset the Soviet bloc, as well as to the hypertrophy of the second or informal economy, with its moonlighting, personalism, and pervasive petty corruption down to "the clerk who hides goods under the counter for friends and relatives or for a bribe" (Verdery 1991:423).

The command structure of state communism in general also acted as a drag on technological innovation and on its uptake into the system. The slow pace of technological change reflects in part a general malaise induced by unrelenting pressure to conform to orders from above. More specifically, however, the structure of the command economy lacked sufficient incentives for innovative behavior. There were few rewards for enterprise managers who introduced new and more efficient production processes or products (Berliner 1976; Gregory and Stuart 1990:213). Furthermore, reduction of labor inputs achieved by improved technologies were unlikely to add to an enterprise's "profits" but would, in conformity with the official labor theory of value, get passed along to the consumer in the form of lower prices (Gregory and Stuart 1990:221). The command structure of the Soviet bloc political economy was particularly incompatible with a transition to high-tech industrialism with its devices that create, store, retrieve, copy, and transmit information at high speeds over national and international networks. The operation of such networks presupposes a large degree of freedom for individuals to exchange information both vertically and horizontally. It also presumes telephone lines and high-speed switching systems that can handle the computer-assisted information flowing in every direction between individuals and organizations. But the command structure of state communism was designed to avoid the rapid exchange of information not subject to censorship and party supervision. Indeed, the low priority assigned to the development of a modern telephone network expressed the insecurity of the Communist party more than a lack of technical know-how and resources. And the same can be said of the practice of putting locks on the few computers used by civilian enterprises and of making the unauthorized possession of a copying machine a crime against the state.

The Nationalist Surge

If only in passing, permit me to suggest that the general infrastructural debacle also goes a long way toward explicating the nationalist and separatist surge that has led to the breakup of the Soviet empire. The redistributive functions of the center were not only discharged badly but unevenly. Profound differences in rates of productivity, GNP, damage to the environment, and rates of population growth permeated the Union. The Central Asian and Transcaucus republics bore the brunt of the infrastructural crisis with rampant unemployment and decreasing per capita consumption of meat and dairy products. Perhaps the most telling statistic here is that in the 1970s–1980s the level of infant mortality increased in Uzbekistan, Turkmenia, and Kazakhstan by 48 per cent, 22 per cent, and 14 per cent, respectively (Illarianov 1990:9). Although the least-developed republics received subsidies from the center, the transfers were obviously insufficient. Convinced that the center was taking out more than it was putting in, the republics with the most developed infrastructures, such as the Baltic group and Ukraine, were convinced that their living standards were being depressed by the center's favoritism toward ethnic Russians and the Russian Republic, and hence that they would advance to Western standards once they were free of the Soviet incubus.

I do not, even in this brief compass, wish to minimize the role of ethnic and linguistic sentiments in mobilizing and sustaining the independence movements. Rather, the point is that these sentiments were not simply sustained by the force of history and tradition but by the stagnant or deteriorating material circumstances in which people found themselves at a particular moment in their history.

So there you have it: the collapse of state communism and the Soviet empire as a case of selection against a political economy that increasingly impeded and degraded the performance of its infrastructure.

"Politics in Command"

Let me point out, in advance of my critics, that the evidence for concluding that the Soviet bloc's collapse is an example of the primacy of infrastructure is not as clear-cut as I would like it to be. One could still argue, following Perlo (1991), that the collapse was the consequence of a bad run of leaders who lacked the requisite managerial skills and determination to hold the system together. Indeed, some may wish to advance the thesis that the history of state communism actually disproves the primacy of infrastructure. Since the Soviet command economy lasted for 70 years, the case shows nothing so much as that infrastructure is the dependent variable and that "politics are in command." In rebuttal, I would maintain that the symptoms of infrastructural deterioration were not present throughout most of this period. Twenty-five to thirty years is more like it, since after World War II, Soviet economic growth was fast enough to warrant Nikita Khrushchev's projection that the communist standard of living would exceed that of the United States by 1970 and that capitalism would be buried before the end of the century (Frankland 1967:149–50). Nonetheless, we are talking about a significant number of years, which I shall not try to discount by appealing to archeological time-scales.

The paradigmatic advantage of the primacy of infrastructure over "politics in command" does not lie simply in the demonstration that, sooner or later, politics that subvert infrastructural performance are selected against. Rather it lies in the additional claim that, under similar infrastructural conditions, structural and symbolic-ideational features evolve along convergent paths, whereas "politics in command" is inherently indifferent to any principled explanation of the direction of change. Thus, the test of the primacy of infrastructure lies not only in the Soviet bloc's collapse, but in the kinds of societies that will replace the discredited communist model. If the collapse is really nonsystemic and accountable only in terms of individual choice and counterchoice, of the exercise of power and the resistance to power, then the forms of social life that will arise from the ruins of communism should diverge widely from each other and from the evolving forms of industrial societies everywhere, not excluding the possibility of a return to Leninist-Stalinist regimes. On the other hand, if the collapse is actually part of a process that is bringing the structural and symbolic-ideational components into systemic alignment with post-smokestack industrial infrastructures, then we should expect to see the industrialized Soviet republics and Eastern Europe converging toward systems similar to those emerging in the advanced industrial societies of Europe, Japan, and the United States. The belief that such a convergence would take place (despite its implications of Marxist determinism [Gellner 1990]) was widely promoted in the West during the 1960s (Kerr 1960; Galbraith 1967; Sorokin 1961; Form 1979) and to a lesser extent in the East (Sakharov 1970). By 1980, however, given the apparently permanent presence of the Soviet Union as an industrial giant and military superpower, the conviction reigned, as much in the East as in the West, that the twain would never meet (Kerr 1983).[5] On the eve of perestroika it was being said in the West that "such claims [for convergence] seem absurd" (Davis and Scase 1985:5). And as late as 1989, a leading reform-minded Soviet economist called convergence a "phantom," insisting that the change in organizational-technological and managerial relations in the Soviet Union "does not attest to the . . . formation of any kind of mixed system" (Shishkov 1989:26). But with elections, privatization, stock markets, "market socialism," and globalization being endorsed throughout the former communist bloc, it is the notion of unblendable systems that has become a phantom.

Marx Again

If Marxism is to maintain any credibility, it must be stripped of most of the theories that lie at the core of its classical canon. But is there anything left to Marxism after one strips away such theoretical ghosts as the implacable miseration of the proletariat; the development of working-class consciousness; the subordination of gender and ethnic interests to class unity; the irreconcilability of class interests; the inevitable triumph of the proletariat; the unblendable natures of capitalism and communism; and the dialectical certainty that communism will replace capitalism? Yes indeed, for there still

---

[5] Returning to take a second look at the relationship between political and economic structures and industrialism after 20 years of the Cold War, Kerr (1983:74) concluded that industrialism was "at least minimally compatible with more than a single economic or political structure—with plan or with market and with mixtures of the two, and with monopoly of and with competition for political power, and with mixtures of the two."

remains the fact that the principle of the primacy of infrastructure is a derivative, if substantially modified version of a fundamental part of the classic Marxist paradigm. I cannot refrain from pointing out that Marx's most famous description of the engine of history applies with uncanny precision to what is taking place in the former Soviet bloc. In the Preface to the Critique of Political Economy, Marx wrote:

> At a certain stage of development the material productive forces of society come into conflict with the existing relations of production or—this merely expresses the same thing in legal terms—with the property relations within the framework of which they have operated hitherto. From forms of development of the productive forces these relations turn into their fetters. Then begins an era of social revolution. [Marx 1970:21]

Thus it is the singularly ironic fate of Marxism that through its materialist core it is able to explain its own demise.

A Disclaimer

Having examined the relationship between the political economy of state communism and some of the main failings of Soviet bloc infrastructures, I wish to dissociate myself from the view that the collapse of state communism proves that capitalism is the "end of history" (Fukuyama 1989) or that "capitalism has won" (Tobin 1991:5). Although the malfunctions of neo-capitalist systems remain less intense than the malfunctions of the Soviet bloc, they are nonetheless a source of great instability and pressure for change. Both systems have created life-threatening environmental hazards and depletions; both are plagued by ethnic and racial conflicts; both have severe housing problems; both suffer from bureaucratic hypertrophy; both are riddled with corruption, misinformation, and deception in high places; both have endangered the survival of the species with their nuclear weaponry; and both are prodigiously wasteful of human energy and talent, as can be seen in the recurrent crises of unemployment and overproduction for which capitalism has yet to find a remedy. A system that is so egregiously flawed cannot represent the end point of history.

It is not merely capitalism's unresolved problems that guarantee the continued evolution of novel sociocultural forms and arrangements in the West as well as in the collapsed Soviet bloc. Massive changes within the capitalist infrastructure associated with declining fertility rates, aging population profiles, environmental hazards, the expansion of service and information-production, robotization, new computer-assisted design and manufacturing techniques, satellite transmissions, jumbo jets, and bioengineering have already elicited a new generation of far-ranging modifications in political economy and symbolic-ideational themes among the leading capitalist countries. These include the unprecedented spread and interpenetration of transnational corporations; the appearance of the firm without a country; the emergence of hetero-consumerism (Colson and Kottak 1990; Levitt 1991) as the world's most popular ideology; the development of supranational trade blocks such as the European Community; and the deepening crisis and uneven development of the Third World. Anthropology will find it increasingly difficult to justify its existence if it categorically rejects attempts to combine the study of the local microcosm with the study of these and other global phenomena.

In conclusion, I would like to offer one additional assurance: it does not follow from the primacy of infrastructure that the material restraints imposed on the rest of social life diminish our freedom to intervene and direct the selection of alternate futures. For along with the restraints come opportunities—opportunities for innovations that can broaden and deepen the benefits of social life for all of humankind. Recognition of the primacy of infrastructure does not diminish the importance of conscious human agency.[6] Rather, it merely increases the importance of having robust theories of history that can guide conscious human choice. If there is one thing that the history of the Soviet bloc demonstrates, it is that conscious interventions and empowerments carried out under the auspices of inadequately developed macro theories of sociocultural evolution readily lead to catastrophic, unintended consequences. It is true that knowledge is always contested, and it is true that by itself, as so many anthropologists have recently maintained, knowledge does not guarantee freedom; but there can be no freedom without it.

BIBLIOGRAPHY

Armstrong, G. Patrick
   1989   Gorbachev's Nightmare. Crossroads 29:21–30.
Berliner, Joseph S.
   1976   The Innovation Decision in Soviet Industry. Cambridge: MIT Press.
Burawoy, Michael
   1990   Marxism as Science: Historical Challenges and Theoretical Growth. American Sociological Review 55:775–793.
Callinicos, Alex
   1991   The Revenge of History: Marxism and the East European Revolutions. Oxford: Polity Press.

---

[6] See Cotieri (1988) for a sustained philosophical analysis of the relation between determinist theories of history and human agency.

Clarke, Simori
  1990 Crisis of Socialism or the Crisis of the State Capital and Class. 42(Winter):19–29.
Cohen, Gerald A.
  1978 Karl Marx's Theory of History: A Defense. Princeton, NJ: Princeton University Press.
  1988 History, Labour and Freedom: Themes from Marx. New York: Oxford University Press.
Colson, Elizabeth, and Conrad Kottak
  1990 Multi-level Linkages and Longitudinal Studies. Paper presented at the 89th annual meeting of the American Anthropological Association, New Orleans, LA.
Davis, Howard, and Richard Scase
  1985 Western Capitalism and State Socialism: An Introduction. Oxford: Basil Blackwell.
Draper, Hal
  1987 The "Dictatorship of the Proletariat" from Marx to Lenin. New York: Monthly Review.
Executive Committee of the Socialist Party of Great Britain
  1990 Socialism Has Not Failed. Socialist Standard 86 (January):2–6.
Feshbach, Murray
  1983 Issues in Soviet Health Problems. *In* Soviet Economy in the 1980s: Problems and Prospects. Selected papers submitted to the Joint Economic Committee, Congress of the United States, December 31, 1982. Washington, DC: Government Printing Office.
Form, William
  1979 Comparative Industrial Sociology and the Convergence Hypothesis. Annual Review of Sociology 5:1–25.
Frankland, Mark
  1967 Khruschev. New York: Stein and Day.
Fukuyama, Francis
  1989 The End of History? National Interest 16 (Summer):3–18.
  1990 A Reply to My Critics. National Interest (Winter):26–28.
Galbraith, John Kenneth
  1967 The New Industrial State. Boston: Houghton Mifflin.
Gellner, Ernest
  1990 The Theory of History: East and West. Slavic Review (April–September):141–150.
Goldman, Marshall I.
  1987 Gorbachev's Challenge: Economic Reform in the Age of High Technology. New York: W. W. Norton.
Gregory, Paul R., and Robert C. Stuart
  1990 Soviet Economic Structure and Performance. 4th ed. New York: Harper and Row.
Harris, Marvin
  1991 Anthropology: Ships That Crash in the Night. *In* Perspectives on Social Science: The Colorado Lectures. Richard Jessor, ed. Pp. 70–114. Boulder, CO: Westview Press.

1992   Cultural Materialism Is Alive and Well. *In* Assessing Anthropology. Robert Borofsky, ed. New York: McGraw-Hill.

Heilbronner, Robert
1990   The World after Communism. Dissent (Fall):429–432.

Hollander, Paul
1990   Communism's Collapse Won't Faze the Marxists in Academe. Chronicle of Higher Education, May 23:1244.

Howe, Irving
1990   Some Dissenting Comments. Dissent (Fall):432–435.

Illarianov, A.
1990   Eurasian Market. Twentieth Century and Peace (June):7–11.

IMF (International Monetary Fund)
1990   The Economy of the USSR: Summary and Recommendations. Washington, DC: World Bank.

Kerr, Clark
1960   Industrialism and Industrial Man: The Problems of Labor and Management in Economic Growth. Cambridge, MA: Harvard University Press.
1983   The Future of Industrial Societies: Convergence or Continuing Diversity? Cambridge, MA: Harvard University Press.

Kuhnert, Caroline
1991   More Power for the Soviets: Perestroika and Energy. Soviet Studies 43(3):491–506.

Levitt, Theodore
1991   Thinking about Management. New York: Free Press.

Marx, Karl
1970   A Contribution to the Critique of Political Economy. New York: International Publishers.

Miller, Richard W.
1981   Productive Forces and the Forces of Change: A Review of Gerald A. Cohen, Karl Marx's Theory of History: A Defense. Philosophical Review (January):91–117.

Niebuhr, R. Gustav
1991   Fatima Fever: Did Mary Prophesy Soviet Goings-On? Wall Street Journal, September 27:1.

Nove, Alec
1989   An Economic History of the U.S.S.R. London: Penguin Books.

Perlo, Victor
1991   The Economic and Political Crisis in the USSR. Political Affairs 70 (August):10–18.

Sakharov, Andrei
1970   Progress, Coexistence, Intellectual Freedom. New York: W. W. Norton.

Shishkov, I. V.
1989   Perestroika and the Phantom of Convergence. Problems of Economics 32:6–28.

Sorokin, P. A.
1961   Mutual Convergence of the United States and the USSR to the Mixed Sociological Type. Mexico City: Costa-Amic.

Tobin, James
  1991   The Adam Smith Address. Business Economics 26(1):5–17.
Verdery, Katherine
  1991   Theorizing Socialism: A Prologue to the "Transition." American Ethnologist 18:419–439.
Wallich, Paul, and Elizabeth Corcoran
  1991   The Analytical Economist: Don't Write Off Marx. Scientific American 264(2):135.

QUERIES

- Summarize the various explanations for the collapse of the Soviet Union. What is Harris's response to those explanations?
- Does the "crisis of Marxism" discredit cultural materialism? What is Harris's answer?
- Given the causal primacy of infrastructure in the theory of cultural materialism, does Harris consider the realms of structure and superstructure to be irrelevant?
- Summarize the evidence Harris presents regarding the collapse of Soviet infrastructure. What were some of its consequences in reference to the mode of production and mode of reproduction?
- How did the structural components of Soviet state communism impede and worsen declines in infrastructure?
- Harris concludes by arguing that the "primacy of infrastructure . . . [does not] . . . diminish our freedom to intervene and direct the selection of alternate futures." Explain Harris's position.

CONNECTIONS

- In the second paragraph of the article, Harris criticizes anthropologists who interpret cultural patterns "exclusively in terms of relativized 'local knowledge'"—a swipe at the interpretive anthropologist Clifford Geertz who wrote a 1983 book titled *Local Knowledge: Further Essays in Interpretive Anthropology* (see Moore 2008:259–72). Why does Harris think that the theory of cultural materialism is more useful than Geertz's notion of "local knowledge"? How would Geertz respond?
- Despite both being materialist theories of human culture, in what ways does Harris's theory of cultural materialism differ from White's theory of cultural evolution?

16

Eleanor Burke Leacock

INTRODUCTION

The following article by American anthropologist Eleanor Burke Leacock (1922–1987) exemplifies her theoretical position characterized by Marxist feminism. Leacock's initial research was among the Montagnais-Naskapi of Labrador, and her work focused on the role of private property vs. communal ownership in this hunting society (see Moore 2008:219–21). While such issues had been extensively discussed by Frederich Engels and Karl Marx, it simply was too dangerous to mention Marxist theorists during the red-baiting of the 1950s McCarthy era. Only later was it possible to openly articulate Marxist theoretical positions without professional consequences, and Leacock articulated her position in a series of influential articles and book chapters.

Although Leacock's research considered a variety of ethnographic cases and issues, she most consistently considered the transformation of gender roles in traditional societies altered by capitalism. In this she extended an analytical line not only found in Marx and Engels, but also more broadly in Lewis Henry Morgan's *Ancient Society*: changes in property relationships have corresponding consequences for social structure. In this Leacock's position is thus a form of materialist explanation.

In the article "Women's Status in Egalitarian Society: Implications for Social Evolution," Leacock criticizes anthropologists for assuming that the societies they study were unaffected by historical processes, treating societies like the Montagnais-Naskapi as if they were unchanging representatives of a pristine, primitive past. More specifically, Leacock challenges the conclusion that women's status was inferior to men's status in all human societies. Drawing on her own ethnographic and historical research, Leacock argues that women's status among the Montagnais-Naskapi deteriorated as that society became enmeshed in capitalism. Prior to that, women's work was valued, and they controlled resources. Women's roles were different from men's but not less valued. Yet this changed as the Montagnais-Naskapi relied on the income from fur trading. Work shifted from producing for consumption to producing for commodity exchange, and in the process women's work was undervalued, gender roles were dichotomized, and women were deprived of autonomy. In the case of the Montagnais-Naskapi this was accompanied by Jesuit missionaries who undermined women's status as they converted natives to a patriarchal Catholicism.

Nor was this only true of the Montagnais-Naskapi, as Leacock shows that similar processes occurred among other band societies. Women's inferior status was a historical creation, not a universal pattern among egalitarian band societies. As Leacock concludes, anthropologists should not assume that the patterned inequalities in developed societies are present in incipient form in egalitarian band societies. Rather, gender inequalities are created when property relations change and the divisions between men and women become hierarchical.

PRIMARY TEXT: *WOMEN'S STATUS IN EGALITARIAN SOCIETY: IMPLICATIONS FOR SOCIAL EVOLUTION*

From *Current Anthropology*, Vol. 19(2), 1978, pp. 247–275. Reprinted with permission of the University of Chicago Press.

The analysis of women's status in egalitarian society is inseparable from the analysis of egalitarian social-economic structure as a whole, and concepts based on the hierarchical structure of our society distort both. To see relations of power and property that characterize our society as present in band societies, although extremely weak, obscures the qualitatively different relations that obtained when, in place of dyadic lines of dependency, each individual was dependent upon the group as a whole, "public" and "private" spheres were not dichotomized, and decisions were made by and large by those who would be carrying them out.

Assumptions of female subservience in egalitarian society both derive from and perpetuate a view of such society as merely an incipient form of our own. This problem, along with ethnocentric reporting of data, leads to contradictory ethnographic accounts of women's status among hunter-gatherers, as illustrated by material on Australian Aborigines and on the Ojibwa. Similar problems obtain for the more elaborated but still egalitarian Iroquois.

The failure to deal historically with changes in egalitarian societies as they became involved in the "capitalist world system," recently discussed by Wallerstein, further compounds problems of analyzing their structure. As a result of these various difficulties, the fundamental transformation in women's status that accompanied ranking and hierarchy is commonly obscured. However, an understanding of egalitarian society as based on production for use and control by the producers over their work lays the basis for examining the linked processes proposed by Engels, whereby specialization of labor and production for exchange led to private property, class differences, and the subservience of women in the economic family unit.

The analysis of women's status in egalitarian society is inseparable from the analysis of egalitarian social-economic structure as a whole, and concepts based on the hierarchical structure of our society distort both. I shall argue that the tendency to attribute to band societies the relations of power and property characteristic of our own obscures the qualitatively different relations that obtained when ties of economic dependency linked the individual directly with the group as a whole, when public and private spheres were not dichotomized, and when decisions were made by and large by those who would be carrying them out. I shall attempt to show that a historical approach and an avoidance of ethnocentric phraseology in the study of such societies reveal that their egalitarianism applied as fully to women as to men. Further, I shall point out that this is a fact of great importance to the understanding of social evolution.

Demonstrating that women's status in egalitarian society was qualitatively different from that in our own presents problems at several levels. First, the societies studied by anthropologists are virtually all in some measure incorporated into world economic and political systems that oppress women, and most have been involved in these larger systems for centuries. Anthropologists know this historical reality well, but commonly ignore it when making generalizations about preclass social economic systems.

A second problem follows from the selectivity of research. Too many questions about women have not been asked, or not of the right people, and gaps in ethnographic reports are too readily filled with clichés. To handle women's participation in a given society with brief remarks about food preparation and childcare has until very recently met the requirements for adequate ethnography. Hence a once over lightly of cross-cultural data can readily affirm the virtual universality of the Western ideal for women's status. Ethnocentric interpretation contributes to this affirmation. Women are commonly stated or implied to hold low status in one or another society without benefit of empirical documentation. Casual statements about menstrual blood as polluting and as contributing to women's inferior status may be made without linguistic or other supporting data to demonstrate that this familiarly Western attitude of repugnance actually obtains in the culture under discussion.

A further problem for the analysis of women's status in egalitarian society is theoretical. That women were autonomous in egalitarian society that is, that they held decision-making power over their own lives and activities to the same extent that men did over theirs cannot be understood unless the nature of individual autonomy in general in such society is clear. (I prefer the term "autonomy" to "equality," for equality connotes rights and opportunity specific to class society and confuses similarity with equity. Strictly speaking, who can be, or wants to be, "equal" to anyone else?) Non-class based societies are usually not seen as qualitatively different from those that are class organized when it comes to processes of leadership and decision-making. Differences are seen as purely quantitative, and the possibility that altogether different sets of relationships from those involving economic power might be operating in non-class society is not followed through. Instead, as a result of intellectual habits that stem from Platonic metaphysical traditions, universalistic categories are set up on the basis of individual behavior and are named, counted, described, or otherwise reified by the failure to move on to a discovery of the social-economic processes that lie behind them.

It is difficult to apply the principle that all reality involves interacting processes, and not interacting "essences" or things. Respects may be paid to the concepts of process and conflict, which may then be reified as well. Since these reified concepts are derived from our own culture, it is no accident that hierarchical patterns similar to our own are found to be "incipient" wherever they are not well established. From band to tribe, tribe to chiefdom, chiefdom to state, the development of decision-making processes is seen quantitatively as progressive change toward Western forms of power and control. Fundamental qualitative distinctions between egalitarian and class societies are lost. A hierarchical view of sex roles fits easily into the scheme. That sex roles exist is, after all, a human universal, and to assume that any difference between the sexes necessarily involves hierarchy is seen, not as ethnocentrism, but as common sense.

The reification of the concept "tribe," pointed out by Fried (1968, 1975), affords a good example of what I mean. Fried argues that insofar as tribes exist as culturally and territorially bounded and politically integrated groupings of bands or villages, they are the creatures of colonial relations. However, for want of a clear conception as to what might replace it, the term "tribe" continues in use and fosters the misconception that egalitarian peoples were organized in closed territorially defined units, uniformly obeying the mandates of custom and controlled by the authority, weak though it might be, of a chief and/or council. The structure is not merely "cold" it is positively frozen. In reality, people were far more cosmopolitan than the term "tribesmen" suggests. They moved about, traded and negotiated, and constantly chose among the various alternatives for action.

In relation to the study of sex roles, the core of tribal structure is commonly seen in terms of unilineal agnatic systems that represent formal, jural authority, as counterposed to the "familial" sphere of influence accorded to women. The polarization of public male authority and private female influence is taken as a given of the human condition. Thereby areas in which women exercised socially recognized authority are obscured or downgraded. The reality of the distinction between unilineal and segmenting kinship systems has recently been questioned on the basis of comparison of Melanesian and African data (Barnes 1971; Keesing 1971). It is my contention that the public-private dichotomy is similarly inadequate for understanding societies that are (or were) not structured along class lines. Instead, insofar as social processes of the precolonial world can be reconstructed, the delineation and opposition of public and private spheres can be seen as emergent in many culture areas, where individual families were becoming more or less competitive units in conflict with the communality of family, bands or kin groups. Furthermore, the complex of processes involved, concerning specialization, exchange, and the expenditure of labor on land, together constituted initial steps toward class differentiation. Although the accidents of history caused these processes to become thoroughly entangled with colonial relations throughout the world, some of their essential outlines can still be defined through ethnohistorical research and comparative analysis.

In the case of foraging societies, the control women exercised over their own lives and activities is widely, if not fully, accepted as ethnographic fact. However, assumptions of a somehow lower status and deferential stance toward "dominant" men are made by most writers on the subject. The very existence of different roles for females and males is seen as sufficient explanation, given women's responsibility for childbearing and suckling. The possibility that women and men could be "separate but equal" is seldom considered, albeit not surprisingly, since it seems to tally with the adjuration to women in our society to appreciate the advantages of the liabilities maternity here incurs. That an equal status for women could be interwoven with childbearing is a notion that has only begun to be empirically examined (Draper 1975).

My point is that concepts of band organization must be reexamined if the nature of women's autonomy in foraging societies is to be understood. To describe the band as "familistic" (Service 1966:8) or "only a simple association of families" (Sahlins 1961:324) may serve in a rough and ready way to convey something of the non-hierarchical and informal character of social-economic life among foragers, but it implies a universal "family" to be at the core of all society. Such a view of the band, whether implicit or explicit, leaves no alternative than for sex roles in band society to present a glimmer of what was to develop in class society. It implies historical evolution to be a continuum in which social forms become quantitatively more and more like those we experience, rather than to be constituted by a series of qualitative transformations, in the course of which relations between the sexes could have become altogether different.

To argue the point of sexual egalitarianism, then, involves a combination of theoretical and empirical reexamination. In the following pages, I shall give several examples of what I think is called for. The materials are everywhere at hand; they form the corpus of the ethnographic record.

The Band

As a student of the Montagnais-Naskapi people of the Labrador Peninsula, some 25 years ago, I looked at changing relations to the land and its resources among hunters turned fur-trappers and traders. At that time I confronted the fact that the band as then conceived (Speck 1926:277–78) a rather neat entity, with a leader, a name, and a more or less bounded territory had simply not existed in the past. Missionaries, traders, and government representatives alike bemoaned its absence and did what they could to bring it into existence, while the fur trade itself exerted its inevitable influence. "It would be wrong to infer . . . that increasing dependence on trade has acted to destroy formerly stable social groups," I wrote at that time. Instead, "changes brought about by the fur trade have led to more stable bands with greater formal organization" (Leacock 1954:20). The Jesuit Relations, when analyzed in detail, reveal the 17th century Montagnais-Naskapi band to have been, not a loose collection of families, but a seasonal coalition of smaller groups that hunted cooperatively through most of the winter. These groups, in turn, were made up of several lodge groups that stayed together when they could, but separated when it was necessary to cover wider ranges for hunting. The lodge groups of several families, not individual families, were the basic social-economic units (Leacock 1969; Rogers 1972:133). Among foraging peoples, seasonal patterns of aggregation and dispersal vary according to the ecological features of different areas and the specific technologies employed to exploit them (Cox 1973; Damas 1969). However, that aggregates of several families operate as basic social-economic units which coalesce with and separate from other such units remains constant. These aggregates are highly flexible. Congeniality as well as viable age and sex ratios are fundamental to their makeup; kin ties are important but do not rule out friendships; and when formal kinship is important, as in Australia, the focus is on categorical relationships that define expectations for reciprocity, rather than on genealogical linkages that define status prerogatives.

Distinctions between bands of this sort and bands as they have come to exist may seem slight, but in fact they are profound. The modern band consists of loosely grouped nuclear families that are economically dependent to one extent or another on trade or work outside of the group or on some governmental allowance or missionary provisioning. Therefore the modern band has a chief or leader of some sort to represent its corporate interests in negotiations with governmental, business, or missionary personnel, or individual men, who are accepted by outsiders as heads of nuclear families, take on this role. As an inevitable concomitant of dependence on political and economic relations outside the group, a public domain becomes defined, if but hazily, as counterposed to a private "familial" sphere. Furthermore, the public domain, associated with men, is either the economically and politically more significant one or is rapidly becoming so.

Decision Making in Foraging Society

What is hard to grasp about the structure of the egalitarian band is that leadership as we conceive it is not merely "weak" or "incipient," as is commonly stated, but irrelevant. The very phrases "informal" and "unstable" that are typically applied to band society imply a groping for the "formality" and "stability" of the band as we comfortably construe it and hinder the interpretation of the qualitatively different organizational form, of enormous resiliency, effectiveness, and stability, that preceded the modern band. The fact that consensus, freely arrived at, within and among multi-family units was both essential to everyday living and possibly has implications that we do not usually confront. Individual autonomy was a necessity, and autonomy as a valued principle persists to a striking degree among the descendants of hunter-gatherers. It was linked with a way of life that called for great individual initiative and decisiveness along with the ability to be extremely sensitive to the feelings of lodge-mates. I suggest that personal autonomy was concomitant with the direct dependence of each individual on the group as a whole. Decision making in this context calls for concepts other than ours of leader and led, dominant and deferent, no matter how loosely these are seen to apply.

In egalitarian band society, food and other necessities were procured or manufactured by all able-bodied adults and were directly distributed by their producers (or occasionally, perhaps, by a parallel band member, ritualizing the sharing principle). It is common knowledge that there was no differential access to resources through private land ownership and no specialization of labor beyond that by sex, hence no market system to intervene in the direct relationship between production and distribution. It is not generally recognized, however, that *the direct relation between production and consumption was intimately connected with the dispersal of authority.* Unless some form of control over resources enables persons with authority to withhold them from others, authority is not authority as we know it. Individual prestige and influence must continually validate themselves in daily life, through the wisdom and ability to contribute to group well-being. The tragically bizarre forms personal violence can take among foraging peoples whose economy has been thoroughly and abruptly disrupted, as described recently for the Ik by Turnbull (1972) and for the central and western Australians of an earlier period by Bates (1938), do not vitiate this principle; the bitter quality of collective suicide they portray only underlines it.

The basic principle of egalitarian band society was that people made decisions about the activities for which they were responsible. Consensus was reached within whatever group would be carrying out a collective activity. Infringements upon the rights of others were negotiated by the parties concerned. Men and women, when defined as interest groups according to the sexual division of labor, arbitrated or acted upon differences in "public" ways, such as when women would hold council among the 17th century Montagnais-Naskapi to consider the problem of a lazy man, or would bring a male ceremony to an early conclusion among the Pitjandjara of west-central Australia because they were having to walk too far for food and were ready to move (Tindale 1972:244–45). The negotiation of marriages for young people would seem to be an exception to the principle of autonomy in those societies in which it occurred. However, not only did young people generally have a say in the matter (Lee 1972:358), but divorce was easy and at the desire of either partner.

The dispersal of authority in band societies means that the public-private or jural-familial dichotomy, so important in hierarchically organized society, is not relevant. In keeping with common analytic practice of setting up quantitatively conceived categories for comparative purposes, it could be argued that decisions made by one or several individuals are more private, while decisions that affect larger numbers are more public, and decision-making processes could be tallied and weighted accordingly. My point is that analysis along any such lines continues to mystify actual decision-making processes in egalitarian societies by conceptualizing them in terms of authority and dependence patterns characteristic of our own society.

The Status of Women

With regard to the autonomy of women, nothing in the structure of egalitarian band societies necessitated special deference to men. There were no economic and social liabilities that bound women to be more sensitive to men's needs and feelings than vice versa. This was even true in hunting societies, where women did not furnish a major share of the food. The record of 17th century Montagnais-Naskapi life in the Jesuit Relations makes this clear. Disputes and quarrels among spouses were virtually nonexistent, Le Jeune reported, since each sex carried out its own activities without "meddling" in those of the other. Le Jeune deplored the fact that the Montagnais "imagine that they ought by right of birth, to enjoy the liberty of wild ass colts, rendering no homage to any one whomsoever." Noting that women had "great power," he expressed his disapproval of the fact that men had no apparent inclination to make their wives "obey" them or to enjoin sexual fidelity upon them. He lectured the Indians on this failing, reporting in one instance, "I told him then that he was the master, and that in France women do not rule their husbands." Le Jeune was also distressed by the sharp and ribald joking and teasing into which women entered along with the men. "Their language has the foul odor of the sewers," he wrote. The Relations reflect the program of the Jesuits to "civilize" the Indians, and during the course of the 17th century they attempted to introduce principles of formal authority, lectured the people about obeying newly elected chiefs, and introduced disciplinary measures in the effort to enforce male authority upon women. No data are more illustrative of the distance between hierarchical and egalitarian forms of organization than the Jesuit account of these efforts (Leacock 1975, 1977; Leacock and Goodman 1977).

Nonetheless, runs the argument for universal female subservience to men, the hunt and war, male domains, are associated with power and prestige to the disadvantages of women. What about this assumption?

Answers are at several levels. First, it is necessary to modify the exaggerations of male as hunter and warrior. Women did some individual hunting, as will be discussed below for the Ojibwa, and they participated in hunting drives that were often of great importance. Men did a lot of non-hunting. Warfare was minimal or nonexistent. The association of hunting, war, and masculine assertiveness is not found among hunter-gatherers except, in a limited way, in Australia. Instead, it characterizes horticultural societies in certain areas, notably Melanesia and the Amazon lowlands.

It is also necessary to reexamine the idea that these male activities were in the past more prestigious than the creation of new human beings. I am sympathetic to the scepticism with which women may view the argument that their gift of fertility was as highly valued as or more highly valued than anything men did. Women are too commonly told today to be content with the wondrous ability to give birth and with the presumed propensity for "motherhood" as defined in saccharine terms. They correctly read such exhortations as saying, "Do not fight for a change in status." However, the fact that childbearing is associated with women's present oppression does not mean this was the case in earlier social forms. To the extent that hunting and warring (or, more accurately, sporadic raiding, where it existed) were areas of male ritualization, they were just that: areas of male ritualization. To a greater or lesser extent women participated in the rituals, while to a greater or lesser extent they were also involved in ritual elaborations of generative power, either along with men or separately. To presume the greater importance of male than female participants, or casually to accept the statements to this effect of latter-day male informants, is to miss the basic function of dichotomized sex-symbolism in egalitarian society. Dichotomization made it possible to ritualize the reciprocal roles of females and males in that the group. As ranking began to develop, it became a means of asserting male dominance, and with the full-scale development of classes sex ideologies reinforced inequalities that were basic to exploitative structures. Much is made of Australian Aboriginal society in arguments for universal deference of women toward men. The data need ethnohistorical review, since the vast changes that have taken place in Australia over the last two centuries cannot be ignored in the consideration of ritual life and of male brutality toward women. Disease, outright genocidal practices, and expulsion from their lands reduced the population of native Australians to its lowest point in the 1930s, after which the cessation of direct genocide, the mission distribution of foods, and the control of infant mortality began to permit a population increase. The concomitant intensification of ceremonial life is described as follows by Godelier (1973:13, translation mine):

> This . . . phenomenon, of a politico-religious order, of course expresses the desire of these groups to reaffirm their cultural identity and to resist the destructive pressures of the process of domination and acculturation they are undergoing, which has robbed them of their land and subjected their ancient religious and political practices to erosion and systematic extirpation.

Thus ceremonial elaboration was oriented toward renewed ethnic identification, in the context of oppression. Furthermore, on the reserves, the economic autonomy of women vis-à-vis men was undercut by handouts to men defined as heads of families and by the sporadic opportunities for wage labor open to men. To assume that recent ritual data reflect aboriginal Australian symbolic structures as if unchanged is to be guilty of freezing these people in some timeless "traditional culture" that does not change or develop, but only becomes lost, it is to rob them of their history. Even in their day, Spencer and Gillen (1968:443) noted the probable decline in women's ceremonial participation among the Arunta.

Allusions to male brutality toward women are common for Australia. Not all violence can be blamed on European colonialism, to be sure, yet it is crass ethnocentrism, if not outright racism, to assume that the grim brutality of Europeans toward the Australians they were literally seeking to exterminate was without profound effect. A common response to defeat is to turn hostility inward. The process is reversed when people acquire the political understanding and organizational strength to confront the source of their problems, as has recently been happening among Australian Aborigines.

References to women of recent times fighting back publicly in a spirited style, occasionally going after their husbands with both tongue and fighting club, and publicly haranguing both men and women bespeak a persisting tradition of autonomy (Kaberry 1939:25–26, 181). In relation to "those reciprocal rights and duties that are recognized to be inherent in marriage," Kaberry writes (pp. 142–43):

> I, personally, have seen too many women attack their husbands with a tomahawk or even their own boomerangs, to feel that they are invariably the victims of ill treatment. A man may perhaps try to beat his wife if she has not brought in sufficient food, but I never saw a wife stand by in submission to receive punishment for her culpable conduct. In the quarrel she might even strike the first blow, and if she were clearly in danger of being seriously hurt, then one of the bystanders might intervene, in fact always did within my experience.

Nor did the man's greater strength tell in such a struggle, for the wife "will pack up her goods and chattels and move to the camp of a relative . . . till the loss of an economic partner . . . brings the man to his senses and he attempts a reconciliation" (p. 143). Kaberry concludes that the point to stress about this indispensability of a woman's economic contribution is "not only her great importance in economics, but also her power to utilize this to her own advantage in other spheres of marital life."

A further point also needs stressing: such quarrels are not, as they may first appear, structurally at the same level as similar quarrels in our society. In our case, reciprocity in marital rights and duties is defined in the terms of a social order in which subsistence is gained through paid wage labor, while women supply socially essential but unpaid services within a household. A dichotomy between "public" labor and "private" household service masks the household "slavery" of women. In all societies, women use the resources available to them to manipulate their situation to their advantage as best they can, but they are in a qualitatively different position, structurally, in our society from that in societies where what has been called the "household economy" is the entire economy. References to the autonomy of women when it comes to making decisions about their own lives are common for such societies. Concomitant autonomy of attitude is pointed out by Kaberry, again, for the Kimberley peoples: "The women, as far as I could judge from their attitudes," she writes, "remained regrettably profane in their attitude towards the men." To be sure, they much admired the younger men as they paraded in their ceremonial finery, but "the praise uttered was in terms that suggested that the spectators regarded the men as potential lovers, and not as individuals near unto gods" (p. 230). In summary, Kaberry argues that "there can be no question of identifying the sacred inheritance of the tribe only with the men's ceremonies. Those of the women belong to it also" (p. 277). As for concepts of "pollution," she says, "the women with regard to the men's rituals are profane and uninitiated; the men with regard to the women's ritual are profane and uninitiated" (p. 277).

The record on women's autonomy and lack of special deference among the 17th century Montagnais-Naskapi is unambiguous. Yet this was a society in which the hunt was overwhelmingly important. Women manufactured clothing and other necessities, but furnished much less food than was the usual case with hunter-gatherers. In the 17th century, women as well as men were shamans, although this is apparently no longer remembered. As powerful shamans, they might exhort men to battle. Men held certain special feasts to do with hunting from which women were excluded. Similarly, men were excluded from women's feasts about which we know nothing but that they were held. When a man needed more than public teasing to ensure his good conduct, or in times of crisis, women held their own councils. In relation to warfare, anything but dominance deference behavior is indicated. In historic times, raids were carried on against the Iroquois, who were expanding their territories in search of furs. The fury with which women would enjoin men to do battle and the hideous and protracted intricacies of the torture of captives in which they took the initiative boggle the mind. Getting back at the Iroquois for killing their men-folk was central, however, not "hailing the conquering hero."

Errors, Crude and Subtle

Despite this evidence, relative male dominance and female deference is a constant theme in the ethnographic record. The extent to which data can be skewed by a nonhistorical approach that overlooks centuries old directions of change and by ethnocentric interpretation based on assumptions about public-prestigious males versus private-deferent females becomes apparent when we consider the following two descriptions of hunting society.

In one, women are extremely self-sufficient and independent and "much more versatile than men." They take much pride and interest in their work, especially in the skills of leatherwork and porcupine or quill embroidery. "Girls are urged to do work of such quality that it will excite envy and admiration." The prestige of a good worker spreads fast, and others seek her out to learn from or obtain some of her work. Men listen in on women's discussions in order to hear about "gifted women" they might wish to seek in marriage. Women also gain "public recognition" as midwives and as herbal doctors (also a male occupation). Some women become so interested that "they trade with individuals in distant groups . . . to secure herbs that are not indigenous." They achieve renown as runners or participants in other sports, where they at times compete with, and may win over, men, and occasionally in warfare, where "a girl who qualifies as a warrior is considered as a warrior, and not as a queer girl," by her male colleagues. Women compose songs and dances that may become popular and pass down through the generations, and they make fine masks used in important bear ceremonials. Young girls often accompany their fathers on hunting trips, so they commonly learn men's as well as women's skills. There are more variations in women's lives than in men's, and many women at some time in their lives support themselves by hunting, in mother-daughter, sister-sister, or grandmother-daughter pairs. Some support disabled husbands for a while in this way. If need be, women who are resourceful can make their own canoes. On the whole "women who adopt men's work are characteristically resourceful and untroubled." Women actively pursue, choose, and desert husbands or lovers, or choose to remain unmarried for long periods of time. Too open, casual, or disruptive promiscuity is frowned upon, and there is some feeling against an unmarried girl's having a baby. However, should she or the child's father not wish to marry, a woman with a child has little trouble finding a husband if she wants one.

Women have visions that bring them supernatural powers more easily than do men; visions have to be induced in boys through isolation and repeated fasting. Elder women spend long hours in winter evenings telling stories about women, some factual, some semi-historical, and some legendary.

By contrast, the second description deals with a hunting society in which women are "inferior" and lack "distinct training," in which the generalization is made "that any man is intrinsically and vastly superior to any woman," and in which women are taught to be "recipients of male favors, economic and sexual, and are supposed to be ignored by men." Men's activities are widely spoken of and publicized, while women's tasks are "unpublished"; the "mythology occupies itself with the pursuits and rewards of men." "Artistic women, in marked contrast to gifted men, are given no title nor are they regarded with the awe that indicates general respect." Instead, women "fall into the role of onlookers who watch and admire [men] with bated breath." "No individual woman is distinctive" in the world of men, and although women "discuss the merits of their work just as men do the merits of theirs, . . . these discussions and boasts are not formal, as the men's are; they belong to the level of gossip." A double standard with regard to sex is enjoined on women. Attention is paid to the adolescent activities of boys, while girls, at their first menses, are isolated as full of "maleficent power."

The latter society sounds quite familiar, but one may wonder about the first. The trick is that the two accounts not only describe the same people, but are taken, selectively, from the same monograph, *The Ojibwa Woman*, by Ruth Landes (1938:viii, 5, 11, 18–19, 23–25, 42, 128–32, 136, 140, 180). I regret being critical of a study that offers full documentation of women's activities and interests, but Landes has undermined her own contribution to the understanding of sex roles in a hunting society through the downgrading of women that is built into unexamined and ethnocentric phraseology.

Unacknowledged contradictions abound in her account. Landes is clear and unequivocal about the resourcefulness of women and the fact that they are allowed greater latitude in their activities than men, but then ascribes this to "the general atmosphere of cultural indifference which surrounds them" and "the sketchy and negatively phrased ideals with which tradition makes a pretense of providing them" (p. 181). In another context, however, she speaks of women who "become self-conscious in 'terms of their work'" and "develop a self-respect which finds satisfaction in the recognition accorded it." She calls this bringing "men's motivations into women's work" and pursuing "feminine occupations as a masculine careerist would" (pp. 154–55). Women are "not trained to these attitudes" of competitive striving and shame in defeat while learning female skills, Landes writes, but learn them in games where the emphases "are the same for boys and girls, for men and women," and both "feel that their self-respect hangs upon the outcome of the game" (pp. 23, 27, 155). Yet in another context, she states, "girls are urged to do work of such quality that it will excite admiration and envy" (p. 19). Furthermore, in the context of case examples of renowned women, Landes makes a non-sex-linked statement about abilities, writing that "individual differences in ability are clearly recognized by the people, and include such careful distinctions as that of small ability hitched to great ambition, or that of potentially great ability confined by small ambition" (p. 27).

Girls, Landes writes, are given "protective" names like "Shining of the Thunderbird," while boys are given names with more "vocational promise" like "Crashing Thunder" (p. 13). Then she writes, without comment, of the shaman "Thunder Woman" (pp. 29, 37), of the woman warrior "Chief Earth Woman" (p. 141), and of "Iron Woman," a shaman who was taught by her "medicine" father and her grandfather and who defeated "even the best men at games of chance and skill (pp. 26–27, 62–63, 137).

The basic division of labor, Landes writes, "is in the assignment to the men of hunting and securing raw materials, and the assignment to the women of manufacturing the raw materials" (pp. 130–31). Men's work is less varied than women's, "but it is appraised culturally as infinitely more interesting and honorable" (p. 131). "Women's work is conventionally ignored" by men (p. 18). How, then, does Landes handle the interest shown in women's work by both women and men? She writes that "excellence of handiwork excites the *informal* attention of women as widely as the boy's talent in hunting excites the attention of men" (pp. 18–19, italics added); that a man may brag of his wife's handiwork, which "had led him to walk many miles" to claim her, "in an *unguarded moment*" (p. 11, italics added); and that men learn about gifted workers that they might want to seek in marriage "from *eavesdropping* upon the *chatter* of their own women folk" (p. 19, italics added). The "private" and less prestigious world of women thus having been established, Landes later implies another common stereotype that of women as "passive" vis-à-vis men in relation to sex: "Men seem to be more articulate than women about love. It is men who are said to be proud of their wives, not women of their husbands . . ." (p. 120). I am not suggesting that Landes did not record statements from both men and women about the greater importance of men's work, as well as statements to the contrary. In fact, when she was in the field, men's work was more important. The reciprocity of the sexual division of labor had long since given way to considerable dependence upon trade goods. "Since the advent of the traders," Landes writes, "Ojibwa men have learned how to barter. They trade furs and meat which they have secured in hunting, and since the men, rather than the women, possessed the materials desired by the Whites, they became the traders" (p. 134). She describes the men returning from the post and showing "the results of their trade; ammunition, weapons, traps and tobacco for themselves; yard print, ribbons and beads for the women and children; candy, fruit, whiskey for all" (p. 17). The fact that women remained as autonomous as they did among the Ojibwa was apparently related to the fact that hunting continued to be the main source of food and women could and did often support themselves and their families by hunting. Furthermore, "Today [1932–33], when rice and berries and maple sugar are commanding some White attention, the women also are learning to function as dealers" (p. 134).

Landes's downgrading of women's status among the Ojibwa, in the face of her own evidence to the contrary, flows in part from contradictions due to the changes taking place in women's social-economic position[1] and in part from her lack of a critical and historical orientation toward her material. Nonetheless, Landes deserves credit for making available such full material on women that explicit criticism of her work is possible.

Iroquois materials offer similar contradictions. Horticultural but still egalitarian, Iroquois society of the 17th and 18th centuries is well known for the high status of its women. Lands were handed down in matrilineages, and the matrons managed the economic affairs of the communal "long houses," arranged marriages, nominated and deposed the sachems of the intertribal council, and participated in equal numbers with men as influential "Keepers of the Faith." Postmarital residence was uxorilocal, and a woman could divorce a man who did not please her with little ceremony, sending him back to his own family. Women's value was expressed in the fact that a murdered woman called for twice the compensation of a murdered man.

Yet one can have one's choice among contradictory statements about the status of Iroquois women. In the early 18th century, Lafitau wrote of Iroquois women (or perhaps of the similar Huron), "all real authority is vested

---

[1] For studies of comparable changes in women's status, cf. Hamamsy (1957) and Leacock (1955).

in them. . . . They are the soul of the Councils, the arbiters of peace and of war" (Brown 1970:153). On the other hand, there is the more commonly quoted sentence of none other than Morgan himself: "The Indian regarded woman as the inferior, the dependent, and the servant of man, and from nature and habit, she actually considered herself to be so" (1954:315; cited, for example, in Goldberg 1973:40, 58, 241; Divale 1976:202).

The contrast between the two generalizations is partly a matter of the period. Morgan was working with Iroquois informants in the 19th century, when the long house was but a memory and the Iroquois lived in nuclear families largely supported by wage-earning men. Morgan, however, later quoted Rev. A. Wright on the high position of women among the Seneca: "The women were the great power among the clans, as every where else. They did not hesitate, when occasion required, to 'knock off the horns,' as it was technically called, from the head of a chief and send him back to the ranks of the warriors" (1974:464).

During the period between the *League of the Iroquois* and *Ancient Society*, Morgan was developing his thinking on human social evolution and on the decline in women's relative status with the advent of "civilization." "The mother-right and gyneocracy among the Iroquois . . . is not overdrawn," he wrote later. "We may see in this an ancient phase of human life which has had a wide presence in the tribes of mankind. . . . Not until after civilization had begun among the Greeks, and gentile society was superseded by political society, was the influence of the old order of society overthrown" (1965:66). With monogamy, the woman "was now isolated from her gentile kindred, living in the separate and exclusive house of her husband. Her new condition tended to subvert and destroy the power and influence which descent in the female line and the joint-tenement houses had created" (p. 128).

Yet this is not the end of the matter, for Morgan continued (p. 128):

> But this influence of the woman did not reach out ward to the affairs of the gens, phratry, or tribe, but seems to have commenced and ended with the household. This view is quite consistent with the life of patient drudgery and of general subordination to the husband which the Iroquois wife cheerfully accepted as the portion of her sex.

The question is how such a characterization squares with the description of Wright, who lived many years with the Seneca (Morgan 1965:65–66):

> Usually, the female portion ruled the house, and were doubtless clannish enough about it. The stores were in common; but woe to the luckless husband or lover who was too shiftless to do his share of the providing. No matter how many children, or what ever goods he might have in the house, he might at any time be ordered to pick up his blanket and budge; and after such orders it would not be healthful for him to disobey; the house would be too hot for him; and unless saved by the intercession of some aunt or grandmother, he must retreat to his own clan.

An explanation comes readily to mind in terms of the familiar discrepancy between ideal and real wifely roles in our society. Ideally, the wife is the patient and cheerful "helpmeet" in an entrepreneurial nuclear family. A common reality, behind an acceptable public façade, may be a frustrated wife bolstering up, manipulating, and dominating an emotionally dependent husband. Hence an assumption of male dominance as a cultural ideal and the "henpecked husband" as an alternative reality in societies where women's private "power" is constrained by exclusion from public authority is projected into much ethnography. Furthermore, variations on the theme can be observed in erstwhile egalitarian societies in which trade, various forms of sharecropping, wage work, or outright slavery have been important in recent times. These economic relations transform household collectives that were largely controlled by women and that took communal responsibility for raising children; women and children become dependent upon individual men. However, when the previous structures of such societies are reconstructed and the range of decisions made by women is considered, women's autonomous and public role emerges. Their status was not as literal "equals" of men (a point that has caused much confusion), but as what they were—female persons, with their own rights, duties, and responsibilities, which were complementary to and in no way secondary to those of men.

Women's status in Iroquois society was not based on their economic contribution per se. Women make an essential economic contribution in all societies, but their status depends on how this contribution is structured. The issue is whether they control the conditions of their work and the dispensation of the goods they produce. In egalitarian societies, women are limited by the same technological and ecological considerations as men are, but there is no socially defined group that directs their activities. Brown (1970) documents this point for the Iroquois, and its ramifications have been explored by other researchers (Caulfield 1977; Sanday 1974; Sacks 1975; Schlegel 1977).

Iroquois matrons preserved, stored, and dispensed the corn, meat, fish, berries, squashes, and fats that were buried in special pits or kept in the long house. Brown notes (p. 162) that women's control over the dispensation of the foods they produced, and meat as well, gave them the de facto power to veto declarations of war and to intervene in order to bring about peace: "By supplying the essential provisions for male activities—the hunt, the warpath, and the Council—they were able to control these to some degree." Women also guarded the "tribal public treasure" kept in the long house, the wampum, quill and feather work, and furs—the latter, I would add, new forms of wealth that would be their undoing. The point to be stressed is that this was "household management" of an altogether different order from management of the nuclear or extended family in patriarchal societies. In the latter, women may cajole, manipulate, or browbeat men, but always behind the public façade; in the former case, *"household management" was itself the management of the "public" economy.*

The point that household management had a public character in egalitarian society was made by Engels (1972:137); it was not understood by Morgan. Like most anthropologists today, Morgan saw the status of women in Iroquois society as qualitatively different from what it later became.

Indeed, to pursue Morgan's views on Iroquois women is interesting. Despite his contribution to the understanding of historical factors underlying women's changing status, his *League of the Iroquois* is hardly free of derogatory innuendos with regard to them. From reading the *League* alone, one would not know that the matrons nominated the sachems, and their role as providers is dispensed with in the statement that "the warrior despised the toil of husbandry and held all labor beneath him" (1954:320), although Morgan elsewhere refers to how hard the men worked at hunting. Ignoring women's agriculture, he writes as if the Iroquois were primarily hunters. Without the influence of cities, he states, Iroquois institutions "would have lasted until the people had abandoned the hunter state; until they had given up the chase for agriculture, the arts of war for those of industry" (p. 13). When he describes women's formal participation in tribal affairs, he writes, "Such was the spirit of the Iroquois system of government, that the influence of the inferior chiefs, the warriors, and *even* of the women would make itself felt" (p. 66, italics added); and "If a band of warriors became interested in the passing question, they held a council apart, and having given it full consideration, appointed an orator to communicate their views to the sachems. . . . In like manner would the chiefs, and *even* the women proceed" (p. 101, italics added). Richards (1957) argues that "the aboriginal matriarchy pictured by Lafitau, Morgan, and Hewitt was . . . a mistake" and that the status of Iroquois women had increased by 1784, the beginning of reservation life. Her documentation reveals, however, not an increase in status, but a change from the informality of a fully egalitarian society to the formalization of powers necessary for handling a new and complicated set of political and economic conditions.

Richards takes up two of women's formal powers, the right to dispose of war captives and the right to decide about marriage. On the basis of incidents in the Jesuit Relations and other early sources, she concludes (p. 40) that there was "a gradual increase in the decision-making power of the women and a corresponding loss by the men" as a "product of a long continued contact situation." Richards presents eleven incidents pertaining to the disposition of war captives, eight between 1637 and 1655, one in 1724, and two in 1781. She states (p. 38) that "women in the early period had little if any decision making power," that later they shared power with the men in their families, subject to acceptance by the captors of the prisoner and the council, and that later still "they were able to intervene and even actually instigate the capture of an individual though it was still necessary to complete the formality of obtaining council approval." However, among the eight cases in the first period, several indicate the active and successful intervention by a woman on behalf of a captive, concluded with the formal presentation of wampum to the council, and there is an instance in which a woman insists on the death of a captive given her to replace her dead brother, in spite of the council's wish to the contrary.

True, in no case do women exercise power equivalent to that held by bodies of men in patriarchal class-based societies. Instead, the cases illustrate the flexibility of decision-making processes characteristic of egalitarian societies. The captors, the council, and interested individuals all had a say in the disposition of captives, and individual women or men apparently won or lost according to the depth of their conviction and the persuasiveness with which they presented their case. What is of significance to the present line of argument is that in all instances, scattered as they are over time and among different Iroquois peoples, women operated formally and publicly in their own interest, with ceremonial gift giving, use of the arts of rhetoric, and other public display. Richards (p. 41) quotes Radisson's report of his return from a war foray; his adoptive mother, he says, "comes to meet me, leaping and singing. . . . Shee takes the woman slave that I had and would not that any should medle with her. But my brother's prisoner was burned ye same day." Radisson's mother had first claimed him in the following fashion: "The old woman followed me, speaking aloud, whom they answered with a loud ho, then shee tooke her girdle and about me she tyed it, so brought me to her cottage."

In relation to marriage decisions in the earlier period, Richards cites several examples in which matrons did not have the clear-cut power to decide on spouses for their sons and daughters. However, the early records instead indicate that young women lived in dormitories, took lovers, experimented with trial marriages, and made the decisions about whom they were going to marry, albeit with the advice and formal recognition of their parents. Cartier wrote of this "very bad" custom for the girls, who "after they are of an age to marry . . . are all put into a common house, abandoned to every body who desires them until they have found their match" (Richards 1957:42). Other early accounts report both parents as involved in selecting spouses for their children, but girls as having the right to reject a suitor after trying him out (pp. 40, 43). Marriage arrangements were apparently flexible and included both polygyny and polyandry.

The fact that matrons' powers over disposition of war captives and over marriage became more clear-cut with the formalization of the Iroquois constitution betokens not an increase in power, but a formal recognition of prestige and influence that had long operated. With relation to marriage, in a society where consensus was essential, the young were influenced rather than ordered by their elders with regard to the conduct of their personal lives. However, the formal codification of women's social position took place in a situation in which their autonomy was already undermined. The subsequent history of the Iroquois polity involved a temporary strengthening of the "public sphere" represented by the confederacy at the point at which it was being supplanted by colonial rule. The longhouse communities were replaced by settlements of nuclear family units; what remained were some of the interpersonal styles and traditions of cooperation and personal autonomy.

Transition

Like the Iroquois, societies around the world have been transformed by the economic system that emerged in Europe in what Wallerstein terms "the 'long' sixteenth century" of 1450–1640 (1974:40–67). Unfortunately, this fact has been obscured in anthropology by the practice of separating the "internal" functioning of societies from their total economic and political contexts, in order to reconstruct supposedly "traditional" cultures through deletion of "modern" involvements. Wallerstein's article is not specifically directed at anthropologists, but his criticism of ahistorical methods (p. 389) is apt: "The crucial issue when comparing 'stages' is to determine the units of which the 'stages' are synchronic portraits (or 'ideal types'). . . . And the fundamental error of ahistorical social science (including ahistorical versions of Marxism) is to reify parts of the totality into such units and then to compare reified structures." To be effective in the interpretation of history, stages must be of total social systems.

Wallerstein distinguishes social systems as "mini-systems" or "world-systems." A mini-system is "an entity that has within it a complete division of labor, and a single cultural framework," such as "are found only in very simple agricultural or hunting and gathering societies" (p. 390). He continues: "Such mini-systems no longer exist in the world. Furthermore, there were fewer in the past than is often asserted, since any such system that became tied to an empire by the payment of tribute as 'protection costs' ceased by that fact to be a 'system,' no longer having a self-contained division of labor." Other factors that have been undermining the self contained division of labor of mini-systems for centuries are trade, involvement in raiding or being raided for slaves (in the New World as well as in Africa), taxation of various kinds (often as an incentive to wage work), and wage labor, often entailing men's absence from home villages for long periods. In all cases, missionizing played an important role in urging people toward an individualized work ethic and a nuclear family form. Since mini-systems no longer exist, says Wallerstein, social analysis must take into account that "the only kind of social system is a world-system, . . . a unit with a single division of labor and multiple cultural systems." This world-system is "the capitalist world economy."

Recognition of this fact has serious implications for the cross-cultural study of women, since involvements with a developing capitalist world economy have had profound effects on their relation to the production and distribution of basic group needs, hence to sources of decision-making power. The practice of stacking contemporary peoples in "historical" layers as hunter-gatherers, simple agriculturalists, and advanced agriculturalists with domestication does, it is true, yield some insight into the nature of women's decline in status, since a people's involvement in the world-system starts within each "layer" from a different basis. Furthermore, cultural traditions can be remarkably strong, and people can wage stiff battles for those they value. Hence the method of comparing near-contemporary cultures can be used with care to suggest historical trends (see, e.g., Sacks 1976). However, socioeconomic systems separated from the economic and political constraints that in part define them cannot be treated as direct representations of sex-role definitions in contrasting societies.

Two recent books, *Woman, Culture, and Society* (Rosaldo and Lamphere 1974) and *Women and Men* (Friedl 1975), share an ahistorical orientation and assume from recent and contemporary evidence the universality of male dominance and the cultural devaluation of women. The assumption is neither documented nor argued on the basis of ethnohistorical materials. Instead, 19th century concepts of matriarchal power incorrectly ascribed to Marx and Engels (Friedl 1975:4) or Morgan (Rosaldo and Lamphere 1974:2)—are cited briefly as inadequate, and the alternative of women's equal prestige and autonomy in egalitarian societies is given but passing reference and subsequently ignored (Friedl 1975:47; Rosaldo and Lamphere 1974:3). Yet the authors eschew simplistic psychobiological explanations for an assumed universal male dominance and see the structure of women's position as critical to relative subordination or autonomy in different facets of cultural life, making for an open-ended future according to structural changes.

Friedl offers thoughtful discussions of women's participation in the production and control of food and goods in a variety of cultures, but with no reference to the fact that both ethnohistorical and recent materials indicate a general decline in women's control with the advent of trade (certain notable exceptions do not pertain to the peoples she describes). Rosaldo and Lamphere (1974:9) write of the papers in their book that they "establish that women's role in social processes is far greater than has previously been recognized" and that they show that "women, like men, are social actors who work in structured ways to achieve desired ends" and who "have a good deal more power than conventional theorists have assumed." However, they reveal their entrapment in the anthropological ethos that sees contemporary Third World peoples as virtually unchanged representatives of the past in stating (p. 14) that "the papers . . . do not, on the whole, address questions concerning female roles today." With the exception of a paper on the 19th-century Mende of Sierra Leone, the empirical papers do treat "female roles today" among the Igbo and Ijaw of Nigeria, the Mbum Kpau of Tchad, the Javanese and other Indonesian groups, Lake Atitlán villagers in Guatemala, and people of rural Montenegro, pre- and post-revolutionary China, and urban black communities in the United States. By what fiat are such peoples removed from the world of today?

The upshot of an ahistorical perspective is to see giving birth and suckling as in and of themselves furnishing the basis for a presumed past subordination, though subject to change in the future. Since the division of labor by sex was central to the evolution of cultural life, it is easy to fall into the trap; women bear children; the early division of labor is related to this fact, as is women's present subordination; hence there has been a quantitative but not a qualitative shift in women's status relative to men, which took place as egalitarian social forms were transmuted into hierarchical ones. The structural implications of the fact that, when labor is not specialized beyond the division by sex, goods are completely shared within a band or village collective are ignored, as is the concomitant control by every member of the group over the distribution of the resources and products that each acquires or manufactures. Thereby the source of transformation in women's status is bypassed: the development of trade and specialization to the point that relations of dependence emerge outside of the band, village, or kin collective, undermine individual control and personal autonomy, and lay the basis for hierarchy.

Brown (1970) contrasts the public control exercised by Iroquois women, based on their responsibility for the collective household and its stores, with women's loss of such control, and concomitant loss of status, among the centralized and hierarchical Bemba. In comparative studies, Sacks (1975) and Sanday (1974) affirm the relationship between control of production and distribution by women and their "public" participation and status. Goldhamer (1973) shows the variability in women's control over the products of their labor in the New Guinea highlands and the significance of these variations to their status.

For example, among the Mae Enga women are responsible for the daily allocation of their produce, but "men retain the 'right and duty' involved in the important distribution of pigs, pork, and produce for prestation, trade and debt payments" (Goldhamer 1973:6). By contrast, among the Tor of West Irian, "men say that it is women's total control over the food supply that affords them the 'exceptionally high position' that prevails throughout the district" (p. 10). Food presentation may be a "public" or political act or a private service, according to the structural setting. Among the Tor, as among the Iroquois of the past, women's dispensation of food to strangers is a public act; it sets the stage for the reception of newcomers. "The women's expressed attitude toward strangers coming into the villages determines how they will be received by the men" (p. 10). By contrast, Bemba women dispense food as a family service that redounds to the husband's stature and enjoins obligations to him on the part of the recipients in the same way as does chiefly extending of hospitality. Among the Mae Enga, women's labor furnishes produce that is consumed by the pigs which are distributed in political negotiations by men.

The relatively higher status of women among the Iroquois and Tor, where they control their work and its distribution, than among the Mae Enga and especially the Bemba, where they do not, suggests that preliminary phases in the process of class development did in fact accompany women's decline in status, as Engels originally proposed. The link between women's reduced status, on the one hand, and the growth of private property and economic classes, on the other, was in Engels's view the emergence of the individual family as an independent economic unit. Taking shape within and subverting the former collective economy, the family as an economic unit transformed women's work from public production to private household service. The critical development that triggered the change was the specialization of labor that increasingly replaced the production of goods for use by the production of commodities for exchange and set up economic relationships that lay beyond the control of the producers.

Commodity production, Engels (1972:23) wrote, "undermines the collectivity of production and appropriation" and "elevates appropriation by individuals into the general rule," thereby setting in motion "incorporeal alien powers" that rise up against the producers. The seeds of private property and class exploitation are planted, and the single family as an economic property owning and inheriting unit develops within and destroys the collective. "The division of labor within the family . . . remained the same; and yet it now turned the previous domestic relation upside down simply because the division of labor outside the family had changed" (p. 221). Instead of carrying out public responsibilities in the band or village collective within which goods were distributed, women became dependent on men as the producers of commercially relevant goods. In the context of the individual family, "the woman was degraded and reduced to servitude, . . . a mere instrument for the production of children" (p. 121).

Engels described the process as unfolding through the domestication of animals in the ancient East and the exchange of cattle, which were cared for, and hence came to be owned, by men. Since unequal control over resources and subjugation by class and by sex developed in very different ecological settings in many parts of the world prior to, as well as within, the period of European colonialism, it is important to separate Engels's statement on women's subjugation from the specific context of his discussion. The processes associated with the transformation of goods produced for use to "commodities," produced for future exchange, then become apparent in all world areas. These are: specialization of labor in connection with trade, and warfare to ensure or control trade; intensive work on agricultural land and unequal access to or privatization of prime lands; differences in economic status expressed in categories of "slaves," "rubbish men," perpetual youth, and the like; competition among lineage groups, within which the individual family as an economic unit begins to take shape; the institutionalization of "political" functions connected with warfare and property as separate from "social" functions and the dichotomization of "public" and "private" spheres; and the institutionalization and ideological rationalization of male superiority.

Summary

I have argued that the structure of egalitarian society has been misunderstood as a result of the failure to recognize women's participation in such society as public and autonomous. To conceptualize hunting-gathering bands as loose collections of nuclear families, in which women are bound by dyadic relations of dependency to individual men, projects onto hunter-gatherers the dimensions of our own social structure. Such a concept implies a teleological and unilineal view of social evolution, whereby our society is seen as the full expression of relations that have been present in all society. Ethnohistorical and conceptual reinterpretation of women's roles in hunting-gathering societies reveals that qualitatively different relationships obtained. The band as a whole was the basic economic unit; individuals distributed their own produce; property did not exist as a foundation for individual authority; and decisions were on the whole made by those who would be carrying them out.

Failure to appreciate the structure of egalitarian relations renders more difficult the problem of unraveling the complex processes that initiated class and state formation. Ethnohistorical research indicates that in precolonial horticultural societies where egalitarianism still prevailed, women continued to function publicly in making economic and social decisions, often through councils that mediated their reciprocal relations with men. The comparison of such societies with those characterized by differences in rank and wealth indicates that the main concomitant of women's oppression originally outlined by Engels is indeed found cross-culturally. The transmutation of production for consumption to production of commodities for exchange (usually along with intensive work on land as a commodity for future use) begins to take direct control of their produce out of the hands of the producers and to create new economic ties that undermine the collectivity of the joint households. Women begin to lose control of their production, and the sexual division of labor related to their childbearing ability becomes the basis for their oppression as private dispensers of services in individual households. The process is by no means simple, automatic, or rapid, and where women retain some economic autonomy as traders they retain as well a relatively high status. In West Africa, women were organized to maintain and protect their rights well into the development of economic classes and political states.

The documentation and analysis of women's social roles, then, show that family relations in preclass societies were not merely incipient forms of our own. Social evolution has not been unilineal and quantitative. It has entailed profound qualitative changes in the relations between women and men.

BIBLIOGRAPHY

Bailey, Alfred Goldsworthy
    1969   The Conflict of European and Eastern Algonkian Cultures, 1504–1700. Toronto: University of Toronto Press.
Barnes, John A.
    1971   African Models in the New Guinea Highlands. *In* Melanesia: Readings on a Culture Area. L. L. Langness and John C. Weschler, eds. Scranton, PA: Chandler.
Barwick, Dianne E.
    1974   "And the Lubras are Ladies Now." *In* Woman's Role in Aboriginal Society. Fay Gale, ed. Cartlon, N.S.W.: Excelsis Press.
Basden, G. T.
    1938   Niger Ibos. London: Seely, Service.
    1966   Among the Ibos of Nigeria. New York: Barnes and Noble.
Bates, Daisy
    1938   The Passing of the Aborigines: A Lifetime Spent among the Natives of Australia. London: Murray.
Berndt, Catherine
    1974   Digging Sticks and Spears, or The Two Sex Model. *In* Woman's Role in Aboriginal Society. Fay Gale, ed. Carlton, N.S.W.: Excelsis Press.
Brown, Judith
    1970   Economic Organization and the Position of Women among the Iroquois. Ethnohistory 17:151–167.
Caulfield, Mina
    1977   Universal Sex Oppression? A Critique from Marxist Anthropology. Catalyst (10–11):60–77.
Cox, Bruce, ed.
    1973   Cultural Ecology: Readings on the Canadian Indians and Eskimos. Toronto: McClelland and Stewart.
Damas, David
    1969   Contributions to Anthropology: Band Societies. National Museums of Canada Bulletin 28.

Divale, William T.
1976   Female Status and Cultural Evolution: A Study in Ethnographic Bias. Behavior Science Research 11:169–211.
Draper, Patricia
1975   !Kung Women: Contrasts in Sexual Egalitarianism in Foraging and Sedentary Contexts. *In* Toward an Anthropology of Women. Rayna R. Reiter, ed. New York: Monthly Review Press.
Driver, Harold E.
1962   Indians of North America. Chicago: University of Chicago Press.
Engels, Frederick
1972   The Origin of the Family, Private Property and the State. New York: International.
Faithorn, Elizabeth
1975   The Concept of Pollution among the Kafe of the Papua New Guinea Highlands. *In* Toward an Anthropology of Women. Rayna R. Reiter, ed. New York: Monthly Review.
Fried, Morton H.
1967   The Evolution of Political Society. New York: Random House. .
1968   On the Concepts of "Tribe" and "Tribal Society." Proceedings of the 1967 Annual Spring Meeting, American Ethnological Society, 320.
1975   The Notion of Tribe. Menlo Park, CA: Cummings.
Friedl, Ernestine
1975   Women and Men: An Anthropologist's View. New York: Holt, Rinehart and Winston.
Godelier, Maurice
1973   Modes de production, rapports de parenté et structures démographiques. La Pensée (December):831.
Goldberg, Steven
1973   The Inevitability of Patriarchy. New York: Morrow.
Goldhammer, Florence Kalm
1973   The "Misfit" of Role and Status for the New Guinea Highlands Woman. Paper read at the 72nd annual meeting of the American Anthropological Association.
Hamamsay, Laila
1957   The Role of Women in a Changing Navajo Society. American Anthropologist 59:101–111.
Hart, C. W. and Arnold Pilling
1962   The Tiwi of North Australia. New York: Holt, Rinehart and Winston.
Hartwig M. C.
1972   Aborigines and Racism: An Historical Perspective. *In* Racism: The Australian Experience, vol. 2. F. S. Stevens, ed. New York: Taplinger.
Heizer, R. F. and M. A. Whipple
1971   The California Indians: A Source Book. Berkeley: University of California Press.
Helm, June and Eleanor Leacock
1971   The Hunting Tribes of Subarctic Canada. *In* North American Indians in Historical Perspective. Eleanor Leacock and Nancy Lurie, eds. New York: Random House.

Horner, J.
 1972 Brutality and the Aboriginal People. *In* Racism: The Australian Experience, vol. 2. F. S. Stevens, eds. New York: Taplinger.
Kaberry, Phyllis M.
 1939 Aboriginal Woman, Sacred and Profane. London: Routledge.
Keesing, Roger M.
 1971 Shrines, Ancestors, and Cognatic Descent: The Kwaio and Tallensi. *In* Melanesia: Readings on a Culture Area. L. L. Langness and John C. Weschler, eds. Scranton, PA: Chandler.
Landes, Ruth
 1938 The Ojibwa Woman. New York: Columbia University Press.
Leacock, Eleanor
 1954 The Montagnais "Hunting Territory" and the Fur Trade. American Anthropological Association Memoir 78.
 1955 Matrilocality in a Simple Hunting Economy (Montagnais-Naskapi). Southwestern Journal of Anthropology 11:31–47.
 1969 The Naskapi Band. *In* Contributions to Anthropology: Band Societies. David Damas, ed. National Museums of Canada Bulletin 228.
 1975 Class, Commodity, and the Status of Women. *In* Women Cross-culturally: Change and Challenge. Ruby Rohrlich Leavitt, ed. The Hague: Mouton.
 1977 Women in Egalitarian Society. *In* Becoming Visible: Women in European History. Renate Bridenthal and Claudia Koonz, eds. Boston: Houghton Mifflin.
   In press Modes of Production in Preclass Society: Comments on a Symposium. *In* Modes of Production. James Silverberg, ed. New York: Queens College Press.
Leacock, Eleanor and Jaqueline Goodman
 1977 Montagnais Marriage and the Jesuits in the 17th Century. Western Canadian Journal of Anthropology.
Leacock, Eleanor and June Nash
 1977 Ideologies of Sex, Archetypes, and Stereotypes. Annals of the New York Academy of Sciences 285.
Lee, Richard
 1972 The !Kung Bushmen of Botswana. *In* Hunters and Gatherers Today. M. G. Bicchieri, ed. New York: Holt, Rinehart and Winston.
Levine, Robert
 1966 Sex Roles and Economic Change in Africa. Ethnology 5:186–193.
Lewis, Oscar
 1942 Effects of White Contact upon Blackfoot Culture. Monographs of the American Ethnological Society 6.
Meek, C. K.
 1937 Law and Authority in a Nigerian Tribe. London: Oxford University Press.
Morgan, Lewis Henry
 1954 League of the HoDeNoSauNee or Iroquois, vol. I. New Haven, CT: Human Relations Area Files.
 1965 Houses and House-life of the American Aborigines. Chicago: University of Chicago Press.
 1974 Ancient Society. Gloucester, MA: Peter Smith.

Radcliffe-Brown, A. R.
   1964   The Andaman Islanders. New York: Free Press.
Rattray, R. S.
   1923   The Ashanti. London: Oxford University Press.
Reichard, Gladys A.
   1928   Social Life of the Navajo Indians. New York: Columbia University Press.
Richards, Cara B.
   1957   Matriarchy or Mistake: The Role of Iroquois Women through Time. Pro-
          ceedings of the 1957 Annual Spring Meeting, American Ethnological So-
          ciety, 36–45.
Rogers, Edward S.
   1972   The Mistassini Cree. *In* Hunters and Gatherers Today. M. G. Bicchieri, ed.
          New York: Holt, Rinehart and Winston.
Rosaldo, Michelle Zimbalist and Louise Lamphere, eds.
   1974   Woman, Culture, and Society. Stanford, CA: Stanford University Press.
Sacks, Karen
   1975   Engels Revisited: Women, the Organization of Production, and Private
          Property. *In* Toward an Anthropology of Women. Rayna R. Reiter, ed. New
          York: Monthly Review.
Sahlins, Marshall
   1961   The Segmentary Lineage: An Organization of Predatory Expansion. Amer-
          ican Anthropologist 63:322–345.
Sanday, Peggy
   1974   Female Status in the Public Domain. *In* Women, Culture, and Society.
          Michelle Zimbalist Rosaldo and Louise Lamphere, eds. Stanford, CA:
          Stanford University Press.
Schlegel, Alice, ed.
   1977   Sexual Stratification: A Cross-cultural View. New York: Columbia Univer-
          sity Press.
Service, Elman
   1966   The Hunters. Englewood Cliffs, NJ: Prentice-Hall.
Speck, Frank
   1926   Culture Problems in Northeastern North America. Proceedings of the
          American Philosophical Society 65:273–311.
Spencer, Baldwin and F. J. Gillen
   1968   The Native Tribes of Central Australia. New York: Dover.
Sudarkasa, Niara
   1976   Female Employment and Family Organization in West Africa. *In* New Re-
          search on Women and Sex Roles. Dorothy G. McGuigan, ed. Ann Arbor:
          University of Michigan Center for Continuing Education of Women.
Talbot, P. Amaury
   1912   In the Shadow of the Bush. London: William Heinemann.
Thwaites, R. G., ed.
   1906   The Jesuit Relations and Allied Documents. 71 vols. Cleveland: Burrows.
Tindale, Norman
   1972   The Pitjandjara. *In* Hunters and Gatherers Today. M. G. Bicchieri, ed. New
          York: Holt, Rinehart and Winston.

Turnbull, Colin

1962 The Forest People. Garden City, NY: Doubleday.

1965a The Mbuti Pygmies of the Congo. *In* Peoples of Africa. James L. Gibbs, Jr., ed. New York: Holt, Rinehart and Winston.

1965b The Mbuti Pygmies: An Ethnographic Survey. Anthropological Papers of the American Museum of Natural History 50, Pt. 3.

1972 The Mountain People. New York: Simon and Schuster.

Wallerstein, Immanuel

1974 The Rise and Future Demise of the World Capitalist System: Concepts for Comparative Analysis. Comparative Studies in Society and History 16:387–415.

White, Isobel M.

1974 Aboriginal Women's Status: A Paradox Resolved. *In* Woman's Role in Aboriginal Society. Fay Gale, ed. Carlton, N.S.W.: Excelsis Press.

Women's Bureau, U.S. Department of Labor

1976 The Earnings Gap between Women and Men. Washington, DC: U.S. Government Printing Office.

QUERIES

- What ethnographic evidence does Leacock cite from her research on the Montagnais that indicates the status of women in traditional band societies?
- What is the fundamental change that creates a decline in women's status in band societies?
- Leacock offers an extensive and pointed critique of the images of women embedded in Landes's ethnography, *The Ojibwa Woman.* Summarize Leacock's criticism. How do Landes's unexamined assumptions exemplify anthropologists' descriptions of the status of women in band societies?
- Leacock criticizes Rosaldo and Lamphere, the editors of *Women, Culture and Society* (1974), for stating that the ethnographic case studies in their volume "do not, on the whole, address questions concerning female roles today." What is Leacock's criticism? How does Lamphere and Rosaldo's comment reflect an ahistorical perspective?
- Leacock applies ideas from Engels and Wallerstein to argue that women's status changes as traditional societies are incorporated into global capitalism. What happens?

CONNECTIONS

- Imagine that Leacock was writing a book review of Ruth Benedict's "Cultural Configurations in North America." What do you think Leacock's principle criticism would be?

- Leacock argues that anthropologists failed to acknowledge how "traditional" societies studied in the 19th and 20th centuries were in fact deeply integrated into capitalist systems and global economies. How does this position parallel Eric Wolf's argument in *Europe and the People without History*? (see Moore 2008:350–56, for synopsis).
- Leacock explains the "low-status" of women in band societies as a creation of capitalism. How does this contrast with Sherry Ortner's analysis in "Is Female to Male as Nature Is to Culture?" (see Moore 2008: 311–15).

V

STRUCTURES, SYMBOLS, AND MEANING

17

Claude Lévi-Strauss

INTRODUCTION

The French anthropologist Claude Lévi-Strauss (b. 1908) has been the foremost proponent of a distinctive theoretical position, structuralism. Drawing on his ethnographic investigations among indigenous peoples of South America and an encyclopedic command of anthropological data from the Americas, Lévi-Strauss sought to illuminate the innate organizing principles or deep structures that humans employ to order different types of knowledge (see Moore 2008:231–46). A broad comparative study of different forms of information—as encoded in myth, kinship systems, and exchanges of goods and services—suggests that similar ways of parsing information are used by people from different and historically unconnected cultures.

To use a somewhat trivial but comprehensible example, humans tend to organize very different concepts using polar opposites: up/down, black/white, male/female, good/bad, and so on. There is nothing about these different sets of information regarding vertical position, color, gender, or moral judgment that requires us to conceive these sets of information in bipolar opposition. That so many humans from such different cultures use bipolar opposites suggests the human mind tends to organize data in this way.

In a series of intellectually challenging books and articles published in the mid-20th century, Lévi-Strauss presented detailed examinations of kinship and mythology (for an overview, see Moore 2008:231–36). For example, between 1964 and 1971 he wrote four books on mythology that explored the "logics of myth" (*Mythologiques*), studies that presented an exhaustive corpus of myths and dissected them to expose their underlying conceptual structures. The following article is a more programmatic statement, published in

1955 but outlining the issues Lévi-Strauss developed over the subsequent decades. Arguing that mythology shares some characteristics of other forms of speech—following rules of practice but articulated in specific instances, a distinction the structural linguist Saussure referred to as *langue* and *parole*—Lévi-Strauss insists that myths encode other, almost subterranean levels of meaning.

Since Lévi-Strauss was working before computers were common or analytically flexible, his analytical techniques seem impossibly primitive: elements of myths written out on index cards, shuffled into columns and rows, pinned to two-meter tall boards, or pigeon-holed into massive cabinets filled with cubby-holes in order to arrive at a "three-dimensional" analysis. But if the techniques of data analysis were makeshift and cumbersome, the results were surprising and elegant. For example, his discussion of the Oedipus myth uncovers patterns of complex orders that are not at all evident in the narrative presentations of the tale. Similar patterns are found in the analysis of myths from the American Southwest. In both cases, the basic ways of ordering the myths are not visible on the surface of the narrative, but present in the fundamental ways the humans organize information—based on the innate and deep structures of the mind.

PRIMARY TEXT: *THE STRUCTURAL STUDY OF MYTH*

Reprinted with permission from *The Journal of American Folklore*, Vol. 68 (270), Myth: A Symposium. (Oct.–Dec.,1955), pp. 428–444.

> It would seem that mythological worlds have been built up only to be shattered again, and that new worlds were built from the fragments.[1]

1.0. Despite some recent attempts to renew them, it would seem that during the past twenty years anthropology has more and more turned away from studies in the field of religion. At the same time, and precisely because professional anthropologists' interest has withdrawn from primitive religion, all kinds of amateurs who claim to belong to other disciplines have seized this opportunity to move in, thereby turning into their private playground what we had left as a wasteland. Thus, the prospects for the scientific study of religion have been undermined in two ways.

1.1. The explanation for that situation lies to some extent in the fact that the anthropological study of religion was started by men like Tylor, Frazer, and Durkheim who were psychologically oriented, although not in a posi-

---

[1] Franz Boas, in Introduction to James Teit, Traditions of the Thompson River Indians of British Columbia, Memoirs of the American Folklore Society, VI (1898), 18.

tion to keep up with the progress of psychological research and theory. Therefore, their interpretations soon became vitiated by the outmoded psychological approach which they used as their backing. Although they were undoubtedly right in giving their attention to intellectual processes, the way they handled them remained so coarse as to discredit them altogether. This is much to be regretted since, as Hocart so profoundly noticed in his introduction to a posthumous book recently published,[2] psychological interpretations were withdrawn from the intellectual field only to be introduced again in the field of affectivity, thus adding to "the inherent defects of the psychological school . . . the mistake of deriving clear-cut ideas . . . from vague emotions." Instead of trying to enlarge the framework of our logic to include processes which, whatever their apparent differences, belong to the same kind of intellectual operations, a naive attempt was made to reduce them to inarticulate emotional drives which resulted only in withering our studies.

1.2. Of all the chapters of religious anthropology probably none has tarried to the same extent as studies in the field of mythology. From a theoretical point of view the situation remains very much the same as it was fifty years ago, namely, a picture of chaos. Myths are still widely interpreted in conflicting ways: collective dreams, the outcome of a kind of esthetic play, the foundation of ritual. . . . Mythological figures are considered as personified abstractions, divinized heroes or decayed gods. Whatever the hypothesis, the choice amounts to reducing mythology either to an idle play or to a coarse kind of speculation.

1.3. In order to understand what a myth really is, are we compelled to choose between platitude and sophism? Some claim that human societies merely express, through their mythology, fundamental feelings common to the whole of mankind, such as love, hate, revenge; or that they try to provide some kind of explanations for phenomena which they cannot understand otherwise: astronomical, meteorological, and the like. But why should these societies do it in such elaborate and devious ways, since all of them are also acquainted with positive explanations? On the other hand, psychoanalysts and many anthropologists have shifted the problems to be explained away from the natural or cosmological towards the sociological and psychological fields. But then the interpretation becomes too easy: if a given mythology confers prominence to a certain character, let us say an evil grandmother, it will be claimed that in such a society grandmothers are actually evil and that mythology reflects the social structure and the social relations; but should the actual data be conflicting, it would be readily claimed that the purpose of mythology is to provide an outlet for repressed

---

[2] Hocart, Social Origins (London, 1954), p. 7.

feelings. Whatever the situation may be, a clever dialectic will always find a way to pretend that a meaning has been unraveled.

2.0. Mythology confronts the student with a situation which at first sight could be looked upon as contradictory. On the one hand, it would seem that in the course of a myth anything is likely to happen. There is no logic, no continuity. Any characteristic can be attributed to any subject; every conceivable relation can be met. With myth, everything becomes possible. But on the other hand, this apparent arbitrariness is belied by the astounding similarity between myths collected in widely different regions. Therefore the problem: if the content of a myth is contingent, how are we going to explain that throughout the world myths do resemble one another so much?

2.1. It is precisely this awareness of a basic antinomy pertaining to the nature of myth that may lead us towards its solution. For the contradiction which we face is very similar to that which in earlier times brought considerable worry to the first philosophers concerned with linguistic problems; linguistics could only begin to evolve as a science after this contradiction had been overcome. Ancient philosophers were reasoning about language the way we are about mythology. On the one hand, they did notice that in a given language certain sequences of sounds were associated with definite meanings, and they earnestly aimed at discovering a reason for the linkage between those sounds and that meaning. Their attempt, however, was thwarted from the very beginning by the fact that the same sounds were equally present in other languages though the meaning they conveyed was entirely different. The contradiction was surmounted only by the discovery that it is the combination of sounds, not the sounds in themselves, which provides the significant data.

2.2. Now, it is easy to see that some of the more recent interpretations of mythological thought originated from the same kind of misconception under which those early linguists were laboring. Let us consider, for instance, Jung's idea that a given mythological pattern—the so-called archetype—possesses a certain signification. This is comparable to the long supported error that a sound may possess a certain affinity with a meaning: for instance, the "liquid" semi-vowels with water, the open vowels with things that are big, large, loud, or heavy, etc., a kind of theory which still has its supporter. Whatever emendations the original formulation may now call for, everybody will agree that the Saussurean principle of the arbitrary character of the linguistic signs was a prerequisite for the acceding of linguistics to the scientific level.

2.3. To invite the mythologist to compare his precarious situation with that of the linguist in the prescientific stage is not enough. As a matter of fact we may thus be led only from one difficulty to another. There is a very good reason why myth cannot simply be treated as language if its specific problems are to be solved; myth is language: to be known, myth has to be told; it is a part of human speech. In order to preserve its specificity we should thus put ourselves in a position to show that it is both the same thing as language, and also something different from it. Here, too, the past experience of linguists may help us. For language itself can be analyzed into things which are at the same time similar and different. This is precisely what is expressed in Saussure's distinction between *langue* and *parole*, one being the structural side of language, the other the statistical aspect of it, *langue* belonging to a revertible time, whereas *parole* is non-revertible. If those two levels already exist in language, then a third one can conceivably be isolated.

2.4. We have just distinguished *langue* and *parole* by the different time referents which they use. Keeping this in mind, we may notice that myth uses a third referent which combines the properties of the first two. On the one hand, a myth always refers to events alleged to have taken place in time: before the world was created, or during its first stages—anyway, long ago. But what gives the myth an operative value is that the specific pattern described is everlasting; it explains the present and the past as well as the future. This can be made clear through a comparison between myth and what appears to have largely replaced it in modern societies, namely, politics. When the historian refers to the French Revolution it is always as a sequence of past happenings, a non-revertible series of events the remote consequences of which may still be felt at present. But to the French politician, as well as to his followers, the French Revolution is both a sequence belonging to the past—as to the historian—and an everlasting pattern which can be detected in the present French social structure and which provides a clue for its interpretation, a lead from which to infer the future developments. See, for instance, Michelet who was a politically-minded historian. He describes the French Revolution thus: "This day . . . everything was possible. . . . Future became present . . . that is, no more time, a glimpse of eternity." It is that double structure, altogether historical and anhistorical, which explains that myth, while pertaining to the realm of the *parole* and calling for an explanation as such, as well as to that of the *langue* in which it is expressed, can also be an absolute object on a third level which, though it remains linguistic by nature, is nevertheless distinct from the other two.

2.5. A remark can be introduced at this point which will help to show the singularity of myth among other linguistic phenomena. Myth is the part of language where the formula *traduttore, traditore*[3] reaches its lowest truth-value.

---

[3] Editor's note: Italian phrase paraphrased in English as "the translator is a traitor," which suggests the inherent distortions involved in translation, but a problem according to Lévi-Strauss, not relevant to myth.

From that point of view it should be put in the whole gamut of linguistic expressions at the end opposite to that of poetry, in spite of all the claims which
have been made to prove the contrary. Poetry is a kind of speech which cannot
be translated except at the cost of serious distortions; whereas the mythical
value of the myth remains preserved, even through the worst translation.
Whatever our ignorance of the language and the culture of the people where it
originated, a myth is still felt as a myth by any reader throughout the world. Its
substance does not lie in its style, its original music, or its syntax, but in the
story which it tells. It is language, functioning on an especially high level where
meaning succeeds practically at "taking off from the linguistic ground on
which it keeps on rolling."

2.6. To sum up the discussion at this point, we have so far made the following claims: 1. If there is a meaning to be found in mythology, this cannot reside in the isolated elements which enter into the composition of a
myth, but only in the way those elements are combined. 2. Although myth
belongs to the same category as language, being, as a matter of fact, only
part of it, language in myth unveils specific properties. 3. Those properties
are only to be found above the ordinary linguistic level; that is, they exhibit
more complex features beside those which are to be found in any kind of
linguistic expression.

3.0. If the above three points are granted, at least as a working hypothesis, two consequences will follow: 1. Myth, like the rest of language, is made
up of constituent units. 2. These constituent units presuppose the constituent units present in language when analyzed on other levels, namely,
phonemes, morphemes, and semantemes, but they, nevertheless, differ
from the latter in the same way as they themselves differ from morphemes,
and these from phonemes; they belong to a higher order, a more complex
one. For this reason, we will call them *gross constituent units*.

3.1. How shall we proceed in order to identify and isolate these gross
constituent units? We know that they cannot be found among
phonemes, morphemes, or semantemes, but only on a higher level; otherwise myth would become confused with any other kind of speech.
Therefore, we should look for them on the sentence level. The only
method we can suggest at this stage is to proceed tentatively, by trial and
error, using as a check the principles which serve as a basis for any kind
of structural analysis: economy of explanation; unity of solution; and
ability to reconstruct the whole from a fragment, as well as further stages
from previous ones.

3.2. The technique which has been applied so far by this writer consists
in analyzing each myth individually, breaking down its story into the short-
est possible sentences, and writing each such sentence on an index card
bearing a number corresponding to the unfolding of the story.

3.3. Practically each card will thus show that a certain function is, at a given time, predicated to a given subject. Or, to put it otherwise, each gross constituent unit will consist in a relation.

3.4. However, the above definition remains highly unsatisfactory for two different reasons. In the first place, it is well known to structural linguists that constituent units on all levels are made up of relations and the true difference between our gross units and the others stays unexplained; moreover, we still find ourselves in the realm of a non-revertible time since the numbers of the cards correspond to the unfolding of the informant's speech. Thus, the specific character of mythological time, which as we have seen is both revertible and non-revertible, synchronic and diachronic, remains unaccounted for. Therefrom comes a new hypothesis which constitutes the very core of our argument: the true constituent units of a myth are not the isolated relations but bundles of such relations and it is only as bundles that these relations can be put to use and combined so as to produce a meaning. Relations pertaining to the same bundle may appear diachronically at remote intervals, but when we have succeeded in grouping them together, we have reorganized our myth according to a time referent of a new nature corresponding to the prerequisite of the initial hypothesis, namely, a two-dimensional time referent which is simultaneously diachronic and synchronic and which accordingly integrates the characteristics of the *langue* on one hand, and those of the *parole* on the other. To put it in even more linguistic terms, it is as though a phoneme were always made up of all its variants.

4.0. Two comparisons may help to explain what we have in mind.

4.1. Let us first suppose that archaeologists of the future coming from another planet would one day, when all human life had disappeared from the earth, excavate one of our libraries. Even if they were at first ignorant of our writing, they might succeed in deciphering it—an undertaking which would require, at some early stage, the discovery that the alphabet, as we are in the habit of printing it, should be read from left to right and from top to bottom. However, they would soon find out that a whole category of books did not fit the usual pattern: these would be the orchestra scores on the shelves of the music division. But after trying, without success, to decipher staffs one after the other, from the upper down to the lower, they would probably notice that the same patterns of notes recurred at intervals, either in full or in part, or that some patterns were strongly reminiscent of earlier ones. Hence the hypothesis: what if patterns showing affinity, instead of being considered in succession, were to be treated as one complex pattern and read globally? By getting at what we call *harmony*, they would then find out that an orchestra score, in order to become meaningful, has to be read diachronically along one axis—that is, page after page, and from left to right—and also synchronically along the other axis, all the notes which are written vertically making up one gross constituent unit, i.e. one bundle of relations.

4.2. The other comparison is somewhat different. Let us take an observer ignorant of our playing cards, sitting for a long time with a fortune-teller. He would know something of the visitors: sex, age, look, social situation, etc. in the same way as we know something of the different cultures whose myths we try to study. He would also listen to the séances and keep them recorded so as to be able to go over them and make comparisons—as we do when we listen to myth telling and record it. Mathematicians to whom I have put the problem agree that if the man is bright and if the material available to him is sufficient, he may be able to reconstruct the nature of the deck of cards being used, that is: fifty-two or thirty-two cards according to case, made up of four homologous series consisting of the same units (the individual cards) with only one varying feature, the suit.

4.3. The time has come to give a concrete example of the method we propose. We will use the Oedipus myth which has the advantage of being well-known to every-body and for which no preliminary explanation is therefore needed. By doing so, I am well aware that the Oedipus myth has only reached us under late forms and through literary transfigurations concerned more with esthetic and moral preoccupations than with religious or ritual ones, whatever these may have been. But as will be shown later, this apparently unsatisfactory situation will strengthen our demonstration rather than weaken it.

4.4. The myth will be treated as would be an orchestra score perversely presented as a unilinear series and where our task is to reestablish the correct disposition. As if, for instance, we were confronted with a sequence of the type: 1,2,4,7,8,2,3,4,6,8,1,4,5,7,8,1,2,5,754,5,6,8 . . . , the assignment being to put all the 1's together, all the 2's, the 3's, etc.; the result is a chart:

1	2		4			7	8
	2	3	4		6		8
1			4	5		7	8
1	2			5		7	
		3	4	5			
					6		8

4.5. We will attempt to perform the same kind of operation on the Oedipus myth, trying out several dispositions until we find one which is in harmony with the principles enumerated under 3.1. Let us suppose, for the sake of argument, that the best arrangement is the following (although it might certainly be improved by the help of a specialist in Greek mythology):

Kadmos seeks his sister Europa ravished by Zeus		Kadmos kills the dragon	
	The Spartoi kill each other		Labdacos (Laios's father) = *lame* (?)
	Oedipus kills his father Laios		Laios (Oedipus's father) = *left-sided* (?)
		Oedipus kills the Sphinx	
Oedipus marries his mother Jocasta	Eteocles kills his brother Polynices		Oedipus = *swollen-foot* (?)
Antigone buries her brother Polynices despite prohibition			

4.6. Thus, we find ourselves confronted with four vertical columns each of which include several relations belonging to the same bundle. Were we to *tell* the myth, we would disregard the columns and read the rows from left to right and from top to bottom. But if we want to *understand* the myth, then we will have to disregard one half of the diachronic dimension (top to bottom) and read from left to right, column after column, each one being considered as a unit.

4.7. All the relations belonging to the same column exhibit one common feature which it is our task to unravel. For instance, all the events grouped in the first column on the left have something to do with blood relations which are over-emphasized, i.e. are subject to a more intimate treatment than they should be. Let us say, then, that the first column has as its common feature the *overrating of blood relations*. It is obvious that the second column expresses the same thing, but inverted: *underrating of blood relations*. The third column refers to monsters being slain. As to the fourth, a word of clarification is needed. The remarkable connotation of the surnames in Oedipus' father-line has often been noticed. However, linguists usually disregard it, since to them the only way to define the meaning of a term is to investigate all the contexts in which it appears, and personal names, precisely because they are used as such, are not accompanied by any context. With the method we propose to follow the objection disappears since the myth itself provides its own context. The meaningful fact is no longer to be looked for in the eventual sense of each name, but in the fact that all the names have a common feature: i.e. that they may eventually mean something and that all these hypothetical meanings (which may well remain hypothetical) exhibit a common feature, namely they refer to *difficulties to walk and to behave straight.*

4.8. What is then the relationship between the two columns on the right? Column three refers to monsters. The dragon is a chthonian being which has to be killed in order that mankind be born from the earth; the sphinx is a monster unwilling to permit men to live. The last unit reproduces the first one which has to do with the *autotochthonous origin* of mankind. Since the monsters are overcome by men, we may thus say that the common feature of the third column is *the denial of the autochthonous origin of man.*

4.9. This immediately helps us to understand the meaning of the fourth column. In mythology it is a universal character of men born from the earth that at the moment they emerge from the depth, they either cannot walk or do it clumsily. This is the case of the chthonian beings in the mythology of the Pueblo: Masauwu, who leads the emergence, and the chthonian Shumaikoli are lame ("bleeding-foot," "sore-foot"). The same happens to the Koskimo of the Kwakiutl after they have been swallowed by the chthonian monster, Tsiakish: when they returned to the surface of the earth "they limped forward or tripped sideways." Then the common feature of the fourth column is: *the persistence of the autochthonous origin of man.* It follows that column four is to column three as column one is to column two. The inability to connect two kinds of relationships is overcome (or rather replaced) by the positive statement that contradictory relationships are identical inasmuch as they are both self-contradictory in a similar way. Although this is still a provisional formulation of the structure of mythical thought, it is sufficient at this stage.

4.10. Turning back to the Oedipus myth, we may now see what it means. The myth has to do with the inability, for a culture which holds the belief that mankind is autochthonous (see, for instance, *Pausanias*, VIII, xxix, 4: vegetals provide a *model* for humans), to find a satisfactory transition between this theory and the knowledge that human beings are actually born from the union of man and woman. Although the problem obviously cannot be solved, the Oedipus myth provides a kind of logical tool which, to phrase it coarsely, replaces the original problem: born from one or born from two? born from different or born from same? By a correlation of this type, the overrating of blood relations is to the underrating of blood relations as the attempt to escape autochthony is to the impossibility to succeed in it. Although experience contradicts theory, social life verifies the cosmology by its similarity of structure. Hence cosmology is true.

4.11.0. Two remarks should be made at this stage.

4.11.1. In order to interpret the myth, we were able to leave aside a point which has until now worried the specialists, namely, that in the earlier (Homeric) versions of the Oedipus myth, some basic elements are lacking, such as Jocasta killing herself and Oedipus piercing his own eyes. These events do not alter the substance of the myth although they can easily be integrated, the first one as a new case of auto-destruction (column three) while the second is another case of crippledness (column four). At the same time there is something significant in these additions since the shift from foot to head is to be correlated with the shift from: autochthonous origin negated to: self-destruction.

4.11.2. Thus, our method eliminates a problem which has been so far one of the main obstacles to the progress of mythological studies, namely, the quest for the *true* version, or the *earlier* one. On the contrary, we define the myth as consisting of all its versions; to put it otherwise: a myth remains the same as long as it is felt as such. A striking example is offered by the fact that our interpretation may take into account, and is certainly applicable to, the Freudian use of the Oedipus myth. Although the Freudian problem has ceased to be that of autochthony *versus* bisexual reproduction, it is still the problem of understanding how *one* can be born from *two*: how is it that we do not have only one procreator, but a mother plus a father? Therefore, not only Sophocles, but Freud himself, should be included among the recorded versions of the Oedipus myth on a par with earlier or seemingly more "authentic" versions.

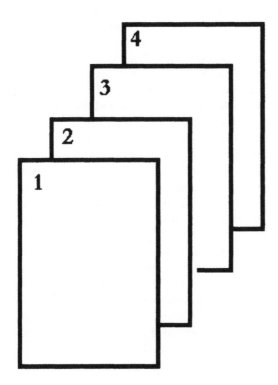

5.0. An important consequence follows. If a myth is made up of all its variants, structural analysis should take all of them into account. Thus, after analyzing all the known variants of the Theban version, we should treat the others in the same way: first, the tales about Labdacos' collateral line including Agavé, Pentheus, and Jocasta herself; the Theban variant about Lycos with Amphion and Zetos as the city founders; more remote variants concerning Dionysos (Oedipus' matrilateral cousin), and Athenian legends where Cecrops takes the place of Kadmos, etc. For each of them a similar chart should be drawn, and then compared and reorganized according to the findings: Cecrops killing the serpent with the parallel episode of Kadmos; abandonment of Dionysos with abandonment of Oedipus; "Swollen Foot" with Dionysos *loxias*, i.e. walking obliquely; Europa's quest with Antiope's; the foundation of Thebes by the Spartoi or by the brothers Amphion and Zetos; Zeus kidnapping Europa and Antiope and the same with Semele; the Theban Oedipus and the Argian Perseus, etc. We will then have several two-dimensional charts, each dealing with a variant, to be organized in a three-dimensional order so that three different readings become possible: left to right, top to bottom, front to back. All of these charts cannot be expected to be identical; but experience shows that any difference to be observed may be correlated with other differences, so that a logical treatment of the whole will allow simplifications, the final outcome being the structural law of the myth.

5.1. One may object at this point that the task is impossible to perform since we can only work with known versions. Is it not possible that a new version might alter the picture? This is true enough if only one or two versions are available, but the objection becomes theoretical as soon as a reasonably large number has been recorded (a number which experience will progressively tell, at least as an approximation). Let us make this point clear by a comparison. If the furniture of a room and the way it is arranged in the room were known to us only through its reflection in two mirrors placed on opposite walls, we would theoretically dispose of an almost infinite number of mirror-images which would provide us with a complete knowledge. However, should the two mirrors be obliquely set, the number of mirror-images would become very small; nevertheless, four or five such images would very likely give us, if not complete information, at least a sufficient coverage so that we would feel sure that no large piece of furniture is missing in our description.

5.2. On the other hand, it cannot be too strongly emphasized that all available variants should be taken into account. If Freudian comments on the Oedipus complex are a part of the Oedipus myth, then questions such as whether Cushing's version of the Zuni origin myth should be retained or discarded become irrelevant. There is no one true version of which all the others are but copies or distortions. Every version belongs to the myth.

5.3. Finally it can be understood why works on general mythology have given discouraging results. This comes from two reasons. First, comparative mythologists have picked up preferred versions instead of using them all. Second, we have seen that the structural analysis of one variant of one myth belonging to one tribe (in some cases, even one village) already requires two dimensions. When we use several variants of the same myth for the same tribe or village, the frame of reference becomes three-dimensional and as soon as we try to enlarge the comparison, the number of dimensions required increases to such an extent that it appears quite impossible to handle them intuitively. The confusions and platitudes which are the outcome of comparative mythology can be explained by the fact that multi-dimensional frames of reference cannot be ignored, or naively replaced by two- or three-dimensional ones. Indeed, progress in comparative mythology depends largely on the cooperation of mathematicians who would undertake to express in symbols multi-dimensional relations which cannot be handled otherwise.

6.0. In order to check this theory,[4] an attempt was made in 1953–1954 towards an exhaustive analysis of all the known versions of the Zuni origin and emergence myth: Cushing 1883, 1896; Stevenson 1904; Parsons 1923; Bunzel 1932; Benedict 1934. Furthermore, a preliminary attempt was made at a comparison of the results with similar myths in other Pueblo tribes, Western and Eastern. Finally, a test was undertaken with Plains mythology. In all cases, it was found that the theory was sound, and light was thrown, not only on North American mythology, but also on a previously unnoticed kind of logical operation, or one known only so far in a wholly different context. The bulk of material which needs to be handled almost at the beginning of the work makes it impossible to enter into details, and we will have to limit ourselves here to a few illustrations.

6.1. An over-simplified chart of the Zuni emergence myth would read as follows:

INCREASE			DEATH
mechanical growth of vegetals	emergence led by Beloved Twins	sibling incest	gods kill children (used as ladders)
food value of wild plants	migration led by the two Newekwe		magical contest with people of the dew (collecting wild food *versus* cultivation)
		sibling sacrificed (to gain victory)	
food value of cultivated plants		sibling adopted (in exchange for corn)	

---

[4] Thanks are due to an unsolicited, but deeply appreciated, grant from the Ford Foundation.

periodical
character of
agricultural work

war against
Kyanakwe
(gardeners
versus hunters)

hunting   war led by two
                     war-gods

salvation of the
tribe (center of
the world found)

warfare   sibling sacrificed
                                     (to avoid flood)

DEATH   PERMANENCY

6.2. As may be seen from a global inspection of the chart, the basic problem consists in discovering a mediation between life and death. For the Pueblo, the problem is especially difficult since they understand the origin of human life on the model of vegetal life (emergence from the earth). They share that belief with the ancient Greeks, and it is not without reason that we chose the Oedipus myth as our first example. But in the American case, the highest form of vegetal life is to be found in agriculture which is periodical in nature, i.e., which consists in an alternation between life and death. If this is disregarded, the contradiction surges at another place: agriculture provides food, therefore life; but hunting provides food and is similar to warfare which means death. Hence there are three different ways of handling the problem. In the Cushing version, the difficulty revolves around an opposition between activities yielding an immediate result (collecting wild food) and activities yielding a delayed result—death has to become integrated so that agriculture can exist. Parsons's version goes from hunting to agriculture, while Stevenson's version operates the other way around. It can be shown that all the differences between these versions can be rigorously correlated with these basic structures. For instance:

		CUSHING	PARSONS	STEVENSON
Gods	⎫	allied, use fiber	Kyanakwe alone,	Gods ⎱ allied, use
	⎬	strings on their	use fiber string	Men ⎰ fiber string
Kyanakwe	⎭	bows (gardeners)		

	VICTORIOUS OVER	VICTORIOUS OVER	VICTORIOUS OVER
Men	alone, use sinew (hunters) (until men shift to fiber)	Gods ⎱ allied, use Men ⎰ sinew string	Kyanakwe alone, use sinew string

Since fiber strings (vegetal) are always superior to sinew strings (animal) and since (to a lesser extent) the gods' alliance is preferable to their antagonism, it follows that in Cushing's version, men begin to be doubly underprivileged (hostile gods, sinew string); in Stevenson, doubly privileged (friendly gods, fiber string); while Parsons's version confronts us with an intermediary situation (friendly gods, but sinew strings since men begin by being hunters). Hence:

	CUSHING	PARSONS	STEVENSON
gods/men	-	+	+
fiber/sinew	-	-	+

6.3. Bunzel's version is from a structural point of view of the same type as Cushing's. However, it differs from both Cushing's and Stevenson's inasmuch as the latter two explain the emergence as a result of man's need to evade his pitiful condition, while Bunzel's version makes it the consequence of a call from the higher powers—hence the inverted sequences of the means resorted to for the emergence: in both Cushing and Stevenson, they go from plants to animals; in Bunzel, from mammals to insects and from insects to plants.

6.4. Among the Western Pueblo the logical approach always remains the same; the starting point and the point of arrival are the simplest ones and ambiguity is met with halfway:

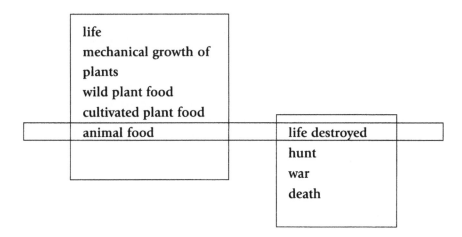

The fact that contradiction appears in the middle of the dialectical process has as its result the production of a double series of dioscuric[5] pairs the purpose of which is to operate a mediation between conflicting terms:

1. 3 divine messengers	2 ceremonial clowns		2 war-gods
2. homogeneous pair: dioscurs (2 brothers)	siblings (brother and sister)	couple (husband and wife)	heterogeneous pair: grandmother/ grandchild

which consists in combinatory variants of the same function; (hence the war attribute of the clowns which has given rise to so many queries).

6.5. Some Central and Eastern Pueblos proceed the other way around. They begin by stating the identity of hunting and cultivation (first corn obtained by Game-Father sowing deer-dewclaws), and they try to derive both life and death from that central notion. Then, instead of extreme terms being simple and intermediary ones duplicated as among the Western groups, the extreme terms become duplicated (i.e., the two sisters of the Eastern Pueblo) while a simple mediating term comes to the foreground (for instance, the Poshaiyanne of the Zia), but endowed with equivocal attributes. Hence the attributes of this "messiah" can be deduced from the place it occupies in the time sequence: good when at the beginning (Zuni, Cushing), equivocal in the middle (Central Pueblo), bad at the end (Zia), except in Bunzel where the sequence is reversed as has been shown.

6.6. By using systematically this kind of structural analysis it becomes possible to organize all the known variants of a myth as a series forming a kind of permutation group, the two variants placed at the far-ends being in a symmetrical, though inverted, relationship to each other.

7.0. Our method not only has the advantage of bringing some kind of order to what was previously chaos; it also enables us to perceive some basic logical processes which are at the root of mythical thought. Three main processes should be distinguished.

7.1.0. The trickster of American mythology has remained so far a problematic figure. Why is it that throughout North America his part is assigned practically everywhere to either coyote or raven? If we keep in mind that mythical thought always works from the awareness of oppositions towards their progressive mediation, the reason for those choices becomes clearer.

---

[5] Editor's note: From the dioscuri, the heavenly twins, Castor and Pollux, born to Leda and Zeus. The dioscuri are famous for their fraternal cooperation, such that when Pollux was granted immortality he convinced Zeus to give a partial and shared grant to his brother Castor, and thus the two brothers spent eternity alternating as divine gods on Olympus and deceased mortals in Hades.

We need only to assume that two opposite terms with no intermediary always tend to be replaced by two equivalent terms which allow a third one as a mediator; then one of the polar terms and the mediator becomes replaced by a new triad and so on. Thus we have:

INITIAL PAIR	FIRST TRIAD	SECOND TRIAD
Life		
	Agriculture	
		Herbivorous animals
		Carrion-eating animals
		(raven; coyote)
	Hunt	
		Prey animals
	War	
Death		

With the unformulated argument: carrion-eating animals are like prey animals (they eat animal food), but they are also like food-plant producers (they do not kill what they eat). Or, to put it otherwise, Pueblo style: ravens are to gardens as prey animals are to herbivorous ones. But it is also clear that herbivorous animals may be called first to act as mediators on the assumption that they are like collectors and gatherers (vegetal-food eaters) while they can be used as animal food though not themselves hunters. Thus we may have mediators of the first order, of the second order, and so on, where each term gives birth to the next by a double process of opposition and correlation.

7.1.1. This kind of process can be followed in the mythology of the Plains where we may order the data according to the sequence:

> Unsuccessful mediator between earth and sky
> (Star husband's wife)
>
> Heterogeneous pair of mediators
> (grandmother/grandchild)
>
> Semi-homogeneous pair of mediators
> (Lodge-Boy and Thrown-away)

While among the Pueblo we have:

> Successful mediator between earth and sky
> (Poshaiyanki)
>
> Semi-homogeneous pair of mediators
> (Uyuyewi and Matsailema)
>
> Homogeneous pair of mediators
> (the Ahaiyuta)

7.1.2. On the other hand, correlations may appear on a transversal axis; (this is true even on the linguistic level; see the manifold connotation of the root *pose* in Tewa according to Parsons: coyote, mist, scalp, etc.). Coyote is intermediary between herbivorous and carnivorous in the same way as mist between sky and earth; scalp between war and hunt (scalp is war-crop); corn smut between wild plants and cultivated plants; garments between "nature" and "culture"; refuse between village and outside; ashes between roof and hearth (chimney). This string of mediators, if one may call them so, not only throws light on whole pieces of North American mythology—why the Dew-God may be at the same time the Game-Master and the giver of raiments and be personified as an "Ash-Boy"; or why the scalps are mist producing; or why the Game-Mother is associated with corn smut; etc.—but it also probably corresponds to a universal way of organizing daily experience. See, for instance, the French for vegetal smut; *nielle*, from Latin *nebula*; the luck-bringing power attributed to refuse (old shoe) and ashes (kissing chimney-sweepers); and compare the American Ash-Boy cycle with the Indo-European Cinderella: both phallic figures (mediator between male and female); master of the dew and of the game; owners of fine raiments; and social bridges (low class marrying into high class); though impossible to interpret through recent diffusion as has been sometimes contended since Ash-Boy and Cinderella are symmetrical but inverted in every detail (while the borrowed Cinderella tale in America—Zuni Turkey-Girl—is parallel to the prototype):

	EUROPE	AMERICA
Sex	female	male
Family Status	double family	no family
Appearance	pretty girl	ugly boy
Sentimental status	nobody likes her	in hopeless love with girl
Transformation	luxuriously clothed with supernatural help	stripped of ugliness with with supernatural help, etc.

7.2.0. Thus, the mediating function of the trickster explains that since its position is halfway between two polar terms he must retain something of that duality, namely an ambiguous and equivocal character. But the trickster figure is not the only conceivable form of mediation; some myths seem to devote themselves to the task of exhausting all the possible solutions to the problem of bridging the gap between two and one. For instance, a comparison between all the variants of the Zuni emergence myth provides us with a series of mediating devices, each of which creates the next one by a process of opposition and correlation:

messiah > dioscurs > trickster > $\begin{array}{c}\text{bisexual}\\\text{being}\end{array}$ > $\begin{array}{c}\text{sibling}\\\text{pair}\end{array}$ > $\begin{array}{c}\text{married}\\\text{couple}\end{array}$ > $\begin{array}{c}\text{grandmother-}\\\text{grandchild}\end{array}$ > $\begin{array}{c}\text{4 terms}\\\text{group}\end{array}$ > triad

In Cushing's version, this dialectic is accompanied by a change from the space dimension (mediating between sky and earth) to the time dimension (mediating between summer and winter, i.e., between birth and death). But while the shift is being made from space to time, the final solution (triad) re-introduces space, since a triad consists in a dioscur pair plus a messiah simultaneously present; and while the point of departure was ostensibly formulated in terms of a space referent (sky and earth) this was nevertheless implicitly conceived in terms of a time referent (first the messiah calls; then the dioscurs descend). Therefore the logic of myth confronts us with a double, reciprocal exchange of functions to which we shall return shortly (7.3).

7.2.1. Not only can we account for the ambiguous character of the trickster, but we may also understand another property of mythical figures the world over, namely, that the same god may be endowed with contradictory attributes; for instance, he may be good and bad at the same time. If we compare the variants of the Hopi myth of the origin of Shalako, we may order them so that the following structure becomes apparent:

(Masauwu: x) $\underset{\sim}{} $ (Muyingwu: Masauwu) $\underset{\sim}{} $ (Shalako: Muyingwu) $\underset{\sim}{} $ (y: Masauwu)

where x and y represent arbitrary values corresponding to the fact that in the two "extreme" variants the god Masauwu, while appearing alone instead of associated with another god, as in variant two, or being absent, as in three, still retains intrinsically a relative value. In variant one, Masauwu (alone) is depicted as helpful to mankind (though not as helpful as he could be), and in version four, harmful to mankind (though not as harmful as he could be); whereas in two, Muyingwu is relatively more helpful than Masauwu, and in three, Shalako more helpful than Muyingwu. We find an identical series when ordering the Keresan variants:

(Poshaiyanki: x) $\underset{\sim}{} $ (Lea: Poshaiyanki) $\underset{\sim}{} $ (Poshaiyanki: Tiamoni) $\underset{\sim}{} $ (y: Poshaiyanki)

7.2.2. This logical framework is particularly interesting since sociologists are already acquainted with it on two other levels: first, with the problem of the pecking order among hens; and second, it also corresponds to what this writer has called general exchange in the field of kinship. By recognizing it also on the level of mythical thought, we may find ourselves in a better position to appraise its basic importance in sociological studies and to give it a more inclusive theoretical interpretation.

7.3.0. Finally, when we have succeeded in organizing a whole series of variants in a kind of permutation group, we are in a position to formulate the law of that group. Although it is not possible at the present stage to come closer than an approximate formulation which will certainly need to be made more accurate in the future, it seems that every myth (considered as the collection of all its variants) corresponds to a formula of the following type:

$$f_x(a) : f_y(b) \simeq f_x(b) : f_a - 1(y)$$

where, two terms being given as well as two functions of these terms, it is stated that a relation of equivalence still exists between two situations when terms and relations are inverted, under two conditions: 1. that one term be replaced by its contrary; 2. that an inversion be made between the *function* and the *term* value of two elements.

7.3.1. This formula becomes highly significant when we recall that Freud considered that two traumas (and not one as it is so commonly said) are necessary in order to give birth to this individual myth in which a neurosis consists. By trying to apply the formula to the analysis of those traumatisms (and assuming that they correspond to conditions 1 and 2, respectively) we should not only be able to improve it, but would find ourselves in the much desired position of developing side by side the sociological and the psychological aspects of the theory; we may also take it to the laboratory and subject it to experimental verification.

8.0. At this point it seems unfortunate that, with the limited means at the disposal of French anthropological research, no further advance can be made. It should be emphasized that the task of analyzing mythological literature, which is extremely bulky, and of breaking it down into its constituent units, requires team work and secretarial help. A variant of average length needs several hundred cards to be properly analyzed. To discover a suitable pattern of rows and columns for those cards, special devices are needed, consisting of vertical boards about two meters long and one and one-half meters high, where cards can be pigeon-holed and moved at will; in order to build up three-dimensional models enabling one to compare the variants, several such boards are necessary, and this in turn requires a spacious workshop, a kind of commodity particularly unavailable in Western Europe nowadays. Furthermore, as soon as the frame of reference becomes multi-dimensional (which occurs at an early stage, as has been shown in 5.3) the board-system has to be replaced by perforated cards which in turn require I.B.M. equipment, etc. Since there is little hope that such facilities will become available in France in the near future, it is much desired that some American group, better equipped than we are here in Paris, will be induced by this paper to start a project of its own in structural mythology.

8.1.0. Three final remarks may serve as conclusion.

8.1.1. First, the question has often been raised why myths, and more generally oral literature, are so much addicted to duplication, triplication or quadruplication of the same sequence. If our hypotheses are accepted, the answer is obvious: repetition has as its function to make the structure of the myth apparent. For we have seen that the synchro-diachronical structure of the myth permits us to organize it into diachronical sequences (the rows in our tables) which should be read synchronically (the columns). Thus, a myth exhibits a "slated" structure which seeps to the surface, if one may say so, through the repetition process.

8.1.2. However, the slates are not absolutely identical to each other. And since the purpose of myth is to provide a logical model capable of overcoming a contradiction (an impossible achievement if, as it happens, the contradiction is real), a theoretically infinite number of slates will be generated, each one slightly different from the others. Thus, myth grows spiralwise until the intellectual impulse which has originated it is exhausted. Its growth is a continuous process whereas its structure remains discontinuous. If this is the case we should consider that it closely corresponds, in the realm of the spoken word, to the kind of being a crystal is in the realm of physical matter. This analogy may help us understand better the relationship of myth on one hand to both *langue* and *parole* on the other.

8.1.3. Prevalent attempts to explain alleged differences between the so-called "primitive" mind and scientific thought have resorted to qualitative differences between the working processes of the mind in both cases while assuming that the objects to which they were applying themselves remained very much the same. If our interpretation is correct, we are led toward a completely different view, namely, that the kind of logic which is used by mythical thought is as rigorous as that of modern science, and that the difference lies not in the quality of the intellectual process, but in the nature of the things to which it is applied. This is well in agreement with the situation known to prevail in the field of technology: what makes a steel ax superior to a stone one is not that the first one is better made than the second. They are equally well made, but steel is a different thing than stone. In the same way we may be able to show that the same logical processes are put to use in myth as in science, and that man has always been thinking equally well; the improvement lies, not in an alleged progress of man's conscience, but in the discovery of new things to which it may apply its unchangeable abilities.

QUERIES

- What is the distinction between *langue* and *parole*? How does myth exhibit another alternative in the communication of information?

- What are the basic organizing principles associated with the Oedipus myth?
- Typically, the logical differences between science and myth are seen as reflecting a distinction between modern and so-called primitive thought. On what grounds does Lévi-Strauss argue that the underlying logics are similar?

CONNECTIONS

- Given his theory of cultural materialism, how would Marvin Harris respond to Lévi-Strauss's ideas?
- Clifford Geertz argued that cultural behavior—the use of symbols to create and convey meaning—can only be explained in terms of its context, an ethnographic process called "thick description." Is Lévi-Strauss's analysis of myth an example of "thick description"?
- How does Lévi-Strauss's concept of a "structure" differ from Radcliffe-Brown's definition of a social structure?

18

Victor Turner

INTRODUCTION

The following selection touches on a number of issues the British anthropologist Victor Turner (1920–1983) explored over a lengthy anthropological career (for an overview, see Moore 2008:247–58). This brief article addresses multiple dimensions of symbols in ritual practice, matters that Turner illustrates from his research among the Ndembu of Zambia and other ethnographic cases from sub-Saharan Africa, but relevant to human culture wherever it is found.

First, Turner distinguishes "ritual" from other domains of cultural practice, emphasizing ritual's sequential and formal use of symbols directed to influence supernatural forces or entities. Like other forms of cultural practice, ritual involves the use of symbols, but those symbols are used in a specific manner to achieve a desired end.

In the process, rituals employ certain sets of symbols that have characteristic values. Ritual symbols simultaneously convey multiple meanings; ritual symbols are multivocal. Ritual symbols connect different multiple and often distinct meanings through association or analogy. Ritual symbols are powerful condensers of meaning. (For example, the American flag may represent the symbol of U.S. territory, the notion of liberty, the imposition of empire, and so on; for an extended discussion, see Moore 2008:252–54.) Finally, the meanings associated with ritual symbols tend to cluster around two "poles," one dealing with the social and moral order of life, the other associated with individual desires and feelings.

Deploying these symbols in complex ways, rituals convey certain themes about a culture, central principles or moral statements about social life. This takes place in a dynamic social setting, because rituals are dramatic. A central point in Turner's argument is that the meanings of ritual symbols are created and expressed within dynamic social settings or what he calls "cultural and operational contexts." These social dramas are often organized in a "cycle of performances" in which some symbols are dominant and others essentially serve to advance the ritual activity, roughly similar to the way nouns and verbs convey the central meanings of a sentence, but prepositions, articles, and punctuation move the sentence along. In this process, however, the dominant symbols connect with other sets of symbols, resulting in complex and profound meanings.

Sometimes these symbols gain their meanings from binary opposition—God/Satan, Heaven/Hell, Redemption/Damnation, to cite a few obvious examples from Christian rituals. Yet, these ritual symbols, Turner suggests, exhibit a counterintuitive property: the more elaborate a symbol and the more detailed a ritual, the narrower its scope of meaning, while less elaborate symbols and less elaborate rituals tend to have a broader range of meanings. These meanings not only convey morals and norms, but they also concentrate the forces "inherent in the persons, objects, relationships, events, and histories represented by ritual symbols" resulting in the mobilization of "energies as well as messages." Turner concludes with a brief overview of how such ritual symbols are used in a variety of African societies, "traditional" and "modern."

PRIMARY TEXT: *SYMBOLS IN AFRICAN RITUAL*

From *Science* 179 (March 16, 1973), pp. 1100–1105. Reprinted by permission of the American Association for the Advancement of Science.

No one who has lived for long in rural sub-Saharan Africa can fail to be struck by the importance of ritual in the lives of villagers and homesteaders and by the fact that rituals are composed of symbols. A ritual is a stereotyped sequence of activities involving gestures, words, and objects, performed in a sequestered place, and designed to influence preternatural entities or forces on behalf of the actors' goals and interests. Rituals may be seasonal, hallowing a culturally defined moment of change in the climatic cycle or the inauguration of an activity such as planting, harvesting, or moving from winter to summer pasture; or they may be contingent, held in response to an individual or collective crisis. Contingent rituals may be further subdivided into life-crisis ceremonies, which are performed at birth, puberty, marriage, death, and so on to demarcate the passage from one phase to another in the individual's life-cycle, and rituals of affliction, which are performed to placate or exorcise preternatural beings or forces believed to have afflicted villagers with illness, bad luck, gynecological troubles, severe physical injuries, and the like. Other classes of rituals include divinatory rituals; ceremonies performed by political authorities to ensure the health and fertility of human beings, animals, and crops in their territories; initiation into priesthoods devoted to certain deities, into religious associations, or into secret societies; and those accompanying the daily offering of food and libations to deities or ancestral spirits or both. Africa is rich indeed in ritual genres, and each involves many specific performances.

Each rural African society (which is often, though not always, coterminous with a linguistic community) possesses a finite number of distinguishable rituals that may include all or some of the types listed above. At varying intervals, from a year to several decades a society's rituals will be performed, the most important [for example, the symbolic transference of political authority from one generation to another as among the Nyakyusa of Tanzania (Turner 1964:20–51; Wilson 1959:49–69) being performed perhaps the least often. Since societies are processes responsive to change, not fixed structures, new rituals are devised or borrowed, and old ones decline and disappear. Nevertheless, forms survive through flux, and new ritual items, even new ritual configurations, tend more often to be variants of old themes than radical novelties. Thus it is possible for anthropologists to describe the main features of a ritual system, or rather ritual round (successive ritual performances), in those parts of rural Africa where change is occurring slowly.

The Semantic Structure of the Symbol

The ritual symbol is "the smallest unit of ritual which still retains the specific properties of ritual behavior . . . the ultimate unit of specific structure in a ritual context" (Opler 1945:198). This structure is a semantic one (that is, it deals with relationships between signs and symbols and the things to which they refer) and has the following attributes: (i) multiple meanings (significata) actions or objects perceived by the senses in ritual contexts (that is, symbol vehicles) have many meanings; (ii) unification of apparently disparate significata—the essentially distinct significata are interconnected by analogy or by association in fact or thought; (iii) condensation—many ideas, relations between things, actions, interactions, and transactions are represented simultaneously by the symbol vehicle (the ritual use of such a vehicle abridges what would verbally be a lengthy statement or argument); (iv) polarization of significata—the referents assigned by custom to a major ritual symbol tend frequently to be grouped at opposed semantic poles. At one pole of meaning, empirical research has shown that the significata tend to refer to components of the moral and social orders—this might be termed the ideological (or normative) pole of symbolic meaning; at the other, the sensory (or orectic) pole, are concentrated references to phenomena and processes that may be expected to stimulate desires and feelings. Thus, I have shown (1964:21–36) that the mudyi tree, or milk-tree (Diplorrhyncus mlossanibicensis) which is the focal symbol of the girls' puberty ritual of the Ndembu people of northwestern Zambia, at its normative pole represents womanhood, motherhood, the mother-child bond, a novice undergoing initiation into mature womanhood, a specific matrilineage, the principle of matriliny, the process of learning "women's wisdom," the unity and perdurance of Ndembu society, and all of the values and virtues inherent in the various relationships—domestic, legal, and political—controlled by matrilineal descent. Each of these aspects of its normative meaning becomes paramount in a specific episode of the puberty ritual; together, they form a condensed statement of the structural and communal importance of femaleness in Ndembu culture. At its sensory pole, the same symbol stands for breast milk (the tree exudes milky latex—indeed, the significata associated with the sensory pole often have a more or less direct connection with some sensorily perceptible attribute of the symbol), mother's breasts, and the bodily slenderness and mental pliancy of the novice (a young slender sapling of mudyi is used). The tree, situated a short distance from the novice's village, becomes the center of a sequence of ritual episodes rich in symbols (words, objects, and actions) that express important cultural themes.

Ritual Symbols and Cultural Themes

Opler has defined a theme as a part of a limited set of "dynamic affirmations" that "can be identified in every culture" (1945:198). In the "nature, expression, and relationship" of themes is to be found the "key to the character, structure, and direction of the specific culture" (Opler 1945:198). The term "theme" denotes "a postulate or position, declared or implied, and usually controlling behavior or stimulating activity, which is tacitly approved or openly promoted in a society" (Opler 1945:198). Every culture has multiple themes, and most themes have multiple expressions, some of which may be in one or more parts of the institutional culture (Watson 1964:164). Ritual forms an important setting for the expression of themes, and ritual symbols transmit themes. Themes have multiple expressions, and ritual symbols, such as the mudyi tree (and thousands of others in the ethnographic literature of African ritual), have multiple significata (Turner 1971). The major difference between themes and symbols is that themes are postulates or ideas inferred by an observer from the data of a given culture, while ritual symbols are one class of such data. Ritual symbols are multivocal—that is, each symbol expresses not one theme but many themes simultaneously by the same perceptible object or activity (symbol vehicle). Symbols *have* significata, themes may *be* significata.

Themes, in their capacity as significata (including both conceptions and images), may be disparate or grouped, as we have seen, at opposed semantic poles. Thus the mudyi signifies aspects of female bodily imagery (milk, suckling, breasts, girlish slenderness) and conceptions about standards of womanhood and motherhood, as well as the normative ordering of these in relation to group membership, the inheritance of property, and succession to such political offices as chieftainship and village headmanship through matrilineal descent. There are rules of exclusion connected with the mudyi in this ritual context—all that is not concerned with the nurtural, procreative, and esthetic aspects of human femaleness and with their cultural control and structuring, is excluded from the semantic field of mudyi symbolism. This is a field of themes with varying degrees of concreteness, abstraction, and cognitive and orectic quality. The impulse that leads advanced cultures to the economical use of signs in mathematics finds its equivalent here in the use of a single symbol vehicle to represent simultaneously a variety of themes, most of which can be shown to be related, logically or pragmatically, but some of which depend for their association on a sensed likeness between variables rather than on cognitive criteria. One is dealing with a "mathematics" of sociocultural experience rather than with a mathematics of logical relationships.

Ritual symbols differ from other modes of thematic expression, particularly from those unformalized modes that arise in spontaneous behavior and allow for individual choice in expression (Opler 1945:200). Indeed, it might be argued that the more ritualized the expression, the wider the range of themes that may be signified by it. On the other hand, since a ritual symbol may represent disparate, even contradictory themes, the gain in economy may be offset by a loss in clarity of communication. This would be inevitable if such symbols existed in a vacuum, but they exist in cultural and operational contexts that to some extent overcome the loss in intelligibility and to some extent capitalize on it.

Dominant Symbols in Ritual Cycles

Rituals tend to be organized in a cycle of performances (annual, biennial, quinquennial, and so on); even in the case of contingent rituals, each is performed eventually. In each total assemblage, or system, there is a nucleus of dominant symbols, which are characterized by extreme multivocality (having many senses) and a central position in each ritual performance. Associated with this nucleus is a much larger number of enclitic (dependent) symbols. Some of these are univocal, while others, like prepositions in language, become mere relation or function signs that keep the ritual action going (for example, bowings, lustrations, sweepings, and objects indicative of joining or separation). Dominant symbols provide the fixed points of the total system and recur in many of its component rituals. For example, if 15 separate kinds of ritual can be empirically distinguished in a given ritual system, dominant symbol A may be found in 10 of them, B in 7, C in 5, and D in 12. The mudyi tree, for example, is found in boys' and girls' initiation ceremonies, in five rituals concerned with female reproductive disorders, in at least three rituals of the hunters' cults, and in various herbalistic practices of a magical cast. Other dominant symbols of Ndembu rituals, as I have shown elsewhere (1961, 1966, 1969), recur almost as frequently in the ritual round. Each of these symbols, then, has multiple referents, but on each occasion that it is used—usually an episode within a ritual performance—only one or a related few of its referents are drawn to public attention. The process of "selectivity" consists in constructing around the dominant symbol a context of symbolic objects, activities, gestures, social relationships between actors of ritual roles, and verbal behavior (prayers, formulas, chants, songs, recitation of sacred narratives, and so on) that both bracket and underline those of its referents deemed pertinent in the given situation. Thus, only a portion of a dominant symbol's full semantic wealth is deployed in a single kind of ritual or in one of its episodes. The semantic structure of a dominant symbol may be compared with a ratchet wheel, each of whose teeth represents a conception or theme. The ritual context is like a pawl, which engages the notches. The point of engagement represents a meaning that is important in the particular situation. The wheel is the symbol's total meaning, and the complete range is only exposed when the whole cycle of rituals has been performed. Dominant symbols represent sets of fundamental themes. The symbol appears in many rituals, and its meanings are emphasized separately in many episodes. Since the settings in which the themes are ritually presented vary, and since themes are linked in different combinations in each setting, members of the culture who have been exposed to the entire ritual cycle gradually learn, through repetition, variation, and contrast of symbols and themes, what the values, rules, behavioral styles, and cognitive postulates of their culture are. Even more important, they learn in what cultural domains and with what intensity in each domain the themes should apply.

Positional Role of Binary Opposition

The selection of a given theme from a symbol's theme assemblage is a function of positioning—that is, of the manner in which the object or activity assigned symbolic value is placed or arranged vis-à-vis similar objects or activities. One common mode of positioning is binary opposition, the relating of two symbol vehicles whose opposed perceptible qualities or quantities suggest, in terms of the associative rules of the culture, semantic opposition. Thus when a grass hut is made at the Ndembu girls' puberty ceremony for the seclusion of the novice for several months, the two principal laths of the wooden frame are made respectively from mudyi and mukula (blood tree) wood. Both species are dominant symbols. To the Ndembu, mukula represents the husband whom the girl will marry immediately after the puberty rites, and the mudyi stands for the bride, the novice herself. Yet when mukula is considered as a dominant symbol of the total ritual system, it is found to have a wide range (what has aptly been called a "fan") of significata (Turner 1967, 1968). Its primary and sensory meaning is blood—the Ndembu point to the dusky red gum secreted by the tree from cracks in its bark to justify their interpretation. But some bloods, they say, are masculine and some feminine. The former include blood shed by warriors, hunters, and circumcisers in the call of duty; the latter represents blood shown at menstruation and parturition. Another binary opposition within the semantic field of blood is between running blood and coagulating blood. The latter is good, the former is dangerous. Thus, prolonged menstruation means that a woman's blood is ebbing away uselessly; it should coagulate to form fetus and placenta. But since men are the dangerous sex, the blood they cause to flow in hunting and war may be good— that is, beneficial for their own group.

Mukula symbolism is adroitly manipulated in different rituals to express various aspects of the human condition as the Ndembu experience it. For example, in the Nkula ritual, performed to placate the spirit of a dead kinswoman afflicting the female patient with menstrual troubles causing barrenness, mukula and other red symbols are contextually connected with symbols characteristic of the male hunting cults to convey the message: the patient is behaving like a male shedder of blood, not like a female conserver of blood, as she should be. It is her "masculine protest" that the ritual is mainly directed at overcoming and domesticating into the service of her female role (Turner 1968:55–88). Mukula means many other things in other contexts, when used in religious ritual or in magical therapy. But the binary opposition of mudyi to mukula restricts the meaning of mudyi to young mature femininity and that of mukula to young mature masculinity, both of which are foundations of a hut, the prototypical domestic unit. The binding together of the laths taken from these trees is said to represent the sexual and the procreative union of the young couple. If these meanings form the sensory pole of the binary opposition as symbol, then the legitimated union by marriage represents the normative pole. In other words, even the binary opposition does not stand alone; it must be examined in the context of building the novice's seclusion hut and of the symbolic objects comprising the hut and its total meaning. There are, of course, many types of binary opposition. The members of pairs of symbols may be asymmetrical (A > B, A < B); they may be like or unlike but equal in value; they may be antithetical; one may be thought of as the product or offspring of the other; one may be active, the other passive; and so on. In this way, the Ndembu are induced to consider the nature and function of relationships as well as of the variables being related, for nonverbal symbol systems have the equivalents of grammar, syntax, accidence, and parts of speech.

Sometimes binary opposition may appear between complexes of symbol vehicles, each carrying a system of dominant and secondary symbols. Thus, in the circumcision rites of the Wiko, in Zambia one group of masked dancers may mime opposition to another group; each mask and headpiece is already a combination of multivocal symbols. Yet one team may represent protectiveness and the other, aggressiveness. It is, in fact, not uncommon to find complex symbol vehicles, such as statues or shrines, with simple meanings, while simple vehicles, such as marks drawn in white or red clay, may be highly multivocal in almost every ritual situation in which they are used. A simple vehicle, exhibiting some color, shape, texture, or contrast commonly found in one's experience (such as the whiteness of the mudyi or the redness of the mukula), can literally or metaphorically connect a great range of phenomena and ideas. By contrast, a complex vehicle is already committed, at the level of sensory perception, to a host of contrasts that narrow and specify its message. This is probably why the great religious symbol vehicles such as the cross, the lotus, the crescent moon, the ark, and so on are relatively simple, although their significata constitute whole theological systems and control liturgical and architectural structures of immense complexity. One might almost hypothesize that the more complex the ritual (many symbols, complex vehicles), the more particularistic, localized, and socially structured its message; the simpler the ritual (few symbols, simple vehicles), the more universalistic its message. Thus, ecumenical liturgiologists today are recommending that Christian ritual be essentially reduced to the blessing, distribution, and partaking of bread and wine, in order to provide most denominations with a common ground.

Actors Experience Symbols as Powers and as Meanings

The second characteristic of ritual condensation, which compensates in some measure for semantic obscurity, is its efficacy. Ritual is not just a concentration of referents, of messages about values and norms; nor is it simply a set of practical guidelines and a set of symbolic paradigms for everyday action, indicating how spouses should treat each other, how pastoralists should classify and regard cattle, how hunters should behave in different wild habitats, and so on. It is also a fusion of the powers believed to be inherent in the persons, objects, relationships, events, and histories represented by ritual symbols. It is a mobilization of energies as well as messages.[1] In this respect, the objects and activities in point are not merely

---

[1] This problem of the sources of the effectiveness of symbols has been discussed by Lévi-Strauss (1963); Turner (1969:10–43); Munn (1969:178–207).

things that stand for other things or something abstract, they participate in the powers and virtues they represent. I use "virtue" advisedly, for many objects termed symbols are also termed medicines. Thus, scrapings and leaves from such trees as the mudyi and the mukula are pounded together in meal mortars, mixed with water, and given to the afflicted to drink or to wash with. Here there is direct communication of the life-giving powers thought to inhere in certain objects under ritual conditions (a consecrated site, invocations of preternatural entities, and so on). When an object is used analogously, it functions unambiguously as a symbol. Thus, when the mudyi tree is used in puberty rites it clearly represents mother's milk; here the association is through sight, not taste. But when the mudyi is used as medicine in ritual, it is felt that certain qualities of motherhood and nurturing are being communicated physically. In the first case, the mudyi is used because it is "good to think" rather than "good to eat" (Lévi-Strauss 1962); in the second, it is used because it has maternal power. The same objects are used both as powers and symbols, metonymically and metaphorically—it is the context that distinguishes them. The power aspect of a symbol derives from its being a part of a physical whole, the ideational aspect from an analogy between a symbol vehicle and its principal significata.

Each symbol expresses many themes, and each theme is expressed by many symbols. The cultural weave is made up of symbolic warp and thematic weft. This weaving of symbols and themes serves as a rich store of information, not only about the natural environment as perceived and evaluated by the ritual actors, but also about their ethical, esthetic, political, legal, and ludic (the domain of play, sport, and so forth in a culture) ideas, ideals, and rules. Each symbol is a store of information, both for actors and investigators, but in order to specify just which set of themes any particular ritual or ritual episode contains, one must determine the relations between the ritual's symbols and their vehicles, including verbal symbolic behavior. The advantages of communication by means of rituals in nonliterate societies are clearly great, for the individual symbols and the patterned relations between them have a mnemonic function. The symbolic vocabulary and grammar to some extent make up for the lack of written records.

The Semantic Dimensions

Symbols have three especially significant dimensions: the exegetic, the operational, and the positional. The exegetic dimension consists of the explanations given the investigator by actors in the ritual system. Actors of different age, sex, ritual role, status, grade of esoteric knowledge, and so forth provide data of varying richness, explicitness, and internal coherence. The investigator should infer from this information how members of a given society think about ritual. Not all African societies contain persons who are ready to make verbal statements about ritual, and the percentage of those prepared to offer interpretations varies from group to group and within groups. But, as much ethnographic work attests, many African societies are well endowed with exegetes (for example, Wilson 1954; Richards 1956; Griaule 1965; Evans-Pritchard 1956; Douglas 1955; White 1948; Beidelman 1961; Morton-Williams et al. 1966; Beattie 1968).

In the operational dimension, the investigator equates a symbol's meaning with its use—he observes what actors do with it and how they relate to one another in this process. He also records their gestures, expressions, and other nonverbal aspects of behavior and discovers what values they represent—grief, joy, anger, triumph, modesty, and so on. Anthropologists are now studying several genres of nonverbal language, from iconography (the study of symbols whose vehicles picture the conceptions they signify, rather than being arbitrary, conventional signs for them) to kinesics (the study of bodily movements, facial expressions, and so forth as ways of communication or adjuncts and intensifiers of speech). Several of these fall under the rubric of a symbol's operational meaning. Non-exegetical, ritualized speech, such as formalized prayers or invocations, would also fall into this category. Here verbal symbols approximate nonverbal symbols. The investigator is interested not only in the social organization and structure of those individuals who operate with symbols on this level, but also in what persons, categories, and groups are absent from the situation, for formal exclusion would reveal social values and attitudes.

In the positional dimension, the observer finds in the relations between one symbol and other symbols an important source of its meaning. I have shown how binary opposition may, in context, highlight one (or more) of a symbol's many referents by contrasting it with one (or more) of another symbol's referents. When used in a ritual context with three or more other symbols, a particular symbol reveals further facets of its total "meaning." Groups of symbols may be so arrayed as to state a message, in which some symbols function analogously to parts of speech and in which there may be conventional rules of connection. The message is not about specific actions and circumstances, but about the given culture's basic structures of thought, ethics, esthetics, law, and modes of speculation about new experience.

In several African cultures, particularly in West Africa, a complex system of rituals is associated with myths.[2] These tell of the origins of the gods, the cosmos, human types and groups, and the key institutions of culture and society. Some ritual episodes reenact primordial events, drawing on their inherent power to achieve the contemporary goals of the members of the culture (for example, adjustment to puberty and the healing of the sick). Rit-

---

[2] Examples of African cosmological systems may be found in D. Forde (1954). See also T. O. Beidelman (1966) on aspects of Swazi cosmology, Africa 36, 379 (1966).

ual systems are sometimes based on myths. There may coexist with myths and rituals standardized schemata of interpretation that may amount to theological doctrine. But in wide areas of East and Central Africa, there may be few myths connected with rituals and no religious system interrelating myths, rituals, and doctrine. In compensation, there may be much piecemeal exegesis of particular symbols.

Foundations of Meaning

Most African languages have terms for ritual symbol. The Nyakyusa, for example, speak of ififwani (likenesses); the Ndembu use chijikijilu (a landmark, or blaze), which is derived from kujikijila (to blaze a trail or set up a landmark). The first connotes an association, a feeling of likeness between sign and signified, vehicle and concept; the second is a means of connecting known with unknown territory. (The Ndembu compare the ritual symbol to the trail a hunter blazes in order to find his way back from unexplored bush to his village.) Other languages possess similar terms. In societies that do not have myths, the meaning of a symbol is built up by analogy and association of three foundations—nominal, substantial, and artifactual—though in any given instance only one of these might be utilized. The nominal basis is the name of the symbol, an element in an acoustic system; the substantial basis is a symbol's sensorily perceptible physical or chemical properties as recognized by the culture; and its artifactual basis is the technical changing of an object used in ritual by human purposive activity.

For example: At the start of a girl's puberty ritual among the Nyakyusa of Tanzania (Wilson: 1957), she is treated with a "medicine" called undumila. This medicine is also an elaborate symbol. Its nominal basis is the derivation of the term from ukulumila, meaning "to bite, to be painful." The substantial basis is a natural property of the root after which the medicine is named—it is pungent-tasting. As an artifact, the medicine is a composite of several symbolic substances. The total symbol involves action as well as a set of objects. Wilson writes (1957:87) that the root "is pushed through the tip of a funnel or cup made of a leaf of the bark-cloth tree, and salt is poured into the cup. The girl takes the tip of the root in her mouth and pulls it inward with her teeth, thus causing the salt to trickle into her mouth." The root and leaf funnel, together with their ritual use, constitute an artifact. These three bases of significance are substantiated by the Nyakyusa Wilson talked to. One woman told her (Wilson 1957:102): "The pungent root is the penis of the husband, the cup is her vagina, the salt, also pungent, is the semen of her husband. Biting the root and eating the salt is copulation." Another woman confirmed this: "The undumila is put through the leaf of a bark-cloth tree, shaped into a cup, and it is a sign of man and woman, the penis in the vagina. It is similar to the plantains which we give her when we wash her. The plantains are a symbol of the husband. If we do not give her . . . the undumila, she constantly has periods and is barren." A third informant said: "It is the pain of periods that we symbolize in the sharpness of the undumila and salt." Thus undumila is at once a symbol of sexual intercourse, a prophylactic against pain in inter-course and against frequent or painful periods, and (according to other accounts) a ritual defense against those who are "heavy"—that is, those actively engaged in sexual intercourse, especially women who have just conceived. If a heavy person steps over the novice's footprints, the novice will not bear a child, but will menstruate continually. These explanations also demonstrate the multivocality and economy of reference of a single dominant symbol. The same symbol vehicles can represent different, even disparate, processes—marital intercourse and menstrual difficulty—although it may be argued that the Nyakyusa, at an unconscious level, regard a woman's "distaste" for intercourse as a cause of her barrenness or menorrhagia.

Symbols and Cosmologies

Similar examples abound in the ethnography of subsaharan Africa, but in the great West African cultures of the Fon, Ashanti, Yoruba, Dahomeyans, and Dogon, piecemeal exegesis gives way to explicit, complex cosmologies. Among the Dogon, for example, a symbol becomes a fixed point of linkage between animal, vegetable, and mineral kingdoms, which are themselves regarded as parts of *"un gigantesque organisme humaine."* The doctrine of correspondences reigns—everything is a symbol of everything else, whether in ritual context or not. Thus the Dogon establish a correspondence between the different categories of minerals and the organs of the body. The various soils in the area are conceived of as the organs of "the interior of the stomach," rocks are regarded as the bones of the skeleton, and various hues of red clay are likened to the blood. Sometimes these correspondences are remarkably precise: one rock resting on another represents the chest; little white river pebbles stand for the toes of the feet. The same *parole du monde* principles hold true for the relationship between man and the vegetable kingdom. Man is not only the grain of the universe, but each distinct part of a single grain represents part of the human body. In fact, it is only science that has emancipated man from the complex weave of correspondences, based on analogy, metaphor, and mystical participation, and that enables him to regard all relations as problematical, not preordained, until they have been experimentally tested or systematically compared.

The Dogon further conceive of a subtle and finely wrought interplay between speech and the components of personality. The body constitutes a magnet or focus for man's spiritual principles, which nevertheless are capable of sustaining an independent existence. The Dogon contrast visible and invisible ("spiritual") components of the human personality. The body is made up of four elements: water (the blood and bodily fluids), earth (the skeleton), air (breath), and fire (animal warmth). There is a continuous interchange between these internal expressions of the elements and their external aspects. The body has 22 parts: feet, shins, thighs, lumbar region, stomach, chest, arms, neck, and head make up nine parts (it would seem that Dogon reckon double parts, as they do twins, as a unit); the fingers (each counting as a unit), make up ten parts; and the male genitals make up three parts. Further numerical symbolism is involved: there are believed to be eight symbolic grains—representing the principal cereal crops of the region—lodged in the collarbones of each Dogon. These grains represent the mystical bond between man and his crops. The body of speech itself is, like the human body, composed of four elements: water is saliva, without which speech is dry; air gives rise to sound vibrations; earth gives speech its weight and significance; and fire gives speech its warmth. There is not only homology between personality and speech, but also a sort of functional interdependence, for words are selected by the brain, stir up the liver, and rise as steam from the lungs to the clavicles, which decide ultimately whether the speech is to emerge from the mouth.

To the 22 parts of the personality must be added the 48 types of speech, which are divided into two sets of 24. Each set is under the sign of a supernatural being, one of the androgynous twins Nommo and Yourougou. Here I must draw on Griaule (1966) and Dieterlen's (1941, 1963) extensive work on the Dogons' cosmogonic mythology. The twins are the creations of Amma. Yourougou rebelled against Amma and had sexual relations with his mother—he was punished by being changed into a pale fox. Nommo saved the world by an act of self-sacrifice, brought humans, animals, and plants to the earth, and became the lord of speech. Nommo's speech is human and can be heard; the Fox's is silent, a sign language made by his paw marks, and only diviners can interpret it. These myths provide a classification and taxonomy of cosmos and society; explain many details of ritual, including the forms and color symbolism of elaborate masks; and, indeed, determine where and how houses are constructed. Other West African cultures have equally elaborate cosmologies, which are manifested in ritual and divinatory symbolism. Their internal consistency and symmetry may be related to traditions of continuous residence and farming in a single habitat, combined with exposure to trans-Saharan cultural elements, including religious beliefs, for thousands of years—ancient Egyptian, Roman, Christian, Neo-Platonic, Gnostic, Islamic. The history of West Africa contrasts with that of Central Africa, where most societies descend from groups that migrated in a relatively short period of time across several distinct ecological habitats and that were then exposed to several centuries of slave raiding and slave trading. Groups were fragmented and then combined with the social detritus of other societies into new, temporary polities. There were conquests, assimilations, reconquests, the rise and fall of "kingdoms of the savannah," and temporary centralization followed by decentralization into localized clans. Swidden (slash-and-burn) agriculture kept people constantly on the move; hunting and pastoralism compounded the mobility. Because of these circumstances, there was less likelihood of complex, integrated religious and cosmological systems arising in Central Africa than in West Africa. Yet the needs and dangers of social and personal survival provided suitable conditions for the development of rituals as pragmatic instruments (from the standpoint of the actors) for coping with biological change, disease, and natural hazards of all kinds. Social action in response to material pressures was the systematic and systematizing factor. Order, cosmos, came from purpose, not from an elaborate and articulated cosmology. It is an order that accords well with human experience at preindustrial technological levels; even its discrepancies accurately reflect the "facts of life"—in contrast to consistent and harmonious cosmologies whose symbols and myths mask and cloak the basic contradictions between wishes and facts.

The Continuing Efficacy of African Ritual Symbols

Nevertheless, from the comparative viewpoint, there are remarkable similarities among symbols used in ritual throughout sub-Saharan Africa, in spite of differences in cosmological sophistication. The same ideas, analogies, and modes of association underlie symbol formation and manipulation from the Senegal River to the Cape of Good Hope. The same assumptions about powers prevail in kingdoms and nomadic bands. Whether these assemblages of similar symbols represent units of complex orders or the debris of formerly prevalent ones, the symbols remain extraordinarily viable and the themes they represent and embody tenaciously rooted. This may be because they arose in ecological and social experiences of a kind that still prevails in large areas of the continent. Since they are thus sustained and since there is a continuous flux and reflux of people between country and city, it is not surprising that much of the imagery found in the writings of modern African novelists and in the rhetoric of politicians is drawn from ritual symbolism—from which it derives its power to move and channel emotion.

BIBLIOGRAPHY

Beidelman, T. O.
    1961   Right and Left Hand among the Kaguru: A Note on Symbolic Classification. Africa 31:250–257.
    1966   Swazi Royal Ritual. Africa 36:373–405.
Beattie, J.
    1968   Aspects of Nyoro Symbolism. Africa 38:413–442.

Calame-Griaule, G.
  1966 Ethnologie et Langage: Le Parole Chez les Dogon. Paris: Gallimard.
Dieterlen, G.
  1941 Les Ames des Dogon. Paris: Institut d'Ethnologie.
  1963 Le Renard Pale. Paris: Institut d'Ethnologie.
Douglas, M.
  1957 Animals in Lele Religious Symbolism. Africa 27:46–58.
  1968 Dogon Culture. Profane and Arcane. Africa 38:16–25.
Evans-Pritchard, E. E.
  1956 Nuer Religion. Clarendon: Oxford.
Forde D., ed.
  1954 African Worlds. London: Oxford University Press.
Griaule, M.
  1965 Conversations with Ogotemmeli. London: Oxford University Press.
Lévi-Strauss, C.
  1962 Le Totemisme Au-jourd'hui. Paris: Presses Universitaires de France.
  1963 Structural Anthropology. New York: Basic.
Morton-Williams, P., W. Bascom, and E. M. McClelland
  1966 Two Studies of Ifa Divination. Introduction: The Mode of Divination.
        Africa 36:406–431.
Munn, N.
  1969 The Effectiveness of Symbols in Murngin Rite and Myth. *In* Forms of Sym-
        bolic Action. R. F. Spencer, ed. Pp. 178–207. Seattle: University of Wash-
        ington Press.
Opler, M. E.
  1945 Themes as Dynamic Forces in Culture. American Journal of Sociology
        51:198–206.
  1968 The Themal Approach in Cultural Anthropology and Its Application to
        North Indian Data. Southwestern Journal of Anthropology 24:215–227.
Richards, A.
  1956 Chisungu. London: Faber.
Turner V. W.
  1961 Ndembu Divination: Its Symbolism and Techniques. Manchester, Eng-
        land: Manchester University Press.
  1964 Symbols in Ndembu Ritual. *In* Closed Systems and Open Minds: The
        Limits of Naivety in Social Anthropology. M. Gluckman, ed. Pp. 20–51.
        Edinburgh: Oliver & Boyd.
  1966 Colour Classification in Ndembu Ritual. *In* Anthropological Ap-
        proaches to the Study of Religion. M. Banton, ed. Pp. 47–84. London:
        Tavistock.
  1969 Forms of Symbolic Action: Introduction. *In* Forms of Symbolic Action:
        Proceedings of the 1969 Annual Spring Meeting of the American Ethno-
        logical Society. R. F. Spencer, ed. Pp. 3–25. Seattle: University of Wash-
        ington Press.
  1967 The Forest of Symbols. Ithaca, NY: Cornell University Press.
  1968 The Drums of Affliction. Oxford: Clarendon.
  1969 The Ritual Process. Chicago: Aldine.

Watson, J. B.
  1964   Cultural Variation. A Dictionary of the Social Sciences. J. Gould and W. L.
          Kolb, eds. Pp. 163–164. London: Tavistock.
White, C. M. N.
  1948   Notes on Some Metaphysical Concepts of the Balovale Tribes. African
          Studies 7(4):146–156.
Wilson, M.
  1954   Nyakyusa Ritual and Symbolism. American Anthropologist 56:228–241.
  1957   Rituals of Kinship among the Nyakyusa. London: Oxford University
          Press.
  1959   Communal Rituals of the Nyakyusa. London: Oxford University Press.

QUERIES

- What is Turner's definition of a "ritual"?
- According to Turner, what are the four major characteristics of ritual symbols?
- Ritual symbols are powerful condensers of meaning. How does the Ndembu mudyi tree reflect this during female puberty ceremonies?
- What is a cultural "theme"?
- Turner outlines an intriguing hypothesis: the more complex a ritual—incorporating many symbols, for example—the narrower its intended message, while the simpler a ritual—with fewer, simple symbols—the broader its message. Apply this hypothesis to a "traditional" American wedding (formal bridal gown, bridesmaids, church wedding, exchange of rings, etc.). Do you think Turner's hypothesis is correct?

CONNECTIONS

- Contrast Turner's discussion of binary opposition of symbols with Lévi-Strauss's approach to binary oppositions. How does each anthropologist explain these similar patterns?
- What are some of the similarities between Turner's idea of "dominant symbols" and Ortner's concept of "key symbols"?

19

Clifford Geertz

INTRODUCTION

The American anthropologist Clifford Geertz (1926–2006) articulated the position that all ethnography involved multiple acts of interpretation. In Geertz's view, "interpretation" was not an anthropologist's unverifiable opinion of another culture's motives and actions, but rather an informed exposition of how those motives and actions were meaningful in a specific cultural context. Geertz's position was formalized in a 1973 essay, "Thick Description: Toward an Interpretive Theory of Culture," in which he argues "that man is an animal suspended in webs of significance he himself has spun, and I take culture to be those webs, and the analysis of it to be therefore not an experimental science in search of law but an interpretive one in search of meaning." (For an extended discussion of Geertz's theoretical position, see Moore 2008:259–71.)

Articulated in this 1973 essay and maintained over the next thirty years of his career, Geertz's interpretive anthropology is implicit in his 1957 article, "Ritual and Social Change: A Javanese Example." The ethnographic core of the article is a funeral ceremony (slametan) in Java associated with the death of a youth, Paidjan. The slametan combined a mix of Islamic and local practices and beliefs, but this syncretic mix of symbolic actions had become imbued with political overtones. Although he prefaces and concludes this article with a discussion of functionalist approaches to religion (see "Connections" below), Geertz provides a complex and multilayered interpretation of this Javanese funeral—an ethnographic study that exemplifies his later theoretical position.

PRIMARY TEXT: *RITUAL AND SOCIAL CHANGE:*
A JAVANESE EXAMPLE

As in so many areas of anthropological concern, functionalism, either of the sociological sort associated with the name of Radcliffe-Brown or of the social-psychological sort associated with Malinowski, has tended to dominate recent theoretical discussions of the role of religion in society. Stemming originally from Durkheim's *The Elementary Forms of the Religious Life* (1947) and Robertson-Smith's *Lectures on the Religion of the Semites* (1894), the sociological approach (or, as the British anthropologists prefer to call it, the social anthropological approach) emphasizes the manner in which belief and particularly ritual reinforce the traditional social ties between individuals; it stresses the way in which the social structure of a group is strengthened and perpetuated through the ritualistic or mythic symbolization of the underlying social values upon which it rests. The social-psychological approach, of which Frazer and Tylor were perhaps the pioneers but which found its clearest statement in Malinowski's classic *Magic, Science and Religion* (1948), emphasizes what religion does for the individual—how it satisfies both his cognitive and affective demands for a stable, comprehensible, and coercible world, and how it enables him to maintain an inner security in the face of natural contingency. Together, the two approaches have given us an increasingly detailed understanding of the social and psychological "functions" of religion in a wide range of societies.

Where the functional approach has been least impressive, however, is in dealing with social change. As has been noted by several writers (Leach 1954; Merton 1949), the emphasis on systems in balance, on social homeostasis, and on timeless structural pictures, leads to a bias in favor of "well-integrated" societies in a stable equilibrium and to a tendency to emphasize the functional aspects of a people's social usages and customs rather than their dysfunctional implications. In analyses of religion this static, ahistorical approach has led to a somewhat over-conservative view of the role of ritual and belief in social life. Despite cautionary comments by Kluckhohn (1944) and others on the "gain and cost" of various religious practices such as witchcraft, the tendency has been consistently to stress the harmonizing, integrating, and psychologically supportive aspects of religious patterns rather than the disruptive, disintegrative, and psychologically disturbing aspects; to demonstrate the manner in which religion preserves social and psychological structure rather than the manner in which it destroys or transforms it. Where change has been treated, as in Redfield's work on Yucatan

(1941), it has largely been in terms of progressive disintegration: "The changes in culture that in Yucatan appear to 'go along with' lessening isolation and homogeneity are seen to be chiefly three: disorganization of the culture, secularization and individualization" (p. 339). Yet even a passing knowledge of our own religious history makes us hesitate to affirm such a simply "positive" role for religion generally. It is the thesis of this paper that one of the major reasons for the inability of functional theory to cope with change lies in its failure to treat sociological and cultural processes on equal terms; almost inevitably one of the two is either ignored or is sacrificed to become but a simple reflex, a "mirror image," of the other. Either culture is regarded as wholly derivative from the forms of social organization—the approach characteristic of the British structuralists as well as many American sociologists; or the forms of social organization are regarded as behavioral embodiments of cultural patterns—the approach of Malinowski and many American anthropologists. In either case, the lesser term tends to drop out as a dynamic factor and we are left either with an omnibus concept of culture ("that complex whole . . .") or else with a completely comprehensive concept of social structure ("social structure is not an aspect of culture, but the entire culture of a given people handled in a special frame of theory" [Fortes 1953]). In such a situation, the dynamic elements in social change which arise from the failure of cultural patterns to be perfectly congruent with the forms of social organization are largely incapable of formulation. "We functionalists," E. R. Leach has recently remarked, "are not really 'anti-historical' by principle; it is simply that we do not know how to fit historical materials into our framework of concepts" (1954:282).

A revision of the concepts of functional theory so as to make them capable of dealing more effectively with "historical materials" might well begin with an attempt to distinguish analytically between the cultural and social aspects of human life, and to treat them as independently variable yet mutually interdependent factors. Though separable only conceptually, culture and social structure will then be seen to be capable of a wide range of modes of integration with one another, of which the simple isomorphic mode is but a limiting case—a case common only in societies which have been stable over such an extended time as to make possible a close adjustment between social and cultural aspects. In most societies, where change is a characteristic rather than an abnormal occurrence, we shall expect to find more or less radical discontinuities between the two. I would argue that it is in these very discontinuities that we shall find some of the primary driving forces in change.

One of the more useful ways—but far from the only one—of distinguishing between culture and social system is to see the former as an ordered system of meaning and of symbols, in terms of which social interaction takes place; and to see the latter as the pattern of social interaction itself (Parsons and Shils 1951). On the one level there is the framework of beliefs, expressive symbols, and values in terms of which individuals define their world, express their feelings, and make their judgments; on the other level there is the ongoing process of interactive behavior, whose persistent form we call social structure. Culture is the fabric of meaning in terms of which human beings interpret their experience and guide their action; social structure is the form that action takes, the actually existing network of social relations. Culture and social structure are then but different abstractions from the same phenomena. The one considers social action in respect to its meaning for those who carry it out, the other considers it in terms of its contribution to the functioning of some social system.

The nature of the distinction between culture and social system is brought out more clearly when one considers the contrasting sorts of integration characteristic of each of them. This contrast is between what Sorokin (1937) has called "logico-meaningful integration" and what he has called "causal-functional integration." By logico-meaningful integration, characteristic of culture, is meant the sort of integration one finds in a Bach fugue, in Catholic dogma, or in the general theory of relativity; it is a unity of style, of logical implication, of meaning and value. By causal-functional integration, characteristic of the social system, is meant the kind of integration one finds in an organism, where all the parts are united in a single causal web; each part is an element in a reverberating causal ring which "keeps the system going." And because these two types of integration are not identical, because the particular form one of them takes does not directly imply the form the other will take, there is an inherent incongruity and tension between the two and between both of them, and a third element, the pattern of motivational integration within the individual which we usually call personality structure:

> Thus conceived, a social system is only one of three aspects of the structuring of a completely concrete system of social action. The other two are the personality systems of the individual actors and the cultural system which is built into their action. Each of the three must be considered to be an independent focus of the organization of the elements of the action system in the sense that no one of them is theoretically reducible to terms of one or a combination of the other two. Each is indispensable to the other two in the sense that without personalities and culture there would be no social system and so on around the roster of logical possibilities. But this interdependence and interpenetration is a very different matter from reducibility, which would mean that the important properties and processes of one class of system could be theoretically derived from our theoretical knowledge of one or both of the other two. The action frame of reference is common to all three and this fact makes certain "transformations" between them possible. But on the level of theory here attempted they do not constitute a single system, however this might turn out to be on some other theoretical level. (Parsons 1951:6)

I will attempt to demonstrate the utility of this more dynamic function-alist approach by applying it to a particular case of a ritual which failed to function properly. I shall try to show how an approach which does not distinguish the "logico-meaningful" cultural aspects of the ritual pattern from the "causal-functional" social structural aspects is unable to account adequately for this ritual failure, and how an approach which does so distinguish them is able to analyze more explicitly the cause of the trouble. It will further be argued that such an approach is able to avoid the simplistic view of the functional role of religion in society which sees that role merely as structure-conserving, and to substitute for it a more complex conception of the relations between religious belief and practice and secular social life. Historical materials can be fitted into such a conception, and the functional analysis of religion can therefore be widened to deal more adequately with processes of change.

The Setting

The case to be described is that of a funeral held in Modjokuto, a small town in eastern Central Java.[1] A young boy, about ten years of age, who was living with his uncle and aunt, died very suddenly but his death, instead of being followed by the usual hurried, subdued, yet methodically efficient Javanese funeral ceremony and burial routine, brought on an extended period of pronounced social strain and severe psychological tension. The complex of beliefs and rituals which had for generations brought countless Javanese safely through the difficult post-mortem period suddenly failed to work with its accustomed effectiveness. To understand why it failed demands knowledge and understanding of a whole range of social and cultural changes which have taken place in Java since the first decades of this century. This disrupted funeral was in fact but a microcosmic example of the broader conflicts, structural dissolutions, and attempted reintegrations which, in one form or another, are characteristic of contemporary Indonesian society.

The religious tradition of Java, particularly of the peasantry, is a composite of Indian, Islamic, and indigenous Southeast Asian elements (Landon 1949). The rise of large, militaristic kingdoms in the inland rice basins in

---

[1] The names of the town and of all individuals mentioned in this paper are pseudonyms. The field work extended from May 1953 until September 1954, with a two-month gap in July and August of 1953, and was undertaken as part of a cooperative project of six anthropologists and a sociologist under the sponsorship of the Center for International Studies of the Massachusetts Institute of Technology. A full description of the town and of the villages around it, prepared by the entire team, is in the process of publication. I wish to thank Victor Ayoub, Robert Bellah, Hildred Geertz, Arnold Green, Robert Jay, and Elizabeth Tooker for reading and criticizing various drafts of this paper.

the early centuries of the Christian era was associated with the diffusion of Hinduist and Buddhist culture patterns to the island; the expansion of international maritime trade in the port cities of the northern coast in the fifteenth and sixteenth centuries was associated with the diffusion of Islamic patterns. Working their way into the peasant mass, these two world religions became fused with the underlying animistic traditions characteristic of the whole Malaysian culture area. The result was a balanced syncretism of myth and ritual in which Hindu gods and goddesses, Moslem prophets and saints, and local place spirits and demons all found a proper place.

The central ritual form in this syncretism is a communal feast, called the slametan. Slametans, which are given with only slight variations in form and content on almost all occasions of religious significance—at passage points in the life cycle, on calendrical holidays, at certain stages of the crop cycle, on changing one's residence, etc.—are intended to be both offerings to the spirits and commensal mechanisms of social integration for the living. The meal, which consists of specially prepared dishes, each symbolic of a particular religious concept, is cooked by the female members of one nuclear family household and set out on mats in the middle of the living-room. The male head of the household invites the male heads of the eight or ten contiguous households to attend; no close neighbor is ignored in favor of one further away. After a speech by the host explaining the spiritual purpose of the feast and a short Arabic chant, each man takes a few hurried, almost furtive, gulps of food, wraps the remainder of the meal in a banana-leaf basket, and returns home to share it with his family. It is said that the spirits draw their sustenance from the odor of the food, the incense which is burned, and the Moslem prayer; the human participants draw theirs from the material substance of the food and from their social interaction. The result of this quiet, undramatic little ritual is twofold: the spirits are appeased and neighborhood solidarity is strengthened.[2]

The ordinary canons of functional theory are quite adequate for the analysis of such a pattern. It can rather easily be shown that the slametan is well designed both to "tune up the ultimate value attitudes" necessary to the effective integration of a territorially-based social structure, and to fulfill the psychological needs for intellectual coherence and emotional stability characteristic of a peasant population. The Javanese village (once or twice a year, village-wide slametans are held) is essentially a set of geographically contiguous, but rather self-consciously autonomous, nuclear family households whose economic and political interdependence is of roughly the same circumscribed and explicitly defined sort as that demon-

---

[2] A fuller description of the slametan pattern, and of Javanese religion generally, will be found in my contribution to the forthcoming project report on the Modjokuto community study: Geertz, in press.

strated in the slametan. The demands of the labor-intensive rice and dry-crop agricultural process require the perpetuation of specific modes of technical co-operation and enforce a sense of community on the otherwise rather self-contained families—a sense of community which the slametan clearly reinforces. And when we consider the manner in which various conceptual and behavioral elements from Hindu, Buddhism, Islam, and "animism" are reinterpreted and balanced to form a distinctive and nearly homogeneous religious style, the close functional adjustment between the communal feast pattern and the conditions of Javanese rural life is even more readily apparent.

But the fact is that in all but the most isolated parts of Java, both the simple territorial basis of village social integration and the syncretic basis of its cultural homogeneity have been progressively undermined over the past fifty years, Population growth, urbanization, monetization, occupational differentiation, and the like, have combined to weaken the traditional ties of peasant social structure; and the winds of doctrine which have accompanied the appearance of these structural changes have disturbed the simple uniformity of religious belief and practice characteristic of an earlier period. The rise of nationalism, Marxism, and Islamic reform as ideologies, which resulted in part from the increasing complexity of Javanese society, has affected not only the large cities where these creeds first appeared and have always had their greatest strength, but has had a heavy impact on the smaller towns and villages as well. In fact, much of recent Javanese social change is perhaps most aptly characterized as a shift from a situation in which the primary integrative ties between individuals (or between families) are phrased in terms of geographical proximity to one in which they are phrased in terms of ideological like-mindedness.

In the villages and small towns these major ideological changes appeared largely in the guise of a widening split between those who emphasized the Islamic aspects of the indigenous religious syncretism and those who emphasized the Hinduist and animistic elements. It is true that some difference between these variant subtraditions has been present since the arrival of Islam; some individuals have always been particularly skilled in Arabic chanting or particularly learned in Moslem law, while others have been adept at more Hinduistic mystical practices or specialists in local curing techniques. But these contrasts were softened by the easy tolerance of the Javanese for a wide range of religious concepts, so long as basic ritual patterns—i.e., slametans were faithfully supported; whatever social divisiveness they stimulated was largely obscured by the over-riding commonalities of rural and small-town life.

However, the appearance after 1910 of Islamic modernism (as well as vigorous conservative reactions against it) and religious nationalism among the economically and politically sophisticated trading classes of the larger cities strengthened the feeling for Islam as an exclusivist, antisyncretic creed among the more orthodox element of the mass of the population. Similarly, secular nationalism and Marxism, appearing among the civil servants and the expanding proletariat of these cities, strengthened the pre-Islamic (i.e., Hinduist, animist) elements of the syncretic pattern, which these groups tended to prize as a counterweight to puristic Islam and which some of them adopted as a general religious framework in which to set their more specifically political ideas. On the one hand, there arose a more self-conscious Moslem, basing his religious beliefs and practices more explicitly on the international and universalistic doctrines of Mohammed; on the other hand there arose a more self-conscious "nativist," attempting to evolve a generalized religious system out of the material—muting the more Islamic elements—of his inherited religious tradition. And the contrast between the first kind of man, called a santri, and the second, called an abangan, grew steadily more acute, until today it forms the major cultural distinction in the whole of the Modjokuto area.[3]

It is especially in the town that this contrast has come to play a crucial role. The absence of pressures toward interfamilial co-operation exerted by the technical requirements of wet-rice growing, as well as lessened effectiveness of the traditional forms of village government in the face of the complexities of urban living, severely weaken the social supports of the syncretic village pattern. When each man makes his living—as chauffeur, trader, clerk, or laborer more or less independently of how his neighbors make theirs, his sense of the importance of the neighborhood community naturally diminishes. A more differentiated class system, more bureaucratic and impersonal forms of government, greater heterogeneity of social background, all tend to lead to the same result: the de-emphasis of strictly geographical ties in favor of diffusely ideological ones. For the townsman, the distinction between santri and abangan becomes even sharper, for it emerges as his primary point of social reference: it becomes a symbol of his social identity, rather than a mere contrast in belief. The sort of friends he will have, the sort of organizations he will join, the sort of political leadership he will follow, the sort of person he or his son will marry, will all be strongly influenced by the side of this ideological bifurcation which he adopts as his own.

There is thus emerging in the town—though not only in the town—a new pattern of social living organized in terms of an altered framework of cultural classification. Among the elite this new pattern has already become rather highly developed, but among the mass of the townspeople it is still

---

[3] For a description of the role of the santri-abangan distinction in the rural areas of Modjokuto, see Jay (1956). A third religious variant which I have discriminated elsewhere (Geertz 1956, and in press), the prijaji, is mainly confined to upper-class civil servants, teachers, and clerks, and so will not be dealt with here.

in the process of formation. Particularly in the kampongs, the off-the-street neighborhoods in which the common Javanese townsmen live crowded together in a helter-skelter profusion of little bamboo houses, one finds a transitional society in which the traditional forms of rural living are being steadily dissolved and new forms steadily reconstructed. In these enclaves of peasants-come-to-town (or of sons and grandsons of peasants-come-to-town), Redfield's folk culture is being constantly converted into his urban culture, though this latter is not accurately characterized by such negative and residual terms as "secular," "individualized," and "culturally disorganized." What is occurring in the kampongs is not so much a destruction of traditional ways of life, as a construction of a new one; the sharp social conflict characteristic of these lower-class neighborhoods is not simply indicative of a loss of cultural consensus, but rather indicative of a search, not yet entirely successful, for new, more generalized, and flexible patterns of belief and value.

In Modjokuto, as in most of Indonesia, this search is taking place largely within the social context of the mass political parties, as well as in the women's clubs, youth organizations, labor unions, and other sodalities formally or informally linked with them. There are several of these parties (though the recent general election severely reduced their number), each led by educated urban elites—civil servants, teachers, traders, students, and the like—and each competing with the others for the political allegiance of both the half rural, half urban kampong dwellers and of the mass of the peasantry. And almost without exception, they appeal to one or another side of the santri-abangan split. Of this complex of political parties and sodalities, only two are of immediate concern to us here: Masjumi, a huge, Islam-based political party; and Permai, a vigorously anti-Moslem politico-religious cult.

Masjumi is the more or less direct descendent of the pre-war Islamic reform movement. Led, at least in Modjokuto, by modernist santri intellectuals, it stands for a socially conscious, antischolastic, and somewhat puritanical version of back-to-the-Koran Islam. In company with the other Moslem parties, it also supports the institution of an "Islamic State" in Indonesia in place of the present secular republic. However, the meaning of this ideal is not entirely clear. Masjumi's enemies accuse it of pressing for an intolerant, medievalist theocracy in which abangans and non-Moslems will be persecuted and forced to follow exactly the prescripts of the Moslem law, while Masjumi's leaders claim that Islam is intrinsically tolerant and that they only desire a government explicitly based on the Moslem creed, one whose laws will be in consonance with the teachings of the Koran and Hadith. In any case, Masjumi, the country's largest Moslem party, is one of the major spokesmen on both the national and the local levels for the values and aspirations of the santri community.

Permai is not so impressive on a national scale. Though it is a nation-wide party, it is a fairly small one, having strength only in a few fairly circumscribed regions. In the Modjokuto area however, it happened to be of some importance, and what it lacked in national scope it made up in local intensity. Essentially, Permai is a fusion of Marxist politics with abangan religious patterns. It combines a fairly explicit anti-Westernism, anti-capitalism, and anti-imperialism with an attempt to formalize and generalize some of the more characteristic diffuse themes of the peasant religious syncretism. Permai meetings follow both the slametan pattern, complete with incense and symbolic food (but without Islamic chants), and modern parliamentary procedure; Permai pamphlets contain calendrical and numerological divinatory systems and mystical teachings as well as analyses of class conflict; and Permai speeches are concerned with elaborating both religious and political concepts. In Modjokuto, Permai is also a curing cult, with its own special medical practices and spells, a secret password, and cabalistic interpretations of passages in the leaders' social and political writings.

But Permai's most notable characteristic is its strong anti-Moslem stand. Charging that Islam is a foreign import, unsuited to the needs and values of the Javanese, the cult urges a return to "pure" and "original" Javanese beliefs, by which they seem to mean to the indigenous syncretism with the more Islamic elements removed. In line with this, the cult-party has initiated a drive, on both national and local levels, for secular (i.e., non-Islamic) marriage and funeral rites. As the situation stands now, all but Christians and Balinese Hindus must have their marriages legitimatized by means of the Moslem rituals.[4] Funeral rites are an individual concern but, because of the long history of syncretism, they are so deeply involved with Islamic customs that a genuinely non-Islamic funeral tends to be a practical impossibility.

Permai's action on the local level in pursuit of non-Islamic marriage and funeral ceremonies took two forms. One was heavy pressure on local government officials to permit such practices, and the other was heavy pressure on its own members to follow, voluntarily, rituals purified of Islamic elements. In the case of marriage, success was more or less precluded because the local officials' hands were tied by Central Government ordinances, and even highly ideologized members of the cult would not dare an openly "illegitimate" marriage. Without a change in the law, Permai had little chance to alter marriage forms, though a few abortive attempts were made to conduct civil ceremonies under the aegis of abangan-minded village chiefs.

---

[4] Actually, there are two parts to Javanese marriage rites. One, which is part of the general syncretism, is held at the bride's home and involves a slametan and an elaborate ceremonial "meeting" between bride and groom. The other, which is the official ceremony in the eyes of the Government, follows the Moslem law and takes place at the office of the subdistrict religious officer, or Naib. See Geertz, in press.

The case of funerals was somewhat different, for a matter of custom rather than law was involved. During the year I was in the field, the tension between Permai and Masjumi increased very sharply. This was due in part to the imminence of Indonesia's first general elections, and in part to the effects of the cold war. It was also influenced by various special occurrences—such as a report that the national head of Permai had publicly called Mohammed a false prophet; a speech in the nearby regional capital by a Masjumi leader in which he accused Permai of intending to raise a generation of bastards in Indonesia; and a bitter village—chief election largely fought out on santri vs. abangan grounds. As a result, the local subdistrict officer, a worried bureaucrat trapped in the middle, called a meeting of all the village religious officials, or Modins. Among many other duties, a Modin is traditionally responsible for conducting funerals. He directs the whole ritual, instructs the mourners in the technical details of burial, leads the Koran chanting, and reads a set speech to the deceased at the graveside. The subdistrict officer instructed the Modins the majority of whom were village Masjumi leaders—that in the case of the death of a member of Permai, they were merely to note the name and age of the deceased and return home; they were not to participate in the ritual. He warned that if they did not do as he advised, they would be responsible if trouble started and he would not come to their support.

This was the situation on July 17, 1954, when Paidjan, nephew of Karman, an active and ardent member of Permai, died suddenly in the Modjokuto kampong in which I was living.

The Funeral

The mood of a Javanese funeral is not one of hysterical bereavement, unrestrained sobbing, or even of formalized cries of grief for the deceased's departure. Rather, it is a calm, undemonstrative, almost languid letting go, a brief ritualized relinquishment of a relationship no longer possible. Tears are not approved of and certainly not encouraged; the effort is to get the job done, not to linger over the pleasures of grief. The detailed busy-work of the funeral, the politely formal social intercourse with the neighbors pressing in from all sides, the series of commemorative slametans stretched out at intervals for almost three years—the whole momentum of the Javanese ritual system is supposed to carry one through grief without severe emotional disturbance. For the mourner, the funeral and postfuneral ritual is said to produce a feeling of iklas, a kind of willed affectlessness, a detached and static state of "not caring"; for the neighborhood group it is said to produce rukun, "communal harmony."

The actual service is in essence simply another version of the slametan, adapted to the special requirements of interment. When the news of a death is broadcast through the area, everyone in the neighborhood must drop what he is doing and go immediately to the home of the survivors. The women bring bowls of rice, which is cooked up into a slametan; the men begin to cut wooden grave markers and to dig a grave. Soon the Modin arrives and begins to direct activities. The corpse is washed in ceremonially prepared water by the relatives (who unflinchingly hold the body on their laps to demonstrate their affection for the deceased as well as their self-control); then it is wrapped in muslin. About a dozen santris, under the leadership of the Modin, chant Arabic prayers over the body for five or ten minutes; after this it is carried, amid various ritual acts, in a ceremonial procession to the graveyard, where it is interred in prescribed ways. The Modin reads a graveside speech to the deceased, reminding him of his duties as a believing Moslem; and the funeral is over, usually only two or three hours after death. The funeral proper is followed by commemorative slametans in the home of the survivors at three, seven, forty, and one hundred days after death; on the first and second anniversary of death; and, finally, on the thousandth day, when the corpse is considered to have turned to dust and the gap between the living and the dead to have become absolute.

This was the ritual pattern which was called into play when Paidjan died. As soon as dawn broke (death occurred in the early hours of the morning), Karman, the uncle, dispatched a telegram to the boy's parents in a nearby city, telling them in characteristic Javanese fashion that their son was ill. This evasion was intended to soften the impact of death by allowing them to become aware of it more gradually. Javanese feel that emotional damage results not from the severity of a frustration but from the suddenness with which it comes, the degree to which it "surprises" one unprepared for it. It is "shock," not suffering itself, which is feared. Next, in the expectation that the parents would arrive within a few hours, Karman sent for the Modin to begin the ceremony. This was done on the theory that by the time the parents had come little would be left to do but inter the body, and they would thus once more be spared unnecessary stress. By ten o'clock at the very latest it should all be over; a saddening incident, but a ritually muted one.

But when the Modin, as he later told me, arrived at Karman's house and saw the poster displaying Permai's political symbol, he told Karman that he could not perform the ritual. After all, Karman belonged to "another religion" and he, the Modin, did not know the correct burial rituals for it; all he knew was Islam. "I don't want to insult your religion," he said piously, "on the contrary, I hold it in the utmost regard, for there is no intolerance in Islam. But I don't know your ritual. The Christians have their own ritual and their own specialist (the local preacher), but what does Permai do? Do they burn the corpse or what?" (This is a sly allusion to Hindu burial practices; evidently the Modin enjoyed himself hugely in this interchange.) Karman was, the Modin told me, rather upset at all this and evidently surprised, for although he was an active member of Permai, he was a fairly un-sophisticated one. It had evidently never occurred to him that the anti-Moslem-funeral agitation of the party would ever appear as a concrete problem, or that the Modin would actually refuse to officiate. Karman was actually not a bad fellow, the Modin concluded; he was but a dupe of his leaders.

After leaving the now highly agitated Karman, the Modin went directly to the subdistrict officer to ask if he had acted properly. The officer was morally bound to say that he had, and thus fortified the Modin returned home to find Karman and the village policeman, to whom he had gone in desperation, waiting for him. The policeman, a personal friend of Karman's, told the Modin that according to time-honored custom he was supposed to bury everyone with impartiality, never mind whether he happened to agree with their politics. But the Modin, having now been personally supported by the subdistrict officer, insisted that it was no longer his responsibility. However, he suggested, if Karman wished, he could go to the village chief's office and sign a public statement, sealed with the Government stamp and countersigned by the village chief in the presence of two witnesses, declaring that he, Karman, was a true believing Moslem and that he wished the Modin to bury the boy according to Islamic custom. At this suggestion that he officially abandon his religious beliefs, Karman exploded into a rage and stormed from the house, rather uncharacteristic behavior for a Javanese. By the time he arrived home again, at his wit's end about what to do next, he found to his dismay that the news of the boy's death had been broadcast and the entire neighborhood was already gathering for the ceremony.

Like most of the kampongs in the town of Modjokuto, the one in which I lived consisted both of pious santris and ardent abangans (as well as a number of less intense adherents of either side), mixed together in a more or less random manner. In the town, people are forced to live where they can and take whomever they find for neighbors, in contrast to the rural areas where whole neighborhoods, even whole villages, still tend to be made up almost entirely of either abangans or santris. The majority of the santris in the kampong were members of Masjumi and most of the abangans were followers of Permai, and in daily life, social interaction between the two groups was minimal. The abangans, most of whom were either petty artisans or manual laborers, gathered each late afternoon at Karman's roadside coffee shop for the idle twilight conversations which are typical of small town and village life in Java; the santris—tailors, traders and store-keepers for the most part—usually gathered in one or another of the santri-run shops for the same purpose. But despite this lack of close social ties, the demonstration of territorial unity at a funeral was still felt by both groups to be an unavoidable duty; of all the Javanese rituals, the funeral probably carries the greatest obligation on attendance. Everyone who lives within a certain roughly defined radius of the survivors' home is expected to come to the ceremony; and on this occasion everyone did.

With this as background, it is not surprising that when I arrived at Karman's house about eight o'clock, I found two separate clusters of sullen men squatting disconsolately on either side of the yard, a nervous group of whispering women sitting idly inside the house near the still clothed body, and a general air of doubt and uneasiness in place of the usual quiet busyness of slametan preparing, body washing and guest greeting. The abangans were grouped near the house where Karman was crouched, staring blankly off into space, and where Sudjoko and Sastro, the town Chairman and Secretary of Permai (the only nonresidents of the kampong present) sat on chairs, looking vaguely out of place. The santris were crowded together under the narrow shadow of a coconut palm about thirty yards away, chatting quietly to one another about everything but the problem at hand. The almost motionless scene suggested an unlooked-for intermission in a familiar drama, as when a motion picture stops in the mid-action.

After a half hour or so, a few of the abangans began to chip half-heartedly away at pieces of wood to make grave markers and a few women began to construct small flower offerings for want of anything better to do, but it was clear that the ritual was arrested and that no one quite knew what to do next. Tension slowly rose. People nervously watched the sun rise higher and higher in the sky, or glanced at the impassive Karman. Mutterings about the sorry state of affairs began to appear ("everything these days is a political problem," an old, traditionalistic man of about eighty grumbled to me, "you can't even die any more but what it becomes a political problem"). Finally, about 9:30, a young santri tailor named Abu decided to try to do something about the situation before it deteriorated entirely: he stood up and gestured to Karman, the first serious instrumental act which had occurred all morning. And Karman, roused from his meditation, crossed the no-man's-land to talk to him.

As a matter of fact, Abu occupied a rather special position in the kampong. Although he was a pious santri and a loyal Masjumi member, he had more contact with the Permai group because his tailor shop was located directly behind Karman's coffee shop. Though Abu, who stuck to his sewing machine night and day, was not properly a member of this group, he would often exchange comments with them from his work bench about twenty feet away. True, a certain amount of tension existed between him and the Permai people over religious issues. Once, when I was inquiring about their eschatological beliefs, they referred me sarcastically to Abu, saying he was an expert, and they teased him quite openly about what they considered the wholly ridiculous Islamic theories of the after life. Nevertheless, he had something of a social bond with them, and it was perhaps reasonable that he should be the one to try to break the deadlock.

"It is already nearly noon," Abu said, "things can't go straight on like this." He suggested that he send Umar, another of the santris, to see if the Modin could now be induced to come; perhaps things were cooler with him now. Meanwhile, he could get the washing and wrapping of the corpse started himself. Karman replied that he would think about it, and returned to the other side of the yard for a discussion with the two Permai leaders. After a few minutes of vigorous gesturing and nodding, Karman returned and said simply, "all right, that way." "I know how you feel," Abu said, "I'll just do what is absolutely necessary and keep the Islam out as much as possible." He gathered the santris together and they entered the house.

The first requisite was stripping the corpse (which was still lying on the floor, because no one could bring himself to move it). But by now the body was rigid, making it necessary to cut the clothes off with a knife, an unusual procedure which deeply disturbed everyone, especially the women clustered around. The santris finally managed to get the body outside and set up the bathing enclosure. Abu asked for volunteers for the washing; he reminded them that God would consider such an act a good work. But the relatives, who normally would be expected to undertake this task, were by now so deeply shaken and confused that they were unable to bring themselves to hold the boy on their laps in the customary fashion. There was another wait while people looked hopelessly at each other. Finally, Pak Sura, a member of Karman's group but no relative, took the boy on his lap, although he was clearly frightened and kept whispering a protective spell. One reason the Javanese give for their custom of rapid burial is that it is dangerous to have the spirit of the deceased hovering around the house.

Before the washing could begin, however, someone raised the question as to whether one person was enough—wasn't it usually three? No one was quite sure, including Abu; some thought that although it was customary to have three people it was not obligatory, and some thought three a necessary number. After about ten minutes of anxious discussion, a male cousin of the boy and a carpenter, unrelated to him, managed to work up the courage to join Pak Sura. Abu, attempting to act the Modin's role as best he could, sprinkled a few drops of water on the corpse and then it was washed, rather haphazardly and in unsacralized water. When this was finished, however, the procedure was again stalled, for no one knew exactly how to arrange the small cotton pads which, under Moslem law, should plug the body orifices. Karman's wife, sister of the deceased's mother, could evidently take no more, for she broke into a loud, unrestrained wailing, the only demonstration of this sort I witnessed among the dozen or so Javanese funerals I attended. Everyone was further upset by this development, and most of the kampong women made a frantic but unavailing effort to comfort her. Most of the men remained seated in the yard, outwardly calm and inexpressive, but the embarrassed uneasiness which had been present since the beginning seemed to be turning toward fearful desperation. "It is not nice for her to cry that way," several men said to me, "it isn't proper." At this point, the Modin arrived.

However, he was still adamant. Further, he warned Abu that he was courting eternal damnation by his actions. "You will have to answer to God on Judgment Day," he said, "if you make mistakes in the ritual. It will be your responsibility. For a Moslem, burial is a serious matter and must be carried out according to the Law by someone who knows what the Law is, not according to the will of the individual." He then suggested to Sudjoko and Sastro, the Permai leaders, that they take charge of the funeral, for as party "intellectuals" they must certainly know what kind of funeral customs Permai followed. The two leaders, who had not moved from their chairs, considered this as everyone watched expectantly, but they finally refused, with some chagrin, saying they really did not know how to go about it. The Modin shrugged and turned away. One of the bystanders, a friend of Karman's, then suggested that they just take the body out and bury it and forget about the whole ritual; it was extremely dangerous to leave things as they were much longer. I don't know whether this remarkable suggestion would have been followed, for at this juncture the mother and father of the dead child entered the kampong.

They seemed quite composed. They were not unaware of the death, for the father later told me he had suspected as much when he got the telegram; he and his wife had prepared themselves for the worst and were more or less resigned by the time they arrived. When they approached the kampong and saw the whole neighborhood gathered, they knew that their fears were well founded. When Karman's wife, whose weeping had subsided slightly, saw the dead boy's mother come into the yard, she burst free of those who were comforting her and with a shriek rushed to embrace her sister. In what seemed a split second, both women had dissolved into wild hysterics and the crowd had rushed in and pulled them apart, dragging them to houses at opposite sides of the kampong. Their wailing continued in undiminished volume, and nervous comments arose to the effect that they ought to get on with the burial in one fashion or another, before the boy's spirit possessed someone.

But the mother now insisted on seeing the body of her child before it was wrapped. The father at first forbade it, angrily ordering her to stop crying, didn't she know that such behavior would darken the boy's pathway to the other world? But she persisted and so they brought her, stumbling, to where he lay in Karman's house. The women tried to keep her from drawing too close, but she broke loose and began to kiss the boy about the genitals. She was snatched away almost immediately by her husband and the women, though she screamed that she had not yet finished; and they pulled her into the back room where she subsided into a daze. After awhile—the body was finally being wrapped, the Modin having unbent enough to point out where the cotton pads went—she seemed to lose her bearings entirely and began to move about the yard shaking hands with everyone, all strangers to her, and saying "forgive me my faults, forgive me my faults." Again she was forcibly restrained; people said, "calm yourself, think of your other children—do you want to follow your son to the grave?"

The corpse was now wrapped and new suggestions were made that it be taken off immediately to the graveyard. At this point, Abu approached the father, who, he evidently felt, had now displaced Karman as the man legally responsible for the proceedings. Abu explained that the Modin, being a Government official, did not feel free to approach the father himself, but he would like to know: how did he wish the boy to be buried—the Islamic way or what? The father, somewhat bewildered, said, "Of course, the Islamic way. I don't have much of any religion, but I'm not a Christian, and when it comes to death the burial should be the Islamic way. Completely Islamic." Abu explained again that the Modin could not approach the father directly, but that he, being "free," could do as he pleased. He said that he had tried to help as best he could but that he had been careful to do nothing Islamic before the father came. It was too bad, he apologized, about all the tension that was in the air, that political differences had to make so much trouble. But after all, everything had to be "clear" and "legal" about the funeral. It was important for the boy's soul. The santris, somewhat gleefully, now chanted their prayers over the corpse, and it was carried to the grave and buried in the usual manner. The Modin gave the usual graveyard speech, as amended for children, and the funeral was finally completed. None of the relatives or the women went to the graveyard; but when we returned to the house—it was now well after noon—the slametan was finally served, and Paidjan's spirit presumably left the kampong to begin its journey to the other world.

Three days later, in the evening, the first of the commemorative slametans was held, but it turned out that not only were no santris present but that it was as much a Permai political and religious cult meeting as a mourning ritual. Karman started off in the traditional fashion by announcing in high Javanese that this was a slametan in remembrance of the death of Paidjan. Sudjoko, the Permai leader, immediately burst in saying, "No, no, that is wrong. At a third day slametan you just eat and give a long Islamic chant for the dead, and we are certainly not going to do that." He then launched into a long, rambling speech. Everyone, he said, must know the philosophical-religious basis of the country. "Suppose this American (he pointed to me; he was not at all pleased by my presence) came up and asked you: what is the spiritual basis of the country? and you didn't know—wouldn't you be ashamed?"

He went on in this vein, building up a whole rationale for the present national political structure on the basis of a mystical interpretation of President Sukarno's "Five Points" (Monotheism, Social Justice, Humanitarianism, Democracy, and Nationalism)[5] which are the official ideological foundation of

---

[5] For a fuller discussion of President Sukarno's pantjasila ideology and his attempt to root it in general Indonesian values, see Kahin (1952:122–27).

the new republic. Aided by Karman and others, he worked out a micro-macrocosm correspondence theory in which the individual is seen to be but a small replica of the state, and the state but an enlarged image of the individual. If the state is to be ordered, then the individual must also be ordered; each implies the other. As the President's Five Points are at the basis of the state, so the five senses are at the basis of an individual. The process of harmonizing both are the same, and it is this we must be sure we know. The discussion continued for nearly half an hour, ranging widely through religious, philosophical, and political issues (including, evidently for my benefit, a discussion of the Rosenbergs' execution).

We paused for coffee and as Sudjoko was about to begin again, Paidjan's father, who had been sitting quietly and expressionless, began suddenly to talk, softly and with a curiously mechanical tonelessness, almost as if he were reasoning with himself but without much hope of success. "I am sorry for my rough city accent," he said, "but I very much want to say something." He hoped they would forgive him; they could continue their discussion in a moment. "I have been trying to be iklas ("detached," "resigned") about Paidjan's death. I'm convinced that everything that could have been done for him was done and that his death was just an event which simply happened." He said he was still in Modjokuto because he could not yet face the people where he lived, couldn't face having to tell each one of them what had occurred. His wife, he said, was a little more iklas now too. It was hard, though. He kept telling himself it was just the will of God, but it was so hard, for nowadays people didn't agree on things any more; one person tells you one thing and others tell you another. It's hard to know which is right, to know what to believe. He said he appreciated all the Modjokuto people coming to the funeral, and he was sorry it had been all mixed up. "I'm not very religious myself. I'm not Masjumi and I'm not Permai. But I wanted the boy to be buried in the old way. I hope no one's feelings were hurt." He said again he was trying to be iklas, to tell himself it was just the will of God, but it was hard, for things were so confused these days. It was hard to see why the boy should have died. This sort of public expression of one's feelings is extremely unusual—in my experience unique—among Javanese, and in the formalized traditional slametan pattern there is simply no place for it (nor for philosophical or political discussion). Everyone present was rather shaken by the father's talk, and there was a painful silence. Sudjoko finally began to talk again, but this time he described in detail the boy's death. How Paidjan had first gotten a fever and Karman had called him, Sudjoko, to come and say a Permai spell. But the boy did not respond. They finally took him to a male nurse in the hospital, where he was given an injection. But still he worsened. He vomited blood and went into convulsions, which Sudjoko described rather graphically, and then he died. "I don't know why the Permai spell didn't work," he said "it has worked before. This time it didn't. I don't know why; that sort of thing can't be explained no matter how much you think about it. Sometimes it just works and sometimes it just doesn't." There was another silence and then, after about ten minutes more of political discussion, we disbanded. The father returned the next day to his home and I was not invited to any of the later slametans. When I left the field about four months later, Karman's wife had still not entirely re-covered from the experience, the tension between the santris and the aban-gans in the kampong had increased, and everyone wondered what would happen the next time a death occurred in a Permai family.

Analysis

"Of all the sources of religion," wrote Malinowski, "the supreme and fi-nal crisis of life—death—is of the greatest importance" (1948:29). Death, he argued, provokes in the survivors a dual response of love and loathing, a deep-going emotional ambivalence of fascination and fear which threat-ens both the psychological and social foundations of human existence. The survivors are drawn toward the deceased by their affection for him, repelled from him by the dreadful transformation wrought by death. Funeral rites, and the mourning practices which follow them, focus around this paradox-ical desire both to maintain the tie in the face of death and to break the bond immediately and utterly, and to insure the domination of the will to live over the tendency to despair. Mortuary rituals maintain the continuity of human life by preventing the survivors from yielding either to the im-pulse to flee panic-stricken from the scene or to the contrary impulse to fol-low the deceased into the grave:

And here into this play of emotional forces, into this supreme dilemma of life and final death, religion steps in, selecting the positive creed, the comforting view, the culturally valuable belief in immortality, in the spirit independent of the body, and in the continuance of life after death. In the various ceremonies at death, in commemoration and communion with the departed, and worship of ancestral ghosts, religion gives body and form to the saving beliefs. . . . Ex-actly the same function it fulfills also with regard to the whole group. The cer-emonial of death which ties the survivors to the body and rivets them to the place of death, the beliefs in the existence of the spirit, in its beneficent influ-ences or malevolent intentions, in the duties of a series of commemorative or sacrificial ceremonies—in all this religion counteracts the centrifugal forces of fear, dismay, demoralization, and provides the most powerful means of reinte-gration of the group's shaken solidarity and of the re-establishment of its morale. In short, religion here assures the victory of tradition over the mere negative response of thwarted instinct. (ibid.:33-35)

To this sort of theory, a case such as that described above clearly poses some difficult problems. Not only was the victory of tradition and culture over "thwarted instinct" a narrow one at best, but it seemed as if the ritual were tearing the society apart rather than integrating it, were disorganizing personalities rather than healing them. To this the functionalist has a ready answer, which takes one of two forms depending upon whether he follows the Durkheim or the Malinowski tradition: social disintegration or cultural demoralization. Rapid social change has disrupted Javanese society and this is reflected in a disintegrated culture; as the unified state of traditional village society was mirrored in the unified slametan, so the broken society of the kampong is mirrored in the broken slametan of the funeral ritual we have just witnessed. Or, in the alternate phraseology, cultural decay has led to social fragmentation; loss of a vigorous folk tradition has weakened the moral ties between individuals.

It seems to me that there are two things wrong with this argument, no matter in which of the two vocabularies it is stated: it identifies social (or cultural) conflict with social (or cultural) disintegration; it denies independent roles to both culture and social structure, regarding one of the two as a mere epiphenomenon of the other.

In the first place, kampong life is not simply anomic. Though it is marked by vigorous social conflicts, as is our own society, it nevertheless proceeds fairly effectively in most areas. If governmental, economic, familial, stratificatory, and social control institutions functioned as poorly as did Paidjan's funeral, a kampong would indeed be an uncomfortable place in which to live. But though some of the typical symptoms of urban upheaval—such as increased gambling, petty thievery, and prostitution—are to some degree present, kampong social life is clearly not on the verge of collapse; everyday social interaction does not limp along with the suppressed bitterness and deep uncertainty we have seen focused around burial. For most of its members most of the time, a semiurban neighborhood in Modjokuto offers a viable way of life, despite its material disadvantages and its transitional character; and for all the sentimentality which has been lavished on descriptions of rural life in Java, this is probably as much as one could say for the village. As a matter of fact, it is around religious beliefs and practices—slametans, holidays, curing, sorcery, cult groups, etc.—that the most seriously disruptive events seem to cluster. Religion here is somehow the center and source of stress, not merely the reflection of stress elsewhere in the society.[6] Yet it is not a source of stress because commitment to the inherited patterns of belief and ritual has been weakened. The conflict around Paidjan's death

---

[6] For a description of a somewhat disrupted celebration of the end of the Fast holiday, Hari Raya (Id al-fitr) in Modjokuto, which shows many formal similarities to Paidjan's funeral, see Geertz, in press.

took place simply because all the kampong residents did share a common, highly integrated, cultural tradition concerning funerals. There was no argument over whether the slametan pattern was the correct ritual, whether the neighbors were obligated to attend, or whether the supernatural concepts upon which the ritual is based were valid ones. For both santris and abangans in the kampongs, the slametan maintains its force as a genuine sacred symbol; it still provides a meaningful framework for facing death—for most people the only meaningful framework. We cannot attribute the failure of the ritual to secularization, to a growth in skepticism, or to a disinterest in the traditional "saving beliefs," any more than we can attribute it to anomie.

We must rather, I think, ascribe it to a discontinuity between the form of integration existing in the social structural ("causal-functional") dimension and the form of integration existing in the cultural ("logico-meaningful") dimension—a discontinuity which leads not to social and cultural disintegration, but to social and cultural conflict. In more concrete, if somewhat aphoristic terms, the difficulty lies in the fact that socially kampong people are urbanites, while culturally they are still folk.

I have already pointed out that the Javanese kampong represents a transitional sort of society, that its members stand "in between" the more or less fully urbanized elite and the more or less traditionally organized peasantry. The social structural forms in which they participate are for the most part urban ones. The emergence of a highly differentiated occupational structure in place of the almost entirely agricultural one of the countryside; the virtual disappearance of the semihereditary, traditional village government as a personalistic buffer between the individual and the rationalized central government bureaucracy, and its replacement by the more flexible forms of modern parliamentary democracy; the evolution of a multiclass society in which the kampong, unlike the village, is not even a potentially self-sufficient entity, but is only one dependent subpart—all this means that the kampong man lives in a very urban world. Socially, his is a *Gesellschaht* existence.

But on the cultural level—the level of meaning—there is much less of a contrast between the kampong dweller and the villager; much more between him and a member of the urban elite. The patterns of belief, expression, and value to which the kampong man is committed—his world-view, ethos, ethic, or whatever—differ only slightly from those followed by the villager. Amid a radically more complex social environment, he clings noticeably to the symbols which guided him or his parents through life in rural society. And it is this fact which gave rise to the psychological and social tension surrounding Paidjan's funeral.

The disorganization of the ritual resulted from a basic ambiguity in the meaning of the rite for those who participated in it. Most simply stated, this ambiguity lay in the fact that the symbols which compose the slametan had both religious and political significance, were charged with both sacred and profane import. The people who came into Karman's yard, including Karman himself, were not sure whether they were engaged in a sacralized consideration of first and last things or in a secular struggle for power. This is why the old man (he was a graveyard keeper, as a matter of fact) complained to me that dying was nowadays a political problem; why the village policeman accused the Modin not of religious but of political bias for refusing to bury Paidjan; why the unsophisticated Karman was astonished when his ideological commitments suddenly loomed as obstacles to his religious practices; why Abu was torn between his willingness to submerge political differences in the interest of a harmonious funeral and his unwillingness to trifle with his religious beliefs in the interest of his own salvation; why the commemorative rite oscillated between political diatribe and a poignant search for an adequate explanation of what had happened—why, in sum, the slametan religious pattern stumbled when it attempted to "step in" with the "positive creed" and "the culturally valuable belief."

As emphasized earlier, the present severity of the contrast between santri and abangan is in great part due to the rise of nationalist social movements in twentieth-century Indonesia. In the larger cities where these movements were born, they were originally of various sorts: tradesmen's societies to fight Chinese competition; unions of workers to resist plantation exploitation; religious groups trying to redefine ultimate concepts; philosophical discussion clubs attempting to clarify Indonesian metaphysical and moral notions; school associations striving to revivify Indonesian education; co-operative societies trying to work out new forms of economic organization; cultural groups moving toward a renaissance of Indonesian artistic life; and, of course, political parties working to build up effective opposition to Dutch rule. As time wore on, however, the struggle for independence absorbed more and more the energies of all these essentially elite groups. Whatever the distinctive aim of each of them—economic reconstruction, religious reform, artistic renaissance—it became submerged in a diffuse political ideology; all the groups were increasingly concerned with one end as the prerequisite of all further social and cultural progress—freedom. By the time the revolution began in 1945, reformulation of ideas outside the political sphere had noticeably slackened and most aspects of life had become intensely ideologized, a tendency which has continued into the post-war period.

In the villages and small town kampongs, the early, specific phase of nationalism had only a minor effect. But as the movement unified and moved toward eventual triumph, the masses too began to be affected and, as I have pointed out, mainly through the medium of religious symbols. The highly urbanized elite forged their bonds to the peasantry not in terms of complex political and economic theory, which would have had little meaning in a rural context, but in terms of concepts and values already present there. As the major line of demarcation among the elite was between those who took Islamic doctrine as the overall basis of their mass appeal and those who took a generalized philosophical refinement of the indigenous syncretic tradition as such a basis, so in the countryside santri and abangan soon became not simply religious but political categories, denoting the followers of these two diffuse approaches to the organization of the emerging independent society. When the achievement of political freedom strengthened the importance of factional politics in parliamentary government, the santri-abangan distinction became, on the local level at least, one of the primary ideological axes around which the process of party maneuvering took place.

The effect of this development has been to cause political debate and religious propitiation to be carried out in the same vocabulary. A koranic chant becomes an affirmation of political allegiance as well as a paean to God; a burning of incense expresses one's secular ideology as well as one's sacred beliefs. Slametans now tend to be marked by anxious discussions of the various elements in the ritual, of what their "real" significance is; by arguments as to whether a particular practice is essential or optional; by abangan uneasiness when santris lift their eyes to pray and santri uneasiness when abangans recite a protective spell. At death, as we have seen, the traditional symbols tend both to solidify individuals in the face of social loss and to remind them of their differences; to emphasize the broadly human themes of mortality and undeserved suffering and the narrowly social ones of factional opposition and party struggle; to strengthen the values the participants hold in common and to "tune up" their animosities and suspicions. The rituals themselves become matters of political conflict; forms for the sacralization of marriage and death are transformed into important party issues. In such an equivocal cultural setting, the average kampong Javanese finds it increasingly difficult to determine the proper attitude toward a particular event, to choose the meaning of a given symbol appropriate to a given social context.

The corollary of this interference of political meanings with religious meanings also occurs: the interference of religious meanings with political ones. Because the same symbols are used in both political and religious contexts, people often regard party struggle as involving not merely the usual ebb and flow of parliamentary maneuver, the necessary factional give-and-take of democratic government, but involving as well decisions on basic values and ultimates. Kampong people in particular tend to see the open struggle for power explicitly institutionalized in the new republican forms of government as a struggle for the right to establish different brands of essentially religious principles as official: "if the abangans get in, the koranic teachers will be forbidden to hold classes"; "if the santris get in, we shall all have to pray five times a day." The normal conflict involved in electoral striving for office is heightened by the idea that literally everything is at stake: the "if we win, it is our country" idea that the group which gains power has a right, as one man said, "to put his own foundation under the state." Politics thus takes on a kind of sacralized bitterness; and one village election in a suburban Modjokuto village actually had to be held twice because of the intense pressures generated in this way.

The kampong man is, so to speak, caught between his ultimate and his proximate concepts. Because he is forced to formulate his essentially metaphysical ideas, his response to such basic "problems" as fate, suffering, and evil, in the same terms as he states his claims to secular power, his political rights and aspirations, he experiences difficulty in enacting either a socially and psychologically efficient funeral or a smoothly running election.

But a ritual is not just a pattern of meaning; it is also a form of social interaction. Thus, in addition to creating cultural ambiguity, the attempt to bring a religious pattern from a relatively less differentiated rural background into an urban context also gives rise to social conflict, simply because the kind of social integration demonstrated by the pattern is not congruent with the major patterns of integration in the society generally. The way kampong people go about maintaining solidarity in everyday life is quite different from the way the slametan insists that they should go about maintaining it.

As emphasized earlier, the slametan is essentially a territorially based ritual; it assumes the primary tie between families to be that of residential propinquity. One set of neighbors is considered a significant social unit (politically, religiously, economically) as against another set of neighbors; one village as against another village; one village-cluster as against another village-cluster. In the town, this pattern has in large part changed. Significant social groups are defined by a plurality of factors—class, political commitment, occupation, ethnicity, regional origins, religious preference, age, and sex, as well as residence. The new urban form of organization consists of a careful balance of conflicting forces arising out of diverse contexts: class differences are softened by ideological similarities; ethnic conflicts by common economic interests; political opposition, as we have been, by residential intimacy. But in the midst of all this pluralistic checking and balancing, the slametan remains unchanged, blind to the major lines of social and cultural demarcation in urban life. For it, the primary classifying characteristic of an individual is where he lives.

Thus when an occasion arises demanding sacralization—a life-cycle transition, a holiday, a serious illness—the religious form which must be employed acts not with but against the grain of social equilibrium. The slametan ignores those recently devised mechanisms of social insulation which in daily life keep group conflict within fixed bounds, as it also ignores the newly evolved patterns of social integration among opposed groups which balance contradictory tensions in a reasonably effective fashion. People are pressed into an intimacy they would as soon avoid; where the incongruity between the social assumptions of the ritual ("we are all culturally homogeneous peasants together") and what is in fact the case ("we are several different kinds of people who must perforce live together despite our serious value disagreements") leads to a deep uneasiness of which Paidjan's funeral was but an extreme example. In the kampong, the holding of a slametan increasingly serves to remind people that the neighborhood bonds they are strengthening through a dramatic enactment are no longer the bonds which most emphatically hold them together. These latter are ideological, class, occupation and political bonds, divergent ties which are no longer adequately summed up in territorial relationships.

In sum, the disruption of Paidjan's funeral may be traced to a single source: an incongruity between the cultural framework of meaning and the patterning of social interaction, an incongruity due to the persistence in an urban environment of a religious symbol system adjusted to peasant social structure. Static functionalism, of either the sociological or social psychological sort, is unable to isolate this kind of incongruity because it fails to discriminate between logico-meaningful integration and causal-functional integration; because it fails to realize that cultural structure and social structure are not mere reflexes of one another but independent, yet interdependent, variables. The driving forces in social change can be clearly formulated only by a more dynamic form of functionalist theory, one which takes into account the fact that man's need to live in a world to which he can attribute some significance, whose essential import he feels he can grasp, often diverges from his concurrent need to maintain a functioning social organism. A diffuse concept of culture as "learned behavior," a static view of social structure as an equilibrated pattern of interaction, and a stated or unstated assumption that the two must somehow (save in "disorganized" situations) be simple mirror images of one another, is rather too primitive a conceptual apparatus with which to attack such problems as those raised by Paidjan's unfortunate but instructive funeral.

BIBLIOGRAPHY

Durkheim, Emile
    1947   The Elementary Forms of the Religious Life. Glencoe, Ill.: Free Press.
Fortes, Meyer
    1953   The Structure of Unilineal Descent Groups. American Anthropologist
            55:17–41.
Geertz, Clifford
    1956   Religious Belief and Economic Behavior in a Central Javanese Town:
            Some Preliminary Considerations. Economic Development and Cultural
            Change IV:134–158.
    In press. Religion in Modjokuto. (In press, Cambridge, Massachusetts.) Editor's
            note: Subsequently published in 1960 as The Religion of Java. New York:
            Free Press.

Jay, Robert
    1956   Local Government in Rural Central Java. The Far Eastern Quarterly
            XV:215–227.
Kahin, George McTurnan
    1952   Nationalism and Revolution in Indonesia. Ithaca, N.Y.: Cornell Univer-
            sity Press.
Kluckhohn, Clyde
    1944   Navaho Witchcraft. Peabody Museum Papers, No. XXII. Cambridge, Mass.
Landon, K.
    1949   Southeast Asia, Crossroad of Religions. Chicago: University of Chicago
            Press.
Leach, Edmund R.
    1954   Political Systems of Highland Burma. Cambridge, Mass.: Harvard Univer-
            sity Press.
Malinowski, Bronislaw
    1948   Magic, Science and Religion and Other Essays. Glencoe, Ill.: Free Press.
Merton, Robert
    1949   Social Theory and Social Structure. Glencoe, Ill.: Free Press.
Parsons, Talcott
    1951   The Social System. Glencoe, Ill.: Free Press.
Parsons, Talcot and Edward Shils
    1951   Toward a General Theory of Action. Cambridge, Mass.: Harvard Univer-
            sity Press.
Redfield, Robert
    1941   The Folk Culture of Yucatan. Chicago: University of Chicago Press.
Robertson-Smith, W.
    1894   Lectures on the Religion of the Semites. Edinburgh: A. & C. Black.
Sorokin, Peter
    1937   Social and Cultural Dynamics. 3 vols. New York: Bedminster Press.

QUERIES

- What is Geertz's distinction between "culture" and "social-system"?
  How does Geertz define "culture"?
- Citing the ideas of Sorokin, Geertz distinguishes two sorts of integration: "logico-meaningful integration" and "causal-functional integration." The first is characterized by "a unity of style, of logical implication, or meaning and value," whereas the latter is when the elements
  of a system are functionally or organically unified into a single system.
  How does this distinction link to Geertz's definitions of "culture" and
  "social-system"? How does this distinction intersect with Geertz's interpretation of culture?
- In "Thick Description" (see Moore 2008:263–65), Geertz argues that
  anthropology's task is "sorting out the structures of signification" in or-

der to determine "their social ground and import." What were the structures of signification surrounding the slametan for Paidjan on July 17, 1954? Describe the various levels—national/local, political/religious, Islamic/non-Islamic—at which these structures of signification occur.

- When Geertz engages in an "analysis," it is clearly not an analysis based on the search for scientific laws or the testing of hypotheses. What is Geertz's form of analysis? How can we know if it is correct?

CONNECTIONS

- Geertz contrasts his approach to religion with the functionalist approaches of Malinowski. What was Malinowski's theory about the role of religion? How does it differ from Geertz's interpretive approach?
- Geertz notes that structural-functionalist approaches like those outlined by Radcliffe-Brown emphasize "systems in balance" and "'well-integrated' societies in a stable equilibrium"? How does this critique parallel the comments by Victor Turner about Radcliffe-Brown's brand of British social anthropology? (See Moore 2008:249–50.)
- Although Geertz does not use these terms in this article, it is clear that a theory of practice can be applied to this Javanese funeral. As variously discussed by Bourdieu, Ortner, Wolf, and Sahlins (Moore 2008), what are the intersections of structure, history, and agency in the slametan?

20

Mary Douglas

INTRODUCTION

The British anthropologist Mary Douglas (1921–2007) pursued a line of anthropological inquiry that built upon Emile Durkheim's investigations into systems of classification and the bases of social experience (see Moore 2008:272–87). Throughout her distinguished career, Douglas revisited the issues of purity and pollution, seeing those social classifications as symbolic restatements of social order. Citing the phrase by the 19th-century British statesman, Lord Chesterfield, "Dirt is matter in the wrong place," Douglas explored how concepts of purity and pollution represented systems of social classification—often serving as symbolic statements of how members of different societies viewed themselves and the cosmos.

Douglas's initial ethnographic research was among the Lele of the Congo, a tribal society deeply concerned with matters of pollution. This concern is reflected in the following article. In this selection Douglas briefly mentions the dietary prohibitions found in the Old Testament books of Deuteronomy and Leviticus, a topic that she returned to a various points in her career (Moore 2008:275–77, 284–85). In these prohibitions, clean animals are those that are completely within a category; unclean animals are those that cross categories or defy classification. Thus, fish living in water and having scales and fins are clean and edible; shellfish and eels, living in water but lacking scales and fins are unclean and avoided. This system of classification, Douglas argues, in turn reflected a social conception of Jehovah as simultaneous "holy and whole." Animals wholly within their classification were not only edible but also a holy gift from Jehovah to humanity. In contrast, animals that crossed categories were unclean and unholy; they were examples of matter out of place.

The following selection approaches these issues from an unlikely starting point: the ways the Lele classify the scaly anteater or pangolin. As Douglas observes, the pangolin is the only animal associated with a Lele fertility cult, and its special status reflects broader ideas about the difference between humans, animals, and spirits. Humans are different from animals because humans have manners, tend to give birth to single infants (and rarely twins), and occupy the domesticated realms of villages and fields. Animals are naturally voracious, have litters, and shun the human realms. The pangolin, however, is anomalous: an animal with the scaly tail of a fish, but with four legs it uses to climb trees. Even odder, the pangolin "offers" itself to Lele hunters: when the animal is first struck, it rolls into a ball to "play dead" opossum-like, but later uncurls itself so it can be easily killed. The special status of the pangolin, which Douglas describes in detail, derives from the confusion of categories it represents.

PRIMARY TEXT: *ANIMALS IN LELE RELIGIOUS SYMBOLISM*

Originally published in *Africa: Journal of the International African Institute*, Vol. 27, No. 1, (Jan. 1957), pp. 46–58. Reprinted with permission of Edinburgh University Press. www.euppublishing.com.

Lele religious life is organized by a number of cult groups. For a long time they seemed to me to be a collection of quite heterogeneous cults, uncoordinated except for a certain overlap in membership. In one of them, the Diviners' group, entry is by initiation only, though the candidate is supposed to give evidence of a dream summons. In another, the Twin Parents, there is no initiation. Parents of twins have no choice but to pay the fees and become Twin Diviners. In another, the Begetters, candidates must have begotten a child, pay fees and undergo initiation. Members of this group, who have begotten children of both sexes, are qualified for entrance into another group, which makes a cult of the pangolin[1] (Manis tricuspis). Lastly there are Diviners of God (*Bangang banjambi*) who are supposed to acquire their power not by initiation, but by direct communication with supernatural beings, the spirits. The primary objects of all these cults[2] are fertility and good hunting.

The Pangolin cult is the only one in which an animal is the cult object. In the other cults parts of certain animals are reserved to initiates: the head

---

[1] The pangolin is a scaly ant-eater.
[2] The Begetters are an exception, their initiation being mainly a rite de passage. They give indirect support to the other fertility cults by honoring virility and penalizing impotence.

and stomach of the bush pig to Diviners, the chest and young of all animals to the Begetters. Or parts of animals or whole animals may be prohibited to them as a condition of their calling: Twin Parents must not eat the back of any animal; so many animals are prohibited to the Diviners of God that they practise an almost vegetarian austerity.

Regarding these practises the Lele offer very little explanation of the symbolism involved. The different animals are associated traditionally with the different cults. The symbolism of the bush pig is relatively explicit. It is the Diviners' animal, they will say, because it frequents the marshy sources of streams where the spirits abide, and because it produces the largest litters in the animal world. In very few other instances is the symbolism so clearly recognized. In most cases one would be justified in assuming that no symbolism whatever is involved, and that the prohibitions concerning different animals are observed simply as diacritical badges of cult membership.

If this be the correct interpretation of the different observances, one must equally accept the view that there is no single system of thought integrating the various fertility cults. At first I felt obliged to adopt this point of view. Believing the Lele culture to be highly eclectic and capable of assimilating into itself any number of cults of neighbouring tribes, I concluded that the connexion between the various cults was probably only an historical one, and that in the absence of historical or ethnographic data from surrounding areas, it was impossible to take the problem any further.

Although I could never get a direct answer that satisfied me as to why the pangolin should be the object of a fertility cult, I kept receiving odd scraps of disconnected information about it and about other animals in different religious and secular contexts. Gradually I was able to relate these ideas within a broad framework of assumptions about animals and humans. These assumptions are so fundamental to Lele thought that one could almost describe them as unformulated categories through which they unconsciously organize their experience. They could never emerge in reply to direct questions because it was impossible for Lele to suppose that the questioner might take his standpoint on another set of assumptions. Only when I was able to appreciate the kind of implicit connections they made between one set of facts and another, did a framework of metaphysical ideas emerge. Within this it was not difficult to understand the central role of the pangolin, and the significance of other animals in Lele religion. The different cult groups no longer seemed to be disconnected and overlapping, but appeared rather as complementary developments of the same basic theme.

Animals in the Natural Order

The Lele have a clear concept of order in their universe which is based on a few simple categories. The first is the distinction between humans and animals.[3] Humans are mannerly. They observe polite conventions in their dealings with each other and hide themselves when performing their natural functions. Animals satisfy their natural appetites uncontrolled. They are regarded as the 'brute beasts which have no understanding' of the Anglican marriage service. This governing distinction between men and animals testifies to the superiority of mankind. It gives men a kind of moral licence to hunt and kill wild animals without shame or pity.

A subsidiary characteristic of animals is held to be their immense fecundity. In this, animals have the advantage of humans. They give birth to two, three, six or seven of their young at a time. Barrenness in humans is attributed to sorcery: barrenness in animals is not normally envisaged in Lele ideas about them. The set incantation in fertility rites refers to the fecundity of the animals in the forest, and asks why humans should not be so prolific.

The third defining characteristic of animals is their acceptance of their own sphere in the natural order. Most animals run away from the hunter and shun all human con-tact. Sometimes there are individual animals which, contrary to the habit of their kind, disregard the boundary between humans and themselves. Such a deviation from characteristically animal behavior shows them to be not entirely animal, but partly human.[4] Two sets of beliefs account for the fact that some wild animals occasionally attack humans, loiter near villages, even enter them and steal chickens and goats: sorcery and metempsychosis. I do not propose to describe them here.

Apart from these individual deviants, there are whole deviant species. Breeding habits, sleeping, watering, and feeding habits give the Lele categories in which there is consistency among the secondary characteristics, so that different species can be recognized. Carnivorous animals have fur and claws as distinct from vegetarian animals, such as the antelopes with their smooth hides and hoofs.[5] Egg-laying creatures tend to fly with wings. Mam-

---

[3] See my article Social and Religious Symbolism of the Lele of the Kasai, Zaire, ix, 4, 1955, in which I give in detail the various situations of cooking, eating, washing, quarrelling, &c., in which these categories become evident.

[4] Domestic animals and vermin are major exceptions. Before the recent introduction of goats, pigs, and ducks, the only domestic animals which the Lele kept were dogs and chickens. There is a fable which describes how the first ancestors of these, jackal and a partridge, came to throw in their lot with man, and how both dogs and poultry are continually begged by their forest-kin to leave the villages of humans. Conventional attitudes to both of these in a number of situations are consistent with the notion that a domestic animal is essentially an anomaly. For rats, which infest the huts, Lele feel nothing but disgust. In conformity their attitude to other anomalous animals, they never eat dog, domestic rats, or mice, and women extend the avoidance to a number of other rats and to all poultry.

[5] For brevity's sake I use here some terms of our own categorization. Lele use no one word to render 'carnivorous' exactly, but they indicate carnivorous animals by the term hutapok-animals with skins, or 'furry animals'. I do not know any Lele term for 'oviparous' or 'mammalian', but it is clear that the manner of reproduction provides criteria for classification as surely for the Lele as for our zoologists, for their descriptions never fail to mention an animal's breeding habits.

mals are four-footed and walk or climb, and so on. But some species defy classification by the usual means. There are four-footed animals which lay eggs, and mammals which fly like birds, land animals which live in the water, aquatic animals which live on the land.

Avoidances in Connexion with Animals

These problems in animal taxonomy struck me first when I inquired into the food prohibitions observed by women. Some animals they avoid simply because they are anomalous, no ritual sanction being involved. For example, there is a 'flying squirrel', the scaly tail, which women avoid, because they are not sure what it is, bird or animal.[6] I have described elsewhere their self-imposed prohibitions on foods which they consider disgusting apart from any religious symbolism.[7] Here I am concerned with the provisions made in Lele religion for regulating human contact with animals. Restrictions on the contact of women with one species or another is the most usual ritual rule.

A wide diversity of animals are classed as 'spirit animals' (*hut a ngehe*). I could not clarify in what sense these creatures are spirits. In some contexts they are spoken of as if they were spirits or manifestations of spirits. In others they are animals closely associated with spirits. They can be divided according to the restrictions which are imposed on women's contact with them.

Women may never touch the Nile monitor (Varanus niloticus) or the small pangolin (Manis tricuspis). Concerning the pangolin I shall say more below. The Nile monitor is a large aquatic lizard. The Lele describe it as a cousin of the crocodile, but without scales; like a snake with little legs; a lizard, but bigger, swifter, and more vicious than any lizard. Like the crocodile, it is a large, potentially dangerous amphibian.

Women may touch, but never eat, the tortoise and the yellow baboon (Papio cynocephalus kindae). The tortoise is a curious beast. Its shell distinguishes it from other reptiles but, as a four-footed creature, it is anomalous in that it lays eggs. The baboon is interesting in several ways. Unlike other monkeys it is reputed not to be afraid of men, but will stand up to a hunter, strike him, talk, and throw sticks at him. When the troop of baboons goes off from the grass-land to the water, the females pick up their young in their arms, and those which are childless hitch a stone or stick into the crook of their arms, pretending that they too have babies. They go to the water, not merely to drink, but to wash. Moreover, they shelter in deep erosion gullies which are associated by the Lele with spirits who are thought to

---

[6] Significantly, its zoological name is Anomalurus beecroftii.
[7] Zaire, op. cit.

dig them for their own inscrutable purposes. Some of these gullies are very deep and become rushing torrents in the rains. As one of the ordeals of initiation, diviners have to climb down into one of these gullies and carry back mud from the bottom. Baboons, then, are unlike other animals in that they will stand up to a man, they experience barrenness, they wash, and they undergo one of the ordeals of initiation.

There is one animal which women never eat unless they are pregnant. It is the giant rat (Cricetomys dissimilis proparator) which has a white tail and burrows underground. It is associated with the ghosts of the dead, perhaps because of the holes in the ground. The ghosts of the dead are often referred to as *bina hin*, the people down below. The habit of sleeping in a hole also seems to be associated with the spirits. Several of the spirit animals which women have to avoid are characterized as sleeping in holes, but I am not confident about this category, as there are other burrowing animals which are not classed as spirit animals. The porcupine (Hystrix galatea) and the giant pangolin (Manis gigantea) are spirit animals which women may not eat if they are pregnant. The ant-bear (Orycteropus afer), which digs holes to escape from its pursuers, may be eaten by women except during the four months immediately following a certain fertility rite.

Water creatures are all associated with spirits and pregnant women must avoid them. The wild bush pig (Potamochaerus koiropotamus), as I have already said, is a spirit animal because it frequents the streams and breeds prolifically. Pregnant women avoid it. There are two antelopes associated with spirits, which women must avoid during pregnancy. One is the water-chevrotain (Hyemoschus aquaticus) which hides itself by sinking down into the water until only its nostrils appear above the surface. The other is Cephalophus grimmi, whose idiosyncrasy is to sleep in daylight with its eyes wide open, so soundly asleep that a hunter can grab it by the leg. This habit associates it with the spirits, who are supposed to be active at night and asleep in the day. The little antelope is thought to be a servant of the spirits, resting in the day from its labors of the night.

So far as I know, this is the complete list of the animals whose contact with women is normally restricted. There are local variations. In the north crocodiles may be eaten by pregnant women; in the far south women's post-natal food includes squirrels and birds, i.e. animals of above (*hutadiku*) as opposed to ground animals (*hutahin*). In reply to my queries, Lele would merely reiterate the characteristics of the animal in question, as if its oddity would be instantly appreciated by me and would provide sufficient answer to my question.

No doubt the first essential procedure for understanding one's environment is to introduce order into apparent chaos by classifying. But, under any very simple scheme of classification, certain creatures seem to be anomalous. Their irregular behavior is not merely puzzling but even offensive to the dignity of human reason. We find this attitude in our own spontaneous reaction to 'monstrosities' of all kinds.

* * *

The Lele do not turn away their eyes in disgust, but they react to 'unnatural behavior' in animals in somewhat the same way as did the author of Deuteronomy—by prescribing avoidance.

> Every beast that divideth the hoof into two parts, and cheweth the cud, you shall eat. But of them that chew the cud, but divide not the hoof, you shall not eat, such as the camel, the hare and the rock-badger . . . these shall you eat of all that abide in the waters, all that have fins and scales you shall eat. Such as are without fins and scales, you shall not eat. (Deuteronomy xiv:7, Leviticus xi:4–5)

The baboon, the scaly tail, the tortoise, and other animal anomalies are to the Lele as the camel, the hare and the rock-badger to the ancient Hebrews.

The Pangolin

The pangolin is described by the Lele in terms in which there is no mistaking its anomalous character. They say: "In our forest there is an animal with the body and tail of a fish, covered in scales. It has four little legs and it climbs in the trees." If I had not by chance identified it at once as the scaly ant-eater, but had thought of it always as a scaly fish-like monster that ought to abide in the waters, but creeps on the land, its symbolic role would not have eluded me for so long.

Anomalous characteristics, like the scaly tail, would set the pangolin apart but would not explain its association with fertility. The fertility of humans is thought to be controlled by the spirits inhabiting the deepest, dampest parts of the forest. The symbolic connection of water with fertility and with the spirits who control human fertility, is fairly explicit for the Lele. All aquatic things—fishes, water-animals, and water-plants, as well as amphibians—are associated with the spirits and with fertility. Creatures which have the same outward characteristics as aquatics, but live on the land (the pangolin), or which are essentially land animals but frequent the water (the water chevrotain), are also associated with the spirits. In this context the pangolin's association with fertility becomes clear.

According to the Lele, the pangolin is anomalous in other ways. Unlike other animals, it does not shun men but offers itself patiently to the hunter. If you see a pangolin in the forest, you come up quietly behind it and smack it sharply on the back. It falls off the branch and, instead of scuttling away as other animals would do, it curls into a tightly armored ball. You wait quietly until it eventually uncurls and pokes its head out, then you strike it dead. Furthermore, the pangolin reproduces itself after the human rather than the fish or lizard pattern, as one might expect from its appearance. Lele say that, like humans, it gives birth to one child at a time. This in itself is sufficiently unusual to mark the pangolin out from the rest of the animal creation and cause it to be treated as a special kind of link between humans and animals.

In this respect the pangolin would seem to stand towards humans as parents of twins stand towards animals. Parents of twins and triplets are, of course, regarded as anomalous humans who produce their young in the manner of animals.

For a human to be classed with animals in any other connection—because, for instance, of unmannerly behavior—is reprehensible. But to vie with animals in fertility is good. Men do not beget by their own efforts alone, but because the spirits in the forest consent. The parents of twins are considered to have been specially honored by the spirits. They are treated as diviners and are exempt from the initiation which ordinary men must undergo if they wish to acquire magic powers. Twin children are spoken of as spirits and their parents as Twin Diviners (*Bangang bamaayeh*). They pay an entrance fee into their own cult group, and learn 'twin-magic' for fertility and good hunting.

The most striking proof of the high ritual status enjoyed by parents of twins is that the usual ritual disabilities of women are disregarded in the case of a woman who has borne twins. She attends the conferences on twin-magic on exactly the same footing as the men, performs the rites with them, and at her death is supposed to be buried with all the other diviners. This is quite out of character with the normally subordinate position of women in Lele ritual. Parents of twins are regarded as having been selected by the spirits for a special role, mediating between humans and animals and spirits. Pangolins perform a corresponding role in the animal sphere.

Humans, Animals and Spirits

Lele religion is based on certain assumptions about the interrelation of humans, animals, and spirits. Each has a defined sphere, but there is interaction between them. The whole is regarded as a single system. A major disorder in the human sphere is presumed to disturb the relations which ought to exist between all the parts. Major disorders in the other spheres are not expected to occur.

Animals live their lives, each behaving according to its kind. Their sphere does not impinge on the human sphere. No animal will molest a human, enter a human habitation, or steal chickens and goats, unless made to do so by sorcery. Nor will an animal become a victim to a hunter unless the spirits are willing. For their part, humans cannot expect to intervene in animal affairs, even to sight or pursue, still less to kill an animal, unless their relations with the spirits are harmonious. The approval of the spirits is assured if human relations with each other are peaceful and if ritual is correctly performed. The goodwill of the spirits notwithstanding, the hunter's success may be spoilt by sorcery.

The hunt is the point at which the three spheres touch. Its significance far surpasses its primary object—the supply of meat. The whole range of human aspirations—for food, fertility, health, and longevity—is controlled by the spirits and may be thwarted by sorcery. If the hunt fails, the Lele fear that their other enterprises also are in danger. Not only do they feel angry at a wasted day and meatless fare, but they feel anxious for the recovery of the sick, for the efficacy of their medicines, for their whole future prosperity.

In the delicate balance between humans, animals, and spirits, certain humans and certain animals occupy key positions of influence. Among humans, the Begetters' Group honors those who have been blessed with a child. At their initiation rites ribald songs mock the sterile. The Pangolin cult honors those who have been blessed with children of both sexes; the Twin cult honors those who have been blessed with multiple births. The qualification for membership of any of these cults is not something which a man can achieve by his own efforts. He must have been chosen by the spirits for his role as mediator between the human and the supernatural. In theory, the candidates for the Diviners' Group are also believed to have been made aware of their vocation in a dream or by spirit-possession, though in practice men are known to fake this qualification. Once initiated these men have access to magical powers which can be used on behalf of their fellows.

In the animal world certain creatures mediate between animals and humans. Among these the pangolin is pre-eminent. It has the character of a denatured fish: a fish-like creature which lives on dry land, which bears its young after the manner of humans, and which does not run away from humans. In order to see the full significance of its fish-like scales, one should know more of the symbolic role of fish for the Lele.

Fishes belong so completely to the watery element that they cannot survive out of it. Bringing fish out of the water and the forest into the village is an act surrounded with precautionary ritual. Women abstain from sexual intercourse before going fishing. Fish and fishing gear, and certain water-plants, cannot be brought into the village on the day they are taken from the water unless ritual is performed. The woman who is carrying the fish sends a child ahead to fetch a live firebrand with which she touches the fish. The other things are left for one night in the grass-land before being taken into the village.

I might interpret this behavior by saying that they wish to avoid any confusion of the dry and the watery elements, but this would not be a translation of any Lele explanation. If asked why they do it, they reply: 'To prevent an outbreak of coughing and illness', or, 'Otherwise the furry animals (hutapok) will get in and steal our chickens, and coughing will break out among our children.' But these are merely elliptical references to the communion between spirit, animal, and human spheres. The furry animals which steal chickens and cause illness are not ordinary carnivorous animals, but sorcerers' familiars, whose access to the sphere of living humans is made more difficult if the proper distinctions between human and animal, day and night, water and land, are correctly observed.[8]

In accordance with the symbolism relating fishes with fertility and with spirits, pregnant women and novices for initiation must totally avoid eating fish. Certain fishes are more specially associated with spirits than others, and diviners are supposed to avoid eating them. Fishes do nothing to bridge the gap between human society and the creatures of the forest. Unprepared contact with them is potentially dangerous and is hedged with ritual. People in a marginal ritual condition avoid them altogether. But pangolins, part fish, part animal, friendly to humans, are apt for a mediatory role. This, I suggest, is the context of the underlying assumptions by means of which the Lele cult of pangolins is intelligible to themselves. This is why killing and eating pangolins, with proper ritual observances, are believed to bring animals in droves to the hunter's arrows and babies to women.

Pangolin Ritual

In a village of forty men and fifty women, all the adult male pagans save one were Begetters, sixteen were initiated Diviners, three men and their wives were Twin Parents, four men were Pangolin initiates. I was present and able to record the results of a number of hunts in the dry season of 1953.

All the villages to the north, and many to the south of my village had adopted a new anti-sorcery cult, Kabengabenga, which was sweeping across the whole Kasai district. It promised hunting success, health, and long life to its initiates by threatening automatic death to anyone who attempted sorcery after initiation. Men and women in Kabengabenga villages brought pressure to bear on their kinsmen in other villages to follow their example and rid themselves of sorcery, and those who hesitated were accused by the initiates of culpable neglect if any of their kinsmen fell ill or died. Deaths in Kabengabenga villages were attributed to the boomerang action of the cult magic, so that anyone who died was held to be convicted of attempted sorcery. The mission and the Administration had taken strong action to stop the spread of the Kabengabenga cult, and in our own village the young Christians threatened to run away if the village were initiated.

---

[8] I have given an outline of the most important of these distinctions as they appear in ritual, in The Lele of the Kasai, in African Worlds, ed. Daryll Forde, 1954.

Tension was running high in the village. Hunting failures, personal or communal, were attributed to sorcery; so also was sickness. Scarcely a night passed without someone shouting warnings to unnamed sorcerers to desist, to leave the sick to recover, to leave the hunter in peace to kill his quarry. They were begged to consider the reputation of the village in the eyes of other villages. One old man declared: "The villages to the north and the villages to the south have taken Kabengabenga. They are all watching us. They used to say: 'The men of Lubello kill quantities of game, without taking Kabengabenga.' Now we go out hunting, and we come back empty-handed. That is a disgrace. They watch us and say we have sorcerers in our midst."

Alternative explanations for misfortunes were offered. The senior Pan-golin man said that after a strange woman had entered the village recently, it was discovered that she had borne twins; no twin-rites had been performed to prevent her entry from spoiling the village; the twin-parents should now perform rites and send the village on a hunt that would make good the breach of the twin-ritual.

On 6 August the twin-parents duly consulted together. A twin-parent is supposed to be an 'owner' of the village (*muna bola*) in the sense that his or her anger would render hunting fruitless unless a rite of blessing were performed. One of them, therefore, drew attention to her ulcerated leg, and protested that, in spite of the callous disregard of others in the village, she held no grudge against them for their neglect. If she had been heard to complain, it was in pain, not in anger. She performed the ritual of blessing. Instructions were given for a hunt for the next day.

7 August. The hunt was moderately successful; although four duikers escaped, two small "blue duikers," one water chevrotain, and one young bay duiker were killed. The success was attributed to the performance of the twin-ritual.

There was no more communal hunting until 12 August. Individual hunters complained of their lack of success, and considered the village to be 'bad'. The senior official diviner of the village, the *ilumbi*, was informally approached and asked to take up his magic for the next hunt. It required some courage and tact to ask him to do this, as he was widely thought to be the sorcerer responsible for the bad condition of the village. On the eve of the hunt, he ordered those who had quarreled to pay fines, and announced that he would do magic. Before the hunt one of the Pangolin men spoke a blessing, in case his grief at the obstinate and rude behavior of the young Christians should spoil the hunt. They drew three covers, saw little game, killed only one adult and one young 'blue duiker'—a quite negligible bag. The ilumbi felt discredited. He announced that the animals which he had seen by divination had been escaping behind the hunters; next time he would do different magic.

13 August. In the dawn an old man got up and harangued the sorcerers, asking what they ate if they didn't like animal meat? Dogs? People? What? He warned them that he did not consent to the illness of children in the village.

During the day it transpired that the twin-ritual was still outstanding. The village had been tricked into believing that the successful hunt on 7 August had been the result of twin-rituals whereas, in fact, the junior ilumbi, himself a twin-parent, had persuaded the others to let him try a 'spirit magic' which had been highly successful a month earlier. Everyone was angry at the deception. The senior Pangolin man, who had originally diagnosed that a breach of twin-ritual had "spoilt the village", declared that if only the twin-parents had been frank, the diviners themselves would have stepped in to perform the necessary twin-rites. Twins (*mayehe*) and spirits (*mingehe*) are all the same, he said, and initiated diviners do not need to beget twins in order to do twin-rites. Angriest of all was the senior ilumbi, hurt in his pride of magic, who now saw the reason for the failure of the hunt he had arranged on 12 August. More serious than being made to look a fool, he had looked like a sorcerer chasing away the game. In the next village the ilumbi had been hounded out for failure to produce game, and in the old days he would have been made to take the poison ordeal. He was obliged to dissemble his anger, as the village could be 'spoilt' by the ill will of any of its ritual officers.

In the next week men refused to go on a communal hunt as the village seemed obviously 'bad', i.e. infected with sorcery. Individual hunters had some success: a duiker was caught in a trap, a man chanced on a wild sow just after she had farrowed and easily shot her and killed her young; and a large harnessed bush-buck was shot. In spite of these successes, there was an atmosphere of frustration and acrimony in the village.

On 24 and 27 August the women went on two long fishing expeditions. While they were away there was little food, and work in the village just ticked over till their return. On 28th two pangolins were killed. When the women came back the atmosphere in the village had changed overnight to one of general rejoicing. The village evidently was felt to be vindicated in the eyes of its Kabengabenga critics. A neighboring village asked to be allowed to send a candidate for initiation into the Pangolin cult. Among the ritual specialists annoyance about the overdue twin-rite still rankled, but the Pangolin rites had to take precedence now.

The junior Pangolin man announced on behalf of the initiates that the village was "tied" (*kanda*), that is, that sexual intercourse was banned until after the eating of the pangolin and the shedding of animal blood in the hunt that should follow the feast. Etiquette appropriate to the presence of a chief in the village was to be observed. He used the words: "*Kum ma wa*": The master is dead. Let no one fight. "*Kum*" can be translated as master or chief. Unfortunately a quarrel between children dancing broke out, adults took sides, and blows were struck. A fine had to be paid to the Pangolin group for this breach of ritual peace.

29 August. A meeting was called. The village was in a ferment because a man had been caught seducing the wife of the senior Pangolin man. The latter refused to carry on with the Pangolin initiation and feast.

30 August. There was a spate of early-morning speeches. The senior Pangolin man was reproached for turning household affairs into village affairs, and for making the village suffer for his private wrong. Someone pointed out that if the pangolins were left to rot, the people of the next village, who wanted their candidate vested with Pangolin power, would think we had refused to eat the pangolin to spite them. All those who had quarreled were roundly taken to task in public speeches. All were convinced that to go hunting while the senior Pangolin man was feeling angry would be useless.

31 August. Village opinion, originally sympathetic to the senior Pangolin man, now turned against him. He was insisting that full adultery damages should be paid before he proceeded with the Pangolin rites. There was anxiety lest the pangolins should go bad; they had already been dead five days. If they were to go bad without being eaten with proper ritual, the whole village would go 'hard' and suffer for a long time, until Pangolin magic had been done again. Repeated injunctions were made to keep the peace until the pangolin hunt. Two more cases of fighting occurred.

2 September. Fines for fighting were all paid up, and the major part of the adultery damages had been given. Ritual was performed to make the way clear for hunting the next day. The two ilumbi, the four Pangolin men, and the twin-parents met and agreed to do two rites: twin-ritual and Pangolin ritual, for the hunt.

3 September. Before the hunt, two twin-parents aired their grievances; one on account of her ulcerated leg, which she felt no one took trouble to diagnose and cure; the other complained that her husband had abandoned her for a new young wife. Her husband's colleagues replied for him that it was nonsense to suppose that a man would leave a woman through whom he had attained three of God's callings or vocations (*mapok manjambi*). He was, through her, an initiate of the Begetters, of Twins and of the Pangolin. She was reminded of the danger to the village if a woman who was in these three senses one of its 'owners' were allowed to nurse her anger.

The hunt that followed this concerted ritual effort was a failure. Seven animals in all were seen, but only two small duikers were killed. There was great anger and agreement that the village was bad. However, blood had been shed and the Pangolin feast could proceed. After the Pangolin rites had been performed, people assured each other, we should all see great quantities of game being brought back. The pangolin would draw animals to the village. The next day was fixed for the feast.

That very afternoon a third pangolin was killed. There was great satisfaction. "Just as we were saying 'Tomorrow we shall eat pangolin, and invest new members' . . . behold, another pangolin comes into the village!" They spoke as if the pangolin had died voluntarily, as if it had elected to be the object of Pangolin ritual and to offer itself for the feast of initiates; as if it had honored this village by choosing it.

At night the junior Pangolin man announced that no one was to fight, above all no one was to fight secretly. "If you must fight, do it openly and pay up. He who fights tonight, let him be rich. The fine will be twenty raffia cloths."

5 September. The Pangolin feast and initiation rite were eventually held. I was unfortunately unable to see the rites. I was told that emphasis was laid on the chiefship of the pangolin. We call him kum, they said, because he makes women conceive. They expressed shame and embarrassment at having eaten a kum. No one is allowed to see the pangolins being roasted over the fire. The tongues, necks, ribs, and stomachs were not eaten, but buried under a palm-tree whose wine thenceforth becomes the sole prerogative of the Begetters. Apparently the new initiate was made to eat some of the flesh of the first two pangolins which were in process of decay; the more rotten parts, together with the scales and bones, were given to the dogs. The senior initiates ate the flesh of the more recently killed animal. All were confident that the hunt on the following day would be successful.

6 September. The hunt went off in good heart, twenty men and eight dogs. It was an abject failure. Powerful sorcery was evidently at work, since all ritual had been duly performed. People discussed the possible significance of a leopard that had been heard to bark in the precincts of the village that night, and of leopard tracks that had been seen on the way to the hunt. The leopard is one of the forms which the ilumbi is supposed to be able to take, and the ilumbi was suspected of having gone ahead of the hunters in leopard's guise, and scared off the game. The ilumbi himself, realizing that suspicions of sorcery were again directed at him, suggested that he would gladly go with the rest of the village to take Kabengabenga magic, if only the Christians did not hold such strong objections. He evidently saw it as a means of clearing his own name. In his youth he had twice taken the poison ordeal and confounded his accusers. He also suggested to me privately that he might leave the village and live elsewhere, as his enemies had never forgiven him for the disputes over women in which he had been embroiled.

In the meanwhile, the village was still 'tied': the ban on sexual intercourse had not been lifted since 28 August, and could not be until blood had been shed in a hunt following the feast of Pangolin initiates.

9 September. A hunt took place in which one small duiker was killed. The ritual requirement was fulfilled, and the ban on sexual intercourse was lifted, but from every other point of view it was felt to have been a failure.

Accuracy of Lele Observation of Animals

Writing strictly from the point of view of religious symbolism it is not relevant to ask how accurate is Lele observation of animal behavior. A symbol based on mistaken information can be fully effective as a symbol, so long as the fable in question is well known. The dove, it would seem, can be one of the most relentlessly savage of birds.[9] The pelican does not nourish its young from its own living flesh. Yet the one bird has provided a symbol of peace, and the other of maternal devotion, for centuries.

However, it would be interesting to know whether the symbolism described above is based on fables or not. I must confess that I was able only with great difficulty to identify most of the animals. Many of the rarer ones I never saw alive or dead and in any case should not have been able to recognize them at sight. I was fortunate in securing the kind collaboration of Monsieur A. J. Jobaert, Warden of the Muene Ditu Game Reserve, who knew the Kasai and several of the local languages well. By sending him the native names in two local languages, together with a description, I obtained translations into French, Latin, and English, and these names were checked again by Mr. R. B. Freeman, the Reader in Taxonomy at University College, London. My remarks are based on identification obtained in this roundabout and unreliable way. The point I thought it most important to check was whether the Lele are right in considering the breeding habits of pangolins anomalous: first, do pangolins give birth to their young one at a time? Second, how unusual is this among the smaller mammals? In pursuing this inquiry I was interested to find how little scientifically tested knowledge there is concerning the manner of reproduction of mammals, common and uncommon. Such information as is available serves to justify the Lele in both these views.[10]

One interesting point that I am still unable to elucidate is the principle on which the Lele discriminate between the small pangolin (Manis tricuspis) which they call *luwawa*, and the giant pangolin (Manis gigantea) which they call *yolabondu*, making a major cult of the first but not of the second. Zoologists may be able to give information about the distribution and habits of the two species which may throw light on the question. It may require an historical solution, since pangolin cults are found in other parts of the Congo.[11]

---

9 Lorenz, King Solomon's Ring.
10 S. A. Asdell, Patterns of Mammalian Reproduction, 1946, p. 184.
11 D. Biebuyck, Repartitions et droits du Pangolin chez les Balega, Zaire, vii, 9 Nov.

QUERIES

- What categories do the Lele use to conceptualize their universe?
- Discuss the different prohibitions on contacts between Lele women and certain animals. How do these prohibitions focus on "category-anomalous" animals?
- Douglas compares the Lele prohibitions about animals to Old Testament dietary restrictions. How are they similar in principle?
- Why are the parents of twin children given special ritual attention in Lele society?
- What characterizes the pangolin as a special class of animal in Lele culture?
- In the later section of the article, Douglas summarizes an ethnographic case involving "Pangolin Ritual." Summarize this case, paying attention to the Kabengabenga antisorcery cult, tensions within the village, scarce hunting, and the death and consumption of the pangolin.

CONNECTIONS

- How do the unformulated categories the Lele employ to "unconsciously organize their existence," as described by Douglas, exemplify Emile Durkheim's ideas about the social basis of the categories of understanding?
- Contrast Douglas's discussion of Lele prohibitions to Ortner's analysis in "Sherpa Purity." What are some conceptual principles similar in both cases?
- How does Douglas's account of "Pangolin Ritual" represent an example of what Clifford Geertz called "thick description"?

VI

STRUCTURES, PRACTICE, AGENCY, AND POWER

21

James W. Fernandez

INTRODUCTION

Over the last four decades, the American anthropologist James W. Fernandez (b. 1930) has developed a body of writing that illuminates the shifting meanings associated with symbols in the course of complex cultural practice. These theoretical concerns are directly derived from his ethnographic investigations, first among the Fang of West Africa and then in the mountainous Asturias province in northern Spain (see Moore 2008:295–306). In his investigations, Fernandez consistently has been interested in the fluid meanings of symbols as they are bent to opposing purposes and deployed for sometimes contradictory goals. Fernandez has referred to this as "the play of tropes" (for discussion, see Moore 2008:299–301). The Oxford English Dictionary defines "trope" as "a figure of speech which consists in the use of a word or phrase in a sense other than that which is proper to it." In Fernandez's theory a trope becomes a metaphorical statement about human existence and a guideline that people follow in their existence. For example, in the aftermath of the World Trade Center bombings, then-President George W. Bush announced in a speech of September 20, 2001, that the United States was engaged in a "war on terror." The phrase "war on terror" is a trope: it metaphorically describes human actions—for example, "the war" was not accompanied by a Congressional authorization that a state of war existed, although certainly military force was used. Simultaneously, the phrase "war on terror" became the basis for action—for example, justifying the suspension of habeas corpus to "enemy combatants" held in the prisons at Guantanamo Bay—because the United States was "at war."

This play of tropes, in Fernandez's view, leads to the core of human experience. If culture is based on symbols—or as Clifford Geertz would argue, if culture is an enacted public document—then understanding how meaning is created and conveyed is central. If symbols have multiple and inconsistent meanings, then how are such different meanings conveyed? The answer, Fernandez argues, is in the very setting in which those symbols are being used. Symbols never have single, simple meanings. That point raises additional issues about how symbols enhance or derail efforts at social cohesion.

And finally, it suggests that anthropologists cannot broadly generalize, using terms like "The Trobriand Islanders believe X" or "The Nuer think such and such." One of the implications from Fernandez's ethnography is that culture is never a uniformly held or unanimous set of meanings. Ethnography must be alert to those multifaceted meanings. In this, one can loosely classify Fernandez's idea of "the play of tropes" as a late 20th century, postmodernist theoretical position (see Moore 2008:295–97), but one that ultimately derives from his ethnographic attempts to understand Bwiti.

PRIMARY TEXT: *SYMBOLIC CONSENSUS IN A FANG REFORMATIVE CULT*

The concepts of "consensus" and "symbol," like the proverb to non-literate peoples, appear to be for many students of human behavior work horses of theoretical discourse. Like the proverb, however, these concepts are ambiguous and almost always carry more weight than is analytically useful. Symbols surround us and when, for example, White argues that "all culture depends upon the symbol" (1944:235) we readily assent to their importance if we do not quite still grasp their meaning. As for consensus, we see its consequences clearly enough. But, beyond the raising of hands or some other significant statement of allegiance and cohesion, do we really understand what is taking place in acts of consensus? In fact, culture is not something of which everyone carries an equal burden, and the study of symbolic consensus can demonstrate the disparate portions which culture-carriers appropriate or are assigned, and the dynamic consequences that proceed therefrom.

In an attempt to contribute to the understanding of these two terms and their relationship, I propose to employ them in discussing the religious ritual of an African reformative cult. I shall avoid such rubrics as "common value attitudes," or "shared frame of reference," or "collective representations." In examining certain features of the cult, I shall keep in mind Sapir's argument that communication is identical with the cultural process and his catch phrase—"the essence of culture is understanding" (1931:78). I shall, in part, dispute and, in part, qualify Park's long-standing contention that "communication operates primarily as an integrating and socializing principle" (1938:195). The distinction between signals, signs, and symbols will be integral to the discussion.

The reformative cult in question, Bwiti, appears among the Fang peoples of northern Gabon and the Spanish African territory, Rio Muni. It is a minority movement and not more than 10 per cent of the population are involved. When first in evidence at the turn of the century and until the Second World War the cult represented a reworking of the Fang ancestral cult, bieri. This was accomplished by the borrowing, almost entirely within the African tradition, of elements of ritual and belief from the ancestor cults of adjacent Northwestern Bantu peoples whom the Fang had been historically displacing in southwestern migration. There is a similarity of features in the ancestral cults of all the Gabonese Bantu but sufficient difference in detail as to provoke attention and elicit comparison. In the eyes of Fang reformatists the cult life of the southern Gabonese peoples, most notably the Metsogo and the Baloumbo, was more elaborate and more dramatic. In the context of the increasing frustration and religious limitations of colonial controls, it was more effective in establishing contact with ancestral forces, themselves increasingly distant and increasingly compromised by lower and higher powers: witchcraft on the one hand, and God and the saints of Catholic Christianity on the other. It is only in the last 20 years, however, that a direct coming-to-terms with missionary Christianity has been attempted. But syncretism in this phase has been rapid. Many Christian elements have been incorporated. A Christian calendar has been adopted.

As is typical in almost all the African religious movements, fission is frequent and has produced polymorphism: (Veciana 1957:11) a variety of sub-cults. There are five main sub-cults of Bwiti among the Fang. The data here is taken from the principal sub-cult—Dissoumba of Asumege Ening, which separated from the parent tradition in the late 1930's and by 1960 was the major cult. It is found primarily in Gabon.

It is useful in categorizing African religious movements to think of two continuums on a bi-axial coordinate system (Fernandez 1964). On one continuum we mark the tendency toward nativism or the return to African tradition, on the one hand, and separatism or the acceptance of imported, usually Christian, elements on the other. The second continuum marks realism-rationalism, that is the instrumental search for satisfaction on the one pole as against the elaboration of a projective system, the search for expressive satisfactions on the other. At the present time, Bwiti, as a reformative movement compared with other African religious movements, occupies

a median position on both continuums. It is more nativistic than Kimban-
guisme (Raymaekers 1959); less nativistic than the Shembe movement in
South Africa (Sundkler 1961); more instrumental than either of these two
movements but much more concerned with expressive satisfactions than
the National Church of Nigeria and the Cameroons (Parrinder 1953) or any
of the "rebel" churches described for Uganda by Welbourne (1961). The
Asumege Ening branch of the Bwiti cult with which we are concerned here
is more nativistic and more expressive than all but one of the other Bwiti
sub-cults. It frequently re-introduces by-gone Fang rituals and it has elaborated a complex cosmology and liturgy with which it is preoccupied.

Bwiti, like revitalization movements in general (Wallace 1956:265), and
reformative movements in particular, is characterized in its leadership by a
deliberate, organized, conscious effort to construct a more satisfying culture. Leaders of the cult give evidence of this, for they sometimes visit
Catholic or Protestant services or other cults with the express intention of
discovering materials suitable for the further elaboration of their own cult
life. Asumege Ening in Fang means "beginning of life," and cult leaders frequently detail their responsibilities in the idiom of reconstruction. They are
aware that they are re-building in a new way something which has been destroyed. Not all the members of the cult, it is to be remarked, take this
"promethean" view of their responsibilities to the culture of the cult, and
what remains to be seen below is the extent to which they are "conscious"
of reconstructive revitalization. We must also keep in mind for the purposes
of the ensuing discussion that this conscious search results in a rapid
turnover of beliefs and liturgical elements. The dynamic of the symbol system is intensive; this is not unusual for revitalization movements, though
unusual for religion in general which tends in its "church" as opposed to its
"sect" form, to be fairly conservative in this respect.

The observations on the behavior of cult members in respect to their symbol system detailed here are based on participation in the life of two cult
houses (aba eboka): six months were spent in a peripheral, recently
founded Asumege Ening house in Sougoudzap, Woleu-Ntem, northern
Gabon; and three months were spent in a founding house in Kougouleu,
Kango, central Gabon. The latter was a point of origination for most but not
all of the practices of the former. There were eleven members in the
Sougoudzap cult house, six men and five women. At Kougouleu, 42 participants, 18 men and 24 women, danced the religion that calls the ancestors
back from the deep forest, steps over death and discovers God (Zame ye
Mebege) and his sister (Nyingwan Mebege). Direct inquiry as to the meaning of cult symbolism was not pursued throughout this period but in both
cases at a quiescent period of cult life. Observations in periods of turmoil
complement this more intensive research. Twenty full members of the cult
with whom the ethnographer had established fairly confidential relation-

ship were queried extensively, and it is the views of these 20 that we refer to here below. They represented all echelons of the cult.[1]

On the face of it, consensus prevailed in both of these cult houses, for all participants who were queried emphatically subscribed to the efficacy of the ritual involved. All informants believed that participation in the night-long ritual led to a state of nlem mvore (one-heartedness), uniting all members of the cult. It seems appropriate to take this achievement of nlem mvore as the achievement of consensus. Informants frequently characterized this state as one in which bot ba wogan (people understand each other). Since this common understanding is obtained by ritual means, that is, apparently, by the ritual manipulation of symbols, and is itself achieved by a particular ritual, we may wish to call nlem mvore symbolic consensus. In any case, the state of nlem mvore indicates a high degree of social solidarity among cult participants. The degree to which understanding prevails among the membership in any logico-meaningful sense remains to be examined.

The achievement of this state, it must be pointed out, is remarkable both from the perspective of the Fang as well as that of the ethnographer. This is so because the growth of economic individualism and the abandonment of old ceremonial institutions has meant a great increase, in contemporary Fang life, of mutual distrust and suspicion unalleviated by the traditional forms of ritual reintegration. This has been especially the case within the kin group (mvoga-bot, village of patrilineally related people) where the traditional high expectation of solidarity has been most painfully disabused.[2] Cult members boast of the achievement of nlem mvore as one of the great virtues of Bwiti. Naturally enough, Fang outside the cult, recognizing their own contemporary problems in fraternal interrelationships, are frankly skeptical that anything approaching "one heart" can any longer be obtained in Fang affairs. If we regard the penetration of "one heartedness" into social relationships outside the specific ceremonial context, a two-to-three-day period occurring several times a month, we find some reason for this skepticism. The members of Bwiti (banzie) themselves recognize that the ritual achievement of nlem mvore is not pervasive in their interrelationships outside the ceremonial period. But they explain that it is the building up of

---

[1] The social structure of the cult is, in contrast to traditional Fang life, clearly hierarchical, and the spiritual progress of the individual member is three-phased. A member passes progressively from the stage of neophyte (mwan) to adept (banzie) to knowledgeable director and initiator of ceremonies (yemba and nyiman akombo).

[2] It is not only those who have some lineage or clan relationship who dance Bwiti together. In no case of a cult of any size (over 25 members) were more than 40 percent of the male members drawn from the same clan. In view of the fact that there is reinterpreted ancestor worship in the cult this has posed problems. The answer has been to generalize the conception of spirits whenever obeisance to them is demanded within the ceremonial progress. Attention to particular lineage linked ancestor spirits usually takes place outside the chapel.

"bad-heartedness" (nlem abe) in between times that provides one important reason for holding the Bwiti ceremonies again. In any case we are not
concerned with the state of consensus outside the ceremonial context.
Within it, participants maintain, it is effectively achieved.

The state of nlem mvore is ritually obtained in the following manner. Cult
ritual commences at six in the evening and concludes at six in the morning.
Dancing is continuous after 9:00 p.m. when preliminary ceremonies have
purified the chapel, except for a lull at midnight and at 3:00 a.m. when
prayers are addressed directly to the ancestors and to God. An alkaloid intoxicant, eboga (Tabernenthes eboka), is taken in moderate amounts to
achieve an ecstatic state, though alienation is rarely so complete as to produce possession. In fact, and this is an anomaly in African religious movements, possession is regarded as impeding proper ritual development—it is
considered unaesthetic. Nevertheless, the intoxicant is taken, to translate directly from the Fang, "in order to make the body light and to enable the soul
to fly." The spiritual world—mam ye esi ayat—does not, in this cult, come to
possess the worshipper. It is, rather, the worshipper who must leave himself
in order to make contact with the unseen.

The ritual—its Christian influences will be noted—is two-phased. From
six until midnight the members of Bwiti dance creation and birth: the creation of the world and the creation of man, as well as the birth of Adam and
the birth of Christ are all thematically developed in the song and dance but
are not systematically distinguished. These themes are not, in other words,
presented serially but simultaneously. Hence, analysis must consider levels
of meaning at any given moment of the ritual. Members of the cult, as we
shall point out, differ in the extent to which they appreciate and achieve
logico-aesthetic integration of these various levels of meaning.

After midnight we witness dancing representing death and destruction:
the destruction of man's hopes in a benign world, the death of Christ, the
expulsion from paradise, the flight from the savannah into the rain forest (a
symbolic re-creation of the actual Fang migration experience), and the passage from day into night. It is also after midnight that the membership establishes reunion—esamba—with the ancestor spirits which have been attracted into the cult house from the deep forest. It is in this reunion that the
distinction between the living and the dead, and more important for us
here, the distinction between the individual living cult members, is obliter-
ated. All become nlem myore—one heart.

One particular ritual symbolizes this achievement. In the early hours of
the morning the membership, carrying small pitch torches, line up in single file, closely compressed. In company to the subdued strumming of the
native harp, ngombi, they file out of the chapel into the village, thence into
the forest following a network of narrow cleared paths. They go out, it is
said, in search for those lingering ancestors who have not responded to the

dramatic invitations extended to them from the cult house previously in the evening. After brief circulation in the forest they return to the cult house, maintaining the prescribed decorum. Here the leader, separating the harp player from the line, begins to turn it into a tighter and tighter circle. Shortly, all members are folded into a solid mass with torches held high above their heads where the individual flames unite in a single fire. They intone a low sign of satisfaction. "One-heartedness" is achieved.

This ritual is profoundly significant to the membership and, we repeat, all of the members among whom intensive research was carried forth testified to its efficacy. It does something for them which they find satisfying. It accomplishes for them a change of state—a cessation of felt deprivation and anxiety if one wishes—even if this only be temporary.

At this point, however, the data from extensive discussion with the 20 cult members in question reminds us of the fact of variation in the individual interpretation of commonly experienced phenomena. The field notes of any anthropologist regularly betray this fact of variation and we are quite accustomed to it though it may constitute an inconvenience in the face of such unitary terms as society and culture and a difficult-to-suppress tendency to think in terms of the group mind. It is a fact of field work that bears closer scrutiny than we have heretofore given it. In any case the individual data from the 20 members of Bwiti call into question the nature of the consensus that seems to have been so clearly established among them.

While all cult members recognized that the commonality of one heart was a remarkable consequence of cult ritual, only half of these informants recognized that the particular ritual described above symbolized the creation of nlem mvore. Moreover, it appears that the cult in the eyes of the members queried had a number of manifest functions and that these members differ in assigning priorities to, or even recognizing, these various functions. Of the 20 cult members, seven said that the main purpose of the ritual was to find and establish proper relationship with the Christian God who lies behind death and of whom the Fang had no traditional knowledge. Eight said that the main purpose of the cult was to reestablish contact with the abandoned ancestors and regain their tutelary blessing. The remaining three informants declared the purpose of the cult ritual to be various: guaranteeing the well-being and tranquility (mvwaa) of the village, demonstrating to the European the validity of an African religion, and curing the individual illnesses of the worshippers.

A careful consultation with cult members turns up, therefore, considerable variance in the rationale of their participation. It should not be presumed, of course, that members have but one reason for participation. In fact, prolonged discussion with the individual informant almost always turned up a number of objectives to be reached through cult ritual. And though the individual may give priority to one, he will usually concede the validity of another's reasons for participation. What we find, ideologically, in the cult, then, is a congeries of purposes. Individuals select among these purposes apparently those that most suit their temperaments and most speak to their condition.

If we should ask how it is that cooperative participation continues in cult ritual despite a lack of consensus at this level, the obvious answer is that a cult rationale or charter is rarely explicitly stated, or if stated is phrased in such general terms as not to offend or exclude the particular purposes of various individuals. Secondly, and this is particularly true for the older cult house at Kougouleu, the participants rarely discuss or debate the rationale and are content that it should be taken for granted. Only cult leaders concern themselves with such matters, in competition with other cult leaders for membership—and in discussion with the ethnographer. In the Kougouleu cult we may even speak of a patterned avoidance of such ideological issues. Of such issues it is said: "We speak here with one voice," (nkin da) and the inquiry is then referred to the leader of the cult. It may even be argued that this patterned avoidance is a greater guarantee of integration and ongoing participation in cult life than the occasional expressions of egalitarian tolerance one gets from participants when they are confronted, usually by the ethnographer, with evidence of other, differing rationales.

These facts bring to mind Malinowski's concise definition of an institution as a group of people united by a purpose into an organization capable of achieving that purpose (1944:39 ff.). Malinowski also speaks of the institutional charter as a set of ideas validating the purpose to be achieved. Integration in the cult is high, if we mean by that the degree to which participants fulfill their ritual role expectations and claim to derive satisfaction in so doing. Yet it is difficult to say that they are by consensus united around any given purpose or even that the articulation of a purpose in the form of the charter is felt necessary to the majority of participants. Perhaps one should speak of the purpose as a feeling of satisfaction offered through social solidarity, but a feeling is not a purpose until articulated to be so and it is only the ethnographer and not the Fang who could make such a statement. In short, Malinowski's definition of an institution in terms of a purpose seems too greatly to intellectualize the nature of integration that obtains within the institutions discussed here. The difficulty to which we shall return arises from the fact that we are dealing with two different kinds of integration—social and cultural.

The same ideological variability accompanying ritual behavior is, as we have already indicated, evident in respect to the ritual symbols involved. It is well accepted that a common system of symbols interpreted in a common way is a prime requisite for an integrated social system. It may be said that confidence in the appropriateness of one's own behavior, and security in the interpretation of others' behavior is obtained, in part, according to the symbols which accompany that behavior. In checking with informants we again find, however, considerable variation as to the interpretation of the key symbols involved. We are led to observe that in respect to this syncretistic social system, though common symbols are indeed necessary for integration, interpretation of these symbols in a common way is not a prime requisite.

One of the key symbols, for example, is the native harp (ngombi)—the central instrument in cult activity and the symbol which is borne out into the forest in search of the ancestors in the procession we have already described. We find again a congeries of meanings attached to this symbol. Three informants, although recognizing its importance in cult ritual, see no meaning in it whatsoever. Most informants saw it as symbolic of the female principle of the universe—Nyingwan Mebege—the sister of God, though one informant regarded it as symbolic of God, the voice of God-Zame ye Mebege. They said things like, "In this harp we see Nyingwan Mebege. She speaks to us through its music and it conveys our prayers and thoughts to her"; or, "In this harp Nyingwan Mebe comes among us." Half of these informants also gave elaborate interpretations of the various parts of the harp. The sounding box covered with antelope skin is symbolic of the stomach of the female principle, the source of all life. The support arm of the harp with its eight keys represents the backbone. The eight strings themselves are the sinews of the spiritual body of Nyingwan Mebege, and communicate, as do the sinews in the body, endurance and flexibility to the members.

These symbolic interpretations of the meaning of the harp are themselves shallow when compared to the elaborations provided by cult leaders, particularly the leader of the Kougoulou cult, a man of impressive mythopoeic imagination. In him the various elements of the harp are fully explained and achieve logico-meaningful integration of a high order. He points out that the two basic sexual colors, white male and red female, which are painted on the right and left side of the sounding box represent that sexual union which is the source of vitality, the essence of the female principle. The support arm, which is the backbone, is representative of male potency since it is the backbone that gives to the male his sexual vigor. Thus the conjunction of support arm and sound box, backbone and stomach, also express sexual union. The integration of symbolic meanings into a meaningful configuration is further achieved in this man's mind by reference to the eight strings of the harp. The four cords of highest pitch are the feminine cords, those four of lowest pitch are masculine cords. As the harp is played, masculine and feminine tones intermingle in another manifestation of that union which is the source of vitality (ening). It may be remarked that this man's facility in discovering and adducing complex symbolic meanings in the various paraphernalia and phenomena which accompany cult ritual is one source of the respect which validates his authority. What needs explaining is why the range of interpretations known to him are not equally well known to his followers.

This variation in the interpretation of symbols is encountered in varying degrees with all the symbols of this syncretist ritual system. We may place symbols, therefore, on a continuum ranging from those whose meanings are patent to those which are either esoteric or apprehended but not understood. At the same time, we recognize that the individual members of the cult differ in their appraisal of any given symbol. A symbol whose meanings are quite patent to most members of the cult will be more elaborately interpreted by certain members, cult leaders particularly, as in the case of the harp. Two more examples will be helpful in making the point.

Three kinds of fire are kept burning in the cult house during the all-night ceremonies. Most common is a pitch "lamp" (otsa)—a cylinder of bark five to eight inches in diameter and ten to fifteen inches deep filled with the pitch of the okoume tree (Okoumea Kleineana) and set afire. The "lamps," of which there are usually two or three in the house, if properly tended, will burn ten hours or as long as the ceremonies last. On special ceremonial occasions, the climatic phase of a ritual cycle, for example, a small bonfire (mewuba) is kept burning in the exact center of the cult house. A third kind of fire occasionally employed is a long raffia torch (nduan) which burns vigorously and is swooped and swung by a dancer throughout the cult house. The intention of the torch is to purify the cult house and to put witches and other evil spirits to flight.

Fire was understood as a weapon against the infiltration of witches by all informants. Five, however, did not seem to recognize its capacity to purify and make clean. Members of the upper echelon, nima na kombo, kombo and yemba, were privy to fuller meanings of the pitch lamp and the bonfire. The pitch lamp, they pointed out, is symbolic of the life of man. All men are shells, husks in which the pitch, the vital substance of life, burns away until it finally burns out. These pitch lamps should remind the membership of life and death and the attempt to leap over beyond death which is one of the principal objects of cult practice.

In some cult houses, notably at Bifun near Lambarene, though not in the two houses whose participants' views we are examining here, the spirit of man is created in a fire in the early moments of the evening by use of a mock forge with bellows and other traditional paraphernalia of iron-working (nkom, nzong). A dancer sitting to one side of the fire suddenly rises, quavers as the bellows work, and, drawing himself up, jumps over the fire. He is created. His death can be represented at any appropriate moment in the ritual by his jumping back over the fire. In cults who follow these practices the fire itself is commonly associated with the Holy Spirit—the red of the fire is the blood of Nyingwan Mebege, the sister of God, the spiritual source of vitality. The heat of the fire symbolizes God himself, the terrifying and the untouchable. The bellows, together with the ceramic fire nozzle, represent the male organ.

Another very common symbol is the rattle (tchoke), which is held in the right hand in company with a raffia brush, symbolic of the female organ, held in the left. In the process of the various dances these two rhythm instruments are brought together in such a way as to symbolize the sexual act.

All informants recognized that the tchoke was symbolic of the male member—its iconic qualities are fairly obvious. But only half of the informants recognized that the periodic shaking of the tchoke together with the raffia broom at certain ritual junctures was symbolic of sexual union and was intended to add power and force to ritual development—to give to the individual cult member the fertility he sought, the capacity to create his own world in true patriarchal patrilineal fashion.

It will be clear that we have presented here only the most contextually relevant linkages for some of the symbols manipulated in the ritual. In fact, a patient examination of these symbols in the presence of a sensitive informant and in the context of all Fang tradition would reveal a much broader range of associations and interpretations—each symbol gathering unto itself a congeries of meanings—the product of all the situations in which it had appeared in Fang life and of associations both accidental and intentional which have attached themselves to it. Turner has demonstrated for the Ndembu what a subtle web of associations commonplace ritual symbols can call up (1961a, 1961b). Our purpose here, however, has been to demonstrate a variability in the interpretation of these symbols and a variability in the degree to which various culture carriers make out configurations in the relationships between various symbols, engage, in other words, in logico-meaningful integration.

* * *

The banzie regard the making out of configurative relationships and associations between symbols and between symbols and other events, beliefs, and items in experience with some awe. It is a form of penetration of the unseen and mysterious (asok engang), which was accomplished in former days also by diviners, by the eldest members of the ancestor cult (bieri), in the presence of the craniums of the ancestors (nkukweng), or at times of initiation into the cult. Thus it is said of the leader of the Kougoulou cult house, something of whose elaborate symbolic interpretations we have suggested above, that he is a man who sees far and has died often; he is familiar with the grave and all that exists there and shapes our lives here.

The data presented above confronts us with the fact that within such highly patterned behavior as ritual different cultural perspectives are in existence.

Common symbols carry different weightings for different participants. Symbols which are elaborately expressive for some, conjuring up conceptions basic to the cult world-view, are simply situation referential for others—that is, insofar as they are signaled out for attention they refer back to the ritual itself out of which they sprang rather than to meanings beyond ritual activity. What are symbols for some informants, in effect, are signs or signals for others—simply clues to the conduct of ritual activity rather than expressive of cultural dimensions associated with but beyond that activity. The cult harp, the fire, the rattle to which some cult members lend complex meanings to others are much more matter-of-factly experienced as the necessary paraphernalia of ritual activity, without which that activity could not go on, but otherwise not especially meaningful.

If research into the views of cult members shows that the significance and "symbolicness" of their ritual behavior is differentially interpreted, what can it mean, then, to speak of symbolic representations with any implication that they are collective? If we take Tylor's working definition of culture as repeated activities and shared ideas, the repeated activity of the ritual is obvious enough but we become more skeptical about the ideas shared. We become aware of the range of cultural ambiguities involved in social interaction.

No doubt, as behavior goes, ritual is a special case. We are forced, it seems, to recognize the relevance of Leach's observation as to "the essential vagueness of all ritual statements" (1954:286). The remarkable integrative effect of ritual, he maintains, rests in the fact that it can bring together in repeated activity persons who have quite a variant interpretation of the meaning of that activity. Ritual can achieve integration on the social level of interaction, between participants who on the cultural level—the ideological level of beliefs, rationales, interpretation of symbols—in fact, lack consensus. Ritual is, it is true, a special category of behavior; but the data we derive from it may have more general applicability, for the specialness of ritual lies only in the fact that it is a more tightly patterned and repetitive form of non-random behavior. We should not be prevented from generalizing upon its behavioral characteristics because of a Durkheimian commitment to a sacred-profane dichotomy. The analysis of ritual should impel us to ask questions about the essential vagueness of all social statements. Reflection on this problem puts one in mind of Sumner's tendency to expand the definition of ritual to include practically every instance of regularized behavior and to define it, finally, as "that process by which mores are developed and established" (1906:67).

What remains of interest is that such highly regularized activity betrays such variable perspectives on the meanings involved. This is a paradox which challenges explanation. If it is not to defeat it we must adopt some analytic distinction between activity and meaning. The principle that can be suggested at this point is that the more rigorously regularized social inter-action becomes, the more highly trained the participants in carrying out an increasingly alternative free interaction, the greater possibility there is that the symbolic dimension of this interaction should have variable interpreta-tion. This may be for two reasons. The participants are assured of solidarity in the forms of social interaction and need no longer seek it in cultural forms. If, in other words, coexistence is guaranteed socially, coherence need not be sought culturally. Participants may reflect this state of affairs by ei-ther manifesting a disinterest in cultural meanings or by prohibiting the gratuitous interpretation of these meanings. We find both these reactions in the syncretist cult examined here. There is very little discussion of cultural meanings within the cult except on the part of the cult leader. For all speak with one voice!

Social and Cultural Consensus

An explanation such as the above forces a return to the concepts of symbol and consensus upon which it is based. We see the utility of distinguishing be-tween signal, sign and symbol, on the one hand, and between two kinds of consensus, social and cultural, on the other. Taking the latter distinction first, the reader will be aware that we have employed the phrase "symbolic con-sensus" in two different ways. We have discussed the ritual achievement of so-cial solidarity (nlem mvore—one-heartedness) as the symbolic achievement of solidarity. We have also examined the meanings for the participant of cer-tain symbols manipulated in this ritual. This examination exposed lack of consensus. We must, it seems, recognize the existence of consensus at two lev-els, exactly as we must distinguish between social and cultural systems. Geertz (1957:34) following Parsons (1951:6) has made clear the value of two ana-lytic perspectives: the social or causal-functional, on the one hand; the cul-tural or logico-meaningful, on the other. Integration in these two systems, Parsons argued, is not of the same type and there is, in fact, tension between them. Parsons elsewhere in a footnote to the elaboration of his system em-ploys as we have the distinction between co-existence and coherence.

> Systems of action are functional systems; cultural systems are symbolic systems in which the components have logical or meaningful rather than functional rela-tionships with one another. Hence the imperatives which are characteristic of the two classes of system are different. In systems of action the imperatives which im-pose certain adaptations on the components result from the empirical possibili-ties or necessities of co-existence which we designate as scarcity and from the properties of the actor as an organism: in cultural systems the internal imperatives are independent of the compatibilities or incompatibilities of coexistence. In cul-tural systems the systemic feature is coherence; the components of the cultural sys-tem are either logically consistent or meaningfully congruous. (1953:173)

Following this approach in which it becomes clear that the requirements of social co-existence are not the same as cultural coherence, logical consistency and aesthetic congruity, it is not only convenient but necessary to distinguish between social and cultural consensus.

Social consensus we may define as an acceptance of the necessity for interaction and, following Max Weber's definition of the social situation as one in which people orient their actions toward one another, the agreement to orient action towards one another. This acceptance and agreement involves the acceptance of a certain set of signals and signs which give direction and orientation to this interaction permitting the coordination and co-existence of the various participants. A good example of social consensus is found in ritual action. In the example we have discussed here the individuals involved hold largely private and in abeyance a logico-meaningful perspective or judgment. They do so for the sake of a social-satisfaction—the satisfaction of orienting their activity towards each other with the resulting psycho-biological benefits whatever these may be—the security of acceptance, exaltation, esprit de corps, morale, well-being, enthusiasm or exstasis. To some degree in every social situation and to a considerable degree in the example explored here, the individual must ignore or play hob with his own meanings for the sake of social consensus. He must be ready to interact and cooperate with others whether he understands or agrees with them in any intellectual sense or not. He does this for the sake of what Malinowski has called the satisfaction of "phatic communion" as opposed to logico-meaningful satisfactions (1923:315).[3]

Cultural consensus is an understanding that one holds symbolic meanings in common. This recognition is obtained by explicit communication, discussion, and debate. The tension between this form of consensus and social consensus is illustrated in the ritual situation analyzed. Despite the achievement of social consensus (nlem mvore, one heart) we do not find among the informants queried a high degree of cultural consensus nor a concern with achieving it. In point of fact, we find a resistance towards the raising of logico-meaningful matters and a feeling that too great a concern with consensus at that level might actually interfere with social consensus—the readiness to orient actions toward one another and engage in ritual activity.

Given the dynamism of cult life, it is not difficult to understand why a pre-occupation with logico-meaningful matters in lower echelon cult members is perceived by cult leaders as a threat to their cult—an attempt to set

---

[3] Malinowski is discussing that use of language in which meaning is not primary. In "phatic communion," words are used rather to "fulfill a social function and that is their principal aim but they are neither the result of intellectual reflection nor do they necessarily arouse reflection in the listener . . . each utterance is an act serving a direct aim of binding hearer to speaker by a tie of some social sentiment or other. Once more language appears to us in this function not as an instrument of reflection of thought but as a mode of action" (1923:315).

up a new group. In fact, it often indicates such intention, for divisive elements often make their case by reference to the logic or meanings evident in the ritual and its symbols.

Field data on the peripheral chapter of Bwiti where the ritual and ceremony had not been fully regularized so that ritual acts were not well coordinated and signals and signs not well learned give us just such a situation. Cult life in the Bwiti chapter in Sougoudzap, Woleu-Ntem, northern Gabon was entirely disrupted during the fall of 1959 because of an ideological dispute as to the use and meaning of certain symbols in ritual. In this case the elderly leader of the cult persisted in certain pre-war practices: styles of ceremonial garb, use of the chest drum for dancing, two stages of initiation, a limited song cycle. For more than two years younger members of the cult susceptible to syncretisms and innovations emanating from central Gabon fretted under what they evidently regarded as an outmoded symbol system. From time to time they suggested modifications to the elderly leader and occasionally changes were incorporated at their suggestion. But no open criticism or discussion of the differing cultural perspectives took place. Cult life went on as usual and the ritual achievement of solidarity—the affirmation of social consensus—continued. Finally, the occasion of an initiation brought forth the impending ideological dispute. The cult leader was openly questioned on the meanings of the various symbols he planned to employ and openly contradicted when he proffered his explanations. Offended at this contradiction, he invited the dissidents to follow Bwiti elsewhere—where the "red path of eboga" was more to their liking. Thereupon, three-fourths of his membership abandoned his chapel, undertaking an arduous weekly journey of 21 kilometers to another and more progressive cult house. The old man was left with the immediate members of his family and a few dependents who, unconcerned by ideological matters, continued to seek the satisfactions of social consensus in as convenient a way as practicable. Eventually, the dissidents returned to the village and built their own chapel. The elderly leader and his family after a period of time joined the dissidents and submitted to their ritual forms. In the face of a more active and socially satisfying cult house in the same village, his remaining dependents had abandoned him for the new cult. Soon his own ceremonies began to seem a solitary and pale reflection of greater activity at the other end of the village. The satisfactions of social consensus were so manifestly greater in the new cult that the closing of his own cult house was inevitable. The ideological problems of cultural consensus were forgotten in pursuit of those psychobiological satisfactions which a massively coordinated ritual can so richly afford.

Several things must be said further about this occurrence. First, Bwiti, as we have remarked, is a highly decentralized religious movement. The vitality of any particular cult chapel depends upon the ability of its leadership to interest the membership in cult activity. They have no other guarantee that their membership will not abandon them for another more attractive chapel. In some cults this can mean a high emphasis upon innovation and novelty in the symbolic accompaniments of ritual interaction. Balandier has remarked upon 'such an emphasis upon novel symbolic forms in the Bwiti cults he visited (1955:221).

It is understood in all the cults, however, that this innovation is the responsibility of the leadership—of those men, in other words, who have retired from the strenuous activity of the all-night dance cycle, and who sit in the back of the chapel to observe and discipline the orderly ritual progression of this cycle. The members of Bwiti make an important distinction between the active-dancing-members of the cult (banzie) and the passive leadership (nima na kombo—those who create). The latter have already danced much, died often, and seen far, and they have every right in their acquired otiosity to scrutinize the ritual symbols in a meaningful manner. This is, however, entirely inappropriate in active, dancing members of the cult. Thus, attempts at innovation stemming from them are usually interpreted as divisive in intent. Discussion of the meaning of the symbol system, though this could be easily justified by the ambiguities and uncertainties created by rapid turnover in this system, are usually suspect for the same reason. The failure of the elderly leader in the above case was obviously a failure of innovation. But the attempt by his membership to discuss the meaning of symbols was interpreted by him as a threat to his authority and his right to arbitrate such cultural matters. Some cults, it is true, do readily admit to discussion of ideological matters and all, at the moment of initiation, make some attempt to acquaint the new members with the esoteric— the ritual symbols and their meaning. But it is remarkable the extent to which, among an egalitarian people like the Fang, this discussion is carried on in the form of a didactic lesson from the leadership. Rarely is there a concerted and sincere attempt made to make sure that substantial cultural consensus exists throughout the membership—that the lesson is truly learned.

*   *   *

The treatment of these important details should not allow us to forget the fundamental tension between social consensus and cultural consensus which we are seeking to demonstrate. One may argue that in the reformative cult situation a rapid turnover of symbols makes cultural consensus particularly difficult of achievement. In the syncretistic process the awareness and articulation with other cultural systems in the interest of synthesis is such that old symbols are constantly replaced or acquire new dimensions. Cult leaders validate their authority by producing new symbolic forms and this clearly acts to increase the variation in symbolic interpretation on the part of participants. In such a situation the variability in symbolic interpretations can threaten social interaction if made explicit through attempts at cultural consensus. Particularly in the context of turmoil and anxiety of a society in transition, like the Fang, where role expectations are frequently frustrated and where, therefore, the compensatory satisfactions of social interaction even in ritual form are to be highly valued would the substantial consideration of cult symbols be seen as divisive and destructive. This is so even though the fact of disintegration in Fang society at large has produced a search for meaningful "signs" and symbols. Such are the factors at work in the syncretist cult situation we have described. They provide for a notable tension between society and culture because of lag in one or the other; in this case, social lag.

But the tension we are discussing, though more clear-cut here, is not limited to such a transitional situation. It is certainly more general in human behavior. It is the product, first, of the idiosyncratic experience of every culture carrier who possesses private as well as public symbols as well as private and public meanings for every symbol singled out for his attention by his enculturation (Leach 1958:150–52). Secondly, it is the product of the inevitable division of labor and structural differentiation produced in any social structure. The understanding of their field of behavior in terms of the meanings available to them are different for those in dominant as against those in subordinate positions. For these and other reasons persons who agree to interact and orient their behavior one towards another may yet evidence substantial lack of agreement about the meanings of the symbols manipulated in that interaction. We find men agreeing to interact—agreeing to coexist—even though they, in effect and to various degrees disagree about much of the meaning of that interaction. It is a much harder thing in human affairs, it appears, to subject that behavior to scrutiny at the cultural level in search of logical coherence and aesthetic compatability: to agree to disagree, in other words, in a thoroughly intellectual way about the meaning of behavior that is already effectively coordinated.

Social Signals, Signs, and Cultural Symbols

We have said that social consensus rests upon the acceptance of a set of signals and signs and an agreement about their significance in the sense that there is acceptance of the appropriateness of these signals and signs as orienters of interaction in a specific social situation and a commonality of response to them. Cultural consensus, we have said, rests upon agreement as to the meanings of the symbols which accompany interaction. What follows and what needs to be discussed is the simplification that social consensus is consensus in respect to signals and cultural consensus a consensus in respect to symbols. Signs, as we define them here, occupy an intermediary relationship between the two spheres—social and cultural—with a foot in both.

The vessel of such an argument as this is easily foundered, however, on a congeries of resurgent problems. The most persistent of these are the problem of meaning and the problem of the distinction between signals, signs, and symbols. In respect to the perennial problem of meaning we limit ourselves to saying that the significance of a social signal lies in the action it stimulates; the orientation of behavior made to it in the process of interaction in the social situation in which it belongs. The meaning of a cultural symbol (it goes against the grain to talk about the significance of symbols), lies in the cognitive interpretation given to it by culture carriers in a much wider set of circumstances than its customary context. The meaning of a red traffic signal, for example, is not the same in terms of behavior if presented when one is seated in one's living room. In its context it means stop, but that is entirely inappropriate behavior in one's living room. There is no call for such a sign and it cannot imply or require any useful succeeding action in the living room situation. The American flag is significant in orienting behavior on the parade ground but it has meaning as well. We can interpret this manifold meaning equally well in the living room. It means the United States of America and its 50 states, and has developed through many historic stages and stands for purity, valor and unity. In other words, the symbol as opposed to the signal has acquired a meaning involving associations beyond its significance within the social context where it customarily appears. Symbols may thus function in many disparate contexts. Morris, quoting Yerkes, has pointed out that the signal and sign, unlike the symbol, sooner or later lose their "meaning" apart from their context. The symbol is, therefore, more autonomous (Morris 1955:23–27). Similarly, Sapir speaking of two basic types of symbols points out that they both begin with situations in which a sign is dissociated from its context (1934:494). Parsons in the same vein recognizes this "autonomy," which he calls abstraction or generalization, in speaking of diffusion as a cultural problem not a social problem. "Thus symbols differ from need-dispositions and role expectations in that they are transmissable from one action system to another" (1951:159). Parsons needs but does not make a successful working distinction between signal, sign and symbol orientations in his social system. We can understand the quotation above more easily if we see need dispositions and role expectations as signal and sign oriented features of the social system.

Beyond this matter of autonomy, however, the student rapidly discovers that clear discussion of symbolism is hampered because the term has been employed to "cover a great variety of apparently dissimilar modes of behavior" (Sapir 1934:492). We may note one sign-symbol distinction frequently employed which must be brought in line with our own signal-sign-symbol distinction. In this perspective signs in behavior are primarily genetic in origin and are subjective expressions of internal states of the communicating organism. Thus Kroeber:

> Signs are primarily genetic in origin . . . they convey information to recipient individuals only as to the condition of the sign-producing individual. They alert one organism as to the condition of another. . . . True symbols, however, can convey information on other matters than the condition of the communicating organism. Such external information can fairly be called objective as compared with the essentially subjective nature of what is communicated by non-symbolic signs. (1952:753)

This definition confronts natural signs only which are more akin to what has been called a "symptom" than to signals as understood here. We speak of signals in the conventional sense as items of communication which give orientation, like a traffic light, to action but whose significance is limited to the specific interaction situation and which evoke no meaning outside that situation.

The signals and signs which we have singled out in cult life are, it is true, symbols in the sense congenial to Kroeber in that their meaning is not natural or intrinsic to them in their situation but has been assigned arbitrarily by those who have developed the ritual of the cult. Thereafter, however, they function for a good many members of the cult merely as signals, that is, not as having special meanings in and of themselves but as having significance only in relation to the specific context of the situation—in this case the ritual situation—in which they function.

In psychological terms what seems to be involved with many participants in the ritual is a short-circuiting of behavior in respect to symbols. Whereas, as is frequently the case with Bwiti, the meaning of the symbols has been originally explained to the participants, this verbal mediation with its host of associations is forgotten or repressed and these participants become directly accustomed to a stimulus-motor response.[4] They see the "symbol become signal" and rather than going through the cerebral routine of explaining it they simply orient themselves towards it with the appropriate action. Symbols become signals in ritual if when sensed they no longer evoke explanations and associations but lead rather directly to highly patterned behavior. To a good many members of Bwiti, as we have suggested, ritual activity in respect to symbols is primarily a matter of stimulus-motor response and response chaining. For some, however, frequently those less

---

[4] Fairly complicated patterns of stimulus-motor activity, of course, can be learned without benefit of verbal mediation and pre-neophyte children and young people spend a long enough period as cult spectators to learn the appropriate behavior patterns without extensive instruction.

involved with ritual activity, the explanations, and associations, the verbal mediation is important and what are signals or signs to many members are symbols to them. It may be said that these people fully participate in the culture of their cult though they may not be fully participant in ritual interaction. They deal in symbolic meanings, with the wealth of possible configurations they suggest, which enables them cognitively to construct a universe and reshape it at will.

If we follow Kroeber's definition that signals are genetic and subjective we are obliged to speak of the social and cultural use of "symbols" and we risk sweeping over with the same term the distinction we are seeking to point up. This distinction, however, did not escape White in his classic article on symboling.

> That which is a symbol in the context of origination becomes a sign in use thereafter. Things may be signs or symbols to man. They can be only signs to other creatures. (1940:233)

It is true, referring to Kroeber once again, that the manipulation of signals and signs in the process of ritual interaction serves not only to orient action but also to alert participants to the emotional state of another or the others. Signals and signs can be, in other words, expressively manipulated and, in fact, the ritual we have described has powerful affective content and, hence, important impact on the attitudes of the participants. The distinction between signs and symbols which Kroeber suggests is that the essential function of signs is emotive and symbols cognitive. But this seems too simple a distinction and symbols are not to be excluded from an emotive function. The American flag or the Cross or the Cult Harp may be, for those who interpret them symbolically, abundantly productive of emotion as well. While an interpretation of these symbols in logico-meaningful fashion in the manner of our cult leader will help to locate the individual in his universe—contributing to his cognitive map—they also produce emotion usually because like signs and signals they carry with them, in the Durkheimian sense, affective references to the interaction situation in which they most customarily occur—in all these cases a ritual situation with the heightened emotion and exaltation characteristic of it. For Parsons, in fact, the most important starting point for any discussion of symbolism is the recognition "that every symbol has both expressive and cognitive meanings references" (1953:80).

The more closely we scrutinize the signal sign-symbol relationship, therefore, the more careful we become in suggesting a clear dichotomy. We are led to observe that all signals have symbol potential and all symbols act to one degree or another as signals. Signals appearing out of their context may assume dimensions of meaning. Clearly a college boy who has hung a parking sign on his wall has made of it a symbol. Levy-Bruhl gives us many examples of the way in which natural signals appearing outside their customary context suddenly assume symbolic import for the "primitive" (1938). He characteristically suggests that the "primitive" is particularly susceptible to the portentous investment of signals—to the elaboration of symbols out of signs.

We see the close signal-symbol relationship in the research on which we are reporting. What was substantially a symbol to some cult members was a sign to others, significant only within the context of cult activity and meaningless outside it or at best, when brought up in discussion, re-referential, referring only back to cult activity. The range of variability of the interpretation of various symbols was thus quite great. For some the cult-harp was a fully autonomous symbol with a full weighting of associated meanings. For others it was almost exclusively a ritual object—a necessary element in the coordination of ritual interaction but otherwise not particularly meaningful in a cognitive sense. For some it was not even especially meaningful in an expressive sense. These facts remind us that the connection between signals, signs, and symbols is an intimate one. Perhaps signals and symbols are best treated, as Morris does in his science of semiotic, as polar varieties of sign (1955:27). In line with our thinking here a different distinction would be clearer. Our argument suggests a three part distinction between social signals, signs, and cultural symbols according to their autonomy from the situation in which they usually appear: their ability, in other words, to function in many slots in many different contexts. A signal is something singled out to stand for and thus simplify a condition of the larger situation of which it is a part. Socially it is used exclusively to coordinate and orient activity in that situation. A sign has much of the characteristics of signals as stated but is sufficiently free of its context to have superadded expressive meanings—inarticulated and therefore merely pregnant—which give it in its "mystery" high affective content. A symbol obtains to cognitive meaning rather than significance by its greater abstraction and in the fact that it elicits explicitly articulated associations though it may also give some orientation for action. The more it is verbally articulated, it seems, the more it loses affective content: "emotionally denuded" is Sapir's term. It may be mentioned that our term sign corresponds to his "condensation symbol"; our term symbol to his "referential symbolism" (1934:494).

In effect, then, a symbol is only a more abstracted and more intentionally interpreted signal which stimulates largely cerebral and verbal rather than gross motor behavior. They both, after all, come into being—are singled out—from a diffuse background in the interaction process though symbols because of the greater intellection involved may obtain to either greater complexity or greater definiteness. Signs, midway between signals and symbols, have multiple and often ambiguous meanings which are, perhaps because of this intermediary position, especially emotion producing. This is a consequence of their appearance in many contexts: autonomous relative to signals, mysteriously inexplicit relative to symbols. We are not suggesting by the term autonomy that either signs or symbols have an innate meaning which exists apart from the contexts in which they have appeared.

In our own example we see the intimacy of the signal-sign-symbol distinction, then, in the fact that what is in effect a symbol to some participants in the cult is a sign or signal to others and, at the same time what in one context is treated by one person as a symbol with autonomous superadded meanings of its own in another behavioral context, usually of ritual action, is treated by him, despite its potential meanings, as a sign or simply as a signal. When on rare occasions the leader of the cult is dancing, the cult harp acts primarily as a signal in coordinating his interaction rather than as a symbol. The subtle interpenetration of signal, sign, and symbol behavior and its manifestation in the interpenetration of society and culture produces caution in the use of the analytic perspective being employed here. It does not counter its utility for it gives us, as has been emphasized, an important grasp of the fundamental tensions which lie behind social and cultural dynamics.

Since we are dealing with symbols of a religious movement the usual understanding of religious symbolism may seem to be at variance with the distinctions proposed here. The customary notion of a religious symbol as having a non-empirical referent, however, is entirely in keeping with the distinction we propose in so far as it suggests that symbolism and signs of all kinds, religious or not, possess meanings which are not simply a function of the particular social situations in which they appear. They refer beyond these situations. This "reference beyond" is what we are to understand in those who discuss religious or mythological symbolism when they tell us that these symbols are invested with transcendent meanings, that they are a coincidence of the particular and the universal, that they are "man's way of expressing the quintessence of his experience" past and present, (May 1960: 34), and that they "revive the communication, indeed communion of present man with his mythical or perennial sources of life" (Kahler 1960:63).

It is well to point out that the consensus as regards specifically religious symbols in the syncretist cult data has the same variability as for other symbolism. Once again if we take the cult harp we find the majority understanding this as referring to the female deity, Nyingwan Mebege, and its music her compassion—understanding it as a strictly religious symbol. Still there are some cult participants who do not understand this non-empirical reference of religious type and some who treat it almost as a signal, or rather, as the harp is played in a number of modes, a set of signals. Ritual action proceeds according to directions given by the harp.

Therefore, we say that social signals are the guideposts and direction givers of social interaction systems. They are the "points de repere" of causal-functional relationships. They coordinate concrete coexistence. Cultural symbols are the summary points, the surface features referring to deeper systems of logico-aesthetic meaning which are not concretely present with them but are called up by them in association and explanation. Between these two elements of communication lie emotionally pregnant signs. It appears, thus, that the tension between society and culture, between causal-functional systems and logico-meaningful systems is not only a consequence of their inevitable incongruities but can be summed up in the tension between the symbol and the signal—the one immediate, dependent, imbedded in the existential situation of coexistence and co-ordinated interaction, the other autonomous with super-added meanings forever pulling the culture carrier's attention beyond his immediate situation to the larger implications of his actions—creating in him in other words self-awareness (Hallowell 1959:50–51). This tension between signal and symbol is often embodied in the sign.

Conclusion

In an influential article on "Communication and Culture" Park argued that "communication operates primarily as an integrating and socializing principle" (1938:195). The data we have presented from the Gabon reformative cult of Bwiti shows us one area in which effective communication is resisted, in this case, in favor of ongoing ritual activity. We find in this cult variable interpretation of the "symbols" involved in ritual interaction while, at the same time, unanimous recognition of the effectiveness of the ritual. It achieves the kind of cohesiveness and solidarity the Fang call nlem mvore (one-heartedness). The ritual at once attracts the participants to it by the sheer interest they have in its forms, and exerts this cohesive influence upon them through their participation in these forms of ritual interaction. Yet while there is a rather elaborate symbol system manipulated in this ritual there is resistance towards attempting to establish consensus about the meaning of these symbols. "All participants speak with one voice," it is said, "and that voice is the voice of the leader." Apparently communication between members about such matters is felt to threaten the cohesiveness and integration obtained by the ritual.

The fact that we find manifest acceptance of the ritual activity and the signals and signs that accompany and give direction to it, yet resistance to explorations of symbolic meanings leads to the distinction between social and cultural consensus—the first agreement in respect to the interaction requirements of signals and signs, the second agreement as to the meanings of symbols. We note an incongruity and a tension between these two forms of consensus. Paradoxically a high degree of social integration in the sense of agreement about signals and signs and smooth coordination of interaction does not necessarily imply a high degree of cultural consensus. In fact, the more perfectly coordinated social interaction should be the greater opportunity there may be for variable interpretations of that activity and hence lack of cultural consensus. It is almost as if cultural consensus is sought in lieu of social consensus. Where high social consensus is evident further attempts at the achievement of cultural consensus may be felt to pose, as in the case studied here, too many uncertainties and threats to the cohesiveness already established. White has pointed out that what are in origin symbols often become merely signs. Our data seems to indicate that once this occurs there is a resistance to building them again towards the status of symbols. The, at first blush, paradoxical proposition of high social consensus-low cultural consensus is supported in recent work by Downing showing that the greater the cohesiveness of a group the less influence it has on its members' judgments (1958:164–65). It also follows as a proposition from what has been said that if concern with symbolic meaning decreases with effective increase in the coordination of social interaction, then in transitional periods of low social cohesion the concern with symbols will be high. People will be looking for signs and anxious to interpret their meaning. To such inclinations must be traced the origin of Bwiti in the first place.

Park (1938) has a Deweyian vision of society as a moral order and he maintains that in the long run greater intimacy brings with it greater self-awareness and a more profound understanding each of the other. Communication in such a cohesive situation acts to humanize social relationships and to substitute a moral order for one that is only symbiotic. The vision is compelling but it may be only academic. The prospect of men both acting together socially and thinking together culturally in entire mutuality cannot fail to inspire, but it cannot cause us to forget the degree to which men value acting together and distrust thinking together about the meaning of that action. It cannot cause us to forget that the gut-feeling of moral community created by coordinated interaction such as ritual may be actually threatened by an attempt to achieve moral community on the cultural level where the symbolic dimensions of interaction must be made explicit. A gratuitous but relevant reference to French and English politics makes the point *"en gros."* The instability of the pre-Gaullist French and the stability of the English rests on the degree to which they strive to achieve a correspondence between social and cultural consensus. The French strive to consciously and rationally interpret their political activity with dynamic results. As regards the British we are struck by two things. The first is the concept of the loyal opposition—which is, as far as it goes, the institutionalization of the agreement to disagree on the cultural level. The second is summed up for the great majority in Walter Bagehot's thesis that the true source of strength in the government of England is the apathy of the population. "The best English people keep their minds in a state of decorous dullness" (1948: xv). Whatever may be said of Bagehot's English, to such a mental state as he describes aspire the majority of participants in the ritual we have examined. In contrast all these members of the cult keep their bodies in a state of intense kinesthetic participation.

Other visions than Park's appear in relation to the materials we have discussed. Malinowski (1923) in his discussion of the problem of meaning in primitive languages suggests that the relatively meaningless use of language which he calls "phatic communion" is a primitive trait, though plentiful enough in modern societies. We are becoming, he implies, increasingly reflective and thoughtful—increasingly concerned with the meaning of symbols and hence with more and more substantial forms of communication. In one respect this optimism is not shared by May who from a psychoanalyst's perspective feels that what he calls "transcendent symbols" (our signs) have lost their power to grasp and convey meaning. "They have been replaced by signs and techniques borrowed from the scientific and mechanical spheres" (1960:28). And this has been done to the great detriment of man's ability, he says, to come to terms with himself and the human situation.

Finally we have Durkheim's vision as set forth in *The Elementary Forms of the Religious Life* (1915) [and later presented more precisely (1960)] that men will become increasingly obliged to respond to the impersonal demands of the organic collectivity and deal in the more and more explicit and abstract. Man's activity will become more and more rational and more and more strictly attentive to collective representations (1960:338–39)]. But Durkheim lacks the concept of culture which set against society would have given him a more revealing dualism than the personal-impersonal, individual-collectivity, sacred and profane dualism he pursued. We cannot share his vision automatically that man's communication moves towards an ever more rational commerce in collective representations. We repeat that a more coordinated social life may actually mean for the majority of participants a less explicit commerce in collective representations. The collectivity may feel itself best served by social and not cultural consensus.

Whatever may be said about these pronouncements on the human condition we find them reflecting one of the main points we have been arguing: namely that there is a changing, therefore, dynamic relation between attention to signal and sign systems and attention to symbol systems. They suggest the importance of what might be called signal, sign, symbol research. In pursuing this research we come to recognize the fundamental tension between society and culture—between the two fundamental and complementary perspectives in the study of human behavior (Kroeber and Parsons 1958).

There are difficulties in such study. But even Radcliffe-Brown who was ever suspicious of explanations of what natives mean affirmed that there are methods of determining with some fair degree of probability the meanings of rites and other symbols (1952:143). He does not tell us what this may be. We see it as the obligation to study the comparative weightings given to and tensions between signal, sign, and symbol reactions—significance and meaning—in social systems. We must ask questions of the kind: how much symbolic elaboration is possible in any system; is there such a thing as an over-elaborated symbol system; to what extent and at what level and how does the awareness of symbolic meanings interfere with coordinated social interaction (sign and signal behavior)? How is significance and meaning distributed in social systems? Under what circumstances do signals become signs and signals symbols and vice versa? All these questions which have not been actively pursued in anthropology demand that we understand when in human behavior we are talking about symbols and when we are talking about signs and signals and, equally important, what is meant when we speak about consensus. Of general importance in the study of behavior, these distinctions are inescapably relevant in the analysis of ritual.

The data presented here I think produces a useful caution. It has been necessary to point out that culture, logico-meaningful integration in respect to symbols, has been sacrificed among the majority of our informants for the sake of ongoing social interaction. In counterpart there is an elaborate symbolic, logical, and aesthetic structure in the Bwiti cult. But this has been elaborated and is articulated by cult leaders and not by participants. For these few cult leaders at least cultural consensus is important and they well recognize that difference which Whitehead has pointed out between "the comparative emptiness of presentational immediacy" and the deep meaning created by symbolic representation and symbolic truth (1927:47). But a strong resistance to meaning remains. Such data may be salutary for anthropologists who live in an occupational subculture which sets high value upon cultural consensus. We may tend to overlook the obvious fact that there are many situations in which ignorance is institutionalized and in which social consensus, the so-called existential continuum of uninterpreted interaction, is more highly valued.[5] We may always be too persuaded by the Cartesian premise and overlook a very widespread postulate, "I participate therefore I am!"

---

[5] The emphasis on social consensus has been remarked as a prime characteristic of African religious movements. For example Baeta discussing Prophetism in Ghana (1962) singles out, from his Protestant perspective, their "neglect of theological study." "There is a general tendency to exalt blind faith rather than encourage intellectual and spiritual wrestling with religious problems" (1962:132). And Balandier (1955:275) sees as a prime characteristic of equatorial religious movements a "reaction a l'encontre de toutes les forces suscitant et developpant la rationalisation."

BIBLIOGRAPHY

Baeta, C. G.
1962 Prophetism in Ghana. London: SCM Press.
Bagehot, W.
1948 Physics and Politics. New York: Alfred Knopf.
Balandier, G
1955 Sociologie actuelle de l'Afrique noire. Presses Universitaires de France.
Ball, H., G. Simpson, and K. Ikeda
1962 Law and Social Change: Sumner Reconsidered. American Journal of Sociology LXVII:532–540.
Downing, J.
1958 Cohesiveness, Perception and Values. Human Relations XI:157–166.
Durkheim, E.
1915 The elementary Forms of the Religious Life. New York: Macmillan.
1960 The Dualism of Human Nature and its Social Conditions. *In* Essays in Sociology and Philosophy by Emile Durkheim et al. Kurt H. Wolff, ed. Columbus: Ohio University Press.
Fernandez, J.
1964 The Idea and Symbol of the Saviour in a Gabon Syncretist Cult. International Review of Missions LIII:281–289.
1965 African Religious Movements—Types and Dynamics. Journal of Modern African Studies III 4:418–446.
Fernandez, J. and P. Bekale
1962 Christian Acculturation and Fang Witchcraft. Cahiers d'Etudes Africaines 6:244–270.
Geertz, C.
1957 Ritual and Social Change: A Javanese Example. American Anthropologist 59:32–54.
Greenberg, J.
1959 Language and Evolution. *In* Evolution and Anthropology: A Centennial Appraisal. Betty J. Meggers, ed. Washington, DC: Anthropological Society of Washington.
Hallowell, A.
1955 The Self and Its Behavioral Environment. *In* Culture and Experience. Philadelphia: University of Pennsylvania Press.
1959 Behavioral Evolution and the Emergence of the Self. *In* Evolution and Anthropology: A Centennial Appraisal. Betty J. Meggers, ed. Washington, DC: Anthropological Society of Washington.
Johnson, F. E.
1955 Religious Symbolism. New York: Harper.
Kahler, E.
1960 The Nature of the Symbol. *In* Symbolism in Religion and Literature. Rollo May, ed. New York: George Braziller.
Kroeber, A.
1952 Signs and Symbol in Bee Communications. Proceedings of the National Academy of Science 38:753–757.

Kroeber, A. and T. Parsons
   1958   The Concepts of Culture and of Social System. American Sociological Review 23:582–583.
Leach, E.
   1954   Political Systems of Highland Burma. Cambridge, MA: Harvard University Press.
   1958   Magical Hair. *In* The Journal of the Royal Anthropological Institute, vol. 88, Part II, July–December, 147–164.
Lévy-Bruhl, L.
   1938   L'Experience mystique et les symboles chez les primitifs. Paris: Payot et cie.
Malinowski, B.
   1923   The Problem of Meaning in Primitive Languages. *In* The Meaning of Meaning. C. K. Ogden and I. A. Richards, eds. London: Harcourt Brace and Co.
   1944   A Scientific Theory of Culture. Chapel Hill: University of North Carolina Press.
May, R.
   1960   The Significance of Symbols. *In* Symbolism in Religion and Literature. Rollo May, ed. New York: George Braziller.
Morris, C.
   1955   Signs Language and Behaviour. New York: George Braziller.
Park, R.
   1938   Reflections on Communication and Culture. American Journal of Sociology XLIV:187–205.
Parrinder, G.
   1953   Religion in an African City. London: SCM Press.
Parsons, T.
   1951   The Social System. Glencoe, IL: Free Press.
   1953   Working Papers in the Theory of Action. Glencoe, IL: Free Press.
Parsons, T. and E. Shils, eds.
   1954   Toward a General Theory of Action. Cambridge: Harvard University Press.
Radcliffe-Brown, A. R.
   1952   Structure and Function in Primitive Society. Glencoe, IL: Free Press.
Raymaekers, P.
   1959   L'Eglise de Jesus Christ sur la terre par le prophete Simon Kimbangu. Zaire XIII:7, 674–756.
Sapir, E.
   1931   Communication. *In* Encyclopedia of the Social Sciences IV:78–80.
   1934   Symbolism. *In* Encyclopedia of the Social Sciences XIV:492–495.
Stein, L.
   1955   What is a Symbol Supposed to be? Journal of Analytical Psychology II:73–84.
Sumner, W.
   1906   Folkways. New York: Ginn and Co.
Sundkler, B.
   1961   Bantu Prophets in South Africa. London: International African Institute.

Turner, V.
1961a Ndembu Divination, its Symbolism and Techniques. The Rhodes-Livingston Papers #31. Manchester, England.
1961b Ritual Symbolism, Morality and Social Structure among the Ndembu. Rhodes-Livingston Journal 30:1-10.
1962 Ndembu Circumcision Ritual. *In* Essays on the Ritual of Social Relations Max Gluckman, ed. Manchester: Manchester University Press.
Veciana-Vilaldach, A. de
1957 La Secta del Bwiti en la Guinea Espanola. Madrid: Instituto de Estudios Africanos.
Wallace, A.
1956 Revitalization Movements. American Anthropologist 58:264-281.
Welbourne, F.
1961 East African Rebels, a Study of Some Independent Churches. London: SCM Press.
White, L.
1940 The Symbol: The Origin and Basis of Human Behaviour. Philosophy of Science 7:451-463.
Whitehead, A.
1927 Symbolism: Its Meaning and Effect. New York: Macmillan.
Wilson, M.
1957 Rituals of Kinship among the Nyakyusa. London: International African Institute.
1959 Communal Rituals of the Nyakyusa. London: International African Institute.

QUERIES

- Like other revitalization movements, Bwiti is an attempt to create "a more satisfying culture." Based on Fernandez's article, what are examples of that attempt?
- What is the distinction between "social consensus" and "cultural consensus"?
- How is the achievement of "one-heartedness" (nlem-mvore) in Bwiti an example of "symbolic consensus"? How is nlem-vore attained?
- Why does Fernandez argue that symbols are not always points of unity and consensus for members of a culture?
- Define Fernandez's distinctions between "signals," "signs," and "symbols."

CONNECTIONS

- Applying Ortner's criteria for identifying "key symbols," what are some key symbols used during the Bwiti rituals?

- Review Fernandez's discussion of the ideological dispute that erupted in the fall of 1959 in the Bwiti chapter in Sougoudzap (pp. 375–76). How does this event parallel the disruption of cultural consensus discussed by Clifford Geertz in "Ritual and Social Change: A Javanese Example"?
- In contrast to Durkheim's ideas in "Elementary Forms of the Religious Life" that collective representations are shared uniformly by members of a society, why does Fernandez suggest that individuals may emphasize social consensus over the cultural consensus?

22

Sherry B. Ortner

INTRODUCTION

The following article by American anthropologist Sherry B. Ortner (b. 1941) was published early in her career, but it marks a theoretical theme subsequently developed in her research: the importance of symbolic systems as models of and models for human social life (for an extended overview, see Moore 2008:307–24). This article was published during 1973 in the journal *American Anthropologist*; since then Ortner continued her ethnographic research in the Himalayas, incorporated feminism into her anthropological concerns, and developed a robust theory of practice into her work, most recently focusing on U.S. society. Nevertheless, "Key Symbols" represents an early and fundamental theoretical statement in Sherry Ortner's work.

In "Key Symbols" Ortner argues that certain symbols are of central significance in human societies, representations and conceptions that are pivotal for a society's conceptual order. Key symbols are not universal—they vary between societies—and a society usually has multiple key symbols. But certain symbols are key, while others are not (the U.S. flag may be a key symbol in American society; a semicolon is not). Some key symbols are catalysts for a constellation of meanings; these Ortner calls "summarizing symbols." Other key symbols are used to make distinctions or classifications; these are "elaborating symbols." In turn, elaborating symbols include two subsets: root metaphors, the conceptual bases of elaboration, and key scenarios, idealized patterns for action.

In Ortner's analysis, key symbols are integral to human social action and exist in the midst of controversy. Often surrounded by prohibitions and special treatments, key symbols show up in a variety of social settings, and conceptually rich—and sometimes contradictory—associations and interpretations may cluster around key symbols. In this, "Key Symbols" foreshadows Ortner's later interest in agency, structure and history (see Moore 2008:317-23). Key symbols are in the thick of social action, and thus central to ethnographic scrutiny.

PRIMARY TEXT: *ON KEY SYMBOLS*

It is by no means a novel idea that each culture has certain key elements which, in an ill-defined way, are crucial to its distinctive organization. Since the publication of Benedict's *Patterns of Culture* in 1934, the notion of such key elements has persisted in American anthropology under a variety of rubrics: "themes" (e.g., Opler 1945; Cohen 1948), "focal values" (Albert 1956), "dominant values" (DuBois 1955), "integrative concepts" (DuBois 1936), "dominant orientations" (Kluckhohn 1950), and so forth. We can also find this idea sneaking namelessly into British social anthropological writing; the best example of this is Lienhardt's (1961) discussion of cattle in Dinka culture (and I say culture rather than society advisedly). Even Evans-Pritchard has said,

> as every experienced field-worker knows, the most difficult task in social anthropological field work is to determine the meanings of a few key words, upon an understanding of which the success of the whole investigation depends. [1962:80]

Recently, as the focus in the study of meaning systems has shifted to the symbolic units which formulate meaning, the interest in these key elements of cultures has become specified as the interest in key symbols. Schneider (1968) calls them "core symbols" in his study of American kinship; Turner (1967) calls them "dominant symbols" in his study of Ndembu ritual; I called them "key symbols" in my study of Sherpa social relations (Ortner 1970).

The primary question of course is what do we mean by "key"? But I will postpone considering this problem until I have discussed the various usages of the notion of key symbols in the literature of symbolic analysis.

Two methodological approaches to establishing certain symbols as "core" or "key" to a cultural system have been employed. The first approach, less commonly used, involves analyzing the system (or domains thereof) for its underlying elements—cognitive distinctions, value orientations, etc.—then looking about in the culture for some figure or image which seems to formulate, in relatively pure form, the underlying orientations exposed in the analysis. The best example of this approach in the current literature is David Schneider's (1968) analysis of American kinship; Schneider first analyzes the kinship system for its basic components—nature and law—and then decides that conjugal sexual intercourse is the form which, given its meaning in the culture, expresses this opposition most succinctly and meaningfully. Schneider expresses his debt to Ruth Benedict, and this debt turns out to be quite specific, since the other major work which embodies this method is Benedict's *The Chrysanthemum and the Sword* (1967). The sword and the chrysanthemum were chosen by Benedict from the repertoire of Japanese symbols as most succinctly, or perhaps most poetically, representing the tension in the Japanese value system which she postulated. She did not arrive at this tension through an analysis of the meanings of chrysanthemums and swords in the culture; she first established the tension in Japanese culture through analysis of various symbolic systems, then chose these two items from the repertoire of Japanese symbols to sum up the opposition.

In the second, more commonly employed approach, the investigator observes something which seems to be an object of cultural interest, and analyzes it for its meanings. The observation that some symbol is a focus of cultural interest need not be very mysterious or intuitive. I offer here five reasonably reliable indicators of cultural interest, and there are probably more. Most key symbols, I venture to suggest, will be signaled by more than one of these indicators:

(1) The natives tell us that X is culturally important.
(2) The natives seem positively or negatively aroused about X, rather than indifferent.
(3) X comes up in many different contexts. These contexts may be behavioral or systemic: X comes up in many different kinds of action situation or conversation, or X comes up in many different symbolic domains (myth, ritual, art, formal rhetoric, etc.).
(4) There is greater cultural elaboration surrounding X, e.g., elaboration of vocabulary, or elaboration of details of X's nature, compared with similar phenomena in the culture.
(5) There are greater cultural restrictions surrounding X, either in sheer number of rules, or severity of sanctions regarding its misuse.

As I said, there may be more indicators even than these of the key status of a symbol in a culture, but any of these should be enough to point even the most insensitive fieldworker in the right direction. I should also add that I am not assuming that there is only one key symbol to every culture; cultures are of course a product of the interplay of many basic orientations, some quite conflicting. But all of them will be expressed somewhere in the public system, because the public symbol system is ultimately the only source from which the natives themselves discover, rediscover, and transform their own culture, generation after generation.

It remains for us now to sort out the bewildering array of phenomena to which various investigators have been led to assign implicitly or explicitly the status of key cultural symbol. Anything by definition can be a symbol, i.e., a vehicle for cultural meaning, and it seems from a survey of the literature that almost anything can be key. Omitting the symbols established by the first approach cited above, which have a different epistemological status, we can cite from the anthropological literature such things as cattle among the Dinka and Nuer, the Naven ritual of the Iatmul, the Australian churinga, the slametan of the Javanese, the potlatch of the northwest coast, the forked stick of Ndembu rituals, and from my own research, the wheel-image in Tibet and food among the Sherpas. We could also add such intuitive examples as the cross of Christianity, the American flag, the motorcycle for the Hell's Angels, "work" in the Protestant ethic, and so on.

The list is a jumble—things and abstractions, nouns and verbs, single items and whole events. I should like to propose a way of subdividing and ordering the set, in terms of the ways in which the symbols operate in relation to cultural thought and action.

The first major breakdown among the various types of symbols is along a continuum whose two ends I call "summarizing" vs. "elaborating." I stress that it is a continuum, but I work with the ideal types at the two ends.

Summarizing symbols, first, are those symbols which are seen as summing up, expressing, representing for the participants in an emotionally powerful and relatively undifferentiated way, what the system means to them. This category is essentially the category of sacred symbols in the broadest sense, and includes all those items which are objects of reverence and/or catalysts of emotion—the flag, the cross, the churinga, the forked stick, the motorcycle, etc. The American flag, for example, for certain Americans, stands for something called "the American way," a conglomerate of ideas and feelings including theoretically) democracy, free enterprise, hard work, competition, progress, national superiority, freedom, etc. And it stands for them all at once. It does not encourage reflection on the logical relations among these ideas, nor on the logical consequences of them as they are played out in social actuality, over time and history. On the contrary, the flag encourages a sort of all-or-nothing allegiance to the whole package, best summed up on a billboard I saw recently: "Our flag, love it or leave." And this is the point about summarizing symbols in general—they operate to compound and synthesize a complex system of ideas, to "summarize" them under a unitary form which, in an old-fashioned way, "stands for" the system as a whole.

Elaborating symbols, on the other hand, work in the opposite direction, providing vehicles for sorting out complex and undifferentiated feelings and ideas, making them comprehensible to oneself, communicable to others, and translatable into orderly action. Elaborating symbols are accorded central status in the culture on the basis of their capacity to order experience; they are essentially analytic. Rarely are these symbols sacred in the conventional sense of being objects of respect or foci of emotion; their key status is indicated primarily by their recurrence in cultural behavior or cultural symbolic systems.

Symbols can be seen as having elaborating power in two modes. They may have primarily conceptual elaborating power, that is, they are valued as a source of categories for conceptualizing the order of the world. Or they may have primarily action elaborating power; that is, they are valued as implying mechanisms for successful social action. These two modes reflect what I see as the two basic and of course interrelated functions of culture in general: to provide for its members "orientations," i.e., cognitive and affective categories; and "strategies," i.e., programs for orderly social action in relation to culturally defined goals.

Symbols with great conceptual elaborating power are what Stephen Pepper (1942) has called "root metaphors," and indeed in this realm the basic mechanism is the metaphor. It is felt in the culture that many aspects of experience can be likened to, and illuminated by the comparison with, the symbol itself. In Pepper's terms, the symbol provides a set of categories for conceptualizing other aspects of experience, or, if this point is stated too unidirectionally for some tastes, we may say that the root metaphor formulates the unity of cultural orientation underlying many aspects of experience, by virtue of the fact that those many aspects of experience can be likened to it.

One of the best examples of a cultural root metaphor in the anthropological literature is found in Godfrey Lienhardt's discussion of the role of cattle in Dinka thought. Cows provide for the Dinka an almost endless set of categories for conceptualizing and responding to the subtleties of experience. For example:

The Dinkas' very perception of colour, light, and shade in the world around them is . . . inextricably connected with their recognition of colour-configurations in their cattle. If their cattle-colour vocabulary were taken away, they would have scarcely any way of describing visual experience in terms of colour, light and darkness. [1961:13]

More important for Lienhardt's thesis is the Dinka conceptualization of the structure of their own society on analogy with the physical structure of the bull. "'The people are put together, as a bull is put together,' said a Dinka chief on one occasion" (Ibid.:23), and indeed the formally prescribed division of the meat of a sacrificed bull is a most graphic representation of the statuses, functions, and interrelationships of the major social categories of Dinka society, as the Dinka themselves represent the situation.

In fact, as Mary Douglas points out, the living organism in one form or another functions as a root metaphor in many cultures, as a source of categories for conceptualizing social phenomena (1966). In mechanized society, on the other hand, one root metaphor for the social process is the machine, and in recent times the computer represents a crucial modification upon this root metaphor. But the social is not the only aspect of experience which root-metaphor type symbols are used to illuminate; for example, much of greater Indo-Tibetan cosmology—the forms and processes of life, space, and time—is developed on analogy with the quite simple image of the wheel (Ortner 1966).

A root metaphor, then, is one type of key symbol in the elaborating mode, i.e., a symbol which operates to sort out experience, to place it in cultural categories, and to help us think about how it all hangs together. They are symbols which are "good to think," not exactly in the Lévi-Straussian sense, but in that one can conceptualize the interrelationships among phenomena by analogy to the interrelations among the parts of the root metaphor.[1]

The other major type of elaborating symbol is valued primarily because it implies clear-cut modes of action appropriate to correct and successful living in the culture. Every culture, of course, embodies some vision of success, or the good life, but the cultural variation occurs in how success is defined, and, given that, what are considered the best ways of achieving it. "Key scenarios," as I call the type of key symbol in this category, are culturally valued in that they formulate the culture's basic means-ends relationships in actable forms.

An example of a key scenario from American culture would be the Horatio Alger myth. The scenario runs: poor boy of low status, but with total faith in the American system, works very hard and ultimately becomes rich and powerful. The myth formulates both the American conception of success—wealth and power and suggests that there is a simple (but not easy) way of achieving them—single-minded hard work. This scenario may be contrasted with ones from other cultures which present other actions as the most effective means of achieving wealth and power, or which formulate wealth and

---

[1] While I am not using the phrase "good to think" precisely in the way in which Lévi-Strauss uses it, there is obviously some parallel between my discussion of root metaphors and Lévi-Strauss's discussion of "the science of the concrete" (1966).

power as appropriate goals only for certain segments of the society, or, of course, those which do not define cultural success in terms of wealth and power at all. In any case, the point is that every culture has a number of such key scenarios which both formulate appropriate goals and suggest effective action for achieving them; which formulate, in other words, key cultural strategies.

This category of key symbols may also include rituals; Singer seems to be making the point of rituals as scenarios when he writes of "cultural performances" (1958), in which both valued end states and effective means for achieving them are dramatized for all to see. Thus this category would include naven, the slametan, the potlatch, and others. The category could also include individual elements of rituals—objects, roles, action sequences—insofar as they refer to or epitomize the ritual as a whole, which is why one can have actions, objects, and whole events in the same category.

Further, scenarios as key symbols may include not only formal, usually named events, but also all those cultural sequences of action which we can observe enacted and reenacted according to unarticulated formulae in the normal course of daily life. An example of such a scenario from Sherpa culture would be the hospitality scenario, in which any individual in the role of host feeds a guest and thereby renders him voluntarily cooperative vis-á-vis oneself. The scenario formulates both the ideally valued (though infrequently attained) mode of social relations in the culture—voluntary cooperation—and, given certain cultural assumptions about the effects of food on people, the most effective way of establishing those kinds of relations. Once again then, the scenario is culturally valued—indicated in this case by the fact that it is played and replayed in the most diverse sorts of social contexts—because it suggests a clear-cut strategy for arriving at culturally defined success.

I have been discussing the category of key symbols which I called "elaborating" symbols, symbols valued for their contribution to the sorting out of experience. This class includes both root metaphors which provide categories for the ordering of conceptual experience, and key scenarios which provide strategies for organizing action experience. While for purposes of this discussion I have been led by the data to separate thought from action, I must hasten to put the pieces back together again. For my view is that ultimately both kinds of symbols have both types of referents. Root metaphors, by establishing a certain view of the world, implicitly suggest certain valid and effective ways of acting upon it; key scenarios, by prescribing certain culturally effective courses of action, embody and rest upon certain assumptions about the nature of reality. Even summarizing symbols, while primarily functioning to compound rather than sort out experience, are seen as both formulating basic orientations and implying, though much less systematically than scenarios, certain modes of action.

One question which might be raised at this point is how we are to understand the logical relationships among the types of key symbols I have distinguished. As the scheme stands now, it has the following unbalanced structure:

summarizing vs. elaborating

↙   ↘

root   key
metaphor   scenario

I would argue that this asymmetry follows from the content of the types: the meaning-content of summarizing or sacred symbols is by definition clustered, condensed, relatively undifferentiated, "thick," while the meaning-content of elaborating symbols is by definition relatively clear, orderly, differentiated, articulate. Thus it is possible to make distinctions among the different ordering functions of elaborating symbols, while the denseness of meaning of summarizing symbols renders them relatively resistant to subdivision and ordering by types. Nonetheless, in the interest of systematic analysis, we may raise the question of whether such subdivisions are possible, and in particular whether the thought/action distinction which subdivides elaborating symbols (into root metaphors and key scenarios) also crosscuts and subdivides summarizing symbols.

The important mode of operation of summarizing symbols, it will be recalled, is its focusing power, its drawing-together, intensifying, catalyzing impact upon the respondent. Thus we must ask whether some summarizing symbols primarily operate to catalyze thought or in any case internal states of the actor, while others primarily operate to catalyze overt action on the part of the actor. Now it does seem possible, for example, to see the cross or some other religious symbol as primarily focusing and intensifying inner attitude, with no particular implied public action, while the flag or some other political symbol is primarily geared to focusing and catalyzing overt action in the public world. Yet, intuitively at least, this distinction seems relatively weak and unconvincing compared to the easily formulated and grasped distinction between the two types of elaborating symbols: static formal images serving metaphor functions for thought (root metaphors), and dramatic, phased action sequences serving scenario functions for action (key scenarios). Of course, as I said, root metaphors may imply particular modes of, or at least a restricted set of possible modes of, action; and key scenarios presuppose certain orderly assumptions of thought. But the distinction—the former geared primarily to thought, the latter to action—remains sharp.

Summarizing symbols, on the other hand, speak primarily to attitudes, to a crystallization of commitment. And, in the mode of commitment, the thought/action distinction is not particularly relevant. There may certainly be consequences for thought and action as a result of a crystallized commitment, but commitment itself is neither thought nor action. The point perhaps illuminates the generally sacred status of summarizing symbols, for they are speaking to a more diffuse mode of orientation in the actor, a broader context of attitude within which particular modes of thinking and acting are formulated.[2]

This is not to say that nothing analytic may be said about summarizing symbols beyond the fact that they catalyze feeling; there are a number of possible ways of subdividing the catalog of sacred symbols in the world, some no doubt more useful or illuminated than others. My point is merely that the particular factor which subdivides elaborating symbols—the thought/action distinction—does not serve very powerfully to subdivide the category of summarizing symbols, since the summarizing symbol is speaking to a different level of response, the level of attitude and commitment.

We are now in a position to return to the question of "key" or central status. Why are we justified in calling a particular symbol "key"? The indicators provided earlier for at least provisionally regarding certain symbols as key to a particular culture were all based on the assumption that keyness has public (though not necessarily conscious) manifestation in the culture itself, available to the observer in the field, or at least available when one reflects upon one's observations. But the fact of public cultural concern or focus of interest is not why a symbol is key; it is only a signal that the symbol is playing some key role in relation to other elements of the cultural system of thought. The issue of keyness, in short, has to do with the internal organization of the system of cultural meaning, as that system functions for actors leading their lives in the culture.

Broadly speaking, the two types of key symbols distinguished above, defined in terms of how they act upon or are manipulated by cultural actors, also indicate the two broad modes of "keyness" from a systemic point of view, defined in terms of the role such symbols are playing in the system; that is, a given summarizing symbol is "key" to the system insofar as the meanings which it formulates are logically or affectively prior to other meanings of the system. By "logically or affectively prior" I mean simply that many other cultural ideas and attitudes presuppose, and make sense only in the context of, those meanings formulated by the symbol. The key role of an elaborating symbol, by contrast, derives not so much from the status of its particular substantive meanings, but from its formal or organizational role in relation to the system; that is, we say such a symbol is "key"

---

to the system insofar as it extensively and systematically formulates relationships—parallels, isomorphisms, complementarities, and so forth—between a wide range of diverse cultural elements.

This contrast between the two modes of "keyness" may be summed up in various ways, all of which oversimplify to some extent, but which nonetheless give perspective on the point. (1) "Content versus form": The keyness of a summarizing symbol derives from its particular substantive meanings (content) and their logical priority in relation to other meanings of the system. The keyness of an elaborating symbol derives from its formal properties, and their culturally postulated power to formulate widely applicable modes of organizing cultural phenomena. (2) "Quality versus quantity": The keyness of a summarizing symbol derives from the relative fundamentality (or ultimacy) of the meanings which it formulates, relative to other meanings of the system. The keyness of an elaborating symbol derives from the broadness of its scope, the extent to which it systematically draws relationships between a wide range of diverse cultural elements. (3) "Vertical versus lateral": The keyness of a summarizing symbol derives from its ability to relate lower-order meanings to higher-order assumptions, or to "ground" more surface-level meanings to their deeper bases. (The issue here is degree of generality of meaning. Whether more general meanings are termed "higher" or "deeper," "ultimate" or "fundamental," by a particular cultural analyst seems a matter of personal preference.) The keyness of an elaborating symbol by contrast derives from its ability to interconnect disparate elements at essentially the same level, by virtue of its ability to manifest (or bring into relief) their formal similarities.

All of these terminological contrasts—form/content, quantity/quality, lateral/vertical—are really perspectives upon the same basic contrast, for which we have no more general term; that is, when we say a summarizing symbol is "key" to the system, we mean that its substantive meanings have certain kinds of priority relative to other meanings of the system. When we say an elaborating symbol is key to the system, we refer to the power of its formal or organizational role in relation to the system.

But at this point we must stop short of reifying the distinctions, for, in practice, the contrast between the two broad types of key symbols and the two modes of "keyness" may break down. It seems empirically to be the case that an elaborating symbol which is accorded wide-ranging applicability in the culture—played in many contexts, or applied to many different sorts of forms is generally not only formally apt but also substantively referential to high level values, ideas, cognitive assertions, and so forth. Indeed, insofar as such high level formulations are made, a key elaborating symbol of a culture may move into the sacred mode and operate in much the same way as does a summarizing symbol. And, on the other hand, some summarizing symbols may play important ordering functions, as when they relate the respondent not merely to a cluster of high level assumptions and values, but to a particular scenario which may be replayed in ongoing life. (One may think, for example, of the Christian cross evoking, among other things, not only a general sense of God's purpose and support, but also the particular scenario of Christ's martyrdom.)

Thus we are brought to an important point, namely, that we are distinguishing not only types of symbols, but types of symbolic functions. These functions may be performed by any given symbol—at different times, or in different contexts, or even simultaneously by different "levels" of its meaning. While there are many examples of summarizing and elaborating symbols in their relatively pure forms, the kinds of functions or operations these symbols perform may also be seen as aspects of any given symbols.

To summarize the original scheme briefly, key symbols may be discovered by virtue of a number of reliable indicators which point to cultural focus of interest. They are of two broad types, summarizing and elaborating. Summarizing symbols are primarily objects of attention and cultural respect; they synthesize or "collapse" complex experience, and relate the respondent to the grounds of the system as a whole. They include most importantly sacred symbols in the traditional sense. Elaborating symbols, on the other hand, are symbols valued for their contribution to the ordering or "sorting out" of experience. Within this are symbols valued primarily for the ordering of conceptual experience, i.e., for providing cultural "orientations," and those valued primarily for the ordering of action, i.e., for providing cultural "strategies." The former includes what Pepper calls "root metaphors," the latter includes key scenarios, or elements of scenarios which are crucial to the means-end relationship postulated in the complete scenario.[3]

This scheme also suggests, at least by the choices of terms, the modes of symbolic analysis relevant to the different types of key symbols. The first type (summarizing symbols) suggests a range of questions pertaining to the cultural conversion of complex ideas into various kinds of relatively undifferentiated commitment—patriotism, for example, or faith. The second type (root metaphors) suggests questions applicable to the analysis of metaphor in the broadest sense, questions of how thought proceeds and organizes itself through analogies, models, images, and so forth. And the third type (key scenarios) suggests dramatistic modes of analysis, in which one raises questions concerning the restructuring of attitudes and relationships as a result of enacting particular culturally provided sequences of stylized actions.

---

[3] There are a number of schemes in the literature of semiotics to which this scheme may be compared, although none are isomorphic with it. Probably the closest is the tripartite scheme derived from philosophical psychology, which divides the symbolic functions into the affective, the cognitive, and the conative (cf. Miller 1964).

This article has been frankly programmatic; I am in the process of implementing some of its ideas in a monograph on Sherpa social and religious relations. Here I have simply been concerned to show that, although a method of cultural analysis via key symbols has been for the most part unarticulated, there is at least incipiently method in such analysis. It is worth our while to try to systematize this method, for it may be our most powerful entree to the distinctiveness and variability of human cultures.

BIBLIOGRAPHY

Albert, Ethel
    1956   The Classification of Values: A Method and Illustration. American Anthropologist 58:221–248.
Benedict, Ruth
    1934   Patterns of Culture. Boston: Houghton-Mifflin.
    1967   The Chrysanthemum and the Sword. Cleveland: World.
Cohen, A. K.
    1948   On the Place of "Themes" and Kindred Concepts in Social Theory. American Anthropologist 50:436–443.
Douglas, Mary
    1966   Purity and Danger. New York: Praeger.
DuBois, Cora
    1936   The Wealth Concept as an Integrative Factor in Tolowa-Tututni Culture. *In* Essays in Anthropology Presented to A. L. Kroeber. Robert Lowie, ed. Berkeley: University of California Press.
    1955   The Dominant Value Profile of American Culture. American Anthropologist 57:1232–1239.
Evans-Pritchard, E. E.
    1962   Social Anthropology and Other Essays. New York: Free Press.
Geertz, Clifford
    1966   Religion as a Cultural System. *In* Anthropological Approaches to the Study of Religion. Michael Banton, ed. ASA Monographs 3. London: Tavistock.
Kluckhohn, Florence
    1950   Dominant and Substitute Profiles of Cultural Orientation. Social Forces 28:376–393.
Lévi-Strauss, Claude
    1966   The Savage Mind. Chicago: University of Chicago Press.
Lienhardt, Godfrey
    1961   Divinity and Experience. Oxford: Clarendon Press.
Miller, George A.
    1964   Language and Psychology. *In* New Directions in the Study of Language. Eric H. Lenneberg, ed. Cambridge, MA: MIT Press.
Opler, Morris E.
    1945   Themes as Dynamic Forces in Culture. American Journal of Sociology 51:198–206.

Ortner, Sherry B. (Sherry O. Paul)
1966   Tibetan Circles. M.A. thesis, University of Chicago.
1970   Food for Thought: A Key Symbol in Sherpa Culture. Ph.D. thesis, University of Chicago.
Pepper, Stephen
1942   World Hypotheses. Berkeley: University of California Press.
Schneider, David M.
1968   American Kinship. Englewood Cliffs, NJ: Prentice-Hall.
Singer, Milton
1958   The Great Tradition in a Metropolitan Center: Madras. *In* Traditional India: Structure and Change. Milton Singer, ed. Philadelphia: American Folklore Society.
Turner, Victor
1967   The Forest of Symbols. Ithaca, NY: Cornell University Press.

QUERIES

- In "Key Symbols," Ortner distinguishes key symbols from other types of symbols. How can an ethnographer determine which symbols are key symbols in another society?
- What is the fundamental difference between "summarizing" symbols vs. "elaborating" symbols?
- As Ortner notes, the "rags-to-riches" story is a "key scenario" in American society; apply it to different fields of human action. Is it applicable to all fields of human action in American society or are there other, alternative, key scenarios?

CONNECTIONS

- In "Key Symbols," Ortner cites a list of key symbols from the anthropological literature "which have a different epistemological status" compared to other symbols; this list includes the slametan, the potlatch, the "forked stick [chisinga] of the Ndembu," and other famous examples. Who are the anthropologists and what are the ethnographic cases associated with that list?
- How does Ortner's analysis of symbols parallel with and/or diverge from Victor Turner's ideas? (See Moore 2008:247–58, for discussion.)

23

Pierre Bourdieu

INTRODUCTION

The French social scientist Pierre Bourdieu (1933-2002) contributed to a theoretical position that he called "a theory of practice" or *praxis* (see Moore 2008:325-26, 330-34). To oversimplify, a theory of practice contends that culture cannot be reduced to either a system of rules—"In society X, a man must marry his mother's brother's daughter"—or to the cumulative result of individual's freely willed actions—"I married her because I love her." Further, cultural behavior cannot be understood apart from the historical circumstances and traditions that limit or transform the "rules" of a culture and/or the range of individual action. Culture, according to Bourdieu, is actively constructed by social actors who employ a society's rules in light of the historical structures. Culture cannot be reduced to rules, individual action, or historical traditions. Culture involves the interplay of all three domains set into action through cultural practice.

To clarify, we can use the analogy of a game, for example, soccer. There are a set of rules that define the play: the ball cannot be touched with your hands except by the goalie, the ball must remain in bounds, players cannot be offsides, and so on. On the other hand there is individual performance: no one can execute a bicycle kick like the great Brazilian athlete, Pelé. Further, there is the matter of strategy: if your team is winning, you try to pass among your teammates to tire and delay the opposition. Soccer involves each of these domains—rules, individual performance, and strategy—but it is not reducible to any one of those domains. The game of soccer—its *praxis*—is the dynamic outcome of each of those domains. Culture is the same, and anthropology must attend to the complex interplay of rules, individual action, and historical structures.

Bourdieu presented his ideas in *Outline of a Theory of Practice* (original 1972, English translation 1977) and *The Logic of Practice* (original 1980, English translation 1990), but one can see the origins of his ideas in the following selection, "The Berber House of the World Reversed" (for a discussion, see Moore 2008:336–39). Bourdieu outlines how the house of Berber peasant farmers in Algeria become a metaphorical template for numerous sets of associated meanings and actions. At first glance, it might seem that the article is an example of structuralism as practiced by Lévi-Strauss (in fact, Bourdieu later acknowledged that it was written when he was most influenced by Lévi-Strauss and the article was first published in an edited volume honoring Lévi-Strauss). However, if one compares Bourdieu's article with an example of Lévi-Strauss's analysis—such as the article "The Structural Study of Myth"—one can see the points of divergence. Rather than simply identify the oppositions (dark-light) and homologies (dark is to female as light is to male) that are encoded in the Kabyle house, Bourdieu is more interested in the ways such generative schemes—which Bourdieu refers to as *habitus*—become so accepted that culture seems to reflect nature. Thus, the interior of the Kabyle house and the female realm become so tightly associated that this seems "natural," becoming an unquestioned field of social life Bourdieu called *doxa* (see Moore 2008:334–36). In the Berber case, habitus and doxa are enacted and restated in sayings, metaphorical associations reflected in the names of architectural features, but ultimately through human practice.

PRIMARY TEXT: *THE BERBER HOUSE OF THE WORLD REVERSED*

From *The Berber House or the World Reversed*. Originally appeared in *Exhanges et communications: Mélange offerts à Claude Lévi-Strauss àl'occasion de son 60e anniversaire*. The Hague: Mouton, 1970.

The interior of the Kabyle house is rectangular in shape and divided into two parts, at a point two-thirds of the way along its length, by a small lattice-work wall half as high as the house. Of these two parts, the larger is approximately 50 centimeters higher than the other and is covered over by a layer of black clay and cow dung which the women polish with a stone; this part is reserved for human use. The smaller part is paved with flagstones and is occupied by the animals. A door within two wings provides entrance to both rooms. Upon the dividing wall are kept, at one end, the small clay

jars or esparto-grass baskets in which provisions awaiting immediate consumption, such as figs, flour, and leguminous plants, are conserved; at the
other end, near the door the water-jars. Above the stable there is a loft where
next to all kinds of tools and implements, quantities of straw and hay to be
used as animal-fodder are piled up; it is here that the women and children
usually sleep, particularly in winter. Against the gable wall, known as the
wall (or, more exactly, the 'side') of the upper part or of the *kanun*, there is
set a brick-work construction in the recesses and holes of which are kept the
kitchen utensils (ladle, cooking pot, dish used to cook the bannock, and
other earthenware objects blackened by fire) and at each end of which are
placed large jars filled with grain. In front of this construction is to be found
the fireplace; this consists of a circular hollow, two or three centimeters
deep at its center, around which arranged in a triangle three large stones
upon which the cooking is done.

In front of the wall opposite the door stands the weaving-loom. This
wall is usually called by the same name as the outside front wall giving
onto the courtyard (tasga), or else wall of the weaving-loom or opposite
wall, since one is opposite it when one enters. The wall opposite to this,
where the door is, is called wall of darkness, or of sleep, or of the maiden,
or of the tomb; a bench wide enough for a mat to be spread out over it is
set against this wall; the bench is used to shelter the young calf or the sheep
for feast-days and sometimes the wood or the water-pitcher. Clothes, mats
and blankets are hung, during the day, on a peg or on a wooden cross-bar
against the wall of darkness or else they are put under the dividing bench.
Clearly, therefore, the wall of the kanun is opposed to the stable as the top
is to the bottom (*adaynin*, stable comes from the root ada, meaning the
bottom) and the wall of the weaving-loom is opposed to the wall to the
door as the light is to the darkness. One might be tempted to give a strictly
technical explanation to these oppositions since the wall of the weaving-
loom, placed opposite the door or, which is itself turned towards the east,
receives the most light and the stable, is in fact most often built perpen-
dicularly with contour lines in order to facilitate the flow of liquid manure
and dirty water. A number of signs suggest, however that these oppositions
are the center of a whole cluster of parallel oppositions, the necessity of
which is never completely due to technical imperatives or functional requirements.

The dark and nocturnal, lower part of the house, place of objects that are
moist, green or raw—jars of water placed on benches in various parts of the entrance to the stable or against the wall of darkness, wood and green fodder—
natural place also of beings, oxen and cows, donkeys and mules—and place of
natural activities—sleep, the sexual act, giving birth—and the place also of
death, is opposed, as nature is to culture to the light-filled, noble, upper part

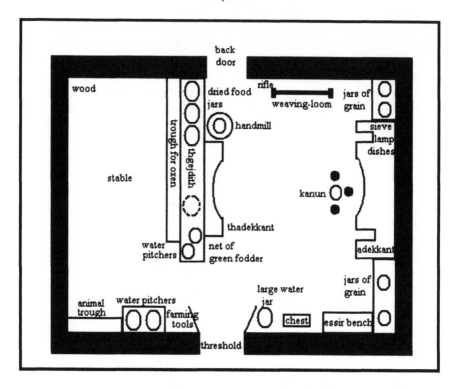

of the house: this is the place of human beings and, in particular, of the guest; it is the place of fire and objects created by fire—lamp, kitchen utensils, rifle— the symbol of the male point of honor (*ennif*) and the protector of female honor (*horma*)—and it is the place of the weaving-loom activities that are carried out in the space of the house: cooking and weaving. These relationships of opposition are expressed through a whole set of convergent signs which establish the relationships at the same time as receiving their meaning from them. Whenever there is a guest to be honored (the verb *qabel* "to honor" also means to face and to face the east), he is made to sit in front of the weaving loom. When a person has been badly received, it is customary for him to say: "He made me sit before his wall of darkness as in a grave," or "His wall of darkness is as dark as a grave." The wall of darkness is also called wall of the invalid and the expression "to keep to the wall" means to be ill and, by extension, to be idle: the bed of the sick person is, in fact, placed next to this wall, particularly in winter. The link between the dark part of the house and death is also shown in the fact that the washing of the dead takes place at the entrance to the stable. It is customary to say that the loft, which is entirely made of wood, is carried by the stable as the corpse is by the bearers, and the word *tha'richth* refers to both the loft and the stretcher which is used to transport the dead. It is therefore obvious that one cannot, without causing offence, invite a guest to sleep in the loft which is opposite to the wall of the weaving-loom like the wall of the tomb.

In front of the wall of the weaving-loom, opposite the door, in the light, is also seated or rather shown off, like the decorated plates which are hung there, the young bride on her wedding-day. When one knows that the umbilical cord of the girl is buried behind the weaving loom and that, in order to protect the virginity of the maiden, she is made to pass through the warp, going from the door towards the weaving-loom, then the magic protection attributed to the weaving-loom becomes evident. In fact, from the point of view of the male members of her family, all of the girl's life is, at it were, summed up in the successive positions that she symbolically occupies in relation to the weaving loom, which is the symbol of male protection: before marriage she is placed behind the weaving-loom, in its shadow, under its protection, as she is placed under the protection of her father and her brothers; on her wedding-day she is seated in front of the weaving-loom with her back to it, with the light upon her, and finally she will sit weaving with her back to the wall of light, behind the loom. "Shame," it is said, "is the maiden," and the son-in-law is called "the veil of shames" since the man's point of honor is the protective "barrier" of female honour.

The low and dark part of the house is also opposed to the high part as the feminine is to the masculine: besides the fact that the division of wok between the sexes, which is based upon the same principle of division as the organization of space, entrusts to the woman the responsibility of most objects which belong to the dark part of the house—water-transport, and the carrying of wood and manure, for instance—the opposition between the upper part and the lower part reproduces within the space of the house the opposition set up between the inside and the outside. This is the opposition between female space and male space, between the house and the garden, the place *par excellence* of the *harem*, i.e., of all which is sacred and forbidden, and a closed and secret space, well protected and sheltered from the intrusions and the gaze of others, and the pace of assembly (*thajma'th*), the mosque, the café, the fields or the market: on the one hand, the privacy of all that is intimate, on the other the open space of social relations; on the one hand, the life of the senses and of the feelings, on the other, the life of relations between man and man, the life of dialogue and exchange. The lower part of the house is the place of the most intimate privacy within the very world of intimacy, that is to say, it is the place of all that pertains to sexuality and procreation. More or less empty during the day, when all activity—which is, of course, exclusively feminine—is based around the fireplace, the dark part is full at night, full of human beings but also full of animals since, unlike the mules and the donkeys, the oxen and the cows never spend the night out of doors; and it is never quite so full as it is during the damp season when the men sleep inside and the oxen and the cows are fed in the stable. It is possible here to establish more directly the relationship which links the fertility of men and of the fields to the dark part of the house and which is a particular instance of the relationship of equivalence between fertility and that which is dark, full (or swollen) or damp, vouched for the whole mythico-ritual system: whilst the grain meant for consumption is, as we have seen, stored in large earthenware jars next to the wall of the upper part, on either side of the fireplace, the grain which is intended for sowing is placed in the dark part of the house, either in sheepskins or in chests placed at the foot of the wall of darkness; or sometimes under the conjugal bed, or in wooden chests placed under the bench which is set against the dividing wall where the wife, who normally sleeps at a lower level, beside the entrance to the stable, rejoins her husband. Once we are aware that birth is always rebirth of the ancestor, since the life circle (which should be called the cycle of generation) turns upon itself every third generation (a proposition which cannot be demonstrated here), it becomes obvious that the dark part of the house may be at the same time and without any contradiction the place of death and of procreation, or of birth as resurrection.

In addition to all this, at the center of the dividing wall, between "the house of the human beings" and the "house of the animals" stands the main pillar, supporting the governing beam and all the framework of the house. Now this governing beam which connects the gables and spreads the protection of the male part of the house to the female part (*asalas alemmas*, a masculine term) is identified explicitly with the mast of the house, whilst the main pillar upon which it rests, which is the trunk of forked tree (*thigejdith*, a feminine term) is identified with the wife (the Beni Khellilui call it "*Mas'uda*" a feminine first name which means "the happy woman"), and their interlocking represents the act of physical union (shown in mural paintings in the form of the union of the beam and the pillar by two superimposed forked trees.) The main beam, which supports the roof, is identified with protector of family honour; sacrifices are often made to it, and it is around this beam that, on a level with the fireplace, is coiled the snake who is the "guardian" of the house. As the symbol of the fertilizing power of man and the symbol also of death followed by resurrection, the snake is sometimes shown (in the Collo region for example) upon earthen jars made by the women and which contain the seed for sowing. The snake is also said to descend sometimes into the house, into the lap of the sterile woman, calling her mother, or to coil itself around the central pillar, growing longer by the length of one coil of its body after each time that it takes suck. In Darna according to Rene Maurnier, the sterile woman ties her belt to the central beam which is where the foreskin is hung and the reed has been used for circumcision; when the beam is heard to crack the Berbers hastily say "may it turn out well," because this presages the death of the chief of the family. At the birth of a boy, the wish is made that "he be the governing beam of the house", and when he carries out his ritual fast for the first time, he takes his first meal on the roof, that is to say, on the central beam (in order, so it is said that he may be able to transport beams).

A number of riddles and sayings explicitly identify the woman with the central pillar. "My father's father's wife carries my fathers' father who carries his daughters"; "The slave strangles his master"; "The woman supports the man"; "The woman is the central pillar." To the young bride one says: "May God make of you the pillar firmly planted in the middle of the house." Another riddle says: "She stands but she has no feet"; a forked tree open at the top and not set upon her feet, she is female nature and, as such, she is fertile or rather, able to be fertilized. Against the central pillar are poled the leather bottles full of hij seeds, and it is here that the marriage is consummated. Thus, as a symbolic summing up of the house, the union of *asalas* and *thigejidth*, which spreads its fertilizing protection over all human marriage, is in a certain way primordial marriage, the marriage of the ancestors which is also, like tillage, the marriage of heaven and earth. "Woman is the foundations, man is the governing beam," says another proverb. Asalas, which a riddle defines as "born in the earth and buried in the sky," fertilizes thigejdith, which is planted in the earth, the place of the ancestors who are the masters of fecundity, and open towards the sky.

Thus, the house is organized according to a set of homologous oppositions: fire:water; cooked:raw; high:low; light:shadow; day:night; male:female; *nif:horma*; fertilizing:able to be fertilized; culture:nature. But in fact the same oppositions exist between the houses as a whole and the rest of the universe. Considered in its relationship with the external world, which is a specifically masculine world of public life and agricultural work, the house, which is the universe of women and the world of intimacy and privacy, is haram, that is to say at once sacred and illicit for every man who does not form part of it (hence the expression used when taking an oath: "May my wife—or my house—become illicit—haram—to me if . . ."). As the place of the sacred or the left-hand side, appertaining to the horma to which are linked all those properties which are associated with the dark part of the house, the house is placed under the safeguard of the masculine point of honor (*nif*) as the dark part of the house is placed under the protection of the main beam. Any violation of the sacred spaces takes on therefore the social significance of a sacrilege: thus, theft in an inhabited house is treated in everyday usage as a very serious fault inasmuch as it is offence to the *nif* of the head of the family and an outrage upon the horma of the house and consequently of all the community. Moreover, when a guest who is not a member of the family is introduced to the women, he gives the mistress of the house a sum of money which is called "the view."

One is not justified in saying that the woman is locked up in the house unless one also observes that the man is kept out of it, at least during the day. As soon as the sun has risen he must, during the summer, be in the fields or at the assembly house; in the winter, if he is not in the field, he has to be at the place of assembly or upon the benches set in the shelter of the pent-roof over the entrance door to the courtyard. Even at night, at least during the dry season, the men and the boys, as soon as they have been circumcised, sleep outside the house, either near the haystacks upon the threshing-floor, beside the donkey and the shackled mule, or upon the fig-dryer, or in the open field, or else, more rarely, in the thajma'th. The man who stays too long in the house during the day is either suspect or ridiculous: he is "the man of the home", as one says of the importunate man who stays amongst the women and who "broods at home like a hen in the hen-house." A man who has respect for himself should let himself be seen, should continuously place himself under the gaze of others and face them (*qabel*). He is a man amongst men (*argaz yer irgazen*). Hence the importance accorded to the games of hour which are a kind of dramatic action, performed in front of others who are knowing spectators, familiar with the text and all the stage business and capable of appreciating the slightest variations. It is not difficult to understand why all biological activities such as eating, sleeping and procreating are excluded from the specifically cultural universe and relegated to the sanctuary of intimacy and the refuge for the secrets of nature which is the house, the woman's world. In opposition to man's work which is performed outside, it is the nature of woman's work to remain hidden ("God conceals it"): "Inside the house, woman is always on the move, she flounders like a fly in whey; outside the house nothing of her work is seen." Two very similar sayings define woman's condition as being that of one who cannot know of any other sojourn than that tomb above the earth which is the house and that subterranean house which is the tomb: "Your house is your tomb"; "Woman has only two dwellings, the house and the tomb."

Thus, the opposition between the house and the assembly of men, between the fields and the market, between private life and public life, or if one prefers, between the full light of the day and the secrecy of the night, overlaps very exactly with the opposition between the dark and nocturnal, lower part of the house and the noble and brightly-lit, upper part. The opposition which is set up between the external world and the house only takes on its full meaning therefore if one of the terms of this relation, that is to say the house, is itself seen as being divided according to the same principles which oppose it to the other term. It is therefore both true and false to say that the external world is opposed to the house as male is to female, or day to night, or fire to water, etc., since the second term of these oppositions divides up each time into itself and its opposites.

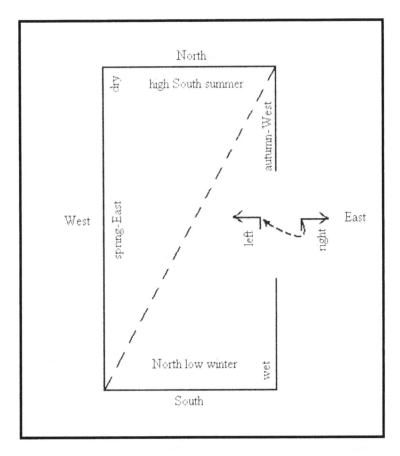

In short the most apparent opposition male (or day, fire, etc)/female (or night, water, etc.) may well mask the opposition: male/female-male/female-female, and in the same way the homology male/female; female-male/female-female. It is obvious from this that the first opposition is but a transformation of the second, which presupposes a change in the field of reference at the end of which the female-female is no longer opposed to the female-male and instead, the group which they form is opposed to a third term: female-male/female-female à female (=female-male + female-female)/male.

As a microcosm organized according to the same oppositions which govern all the universe, the house maintains a relation with the rest of the universe which is that of a homology: but from another point of view, the world is the house taken as a whole in a relation with the rest of the world which is one of opposition, and the principles of which are none other than those which govern the organization of the internal space of the house as much as they do the rest of the world and, more generally all the areas of existence. Thus, the opposition between the world of female life and the

world of the city of men is based upon the same principles as the two systems of oppositions it opposes. It follows from this that the application to
opposed areas of the same principium divisionis, which in fact forms their
very opposition, provides, at the least cost, a surplus of consistence and
does not, in return, result in any confusion between these areas. The structure of the type a:b;b1:b2 is doubtless one of the simplest and most powerful that can be employed in a mythico-ritual system since it cannot oppose without simultaneously uniting (and inversely), while all the time
being capable of integrating in a set order an infinite number of data, by the
simple application of the same principle of division indefinitely repeated.

It also follows from this that each of the two parts of the house (and, by
the same token, all of the objects which are put there and all the activities
which take place there) is in a certain way qualified to two degrees, namely,
firstly as female (nocturnal, dark, etc.) inasmuch as it participates in the
universe of the house, and secondly as male or female, inasmuch as it participates in one or the other of the divisions of this universe. Thus, for example, when the proverb says: "Man is the lamp of the outside and woman
the lamp of the inside," it is to be understood that man is the true light, that
of the day, and woman the light of the darkness, the dark light; moreover,
she is of course, to the moon what man is to the sun. In the same way, when
she works with wool, woman produces the beneficent protection of weaving, the whiteness of which symbolizes happiness; the weaving-loom,
which is the instrument par excellence of female activity and which faces
the east like the plough, its homologue, is at the same time the east of the
internal space of the house with the result that, within the system of the
house, it has a male value as a symbol of protection. Likewise, the fireplace,
which is the navel of the house (itself identified with the womb of the
mother), where smoulder the embers, which is a secret, hidden and female
fire, is the domain of woman who is invested with total authority in all matters concerning the kitchen and the management of the food-stores; she
takes her meals at the fireside whilst man, turned towards the outside, sits
in the middle of the room or in the courtyard. Nevertheless, in all the rites
where they play a part, the fireplace and the stones which surround it derive their potent magic from their participation in the order of fire, of that
which is dry and of the solar heat, whether it is a question of providing protection against the evil eye or against illness or to summon up fine weather.
The house is also endowed with a double significance: if it is true that it is
opposed to the public world as nature is to culture, it is also, in another respect, culture; is it not said of the jackal, the incarnation of all that is savage
in nature, that it does not have a home?

But one of the other of the two systems of opposition which define the
house, either in its internal organization or in its relationship with the outside world, will take prime importance according to whether the house is

considered from the male point of view or the female point of view: whereas, for the man, the house is less a place one goes into than a place from which one goes out, the woman can only confer upon these two movements and the different definitions of the house which form an integral part with them an inverse importance and meaning, since movement towards the outside consists above all for her of acts of expulsion and it is her specific role to be responsible for all movement towards the inside, that is to say, from the threshold towards the fireplace. The significance of the movement towards the outside is never quite so apparent as in the rite performed by the mother, on the seventh day after a birth, "in order that her son be courageous": striding across the threshold, she sets her right foot upon the carding comb and simulates a fight with the first boy she meets. The sallying forth is a specifically male movement which leads towards other men and also towards dangers and threats which it is important to confront like a man, a man as spiky, when it is a question of hounor, as the points of comb. Going out, or more exactly opening (*fatah*), is the equivalent of "being in the morning" (*sebah*). A man who has respect for himself should leave the house at daybreak, morning being the day of the daytime, and the sallying forth from the house, in the morning, being a birth: whence the importance of things encountered which are a potent for the whole day, with the result that, in the case of bad encounters (blacksmith, woman carrying an empty leather bottle, shouts or a quarrel, a deformed being), it is best to "remake one's morning" or "one's going out."

Bearing this in mind, it is not difficult to understand the importance accorded to the direction which the house faces: the front of the house, the one which shelters the head of the family and which contains a stable, is almost always turned towards the east, and the main door—in opposition to the low and narrow door, reserved for the women, which opens in the direction of the garden, at the back of the house is commonly called the door of the east (*thabburth thacherqith*) or else the door of the street, the door of the upper part or the great door. Considering the way in which the villages present themselves and the lower position of the stable, the upper part of the house, with the fireplace is situated in the north, the stable is in the south and the wall of the weaving-loom is in the west. It follows from this that the movement one makes when going towards the house in order to enter it is directed from the east to the west, in opposition to the movement made to come out which, is accordance with the supreme direction, is toward the east, that is to say, towards the height, the light and the good: the ploughman turns his oxen towards the east when he harnesses them, and also when he unharnesses them, and he starts ploughing from west to east; likewise the harvesters arrange themselves opposite the *qibla* and they cut the throat of the sacrificial ox facing the east. Limitless are the acts which are performed in accordance with this principal direction for these are all the acts of importance involving the fertility and the prosperity of the group. It will suffice to note that the verb *qabel* means not only to face, to affront with honour and to receive in a worthy manner, but also to face the east (*lqibla*) and the future (*qabel*).

If we refer back now to the internal organization of the house we will see that its orientation is exactly the inverse of that of the external space, as if it had been obtained by a semi-rotation around the front wall or the threshold taken as an axis. The wall of the weaving-loom, which one faces as soon as one crosses the threshold, and which is lit up directly by the morning sun, is the light of the inside (as the woman is the lamp of the inside), that is to say, the east of the inside symmetrical to the external east, whence it derives its borrowed light. The interior and dark side of the front wall represents the west of the house and is the place of sleep which is left behind when one goes from the door towards the *kanuin*; the door corresponds symbolically to the "door of the year" which is the beginning of the wet season and the agrarian year. Likewise, the two gable walls, the wall of the stable and the wall of the fireplace, take on two opposed meaning depending on which of their sides is being considered: to the external north corresponds the south (and the summer) of the inside, that is to say, the side of the house which is in front of one and on one's right when one goes in facing the weaving-loom; to the external south corresponds the inside north (and the winter), that is to say the stable, which is situated behind and on the left when one goes from the door towards the fireplace. The division of the house into a dark part (the west and north sides) and a light part (the east and south sides) corresponds to the division of the year into a wet season and a dry season. In short, to each exterior side of the wall (*essur*) there corresponds a region of interior space (which the Kabyles refer to as *tharkunt*, which means roughly, the side) which has a symmetrical and inverse sense signification in the system of internal oppositions; each of the two spaces can therefore be defined as the set of movements made to effect the same change of position, that is to say a semi-rotation, in relation to the other, the threshold acting as the axis of rotation.

It is not possible completely to understand the importance and symbolic values attached to the thresholds in the system, unless one is aware that it owes its function as a magic frontier to the fact that it is the place of a logical inversion and that, as the obligatory place of passage and of meeting between the two spaces, which are defined in relation to socially qualified movements of the body and crossings from one place to another, it is logically the place where the world is reversed.

Thus each of the universes has its own east and the two movements that are most pregnant with meaning and magical consequences, the movement from the threshold to the fireplace, which should bring plenitude and whose performance or ritual control is the responsibility of woman, and the movement from the threshold towards the exterior world which, but its in-augural value, contains all that the future holds and especially the future of agrarian work, may be carried out in accordance with the beneficent direc-tion, that is to say from west to east. The twofold orientation in the space of the house means that it is possible both to go in and to go out starting from the right foot, both in the literal and the figurative sense, with all the magical benefit attached to this observance, without there ever being a break in the relation which unites the right to the upper part, to the light and to the good. The semi-rotation of the space around the threshold en-sures then, if we may use the expression, the maximization of the magical benefit since both centripetal and centrifugal movement are performed in a space which is organized in such a way that once comes into it facing the light and one goes out of it facing the light.

The two symmetrical and inverse spaces are not interchangeable but hierar-chized, the internal space being nothing but the inverses image or the mirror-reflection of the male space. It is not by chance that only the direction which the door faces is explicitly prescribed whereas the interior organization of space is never consciously perceived and is even less desired to be so organized by the inhabitants. The orientation of the house is fundamentally defined from the outside, from the point of view of men and, if one may say so, by men and for men, as the place from which men come out. The house is an em-pire within an empire, but one which always remains subordinate because, even though it presents all the properties and all the relations which define the archetypal world, it remains a reverse world, an inverted reflection. "Man is the lamp of the outside and woman the lamp of the inside."

QUERIES

- What are some of the activities and objects associated with the darker, lower portion of a Kabyle house?
- What is *haram*? In what sense is this concept an example of habitus?
- What are the divergent domains of male and female work in Kabyle so-ciety?
- What is the significance of the east? How is this reflected in architectural terms, agricultural practices, and the seating of guests in Berber society?

CONNECTIONS

- Compare Bourdieu's article to Lévi-Strauss's article "The Structural Study of Myth." In what ways are the two writings similar? At what points do they differ?

- How would Marvin Harris react to Bourdieu's article? Would Harris consider these symbolic associations examples of infrastructure, structure, or superstructure?
- Would you consider the Kabyle house an example of what Sherry Ortner called "key symbols"?

24

Eric R. Wolf

INTRODUCTION

The American anthropologist Eric Wolf (1923–1999) had a sustained interest in the dimensions of culture, history, and power over his lengthy career (see Moore 2008:343–64). The following articles by Wolf bracket his career and illustrate the connections and developments of his interest.

In his 1955 "Types of Latin American Peasantry: A Preliminary Discussion," Wolf contrasts two major modes of peasant communities: the closed corporate peasant community and the open peasant community. These two forms of peasant communities—and Wolf briefly discusses five other types—are widespread in Latin America. Wolf's own dissertation research, as a member of Julian Steward's Puerto Rico project (see Moore 2008:197–98), examined an open peasant community of coffee farmers, while he drew on extensive anthropological literature to define the closed corporate peasant community. Wolf's typology of peasant communities was less a tool for classifying peasant communities than it was a comparative device (Marshall Sahlins used a similar tactic in writing about political forms in Oceania [see chapter 25; Moore 2008:368–69].) Wolf shows how peasant communities vary in terms of agriculture, economy, internal social regulations, and their interactions with larger nation-states.

But at a more fundamental level, Wolf argues that peasant societies cannot be understood except in terms of broader historical contexts and power relationships. The anthropologist cannot view such societies as culturally insulated entities, timeless reflections of core values, or functionally integrated systems. Rather, peasant societies always exist in reference to other social forces. There are no peasant villages without urban centers. Peasant economies are always—although varyingly—articulated to national and/or global markets. Peasant social norms are, in part, responses to the threats and opportunities posed by nation-states or colonial governments. And finally, peasant societies only exist given a specific set of historical circumstances: the growing power of city-states, the spread of empires, or the expansion of capitalism. All these issues are embedded in Wolf's 1955 article.

Decades later, Wolf remained interested in those issues. In his 1990 article, "Facing Power—Old Insights, New Questions," Wolf focuses on *power*, a term that has multiple meanings in Western intellectual traditions, and outlines four modes of power; in this article, Wolf concentrates on the relation between tactical/organizational power and structural power. Wolf summarizes three ethnographic research projects—including the Puerto Rico project in which he participated—and points out their respective strengths and weaknesses in identifying power. He also summarizes a variety of ethnographic cases in which power is deployed and employed in differing modes. Just as in his earlier discussion of peasant types, Wolf is not interested in pigeonholing cultural phenomena in discrete categories but, rather, in viewing them as the reflections of broader processes involving human agency, historical contingencies, and cultural traditions (see Moore 2008: 289–94).

PRIMARY TEXT: *TYPES OF LATIN AMERICAN PEASANTRY: A PRELIMINARY DISCUSSION*

The Peasant Type

As anthropology has become increasingly concerned with the study of modern communities, anthropologists have paid increasing attention to the social and cultural characteristics of the peasantry. It will be the purpose of this article to draw up a tentative typology of peasant groups for Latin America, as a basis for further field work and discussion. Such a typology will of necessity raise more questions than can be answered easily at the present time. To date, anthropologists working in Latin America have dealt mainly with groups with "Indian" cultures, and available anthropological literature reflects this major interest. Any projected reorientation of inquiry from typologies based mainly on characteristics of culture content to typologies based on similarities or dissimilarities of structure has implications with which no single writer could expect to cope. This article is therefore provisional in character, and its statements wholly open to discussion.

There have been several recent attempts to draw a line between primitives and peasants. Redfield, for example, has discussed the distinction in the following words (1953:31):

> There were no peasants before the first cities. And those surviving primitive peoples who do not live in terms of the city are not peasants. . . . The peasant is a rural native whose long established order of life takes important account of the city.

Kroeber has also emphasized the relation between the peasant and the city (1948:284):

> Peasants are definitely rural—yet live in relation to market towns; they form a class segment of a larger population which usually contains also urban centers, sometimes metropolitan capitals. They constitute part-societies with part-cultures.
> Peasants thus form "horizontal socio-cultural segments," as this term has been defined by Steward (1950:115).

Redfield further states that the city was made "possible" through the labor of its peasants (1953), and both definitions imply—though they do not state outright—that the city consumes a large part of what the peasant produces. Urban life is impossible without production of an agricultural surplus in the countryside.

Since we are interested less in the generic peasant type than in discriminating between different types of peasants, we must go on to draw distinctions between groups of peasants involved in divergent types of urban culture (for a discussion of differences in urban centers, cf. Beals 1951:8–9; Hoselitz 1953). It is especially important to recognize the effects of the industrial revolution and the growing world market on peasant segments the world over.

These have changed both the cultural characteristics of such segments and the character of their relations with other segments. Peasants everywhere have become involved in market relations of a vastly different order of magnitude than those which prevailed before the advent of industrial culture. Nor can this expansion be understood as a purely unilineal phenomenon. There have been different types of industry and markets, different types of industrial expansion and market growth. These have affected different parts of the world in very different ways. The peasantries found in the world today are the multiple products of such multilineal growth. At the same time, peasants are no longer the primary producers of wealth. Industry and trade rather than agriculture now produce the bulk of the surpluses needed to support segments not directly involved in the processes of production. Various kinds of large scale agricultural enterprises have grown up to compete with the peasant for economic resources and opportunities. This has produced a world-wide "crisis of the peasantry" (Firth 1952: 12), related to the increasingly marginal role of the peasantry within the prevalent economic system.

In choosing a definition of the peasant which would be adequate for our present purpose, we must remember that definitions are tools of thought, and not eternal verities. Firth, for example, defines the term as widely as possible, including not only agriculturists but also fishermen and rural craftsmen (1952:87). Others might be tempted to add independent rubber gatherers and strip miners. For the sake of initial analysis, this writer has found it convenient to consider each of these various kinds of enterprise separately and thus to define the term "peasant" as strictly as possible. Three distinctions may serve as the basis for such a definition. All three are chosen with a view to Latin American conditions, and all seem flexible enough to include varieties which we may discover in the course of our inquiry.

First, let us deal with the peasant only as an agricultural producer. This means that for the purposes of the present article we shall draw a line between peasants, on the one hand, and fishermen, strip miners, rubber gatherers, and livestock keepers, on the other. The economic and cultural implications of livestock keeping, for example, are sufficiently different from those of agriculture to warrant separate treatment. This is especially true in Latin America, where livestock keeping has been carried on mainly on large estates rather than on small holdings.

Second, we should—for our present purpose—distinguish between the peasant who retains effective control of land and the tenant whose control of land is subject to an outside authority. This distinction has some importance in Latin America. Effective control of land by the peasant is generally insured through direct ownership, through undisputed squatter rights, or through customary arrangements governing the rental and use of land. He does not have to pay dues to an outside landowner. Tenants, on the other hand, tend to seek security primarily through acceptance of outside controls over the arrangements of production and distribution, and thus often accept subordinate roles within hierarchically organized networks of relationships. The peasants generally retain much greater control of their processes of production. Outside controls become manifest primarily when they sell their goods on the market. Consideration of tenant segments belongs properly with a discussion of haciendas and plantations rather than with a discussion of the peasantry. This does not mean that in dealing with Latin America we can afford to forget for a moment that large estates overshadowed other forms of landholding for many centuries, or that tenant segments may exert greater ultimate influence on the total sociocultural whole than peasants.

Third, the peasant aims at subsistence, not at reinvestment. The starting point of the peasant is the needs which are defined by his culture. His answer, the production of cash crops for a market, is prompted largely by his inability to meet these needs within the sociocultural segment of which he is a part. He sells cash crops to get money, but this money is used in turn to buy goods and services which he requires to subsist and to maintain his social status, rather than to enlarge his scale of operations. We may thus draw a line between the peasant and another agricultural type whom we call the "farmer." The farmer views agriculture as a business enterprise. He begins his operations with a sum of money which he invests in a farm. The crops produced are sold not only to provide goods and services for the farm operator but to permit amortization and expansion of his business. The aim of the peasant is subsistence. The aim of the farmer is reinvestment (Wolf 1951:60–61).

The term "peasant" indicates a structural relationship, not a particular culture content. By "structural relations" we mean "relatively fixed relations between parts rather than . . . the parts or elements themselves." By "structure," similarly, we mean "the mode in which the parts stand to each other" (Kroeber and Kluckhohn 1952:62, 63). A typology of peasantries should be set up on the basis of regularities in the occurrence of structural relationships rather than on the basis of regularities in the occurrence of similar culture elements. In selecting out certain structural features rather than others to provide a starting point for the formulation of types we may proceed wholly on an empirical basis. The selection of primarily economic criteria would be congruent with the present interest in typologies based on economic and sociopolitical features alone. The functional implications of these features are more clearly understood at present than those of other features of culture, and their dominant role in the development of the organizational framework has been noted empirically in many studies of particular cultures.

In setting up a typology of peasant segments we immediately face the difficulty that peasants are not primitives, that is, the culture of a peasant segment cannot be understood in terms of itself but is a part-culture, related to some larger integral whole. Certain relationships among the features of peasant culture are tied to bodies of relationships outside the peasant culture, yet help determine both its character and continuity. The higher the level of integration of such part-cultures, the greater the weight of such outside determinants. In complex societies certain components of the social superstructure rather than ecology seem increasingly to be determinants of further developments (Steward 1938:262).

This is especially true when we reach the organizational level of the capitalist market, where the relationship of technology and environment is mediated through complicated mechanisms of credit or political control which may originate wholly outside the part-culture under investigation.

We must not only be cognizant of outside factors which affect the culture of the part-culture. We must also account for the manner in which the part-culture is organized into the larger sociocultural whole. Unlike other horizontal sociocultural segments, like traders or businessmen, peasants function primarily within a local setting rather than on an interlocal or nonlocal basis. This produces considerable local variation within a given peasant segment. It means also that the peasantry is integrated into the sociocultural whole primarily through the structure of the community. We must therefore do more than define different kinds of peasants. We must also analyze the manner in which they are integrated with the outside world. In other words, a typology of peasants must include a typology of the kinds of communities in which they live.

The notion of type also implies a notion of history. The functioning of a particular segment depends on the historical interplay of factors which affect it. This point is especially important where we deal with part-cultures which must adapt their internal organization to changes in the total social field of which they are a part. Integration into a larger sociocultural whole is a historical process. We must be able to place part-cultures on the growth curve of the totality of which they form a part. In building a typology, we must take into account the growth curve of our cultural types.

Here we may summarize briefly our several criteria for the construction of a typology of peasant groups. First, it would seem to be advisable to define our subject matter as narrowly as possible. Second, we shall be interested in structure, rather than in culture content. Third, the initial criteria for our types can be primarily economic or sociopolitical, but should of course include as many other features as possible. Fourth, the types should be seen as component parts of larger wholes. The typical phenomena with which we are dealing are probably produced principally by the impact of outside forces on preexisting local cultures. Fifth, some notion of historical trajectory should be included in the formulation of a type.

Two Types of Peasant Part-Cultures

To make our discussion more concrete, let us turn to an analysis of two types of peasant segments. The first type comprises certain groups in the high highlands of Latin America; the second covers peasant groups found in humid low highlands and tropical lowlands. While these types are based on available field reports, they should be interpreted as provisional models for the construction of a typology, and thus subject to future revision.

Our first type (1) comprises peasants practicing intensive cultivation in the high highlands of Nuclear America. While some production is carried on to cover immediate subsistence needs, these peasants must sell a little cash produce to buy goods produced elsewhere (Pozas 1952:311). Production is largely unsupported by fluid capital. It flows into a system of village markets which is highly congruent with such a marginal economy.

The geographical area in which this type of peasant prevails formed the core area of Spanish colonial America. It supported the bulk of Spanish settlement, furnished the labor force required by Spanish enterprises, and provided the mineral wealth which served as the driving force of Spanish colonization. Integration of this peasantry into the colonial structure was achieved typically through the formation of communities which inhibited direct contact between the individual and the outside world but interposed between them an organized communal structure. This structure we shall call here the "corporate" community. It has shown a high degree of persistence, which has been challenged successfully only in recent years when alternative structures are encroaching upon it. Anthropologists have studied a number of such communities in highland Peru and Mexico.

The reader will be tempted immediately to characterize this type of community as "Indian" and perhaps to ask if we are not dealing here with a survival from pre-Columbian times. Since structure rather than culture content is our main concern here, we shall emphasize the features of organization which may make this type of community like corporate communities elsewhere, rather than characterize it in purely ethnographic terms. Moreover, it is necessary to explain the persistence of any survival over a period of three hundred years. As we hope to show below, persistence of "Indian" culture content seems to have depended primarily on maintenance of this structure. Where the structure collapsed, traditional cultural forms quickly gave way to new alternatives of outside derivation.

The distinctive characteristic of the corporate peasant community is that it represents a bounded social system with clear-cut limits, in relation to both outsiders and insiders. It has structural identity over time. Seen from the outside, the community as a whole carries on a series of activities and upholds certain "collective representations." Seen from within, it defines the rights and duties of its members and prescribes large segments of their behavior.

Fortes recently analyzed groupings of a corporate character based on kinship (1953:25–29). The corporate peasant community resembles these other units in its corporate character but is no longer held together by kinship. It may once have been based on kinship units of a peculiar type (see Kirchhoff 1949:293), and features of kinship organization persist, such as a tendency toward local endogamy (for Mesoamerica, cf. Redfield and Tax 1952:31; for the Quechua, cf. Mishkin 1946:453) or in occasionally differential rights of old and new settlers. Nevertheless, the corporate community in Latin America represents the end product of a long process of reorganization which began in pre-Columbian times and was carried through under Spanish rule. As a result of the conquest any kinship feature which this type of community may have had was relegated to secondary importance. Members of the community were made co-owners of a landholding corporation (Garcia 1948:269), a co-ownership which implied systematic participation in communal political and religious affairs.

Several considerations may have prompted Crown policy toward such communities. First, the corporate community performing joint labor services for an overlord was a widespread characteristic of European economic feudalism. In trying to curtail the political power of a potential new landholding class in the Spanish colonies the Crown took over management of Indian communities in order to deny the conquerors direct managerial control over labor. The Crown attempted to act as a go-between and labor contractor for both peasant community and landowner. Second, the corporate community fitted well into the political structure of the Spanish dynastic state, which attempted to incorporate each subcultural group and to define its radius of activity by law (Wolf 1953:100–101). This enabled the Crown to marshal the resources of such a group as an organized unit, and to impose its economic, social, and religious controls by a type of indirect rule. Third, the corporate structure of the peasant communities permitted the imposition of communal as well as of individual burdens of forced labor and taxation. This was especially important in view of the heavy loss of labor power through flight or disease. The imposition of the burden on a community rather than on individuals favored maintenance of a steady level of production.

Given this general historical background, what is the distinctive set of relationships characteristic of the corporate peasant community?

The first of these is location on marginal land. Needs within the larger society which might compel the absorption and exploitation of this land are weak or absent, and the existing level of technology and transportation may make such absorption difficult. In other words, the amount of energy required to destroy the existing structure of the corporate community and to reorganize it at present outweighs the capacity of the larger society.

In the corporate peasant community marginal land tends to be exploited by means of a traditional technology involving the members of the community in the continuous physical effort of manual labor.

Marginal location and traditional technology together limit the production power of the community, and thus its ability to produce cash crops for the market. This in turn limits the number of goods brought in from the outside which the community can afford to consume. The community is poor.

Within this economic setting, the corporate structure of the community is retained by community jurisdiction over the free disposal of land. Needless to say, community controls tend to be strongest where land is owned in common and re-allocated among members every year. But even where private property in land is the rule within the community, as is common today, the communal taboo on sale of land to outsiders (cf. Aguirre 1952: 149; Lewis 1951:124; Mishkin 1946:443) severely limits the degree to which factors outside the community can affect the structure of private property and related class differences within the community. Land is thus not a complete commodity. The taboo on sale of land to outsiders may be reinforced by other communal rights, such as gleaning rights or the right to graze cattle on any land within the community after the harvest.

The community possesses a system of power which embraces the male members of the community and makes the achievement of power a matter of community decision rather than a matter of individually achieved status (Redfield and Tax 1952:39; Mishkin 1946:459). This system of power is often tied into a religious system or into a series of interlocking religious systems. The political-religious system as a whole tends to define the boundaries of the community and acts as a rallying point and symbol of collective unity. Prestige within the community is largely related to rising from religious office to office along a prescribed ladder of achievement. Conspicuous consumption is geared to this communally approved system of power and religion rather than to private individual show. This makes individual conspicuous consumption incidental to communal expenditure. Thus the community at one and the same time levels differences of wealth which might intensify class divisions within the community to the detriment of the corporate structure and symbolically reasserts the strength and integrity of its structure before the eyes of its members (Aguirre 1952:242; Mishkin 1946:468).

The existence of such leveling mechanisms does not mean that class divisions within the corporate community do not exist. But it does mean that the class structure must find expression within the boundaries set by the community. The corporate structure acts to impede the mobilization of capital and wealth within the community in terms of the outside world which employs wealth capitalistically. It thus blunts the impact of the main opening wedge calculated to set up new tensions within the community and thus to hasten its disintegration (cf. Aguirre 1952; Carrasco 1952:48).

While striving to guarantee its members some basic livelihood within the confines of the community, the lack of resources and the very need to sustain the system of religion and power economically force the community to enter the outside market. Any imposition of taxes, any increase in expenditures relative to the productive capacity of the community, or the internal growth of the population on a limited amount of land, must result in compensatory economic reactions in the field of production. These may be wage labor, or the development of some specialization which has competitive advantages within the marginal economy of such communities. These may include specializations in trade, as among the Zapotecs, Tarascans, or Collas, or in witchcraft, as among the Killawallas or Kamilis of Bolivia.

In the field of consumption, increases of expenditures relative to the productive capacity of the economic base are met with attempts to decrease expenditure by decreasing consumption. This leads to the establishment of a culturally recognized standard of consumption which consciously excludes cultural alternative (on cultural alternatives, their rejection or acceptance, cf. Linton 1936:282–83). By reducing alternative items of consumption, along with the kinds of behavior and ideal norms which make use of these items of consumption, the community reduces the threat to its integrity. Moore and Tumin have called this kind of reaction ignorance with a "structural function" (1949:788).

In other words, we are dealing here not merely with a lack of knowledge, an absence of information, but with a defensive ignorance, an active denial of outside alternatives which, if accepted, might threaten the corporate structure (Beals's "rejection pattern" [1952:229]; Mishkin 1946:443). Unwillingness to admit outsiders as competitors for land or as carriers of cultural alternatives may account for the prevalent tendency toward community endogamy (Redfield and Tax 1952:31; Mishkin 1946:453).

Related to the need to maintain a steady state by decreasing expenditures is the conscious effort to eat and consume less by "pulling in one's belt," while working more. This "exploitation of the self" is culturally institutionalized in what might be called a "cult of poverty." Hard work and poverty as well as behavior symbolic of these, such as going barefoot or wearing "Indian" clothes (cf. Tumin 1952:85–94), are extolled, and laziness and greed and behavior associated with these vices are denounced (Carrasco 1952:47).

The increase in output and concomitant restriction of consumption is carried out primarily within the nuclear family. The family thus acquires special importance in this kind of community, especially in a modern setting (Redfield and Tax 1952:33; Mishkin 1946:449–51). This is primarily because

> on the typical family farm . . . the farmer himself cannot tell you what part of his income comes to him in his capacity as a worker, what in his capacity as a capitalist who has provided tools and implements, or finally what in his capacity as owner of land. In fact, he is not able to tell you how much of his total income stems from his own labors and how much comes from the varied, but important efforts of his wife and children. (Samuelson 1948:761)

The family does not carry on cost-accounting. It does not know how much its labor is worth. Labor is not a commodity for it; it does not sell labor within the family. No money changes hands within the family. It acts as a unit of consumption and it can cut its consumption as a unit. The family is thus the ideal unit for the restriction of consumption and the increase of unpaid performance of work.

The economy of the corporate community is congruent, if not structurally linked, with a marketing system of a peculiar sort. Lack of money resources requires that sales and purchases in the market be small. The highland village markets fit groups with low incomes which can buy only a little at a time (for Mexico, cf. Foster 1948:154; for the Quechua, cf. Mishkin 1946:436). Such markets bring together a much larger supply of articles than merchants of any one community could afford to keep continuously in their stores (Whetten 1948:359). Most goods in such markets are homemade or locally grown (Whetten 1948:358; Mishkin 1946:437). Local producers thus acquire the needed supplementary income, while the character of the commodities offered for sale reinforces the traditional pattern of consumption. Specialization on the part of villages is evident throughout (Whetten 1948; Foster 1948; Mishkin 1946:434). Regular market days in regional sequence making for a wider exchange of local produce (Whetten 1948; Mishkin 1946:436; Valcarcel 1946:477-79) may be due to the fact that villages producing similar products must find outlets far away, as well as to exchanges of produce between highlands and lowlands. The fact that the goods carried are produced in order to obtain small amounts of needed cash in order to purchase other needed goods is evident in the very high percentage of dealings between producer and ultimate consumer. The market is in fact a means of bringing the two into contact (Whetten 1948:359; Foster 1948; Mishkin 1946). The role of the nuclear family in production and in the "exploitation of the self" is evident in the high percentage of goods in whose production the individual or the nuclear family completes an entire production cycle (Foster 1948).

Paralleling the mechanisms of control which are primarily economic in origin are psychological mechanisms like institutionalized envy, which may find expression in various manifestations such as gossip, attacks of the evil eye, or in the fear and practice of witchcraft. The communal organization of the corporate community has often been romanticized; it is sometimes assumed that a communal structure makes for the absence of divisive tensions. Lewis has demonstrated that there is no necessary correlation between communal structure and pervasive good-will among the members of the community (Lewis 1951:428-29). Quite the contrary, it would seem that some form of institutionalized envy plays an important part in such communities (Gillin 1952:208). Kluckhohn has shown that fear of witchcraft acts as an effective leveler in Navaho society (1944:67-68). A similar relationship obtains in the type of community which we are discussing. Here witchcraft, as well as milder forms of institutionalized envy, have an integrative effect in restraining nontraditional behavior, as long as social relationships suffer no serious disruption. It minimizes disruptive phenomena such as economic mobility, abuse of ascribed power, or individual conspicuous show of wealth. On the individual plane, it thus acts to maintain the individual in equilibrium with his neighbors. On the social plane, it reduces the disruptive influences of outside society.

The need to keep social relationships in equilibrium in order to maintain the steady state of the corporate community is internalized in the individual as strong conscious efforts to adhere to the traditional roles, roles which were successful in maintaining the steady state in the past. Hence there appears a strong tendency on the social psychological level to stress "uninterrupted routine practice of traditional patterns" (Gillin 1952:206). Such a psychological emphasis would tend to act against overt expressions of individual autonomy, and set up in individuals strong fears against being thrown out of equilibrium (Gillin 1952:208).

An individual thus carries the culture of such a community, not merely passively as a social inheritance inherited and accepted automatically, but actively. Adherence to the culture validates membership in an existing society and acts as a passport to participation in the life of the community. The particular traits held help the individual remain within the equilibrium of relationships which maintain the community. Corporate communities produce "distinctive cultural, linguistic, and other social attributes," which Beals has aptly called "plural cultures" (1953:333); tenacious defense of this plurality maintains the integrity of such communities.

It is needless to add that any aspect relates to any other, and that changes in one would vitally affect the rest. Thus the employment of traditional technology keeps the land marginal from the point of view of the larger society, keeps the community poor, forces a search for supplementary sources of income, and requires high expenditures of physical labor within the nuclear family. The technology is in turn maintained by the need to adhere to traditional roles in order to validate one's membership in the community, and this adherence is produced by the conscious denial of alternative forms of behavior, by institutionalized envy, and by the fear of being thrown out of equilibrium with one's neighbor. The various aspects enumerated thus exhibit a very high degree of covariance.

The second type (2) which we shall discuss comprises peasants who regularly sell a cash crop constituting probably between 50 and 75 per cent of their total production. Geographically, this type of peasant is distributed over humid low highlands and tropical lowlands. Present-day use of their environments has been dictated by a shift in demand on the world market for crops from the American tropics during the latter part of the nineteenth century and the early part of the twentieth. On the whole, production for the market by this type of peasant has been in an ascendant phase, though often threatened by intermittent periods of decline and depression.

In seasonally rainy tropical lowlands, these peasants may raise sugar cane. In chronically rainy lowlands, such as northern Colombia or Venezuela or coastal Ecuador, they have tended to grow cocoa or bananas.

The development of this peasant segment has been most impressive in humid low highlands, where the standard crop is coffee (Platt 1943:498). This crop is easily grown on both small and large holdings, as is the case in Colombia, Guatemala, Costa Rica, and parts of the West Indies.

Such cash crop production requires outside capitalization. The amount and kind of capitalization will have important ramifications throughout the particular local adaptation made. Peasants of this type receive such capitalization from the outside, but mainly on a traditional, small-scale, intermittent and speculative basis. Investments are not made either to stabilize the market or to reorganize the apparatus of production and distribution of the peasantry. Few peasant groups of this type have been studied fully by anthropologists, and any discussion of them must to some extent remain conjectural until further work adds to our knowledge. For the construction of this type the writer has relied largely on his own field work in Puerto Rico (Wolf 1951) and on insights gained from studies made in southern Brazil (Herrmann 1950; Pierson and others 1951).

The typical structure which serves to integrate this type of peasant segment with other segments and with the larger sociocultural whole we shall here call the "open" community. The open community differs from the corporate peasant community in a number of ways. The corporate peasant community is composed primarily of one subculture, the peasantry. The open community comprises a number of subcultures of which the peasantry is only one, although the most important functional segment. The corporate community emphasizes resistance to influences from without which might threaten its integrity. The open community, on the other hand, emphasizes continuous interaction with the outside world and ties its fortunes to outside demands. The corporate community frowns on individual accumulation and display of wealth and strives to reduce the effects of such accumulation on the communal structure. It resists reshaping of relationships; it defends the traditional equilibrium. The open-ended community permits and expects individual accumulation and display of wealth during periods of rising outside demand and allows this new wealth much influence in the periodic reshaping of social ties.

Historically, the open peasant community arose in response to the rising demand for cash crops which accompanied the development of capitalism in Europe. In a sense, it represents the offshoot of a growing type of society which multiplied its wealth by budding off to form new communities to produce new wealth in their turn. Many peasant communities were established in Latin America by settlers who brought to the New World cultural patterns of consumption and production which from the outset involved them in relations with an outside market. Being a Spaniard or Portuguese meant more than merely speaking Spanish or Portuguese or adhering to certain kinds of traditional behavior and ideal norms. It implied participation in a complex system of hierarchical relationships and prestige which required the consumption of goods that could be produced only by means of a complicated division of labor and had to be acquired in the market. No amount of Indian blankets delivered as tribute could make up for the status gained by the possession of one shirt of Castilian silk, or for a small ruffle of Cambrai lace. Prestige goods as well as necessities like iron could only be bought with money, and the need for money drove people to produce for an outside market. The demand for European goods by Spanish colonists was enormous and in turn caused heavy alterations in the economic structure of the mother country (Sombart 1928, I, Pt. 2:780–81). In the establishment of the open community, therefore, the character of the outside society was a major determinant from the beginning.

It would be a mistake, moreover, to visualize the development of the world market in terms of continuous and even expansion, and to suppose therefore that the line of development of particular peasant communities always leads from lesser involvement in the market to more involvement. This line of reasoning would seem to be especially out of place in the case of Latin America where the isolation and homogeneity of the "folk" are often secondary, that is to say, follow in time after a stage of much contact and heterogeneity. Redfield has recognized aspects of this problem in his recent category of "remade folk" (1953:47). Such a category should cover not only the Yucatecan Indians who fled into the isolation of the bush but also groups of settlers with a culture of basically Iberian derivation which were once in the mainstream of commercial development, only to be left behind on its poverty-stricken margins (cf., e.g., the Spanish settlements at Culiacgn, New Galicia, described by Mota [1940:99–1021], and Chiapa Real, Chiapas, described by Gage [1929:151–531]).

Latin America has been involved in major shifts and fluctuations of the market since the period of initial European conquest. It would appear, for example, that a rapid expansion of commercial development in New Spain during the sixteenth century was followed by a "century of depression" in the seventeenth (cf. Borah 1951; Chevalier 1952:xii, 54). The slack was taken up again in the eighteenth century, with renewed shrinkage and disintegration of the market in the early part of the nineteenth. During the second part of the nineteenth century and the beginning of the twentieth, many Latin American countries were repeatedly caught up in speculative booms of cash crop production for foreign markets, often with disastrous results in the case of market failure. Entire communities might find their market gone overnight, and revert to the production of subsistence crops for their own use.

Two things seem clear from this discussion. First, in dealing with present day Latin America it would seem advisable to beware of treating production for subsistence and production for the market as two progressive stages of development. Rather, we must allow for the cyclical alternation of the two kinds of production within the same community and realize that from the point of view of the community both kinds may be alternative responses to changes in conditions of the outside market. This means that a synchronic study of such a community is insufficient, because it cannot reveal how the community can adapt to such seemingly radical changes. Second, we must look for the mechanisms which make such changes possible.

In the corporate peasant community, the relationships of individuals and kin groups within the community are bounded by a common structure. We have seen that the community aims primarily at maintaining an equilibrium of roles within the community in an effort to keep intact its outer boundary. Maintenance of the outer boundary reacts in turn on the stability of the equilibrium within it. The open community lacks such a formalized corporate structure. It neither limits its membership nor insists on a defensive boundary. Quite the contrary, it permits free permeation by outside influences.

In contrast to the corporate peasant community where the community retains the right to review and revise individual decisions, the open community lends itself to rapid shifts in production because it is possible to mobilize the peasant and to orient him rapidly toward the expanding market. Land is usually owned privately. Decisions for change can be made by individual families. Property can be mortgaged, or pawned in return for capital. The community qua community cannot interfere in such change.

As in the corporate peasant community, land tends to be marginal and technology primitive. Yet functionally both land and technology are elements in a different complex of relationships. The buyers of peasant produce have an interest in the continued "backwardness" of the peasant. Reorganization of his productive apparatus would absorb capital and credit which can be spent better in expanding the market by buying means of transportation, engaging middlemen, etc. Moreover, by keeping the productive apparatus unchanged, the buyer can reduce the risk of having his capital tied up in the means of production of the peasant holding, if and when the bottom drops out of the market. The buyers of peasant produce thus trade increasing productivity per man-hour for the lessened risks of investment. We may say that the marginality of land and the poor technology are here a function of the speculative market. In the case of need, the investor merely withdraws credit, while the peasant returns to subsistence production by means of his traditional technology.

The fact that cash crop production can be undertaken on peasant holdings without materially reorganizing the productive apparatus implies furthermore that the amount of cash crop produced by each peasant will tend to be small, as will be the income which he receives after paying off all obligations. This does not mean that the aggregate amounts of such production cannot

reach respectable sums, nor that the amounts of profit accruing to middlemen from involvement in such production need be low.

In this cycle of subsistence crops and cash crops, subsistence crops guarantee a stable minimum livelihood, where cash crops promise higher
money returns but involve the family in the hazards of the fluctuating market. The peasant is always concerned with the problem of striking some sort
of balance between subsistence production and cash crop production. Preceding cycles of cash crop production have enabled him to buy goods and
services which he cannot afford if he produces only for his own subsistence.
Yet an all-out effort to increase his ability to buy more goods and services
of this kind may spell his end as an independent agricultural producer. His
tendency is thus to rely on a basic minimum of subsistence production and
to expand his cash purchases only slowly. Usually he can rely on traditional
norms of consumption which define a decent standard of living in terms of
a fixed number of culturally standardized needs. Such needs are of course
not only economic but may include standardized expenditures for religious
or recreational purposes, or for hospitality (cf. Wolf 1951:64). Nor are these
needs static. Viewing the expansion of the market from the point of view of
subsistence, however, permits the peasant to expand his consumption only
slowly.

> In cutting down on money expenditures, he defers purchases of new goods, and
> distributes his purchases over a long period of time. The peasant standard of liv-
> ing is undergoing change but the rate of that change is slow (Wolf 1951:65).

The cultural yardstick enables him to limit the rate of expansion but also
permits him to retrench when he has overextended himself economically.
As in the corporate peasant community, the unit within which consumption can best be restricted while output is stepped up is again the nuclear
family.

This modus operandi reacts back on his technology and on his ability to
increase his cash income. The buyer of peasant produce knows that the peasant will be slow in expanding his demand for money. He can therefore count
on accumulating his largest share of gain during the initial phase of a growing market, a factor which adds to the speculative character of the economy.

Peasants who are forced overnight to reorient their production from the
production of subsistence crops for their own use to cash crop production
are rarely able to generate the needed capital themselves. It must be
pumped into the peasant segment from without, either from another segment within the community, or from outside the community altogether.
The result is that when cash crop production grows important, there is a
tightening of bonds between town and country. Urban families become
concerned with the production and distribution of cash crops and tie their

own fate to the fate of the cash crop. In a society subject to frequent fluctuations of the market but possessed of little fluid capital, there are few formal institutional mechanisms for insuring the flow of capital into peasant production. In a more highly capitalized society, the stock market functions as an impersonal governor of relationships between investors. Corporations form, merge, or dissolve according to the dictates of this governor. In a society where capital accumulation is low, the structure of incorporation tends to be weak or lacking. More important are the informal alliances of families and clients which polarize wealth and power at any given time. Expansion of the market tends to involve the peasant in one or the other of these blocs of family power in town. These blocs, in turn, permit the rapid diffusion of capital into the countryside, since credit is guaranteed by personal relationships between creditor and debtor. Peasant allegiance then acts further to reinforce the social and political position of a given family bloc within the urban sector.

When the market fails, peasants and urban patrons both tend to be caught in the same downward movement. Open communities of the type we are analyzing here are therefore marked by the repeated "circulation of the elite." Blocs of wealth and power form, only to break up and be replaced by similar blocs coming to the fore. The great concern with status is related to this type of mobility. Status on the social plane measures the position in the trajectory of the family on the economic plane. To put it in somewhat oversimplified terms, status in such a society represents the "credit rating" of the family. The economic circulation of the elite thus takes the form of shifts in social status. Such shifts in social and economic position always involve an urban and a rural aspect. If the family cannot find alternate economic supports, it loses prestige within the urban sector, and is sooner or later abandoned by its peasant clientele who must needs seek other urban patrons.

We are thus dealing with a type of community which is continuously faced with alignments, circulation and realignments, both on the socioeconomic and political level. Since social, economic, and political arrangements are based primarily on personal ties, such fluctuations act to redefine personal relationships, and such personal relationships are in turn watched closely for indices of readjustment. Relations between two individuals do not symbolize merely the respective statuses and roles of the two concerned; they involve a whole series of relations which must be evaluated and readjusted if there is any indication of change. This "overloading" of personal relations produces two types of behavior: behavior calculated to retain social status, and a type of behavior which for want of a better term might be called "redefining" behavior, behavior aimed at altering the existing state of personal relationships. Both types will be present in any given social situation, but the dominance of one over the other will be determined by the relative stability or instability of the economic base. Status behavior is loaded with a fierce consciousness of the symbols of status, while "redefining" behavior aims at testing the social limits through such varied mechanisms as humor, invitations to share drinks or meals, visiting, assertions of individual worth, proposals of marriage, and so forth. The most important of these types of behavior, quite absent in the corporate community, consists in the ostentatious exhibition of commodities purchased with money.

This type of redefining behavior ramifies through other aspects of the culture. Wealth is its prerequisite. It is therefore most obvious in the ascendant phases of the economic cycle, rather than when the cycle is leveling off. Such accumulation of goods and the behavior associated with it serves as a challenge to existing relations with kin folk, both real and fictitious, since it is usually associated with a reduction in relations of reciprocal aid and hospitality on which these ties are based.

This disruption of social ties through accumulation is inhibited in the corporate peasant community, but can go on unchecked in the type of community which we are considering. Here forms of envy such as witchcraft are often present, but not institutionalized as in the first type of community. Rather, fear of witchcraft conforms to the hypothesis proposed by Passin (1942:15) that in any society where there is a widespread evasion of a cultural obligation which results in the diffusion of tension and hostility between people, and further if this hostility is not expressed in overt physical strife, . . . sorcery or related non-physical techniques will be brought into play.

Fear of witchcraft in such a community may be interpreted as a product of guilt on the part of the individual who is himself disrupting ties which are valued, coupled with a vague anxiety about the loss of stable definitions of situations in terms of clear-cut status. At the same time, the new possessions and their conspicuous show serves not only to redefine status and thus to reduce anxiety but also as a means of expressing hostility against those who do not own the same goods (cf. Kluckhohn 1944:67, fn. 96). The "invidious" comparisons produced by this hostility in turn produce an increase in the rate of accumulation.

Suggestions for Further Research

The two model types discussed above by no means exhaust the variety of peasant segments to be found in Latin America. They were singled out for consideration because I felt most competent to deal with them in terms of both time and field experience.

*   *   *

In summary, this article has made an attempt to distinguish among several types of peasantry in Latin America. These types are based on cultural structure rather than on culture content. Peasant cultures are seen as part-cultures within larger sociocultural wholes. The character of the larger whole and the mode of integration of the part-culture with it have been given primary weight in constructing the typology. The types suggested remain wholly provisional.

BIBLIOGRAPHY

Aguirre Beltrán, Gonzalo
  1952 Problemas de la población indígena de la cuenca del Tepalcatepec. Memorias del Instituto Nacional Indigenista 3. México, D. F.
Armstrong, John M.
  1949 A Mexican Community: A Study of the Cultural Determinants of Migration. Ph.D. dissertation, Yale University.
Beals, Ralph L.
  1951 Urbanism, Urbanization and Acculturation. American Anthropologist 53:1-10.
  1952 Notes on Acculturation. In Heritage of Conquest Sol Tax, ed. Pp. 225-231. Glencoe, IL: Free Press.
  1953 Social Stratification in Latin America. American Journal of Sociology 58:327-339.
Borah, Woodrow
  1951 New Spain's Century of Depression. Ibero-Americana 35. Berkeley: University of California Press.
Bowman, Isaiah
  1931 The Pioneer Fringe. American Geographical Society Special Publication 13. New York.
Carrasoco Pizana, Perdro
  1952 Tarascan Folk Religion: An Analysis of Economic, Social and Religious Interactions. Middle American Research Institute Publication 17:1-64. Tulane University, New Orleans.
Chevalier, François
  1952 La formation des grands domaines au Mexique: Terre et Société aux XVIe-XVIIe Siecles. Travaux et Mémoires de 1'Institut d'Ethnologie 56. Paris.
Firth, Raymond
  1952 Elements of Social Organization. London: Watts.
Fortes, Meyer
  1953 The Structure of Unilineal Descent Groups. American Anthropologist 55:17-41.
Foster, George M.
  1948 The Folk Economy of Rural Mexico with Special Reference to Marketing. Journal of Marketing 12:153-162.
Gage, Thomas
  1929 [1648] A New Survey of the West Indies, the English American. Argonaut Series. New York: McBride.
García, Antonio
  1948 Regimenes Indigenas de salariado. America Indigena 8:249-287.

Gillin, John
  1952 Ethos and Cultural Aspects of Personality. *In* Heritage of Conquest. Sol
      Tax, ed. Pp. 193–212. Glencoe, IL: Free Press.
Hermann, Lucila
  1950 Classe Media em Guarantigueth. Materiales para el Estudio de la Clase
      Media en la America Latina 3:18–59. Publicaciones de la Oficina de Cien-
      cias Sociales, Union Panamericana, Washington, DC.
Hoselitz, Berte
  1953 The Role of Cities in the Economic Growth of Underdeveloped Countries.
      Journal of Political Economy 61:195–208.
Humphrey, Normand
  1948 The Cultural Background of the Mexican Immigrant. Rural Sociology
      13:239–255.
Hutchinson, Harry W.
  1952 Race Relations in a Rural Community of the Bahian Reconcavo. *In* Race
      and Class in Rural Brazil. Charles Wagley, ed. Pp. 16–46. Paris: UNESCO.
Kirchoff, Paul
  1949 The Social and Political Organization of the Andean Peoples. *In* Hand-
      book of South American Indians. Vol. 5. Julian Steward, ed. Pp. 293–311.
      Washington, DC: Smithsonian Institution.
Kluckhohn, Clyde
  1944 Navaho Witchcraft. Papers of the Peabody Museum of American Archae-
      ology and Ethnology, Harvard University 22, No. 2. Cambridge, Mass.
Kroeber, Alfred L.
  1948 Anthropology. New York: Harcourt-Brace.
Kroeber, Alfred L. and Clyde Kluckhohn
  1952 Culture. Papers of the Peabody Museum of American Archaeology and
      Ethnology, Harvard University 47, No. 1. Cambridge, Mass.
Leonard, Olen E.
  1952 Bolivia. Washington, DC: Scarecrow Press.
Lewis, Oscar
  1951 Life in a Mexican Village: Tepoztlán Revisited. Urbana: University of Illi-
      nois Press.
Linton, Ralph
  1936 The Study of Man. New York: Appleton-Century.
Mintz, Sidney W.
  1953 The Culture History of a Puerto Rican Sugar Cane Plantation, 1876–1949.
      Hispanic American Historical Review 33:224–251.
Mishkin, Bernard
  1946 The Contemporary Quechua. *In* Handbook of South American Indians.
      Vol. 2. Julian Steward, ed. Pp. 411–76. Washington, DC: Smithsonian In-
      stitution.
Moore, Wilbert E. and Melvin M. Tumin
  1949 Some Social Functions of Ignorance. American Sociological Review 14:
      787–795.

Mota Escobar, Alonso de la
1940[1601-31]   Descripción Geográfica de los Reinos de Nueva Galicia, Nueva
        Vizcaya y Nuevo León. México, D. F., Editorial Pedro Robredo.
Parsons, James
1949   Antioquia Colonization in Western Colombia. Ibero-Americana 32.
        Berkeley: University of California Press.
Passin, Herbert
1942   Sorcery as a Phase of Tarahumara Economic Relations. Man 42:11-15.
Pierson, Donald et al.
1951   Cruz das Almas: a Brazilian Village. Institute of Social Anthropology Pub-
        lication 12. Washington, DC: Smithsonian Institution.
Platt, Robert
1943   Latin America: Countrysides and United Regions. New York: Whittlesey
        House.
Pozas, Ricardo
1952   La situation économique et financiere de l'Indien Américain. Civilization
        2:309-329.
Redfield, Robert
1953   The Primitive World and Its Transformations. Ithaca, NY: Cornell Univer-
        sity Press.
Redfield, Robert and Sol Tax
1952   General Characteristics of Present-day Mesoamerican Indian Society.
        In Heritage of Conquest. Sol Tax, ed. Pp. 31-39. Glencoe, IL: Free Press.
Samuelson, Paul A.
1948   Economics: An Introductory Analysis. New York: McGraw-Hill.
Service, Elman
        In press Ms. Tobati: A Paraguayan Community.
Smith, T. Lynn et al.
1945   Tabio: A Study in Rural Social Organization. Washington, DC: Office of
        Foreign Agricultural Relations, U.S. Department of Agriculture.
1946   Brazil: People and Institutions. Baton Rouge: Louisiana State University
        Press.
Sombart, Werner
1928   Der moderne kapitalismus. 2 vols. München-Leipzig: Duncker and Hum-
        blot.
Steward, Julian
1938   Basin-plateau Aboriginal Sociopolitical Groups. Bureau of American Eth-
        nology Bulletin 120. Washington, DC: Smithsonian Institution.
1950   Area Research: Theory and Practice. Social Science Research Council Bul-
        letin 63. New York.
Steward, Julian, ed.
1946-51   Handbook of South American Indians. Bureau of American Ethnol-
        ogy Bulletin 143. Washington, DC: Smithsonian Institution.
Tax, Sol, ed.
1952   Heritage of Conquest. Glencoe, IL: Free Press.

Taylor, Paul S.
  1933   A Spanish-American Peasant Community: Arandas in Jalisco, Mexico.
         Ibero-Americana 4. Berkeley: University of California Press.
Tumin, Melvin
  1952   Caste in a Peasant Society. Princeton, NJ: Princeton University Press.
Valcarcel, Luis
  1946   Indian Markets and Fairs in Peru. *In* Handbook of South American Indi-
         ans. Vol. 2. Julian Steward, ed. Pp. 477–482. Washington, DC: Smithson-
         ian Institution.
Whetten, Nathan
  1948   Rural Mexico. Chicago: University of Chicago Press.
Willems, Emilio
  1942   Some Aspects of Cultural Conflict and Acculturation in Southern Rural
         Brazil. Rural Sociology 7:375–384.
  1944   Acculturation and the Horse Complex among German-Brasilians. Ameri-
         can Anthropologist 46:153–161.
  1945   El problema rural Brasileiño desde el punto de vista antropológico. Jor-
         nadas 33. México, D. F.: Colegio de México, Centro de Estudios Sociales.
Williams, Eric
  1944   Capitalism and Slavery. Chapel Hill: University of North Carolina.
Wolf, Eric
  1951   Culture Change and Culture Stability in a Puerto Rican Coffee Commu-
         nity. Ph.D. dissertation, Columbia University.
  1953   La formacion de la nación: un ensayo de formulación. Ciencias Sociales
         4:50–62, 98–111, 146–171.

QUERIES

- What are the basic characteristics of "structural relations" that define peasant societies?
- What differentiates "closed corporate" and "open" peasant societies?
- Wolf discusses a series of external variables that structure peasant communities, such as quality of arable land, access to technology, and the demands of the outside market or larger nation-state. Discuss some of the internal features that characterize closed and open peasant communities such as the political-religious system, the cult of poverty, and institutionalized envy.

CONNECTIONS

- In "Types of Latin American Peasantry," Wolf observes, "the culture of a peasant segment cannot be understood in terms of itself but is a part-culture, related to some larger integral whole." How would this contrast with Ruth Benedict's idea that cultures are "more or less coherent wholes"? Does this mean that peasants do not "have" culture?

PRIMARY TEXT: *DISTINGUISHED LECTURE: FACING POWER—OLD INSIGHTS, NEW QUESTIONS*

Reprinted by permission of the American Anthropological Association from *American Anthropologist*, Vol. 92 (3), Sep., 1990, pp. 586–596. www.aaanet.org. Not for sale or further reproduction.

In this essay I engage the problem of power and the issues that it poses for anthropology. I argue that we actually know a great deal about power, but have been timid in building upon what we know. This has implications for both theory and method, for assessing the insights of the past and for raising new questions.

The very term makes many of us uncomfortable. It is certainly one of the most loaded and polymorphous words in our repertoire. The Romance, Germanic, and Slavic languages, at least, conflate a multitude of meanings in speaking about pouvoir or potere, Macht, or mogushchestvo. Such words allow us to speak about power as if it meant the same thing to all of us. At the same time, we often speak of power as if all phenomena involving it were somehow reducible to a common core, some inner essence. This conjures up monstrous images of power, Hobbes's Leviathan or Bertrand de Jouvenel's Minotaur, but it leads away from specifying different kinds of power implicated in different kinds of relationships.

I argue instead that it is useful to think of four different modes of power. One is power as the attribute of the person, as potency or capability, the basic Nietzschean idea of power (Kaufmann 1968). Speaking of power in this sense draws attention to the endowment of persons in the play of power, but tells us little about the form and direction of that play. The second kind of power can be understood as the ability of an ego to impose its will on an alter, in social action, in interpersonal relations. This draws attention to the sequences of interactions and transactions among people, but it does not address the nature of the arena in which the interactions go forward. That comes into view more sharply when we focus on power in the third mode, as power that controls the settings in which people may show forth their potentialities and interact with others. I first came across this phrasing of power in anthropology when Richard Adams sought to define power not in interpersonal terms, but as the control that one actor or "operating unit" (his term) exercises over energy flows that constitute part of the environment of another actor (Adams 1966, 1975). This definition calls attention to the instrumentalities of power and is useful for understanding how "operating units" circumscribe the actions of others within determinate settings. I call this third kind of power tactical or organizational power.

But there is still a fourth mode of power, power that not only operates within settings or domains but that also organizes and orchestrates the settings themselves, and that specifies the distribution and direction of energy flows. I think that this is the kind of power that Marx addressed in speaking about the power of capital to harness and allocate labor power, and it forms the background of Michel Foucault's notion of power as the ability "to structure the possible field of action of others" (Foucault 1984:428). Foucault called this "to govern," in the 16th-century sense of governance, an exercise of "action upon action" (1984:427–28). Foucault himself was primarily interested in this as the power to govern consciousness, but I want to use it as power that structures the political economy. I will refer to this kind of power as structural power. This term rephrases the older notion of "the social relations of production," and is intended to emphasize power to deploy and allocate social labor. These governing relations do not come into view when you think of power primarily in interactional terms. Structural power shapes the social field of action so as to render some kinds of behavior possible, while making others less possible or impossible. As old Georg Friedrich Hegel argued, what occurs in reality has first to be possible.

What capitalist relations of production accomplish, for example, is to make possible the accumulation of capital based on the sale of marketable labor power in a large number of settings around the world. As anthropologists we can follow the flows of capital and labor through ups and downs, advances and retreats, and investigate the ways in which social and cultural arrangements in space and time are drawn into and implicated in the workings of this double whammy. This is not a purely economic relation, but a political one as well: it takes clout to set up, clout to maintain, and clout to defend; and wielding that clout becomes a target for competition or alliance building, resistance or accommodation.

This is the dimension that has been stressed variously in studies of imperialism, dependency, or world-systems. Their questions are why and how some sectors, regions, or nations are able to constrain the options of others, and what coalitions and conflicts occur in the course of this interplay. Some have said that these questions have little relevance to anthropology, in that they don't have enough to say about "real people doing real things," as Sherry Ortner put it (Ortner 1984:114); but it seems to me that they do touch on a lot of what goes on in the real world, that constrains, inhibits, or promotes what people do, or cannot do, within the scenarios we study. The notion of structural power is useful precisely because it allows us to delineate how the forces of the world impinge upon the people we study, without falling back into an anthropological nativism that postulates supposedly isolated societies and uncontaminated cultures, either in the present or in the past. There is no gain in a false romanticism that pretends that "real people doing real things" inhabit self-enclosed and self-sufficient universes.

I address here primarily the relation between tactical (or organizational) power and structural power. I do this because I believe that these concepts can help us to explain the world we inhabit. I think that it is the task of anthropology—or at least the task of some anthropologists—to attempt explanation, and not merely description, descriptive integration, or interpretation. Anthropology can be different things to different people (entertainment, exotic frisson, a "show-and-tell" of differences), but it should not, I submit, be content with James Boon's "shifting collage of contraries threatening (promising) to become unglued" (Boon 1982:237). Writing culture may require literary skill and genre, but a search for explanation requires more: it cannot do without naming and comparing things, and formulating concepts for naming and comparison. I think we must move beyond Geertz's "experience-near" understandings to analytical concepts that allow us to set what we know about X against what we know about Y, in pursuit of explanation. This means that I subscribe to a basically realist position. I think that the world is real, that these realities affect what humans do and that what humans do affects the world, and that we can come to understand the whys and wherefores of this relationship. We need to be professionally suspicious of our categories and models; we should be aware of their historical and cultural contingencies; we can understand a quest for explanation as approximations to truth rather than the truth itself. But I also believe that the search for explanation in anthropology can be cumulative; that knowledge and insights gained in the past can generate new questions, and that new departures can incorporate the accomplishments of the past.

In anthropology we are continuously slaying paradigms, only to see them return to life, as if discovered for the first time. The old-time evolutionism of Morgan and Engels reappeared in ecological guise in the forties and fifties. The Boasian insistence that we must understand the ways "that people actually think about their own culture and institutions" (Goldman 1975:15) has resurfaced in the anthropology of cognition and symbolism, now often played as a dissonant quartet in the format of deconstructionism. Diffusionism grew exhausted after biting too deeply into the seductive apple of trait-list collecting, but sprang back to life in the studies of acculturation, interaction spheres, and world-systems. Functionalism overreached itself by claiming to depict organic unities, but returned in systems theory as well as in other disguises. Culture-and-personality studies advanced notions of "basic personality structure" and "national character," without paying heed to history, cultural heterogeneity, or the role of hegemony in shaping uniformities; but suspiciously similar characterizations of modern nations and "ethnic groups" continue to appear. The varieties of ecological anthropology and the various Marxisms are being told by both user-friendly and unfriendly folk that what they need is "the concept of culture." We are all familiar, I trust, with Robert Lowie's image of "diffusionism laying the axe to evolutionism." As each successive approach carries the ax to its predecessors, anthropology comes to resemble a project in intellectual deforestation.

I do not think that this is either necessary or desirable. I think that anthropology can be cumulative, that we can use the work of our predecessors to raise new questions.

Three Projects

Some of anthropology's older insights into power can be the basis for new inquiry. I want to briefly review three projects that sought to understand what happens to people in the modern world and in the process raised questions about power, both tactical and structural. These projects yielded substantial bodies of data and theory; they opened up perspectives that reached beyond their scope of inquiry; and all were criticized in their time and subjected to reevaluation thereafter. All three were efforts toward an explanatory anthropology.

The first of these projects is the study of Puerto Rico in 1948–1949, directed by Julian Steward; the results are in the collective work, *The People of Puerto Rico* (Steward et al. 1956). The original thrust of the project stemmed from Steward's attack on the assumptions of a unitary national culture and national character which then dominated the field of culture-and-personality. The project aimed instead at exhibiting the heterogeneity of a national society. It was also a rejection of the model in which a single community was made to stand for an entire nation. It depicted Puerto Rico as a structure of varied localities and regions, clamped together by island wide institutions and the activities of an insular upper class, a system of heterogeneous parts and levels. The project was especially innovative in trying to find out how this complex arrangement developed historically, by tracing out the historical causes and courses of crop production on the island, and then following out the differential implications of that development in four representative communities. It promised to pay attention to the institutions connecting localities, regions, and nation, but actually confined itself to looking at these institutions primarily in terms of their local effects. It did carry out a study of the insular upper class, which was conceived as occupying the apex of linkages to the level of the nation. The project's major shortfall, in terms of its own undertaking, was its failure to take proper account of the rapidly intensifying migration to the nearby U.S. mainland. Too narrow a focus on agricultural ecology prevented it from coming to grips with issues already then becoming manifest on the local level, but prompted and played out upon a much larger stage.

While the Puerto Rico project averted its eyes from the spectacle of migration, another research effort took labor migration to the towns and burgeoning mines of Central Africa as its primary point of reference. This research was carried out under the auspices of the Rhodes-Livingstone Institute, set up in 1937 in what was then Northern Rhodesia and is now Zambia. Its research goal was defined by the first director, Godfrey Wilson, whose own outlook has been characterized as an unconscious effort to combine Marx and Malinowski (Brown 1973:195). Wilson understood the processes affecting Central Africa as an industrial revolution connected to the workings of the world economy. The massive penetration of the mining industry was seen as causal in generating multiple conflicts on the local and regional scene. Then Max Gluckman, the director from 1942 to 1947, drew up a research plan for the Institute which outlined a number of problem-oriented studies, and enlisted a stellar cast of anthropologists to work on such problems as the intersections of native and colonial governance, the role of witchcraft, the effects of labor migration on domestic economy, and the conflicts generated by the tension-ridden interplay of matrilineal descent and patrilocal residence. Dealing with an area of considerable linguistic and cultural diversity, the researchers were able to compare their findings to identify what was variable and what was common in local responses to general processes. But where the project was at its most innovative was in looking at rural locations, mining centers, and towns not as separate social and cultural entities but as interrelated elements caught up in one social field. It thus moved from Wilson's original concern with detribalization as anomic loss toward a more differentiated scenario of variegated responses to the new behavior settings of village, mine, and urban township. In doing so, it opened perspectives that the Puerto Rico project did not address. Its major failing lay in not taking systematic and critical account of the colonial structure in which these settings were embedded.

The third project I want to mention was directed by Richard Adams between 1963 and 1966, to study the national social structure of Guatemala. It is described in the book *Crucifixion by Power* (Adams 1970). The project took account of the intense growth of agricultural production for the market, and placed what was then known about life in localities within that context. Its specific innovation, however, lies in the fact that it engaged the study of national institutions in ways not broached by the two other projects I have referred to. Adams showed how local, regional, and supranational elites contested each other's power, and how regional elites stabilized their command by forging ties at the level of the nation. At that level, however, their power was subject to competition and interference by groups operating on the transnational and international plane. The study of elites was followed by accounts of the development of various institutions: the military, the renascent Guatemalan Church, the expanding interest organizations of the upper sector, and the legal system and legal profession. Adams then showed how these institutions curtailed agrarian and labor demands in the countryside, and produced individualized patron-client ties between the urban poor and their political sponsors in the capital. What the project did not do was to bring together this rich material into a synthesis that might have provided a theoretical model of the nation for further work.

It seems clear now that the three projects all stood on the threshold of a promising new departure in anthropological inquiry, but failed to cross it. They were adventurous, but not adventurous enough. First, in my view, they anticipated a move toward political economy, while not quite taking that next step. The Puerto Rico project, in its concentration on agriculture, failed to come to grips with the political and economic forces that established that agriculture in the first place, and that were already at work in "Operation Bootstrap" to transform the agricultural island into an industrial service station. We did not understand the ways in which island institutions, supposedly "national" but actually interlocked with mainland economics and politics, were battlegrounds for diverse contending interests. Thus, the project also missed an opportunity to deal with the complex interplay of hegemonic and subaltern cultural stances in the Puerto Rican situation. In fact, no one has done so to date; the task remains for the doing.

The Central Africa project was similarly confined by its own presuppositions. Despite its attention to conflicts and contradictions, it remained a captive of the prevailing functionalism, especially when it interpreted disjunctions as mere phases in the restoration of continuity. There was a tendency to take the colonial system as a given and thus to mute both the historical implications of conquest and the cumulative confrontations between Africans and Europeans. New questions now enable us to address these issues. Colonialism overrode the kin-based and tributary polities it encountered. Their members were turned into peasants in the hinterland and into workers in mine and town; peasantization and proletarianization were concomitant processes, often accompanied by force and violence. New ethnic and class identities re-laced older, now decentered ties (Sichone 1989). Yet research has also uncovered a multiplicity of African responses in labor and political organization (Epstein 1958; Ranger 1970), in dance societies (Mitchell 1957; Ranger 1975), in a proliferation of religious movements (Van Binsbergen and Schofeleers 1985; Werbner 1989), in rebellion and resistance (Lan 1985). These studies have reemphasized the role of cultural understandings as integral ingredients of the transformation of labor and power.

Adams's project came very close to a new opening. It embodied an historical perspective, it understood the relations among groups as conflict-ridden processes, and it included the operations of multinational and transnational powers in this dynamic. It did not, however, move toward a political economic model of the entire ensemble—perhaps because Adams's own specific interests lay in developing an evolutionary theory of power. It thus also neglected the complex interplay of cultures in the Guatemalan case. Such a move toward synthesis still awaits the future.

The significance of these three projects lies not only in their own accomplishments but in the new questions they lead us to ask. First, they all call attention to history, but not history as "one damned thing after another," as Leslie White used to say. "History," says Maurice Godelier, "does not explain: it has to be explained" (1977:5). What attention to history allows you to do is to look at processes unfolding, intertwining, spreading out, and dissipating over time. This means rethinking the units of our inquiries— households, localities, regions, national entities—seeing them not as fixed entities, but as problematic: shaped, reshaped, and changing over time. Attention to processes unfolding over time foregrounds organization—the structuring arrangements of social life—but requires us to see these in process and change. Second, the three projects point us to processes operating on a macro-scale, as well as in micro-settings. Puerto Rico was located first in the Hispanic orbit, then in the orbit of the United States. Central Africa was shaped by worldwide industrialization, as well as by the policies of colonial governance. Guatemala has been crucified by external connections and internal effects at the same time. The point continues an older anthropology which spoke first of "culture areas," then of *oikumenes*, interaction spheres, interethnic systems, and symbiotic regions, and that can now entertain "world-systems." Macroscopic history and processes of organization thus become important elements of a new approach. Both involve considerations of power—tactical and structural.

Organization

Organization is key, because it sets up relationships among people through allocation and control of resources and rewards. It draws on tactical power to monopolize or share out liens and claims, to channel action into certain pathways while interdicting the flow of action into others. Some things become possible and likely; others are rendered unlikely. At the same time, organization is always at risk. Since power balances always shift and change, its work is never done; it operates against entropy (Balandier 1970). Even the most successful organization never goes unchallenged. The enactment of power always creates friction—disgruntlement, foot-dragging, escapism, sabotage, protest or outright resistance, a panoply of responses well documented with Malaysian materials by James Scott (1985) in *Weapons of the Weak*.

Granted the importance of the subject, one might ask why anthropology seems to have relinquished the study of organization, so that today you can find the topic more often discussed in the manuals of business management than in our publications. We structure and are structured, we transact, we play out metaphors, but the whole question of organization has fallen into abeyance.

Many of us entered anthropology when there were still required courses in something called "social organization." It dealt with principles of categorization like gender, generation, and rank, and with groupings, such as lineages, clans, age sets, and associations. We can now see in retrospect that this labeling was too static, because organization was then grasped primarily as an outcome, a finished product responding to a cultural script, and not visualized in the active voice, as process, frequently a difficult and conflict-ridden process at that. When the main emphasis was on organizational forms and principles, it was all too easy to understand organization in architectural terms, as providing the building blocks for structure, a reliable edifice of regular and recurrent practices and ideas that rendered social life predictable, and could thus be investigated in the field. There was little concern with tactical power in shaping organizations, maintaining them, destabilizing them, or undoing them.

If an idea is judged by its fruitfulness, then the notion of social structure proved to be a very good idea. It yielded interesting work and productive insights. It is now evident that it also led us to reify organizational results into the building blocks of hypostatized social architectures, for example, in the concept of "the unilineal descent group." That idea was useful in leading us to think synoptically about features of group membership, descent, jural-political solidarity, rights and obligations focused on a common estate, injunctions of "prescriptive altruism," and norms of encompassing morality. Yet it is one thing to use a model to think out the implications of organizational processes, and another to expect unilineal descent groups with all these features to materialize in these terms, as dependably shaped bricks in a social-structural edifice.

How do we get from viewing organization as product or outcome to understanding organization as process? For a start, we could do worse than heed Conrad Arensberg's advice (1972:10–11) to look at "the flow of action," to ask what is going on, why it is going on, who engages in it, with whom, when, and how often. Yet we would now add to this behavior-centered approach a new question: For what and for whom is all this going on, and—indeed—against whom? This question should not be posed merely in interactionist terms. Asking why something is going on and for whom requires a conceptual guess about the forces and effects of the structural power that drives organization and to which organization on all levels must respond. What are the dominant relations through which labor is deployed? What are the organizational implications of kinship alliances, kin coalitions, chiefdoms, or forms of state? Not all organizations or articulations of organization answer to the same functional requisites, or respond to the same underlying dynamic.

Furthermore, it behooves us to think about what is entailed in conceiving organization as a process. This is an underdeveloped area in anthropological thinking. Clearly dyadic contracts, networks of various sizes and shapes, kinship systems, political hierarchies, corporations, and states possess very different organizational potentials. Understanding how all these sets of people and instrumentalities can be aggregated, hooked together, articulated under different kinds of structural power remains a task for the future.

In the pursuit of this task we can build upon the past by using our concepts and models as discovery procedures, not as fixed representations, universally applicable. For example, Michel Verdon developed a strong critique of lineage theory in his book on the Abutia Ewe (Verdon 1983). Yet the critique itself is informed by the questions raised by that theory and by the demands for evidence required for its corroboration. Verdon investigated the characteristics and distribution of domestic units, residential entities, and matrimonial practices, treating these as prerequisites for defining linkages by kinship. He then used the model of lineage theory to pose further queries about the relation of kinship to political synchronization, taking this connection as a problem, rather than an assumption a priori. The model served as a method of inquiry, rather than an archetype.

A similar redefinition of the problem has taken place in the study of chiefdoms, where interest, as Timothy Earle has said, "has shifted from schemes to classify societies as chiefdoms or not, towards consideration of the causes of observed variability" (Earle 1987:279). Social constellations that can be called chiefdoms not only come in many sizes and shapes (Feinman and Neitzel 1984), but they are now understood as "fragile negotiated institutions," both in securing compliance within and in competition with rivals outside. Emphasis in research now falls on the mixes of economic, political, and ideological strategies that chiefdoms employ to these ends, as well as on their variable success in shaping their different historical trajectories (Earle 1989:87). Similarly, where people once simply spoke of "the state," the state is now seen less as a thing than as "a process" (Gailey 1987). A new emphasis on state-making processes takes account both of the "diversity and fluidity of form, function and malfunction" and of "the extent to which all states are internally divided and subject to penetration by conflicting and usually contradictory forces" (Bright and Harding 1984:4).

Signification

Finally, I want to address the issue of power in signification. Anthropology has treated signification mainly in terms of encompassing cultural unities, such as patterns, configurations, ethos, eidos, epistemes, paradigms, cultural structures. These unities, in turn, have been conceptualized primarily as the outcomes of processes of logico-aesthetic integration. Even when the frequently incongruous and disjointed characteristics of culture are admitted, the hope has been—and I quote Geertz—that identifying significant symbols, clusters of such symbols, and clusters of clusters would yield statements of "the underlying regularities of human experience implicit in their formation" (Geertz 1973:408). The appeal is to the efficacy of symbols, to the workings of logics and aesthetics in the movement toward integration or reintegration, as if these cognitive processes were guided by a telos all their own.

I call this approach into question on several grounds. First, I draw on the insight of Anthony Wallace, who in the late 1950s contrasted views of culture that emphasize "the replication of uniformity" with those that acknowledge the problem of "the organization of diversity." He argued that

> all societies are, in a radical sense, plural societies. . . . How do societies ensure that the diverse cognitions of adults and children, males and females, warriors and shamans, slaves and masters articulate to form the equivalence structures that are the substance of social life? [Wallace 1970:110]

This query of Wallace's continues to echo in many quarters: in a feminist anthropology that questions the assumption that men and women share the same cultural understandings; in ethnography from various areas, where "rubbish-men" in Melanesia and "no account people" on the Northwest Coast do not seem to abide by the norms and ideals of Big Men and chiefs; in studies of hierarchical systems in which different strata and segments exhibit different and contending models of logico-aesthetic integration (India furnishes a telling case). We have been told that such divergences are ultimately kept in check and on track by cultural logic, pure and simple. This seems to me unconvincing. It is indeed the case that our informants in the field invoke metaphoric polarities of purity and pollution, well-being and malevolence, yin and yang, life and death. Yet these metaphors are intrinsically polysemic, so abundant in possible signifiers that they can embrace any and all situations. To put them to work in particular scenarios requires that their range be constricted and narrowed down to but a small set of referents. What Lévi-Strauss called "the surplus of signifiers" must be subjected to parsimonious selection before the logic of cultural integration can be actualized. This indexing, as some have called it, is no automatic process, but passes through power and through contentions over power, with all sorts of consequences for signification.

Wallace's insights on the organization of diversity also raise questions about how meaning actually works in social life. He pointed out that participants in social action do not need to understand what meanings lie behind the behavior of their partners in interchange. All they have to know is how to respond appropriately to the cues signaled by others. Issues of meaning need not ever rise into consciousness. This is often the concern only of certain specialists, whose specific job or interest it is to explore the plenitude of possible meanings: people such as shamans, tohunga, or academics. Yet there are also situations in which the mutual signaling of expectations is deranged, where opposite and contradictory interests come to the fore, or where cultural schemata come under challenge. It then becomes apparent that beyond logic and aesthetics, it is power that guarantees—or fails.

Power is implicated in meaning through its role in upholding one version of significance as true, fruitful, or beautiful, against other possibilities that may threaten truth, fruitfulness, or beauty. All cultures, however conceived, carve out significance and try to stabilize it against possible alternatives. In human affairs, things might be different, and often are. Roy Rappaport, in writing on sanctity and ritual (Rappaport 1979), has emphasized the basic arbitrariness of all cultural orders. He argues that they are anchored in postulates that can neither be verified nor falsified, but that must be treated as unquestionable: to make them unquestionable, they are surrounded with sacredness. I would add that there is always the possibility that they might come unstuck. Hence, symbolic work is never done, achieves no final solution. The cultural assertion that the world is shaped in this way and not in some other has to be repeated and enacted, lest it be questioned and denied. The point is well made by Valerio Valeri in his study of *Kingship and Sacrifice in Hawaii*. Ritual, he says, produces sense

> by creating contrasts in the continuum of experience. This implies suppressing certain elements of experience in order to give relevance to others. Thus the creation of conceptual order is also, constitutively, the suppression of aspects of reality. [Valeri 1985:xi]

* * *

I have spoken of different modes of structural power, which work through key relations of governance. Each such mode would appear to require characteristic ways of conceptualizing and categorizing people. In social formations that deploy labor through relations glossed at kinship, people are assigned to networks or bodies of kin that are distinguished by criteria of gender, distinct substances or essences of descent, connections with the dead, differential distributions of myths, rituals, and emblems. Tributary formations hierarchize these criteria and set up distinct social strata, each stratum marked by a distinctive inner substance that also defines its positions and privileges in society. Capitalist formations peel the individual out of encompassing ascriptive bodies and install people as separate actors, free to exchange, truck, or barter in the market, as well as in other provinces of life. The three modes of categorizing social actors, moreover, imply quite different relations to "nature" and cosmos. When one mode enters into conflict with another, it also challenges the fundamental categories that empower its dynamics. Power will then be invoked to assault rival categorical claims. Power is thus never external to signification—it inhabits meaning and is its champion in stabilization and defense.

We owe to social anthropology the insight that the arrangements of a society become most visible when they are challenged by crisis. The role of power also becomes most evident in instances where major organizational transformations put signification under challenge. Let me offer some examples. In their study of the Plains Vision Experience, Patricia Albers and Seymour Parker (1971) contrast the individualized visions of the egalitarian foragers of the Plains periphery with the standardized kin-group-controlled visions of the horticultural village dwellers. Still a third kind of vision, oriented toward war and wealth, emerged among the buffalo-hunting nomads who developed in response to the introduction of horse and gun. As horse pastoralism proved increasingly successful, the horticulturalists became riven by conflicts between the personal-private visions of young men involved in buffalo hunting, and the visions controlled by hereditary groups of kin.

The development of the Merina state in Madagascar gives us another example (see, for example, Berg 1986; Bloch 1986). As the state became increasingly powerful and centralized around an intensified agriculture and ever more elaborate social hierarchy, the royal center also emerged as the hub of the ideational system. Local rites of circumcision, water sprinkling, offerings to honor superiors, and rituals ministering to group icons and talismans were increasingly synchronized and fused with rituals of state.

The royal rituals of Hawaii furnish a third case. Their development was linked to major transformations that affected Hawaii after 1400, when agriculture and aquaculture were extended and intensified (see, for example, Earle 1978; Kirch 1985; Spriggs 1988). Local communities were reorganized; lineages were deconstructed; commoners lost the right to keep genealogies and to attend temples, and were assigned as quasi-tenants to nonlocal subaltern chiefs. Chiefs and aristocrats were raised up, godlike, into a separate endogamous stratum. Conflicts within the elite brought on endemic warfare and attempts at conquest: both fed the cult of human sacrifice. Innovations in myth and ritual portrayed the eruption of war and violence by the coming of outsiders, "sharks upon the land." Sahlins (1985) has offered the notion of a cultural structure to interpret how Hawaiians understood such changes and re-valued their understandings in the course of change. But reference to a cultural structure alone, or even to a dialectic of a structure of meaning with the world, will not yet explain how given forms of significance relate to transformations of agriculture, settlement, sociopolitical organization, and relations of war and peace. To explain what happened in Hawaii or elsewhere, we must take the further step of understanding the consequences of the exercise of power.

I have put forward the case for an anthropology that is not content merely to translate, interpret, or play with a kaleidoscope of cultural fragments, but that seeks explanations for cultural phenomena. We can build upon past efforts and old insights, but we must also find our way to asking new questions. I understand anthropology as a cumulative undertaking, as well as a collective quest that moves in ever expanding circles, a quest that depends upon the contributions of each of us, and for which we are all responsible.

BIBLIOGRAPHY

Adams, Richard N.
    1966   Power and Power Domains. America Latina 9:3–5, 8–11.
    1970   Crucifixion by Power: Essays on Guatemalan Social Structure, 1944–1966. Austin: University of Texas Press.
    1975   Energy and Structure: A Theory of Social Power. Austin: University of Texas Press.
Albers, Patricia, and Seymour Parker
    1971   The Plains Vision Experience: A Study of Power and Privilege. Southwestern Journal of Anthropology 27:203–233.
Arensberg, Conrad M.
    1972   Culture as Behavior: Structure and Emergence. Annual Review of Anthropology 1:1–26. Palo Alto, CA: Annual Reviews.
Balandier, Georges
    1970   Political Anthropology. New York: Random House.
Berg, Gerald M.
    1986   Royal Authority and the Protector System in Nineteenth-Century Imerina. In Madagascar: Society and History. Conrad P. Kottak et al., eds. Pp. 175–192. Durham, NC: Carolina Academic Press.
Bloch, Maurice
    1986   From Blessing to Violence: History and Ideology in the Circumcision Ritual of the Merina of Madagascar. Cambridge: Cambridge University Press.
Boon, James A.
    1982   Other Tribes, Other Scribes: Symbolic Anthropology in the Comparative Study of Cultures, Histories, Religions, and Texts. Cambridge: Cambridge University Press.
Bright, Charles, and Susan Harding, eds.
    1984   Statemaking and Social Movements: Essays in History and Theory. Ann Arbor: University of Michigan Press.
Brown, Richard
    1973   Anthropology and Colonial Rule: Godfrey Wilson and the Rhodes-Livingstone Institute, Northern Rhodesia. In Anthropology and the Colonial Encounter. Talal Asad, ed. Pp. 173–197. London: Ithaca Press.

Earle, Timothy K.
  1978   Economic and Social Organization of a Complex Chiefdom: The Halelea
         District, Kauai, Hawaii. Anthropological Papers, No. 63. Ann Arbor: Mu-
         seum of Anthropology, University of Michigan.
  1987   Chiefdoms in Archaeological and Ethnohistorical Perspective. Annual Re-
         view of Anthropology 16:279–308. Palo Alto, CA: Annual Reviews.
  1989   The Evolution of Chiefdoms. Current Anthropology 30:84–88.
Epstein, A. L.
  1958   Politics in an Urban African Community. Manchester: Manchester Uni-
         versity Press.
Feinman, Gary M., and Jill Neitzel
  1984   Too Many Types: An Overview of Sedentary Prestate Societies in the Amer-
         icas. *In* Advances in Archaeological Method and Theory, vol. 7. Michael B.
         Schiffer, ed. Pp. 39–102. New York: Academic Press.
Foucault, Michel
  1984   The Subject and Power. *In* Art after Modernism: Rethinking Representa-
         tion. Brian Wallis, ed. Pp. 417–432. Boston/New York: David R. Go-
         dine/New Museum of Contemporary Art.
Gailey, Christine Ward
  1987   Kinship to Kingship: Gender Hierarchy and State Formation in the Ton-
         gan Islands. Austin: University of Texas Press.
Geertz, Clifford
  1973   The Interpretation of Cultures. New York: Basic Books.
Godelier, Maurice
  1977   Perspectives in Marxist Anthropology. Cambridge Studies in Social An-
         thropology, No. 18. Cambridge: Cambridge University Press.
Goldman, Irving
  1975   The Mouth of Heaven: An Introduction to Kwakiutl Religious Thought.
         New York: Wiley Interscience.
Kaufmann, Walter
  1968   Nietzsche: Philosopher, Psychologist, Antichrist. Princeton, NJ: Princeton
         University Press.
Kirch, Patrick V.
  1985   Feathered Gods and Fishhooks: An Introduction to Hawaiian Archaeol-
         ogy and Prehistory. Honolulu: University of Hawaii Press.
Lan, David
  1985   Guns and Rain: Guerillas and Spirit Mediums in Zimbabwe. Berkeley:
         University of California Press.
Mitchell, J. Clyde
  1957   The Kalela Dance. Aspects of Social Relationships among Urban Africans
         in Northern Rhodesia. Rhodes-Livingstone Paper No. 27. Manchester:
         Manchester University Press for Rhodes-Livingstone Institute.
Ortner, Sherry B.
  1984   Theory in Anthropology since the Sixties. Comparative Studies in Society
         and History 26:126–166.
Pocock, John G. A.
  1971   Politics, Language and Time: Essays in Political Thought and History. New
         York: Atheneum.

Ranger, Terence O.
1970   The African Voice in Southern Rhodesia, 1898–1930. London: Heine-
        mann.
1975   Dance and Society in Eastern Africa, 1890–1970: The Beni Ngoma. Berke-
        ley: University of California Press.
Rappaport, Roy A.
1979   Ecology, Meaning, and Religion. Richmond, CA: North Atlantic Books.
Sahlins, Marshall D.
1985   Islands of History. Chicago:University of Chicago Press.
Scott, James
1985   Weapons of the Weak: Everyday Forms of Peasant Resistance. New Haven,
        CT: Yale University Press.
Sichone, Owen B.
1989   The Development of an Urban Working-Class Culture on the Rhodesian
        Copperbelt. *In* Domination and Resistance. Daniel Miller, Michael Row-
        lands, and Christopher Tilley, eds. Pp. 290–298. London: Unwin Hyman.
Spriggs, Mathew
1988   The Hawaiian Transformation of Ancestral Polynesian Society: Conceptu-
        alizing Chiefly States. *In* State and Society: The Emergence and Develop-
        ment of Social Hierarchy and Political Centralization. John Gledhill, Bar-
        bara Bender, and Mogens Trolle-Larsen, eds. Pp. 57– 73. London: Unwin
        Hyman.
Steward, Julian H., et al.
1956   The People of Puerto Rico. Urbana: University of Illinois Press.
Valeri, Valerio
1985   Kingship and Sacrifice: Ritual and Society in Ancient Hawaii. Chicago:
        University of Chicago Press.
Van Binsbergen, Wim M. J., and Matthew Schofeleers, eds.
1985   Theoretical Explorations in African Religion. London: Kegan Paul Inter-
        national.
Verdon, Michel
1983   The Abutia Ewe of West Africa: A Chiefdom That Never Was. Studies in
        the Social Sciences, No. 38. Berlin: Mouton.
Wallace, Anthony F. C.
1970[1961]   Culture and Personality. New York: Random House.
Werbner, Richard P.
1989   Ritual Passage, Sacred Journey: The Form, Process and Organization of
        Religious Movement. Washington, DC: Smithsonian Institution Press.

QUERIES

- What are the four modes of power Wolf defines in "Facing Power—Old Insights, New Questions"? Which modes of power does he emphasize in this article?
- Wolf discusses three anthropological projects—Steward's project in Puerto Rico, Max Gluckman's research in Zambia (then northern

Rhodesia), and Adams's investigations in Guatemala—and concludes, "the three projects all stood on the threshold of a promising new departure in anthropological inquiry, but failed to cross it." What was that threshold? What was the failure?

- In his 1999 article, Wolf insists that an anthropological focus on power must consider matters of organization as a process and the creation of meaning (signification). Looking back at his earlier article on Latin American peasants, how does the organization of closed vs. open peasant communities reflect larger processes? How do the values associated with closed vs. open peasant communities (e.g., their respective views on the accumulation of wealth) represent varying creations of meaning?

CONNECTIONS

- Contrast Wolf's discussion of peasant communities with Marshall Sahlins's subsequent observations about translocal communities in the article "Anthropological Enlightenment." Given that emigrant members of Latin American communities now live throughout North America, Europe, and Asia but still may support their home communities and kinfolk, are Wolf's definitions of open and closed peasant communities still useful?

25

Marshall D. Sahlins

INTRODUCTION

The primary texts presented below come from two points in Marshall Sahlins's (b. 1930) distinguished career (for a profile, see Moore 2008:365–84). Separated by thirty-six years, the two essays also occupy distinct but connected theoretical positions.

The first, "Poor Man, Rich Man, Big-Man, Chief: Political Types in Melanesia and Polynesia" is directly influenced by the comparative evolutionary approach to social forms that Sahlins learned as an undergraduate studying with Leslie White at the University of Michigan and as a graduate student at Columbia University. In this 1963 article, Sahlins opposes two broad but distinct patterns of political authority among traditional societies in the Pacific: Melanesian big-men and Polynesian chiefs. While the apparent goal is to define two "types" of political authority, this overlies a more complex and challenging set of questions: How do different sociopolitical systems evolve? What are the factors that lead to the development of segmentary political systems in which authority is achieved and negotiated versus societies in which power is hierarchical and hereditary? More broadly, the theoretical implications of this article are fascinating, not only because of how it illuminates forms of political authority, but also because of how it embodies distinct theoretical positions.

Sahlins's 1963 article is very much a product of its time; compare it to Eric Wolf's "Types of Latin American Peasantry," (see "Queries" below), and you will see a similar analytical approach. Second, Sahlins is obviously influenced by materialist explanations—see the discussions of environment, population size—and yet Sahlins is also interested in what today we might call "agency" and "structure" (for more discussion of this, see Moore 2008: 372–75). The difference between big-men and chiefs is not only a matter of material conditions, but it is also due to the constraints and opportunities that the different systems provide for social actors. A capable politician, trying to act like a chief in a big-man society, is likely to fail. Third, Sahlins raises a series of theoretical points that, although grounded in a specific body of ethnographic data, resonate with issues raised by a number of other anthropological theorists, including White, Douglas, and Wolf.

The 1999 article, "What is Anthropological Enlightenment?: Some Lessons of the Twentieth Century," is a very different essay, reflecting the changes in Sahlins's theoretical ideas over the course of his career. There is no reference to cultural evolution, the type-based comparative method is absent, and the ethnographic reach is global rather than focused on traditional Oceania.

Sahlins offers a broader overview of how anthropological theories are embedded into broader Western intellectual traditions—and how indigenous peoples have confounded anthropological expectations. A central illusion is what Sahlins calls "despondency theory": the conceit that when Western societies change it is "progress," but when other societies change they have "lost" their culture. Sahlins outlines an elegiac theme in 20th-century anthropology, which bemoans the loss of traditional culture—but then points to a surprising late 20th–early 21st-century phenomenon: indigenous culture exists. Modern technologies (such as snowmobiles, ATVs, and small aircraft) are used for hunting and gathering. Eskimo patrilineal clans bind kinfolk dispersed from the Bering Sea to Oakland. Mixteca extended families share resources from the highlands of Oaxaca to Riverside County, California.

Far from being homogenized by globalization, as Sahlins observes, "the world is being re-diversified by indigenous adaptations to the global juggernaut." Of course, the majority of the "traditional" cultures studied by early anthropologists had been affected by Western expansion; the Iroquois Morgan studied were primarily English-speakers by the mid-19th century, a fact overlooked when he classified them as "Lower Barbarians." Far from being deprived of culture or condemned to the inauthentic mimicry of "real" culture, the "continuity of their respective cultural traditions consisted in the different ways they changed." Which is not to say, Sahlins clarifies, that indigenous peoples are never marginalized or impoverished within larger nation-states, but the problem is not some inherent conflict between monetarized economies and traditional culture, but rather "when they cannot find enough money to support their traditional way of life." Finally, Sahlins argues, "culture" is not disappearing. "Now everyone has a culture; only an anthropologist could doubt it." Based on a flawed assumption that traditional cultures were coherent wholes and an anthropology that overlooked history, the view that culture is now an inauthentic pastiche overlooks a key reality: the translocal community.

PRIMARY TEXT: *POOR MAN, RICH MAN, BIG-MAN, CHIEF: POLITICAL TYPES IN MELANESIA AND POLYNESIA*

Reprinted from *Comparative Studies in Society and History*, Vol. 5 (3), April 1963, pp. 285–303. Footnotes modified from the original. Reproduced by permission of Cambridge University Press.

With an eye to their own life goals, the native peoples of Pacific Islands unwittingly present to anthropologists a generous scientific gift: an extended series of experiments in cultural adaptation and evolutionary development. They have compressed their institutions within the confines of infertile coral atolls, expanded them on volcanic islands, created with the means history gave them cultures adapted to the deserts of Australia, the mountains and warm coasts of New Guinea, the rain forests of the Solomon Islands. From the Australian Aborigines, whose hunting and gathering existence duplicates in outline the cultural life of the later Paleolithic, to the great chiefdoms of Hawaii, where society approached the formative levels of the old Fertile Crescent civilizations, almost every general phase in the progress of primitive culture is exemplified.

Where culture so experiments, anthropology finds its laboratories—makes its comparisons.[1]

In the southern and eastern Pacific two contrasting cultural provinces have long evoked anthropological interest: Melanesia, including New Guinea, the Bismarcks, Solomons, and island groups east to Fiji; and Polynesia, consisting in its main portion of the triangular constellation of lands between New Zealand, Easter Island, and the Hawaiian Islands. In and around Fiji, Melanesia and Polynesia intergrade culturally, but west and east of their intersection the two provinces pose broad contrasts in several sectors: in religion, art, kinship groupings, economics, political organization. The differences are the more notable for the underlying similarities from which they emerge.

---

[1] Since Rivers' day, the Pacific has provided ethnographic stimulus to virtually every major ethnological school and interest. From such great landmarks as Rivers' *History of Melanesian Society*, Radcliffe-Brown's *Social Organization of the Australian Tribes*, Malinowski's famous Trobriand studies, especially *Argonauts of the Western Pacific*, Raymond Firth's path-making *Primitive Economics of the New Zealand Maori*, his functionalist classic, *We, the Tikopia*, and Margaret Mead's, *Coming of Age in Samoa*, one can almost read off the history of ethnological theory in the earlier twentieth century. In addition to continuing to provision all these concerns, the Pacific has been the site of much recent evolutionist work (see, for example, Goldman 1955, 1960; Goodenough 1957; Sahlins 1958; Vayda 1959). There are also the outstanding monographs on special subjects ranging from tropical agriculture (Conklin 1957; Freeman 1955) to millenarianism (Worsley 1957).

Melanesia and Polynesia are both agricultural regions in which many of the same crops such as yams, taro, breadfruit, bananas, and coconuts have long been cultivated by many similar techniques. Some recently presented linguistic and archaeological studies indeed suggest that Polynesian cultures originated from an eastern Melanesian hearth during the first millennium B.C.[2] Yet in anthropological annals the Polynesians were to become famous for elaborate forms of rank and chieftainship, whereas most Melanesian societies broke off advance on this front at more rudimentary levels.

It is obviously imprecise, however, to make out the political contrast in broad culture area terms. Within Polynesia, certain of the islands, such as Hawaii, the Society Islands and Tonga, developed unparalleled political momentum. And not all Melanesian polities, on the other side, were constrained and truncated in their evolution. In New Guinea and nearby areas of western Melanesia, small and loosely ordered political groupings are numerous, but in eastern Melanesia, New Caledonia and Fiji for example, political approximations of the Polynesian condition become common. There is more of an upward west to east slope in political development in the southern Pacific than a step-like, quantum progression.[3] It is quite revealing, however, to compare the extremes of this continuum, the western Melanesian underdevelopment against the greater Polynesian chiefdoms. While such comparison does not exhaust the evolutionary variations, it fairly establishes the scope of overall political achievement in this Pacific phylum of cultures.

Measurable along several dimensions, the contrast between developed Polynesian and underdeveloped Melanesian polities is immediately striking for differences in scale. H. Ian Hogbin and Camilla Wedgwood concluded from a survey of Melanesian, (mostly western Melanesian) societies that ordered, independent political bodies in the region typically include seventy to three hundred persons; more recent work in the New Guinea Highlands suggests political groupings of up to a thousand, occasionally a few thousand, people.[4] But in Polynesia sovereignties of two thousand or three thousand are run-of-the-mill, and the most advanced chiefdoms, as in Tonga or Hawaii, might claim ten thousand, even tens of thousand.[5] Varying step by step with such differences in size of the polity are differences in territorial extent: from a few square miles in western Melanesia to tens or even hundreds of square miles in Polynesia. The Polynesian advance in po-

---

[2] This question, however, is presently in debate. See Grace (1955, 1959); Dyen (1960); Suggs (1960); Golson (1961).

[3] There are notable bumps in the geographical gradient. The Trobriand chieftainships off eastern New Guinea will come to mind. But the Trobriand political development is clearly exceptional for western Melanesia.

[4] Hogbin and Wedgwood (1952–53, 1953–54). On New Guinea Highland political scale see among others, Paula Brown (1960).

[5] See the summary account in Sahlins (1958), especially pp. 132–33.

litical scale was supported by advance over Melanesia in political structure. Melanesia presents a great array of social political forms: here political organization is based upon patrilineal descent groups, there on cognatic groups, or men's clubhouses recruiting neighborhood memberships, on a secret ceremonial society, or perhaps on some combination of these structural principles. Yet a general plan can be discerned. The characteristic western Melanesian "tribe," that is, the ethnic-cultural entity, consists of many autonomous kinship-residential groups. Amounting on the ground to a small village or a local cluster of hamlets, each of these is a copy of the others in organization, each tends to be economically self-governing, and each is the equal of the others in political status. The tribal plan is one of politically unintegrated segments—segmental. But the political geometry in Polynesia is pyramidal. Local groups of the order of self-governing Melanesian communities appear in Polynesia as subdivisions of a more inclusive political body. Smaller units are integrated into larger through a system of intergroup ranking, and the network of representative chiefs of the subdivisions amounts to a coordinating political structure. So instead of the Melanesian scheme of small, separate, and equal political blocs, the Polynesian polity is an extensive pyramid of groups capped by the family and following of a paramount chief. (This Polynesian political upshot is often, although not always, facilitated by the development of ranked lineages. Called conical clan by Kirchhoff, at one time ramage by Firth and status lineage by Goldman, the Polynesian ranked lineage is the same in principle as the so-called obok system widely distributed in Central Asia, and it is at least analogous to the Scottish clan, the Chinese clan, certain Central African Bantu lineage systems, the house-groups of Northwest Coast Indians, perhaps even the "tribes" of the Israelites.[6] Genealogical ranking is its distinctive feature: members of the same descent unit are ranked by genealogical distance from the common ancestor; lines of the same group become senior and cadet branches on this principle; related corporate lineages are relatively ranked, again by genealogical priority.)

Here is another criterion of Polynesian political advance: historical performance. Almost all of the native peoples of the South Pacific were brought up against intense European cultural pressure in the late eighteenth and the nineteenth centuries. Yet only the Hawaiians, Tahitians, Tongans, and to a lesser extent the Fijians, successfully defended themselves by evolving countervailing, native-controlled states. Complete with public governments and public law, monarchs and taxes, ministers and minions, these nineteenth century states are testimony to the native Polynesian political genius, to the level and the potential of indigenous political accomplishments.

---

[6] Kirchhoff (1955); Firth (1957); Goldman (1957); Bacon (1958); Fried (1957).

Embedded within the grand differences in political scale, structure and performance is a more personal contrast, one in quality of leadership. An historically particular type of leader-figure, the "big-man" as he is often locally styled, appears in the underdeveloped settings of Melanesia. Another type, a chief properly so-called, is associated with the Polynesian advance.[7] Now these are distinct sociological types, that is to say, differences in the powers, privileges, rights, duties, and obligations of Melanesian big-men and Polynesian chiefs are given by the divergent societal contexts in which they operate. Yet the institutional distinctions cannot help but be manifest also in differences in bearing and character, appearance and manner—in a word, personality. It may be a good way to begin the more rigorous sociological comparison of leadership with a more impressionistic sketch of the contrast in the human dimension. Here I find it useful to apply characterizations—or is it caricature?—from our own history to big-men and chiefs, however much injustice this does to the historically incomparable backgrounds of the Melanesians and Polynesians. The Melanesian big-man seems so thoroughly bourgeois, so reminiscent of the free enterprising rugged individual of our own heritage. He combines with an ostensible interest in the general welfare a more profound measure of self-interested cunning and economic calculation. His gaze, as Veblen might have put it, is fixed unswervingly to the main chance. His every public action is designed to make a competitive and invidious comparison with others, to show a standing above the masses that is product of his own personal manufacture. The historical caricature of the Polynesian chief, however, is feudal rather than capitalist. His appearance, his bearing is almost regal; very likely he just is a big man—"'Can't you see he is a chief? See how big he is?'"[8] In his every public action is a display of the refinements of breeding, in his man-

---

[7] The big-man pattern is very widespread in western Melanesia, although its complete distribution is not yet clear to me. Anthropological descriptions of big-man leadership vary from mere hints of its existence, as among the Orokaiva (Williams 1930), Lesu (Powdermaker 1933) or the interior peoples of northeastern Guadalcanal (Hogbin 1937–38a), to excellent, closely grained analyses, such as Douglas Oliver's account of the Siuai of Bougainville (Oliver 1955). Big-man leadership has been more or less extensively described for the Manus of the Admiralty Islands (Mead 1934, 1937); the To'ambaita of northern Malaita (Hogbin 1939, 1943–44); the Tangu of northeastern New Guinea (Burridge 1960); the Kapauku of Netherlands New Guinea (Pospisil 1958, 1958–60); the Kaoka of Guadalcanal (Hogbin 1933–34, 1937–38); the Seniang District of Malekula (Deacon 1934); the Gawa' of the Huon Gulf area, New Guinea (Hogbin 1951); the Abelam (Kaberry 1940–41, 1941–42) and the Arapesh (Mead 1937a, 1938, 1947) of the Sepik District, New Guinea; the Elema, Orokolo Bay, New Guinea (Williams 1940); the Ngarawapum of the Markham Valley, New Guinea (Read 1946–47,1949–50); the Kiwai of the Fly estuary, New Guinea (Landtman 1927); and a number of other societies, including, in New Guinea Highlands, the Kuma (Reay 1959), the GahukaGama (Read 1952–53, 1959), the Kyaka (Bulmer 1960–61), the Enga (Meggitt 1957, 1957–58), and others. (For an overview of the structural position of New Guinea Highlands' leaders see Barnes (1962).) A partial bibliography on Polynesian chieftainship can be found in Sahlins (1958). The outstanding ethnographic description of Polynesian chieftainship is, of course, Firth's for Tikopia (1950, 1957)—Tikopia, however, is not typical of the more advanced Polynesian chiefdoms with which we are principally concerned here.

[8] Gifford 1929:124.

ner always that *noblesse oblige* of true pedigree and an incontestable right of rule. With his standing not so much a personal achievement as a just social due, he can afford to be, and he is, every inch a chief.

In the several Melanesian tribes in which big-men have come under anthropological scrutiny, local cultural differences modify the expression of their personal powers.[9] But the indicative quality of big-man authority is everywhere the same: it is *personal* power. Big-men do not come to office; they do not succeed to, nor are they installed in, existing positions of leadership over political groups. The attainment of big-man status is rather the outcome of a series of acts which elevate a person above the common herd and attract about him a coterie of loyal, lesser men. It is not accurate to speak of "big-man" as a political title, for it is but an acknowledged standing in interpersonal relations a—"prince among men" so to speak as opposed to "The Prince of Danes". In particular Melanesian tribes the phrase might be "man of importance" or "man of renown", "generous rich-man", or "center-man", as well as "big-man".

A kind of two-sidedness in authority is implied in this series of phrases, a division of the big-man's field of influence into two distinct sectors. "Center man" particularly connotes a cluster of followers gathered about an influential pivot. It socially implies the division of the tribe into political ingroups dominated by outstanding personalities. To the in-group, the big-man presents this sort of picture:

> The place of the leader in the district group [in northern Malaita] is well summed up by his title, which might be translated as "center-man." . . . He was like a banyan, the natives explain, which, though the biggest and tallest in the forest, is still a tree like the rest. But, just because it exceeds all others, the banyan gives support to more lianas and creepers, provides more food for the birds, and gives better protection against sun and rain.[10]

But "man of renown" connotes a broader tribal field in which a man is not so much a leader as he is some sort of hero. This is the side of the big-man facing outward from his own faction, his status among some or all of the other political clusters of the tribe. The political sphere of the big-man

---

[9] Thus the enclavement of the big-man pattern within a segmented lineage organization in the New Guinea Highlands appears to limit the leader's political role and authority in comparison, say, with the Siuai. In the Highlands, intergroup relations are regulated in part by the segmented lineage structure; among the Siuai intergroup relations depend more on contractual arrangements between big-men, which throws these figures more into prominence. (Notable in this connection has been the greater viability of the Siuai big-man than the native Highlands leader in the face of colonial control.) Barnes' (1962) comparison of Highland social structure with the classic segmentary lineage systems of Africa suggests an inverse relation between the formality of the lineage system and the political significance of individual action. Now, if instances such as the Siuai be tacked on to the comparison, the generalization may be further supported and extended: among societies of the tribal level (cf. Sahlins 1961, Service in press), the greater the self-regulation of the political process through a lineage system, the less function that remains to big-men, and the less significant their political authority.

[10] Hogbin 1943–44:258.

divides itself into a small internal sector composed of his personal satel-
lites—rarely over eighty men—and a much larger external sector, the tribal
galaxy consisting of many similar constellations.

As it crosses over from the internal into the external sector, a big-man's
power undergoes qualitative change. Within his faction a Melanesian leader
has true command ability, outside of it only fame and indirect influence. It is
not that the center-man rules his faction by physical force, but his followers do
feel obliged to obey him, and he can usually get what he wants by haranguing
them—public verbal suasion is indeed so often employed by center men that
they have been styled "harangueutans". The orbits of outsiders, however, are set
by their own center-men. "'Do it yourself. I'm not *your* fool,'" would be the
characteristic response to an order issued by a center-man to an outsider
among the Siuai.[11] This fragmentation of true authority presents special political difficulties, particularly in organizing large masses of people for the pros-
ecution of such collective ends as warfare or ceremony. Big-men do instigate
mass action, but only by establishing both extensive renown and special personal relations of compulsion or reciprocity with other center-men.

Politics is in the main personal politiking in these Melanesian societies,
and the size of a leader's faction as well as the extent of his renown are normally set by competition with other ambitious men. Little or no authority
is given by social ascription: leadership is a—creation of followership. "Followers," as it is written of the Kapauku of New Guinea, "stand in various relations to the leader. Their obedience to the headman's decisions is caused
by motivations which reflect their particular relations to the leader."[12] So a
man must be prepared to demonstrate that he possesses the kinds of skills
that command respect—magical powers, gardening prowess, mastery of
oratorical style, perhaps bravery in war and feud. Typically decisive is the
deployment of one's skills and efforts in a certain direction: towards
amassing goods, most often pigs, shell monies and vegetable foods, and
distributing them in ways which build a name for cavalier generosity, if not
for compassion. A faction is developed by informal private assistance to
people of a locale. Tribal rank and renown are developed by great public
giveaways sponsored by the rising big-man, often on behalf of his faction
as well as himself. In different Melanesian tribes, the renown-making public distribution may appear as one side of a delayed exchange of pigs between corporate kinship groups; a marital consideration given a bride's
kinfolk; a set of feasts connected with the erection of a big-man's dwelling,
or of a clubhouse for himself and his faction, or with the purchase of
higher grades of rank in secret societies; the sponsorship of a religious cer-

---

[11] Oliver 1955:408. Compare with the parallel statement for the Kaoka of Guadalcanal in
Hogbin (1937–38:305).
[12] Pospisil 1958:81.

emony; a payment of subsidies and blood compensations to military allies; or perhaps the giveaway is a ceremonial challenge bestowed on another leader in the attempt to out-give and thus outrank him (a potlatch).

The making of the faction, however, is the true making of the Melanesian big-man. It is essential to establish relations of loyalty and obligation on the part of a number of people such that their production can be mobilized for renown-building external distribution. The bigger the faction the greater the renown; once momentum in external distribution has been generated the opposite can also be true. Any ambitious man who can gather a following can launch a societal career. The rising big-man necessarily depends initially on a small core of followers, principally his own household and his closest relatives. Upon these people he can prevail economically: he capitalizes in the first instance on kinship dues and by finessing the relation of reciprocity appropriate among close kinsmen. Often it becomes necessary at an early phase to enlarge one's household. The rising leader goes out of his way to incorporate within his family "strays" of various sorts, people without familial support themselves, such as widows and orphans. Additional wives are especially useful. The more wives a man has the more pigs he has. The relation here is functional, not identical: with more women gardening there will be more food for pigs and more swineherds. A Kiwai Papuan picturesquely put to an anthropologist in pidgin the advantages, economic and political, of polygamy: "'Another woman go garden, another woman go take firewood, another woman go catch fish, another woman cook him—husband he sing out plenty people come kaikai [i.e., come to eat]."'[13] Each new marriage, incidentally, creates for the big-man an additional set of in-laws from whom he can exact economic favors. Finally, a leader's career sustains its upward climb when he is able to link other men and their families to his faction, harnessing their production to his ambition. This is done by calculated generosities, by placing others in gratitude and obligation through helping them in some big way. A common technique is payment of bride-wealth on behalf of young men seeking wives.

The great Malinowski used a phrase in analyzing primitive political economy that felicitously describes just what the big-man is doing: amassing a "fund of power". A big-man is one who can create and use social relations which give him leverage on others' production and the ability to siphon off an excess product—or sometimes he can cut down their consumption in the interest of the siphon. Now although his attention may be given primarily to short-term personal interests, from an objective standpoint the leader acts to promote long-term societal interests. The fund of power provisions activities that involve other groups of the society at large. In the

---

[13] Landtman 1927:168.

greater perspective of that society at large, big-men are indispensable means of creating supralocal organization: in tribes normally fragmented into small independent groups, big-men at least temporarily widen the sphere of ceremony, recreation and art, economic collaboration, of war too. Yet always this greater societal organization depends on the lesser factional organization, particularly on the ceilings on economic mobilization set by relations between center-men and followers. The limits and the weaknesses of the political order in general are the limits and weaknesses of the factional ingroups.

And the personal quality of subordination to a center-man is a serious weakness in factional structure. A personal loyalty has to be made and continually reinforced; if there is discontent it may well be severed. Merely to create a faction takes time and effort, and to hold it, still more effort. The potential rupture of personal links in the factional chain is at the heart of two broad evolutionary shortcomings of western Melanesian political orders.

First, a comparative instability. Shifting dispositions and magnetisms of ambitious men in a region may induce fluctuations in factions, perhaps some overlapping of them, and fluctuations also in the extent of different renowns. The death of a center-man can become a regional political trauma: the death undermines the personally cemented faction, the group dissolves in whole or in part, and the people regroup finally around rising pivotal big-men. Although particular tribal structures in places cushion the disorganization, the big-man political system is generally unstable over short terms: in its super structure it is a flux of rising and falling leaders, in its substructure of enlarging and contracting factions. Secondly, the personal political bond contributes to the containment of evolutionary advance. The possibility of their desertion, it is clear, often inhibits a leader's ability to forceably push up his followers' output, thereby placing constraints on higher political organization, but there is more to it than that. If it is to generate great momentum, a big man's quest for the summits of renown is likely to bring out a contradiction in his relations to followers, so that he finds himself encouraging defection—or worse, an egalitarian rebellion—by encouraging production.

One side of the Melanesian contradiction is the initial economic reciprocity between a center-man and his followers. For his help they give their help, and for goods going out through his hands other goods (often from outside factions) flow back to his followers by the same path. The other side is that a cumulative build-up of renown forces center-men into economic extortion of the faction. Here it is important that not merely his own status, but the standing and perhaps the military security of his people depend on the big man's achievements in public distribution. Established at the head of a sizeable faction, a center-man comes under increasing pressure to extract goods from his followers, to delay reciprocities owing them, and to deflect incoming goods back into external circulation. Success in competition with other big-men particularly undermines internal-factional reciprocities: such success is precisely measurable by the ability to give outsiders more than they can possibly reciprocate. In well delineated big-man polities, we find leaders negating the reciprocal obligations upon which their following had been predicated. Substituting extraction for reciprocity, they must compel their people to "eat the leader's renown," as one Solomon Island group puts it, in return for productive efforts. Some center-men appear more able than others to dam the inevitable tide of discontent that mounts within their factions, perhaps because of charismatic personalities, perhaps because of the particular social organizations in which they operate, but paradoxically the ultimate defense of the center-man's position is some slackening of his drive to enlarge the funds of power. The alternative is much worse. In the anthropological record there are not merely instances of big-man chicanery and of material deprivation of the faction in the interests of renown, but some also of over loading of social relations with followers: the generation of antagonisms, defections, and in extreme cases the violent liquidation of the center-man. Developing internal constraints, the Melanesian big-man political order brakes evolutionary advance at a certain level. It sets ceilings on the intensification of political authority, on the intensification of household production by political means, and on the diversion of household outputs in support of wider political organization. But in Polynesia these constraints were breached, and although Polynesian chiefdoms also found their developmental plateau, it was not before political evolution had been carried above the Melanesian ceilings.

The fundamental defects of the Melanesian plan were overcome in Polynesia. The division between small internal and larger external political sectors, upon which all big-man politics hinged, was suppressed in Polynesia by the growth of an enclaving chiefdom-at-large. A chain of command subordinating lesser chiefs and groups to greater, on the basis of inherent societal rank, made local blocs or personal followings (such as were independent in Melanesia) merely dependent parts of the larger Polynesian chiefdom. So the nexus of the Polynesian chiefdom became an extensive set of offices, a pyramid of higher and lower chiefs holding sway over larger and smaller sections of the polity. Indeed the system of ranked and subdivided lineages (conical clan system), upon which the pyramid was characteristically established, might build up through several orders of inclusion and encompass the whole of an island or group of islands. While the island or the archipelago would normally be divided into several independent chiefdoms, high-order lineage connections between them, as well as kinship ties between their paramount chiefs, provided structural avenues for at least temporary expansion of political scale, for consolidation of great into even greater chiefdoms.[14]

The pivotal paramount chief as well as the chieftains controlling parts of a chiefdom were true office holders and title holders. They were not, like Melanesian big-men, fishers of men: they held positions of authority over permanent groups. The honorifics of Polynesian chiefs likewise did not refer to a standing in interpersonal relations, but to their leadership of political divisions—here "The Prince of Danes" not "the prince among men". In western Melanesia the personal superiorities and inferiorities arising in the intercourse of particular men largely defined the political bodies. In Polynesia there emerged supra-personal structures of leadership and followership, organizations that continued independently of the particular men who occupied positions in them for brief mortal spans.

And these Polynesian chiefs did not make their positions in society— they were installed in societal positions. In several of the islands, men did struggle to office against the will and stratagems of rival aspirants. But then they came to power. Power resided in the office; it was not made by the demonstration of personal superiority. In other islands, Tahiti was famous for it, succession to chieftainship was tightly controlled by inherent rank. The chiefly lineage ruled by virtue of its genealogical connections with divinity, and chiefs were succeeded by first sons, who carried "in the blood" the attributes of leadership. The important comparative point is this: the qualities of command that had to reside in men in Melanesia, that had to be personally demonstrated in order to attract loyal followers, were in Polynesia socially assigned to office and rank. In Polynesia, people of high rank and office *ipso facto* were leaders, and by the same token the qualities of leadership were automatically lacking—theirs was not to question why—

---

[14] Aside from the transitional developments in eastern Melanesia, several western Melanesian societies advanced to a structural position intermediate between underdeveloped Melanesian polities and Polynesian chiefdoms. In these western Melanesian protochiefdoms, an ascribed division of kinship groups (or segments thereof) into chiefly and nonchiefly ranks emerges—as in Sa'a (Ivens 1927), around Buka passage (Blackwood 1935), in Manam Island (Wedgwood 1933–34, 1958–59), Waropen (Held 1957), perhaps Mafulu (Williamson 1912), and several others. The rank system does not go beyond the broad dual division of groups into chiefly and nonchiefly: no pyramid of ranked social political divisions along Polynesian lines is developed. The political unit remains near the average size of the western Melanesian autonomous community. Sway over the kin groups of such a local body falls automatically to a chiefly unit, but chiefs do not hold office title with stipulated rights over corporate sections of society, and further extension of chiefly authority, if any, must be achieved. The Trobriands, which carry this line of chiefly development to its highest point, remain under the same limitations, although it was ordinarily possible for powerful chiefs to integrate settlements of the external sector within their domains (cf. Powell 1960).

among the underlying population. Magical powers such as a Melanesian big-man might acquire to sustain his position, a Polynesian high chief inherited by divine descent as the mana which sanctified his rule and protected his person against the hands of the commonalty. The productive ability the big-man laboriously had to demonstrate was effortlessly given Polynesian chiefs as religious control over agricultural fertility, and upon the ceremonial implementation of it the rest of the people were conceived dependent. Where a Melanesian leader had to master the compelling oratorical style, Polynesian paramounts often had trained "talking chiefs" whose voice was the chiefly command.

In the Polynesian view, a chiefly personage was in the nature of things powerful. But this merely implies the objective observation that his power was of the group rather than of himself. His authority came from the organization, from an organized acquiescence in his privileges and organized means of sustaining them. A kind of paradox resides in evolutionary developments which detach the exercise of authority from the necessity to demonstrate personal superiority: organizational power actually extends the role of personal decision and conscious planning, gives it greater scope, impact, and effectiveness. The growth of a political system such as the Polynesian constitutes advance over Melanesian orders of interpersonal dominance in the human control of human affairs. Especially significant for society at large were privileges accorded Polynesian chiefs which made them greater architects of funds of power than ever was any Melanesian big-man.

Masters of their people and "owners" in a titular sense of group resources, Polynesian chiefs had rights of call upon the labor and agricultural produce of households within their domains. Economic mobilization did not depend on, as it necessarily had for Melanesian big-men, the *de novo* creation by the leader of personal loyalties and economic obligations. A chief need not stoop to obligate this man or that man, need not by a series of individual acts of generosity induce others to support him, for economic leverage over a group was the inherent chiefly due. Consider the implications for the fund of power of the widespread chiefly privilege, related to titular "ownership" of land, of placing an interdiction, a tabu, on the harvest of some crop by way of reserving its use for a collective project. By means of the tabu the chief directs the course of production in a general way: households of his domain must turn to some other means of subsistence. He delivers a stimulus to household production: in the absence of the tabu further labors would not have been necessary. Most significantly, he has generated a politically utilizable agricultural surplus. A subsequent call on this surplus floats chieftainship as a going concern, capitalizes the fund of power. In certain islands, Polynesian chiefs controlled great storehouses which held the goods congealed by chiefly pressures on the commonalty. David Malo, one

of the great native custodians of old Hawaiian lore, felicitously catches the
political significance of the chiefly magazine in his well-known *Hawaiian
Antiquities*:

> It was the practice for kings [i.e., paramount chiefs of individual islands] to
> build storehouses in which to collect food, fish, tapas [bark cloth], malos
> [men's loin cloths], paus [women's loin skirts], and all sorts of goods. These
> storehouses were designed by the Kalaimoku [the chief's principal executive] as
> a means of keeping the people contented, so they would not desert the king.
> They were like the baskets that were used to entrap the hinalea fish. The Iz-
> inalea thought there was something good within the basket, and he hung
> round the outside of it. In the same way the people thought there was food in
> the storehouses, and they kept their eyes on the king. As the rat will not desert
> the pantry . . . where he thinks food is, so the people will not desert the king
> while they think there is food in his storehouse.[15]

Redistribution of the fund of power was the supreme art of Polynesian
politics. By well-planned noblesse oblige the large domain of a paramount
chief was held together, organized at times for massive projects, protected
against other chiefdoms, even further enriched. Uses of the chiefly fund included lavish hospitality and entertainments for outside chiefs and for the
chief's own people, and succor of individuals or the underlying population
at large in times of scarcities—bread and circuses. Chiefs subsidized craft
production, promoting in Polynesia a division of technical labor unparalleled in extent and expertise in most of the Pacific. They supported also
great technical construction, as of irrigation complexes, the further returns
to which swelled the chiefly fund. They initiated large-scale religious construction too, subsidized the great ceremonies, and organized logistic support for extensive military campaigns. Larger and more easily replenished
than their western Melanesian counterparts, Polynesian funds of power permitted greater political regulation of a greater range of social activities on
greater scale.

In the most advanced Polynesian chiefdoms, as in Hawaii and Tahiti, a
significant part of the chiefly fund was deflected away from general redistribution towards the upkeep of the institution of chieftainship. The fund
was siphoned for the support of a permanent administrative establishment.
In some measure, goods and services contributed by the people precipitated
out as the grand houses, assembly places, and temple platforms of chiefly
precincts. In another measure, they were appropriated for the livelihood of
circles of retainers, many of them close kinsmen of the chief, who clustered
about the powerful paramounts. These were not all useless hangers-on.
They were political cadres: supervisors of the stores, talking chiefs, ceremo-

---

[15] Malo 1903:257–58.

nial attendants, high priests who were intimately involved in political rule, envoys to transmit directives through the chiefdom. There were men in these chiefly retinues—in Tahiti and perhaps Hawaii, specialized warrior corps—whose force could be directed internally as a buttress against fragmenting or rebellious elements of the chiefdom. A Tahitian or Hawaiian high chief had more compelling sanctions than the harangue. He controlled a ready physical force, an armed body of executioners, which gave him mastery particularly over the lesser people of the community. While it looks a lot like the big-man's faction again, the differences in functioning of the great Polynesian chief's retinue are more significant than the superficial similarities in appearance. The chief's coterie, for one thing, is economically dependent upon him rather than he upon them. And in deploying the cadres politically in various sections of the chiefdom, or against the lower orders, the great Polynesian chiefs sustained command where the Melanesian big-man, in his external sector, had at best renown.

This is not to say that the advanced Polynesian chiefdoms were free of internal defect, of potential or actual malfunctioning. The large political military apparatus indicates something of the opposite. So does the recent work of Irving Goldman[16] on the intensity of "status rivalry" in Polynesia, especially when it is considered that much of the status rivalry in developed chiefdoms, as the Hawaiian, amounted to popular rebellion against chiefly despotism rather than mere contest for position within the ruling-stratum. This suggests that Polynesian chiefdoms, just as Melanesian big-man orders, generate along with evolutionary development countervailing antiauthority pressures, and that the weight of the latter may ultimately impede further development.

The Polynesian contradiction seems clear enough. On one side, chieftainship is never detached from kinship moorings and kinship economic ethics. Even the greatest Polynesian chiefs were conceived superior kinsmen to the masses, fathers of their people, and generosity was morally incumbent upon them. On the other side, the major Polynesian paramounts seemed inclined to "eat the power of the government too much," as the Tahitians put it, to divert an undue proportion of the general wealth toward the chiefly establishment.[17] The diversion could be accomplished by lowering the customary level of general redistribution, lessening the material returns of chieftainship to the community at large—tradition attributes the great rebellion of Mangarevan commoners to such cause.[18] Or the diversion might—and I suspect more commonly did—consist in greater and more forceful exactions from

---

[16] Goldman 1955, 1957, 1960.

[17] The great Tahitian chiefs were traditionally enjoined not to eat the power of government too much, as well as to practice openhandedness towards the people (Handy 1930:41). Hawaiian high chiefs were given precisely the same advice by counselors (Malo 1903:255).

[18] Buck 1938:70–77, 160, 165.

lesser chiefs and people, increasing returns to the chiefly apparatus without necessarily affecting the level of general redistribution. In either case, the well developed chiefdom creates for itself the dampening paradox of stoking rebellion by funding its authority.[19]

In Hawaii and other islands cycles of political centralization and decentralization may be abstracted from traditional histories. That is, larger chiefdoms periodically fragmented into smaller and then were later reconstituted. Here would be more evidence of a tendency to overtax the political structure. But how to explain the emergence of a developmental stymie, of an inability to sustain political advance beyond a certain level? To point to a chiefly propensity to consume or a Polynesian propensity to rebel is not enough: such propensities are promoted by the very advance of chiefdoms. There is reason to hazard instead that Parkinson's notable law is behind it all: that progressive expansion in political scale entailed more-than-proportionate accretion in the ruling apparatus, unbalancing the flow of wealth in favor of the apparatus. The ensuing unrest then curbs the chiefly impositions, sometimes by reducing chiefdom scale to the nadir of the periodic cycle. Comparison of the requirements of administration in small and large Polynesian chiefdoms helps make the point.

---

[19] The Hawaiian traditions are very clear on the encouragement given rebellion by chiefly exactions—although one of our greatest sources of Hawaiian tradition, David Malo, provides the most sober caveat regarding this kind of evidence. "I do not suppose," he wrote in the preface to Hawaiian Antiquities, "the following history to be free from mistakes, in that material for it has come from oral traditions; consequently it is marred by errors of human judgment and does not approach the accuracy of the word of God."

Malo (1903:258) noted that "Many kings have been put to death by the people because of their oppression of the makaainana (i.e., commoners)." He goes on to list several who "lost their lives on account of their cruel exactions," and follows the list with the statement "It was for this reason that some of the ancient kings had a wholesome fear of the people." The propensity of Hawaiian high chiefs for undue appropriation from commoners is a point made over and over again by Malo (see pp. 85, 87, 88, 258, 267–68). In Fornander's reconstruction of Hawaiian history (from traditions and genealogies) internal rebellions are laid frequently, almost axiomatically, to chiefly extortion and niggardliness (Fornander 1880:40–41, 76–78, 88, 149–50, 270–71). In addition, Fornander at times links appropriation of wealth and ensuing rebellion to the provisioning of the chiefly establishment, as in the following passage: "Scarcity of food, after a while, obliged Kalaniopuu (paramount chief of the island of Hawaii and half brother of Kamehameha I's father) to remove his court (from the Kona district) into the Kohala district, where his headquarters were fixed at Kapaau. Here the same extravagant, laissez-faite, eat and be merry policy continued that had been commenced at Kona, and much grumbling and discontent began to manifest itself among the resident chiefs and cultivators of the land, the 'Makaainan.' Zmakakaloa, a great chief in the Puna district, and Nuuampaahu, a chief of Naalehu in the Kau district, became the heads and rallyingpoints of the discontented. The former resided on his lands in Puna [in the southeast, across the island from Kohala in the northwest], and openly resisted the orders of Kalaniopuu and his extravagant demands for contributions of all kinds of property; the latter was in attendance with the court of Kalaniopuu in Kohala, but was strongly suspected of favouring the growing discontent" (Fornander 1880:200). Aside from the Mangarevan uprising mentioned in the text, there is some evidence for similar revolts in Tonga (Mariner 1827:80; Thomson 1894:29–40) and in Tahiti (Henry 1928:195–96, 297).

A lesser chiefdom, confined say as in the Marquesas Islands to a narrow valley, could be almost personally ruled by a headman in frequent contact with the relatively small population. Melville's partly romanticized—also for its ethnographic details, partly cribbed—account in *Typee* makes this clear enough.[20] But the great Polynesian chiefs had to rule much larger, spatially dispersed, internally organized populations. Hawaii, an island over four thousand square miles with an aboriginal population approaching one hundred thousand, was at times a single chiefdom, at other times divided into two to six independent chiefdoms, and at all times each chiefdom was composed of large subdivisions under powerful subchiefs. Sometimes a chiefdom in the Hawaiian group extended beyond the confines of one of the islands, incorporating part of another through conquest. Now, such extensive chiefdoms would have to be coordinated; they would have to be centrally tapped for a fund of power, buttressed against internal disruption, sometimes massed for distant, perhaps overseas, military engagements. All of this to be implemented by means of communication still at the level of word-of-mouth, and means of transportation consisting of human bodies and canoes. (The extent of certain larger chieftainships, coupled with the limitations of communication and transportation, incidentally suggests another possible source of political unrest: that the burden of provisioning the governing apparatus would tend to fall disproportionately on groups within easiest access of the paramount.[21]) A tendency for the developed chiefdom to proliferate in executive cadres, to grow top-heavy, seems in these circumstances altogether functional, even though the ensuing drain on wealth proves the chiefdom's undoing. Functional also, and likewise a material drain on the chiefdom at large, would be widening distinctions between chiefs and people in style of life. Palatial housing, ornamentation and luxury, finery and ceremony, in brief, conspicuous consumption, however much it seems mere self-interest always has a more decisive social significance. It creates those invidious distinctions between rulers and ruled so conducive to a passive—hence quite economical!—acceptance of authority. Throughout history, inherently more powerful political organizations than the Polynesian, with more assured logistics of rule, have turned to it including in our time some ostensibly revolutionary and proletarian governments, despite every pre-revolutionary protestation of solidarity with the masses and equality for the classes.

In Polynesia then, as in Melanesia, political evolution is eventually short circuited by an overload on the relations between leaders and their people.

---

[20] Or see Handy (1923) and Linton (1939).

[21] On the difficulty of provisioning the Hawaiian paramount's large stablishment see the citation from Fornander above, and also Fornander (1880:100–101; Malo 1903:92–93, et passim). The Hawaiian great chiefs developed the practice of the circuit—like feudal monarchs—often leaving a train of penury behind as they moved in state from district to district of the chiefdom.

The Polynesian tragedy, however, was somewhat the opposite of the Melanesian. In Polynesia, the evolutionary ceiling was set by extraction from the population at large in favor of the chiefly faction, in Melanesia by extraction from the big-man's faction in favor of distribution to the population at large. Most importantly, the Polynesian ceiling was higher. Melanesian big-men and Polynesian chiefs not only reflect different varieties and levels of political evolution, they display in different degrees the capacity to generate and to sustain political progress.

Especially emerging from their juxtaposition is the more decisive impact of Polynesian chiefs on the economy, the chiefs' greater leverage on the output of the several households of society. The success of any primitive political organization is decided here, in the control that can be developed over household economies. For the household is not merely the principal productive unit in primitive societies, it is often quite capable of autonomous direction of its own production, and it is oriented towards production for its own, not societal consumption. The greater potential of Polynesian chieftainship is precisely the greater pressure it could exert on household output, its capacity both to generate a surplus and to deploy it out of the household towards a broader division of labor, cooperative construction, and massive ceremonial and military action. Polynesian chiefs were the more effective means of societal collaboration on economic, political, indeed all cultural fronts. Perhaps we have been too long accustomed to perceive rank and rule from the standpoint of the individuals involved, rather than from the perspective of the total society, as if the secret of the subordination of man to man lay in the personal satisfactions of power. And then the breakdowns too, or the evolutionary limits, have been searched out in men, in "weak" kings or megalomaniacal dictators always, "who is the matter?" An excursion into the field of primitive politics suggests the more fruitful conception that the gains of political developments accrue more decisively to society than to individuals, and the failings as well are of structure not men.

BIBLIOGRAPHY

Bacon, Elizabeth E.
  1958   Obok. Viking Fund Publications in Anthropology No. 25. New York: Wenner-Gren Foundation.
Barnes, J. A.
  1962   African Models in the New Guinea Highlands. Man 62(2):59.
Blackwood, Beatrice
  1935   Both Sides of Buka Passage. Oxford: Clarendon Press.
Bromley, M.
  1960   A Preliminary Report on Law among the Grand Valley Dani of Netherlands New Guinea. Nieuw Guinea Studierz 4:235–259.

Brown, Paula
1960   Chimbu Tribes: Political Organization in the Eastern Highlands of New Guinea. Southwestern Journal of Anthropology 16:22–35.
Buck, Sir Peter H.
1938   Ethnology of Mangareva. Bernice P. Bishop Museum Bulletin 157, Honolulu.
Bulmer, Ralph
1960–61   Political Aspects of the Moka Exchange System among the Kyaka People of the Western Highlands of New Guinea. Oceania 31:113.
Burridge, Kenelm
1960   Mambu: A Melanesian Millennium. London: Methuen & Co.
Conklin, Harold C.
1957   Hanunoó Agriculture. FAO Forestry Development Paper No. 12. Rome: Food and Agricultural Organization of the United Nations.
Deacon, A. Bernard
1934   Malekula: A Vanishing People in the New Hebrides. C. H. Wedgwood, ed. London: Geo. Routledge and Sons.
Dyen, Isidore
1960   Review of the Position of the Polynesian Languages within the Austronesian. MalayoPolynesian Language Family by George W. Grace. Journal of the Polynesian Society 69:180–184.
Firth, Raymond
1950   Primitive Polynesian Economy. New York: Humanities Press.
1957   We, the Tikopia. 2nd ed. London: Allen and Unwin.
Fornander, Abraham
1880   An Account of the Polynesian Race. Vol. II. London: Trübner.
Freeman, J. D.
1955   Iban Agriculture. Colonial Research Studies No. 18. London: Her Majesty's Stationery Office.
Fried, Morton H.
1957   The Classification of Corporate Unilineal Descent Groups. Journal of the Royal Anthropological Institute 87:129.
Gifford, Edward Winslow
1929   Tongan Society. Bernice P. Bishop Museum Bulletin 61, Honolulu.
Goldman, Irving
1955   Status Rivalry and Cultural Evolution in Polynesia. American Anthropologist 57:680–697.
1957   Variations in Polynesian Social Organization. Journal of the Polynesian Society 66:374–390.
1960   The Evolution of Polynesian Societies. In Culture and History. S. Diamond, ed. New York: Columbia University Press.
Golson, Jack
1961   Polynesian Culture History, Journal of the Polynesian Society 70:498–508.
Goodenough, Ward
1957   Oceania and the Problem of Controls in the Study of Cultural and Human Evolution. Journal of the Polynesian Society 66:146–155.

Grace, George
  1955   Subgroupings of Malayo-Polynesian: A Report of Tentative Findings.
         American Anthropologist 57:337–339.
  1959   The Position of the Polynesian Languages within the Austronesian
         Malayo-Polynesian Family. Indiana University Publications in Anthropo-
         logical Linguistics 16.
Handy, E. and S. Craighill
  1923   The Native Culture in the Marquesas. Bernice P. Bishop Museum Bulletin
         9, Honolulu.
  1930   History and Culture in the Society Islands. Bernice P. Bishop Museum
         Bulletin 79, Honolulu.
Held, G. J.
  1957   The Papuas of Waropen. The Hague: Koninklijk Instituut Voor Taal, Land
         En Volkenkunde.
Henry, Teuira
  1928   Ancient Tahiti. Bernice P. Bishop Museum Bulletin 48, Honolulu.
Hogbin, H. Ian
  1933–34   Culture Change in the Solomon Islands: Report of Field Work in
            Guadalcanal and Malaita. Oceania 4:233–267.
  1937–38a Social Advancement in Guadalcanal, Solomon Islands. Oceania 8:289–
            305.
  1937–38b The Hill People of Northeastern Guadalcanal. Oceania 8:62–89.
  1939   Experiments in Civilization. London: Geo. Routledge and Son.
  1943–44   Native Councils and Courts in the Solomon Islands. Oceania 14:
            258–283.
  1951   Transformation Scene: The Changing Culture of a New Guinea Village.
         London: Routledge and Kegan Paul.
Hogbin H. and Camilla H. Wedgwood
  1952–53   Local Groupings in Melanesia. Oceania 23:241–276.
  1953–54   Local Groupings in Melanesia. Oceania 24:58–76.
Ivens, W. G.
  1927   Melanesians of the Southeast Solomon Islands. London: Kegan, Paul,
         Trench, Trübner and Co.
Kaberry, Phyllis M.
  1940–41   The Abelam Tribe, Sepik District, New Guinea: A Preliminary Report.
            Oceania 11:233–258, 345–367.
  1941–42   Law and Political Organization in the Abelam Tribe. Oceania 12:79–
            95, 209–225, 331–363.
Kirchhoff, Paul
  1955   The Principles of Clanship in Human Society. Davidson Anthropological
         Journal 1:1–11.
Landtman, Gunnar
  1927   The Kiwai Papuans of British New Guinea. London: Macmillan.
Linton, Ralph
  1939   Marquesan Culture. In The Individual and His Society. Ralph Linton and
         A. Kardiner, eds. New York: Columbia University Press.
Malo, David
  1903   Hawaiian Antiquities. Honolulu: Hawaiian Gazette Co.

Mariner, William
  1827   An Account of the Natives of the Tonga Islands. John Martin, compiler. Edinburgh: Constable & Co.
Mead, Margaret
  1934   Kinship in the Admiralty Islands. American Museum of Natural History, Anthropological Papers 34:181–358.
  1937a The Manus of the Admiralty Islands. *In* Cooperation and Competition among Primitive Peoples. Margaret Mead, ed. New York and London: McGraw-Hill.
  1937b The Arapesh of New Guinea. *In* Cooperation and Competition among Primitive Peoples. Margaret Mead, ed. New York and London: McGraw-Hill.
  1938   The Mountain Arapesh I. An Importing Culture. American Museum of Natural History, Anthropological Papers 36:139–349.
  1947   The Mountain Arapesh III. Socio-Economic Life. American Museum of Natural History, Anthropological Papers 40:159–232.
Meggitt, Mervyn
  1957   Enga Political Organization: A Preliminary Description. Mankind 5:133–137.
  1957–58 The Enga of the New Guinea Highlands: Some Preliminary Observations. Oceania 28:253–330.
Oliver, Douglas
  1955   A Solomon Islands Society. Cambridge, MA: Harvard University Press.
Pospisil, Leopold
  1958   Kapauku Papuans and Their Law. Yale University Publications in Anthropology, No. 54. New Haven, CT: Yale University Press.
  1958–59 The Kapauku Papuans and Their Kinship Organization. Oceania 30:188–205.
Powdermaker, Hortense
  1933   Life in Lesu. New York: W. W. Norton, 1933.
Powell, H. A.
  1960   Competitive Leadership in Trobriand Political Organization. Journal of the Royal Anthropological Institute 90:118–145.
Read, K. E.
  1946–47 Social Organization in the Markham Valley, New Guinea. Oceania 17:93–118.
  1949–50 The Political System of the Ngarawapum. Oceania 20:185–223.
  1952–53 The Nama Cult of the Central Highlands, New Guinea. Oceania 23:125.
  1959   Leadership and Consensus in a New Guinea Society American Anthropologist 61:425–436.
Reay, Marie
  1959   The Kuma. Melbourne: Melbourne University Press.
Sahlins, Marshall D.
  1958   Social Stratification in Polynesia. American Ethnological Society Monograph. Seattle: University of Washington Press.
  1961   The Segmentary Lineage: An Organization of Predatory Expansion. American Anthropologist 63:322–345.

Service, Elman R.
  1963   Primitive Social Organization: An Evolutionary Perspective. New York: Random House.
Suggs, Robert C.
  1960   Ancient Civilizations of Polynesia. New York: Mentor.
Thomson, Sir Basil
  1894   The Diversions of a Prime Minister. Edinburgh and London: William Blackwood & Sons.
Vayda, Andrew Peter
  1959   Polynesian Cultural Distributions in New Perspective. American Anthropologist 61:817–828.
Wedgwood, Camilla H.
  1933–34   Report on Research in Manam Island, Mandated Territory of New Guinea. Oceania 4:373–403.
  1958–59   Manam Kinship. Oceania 29:239–256.
Williams, F. E.
  1930   Orokaiva Society. Oxford University Press, London: Humphrey Milford.
  1940   Drama of Orolcolo. Oxford: Clarendon Press.
Williamson, Robert W.
  1912   The Mafulu: Mountain People of British New Guinea. London: Macmillan.
Worsley, Peter
  1957   The Trumpet Shall Sound. London: Macgibbon and Kee.

QUERIES

- What distinguishes the organization of political authority among Melanesian big-men societies versus Polynesian chiefdoms?
- Sahlins writes that there "are distinct sociological types . . . differences in the powers, privileges, rights, duties, and obligations of Melanesian big-men and Polynesian chiefs are given by the divergent societal contexts in which they operate." What are those differences?
- "Developing internal constraints," Sahlins writes, "the Melanesian big-man political order brakes evolutionary advance at a certain level. It sets ceilings on the intensification of political authority. . . . But in Polynesia these constraints were breached, and although Polynesian chiefdoms also found their developmental plateau, it was not before political evolution had been carried above the Melanesian ceilings. The fundamental defects of the Melanesian plan were overcome in Polynesia." Given this:
- How could the limits of Melanesian big-man political order be superceded?
- Do you think Sahlins is implying an evolutionary order for these political forms? (To put it crudely, which came first, big-men or chiefs?)
- Is there any ethnographic reason to think that order exists?

CONNECTIONS

- As mentioned in the introduction, Sahlins's article is similar in its organization and comparative method to Eric Wolf's "Types of Latin American Peasantries." What is the analytical strategy Sahlins and Wolf employ?
- Sahlins implies that big-man societies and chiefdoms represent distinct steps in cultural evolution. Is this idea similar to the different forms of government associated with Morgan's "ethnical periods"?
- Compare Sahlins's discussions of leadership strategies in big-man societies versus chiefdoms to Mary Douglas's discussion of leadership strategies in low-grid versus high-grid societies.

PRIMARY TEXT: *WHAT IS ANTHROPOLOGICAL ENLIGHTENMENT? SOME LESSONS OF THE TWENTIETH CENTURY*

Reprinted with permission from the *Annual Review of Anthropology*, Vol. 28, c 1998, pp ix–xiii, by *Annual Reviews*. www.annualreviews.org.

Introduction

Dare to know! But from what intellectual bondage would anthropology need to liberate itself in our times? No doubt from a lot of inherited ideas, including sexism, positivism, geneticism, utilitarianism, and many other such dogmas of the common average native Western folklore posing as universal understandings of the human condition. I do not presume to talk of all these things, but only of the civilizing theory which Kant responded to his famous question, what is Enlightenment? (1983 [1784]). For him, the question became how, by the progressive use of our reason, can we escape from barbarism?

But what kind of progressive anthropology was this? We are still struggling with what seemed like Enlightenment to the philosophers of the eighteenth century but turned out to be a parochial self-consciousness of European expansion and the *mission civilisatrice*. Indeed civilization was a word the philosophes invented to refer to their own society, of course. Following on Condorcet, the perfectibility they thus celebrated became in the nineteenth century a progressive series of stages into which one could fit—or fix—the various non-Western peoples. Nor was the imperialism of the past two centuries, crowned by the recent global victory of capitalism, exactly designed to reduce the enlightened contrasts between the West and the rest. On the contrary, the ideologies of modernization and development that trailed in the wake of Western domination took basic premises from the same old philosophical regime. Even the left critical arguments of dependency and capitalist hegemony could come to equally dim views of the historical capacities of indigenous peoples and the vitalities of their cultures. In too many narratives of Western domination, the indigenous victims appear as neo-historyless peoples: their own agency disappears, more or less with their culture, the moment Europeans irrupt on the scene.

What Is Not Too Enlightening?

Certain illusions born of the Western self-consciousness of civilization have thus proved not too enlightening. Worked up into academic gazes of other peoples, they became main issues with which modern anthropology has contended, sometimes to no avail. In the interest of examining the contention, I briefly examine this anthropological vision of the Other.

First, the set of defects that make up the historyless character of indigenous cultures in obvious contrast to progressiveness of the West. Indeed Margaret Jolly (1992) notes that when we change it's called progress, but when they do—notably when they adopt some of our progressive things— it's a kind of adulteration, a loss of their culture. But then, before we came upon the inhabitants of the Americas, Asia, Australia, or the Pacific islands, they were pristine and aboriginal. It is as if they had no historical relations with other societies, were never forced to adapt their existence, the one to the other. As if they had no experience constructing their own mode of existence out of their dependency on peoples—not to mention imperious forces of nature—over which they had no control. Rather, until Europeans appeared, they were isolated which just means that we weren't there. They were remote and unknown which means they were far from us, and we were unaware of them. (My lamented colleague Sharon Stephens used to introduce her lectures on Vico by noting that though it is often said that Vico lived an obscure life, I'm sure it didn't look that way to him.) Hence, the history of these societies only began when Europeans showed up: an epiphanal moment, qualitatively different from anything that had gone before and culturally devastating. Supposedly the historical difference with everything precolonial was power. Exposed and subjected to Western domination, the less powerful peoples were destined to lose their cultural coherence as well as the pristine innocence for which Europeans, incomplete and sinful progeny of Adam, so desired them. Of course, as Renato Rosaldo (1989) reminds us, the imperialists have no one to blame for their arcadian nostalgias but themselves. Nor should anything I say here be taken as a denial of the terror that Western imperialism has inflicted on so many peoples, or that so many have gone to the wall.

Accordingly, a main academic consequence of the cultural shock and psychological anomie inflicted by the West was the despondency theory that became popular in the midtwentieth century. Despondency theory was the logical precursor of dependency theory. But as it turned out when the surviving victims of imperialism began to seize their own modern history despondency was another not terribly enlightening idea of the power of Western civilization. Here is a good example from A. L. Kroeber's great 1948 textbook, *Anthropology*:

> With primitive tribes, the shock of culture contact is often sudden and severe. Their hunting lands or pastures may be taken away or broken under the plow, their immemorial customs of blood revenge, headhunting, sacrifice, marriage by purchase or polygamy be suppressed. Despondency settles over the tribes. Under the blocking-out of all old established ideals and prestiges, without provision for new values and opportunities to take their place, the resulting universal hopelessness will weigh doubly heavy because it seems to reaffirm inescapable frustration in personal life also. (Kroeber 1948:437–38).

A corollary of despondency theory was that the others would now become just like us—if they survived. Of course the Enlightenment had already prepared this eventuality by insisting on the universality of human reason and progress: a course of development that would be good in all senses of the term for the human species as such and as a whole. The unilinear evolutionism of the nineteenth century was a logical anthropological sequitur to this enlightened sense of universal rationality. Everyone would have to go through the same sequence of development. In his *Primitive Culture* of 1870, E. B. Tylor showed what doom was in store for the appreciation of cultural diversity by endorsing, as an appropriate procedure for constructing the stages of cultural evolution, Dr. Johnson's immortal observation that "one set of savages is like another" (Tylor 1903:1–6). In any case, to get back to other peoples now confronted by Western civilization, Marx likewise supposed that the country that is more developed industrially only shows to the less developed the image of its own future (1967:89). A late classic of the genre was Walt Rostow's *Stages of Economic Growth* (1960), with its unilinear sequence of five developmental stages from "traditional societies" to the "age of high mass consumption." (Rostow must have been among the first to perceive that the culmination of human social evolution was shopping.) Explicitly argued as an alternative to Marxist stages of progress—the book's subtitle was *A Non-Communist Manifesto*—Rostow's thesis had all the character of a mirror image, including the effect of turning left into right. Also shared with many theories of development was Rostow's cheerful sense of cultural tragedy: the necessary disintegration of traditional societies that functioned, in Rostow's scheme, as a

precondition for economic takeoff. A further necessity was the foreign domination that could accomplish this salutary destruction; for otherwise, the
customary relations of traditional production would set a ceiling on economic growth. By its own providential history, Europe had been able to develop itself, but according to Rostow other peoples would have to be
shocked out of their backwardness by an intrusive alien force—guess who?
No revolutionary himself, Rostow could agree with Marx that in order to
make an omelette one must first crack the eggs. Interesting that many peoples now explicitly engaged in defending their culture against national and
international domination the Maya of Guatemala and the Tukanoans of
Columbia, for example (Warren 1992; Watanabe 1995; Jackson 1995) have
distanced themselves both from the national bourgeois Right and the international proletarian Left, refusing the assimilationist pressures that
would sacrifice their ethnicity to either the construction of the nation or the
struggle against capitalist imperialism. Contrary to the evolutionary destiny
the West had foreseen for them, the so-called savages will neither be all
alike nor just like us.

* * *

Finally, what has not been too enlightening is the way anthropology in the
era of late capitalism is made to serve as a redemptive cultural critique a
morally laudable analysis that can amount to using other societies as an al-
ibi for redressing what has been troubling us lately. (There is a deep tradition here: Anthropology was also like that when it was coming of age in
Samoa and elsewhere.) It is as if other peoples had constructed their lives
for our purposes, in answer to racism, sexism, imperialism, and the other
evils of Western society. The problem with such an anthropology of advo-
cacy is not simply that arguments get judged by their morality, but that as a
priori persuasive, morality gets to be the argument. The true and the good
become one. Since the moral value is usually an external attribute supplied
by (and for) the analyst, however, it is too easy to change the signs, which
leads to some curious double bind arguments of the no-win or no-lose variety.

Take the devastating effects of Western capitalist expansion, on one hand,
and on the other the autonomous ordering of these effects by local peoples
according to their own cultural lights. Opposed as they may be as empirical
conclusions, both can be rejected on the same moral grounds and often are.
For to speak of the historical agency of indigenous peoples, true as it may
be, is to ignore the tyranny of the Western world system, thus to conspire
intellectually in its violence and domination. Whereas, to speak of the systematic hegemony of imperialism, true as it may be, is to ignore the peoples' struggles for cultural survival, thus to conspire intellectually in West-

ern violence and domination. Alternatively, we can make both global domination and local autonomy morally persuasive that is, in favor of the peoples by calling the latter resistance. This is a no-lose strategy since the two characterizations, domination and resistance, are contradictory and in some combination will cover any and every historical eventuality. Ever since Gramsci, posing the notion of hegemony has entailed the equal and opposite discovery of the resistance of the oppressed. Just so, the anthropologist who relates the so-called grand narrative of Western domination is also likely to invert it by invoking local discourses of cultural freedom. Cultural differences thrown out the front door by the homogenizing forces of world capitalism creep in the back in the form of an indigenous counterculture, subversion of the dominant discourse, or some such politics (or poetics) of indigenous defiance.

Local societies of the Third and Fourth Worlds do attempt to organize the irresistible forces of the world system according to their own system of the world in various forms and with varying success, depending on the nature of the indigenous culture and the mode of external domination. What is not too enlightening is the way that New Guinea pig feasting, Maori land claims, Zimbabwe medium cults, Brazilian workers' do-it-yourself housing, Fijian exchange customs, and any number of determinate cultural forms are accounted for, to the anthropologist's satisfaction, by their moral-political implications. It is enough to show they are effects of or reactions to imperialist domination, as if their supposed hegemonic or counter-hegemonic functions could specify their cultural contents. An acid bath of instrumentality, the procedure dissolves worlds of cultural diversity into the one indeterminate meaning. It is something like The Terror, as Sartre said of a certain crude materialism: an intellectual purge of the culture forms, marked by an inflexible refusal to differentiate. It consists of taking the actual cultural content for the mere appearance of a more profound and generic function in this case, the political or power—and having thus dissolved the historically substantional in the instrumentally universal, we are pleased to believe we have reduced appearance to truth (Sartre 1963). So nowadays all culture is power. It used to be that everything maintained the social solidarity. Then for a while everything was economic or adaptively advantageous. We seem to be on a great spiritual quest for the purposes of cultural things. Or perhaps it is that those who do not know their own functionalism are condemned to repeat it.

The Indigenous Culture

So let me end what Stephen Greenblatt (1991) called sentimental pessimism, the encompassment of other people's lives in global visions of Western domination. Not that there is no such domination, only that there is also other people's lives. Accordingly, the rest of my paper is a little more upbeat, being a discussion of how several of the problems bequeathed to us by the Enlightenment have been raised to new levels of perplexity by the advance of anthropology, and more particularly by recent ethnographic experiences of indigenous modernities. Many of the peoples who were left for dead or dying by dependency theory we now find adapting their dependencies to cultural theories of their own. Confronted by cultural processes and forms undreamed of in an earlier anthropology, such as the integration of industrial technologies in indigenous sociologies and cosmologies, we are not leaving the twentieth century with the same ideas that got us there.

One of the surprises of late capitalism, for example, is that hunters and gatherers live—many of them—by hunting and gathering. As late as 1966, most people at the famous Man the Hunter conference in Chicago thought they were talking about a way of life as obsolete as that title sounds today. Yet just a dozen years later, Richard Lee, one of the original conveners, remarked at another such conference: "Hunting is real. Hunting exists and hunting and gathering economies exist and this is to me a new fact in the modern world, because twelve years ago at the Man the Hunter conference we were writing an obituary on the hunters" (in Asch 1982:347). What Lee realized has not only been true of hunter-gatherers of Africa or Southeast Asia. All across the northern tier of the planet, scattered through the vast arctic and subarctic stretches of Europe, Siberia, and North America, hunting, fishing and gathering peoples have survived by harnessing industrial technologies to paleolithic purposes.

Nor is the survival of northern hunters a simple function of their isolation, since precisely their subsistence is dependent on modern means of production, transportation, and communication—rifles, snow-machines, motorized vessels and, at least in North America, CB radios and all-terrain vehicles—which means of existence they generally acquire by monetary purchase, which money they have acquired in a variety of ways ranging from public transfer payments and resource royalties to wage labor and commercial fishing. For upwards of 200 years, the Eskimo of Western and Northern Alaska (Yupik and Inupiat) have been engaged with the ever more powerful economic and political forces of world capitalist domination. You would have thought it was enough to undo them, at least culturally: the commercial whaling, fishing, and trapping and trading; the wage labor in jobs ranging from domestic service to construction of the DEW line and the pipeline; the missionization, education, and migration; the dependence on AFDC and Unemployment Compensation. To all this, the past 25 years added the Alaska Native Claims Settlement Act, followed by the formation of regional and local native corporations, followed by the spectacular exploitation of North Slope oil by powerful multinational corporations. If Eskimo have proven to be only pseudo-beneficiaries of these developments, it also seems they are only the pseudo-victims. However, I want to come back later to the Big Theoretical Issues raised by the apparent successes of native Alaskans and other peoples in dominating the capitalist modes of domination. For now I am simply making the point that the Eskimo are still there— and still Eskimo. Anthropological enlightenment begins with how wrong we were about that.

A sense of impending doom attended the concluding chapter of Charles Hughes's ethnography of Gambell Village on St. Lawrence Island in the Bering Sea, a community of Siberian Yupik speakers he studied in 1954–55. The chapter was titled "The Broken Tribe." Indeed "the time has passed," Hughes said, "when entire groups or communities of Eskimo can successfully relate to the mainland economy and social structure" (1960:389). For Hughes, two movements in opposite directions—of mainland Western culture to the island, and of islanders to the mainland—were between them tearing the indigenous society to pieces. The Gambell villagers who moved to the mainland were "no longer Eskimos," Hughes believed, "no longer people who retain a cultural tradition of their own." In the 1950s and 1960s, when young men went off to the U.S. military or to mainland schools under the sponsorship of the missions or the Bureau of Indian Affairs, when the BIA shipped whole families to Anchorage, Seattle, or Oakland under Relocation and Employment Assistance programs, the understanding was they would learn to live like white folks of the species Homo economicus, sever their relations to their villages and their cultures—and never go back. "They perforce have to forsake the overarching structure of Eskimo belief and practice," said Hughes of the Gambell migrants. "In effect, if they are to adjust to the white world, they must become as much like white men as possible. And the more that people move in that direction the more Gambell, as an Eskimo village, disappears from the human scene" (1960:389).

Yet in the 1980s, Gambell was experiencing spectacular growth—from 372 people in 1970 to 522 in 1989—much of it due to returning migrants, come back to resume a "subsistence life style," as a new generation of ethnographers explained, the epitomizing part of what they described as a general cultural "renaissance." Gambell was one of a set of villages, including Wainwright on the North Slope and Unalakleet on the lower Yukon, that an anthropological team headed by Joseph Jorgensen got to know in some depth in the 1980s with a view to determining how these "oil age Eskimos" were dealing with their increasing dependency (Jorgensen 1990; Jorgensen n.d.). Like Richard Nelson, who had first studied Wainwright in the 1960s and mistakenly thought then that the subsistence economy was finished—"subsistence" is a buzzword in Alaskan identity politics, whose meaning in this context would be about equivalent to "traditional custom"—like Nelson and many other ethnographers, the Jorgensen team found that the Eskimo of the 1980s and 1990s had changed very much more and very much less than anyone expected (Jorgensen 1990:5). More, because of the large influx of productive technologies and domestic conveniences; less, because these new techniques were overwhelmingly deployed to the subsistence life style and manipulated through its customary relations of production and distribution. The people's efficiency in hunting, fishing, and gathering was directly proportionate to their dependency on capitalism. But as their own modes of production were kinship-ordered—on Gambell by a still-functioning patrilineal clan system—the effect was an overall florescence of tradition that extended from intensive relations of reciprocity among kinsmen to cosmic relations of reciprocal life-giving between men and animals, passing by way of the revived winter festivals that had classically effected such interchanges. (In the Yukon I have heard these festivals referred to by English-speaking Yupiit as potlatches.) At the same time, instead of the migrant islanders going off to lose their culture, the effect of their stay for longer or shorter periods in Whiteman's Land has been to extend the village of Gambell from its home site in St. Lawrence Island to clansmen as far away as Oregon and California. Among other reasons: increased "subsistence" at home leads to increased "sharing" abroad. A study of one household's "subsistence sharing" by Lynn Robbins showed it was thus connected to 29 other households in Gambell, 23 in the St. Lawrence village of Savoonga, seven in Nome, two in Fairbanks, one in Sitka, two in Oregon, and six in California. The network included 315 people in 70 households, with the majority of gifts going to members of the patriclan. Echoing similar reports from all over Alaska, Jorgensen writes, "In short, there is a determination on the part of Eskimos to maintain traditional Eskimo culture and at the same time to adopt a pragmatic acceptance of the benefits of modern technology" (Jorgensen n.d.:6).

Still, from the point of view of a traditional anthropology—not to mention world-systems and dependency theory, development economics and modernization theory, postmodernism and globalization theory—the question is, how did the Eskimo do that?

Moreover, the Eskimo are not alone. In the discussion that follows I evoke the analogous modern experiences of other societies, with a view toward unpacking some of the issues the Eskimo pose—and thus reconstructing a too traditional anthropology according to the ways the peoples reconstruct their traditional cultures.

The Indignization of Modernity

This is a modern song of Enga people of New Guinea, about capturing the power-knowledge of Europeans, the "Red Men" in local parlance:

When the time comes,
Our youngsters will feed upon their words,
After the Red Men drift away from this land,
Our youngsters, like honey birds,
After the Reds have gone,
Will suck the flowers,
While standing back here.
We will do like them,
We shall feed upon their deeds
Like honey-birds sucking flowers. (Talyaga 1975:n.p.)

Reversing the real relations of exploitation and domination, these verses could easily be mistaken for the wistful fantasies of the powerless. Yet it would be wrong to suppose them motivated by the people's self contempt or a sense of their impending doom. Everything about the modern ethnography of Highland New Guinea indicates that the sentiment of cultural usurpation here—ambiguously figured as honey birds feeding on the powers of banished White men—that this usurpation is the guiding principle of the Highlanders' historical action. Rather than despondency, it is a forward action on modernity, guided by the assurance the Enga will be able to harness the good things of Europeans to the development of their own existence. "Develop-man" is the neo-Melanesian term for development; and it would not be wrong to re-pidginize it back to English as "the development of man," since the project it refers to is the use of foreign wealth in the expansion of feasting, politicking, subsidizing kinship, and other activities that make up the local conception of a human existence (Nihill 1989). This is what the working and warrior youth of Enga are urged to carry on. Rather than the death of tradition, Enga thus express their confidence in a living tradition, a tradition precisely that serves as a means and measure of innovation.

To put the matter anthropologically, which is to say to perceive great things in little ones, this active appropriation by Enga of the European power imposed upon them is a local manifestation of a new planetary organization of culture. Unified by the expansion of Western capitalism over recent centuries, the world is also being re-diversified by indigenous adaptations to the global juggernaut. In some measure, global homogeneity and local differentiation have developed together, the latter as a response to the former in the name of native cultural autonomy. The new planetary organization has been described as "a Culture of cultures," a world cultural system made up of diverse forms of life. As Ulf Hannerz put it: "There is now a world culture, but we had better make sure we understand what this means. It is marked by an organization of diversity rather than a replication of uniformity" (1990:237). Thus, one complement of the new global ecumene is the so-called culturalism of very recent decades: the self-consciousness their "culture," as a value to be lived and defended, that has broken out all around the Third and Fourth Worlds. Ojibway, Hawaiians, Inuit, Tibetans, Amazonian peoples, Australian Aborigines, Maori, Senegalese: Everyone now speaks of their culture, or some near local equivalent, precisely in the context of national or international threats to its existence. This does not mean a simple and nostalgic desire for teepees and tomahawks or some such fetishized repositories of a pristine identity. A "naive attempt to hold peoples hostage to their own histories," such a supposition, Terence Turner remarks, would thereby deprive them of history. What the self-consciousness of "culture" does signify is the demand of the peoples for their own space within the world cultural order. Rather than a refusal of the commodities and relations of the world-system, this more often means what the Enga sang about, a desire to indigenize them. The project is the indigenization of modernity.

So in certain indigenous respects, their engagement with the international capitalist forces has allowed Enga and other New Guinea Highlanders to "develop" their cultural orders, that is, as they understand develop-man: more and better of what they consider good things. Such is a common ethnographic report from the area since the 1960s. Benefiting from the market returns to migratory labor, coffee production, and other cash-cropping, the great inter-clan ceremonial exchanges—hallmark institution of Highlands culture—have flourished in recent decades as never before. Among Enga, Mendi, Siane, and others, the ceremonies have increased in frequency as well as in the magnitude of people engaged and goods transacted. Accordingly big-men are more numerous and powerful. Old clan alliances that had lapsed have been revived. Interpersonal kinship networks have been widened and strengthened. Rather than the antithesis of community, money has thus been the means. High value bank notes replace pearl shells as key exchange valuables, gifts of Toyota land cruisers complement the usual pigs, and large quantities of beer function as initiatory presents (adding certain celebratory dimensions to the customary festivities). Captured in reciprocal obligations and bridewealth payments, "the money which circulates in exchanges is generally not 'consumed' at all," as Andrew Strathern noted of Hageners, "but keeps on circulating, through the momentum of debt and investment" (1979:546). Rena Lederman reports that among modern Mendi people the exchange obligations between clans and personal kin create a demand for modern currency far greater than the demand generated by existing market outlets (1986:231). Hence, from a Mendi point of view, they have the true exchange economy, by contrast to the mere "subsistence system" of white men (1986:236). Now there's a howdy-do.

Tradition and Change

The struggle of non-Western peoples to create their own cultural versions of modernity undoes the received Western opposition of tradition vs. change, custom vs. rationality and most notably its twentieth century version of tradition vs. development. The antithesis was already old by the time the *philosophes* undertook to *écrasez l'infâime*, to destroy entrenched superstition by progressive reason. It had been kicking around advanced European thought at least since Sir Francis Bacon proposed to smash the idols of the cave and the tribe by the exercise of rational empirical wisdom and thus rescue humanity from the metaphysical consequences of Original Sin. In the redemptive vision (version) of modern Development Economics, as we have seen, so-called tradition, being burdened with "irrationalities," is presented as an obstacle to so-called development. The indigenous people's culture is something the matter with them.

Paradoxically, almost all the "traditional" cultures studied by anthropologists, and so described, were in fact neo-traditional, already changed by Western expansion. In some cases this happened so long ago that no one, not even anthropologists, now debates their cultural authenticity. The Iroquois confederacy was by most accounts a post-contact develop-man, as were the Plains Indian cultures that flourished through the acquisition of the horse. For all that, were the Iroquois less Iroquoian or the Sioux less Siouan? Today in Fiji, Wesleyan Christianity is considered "custom of the land." (I recall a recent man-on-the-street interview in a Suva newspaper, in which a Fijian matron, shocked by the nude bathing at tourist resorts, asked "how are we going to keep our traditional customs if people go around like that?") Indeed Margaret Jolly rightly wonders why church hymns and the Christian mass should not be considered "part of Pacific tradition," given that they "have been significantly remade by Pacific peoples, so that Christianity may appear today as more quintessentially a Pacific than a Western faith (1992:53). If Pacific peoples gloss over the distinction—so critical to our own historical sensibility—between the colonial and the precolonial past, it is that they "are more accepting of both indigenous and exogenous elements as constituting their culture." Indeed, since the exogenous elements are culturally indigenized, there is not, for the people concerned, a radical disconformity, let alone an inauthenticity. So-called hybridity is after all a genealogical observation, not a structural determination—perhaps only appropriate to the cosmopolitan intellectuals from whose external vantage such cultural theories are fabricated. Anthropologists have known at least since the work of Boas and his students that cultures are generally foreign in origin and local in pattern. Or if we have forgotten the diffusionists' lessons, we should at least recall the indigenous daily routine of the average American man described some decades ago by Ralph Linton. After breakfast our good man settles down to read the news of the day "imprinted in characters invented by the ancient Semites upon a material invented in China by a process invented in Germany. As he absorbs the accounts of foreign troubles he will, if he is a good conservative citizen, thank a Hebrew deity in an Indo-European tongue that he is 100 percent American" (1936:329).

In *Europe and the Peoples without History*, Eric Wolf (1982) correctly pointed out that most of the world was like that, a mix of the indigenous and the exogenous, by the time Western anthropologists got there. Imperialism had gotten there first. Regrettably, in his effort to convince fellow anthropologists they had never really known the pristine peoples they hankered after, Wolf neglected to draw the complementary conclusion about the cultural differences the ethnographers had nonetheless discovered and described. If the indigenous peoples were not without history, it was because they were not without their culture—which is also why their modern histories have differed.

In the late eighteenth century, the Hawaiian chiefs largely monopolized trade with the British and American vessels stopping for provisions and sandalwood while en route to China with furs from Northwest America. The chiefs, however, had distinctive demands, mainly for unique adornments and domestic furnishings, flashy goods that linked their persons to the sky and overseas sources of divine power, fashionable goods that could also differentiate them from their aristocratic fellows and rivals. Yet their Kwakiutl counterparts on the Northwest Coast were beginning a long economic history of a contrasting kind, demanding standardized items from the fur traders, eventually Hudson's Bay blankets by the tens of thousands. Moreover, rather than hoarding them up as Hawaiian chiefs did their treasures, the Kwakiutl distributed their blankets in potlatches in ways that allowed them to correlate and measure their otherwise distinct claims to superiority. By contrast to the rather mundane woolen blankets, Honolulu traders of Boston firms were sending to America for luxe: "Everything new and elegant will sell at a good profit. Coarse articles are of no use." The letter books of these traders are full of orders for "fine calicoes and cambricks," silks, scarves "in handsome patterns," superfine broadcloths, cashmeres: a whole catalogue of Polynesian splendors in European idiom—commodities, moreover, from which the people in general were excluded. Unlike the Kwakiutl chiefs who were fashioning their preeminence out of common cloth, the Hawaiian elite were bent on unique projects of economic aggrandizement. But then, the Hawaiian chiefs were all more or less closely descended from the gods, and the main issue between them was how to turn these quantitative differences of genealogy into qualitative distinctions of standing. The Kwakiutl chiefs already represented distinct and unrelated lineages, with different divine origins and powers. As heirs of unique ancestors and treasures, they used stock European goods in public fashion to turn their qualitative differences in genealogy into quantitative measures of rank. Accordingly the politics, economics, and destinies of Hawaiians and Kwakiutl acquired different forms and fates in the nineteenth century (Sahlins 1988). The continuity of their respective cultural traditions consisted in the different ways they changed.

* * *

Money and Markets, Moralities and Mentalities

Eskimo culture, Western techniques. Or as the Yukon village leader said to the anthropologist:

> We take whatever technology works and shape it to our purposes and uses. . . . Apparently that bothers people who want us to remain pristine, or to admit to our contradictions of wanting technology and controlling and preserving the resources of our own use. . . . Why not? We have always accepted and reshaped technology that works for our own purposes. (Jorgensen 1990:69)

I have already mentioned the snowmachines, CB radios, all-terrain four-wheelers, rifles and powered 18' and 32' fishing vessels, but I forgot the Eskimo subsistence airplanes. The anthropologist Steve Langdon tells of five of them owned by the Yupik villagers of Togiak (in Bristol Bay). These planes were used "primarily to 1) extend subsistence range to areas where caribou are located and 2) provide on demand transportation for visiting relatives in nearby villages, objectives totally in congruence with the subsistence-based foundation of the community" (1991:284–85). Such modern modes of paleolithic production bring obvious efficiencies to the subsistence economy— and some not so obvious, such as relief from the necessity of catching, processing, and storing the 5,000 chum salmon required to feed a dog team over the winter. But they also make it possible to engage more effectively in the market economy on which wild food-getting depends, affording the mobility or stability to intermittently hunt money also—when and where (and if) the opportunity presents itself. Contrary to the general opinions of the past two centuries, however, Yupik relations to animals have remained altogether distinct from the capitalist relations of production that provided them with the necessary hunting gear. Chase Hensel quotes John Active, a Yupik man who works at the public radio and television station at Bethel—the year of the interview is 1992:

> The animals, birds and plants have an awareness, and we treat them with the same respect we have for ourselves. The non-Natives refer to these animals as "game." Hunting for them is a game. We do not play games with animals. When we bring animals into our houses, we treat them as guests. . . . We thank

them for having been caught and believe their spirits will return to their gods
and report about how they are cared for. [The "gods" are apparently species
spirit masters, as in the widespread northern cosmology.] If the animals are
treated well, then those gods will provide more of the same. . . . Our ancestors
didn't learn that from your book [the Bible]. (Hensel 1992:71)

It is not simply that Eskimo cultures—or other northern groups such as
Dené and James Bay Cree, of whom similar recent observations have been
made—it is not simply that they have persisted in spite of capitalism or because the people have resisted it. This is not so much the culture of resistance as it is the resistance of culture. Involving the assimilation of the foreign in the logics of the familiar—a change in the contexts of the foreign
forms or forces, which also changes their values—cultural subversion is in
the nature of intercultural relations. Inherent in meaningful action, such resistance of culture is the more inclusive form of historical differentiation,
neither requiring an intentional politics of cultural opposition nor confined
to the reactions of the colonially oppressed. (All this was worked out in the
theoretical line that leads from the refinements of Boasian diffusion by
Benedictian patterns of culture, a development previously noticed here,
through Batesonian culture contact schismogenesis to the similar structural
dialectics of Lévi-Strauss's *Mythologiques*.) Yet even the subjects of Western
domination and dependency relations act in the world as social-historical
beings, so their experience of capitalism is mediated by the *habitus* of an indigenous form of life. In the upshot, the capitalist forces are played out in
the schemata of a different cultural universe. Of course it is true that their
too classic dependency could do in people like the Yupik. On the other
hand, as Durkheim said, a science of the future has no subject matter. In the
meantime, the apparent cultural mystification of dependency produces an
empirical critique of the orthodoxy that money, markets, and the relations
of commodity production are incompatible with the organizations of the
so-called traditional societies.

Marx says that money destroys the archaic community because money
becomes the community. As if, Freud complained, a person suddenly got a
psyche when he drew his first paycheck. In a book called *Money and the
Morality of Exchange*, Maurice Bloch and Jonathan Parry collect a number of
examples to the contrary, from a variety of societies. As against the idea that
money gives rise to particular world view—the unsociable, impersonal, and
contractual one we associate with it—they emphasize "how an existing
world view gives rise to particular ways of representing money" (1989:19).
At issue is the structural position money is accorded in the cultural totality.
The famous statements of Marx, Simmel and company about the destructive effects of markets and money on community, presuppose a separate
"economic" domain, as Bloch and Parry point out—an amoral sphere of

transaction separated from the generosities of kith and kin. But where there is no structural opposition between the relationships of economy and sociability, where material transactions are ordered by social relations rather than vice versa, then the amorality we attribute to money need not obtain.

So in general, one of the Big Surprises of "late capitalism" is that "traditional" cultures are not inevitably incompatible with it nor vulnerable to it. Certainly the recent ethnographers of the Alaskan and Canadian north have had great academic sport with the classic 1950s and 1960s arguments of Service and Murphy and Steward to the effect that commercial trade will be the end of indigenous culture for hunters and trappers. Debt peonage, the breakup of larger communities and collective efforts, disintegration of extended kinship networks, reduction of kinship to nuclearization, the decline of food-sharing and other reciprocities, privatization of property, the development of economic inequalities and overall individualism, such were the forecasts of hunters' fate. The final phase, according to Murphy and Steward, would be marked by "assimilation of the Indians as a local subculture of the national sociocultural system" and perhaps eventually in a" virtual loss of identity as Indians" (1956:350). To summarily categorize the contrary modern findings among northern hunters, however, their long, intensive and varied engagements with the international market economy have not fundamentally altered their customary organizations of production, modes of ownership and resource control, division of labor, or patterns of distribution and consumption; nor have their extended kinship and community bonds been dissolved or the economic and social obligations thereof fallen off; neither have social (cum "spiritual") relations to nature disappeared; and they have not lost their cultural identities, not even when they live in white folks' towns (Fienup-Riordan 1983, 1986; Wenzel 1991).

To put it another way, dependency is real but it is not the internal organization of Cree, Inuit or Yupik existence. The loss of traditional skills—dog sledding, kayak-making, hunting methods and much, much more—makes their dependency all the more serious. But the real problem this poses for the people is not the unlivable contradiction between the money economy and the traditional way of life. The big problems come when they cannot find enough money to support their traditional way of life. For if one calculated, as some anthropologists have, how much income from government transfer funds and commercial trade is devoted to subsidizing the indigenous modes of production, then the internal economy clearly subsumes and integrates the external (Langdon 1986). Within the villages, moreover, the greater a person's or family's successes in the money economy, the more they participate in the indigenous order (Lonner 1986; Wolfe 1986). Sharing with kinsmen increases with monetary income, typically via the advantages money gives in hunting and gathering. But then, studies also show that the people with the greatest outside experience in education or employment are as much or more engaged as anyone in the local subsistence culture (Kruse 1986). If this helps explain why seemingly acculturated people are commonly traditional leaders, it also invites the question of why they ever came back to the village—which leads to another area of enlightenment offered by the indigenization of modernity:

Reversing Center and Periphery

Cities are the favored places of *merantu*, the customary journeys of Menangkabau and other Indonesian men beyond the cultural bounds, whence they return with booty and stories worthy of their manhood. The Malay community in Mecca is second in size only to the Arabs. Some remain on the haj for 10 years or more; some are delayed for years returning via Africa or India (Provencher 1976). The Mexican villagers working in Redwood City, California, and the Samoans in San Francisco likewise intend to return, an eventuality for which they prepare by sending money back to relatives, by periodic visits to their native places, by sending their children home for visits or schooling, and otherwise maintaining their natal ties and building their local status. But how is it that Oaxacans, Samoans, Africans, Filipinos, Peruvians, Thais—the millions of people now cycling between the "peripherae" and metropolitan centers of the modem world-system are content to return to a bucolic existence "after they've seen Paris?" Is it not true that *Stadt Luft macht Frei*?[22] Or if not free, proletarians forever? Well, apparently not always, however true in an earlier European history. Today the huge phenomenon of circular migration is creating a new kind of cultural formation: a determinate community without entity, extending transculturally and often transnationally from a rural center in the Third World to "homes abroad" in the metropolis, the whole united by the to-and-fro of goods, ideas and people on the move. "The geographic village is small," writes Uzzell of Oaxacan campesinos, "the social village spreads over thousands of miles" (1979:343).

Taking shape as urban ethnic outposts of rural "tribal" or peasant homelands, these synthetic formations were for a long time unrecognized as such by the Western social scientists studying them. Or rather in studying urbanization, migration, remittance dependency, labor recruitment, or ethnic formation, Western researchers presented a spectacle something like the blind men and the elephant, each satisfied to describe the translocal cultural whole in terms of one or another of its aspects. No doubt the Euro-American history of urbanization had a stranglehold on the anthropological imagination. The general presumption was that urbanization must everywhere put an end to

---

[22] Editor's note: A German saying that "City air makes one free" referring to the liberating escape from rural life.

"the idiocy of rural life." By the very nature of the city as a complex social and industrial system, relations between people would become impersonal, utilitarian, secular, individualized, and otherwise disenchanted and detribalized. Such was the trend in Robert Redfield's "folk-urban continuum." As the beginning and end of a qualitative change, countryside and city were structurally distinct and opposed ways of life. "After the rise of cities," Redfield wrote, "men became something different to what they had been before" (1953:ix). British social anthropology of the period was hung up on the same dualist a priori. Gluckman was the father of the African version: "The African in the rural area and in town is two different men" (1960:69).

But enlightenment was soon in coming. Explicitly taking on the folk-urban continuum, Edward Bruner demonstrated the continuity of identity, kinship, and custom between Toba Batak villages of highland Sumatra and their urban relatives in Medan. "Examined from the structural point of view, the Toba Batak communities in village and city are part of one social and ceremonial system" (1961:5–15). Speaking more widely of Southeast Asia, Bruner wrote that "contrary to traditional theory, we find in many Asian cities that society does not become secularized, the individual does not become isolated, kinship organizations do not break down, nor do the social relationships in the urban environment become impersonal, superficial and utilitarian" (1961:508). By the mid-1970s such observations had become common in the Latin American homeland of the folk-urban continuum as well as in ethnographies by Gluckman's colleagues and others throughout sub-Sahara Africa. And as the gestalt shifted from the antithesis of the rural-urban to the synthesis of the translocal cultural order, study after study groped for a suitable terminology. The scholars spoke variously of "a bilocal society," "a single social and resource system," "a non-territorial community network," "a common social field" uniting countryside and city, "a social structure that encompasses both donor and host locations," "a single social field in which there is a substantial circulation of members," or some new species of the like (Ryan 1993:326; Ross and Weisner 1977:361; Trager 1988:194; Uzzell 1979:343; Bartle 1981:105).

What any and all of these descriptions express is the structural complementarity of the indigenous homeland and the metropolitan "homes abroad," their interdependence as sources of cultural value and means of social reproduction. Symbolically focused on the homeland, whence its members derive their identity and their destiny, the translocal community is strategically dependent on its urban outliers for material wherewithal. The rural order itself extends into the city, inasmuch as the migrant folk are transitively associated with each other on the bases of their relationships at home. Kinship, community, and tribal affiliations acquire new functions, and perhaps new forms, as relations of migration: They organize the movements of people and resources, the care of homeland dependents, the provision of urban housing and employment. Since people conceive their social being as well as their future in their native place, the material flows generally favor the home-land people. The indigenous order is sustained by earnings and commodities acquired in the foreign commercial sector. But should we speak of "remit-tances" as the foreign economic experts do? This flow of money and goods is better understood by the norms of "reciprocity," Epeli Hau'ofa argues, since it reflects the migrants' obligations to homeland kin, even as it secures their rights in their native place (Hau'ota 1993). "Reciprocity" as opposed to "re-mittances" appropriately shifts the analytic perspective from a geographic vil-lage that is small to a social village spread over thousands of miles, and rather than lament the fate of a village that lives on "remittances," one might with Graeme Hugo commend its success in reversing "the parasitic function tradi-tionally ascribed to cities" (1978:264). In spanning the historic divide be-tween traditional and modern, the developmental distance between center and periphery, and the structural opposition of townsmen and tribesmen, the translocal community deceives a considerable body of enlightened Western social science.

Culture Is Not Disappearing

Of course it is possible that the translocal community will soon disap-pear as a cultural form. If the migrants settle permanently abroad, the struc-ture might have a sort of generational half-life, the attachments to the homeland dissolving with each city-born or foreign-born generation. Still, in parts of Indonesia, Africa, and elsewhere, circular migration has been go-ing on for many generations. Reports from Nairobi in the 1980s echo ob-servations in Java from 1916: The migrants were not being proletarianized (Elkan 1985; Parkin 1975). From a large review of anthropological litera-ture on culture and development, Michael Kearney recently concluded just that: "migrants have not been proletarianized in any deeply ideological sense" (1986:352). However, the longevity of the form is not the issue I am concerned with here. What is of more interest is the ongoing creation of new forms in the modern world Culture of cultures. No one can deny that the world has seen an overall decrease of cultural diversity in the past five centuries. Indeed, anthropology was born out of the consciousness of the decrease as much as the appreciation of the diversity. There is no special rea-son now to panic about the death of culture.

Suppose for argument's sake we agree that Malinowski's *Argonauts of the Western Pacific* was the beginning of modern professional ethnography. If so, it is sobering to reflect it opens with these words:

> Ethnology is in the sadly ludicrous, not to say tragic, position, that at the very moment when it begins to put the workshop in order, to forge its proper tools, to start ready for work on its appointed task, the material of its study melts

away with hopeless rapidity. Just now, when the methods and aims of scientific field ethnology have taken shape, when men [n.b.] fully trained for the work have begun to travel into savage countries and study their inhabitants—these die away under our very eyes. (1922:xv)

Past objects? Yes, history studies these. But how many academic disciplines other than high-energy physics originated as the study of disappearing objects? And nowadays the disintegration of the cultural object seems to many anthropologists worse than ever. Confronted by the apparent disappearance of the old anthropology-cultures, the wreckage of coherent logics and definite boundaries appreciably effected by the passage of the World System, they are tempted to succumb to a postmodern panic about the possibility that anything like "a culture" actually exists. This panic just when all about them the peoples are talking up their "culture." Now everyone has a culture; only the anthropologists could doubt it. But why lose our nerve? Presented by history with a novel set of cultural structures, practices, and politics, anthropology should take the opportunity to renew itself. The discipline seems as well off as it ever was, with cultures disappearing just as we were learning how to perceive them, and then reappearing in ways we had never imagined.

The best modern heirs of the Enlightenment *philosophes* know this. I mean, for example, the West African francophone intellectuals who argue, with Paul Hountondji (1994), that "culture is not only a heritage, it is a project." Yet it is, as Abdou Toure (1994) insists, an African project, or set of projects, and precisely not the universal march of reason proclaimed by the eighteenth century and still worshiped in the development religions of the twentieth:

> That which the minority of [elite] leaders has voluntarily forgotten is Culture as a philosophy of life, and as an inexhaustible reservoir of responses to the world's challenges. And it is because they brush aside this culture that they're able to reason lightly in terms of development while implying a scale of values, norms of conduct or models of behavior transmissible from one society to another!

Toure's conclusion is that Africa is no longer subjected to the Western model of development for the simple reason that there is no longer a model of any worth. Finally—enlightenment.

BIBLIOGRAPHY

Asch, M. I.
1982   Dené Self-determination and the Study of Hunter-gatherers in the Modern World. *In* Politics and History in Band Societies. Eleanor Leacock and R. Lee, eds. Pp. 347–372. Cambridge, UK: Cambridge University Press.

Barrow, J.
    1805   Travels in China. Philadelphia: W. F. McLaughlin.
Bartle, P. F. V.
    1981   Cyclical Migration and the Extended Community: A West African exam-
            ple. *In* Frontiers in Migration Analysis. R. E. Mandal, ed. Pp. 107–139.
            New Delhi: Concept.
Bloch, M., and J. Parry, eds.
    1989   Money and the Morality of Exchange. Cambridge, UK: Cambridge Uni-
            versity Press.
Boeke, J. H.
    1942   The Structure of Netherlands Indian Economy. New York: Institute of Pa-
            cific Relations.
Bruner, E. M.
    1961   Urbanization and Ethnic Identity in North Sumatra. American Anthro-
            pologist 3:508–521.
Chow, T.
    1960   The May Fourth Movement. Cambridge, MA: Harvard University Press.
Cranmer-Byng, J. L.
    1962   An Embassy to China: Being the Journal Kept by Lord Macartney during
            His Embassy to the Emperor Ch 'ien-lung, 1793–94. London: Longmans.
Elkan, W.
    1985   Is a Proletariat Emerging in Nairobi? *In* Circulation in Third World Coun-
            tries. R. M. Prothero and M. Chapman, eds. Pp. 367–379. London: Rout-
            ledge & Kegan Paul.
Fienup-Riordan, A.
    1983   The Nelson Island Eskimo. Anchorage: Alaska Pacific University Press.
    1986   When Our Bad Season Comes. Alaska Anthropological Association
            Monograph Series, No. 1.
Gluckman, M.
    1960   Tribalism in Modern British Central Africa. Cahiers d'Études Africaines
            1:55–70.
Greenblatt, S.
    1991   Marvelous Possessions: The Wonder of the New World. Chicago: Univer-
            sity of Chicago Press.
Hannerz, U.
    1990   Cosmopolitans and Locals in World Culture. *In* Global Culture. M. Feath-
            erstone, ed. Pp. 237–251. London: Sage.
Hau'ota, E.
    1993   New Oceania: Rediscovering Our Sea of Islands. Suva, Fiji: School of Soc.
            Econ. Dev., University of South Pacific.
Hensel, C.
    1992   Telling Our Selves: Ethnicity and Discourse in Southwestern Alaska. New
            York: Oxford University Press.
Hountondji, P.
    1994   Culture and Development in Africa: Lifestyles, Modes of Thought and Forms
            of Social Organization. Presented at World Comm. Cult. Dev., June 8. UN-
            ESCO, CCD-IV/94REG, INF.9, Paris.

Lightning Source UK Ltd.
Milton Keynes UK
UKHW04f0307061018
329995UK00001B/85/P